D0741988

JKTalley

The Emergence of Sociological Theory

The Dorsey Series in Sociology

Advisory Editor
ROBIN M. WILLIAMS, JR.
Cornell University

Consulting Editor
CHARLES M. BONJEAN
The University of Texas at Austin

The Emergence of Sociological Theory

JONATHAN H. TURNER
University of California at Riverside

LEONARD BEEGHLEY
University of Florida

1981

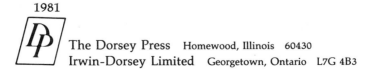

The Dorsey Press   Homewood, Illinois   60430
Irwin-Dorsey Limited   Georgetown, Ontario   L7G 4B3

© THE DORSEY PRESS, 1981

All rights reserved. No part of this publication may be
reproduced, stored in a retrieval system, or transmitted,
in any form or by any means, electronic, mechanical,
photocopying, recording, or otherwise, without the prior
written permission of the publisher.

ISBN 0–256–02416–2
Library of Congress Catalog Card No. 80–70153

Printed in the United States of America

1 2 3 4 5 6 7 8 9 0 K 8 7 6 5 4 3 2 1

To the memory of TALCOTT PARSONS, whose
The Structure of Social Action and later
works demonstrate the importance of
social theory that builds upon the
accomplishments of the early masters.

PREFACE

In this book, we have attempted to understand the initial emergence and subsequent development of sociological theory. In particular, we have focused on sociology's first 100 years as a scientific discipline—from 1830 to 1930. Our efforts have been guided by several intellectual commitments which should be outlined at the outset. First, we are primarily concerned with the emergence of sociological *theory*, and hence, many topics that might be covered in a history of sociology and social thought are not included in these pages. Second, in our concern with theory, we have examined those scholars who contributed the most to the development of abstract concepts, models, and propositions in sociology. Other pioneers in sociology who contributed only to other facets of the discipline, such as the development of research techniques or the formation of professional associations, or those whose ideas have not withstood scrutiny, are omitted from our analysis. Third, because we have emphasized the theoretical content of a scholar's work, our concern is not with the history of social thought, but with the origins and development of theoretical concepts and propositions. Personal biographies of scholars, analyses of the "moods of the time," and other topics that are best included in a "sociology of knowledge" are not prominent in the pages to follow. This kind of work has been more ably performed by others—such as Robert Nisbet and Lewis Coser, to name only two who are more competent than we are in this area. Our goal has been to understand the intellectual connections among purely theoretical ideas in sociology. To do so, we have ventured back into the 18th century, but only to the extent that 18th-century social thought directly influenced the emergence of theory between 1830 and 1930.

These intellectual commitments may appear as constraints, but they also have allowed us to analyze the first 100 years of sociological theory in depth and with great intensity. This analysis deals with three related questions. First, what are the intellectual origins of key concepts, models, and propositions of sociology's first great theorists? Second, what is the profile and nature of the basic works of the early theorists? And third, what is the enduring theoretical legacy of the early theorists? Thus, for each scholar covered in the pages to follow, our analysis is divided into three parts: the origins of his ideas, the nature of his basic works, and the legacy of abstract models and principles that he has provided modern sociological theory.

This last issue is of great importance, since it is our feeling that the purely theoretical legacy of the early masters has not been fully appreciated or utilized. By presenting their ideas more formally, we hope to demonstrate the power of early theory and to excite others to use their concepts and propositions more self-consciously. Sociology has not, we feel, "stood on the shoulders of giants"; rather, it has stood in their shadow, primarily because sociologists have yet to extract the essence of the giants' theories. It is to this goal that this book is dedicated.

Jonathan H. Turner
Leonard Beeghley

ACKNOWLEDGMENTS

Our first acknowledgment goes to one who is primarily responsible for the chapters on Vilfredo Pareto: Charles Powers should be considered the senior author of these three chapters.

Both of us owe a long-standing debt to Talcott Parsons, from whom we never took a course, but whose breadth of knowledge and commitment to sociology as a theoretical enterprise has long served to inspire our efforts. We have come to disagree with Parson's theoretical strategy, but never with his lifelong goal: to develop sociology as a theoretical, and hence scientific, enterprise. For this reason, we have dedicated the book to his memory.

We also wish to thank several individuals who reviewed all or significant parts of a very rough manuscript. They have done much to improve its quality. These reviewers were: Nicholas Mullins, Giles Gobetz, and Robin Williams.

Finally, we want to thank our tireless typist and friend, Clara Dean. For all but one year of the senior author's academic life, she has typed his work, corrected his spelling, and caught errors in his footnotes. I owe her a long-standing debt.

CONTENTS

PART II
THE MATURING TRADITION IN EUROPE

ogy." Durkheim's Theoretical Models: *Durkheim's Overall Model of Social Reality. Durkheim's Specific Causal Models.* Durkheim's Theoretical Principles: *Principles of System Differentiation. Principles of System Integration. Principles of Deviance. Principles of System Mal-integration.*

1

SOCIAL THOUGHT AND
SOCIOLOGICAL THEORY

People have thought about their world for untold centuries. Whether as religious leaders, secular philosophers, or political authorities, speculation about the nature of humans and the social universe is ancient. While observations on social matters were often precise, it was not until the 18th century that social thought took on a scientific character and began to seek the laws of society guiding human behavior.[1] And, by the beginning of the 19th century, the merger of social thought and science was complete, leading Auguste Comte to advocate a "science of society" which he first termed *social physics* and then *sociology*.

The emergence of sociology, then, must be traced to the beginnings of the last century. Sociology did not, however, immediately capture the imagination of scientists and intellectuals, nor did it win converts among academics. Indeed, it was often seen as an intrusion into, or a threat to, more established disciplines, such as law, morals, philosophy, economics, and even psychology. The 19th century is thus a period in which sociology fought for recognition as a unique science and for admission into academic circles. Some scholars successfully waged the battle and became prominent academics, as was the case for such intellectual giants as Max Weber, Émile Durkheim, and George Herbert Mead. Others, such as Herbert Spencer, achieved immense popularity outside academic circles. Some, like Georg Simmel, experienced considerable discrimination in the academic community. And still others, such as

---

[1] For some relevant summaries of pre-19th-century social thought, see Howard Becker and Harry Elmer Barnes, *Social Thought from Lore to Science* (New York: Dover, 1938); and Robert A. Nisbet, *The Social Philosophers: Community and Conflict in Western Thought* (New York: Thomas Y. Crowell, 1973).

1

Karl Marx, never saw themselves as sociologists or as scientists and never became a part of established intellectual or scientific circles.

The founding figures of sociology were thus a diverse group, situated in different positions in varying social contexts. But they all had one feature in common: a desire to understand how society works. In their own way, they all were to ask the fundamental question of sociological theory: How and why are patterns of social organization created, maintained, and changed? In addressing this question, scholars of the 19th and early 20th centuries made the tentative efforts to realize the goals of all science: to create theory.

To appreciate their genius, then, we must come to understand what theory is. These scholars live with us today because they all had a sense for the goals of theory and, hence, science: to explain why events in the social world occur and why social forms should exist. For ultimately, science seeks to answer the question "Why?" And the vehicle for answering this question is theory.

THEORY AND SCIENCE

Theory seeks to explain why phenomena exist and why they reveal certain processes and properties. Sociological theory thus attempts to understand those properties of, and processes involved in, creating, maintaining, and changing patterns of social organization. Theory is constructed from a number of key elements, the most critical of which are (1) definitions of concepts and (2) the organization of concepts.

Concepts as the Building Blocks of Theory[2]

Theories are built from concepts. Most generally, concepts denote or point to phenomena; in so doing they isolate features of the world that are considered, for the moment at hand, important. For example, notions of atoms, protons, neutrons, and the like are concepts, pointing to and isolating phenomena for certain analytical purposes. Familiar sociological concepts would include group, formal organization, power, stratification, interaction, norm, role, status, and socialization. Each term is a concept that embraces aspects of the social world which are considered essential for a particular purpose.

Concepts are constructed from definitions. A definition is a system

---

[2] This section is an adapted version of pp. 2–5 of Jonathan H. Turner, *The Structure of Sociological Theory*, rev. ed. (Homewood, Ill.: Dorsey Press, 1978). © 1978 by The Dorsey Press.

of terms, such as the sentences of a language, the symbols of logic, or the notation of mathematics, that inform investigators as to the phenomenon denoted by a concept. For example, the concept "conflict" only has meaning when it is defined. One possible definition might be: Conflict equals interactions among social units in which one unit seeks to prevent the other from realizing its goals. Such a definition allows scientists to visualize the phenomenon that is denoted by the concept. It allows them, they hope, to "see the same thing" and to understand what it is that is being studied.

The concepts of theory reveal a special characteristic: *abstractness*. Some concepts pertain to concrete phenomena at specific times and locations. Other more abstract concepts point to phenomena that are not related to concrete times or locations. For example, in the context of small-group research, *concrete concepts* would refer to the persistent interactions of particular individuals, whereas an *abstract* conceptualization of such phenomena might refer to those general properties of face-to-face groups that are not tied to particular individuals interacting at a specified time and location. Abstract concepts are thus not tied to a specific context, whereas concrete concepts are. In building theory, abstract concepts are crucial. They transcend particular events or situations and point to the common properties of events and situations.

When used to build theory, two general types of concepts can be distinguished: (1) those that simply label phenomena and (2) those that refer to phenomena that differ in degree. Concepts that merely label phenomena would include such commonly employed abstractions as dog, cat, group, social class, star, and the like. When stated in this way, none of these concepts reveal the ways in which the phenomena they denote vary in terms of properties such as size, weight, density, velocity, cohesiveness, or any of the many criteria used to inform investigators about differences in degree among phenomena. It is for this reason that scientific theory typically utilizes concepts that refer to the *variable properties* of such phenomena as dogs, cats, groups, social classes, and stars. These kinds of concepts allow investigators to distinguish different events and situations from each other in terms of the degree to which they reveal some important property, such as size, weight, density, cohesiveness, and the like. For example, to note that an aggregate of people is a "group" does not indicate what type of group it is or how it compares with other groups in terms of such criteria as size, differentiation, and cohesiveness. Thus, the concepts of scientific theory should denote the *variable* features of the world. For, indeed, to understand events requires that scientists visualize how variation in one phenomenon is related to

4

variation in another. However, this transformation of concepts into full-blown theory requires their organization into theoretical formats.

Formats and the Organization of Concepts[3]

To be useful in explanation—that is, in answering the question "Why?"—concepts must be related to each other. An abstract concept by itself simply indicates that a class of phenomena exists and reveals certain variable properties. The key to understanding the world, however, lies in visualizing *relationships* among phenomena. How are the properties of one phenomenon connected to those of another? For example, how is conflict related to group organization? How is deviance related to value consensus? How is the size of a population related to rates of interaction? All science employs two ways of relating concepts to each other: (1) classifications and (2) propositions.

Classification and Typology. One way to understand the relationships among phenomena is to see them as parts of a larger whole. The object of this procedure is to visualize a phenomenon as an element within a system of related phenomena. For example, the periodic table in chemistry or the Linnean classification of species in biology allows us to visualize the "place" or "location" of phenomena in relation to other phenomena of a particular type—in these instances, basic chemical elements and forms of life, respectively. Much of sociological inquiry, especially that of the early sociologists, involved classification of various social phenomena—such as religious rituals, kinship patterns, legal codes, and the like—as parts of a particular societal type. By emphasizing that certain social phenomena "go together" or "occur together" in certain types of societies, a new level of understanding was believed to be achieved.

Yet as useful as typologies are in allowing investigators to visualize

---

[3] For relevant introductory works, see Paul Davidson Reynolds, *A Primer in Theory Construction* (Indianapolis, Ind.: Bobbs-Merrill, 1971); Arthur L. Stinchcombe, *Constructing Social Theories* (New York: Harcourt, Brace, and World, 1968), pp. 3–56; Karl R. Popper, *The Logic of Scientific Discovery* (New York: Harper & Row, 1959); David Willer and Murray Webster, Jr., "Theoretical Concepts and Observables," *American Sociological Review* 35 (August 1970): 748–57; Hans Zetterberg, *On Theory and Verification in Sociology*, 3d ed. (Totowa, N.J.: Bedminister Press, 1965); Gerald Hage, *Techniques and Problems of Theory Construction in Sociology* (New York: John Wiley, 1972); Walter L. Wallace, *The Logic of Science in Sociology* (Chicago: Aldine, 1971); Robert Dubin, *Theory Building* (New York: Free Press, 1969); Jack Gibbs, *Sociological Theory Construction* (Hinsdale, Ill.: Dryden Press, 1972); Herbert M. Blalock, Jr., *Theory Construction: From Verbal to Mathematical Formulations* (Englewood Cliffs, N.J.: Prentice-Hall, 1969); and Nicholas C. Mullins, *The Art of Theory: Construction and Use* (New York: Harper & Row, 1971).

how phenomena "fit together," it is not clear that classificatory explanations adequately answer the question: Why? Why do the parts of a typology go together or fit into a particular configuration? In biology, for instance, the classification of species was well developed by the early 1800s, and yet it did not answer the questions: Why are there distinctive animal and plant species in the world? Why are these patterns of classification evident? What accounts for the origin, maintenance, and alteration of species? These kinds of questions led scholars to search for the laws of evolution, culminating in Wallace's and Darwin's theories and, with these theories, greater understanding as to why distinguishable and classifiable species should exist.

Similarly, in the nascent social sciences of the last century, a number of scholars had created a typology of modern societies, isolating their typical or modal features. As useful as these typologies were, however, many scholars felt intellectually unfulfilled and began to ask: "Why do these features emerge and bear certain relations to each other?" In asking this question—whether the inquirer was Comte, Spencer, Marx, Durkheim, Pareto, Weber, or any number of prominent thinkers of the time—a different kind of scientific explanation was initiated. And indeed, some of the first theoretical insights of the fledgling discipline of sociology came from those scholars who asked why the typologies of modern societies should reveal their particular profiles and configurations.

There can be little doubt that typological explanations are often a necessary stimulus for other types of scientific explanations. Until one knows the pattern or configuration of phenomena, it is often impossible to know what requires further explanation. So it was with the Linnean classification system and the theory of evolution; and to some extent, so it was for theoretical explanations of societal types. As scholars move beyond classification they can proceed in either of two directions: (1) they can search for causal factors behind phenomena or (2) they can seek the underlying principles exhibited in phenomena. These two directions are not mutually exclusive, since they involve explanation by "propositions." Yet, although these two propositional modes of explanation look for relationships among phenomena, pursuit of one mode yields a different type of explanation than the other.

Propositions.   A proposition relates phenomena to each other by indicating how variation in one accounts for variation in another. Thus, in contrast to a classification scheme where phenomena are simply described and placed together in a pattern or configuration, a proposition tries to account for the variable properties in this pattern by demonstrating how alterations in one phenomenon account for alterations in another.

For example, a classification of modern societies might emphasize that secular (as opposed to religious) values and industrial modes of production "go together." A typology thus emphasizes that a modern society can be seen as typified by these two elements, whereas a proposition seeks to explain why these two elements—secular values and industrialism—should typically occur together by linking them to variations in other phenomena. Theory, then, must ultimately move beyond classificatory to propositional explanation.

In simplest terms, *causal* explanations seek to understand an event in terms of an antecedent event. Variations in a phenomenon occurring prior to a second phenomenon are seen to cause the variations in this second phenomenon. For example, a causal explanation of industrialization would stress the importance of such antecedent variables as money markets, levels of technology, resource levels, urbanization of labor, and other variables seen to produce industrial modes of economic production.[4] At times, causal explanations become quite complex, tracing the connections among a number of variables. For example, one might argue that a decline in agricultural activity can be seen as causing the displacement of workers who migrate to urban areas. Then, along with other events which reveal their own separate causes, the large urban labor pool can be seen to cause industrialization.

Causal explanations are often expressed as *theoretical models*. In some ways a model is like a classification scheme or typology in that it presents a series of phenomena as fitting together within a larger system or configuration. A causal model is much different than a typology, however, in that the elements are not just classified but causally linked. Variables are seen to have causal significance for each other, with degrees of variation in one phenomenon being caused by variations in an antecedent phenomenon. As we will come to appreciate, much of early sociological theorizing involved constructing causal models of social phenomena.

Axiomatic explanations are different from either classificatory or causal explanations. These are explanations in terms of the underlying principles of phenomena rather than in terms of either antecedent causes or broader configurations. The abstract propositions of axiomatic systems state the basic nature of a relationship among phenomena, without regard to causality. For example, Albert Einstein's famous formula, $E = mc^2$, does not state the causal relations between energy or matter, nor does it classify phenomena. It simply states that in the physical world there is

---

[4] The details, or accuracy, of the variables presented here are not at issue. Obviously, these examples oversimplify.

a fundamental relationship among energy, matter, and light; moreover, this relationship is capable of expression as a proposition (in this case, as an equation that is a type of proposition). Many early sociological theorists similarly expressed their ideas as abstract principles, without regard to causality. They simply asserted that, in the social world, certain phenomena are fundamentally related and that this relationship can be expressed as an abstract principle or proposition. For example, although the French sociologist Émile Durkheim was vitally interested in causality, he also presented many sociological principles, such as, the greater the structural differentiation of a social system, the more general and abstract are its values. Such a proposition asserts a fundamental relationship in the social universe between differentiation of roles and the specificity of values, without necessarily positing the direction of causality.[5] Or, to take another example, the early German sociologist Georg Simmel was to offer the following principle: the greater the degree of conflict between social units, the greater each unit's respective level of solidarity. Such a statement argues that there is a basic relationship between conflict and solidarity, but it does not trace out causal connections of events.[6]

Thus, axiomatic theory begins with an abstract principle, called an *axiom*, that states a basic relationship among phenomena.[7] Then, from this axiom or abstract principle, specific propositions are logically deduced. The goal of such deductions is to apply the abstract principle to a specific set of events. For example, if two warring nations become highly nationalistic, we might argue that this specific empirical event, involving particular nations at a given point in history, represents an illustration of Simmel's abstract principle: the greater the degree of conflict between two units, the greater the units' respective level of solidarity. Or, to illustrate further, Durkheim's principle might be used to explain why values become secular and less binding in industrial societies, since industrial societies are an example of a highly differentiated system. The key to using abstract axioms to explain specific, empirical events is to make logically precise deductions from the axioms to the empirical regularity that is to be explained. For without logical deductions, it is not clear if the abstract axiom does indeed apply to the specific events to be explained.

---

[5] He also felt there was a causal relation between these, although this relationship was never specified clearly. And as we will argue in a later chapter, it is this relationship between differentiation and values, rather than causality, that marks Durkheim's contribution.

[6] These could be traced out, but Simmel did not do so.

[7] Axiomatic theory usually begins with a number of such axioms.

The process of using deductions from axioms to empirical regularities is often termed the *covering law* form of theoretical explanation.[8] To a great extent, the more advanced sciences such as physics employ this theoretical format. To subsume a less abstract statement under a more abstract one—in other words, to "cover" the less abstract with the more—is to explain the lower order proposition. In fact, the first self-conscious sociologist, Auguste Comte, preferred the term *social physics* to describe sociology; and he only reluctantly used the term *sociology*. From its beginnings, then, scholars of social physics have held the covering law vision of theoretical explanation.

In sum, we can visualize three different approaches to theoretical explanations: classification, causal modeling, and axiomatic. Causal and axiomatic explanations employ propositions that state how variations in phenomena are related, whereas classification simply describes the fact that phenomena are part of a larger configuration. Figure 1–1 diagrammatically represents these three theoretical formats.[9]

THEORY AND THE EMERGENCE OF SOCIOLOGY

We have emphasized what theory is for a simple reason: a knowledge of just what constitutes theoretical explanation provides a criterion for analyzing and assessing the thought of early sociologists. In many ways, we are simply asserting what sociologists implicitly do all the time: consider certain early scholars more significant than others in terms of the power of their theoretical explanations. Why, for example, do we still read and learn from Marx, Durkheim, Mead, or other giants of sociology's past? These and other scholars are read because they are seen to present theoretical explanations of social events that are still useful. Other scholars of the last century, such as William Graham Sumner, Lester Ward, and Albion Small, are not read today because the theoretical power of their ideas is not believed to be great.

These considerations stress the basic theme of the chapters to follow: the need to assess the founders of sociology in terms of their *theoretical* contributions. Our interest is not to present a comprehensive history of ideas or to see the guiding "mood of the times" that influenced the emergence of sociological theory. Rather, our concern is with examining those scholars who, directly or indirectly through their influence

---

[8] For a good summary of this position and of the relevant references, see George C. Homans, *The Nature of Social Science* (New York: Harcourt, Brace, and World, 1967).

[9] An expanded version of a table in Turner, *Structure of Sociological Theory*, p. 9.

FIGURE 1–1
Types of Theoretical Explanation

A. Classification

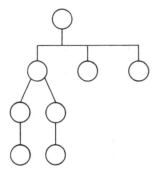

Explanation = Seeing elements as part of a larger configuration of elements without reference to causality

B. Causal modeling

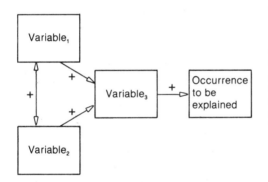

Explanation = Tracing of causal connections among those variables accounting for as much of—and, it is hoped, all—the variation in the occurrence of interest

C. Axiomatic

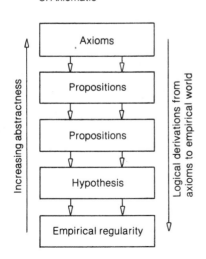

Explanation = Subsumption of empirical regularity under one or more abstract axioms

on others, have made an enduring impact on sociologists' capacity to explain events in the social universe.

Many others have documented with considerable insight such matters as the history of the times in which sociology first emerged, the biographies of ideas of sociology's first masters, and the broad trends in the movement of ideas.[10] In light of the quality of these efforts, it seems redundant to undertake this form of presentation. And hence, in the chapters to follow, we will examine various scholars as *sociological theorists*, and in so doing, we will not attempt to present either a history of social thought or an analysis of the biographical and other conditions that influenced the development of certain ideas.

We thus place particular emphasis on the major concepts, models, and principles of various scholars. These considerations have dictated a particular organization in our analysis of early sociological thinkers:

1. An emphasis on abstract concepts dictates, we feel, a concern with the reasons behind a scholar's selection of certain critical concepts. Hence, we will examine the origins of a thinker's ideas, with the stress on the sources of key concepts. In this way we will be able to examine, to a limited degree, some thinkers of the 18th century and the less-central scholars of the 19th century. As we will come to appreciate, most of sociology's first great scholars had the ability to take ideas from others and combine them in unique and creative ways.

2. An emphasis on concepts, models, and principles requires an appreciation of the specific works in which a theorist's ideas appear. Hence, we will also attempt to summarize in great detail the contents and basic line of argument in the theoretically important works of key theorists. We will not analyze, however, those works that do not contain abstract concepts and that do not reveal either theoretical models or principles.

3. An emphasis on models and principles will lead us to isolate the formal models and theoretical principles that are often buried in the discursive arguments of specific works. It is in these abstract theoretical models and principles, we will argue, that the enduring theoretical contribution of a scholar resides.

---

[10] For examples, see Lewis A. Coser, *Masters of Sociological Thought* (New York: Harcourt Brace Jovanovich, 1977); Robert A. Nisbet, *The Sociological Tradition* (New York: Basic Books, 1966); Clinton Joyce Jesser, *Social Theory Revisited* (Hinsdale, Ill.: Dryden Press, 1975); Nicholas S. Timasheff and George A. Theodorsen, *Sociological Theroy: Its Nature and Growth*, 4th ed. (New York: Random House, 1976).

Our analysis, then, will be organized around these three considerations. Those scholars who have introduced important concepts and who have presented suggestive models and powerful theoretical principles are the most responsible for the emergence of sociological theory. And they deserve our detailed analysis. In discussing the scholars most responsible for the emergence of sociological theory, however, we are confronted with an initial problem of boundaries: Where do we begin and end our analysis? Who are the important figures in the emergence of theory, as opposed to its continuation? Where does the past era of theory end and the modern period begin? Our answer to these questions is somewhat arbitrary: sociology begins as a self-conscious science in the early 1800s with the work of Auguste Comte, and its formative years end in the second decade of the 20th century. By 1930, we believe, the theoretical legacy of sociology's founding theoreticians was evident. Subsequent theoretical work is different in nature and tone, being the product of a more-secure and respected discipline called *sociology*. This post-1930 theorizing is thus "modern" and belongs in a different category than that of the 19th and early 20th centuries.

REVERENCE AND IRREVERENCE IN ASSESSING THE FIRST MASTERS

Any work that employs a set of criteria in assessing sociological theory will expose some ideas to be more significant, in terms of these criteria, than others. For our purposes, those scholars from 1820 to 1930 who have presented sociology with useful (1) abstract concepts, (2) abstract causal models, or (3) abstract principles will be considered more important than others. Yet we should make explicit another consideration in our analysis of sociology's first theorists: Not only will propositions be considered superior to classificatory statements, but also, theoretical principles will be viewed as better theory than causal models. Thus, regardless of whatever else a thinker may have contributed to sociology, the most important contribution is the development of theoretical principles. We are not, of course, denying the importance of concept-formation, classification, or modeling, but only stressing that the goal of science is ultimately the development of abstract principles. This point of view is, no doubt, highly controversial, and thus, we should pause briefly to offer a defense.[11]

As we have argued, a causal model is more likely than a typology to

---

[11] For a related line of argument, see David Willer and Judith Willer, *Systematic Empiricism: Critique of a Pseudo Science* (Englewood Cliffs, N.J.: Prentice-Hall, 1973).

answer the question "Why?" But even causal models that seek to become abstract will remain tied to specific classes of events in particular types of systems. For example, a causal model of the emergence of bureaucracy is abstract in that it may examine all bureaucracies and try to enumerate general types of conditions that cause bureaucracies to emerge. Yet the model is still about a limited social form, bureaucracy, and does not examine other social forms. Moreover, bureaucracy itself has been, when seen from the total span of human history, a comparatively recent development—perhaps being only 7,000 years old. And there is no reason to suppose that such a form will still exist 7,000 years into the future. Thus, a model of bureaucracy is enormously useful in allowing investigators to understand, and perhaps predict, the occurrence and profile of specific classes of empirical events—in our example, bureaucratization. But there are limits to how abstract a causal model can become. If it becomes too abstract, it loses much of its utility to connect classes of events to each other in terms of causal relations. And it is in this capacity to connect events that the particular strengths of modeling reside.

Theoretical principles, however, do not suffer from this limitation, and in fact, the more abstract they become, the more explanatory power they will have over a wider range of phenomena. For example, if we could develop a series of abstract principles on "structural differentiation" in the social world, then we could, through the vehicle of axiomatic theory, achieve understanding of not just bureaucratization, but also differentiation in groups, communities, and other social forms. Of course, causality would not be immediately evident, and thus, we might want to supplement an axiomatic explanation of differentiation in a particular historical period or specific empirical system with a causal model. But we are arguing that principles are more enduring forms of theory than models, because ultimately the latter must be connected to specific classes of events in particular times and places. An emphasis on theoretical principles does not present this limitation, and indeed, the goal is to increase the number of classes or cases covered by an abstract law. Of course, abstract principles are only useful when deductions from them to specific events are possible, but the logic of axiomatic theory does not require the explanatory principle to remain tied to particular classes of empirical phenomena.

This line of argument goes against much current theorizing in sociology which involves a considerable amount of classification and causal modeling. Many analyses of the emergence of sociological theory, therefore, tend to hold in high esteem a number of scholars who presented typologies or causal models of specific historical events. We often revere these scholars because they have provided key insights into particular phenomena of contemporary interest. Conversely, other scholars who presented abstract principles have received less attention, or as is often the case, the typologies and models in their schemes are given more attention than their theoretical principles. Indeed, retrospective looks at past thinkers' work are frequently so concerned with isolating discrete concepts, typologies, or models that the more enduring theoretical principles of a scholar are ignored or not even seen. Our effort in this book will attempt to correct for this tendency by making explicit the theoretical principles of sociology's founding theorists.

But as we do so, some scholars who are currently held in high esteem *as theorists* will be seen as less significant than is presently thought, primarily because their work does not contain abstract theoretical principles. This assessment does not mean that these scholars are less notable *as sociologists*, since empirical observation, historical description, model building, concept formation, and typologizing are extremely important parts of the sociological enterprise. But in a work on sociological theory, our assessment must be in terms of a theoretical criterion—that is, based on those propositions that provide for the explanation of a broad range of social phenomena.

In the chapters to follow, then, some scholars will be seen as less important to the development of sociological theory than typically has been the case. Conversely, others will be given more reverence than previously. And as we will come to see, some of sociology's early masters had a vision of what theory in science *should be* which was superior not just to that of their contemporaries, but also to that which prevails in modern sociology. An implicit theme, therefore, of this book is that modern sociology has often lost the vision of its early masters or has adopted the less theoretically important views of its founders. To delve into the emergence of sociological theory is thus to seek redirection and reinspiration from those who saw that a theory of the social universe must ultimately seek the basic theoretical principles guiding the operation of this universe.

PART I

The Birth of the Sociological Tradition

2

AUGUSTE COMTE AND THE BEGINNINGS OF SOCIOLOGICAL THEORY

Auguste Comte is often given credit for being the founder of sociology, for he coined the term *sociology* and became the most forceful advocate in the early decades of the 19th century for a science of society. Yet new ideas are typically extensions, modifications, and codifications of ideas developed by a scholar's predecessors and contemporaries. Such is the case with Comte's work, which is often criticized for being "unoriginal" or for being a simple restatement of ideas developed by others. To some extent, this charge is true, but as we will see in later chapters, it is also true of Spencer, Marx, Durkheim, Mead, or any number of sociology's great masters. Ideas are not created in an intellectual and social vacuum, for the "great minds" of human history have often been the ones who gave the most articulate expression to ideas that had earlier been debated and discussed by others.

These facts should not diminish our estimation of a scholar. To extend ideas in small but critical ways is often all that is needed to make an important intellectual breakthrough. Curiously, Comte's contribution is frequently downgraded because he is seen to have "only" articulated the ideas of his master, Saint-Simon, and the cumulative legacy of the 18th century. Far from being an indictment, this event in the early 19th century should be viewed as a major achievement. For in articulating Saint-Simon's and others' ideas, Comte extended them in subtle, and yet important, ways. The result was the formal emergence of sociology and sociological theory.

This emergence represents a fascinating story, and thus, we should seek to understand the general conditions that produced Comte's great

17

synthesis of ideas and advocacy for a science of society. In this chapter, therefore, we will first examine the origins of Comte's ideas. Then, only after this task is completed, we will explore Comte's basic works and their implications for the development of sociological theory. In following this course, we are delving back into the origins of sociology as an intellectual enterprise. And as we will discover, the original vision of this enterprise was for a discipline that sought to discover the laws of human organization—a point of emphasis that has been periodically obscured ever since. The emergence of sociology and sociological theorizing are thus concomitant events, forged in the creative imagination of sociology's founder; Auguste Comte.

THE ORIGINS OF SOCIOLOGICAL THEORY

New ideas typically emerge in times of change, turmoil, and conflict. Although "social thought" is as old as human existence, scientifically oriented social thought emerged only after great scientific achievements in the 16th and 17th centuries—achievements that dramatically altered people's conception of the physical universe and how it was to be understood. But sociology is the result of more than the scientific revolution; it emerged out of the tumultuous period in which the new discoveries about the operation of the physical world were accompanied by dramatic changes in patterns of social organization.[1]

The word *revolution* has perhaps become overused in commentaries. Yet this term captures the dramatic nature of changes in the social, moral, and intellectual fabric of European society in the 16th and 17th centuries. For the term revolution denotes the decisive and radical nature of change, although this change often took many decades to be fully realized. Thus, the economic, political, religious, and intellectual revolutions of post-Renaissance Europe are not so much sudden transformations as evolutionary processes that nevertheless altered decisively the nature of the social world. Even the most cataclysmic of events, the French

---

[1] Robert A. Nisbet in his *The Sociological Tradition* (New York: Basic Books, 1966), chap. 2, has presented this line of argument under "The Two Revolutions." While this discussion owes much to Nisbet's work, there are great differences in emphasis between this discussion and Nisbet's. For other interesting discussions of this period, see Ernst Cassirer, *The Philosophy of the Enlightenment* (Boston Beacon Press, 1955; originally published in 1932); R. V. Sampson, *Progress and the Age of Reason* (Cambridge: Harvard University Press; 1956); J. Salwyn Schapiro, *Condorcet and the Rise of Liberalism* (New York: Octagon Books, 1963), chaps. 1–3; and E. J. Hobsbawn, *The Age of Revolution* (New York: Mentor, 1967).

Revolution of 1789, was only the culmination of economic, social, political, and intellectual changes in the 18th-century France.

Sociology thus emerged in a period of change in the nature of the social order and in the context of intellectual discourse. These changes, like all events in the social world, were intimately interconnected, but we shall discuss them as if they were separate revolutions. Such artificial separation can give us a better sense for the dramatic nature of events in the century before Comte's great synthesis and advocacy. We will, therefore, see sociology as emerging out of three great revolutions: (1) the economic revolution, (2) the political revolution, and (3) the intellectual revolution. These three "revolutions" best reflect and signal the fundamental reorganization in all social arrangements in the century before Comte.

The Economic Revolution

During much of the 18th century, the last remnants of the old economic order were crumbling under the impact of the commercial and industrial revolutions. Much of the feudal order had been eliminated with the expansion of trade during the 17th century. Yet economic activity in the 18th century had become greatly restricted by guilds which controlled labor's access to skilled occupations and by chartered corporations which restrained trade and production.

The 18th century saw the growth of free labor and more competitive manufacturing. The cotton industry was the first to break the hold of the guilds and chartered corporations, but with each decade, other industries were subjected to the liberating effects of free labor, free trade, and free production. By the time large-scale industry emerged, first in England, then in France, and later in Germany, the economic reorganization of Europe had been achieved. Large-scale industry and manufacture simply accelerated the transformations in society that had been occurring for decades.

These transformations involved a profound reorganization of society. Labor was liberated from the land; wealth and capital existed independently of the large noble estates; large-scale industry accelerated urbanization of the population; the extension of competitive industry hastened the development of new technologies; increased production encouraged the expansion of markets and world trade for securing raw resources and selling finished goods; religious organizations lost much of their authority in the face of secular economic activities; family structure was altered as people moved from the land to urban areas; law became as concerned with regularizing the new economic processes as in preserving the privilege of the nobility; and the old political regimes legitimated by "divine rights" successively became less tenable.

Thus, the emergence of a capitalist economic system inexorably destroyed the last remnants of the feudal order and the transitional mercantile order of restrictive guilds and chartered corporations. Such economic changes greatly altered the way people lived, created new social classes, such as the bourgeoisie and urban proletariat, and led not only to a revolution of ideas but also to a series of political revolutions. As we will see in the next chapter on Herbert Spencer, these changes were less traumatic in England than in France, where the full brunt of these economic forces clashed with the Old Regime. It was in this volatile mixture of economic changes, coupled with the scientific revolution of the 16th and 17th centuries, that political and intellectual revolutions were to be spawned. And out of these combined revolutions, sociology was to emerge.

The Political Revolution

The Revolution of 1789 marked a dramatic transformation in French society. The Revolution and the century of political turmoil that followed provided early French sociologists with their basic intellectual problem: how to use the "laws of social organization" to create a new social order. Yet, in many ways, the French Revolution was merely the violent culmination of changes that had been occurring in France and elsewhere in Europe for the entire 18th century.

By the time of the French Revolution, the old feudal system was merely a skeleton. Peasants were often landowners, although many engaged in the French equivalent of tenant farming and were subject to excessive taxation. The old landed aristocracy had lost much of its wealth through indolence, incompetence, and unwillingness to pursue lucrative, and yet low-status, occupations. Indeed, many of the nobility lived in genteel poverty behind the walls of their disintegrating estates. And as they fell into severe financial hardship, the affluent bourgeoisie were all too willing to purchase the land. Indeed by 1789, the bourgeoisie had purchased their way into the ranks of the nobility as the financially pressed monarchy sold titles to upwardly mobile families. Thus by the time of the Revolution, the traditional aristocracy was in a less-advantageous position, many downtrodden peasants were landholders, the affluent bourgeoisie were buying their way into the halls of power and prestige, and the monarchy was increasingly dependent upon the bourgeoisie for financial support.

The structure of the state best reflects these changes in the old feudal order. By the end of the 18th century, the French monarchy had become almost functionless. It had, of course, centralized government through the suppression of old centers of feudal power, but its monarchs were now lazy, indolent, and incompetent. The real power of the monarchy increasingly belonged to the professional administrators in the state bureaucracy, most of whom had been recruited from the bourgeoisie. The various magistrates were virtually all recruited from the bourgeoisie, and the independent financiers, particularly the Farmers General, had assumed many of the tax-collecting functions of government. In exchange for a fixed sum of money, the monarchy had contracted to the financiers the right to collect taxes, with the result that the financiers collected all that the traffic could bear, and in the process, generated enormous resentment and hostility in the population. With their excessive profits, the financiers became the major bankers of the monarchy, with the king, nobility, church, guild master, merchant, and monopolistic corporate manufacturer often coming to them for loans.

Thus when the violent revolution came, it hit a vulnerable political system which had been in decline for most of the 18th century. The ease with which it crumbled highlighted its vulnerability, while the political instability that followed revealed the extent to which the ascendance of the bourgeoisie and large-scale industrialists had been incomplete. In other societies where sociology was also to emerge, this transition to industrial capitalism and new political forms was less tumultuous. Particularly in England, the political revolution was more evolutionary than revolutionary, creating a sociology that was distinctly different from that in France (see next chapter).

The political and economic changes of the 18th century were accompanied by intensified intellectual activity. Reacting to economic and political changes, and the concomitant reorganization of social life, much of the 18th century was consumed by intellectual ferment. On the one hand, these intellectuals reflected the changes occurring around them, and yet, on the other hand, their forceful advocacy helped cause these changes. Whether physiocrats like Adam Smith in England or philosophers like Voltaire and Rousseau in France, social thinkers in the 18th century began to exert a powerful influence on public opinion, and in the process, they helped accelerate the very changes to which their work had initially represented a response. It is this influence of ideas and ideology on social events in the 18th century that makes the social thought of the times a true intellectual revolution.

The Intellectual Revolution

The intellectual revolution of the 18th century is commonly referred to as the *Enlightenment*. As we will explore in more detail in the next chapter, the Enlightenment in England and Scotland was dominated by a group of thinkers who argued for a vision of human beings and society that both reflected and justified the industrial capitalism that first emerged in the British Isles. For scholars such as Adam Smith, individuals are to be free of external constraint and allowed to compete, thereby creating a better society. In France, the Enlightenment is often termed the *Age of Reason* and was dominated by a group of scholars known as the "philosophes." And it is out of the intellectual ferment generated by the French philosophes that sociology was born.

Although the Enlightenment was fueled by the political, social, and economic changes of the 18th century, it derived considerable inspiration from the scientific revolution of the 16th and 17th centuries. Through a long and often acrimonious route, the scientific revolution reached a symbolic peak, at least in the eye of thinkers in the 18th century, with Newtonian physics. The post-Newtonian view of science was dramatically different than previous views. The old dualism between reason and the senses had broken down, and for the first time, it could be confidently asserted that the world of reason and the world of phenomena formed a single unity. Through concepts, speculation, and logic, the facts of the empirical world could be understood; and through the accumulation of facts, reason could be disciplined and kept from fanciful flights of speculation.

The world was thus viewed as orderly, and it was now possible to understand its complexity through the use of reason and the collection of facts. Newton's principle of gravity was hailed as the model for this reconciliation between reason and the senses. Physics was to become the vision of how scientific inquiry and theory should be conducted. And increasingly, the individual and society were drawn into the orbit of the new view of science. This gradual inclusion of the individual and society into the realm of science represented a startling break with the past, since heretofore these phenomena had been considered to be in the domain of morals, ethics, and religion. Indeed, much of the philosophes' intellectual effort involved the emancipation of thought about humans from religious speculation, and while the philosophes were far from scientific, they performed the essential function of placing speculation about the human condition in the realm of reason. Indeed, as can be seen in their statements on universal human rights, laws, and on the natural order, much of their work consisted of attacks on established authority in both the church and state. From notions of "natural law," it was to be but a short step to consideration of the laws of human organization. And many of the less shrill and polemical of the philosophes—first Montesquieu, then Turgot and Condorcet—were to actually make this short step and seek to understand the social order in terms of principles that they felt were the equivalent in the social realm of Newton's law of gravitation.

The philosophes' view of human beings and society was greatly influenced by the social conditions around them. They were vehemently opposed to the Old Regime in France and highly supportive of the interest of the bourgeoisie in free trade, free commerce, free industry, free labor, and free opinion. And in fact, the large and literate bourgeoisie formed the reading public that bought the books, papers, and pamphlets of the philosophes. Thus, their concern with the "laws of the human condition" was as much, and probably more, influenced by their moral, political, and ideological commitments as by a dispassionate search for scientific laws. Yet, it would be mistaken to ignore the extent to which the philosophes raised the possibility of a science of society molded after the image of science in physics and biology.

The basic thesis of all philosophes, whether Voltaire, Rousseau, Condorcet, Diderot, or others, was that humans have certain "natural rights" which were violated by the existing institutional arrangements. It would be necessary, therefore, to dismantle the existing order and substitute a new order that was considered to be more compatible with the essence and basic needs of humankind. The transformation was to occur through enlightened and progressive legislation, although ironically the philosophes were to stand in horror as their names and ideas were used to justify the violent Revolution of 1789.

In almost all of the philosophes' formulations was a vision of human progress. Humanity was seen to be marching in a direction and was considered to be governed by a "law of progress" that was as fundamental as the law of gravitation in the physical world. In particular, those who were to exert the most influence on Auguste Comte—Turgot, Condorcet, and Saint-Simon—built their intellectual schemes around a law of progress. Thus, the philosophes were, on the one hand, decidedly unscientific in their moral advocacy, but they offered at least the rhetoric of post-

Newtonian science in their search for the natural laws of human order and in their formulation of the law of progress. It is out of these somewhat contradictory tendencies that sociology emerged in the work of Auguste Comte, who sought to reconcile the seeming contradiction between moral advocacy and detached scientific observation.

The more enlightened of the philosophes, men such as Montesquieu, Turgot, and Condorcet, were to present the broad contours of this reconciliation to Comte: the laws of human organization, particularly the law of progressive development, can be used as tools to create a better society. It is with this mixture of concerns—moral action, progress, and scientific laws—that the Age of Reason ended and the 19th century began. It is from this intellectual milieu, as it was influenced by social, economic, and political conditions, that Comte was to pull diverse and often contradictory elements and forge a forceful statement on the nature of a science of society. But before examining the specifics of Comte's thought, we should first examine the scholars from whom Comte took the most important concepts.

THE INTELLECTUAL ORIGINS OF COMTE'S THOUGHT

Auguste Comte's sociology emerged from the economic, political, and social conditions of postrevolutionary France. No social thinker could ignore the oscillating political situation in France during the first half of the 19th century or the profound changes in social organization that accompanied the growth of large-scale industry. Yet, despite the influence of these forces, the content of Comte's sociology represents a selective borrowing of ideas from the Enlightenment of the 18th century. Comte absorbed, no doubt, the general thrust of the philosophes' advocacy, but he appears to have borrowed and then synthesized concepts from four major figures: (1) Charles Montesquieu, (2) Jacques Turgot, (3) Jean Condorcet, and (4) Henri Saint-Simon. In addition, Comte seems to have been influenced by the liberal tradition of Adam Smith and the physiocrats as well as by the reactionary traditionalism of such scholars as de Maistre and de Bonald.[2] In our review of the origins of Comte's thought, then, we will focus primarily on the influence of Montesquieu, Turgot, Condorcet, and Saint-Simon, with a brief mention of the traditional and liberal elements in Comte's thinking.

---

[2] Lewis Coser's *Masters of Sociological Thought* (New York: Harcourt Brace and Jovanovich, 1978), pp. 25–27, is the first work to bring this line of influence to our attention.

Montesquieu and Comte

In Chapter 15, when we examine the culmination of French sociology in the work of Émile Durkheim, Charles Montesquieu's ideas will be explored in more detail. For the present, we will stress those key concepts that Comte borrowed from Montesquieu. Written in the first half of the 18th century, Montesquieu's *The Spirit of Laws* can be considered one of the first sociological works in both style and tone.[3] Indeed, if we wanted to push back 75 years the founding of sociology, we could view *The Spirit* as the first distinctly sociological work. There are, however, too many problems with Montesquieu's great work for it to represent a founding effort. Its significance resides more in the influence it had upon scholars of the next century, particularly Comte and Durkheim (see Chapters 15 to 17).

In *The Spirit*, Montesquieu argued that society must be considered to be a "thing." As a thing, its properties could be discovered by observation and analysis. Thus, for Montesquieu, morals, manners, and customs, as well as social structures, are amenable to investigation in the same way as are things or phenomena in physics and chemistry. Comte's concern with "social facts," and later, Durkheim's proclamation that sociology is the study of social facts, can both be traced to Montesquieu's particular emphasis on society as a thing.

As a thing, Montesquieu argued, society can be understood by discovering the "laws" of human organization. Montesquieu was not, as we emphasize in Chapter 15, completely clear on this point, but the thrust of his argument appears to have been that the laws of society are discoverable in the same way that Newton had, in Montesquieu's mind, uncovered the laws of physical matter. This point was to become extremely important in Comte's sociology. Indeed, Comte was to prefer the label *social physics* to *sociology*. In this way Comte could stress that social science, like the physical sciences, must involve a search for the laws of social structure and change.

Montesquieu also viewed scientific laws as a hierarchy—a notion that, along with Saint-Simon's emphasis, was to intrigue Comte. Sciences that are low in the hierarchy, such as physics, will reveal deterministic laws, as was the case for Newton's principle of gravitation. Sciences that are higher in the hierarchy will, Montesquieu argued, be typified by less determinative laws. The laws of society, therefore, will be more probabilistic. In this way, Montesquieu was able to retain a vision of

---

[3] Charles Montesquieu, *The Spirit of Laws*, vol. 1 and 2 (London: The Colonial Press, 1900; originally published in 1748).

human freedom and initiative within the context of a scientific inquiry. Comte appears to have accepted much of this argument, for he was to stress that the complexity of social phenomena renders strictly determinative laws difficult to discover. For Comte, sociological laws would capture the basic tendencies and directions of social phenomena.

Montesquieu's *The Spirit* also developed a typology of governmental forms. Much of this work is devoted to analyzing the structure and "spirit" (cultural ideas) of three basic governmental forms: republic, monarchy, and despotism. The details of this analysis are less important than the general thrust of Montesquieu's argument. First, there is an implicit developmental sequence in Montesquieu's argument, although not to the degree evident in the next generation of social thinkers, such as Turgot and Condorcet. Secondly, Montesquieu's abstract typology was constructed to capture the diversity of empirical systems in the world and throughout history. Thus, by developing a typology with an implicit developmental sequence, a better sense for the operation of phenomena was believed to be achieved—a point of emphasis that was to be central to Comte's scheme. And thirdly, Montesquieu's separate analysis of the "spirit of a nation" and its relation to structural variables, especially political structures, was adopted by Comte in his analysis of societal stages that reveal both "spiritual" (ideas) and "temporal" (structural) components.

In sum, then, Montesquieu laid much of the intellectual foundation upon which Comte was to build his scheme. The emphasis on society as a thing, the concern for laws, the stress on hierarchies of laws, the implicit developmental view of political structures, the belief that empirical diversity can be simplified through analytical typologies, and the recognition that the social world is composed of interdependent cultural and structural forces were all to find their way into Comtean sociology, as well as the sociology of Comte's intellectual successors, such as Durkheim. But Montesquieu's ideas were transformed in Comte's mind under the influence of other 18th-century scholars, particularly Turgot, Condorcet, and Adam Smith.

Turgot and Comte

Jacques Turgot was one of the more influential thinkers of the 18th-century Enlightenment. As a scholar, and for a short time as the finance minister of France, Turgot's ideas exerted considerable influence within and outside intellectual circles. Like that of many scholars of his time, Turgot's work was not published in the conventional sense, but initially appeared as a series of lectures or discourses that were, no doubt, informally distributed. Only later, in the early 19th century, were many of Turgot's works to be edited and published.[4] Yet Turgot's ideas were well known to his contemporaries as well as his successors, particularly Condorcet, Saint-Simon, and Comte.

In 1750, Turgot presented two discourses at the Sorbonne; and it is from this date that he established himself as a major social thinker. The first discourse was delivered in July and was entitled "The Advantages which the Establishment of Christianity has Procured for the Human Race."[5] The second discourse was given on December 11, 1750, and was entitled "Philosophical Review of the Successive Advances of the Human Mind."[6] While the first discourse is often discounted in sociological circles, it presented a line of reasoning that was to be reflected in Comte's writings. Basically, Turgot argued that religion performed some valuable services for human progress, and while religion is no longer an important ingredient in human development, it made subsequent progress possible. For had Christianity not existed, basic and fundamental events such as the preservation of classical literature, the abolishment of cruel treatment of children, the eradication of extreme and punitive laws, and other necessary conditions for further progress would not have been achieved. Comte was to take this idea and emphasized that each stage of human evolution, particularly the religious or theological, must reach its zenith, thereby laying the conditions necessary for the next stage of human development.

The second 1750 discourse influenced Comte and other sociologically inclined thinkers more directly. In this discourse, Turgot argued that because humans are basically alike, their perceptions of, and responses to, situations will be similar, and hence, they will all evolve along the same evolutionary path. Humanity, he argued, is like an individual in that it grows and develops in a similar way. Thus, the human race will be typified by a slow advancement from a less-developed to a more-developed state. Naturally, many conditions will influence the rate of

---

[4] Du Pont de Nemours, for example, published a nine-volume edition of Turgot's work between 1808 and 1811 which, while deficient in many respects, brought Turgot's diverse pamphlets, discourses, letters, anonymously published articles, private memoranda, and so on together for the first time. Comte certainly must have read this work, although it is likely that he also read many of the original articles and discourses in their unedited form. See also W. Walker Stephens, ed., *The Life and Writings of Turgot* (London: Green and Co., 1895).

[5] See Du Pont de Nemours.

[6] Reprinted in English in Ronald L. Meek, ed. and trans., *Turgot on Progress, Sociology and Economics* (Cambridge: Cambridge University Press, 1973).

growth, or progress, for a particular people. Hence, progress will be uneven, with some peoples at one stage of growth and others at a more advanced stage. But in the end, all humanity will reach a "stage of perfection." Comte saw much in this line of argument, since it implicitly accounted for variations and diversity among the populations of the world. Populations differ because their societies are at different stages in a single and unified developmental process.

In this second discourse, Turgot also presented a rather sophisticated version of economic determinism. Change occurs as a result of economic forces that inevitably produce alterations in society. For example, the invention of agriculture produces an economic surplus which, in turn, allows for the expansion of the division of labor. Part of this expansion involves commercial activity, which encourages innovations in shipbuilding, with the extensive use of ships causing advances in navigation, astronomy, and geography. The expansion of trade creates towns and cities which preserve the arts and sciences, thereby encouraging the advance of technologies. Thus, Turgot saw progress in more than a moralistic or metaphorical sense; he recognized that structural changes in one area of a social system, especially in economic activity, create pressures for other changes, with these pressures causing further changes, and so on. This mode of analysis was to anticipate by one hundred years Marx's economic determinism and it was to influence evolutionary theorizing in France for 150 years.

Turgot's next works made more explicit the themes developed in these two early discourses. *On Universal History*[7] and *On Political Geography*[8] were apparently written near the end of Turgot's stay at the Sorbonne, perhaps around 1755. *On Political Geography* is most noteworthy for its formulation of the three stages of human progress— an idea that was to become a central part of Comte's view of human evolution. Moreover, the notion of universal stages is used not only to explain human development, but also to account for the diversity of human societies—an analytical tactic similar to that used by Montesquieu. All societies of the world are, Turgot argued, at one of three stages, whether "hunters, shepherds, or husbandmen." *On Universal History* developed even further the notion of three stages, presenting a number of ideas that were to become central to Comte's sociology. First, Turgot divided evolution into "mental" and "structural" progression so that development involves change in economic and social structures as well as in idea systems. Secondly, the progress of society is

[7] Ibid.
[8] Du Pont.

explicitly viewed as the result of internal structural and cultural forces rather than as a result of intervention by a Deity. Thirdly, change and progress are thus understandable in terms of abstract laws that depict the nature of stasis and change in social systems. And fourthly, Turgot's empirical descriptions of what we would now call hunting, horticultural, and agrarian societies are highly detailed and filled with discussion of how structural and cultural conditions at one point in time create pressures for new structures and ideas at the next point in time.

Later in his career, probably during the 1760s, Turgot turned his analytical attention increasingly to economic matters. Around 1766, Turgot formulated his *Reflections on the Formation and Distribution of Wealth*[9] which parallels and, to some extent, anticipates the ideas developed by the physiocrats in England. Turgot's advocacy of free trade, his analysis of the ways in which supply and demand influence prices, and his recognition of the importance of entrepreneurs to economic development are extremely sophisticated for his time. And out of this analysis, an implicit fourth stage of development is introduced: as capital increasingly becomes concentrated in the hands of entrepreneurs in advanced agricultural societies, a commercial type of society is created. Much of Turgot's description of the transition to, and the arrangements in, this commercial stage were to be restated by Marx, Spencer, and Comte in the 19th century, although it was only Comte who was to be directly influenced by Turgot's economic analyses. Yet Comte was never to expand upon Turgot's great insights into the importance of economic variables on the organization and change of society. Only the emphasis on entrepreneurial activity in industrial societies was to be retained—a fact which, in the end, was to make Comte's analysis of structural change superficial in comparison to that of Turgot, Spencer, and Marx.

In sum, then, Turgot dramatically altered the course of social thought in the 18th century. Extending Montesquieu's ideas in subtle but nevertheless important ways, he developed a mode of analysis that influenced Comte both directly and indirectly. The idea of three stages of progress, the notion that structures at one stage create the necessary conditions for the next, and the stress on the lawlike nature of progress, all became an integral part of Comte's sociology. Much of Turgot's influence on Comte, however, may have been indirect, working its way through Condorcet, whose work was greatly affected by Turgot.[10]

---

[9] See, Meek, *Turgot on Progress*, for an English translation.

[10] Indeed, Condorcet wrote a *Life of Turgot* in 1786 which Comte, no doubt, read with interest.

Condorcet and Comte

Jean Condorcet was a student, friend, and great admirer of Turgot, and thus, it is not surprising that Condorcet's work represents an elaboration of ideas developed by Turgot. Throughout Condorcet's career, which flowered during and then floundered after the French Revolution, he concerned himself with the relation of ideas to social action. In particular, he emphasized the importance of science as a means for the infinite perfectability of the human race. The culmination of his intellectual career was the short and powerful *Sketch for a Historical Picture of the Progress of the Human Mind*,[11] which was written while Condorcet was in hiding from an unfavorable political climate.

Progress of the Human Mind was written in haste by a man who knew he would soon die, and yet, it is by far his best work. In its hurried passage, he traced ten stages of human development, stressing the progression of ideas from the emergence of language and simple customs to the development and elaboration of science. Condorcet felt that with the development of science and its extension to the understanding of society, humans could now direct their future toward "infinite perfectability." Human progress, Condorcet argued, "is subject to the same general laws that can be observed in the development of the faculties of the individual," and once these faculties are fully developed, "the perfectability of man is truly indefinite; and that the progress of this perfectability, from now onwards independent of any power that might wish to halt it, has no other limit than the duration of the glove upon which nature has cast us."[12]

The historical details of Condorcet's account are little better than Turgot's, but there are several important changes in emphasis that were to influence Comte's thinking. First, Condorcet's stress on the movement of ideas was to be retained in Comte's view of progress. Second, the emphasis on science as representing a kind of intellectual take-off point for human progress was to be retained in Comte. And third, the almost religious faith in science as the tool for constructing the "good society" was to become central to Comte's advocacy. Thus, Comte's great synthesis was to take elements from both Turgot's and Condorcet's related schemes. Turgot's law of the three stages of progress was to be retained in favor of Condorcet's ten stages, but Condorcet's emphasis on ideas

---

[11] Marquis de Condorcet, *Sketch for a Historical Picture of the Progress of the Human Mind* (London: Weidenfeld and Nicolson, 1955; originally published in 1794; translated into English in 1795).

[12] Ibid., p. 4.

and on the use of science to realize the laws of progress was to be preserved.

Yet, Comte's synthesis was, in some respects, merely an extension of ideas that his master, Saint-Simon, had developed in rough form. And to understand fully the origins of Comte's thought, and hence the emergence of sociology, we must explore the volatile relationship between Saint-Simon and Comte. For it was from their interaction that sociology was officially born.

Saint-Simon and Comte

In many ways, Claude-Henri de Saint-Simon represented a bridge between the 18th century and the early 19th century. Born into an aristocratic family, Saint-Simon initially pursued a nonacademic career. He fought with the French in the American Revolution, traveled the world, proposed a number of engineering projects, including the Panama Canal, was politically active during the French Revolution, became a land speculator in the aftermath of the 1789 Revolution, and amassed and then lost a large fortune. Only late in life, at the turn of the century, did Saint-Simon become a dedicated scholar.[13]

The relationship between Saint-Simon's and Comte's ideas has been debated ever since their violent quarrel and separation in 1824. Just what part of Saint-Simon's work is Comte's, and vice versa, will never be completely determined. But it is clear that between 1800 and 1817, Saint-Simon's ideas were not influenced by Comte. For it was not until 1817 that the young Comte joined the aging Saint-Simon as a secretary, student, and collaborator. In seven years between 1817 and 1824, Comte's and Saint-Simon's ideas were intermingled, but we can see in the pre-1817 works of Saint-Simon many of the ideas that were to become a part of Comte's sociology.[14] The most reasonable interpretation of

---

[13] See Keith Taylor, *Henri Saint-Simon* (London: Croom Helm, 1975), pp. 13–29, for a concise biographical sketch of Saint-Simon.

[14] The most important of these works are *Letters from an Inhabitant of Geneva* (1803), *Introduction to the Scientific Studies of the Nineteenth Century* (1807–8), *Essays on the Science of Man* (1813), and *The Reorganization of the European Community* (1814). Unfortunately, much of Saint-Simon is unavailable in convenient English translations.

For convenient secondary works where portions of the above appear, see F. M. H. Markham, *Henri Comte de Saint-Simon* (New York: Macmillan, 1952) and Taylor, *Henri Saint-Simon*. (The Markham book has been reissued by Harper Torchbooks, 1964.) For interesting commentaries, see G. G. Iggers, *The Political Philosophy of Saint-Simon* (Hague: Mouton, 1958); F. E. Manuel, *The New World of Henri de Saint-Simon* (Cambridge: Cambridge University Press, 1956); and Alvin Gouldner, *Socialism and Saint-Simon* (Yellow Springs, Oh.: Collier Books, 1962).

their collaboration is that Comte took many of the crude and unsystematic ideas of Saint-Simon, refined and polished them in accordance with his greater grasp of history and science, and extended them in small but critical ways in light of his exposure to Montesquieu, Turgot, Condorcet, Adam Smith, and the traditionalists. To appreciate Saint-Simon's unique contribution to the emergence of sociology, then, we must first examine the period between 1800 and 1817, and then the post-1817 work, with speculation on the contribution by Comte to these later works.

Saint-Simon's Early Work, 1800–1817. Saint-Simon had read Condorcet carefully and concluded that the scientific revolution had set the stage for a science of social organization.[15] He argued in his first works that the study of humankind and society must be a "positive" science, based upon empirical observation. Like many others of this period, Saint-Simon saw the study of society as a branch of physiology, since society is a type of organic phenomenon. Like the growth of any organic body, society is governed by natural laws of development which are to be revealed by scientific observation. As an *organism*, then, the study of society would involve investigation of social *organi*zation, with particular emphasis on the nature of growth, order, stability, and abnormal pathologies.[16]

Saint-Simon saw that such a viewpoint argued for a three-part program: (1) "a series of observations on the course of civilization" must be the starting point of the new science; (2) from these observations, the laws of social organization would be revealed; and (3) on the basis of these laws, humans could construct the best form of social organization. From a rather naive and ignorant view of history,[17] Saint-Simon developed a law of history in which ideas move from a polytheistic stage to a Christian theism, and then to a positivistic stage. In Saint-Simon's eye, each set of ideas in human history had been essential to maintaining social order, and with each transition, there was a period of crisis. The transition to positivism, therefore, revolved around the collapse of the feudal order, and its religious underpinnings, and the incomplete establishment of an industrial order in European societies, with its positivistic culture of science.

---

[15] Saint-Simon gave Condorcet explict credit for many of his ideas.

[16] The French word for organizations means both "organization" and "organic structure." Saint-Simon initially used the term to refer to the organic structure of humans and animals, and then extended it to apply to the structure of society.

[17] See, for an interesting commentary, Walter M. Simon, "Ignorance is Bliss: Saint-Simon and the Writing of History," *International Review of Philosophy* 14 nos. 3 and 4 (1960):357–83.

In analyzing this crisis in European society, Saint-Simon noted that scientific observations first penetrated astronomy, then physics and chemistry, and now physiology, including both biological and social organs.[18] It is with the application of the scientific method to social organization that the decline of the traditional order must give way to a new system of ideas. Transitional attempts to restore order, such as the "legal-metaphysical" ideas of the 18th century, must give way to a "terrestrial morality" based upon the ideas of positivism—that is, the use of observations to formulate, test, and implement the laws of social organization.[19]

Founded on a terrestrial morality, this new order was to be the result of a collaboration of scientists and industrialists. In Saint-Simon's early thought, scientists were to be the theoreticians, while industrialists were to be the engineers who performed many of the practical tasks of reconstructing society. Indeed, scientists and industrialists were to be the new priests for the secular religion of positivism. Saint-Simon's thought on social reorganization, however, was to undergo considerable change between 1814 and 1825, when he fell ill and died. Yet the broad contours of his thought were evident before Comte joined him in 1817. But the increasingly political and religious tone of Saint-Simon's writings were to alienate the young Comte, who saw the more detailed study of history and the movement of ideas as necessary for the formulation of the scientific laws of social organization. Ironically, Comte's own work was, later in his career, to take on the same religious fervor and extremes as Saint-Simon's last efforts.

Comte's early sociological work owed much to Saint-Simon's initial period of intellectual activity. The law of the three stages was to become even more prominent; the recognition of the successive penetration of positivism into astronomy, physics, chemistry, and biology was to be translated into a hierarchy of sciences, with physics at the bottom and sociology at the top; and the belief that sociology could be used to reconstruct industrial society was to be part of Comte's program. Comte was, however, to reject much of Saint-Simon's argument. In particular, he did not accept the study of social organization as a part of physiology; on the contrary, he was to argue that sociology is a distinct science with its own unique principles. In this vein, he also rejected Saint-Simon's belief that one law of all the universe could be discovered; instead, Comte recognized that each science has its own unique subject matter,

---

[18] See Peyton V. Lyon, "Saint-Simon and the Origins of Scientism and Historicism," *Canadian Journal of Economics and Political Science* 27 (February 1961):55–63.

[19] These ideas begin to overlap with Saint-Simon's collaboration with Comte.

which can be fully understood only in terms of its own laws and principles. But these objections aside, much of Comte's early work represented the elaboration of ideas developed and then abandoned by Saint-Simon as the aging scholar became increasingly absorbed in the task of reconstructing society.

Saint-Simon's Later Work. After 1814, Saint-Simon turned increasingly to political and economic commentary. He established and edited a series of periodicals which were used to propagate his ideas on the use of scientists and industrialists to reconstruct society.[20] Saint-Simon's terrestrial morality thus became elaborated into a plan for political, economic, and social reform.

The emphasis was on "terrestrial" because Saint-Simon had argued that the old supernatural basis for achieving order could no longer prevail in the positivistic age. Yet by his death, Saint-Simon recognized that a "religious sense" and "feeling" are essential to the social order. People must have faith and believe in a common set of ideas—a theme that was to mark all French sociology in the 19th century. The goal of terrestrial morality, therefore, is to create the functional equivalent of religion with positivism. Scientists and artists are to be the priests and the "spiritual" leaders,[21] while industrialists are to be the "temporal" leaders and to implement the spiritual program through the application of scientific methods to production and the organization of labor.

For Saint-Simon, terrestrial morality had a spiritual and a temporal component. Spiritual leaders give a sense of direction and a new religious sense to societal activity. Temporal leaders assure the organization of industry in ways that destroy hereditary privilege and give people an equal chance to realize their full potential. The key to Saint-Simon's program, then, was to use science as the functional equivalent of religion and to destroy the idle classes so that each person worked to his or her full potential. While Saint-Simon visualized considerable control of economic and social activity by government (in order to prevent exploi-

---

[20] All of these journals were short-lived, but they eventually gave Saint-Simon some degree of recognition as a publicist. These journals included *The Industry* (1816–18), *The Political* (1819), *The Organizer* (1819–20), *On the Industrial System* (1821–22, these were actually a series of brochures), *Disasters of Industry* (1823–24), and *Literary, Philosophic, and Industrial Opinions* (1825). From the latter, a portion on religion was published separately in book form as *New Christianity*, Saint-Simon's last major statement on science and the social order. Another important work of this last period was *On Social Organization*. In all of these works there is a clear change in tone and mood; Saint-Simon is now the activist rather than the detached scholar.

[21] Saint-Simon was initially anti-Christian, but with *New Christianity* he changed his position so that the new spiritual heads of society are "true Christians" in that they capture and advocate the implementation of the "Christian spirit."

tation of workers by the "idle"), he also believed that people should be free to realize their potential. Thus, Saint-Simon's doctrine is a mixture of free-enterprise economics and a tempered but heavy dose of governmental control (a point of emphasis that has often led commentators to place him in the socialist camp).

Saint-Simon's specific political, educational, and social programs were, even for his time, naive and utopian, but they nevertheless set into motion an entire intellectual movement after his death. Auguste Comte, however, was highly critical of Saint-Simon's later writings, and he waged intellectual war with the Saint-Simonians after 1825. While Comte wrote much of Saint-Simon's work between 1817 and 1824, Comte's contribution is recognizable because it is more academic and reasoned than is Saint-Simon's advocacy.[22] Yet as we will come to see, Comte's own work took on the same religious extremes as Saint-Simon's. Thus, Comte clearly accepted in delayed and subliminal form much of Saint-Simon's advocacy for the use of science as a functional substitute for religion.

But Comte's real contribution comes not from Saint-Simon's political commentary but from his systematization of Saint-Simon's early historical and scientific work, for it was out of this effort that sociology as a self-conscious discipline first emerged.

Liberal and Conservative Trends in Comte's Thought

We can see that Saint-Simon's work revealed both liberal and conservative elements. He advocated change and individual freedom, and yet, he desired that change produce a new social order and that individual freedom be subordinated to the collective interests of society. Comte's work also revealed this mixture of liberal and conservative elements in that the ideas of economic liberals, such as Adam Smith, and conservatives or traditionalists like de Maistre and de Bonald all played a part in Comte's intellectual scheme.

Liberal Elements in Comte's Thought. In England, Adam Smith had the most decisive effect on social thought in his advocacy of an economic system consisting of free and competitive markets. His *Wealth of Nations* (1776), however, is more than a simple model of early capitalism; the fifth book reveals a theory of moral sentiments and raises a question that was to concern Comte and later Durkheim: how can society be held together at the same time that the division of labor compartmen-

---

[22] For example, Comte wrote much of *The Organizer* (1819–20), especially the historical and scientific sections.

talizes individuals? For Smith, this dilemma was not insurmountable; whereas for French sociologists who had experienced the disintegrating effects of the Revolution and its aftermath, the splitting of society into diverse occupations posed a real intellectual problem. For French sociologists, the solution to this liberal dilemma involved the creation of a strong state that coordinated activities, preserved individual liberties, and fostered a set of unifying values and beliefs.

Comte also absorbed liberal ideas from the French followers of Adam Smith, particularly Jean-Baptiste Say who had seen the creative role played by entrepreneurs in the organization of other economic elements (land, labor, capital). Saint-Simon appears to have had a notion of entrepreneurship in mind in his proposal that the details of societal reconstruction be left to "industrialists," but Say's explicit formulation of the creative coordination of labor and capital by those with "industry" was to influence explicitly Comte's vision of how a better society could be created by entrepreneurs.[23]

Traditional Elements in Comte's Thought. Saint-Simon had attacked those who, in the turmoil of the Revolution, wanted to return to the old regime. Writing outside France, such Catholic scholars as de Maistre and de Bonald argued that the Revolution had destroyed the structural and moral fibre of society.[24] Religious authority had not been replaced by an alternative; the order achieved from the old social hierarchies had not been reestablished; and the cohesiveness provided by local communities and groups had been allowed to disintegrate. Both Saint-Simon and Comte, as well as an entire generation of French thinkers, agreed with the traditionalist's diagnosis of the problem, but disagreed with the proposed solution. For the traditionalists, the reinstatement of religion, hierarchy, and traditional local groupings (on the feudal model) was the solution.

Although Comte became an atheist in his early teens, he had been reared as a Catholic, and hence, he shared with many of the traditionalists a concern about order and spiritual unity. But Comte had also been influenced by the Enlightenment and liberal economic doctrines, and thus he saw that a return to the old order was not possible. Rather, it is necessary to create the functional equivalent of religious authority and to reestablish nonascriptive hierarchies and communities that would give people an equal chance to realize their full potential. For Comte,

---

[23] Naturally, Say and Saint-Simon did not explicitly use the concept "entrepreneurs." But they clearly grasped the essence of this economic function.

[24] See Robert A. Nisbet, *Tradition and Revolt* (New York: Random House, 1968).

then, the religious element is to be secular and positivistic; hierarchies are to be based on ability and achievement rather than on ascriptive privilege; and community is to be re-created through the solidarity of industrial groups. Comte was thus to give the traditionalist's concerns a liberal slant, although his last works were decidedly authoritarian in tone—perhaps revealing the extent to which the traditionalist's ideas had remained with Comte.

In reviewing the massive economic, political, and intellectual changes of the 18th century, as well as the specific thinkers who preceded Comte, we can see that the emergence of sociology was probably inevitable. Science had become too widespread to be suppressed by a return to religious orthodoxy, and the economic and political transformations of society under the impact of industrialization and urbanization were in need of explanation. All that was necessary was for one scholar to take that final step and seek to create a science of society. Drawing from the leads provided by his predecessors, Auguste Comte took this final step. And in so doing, he gave the science of society a name and a vision of how it should construct theory.

THE BASIC WORKS OF AUGUSTE COMTE

Auguste Comte's works can be divided into two distinct phases: (1) the early scientific stage between 1820 and 1842 and (2) the moralistic and quasi-religious phase which began in the later 1830s and culminated between 1851 and 1854. The scientific phase involved the publication of several important articles, and then between 1830 and 1842, the five volumes of *The Course of Positive Philosophy*[25] where the science of society was formally established. The second period in Comte's life is marked by personal tragedy and frustration; it was during this period that he wrote *System of Positive Polity*[26] which represented his moralistic view of how society should be reconstructed. Despite the excessive moral preachings of this work, its vision of science as the tool for reconstructing society was to be an important element in sociology's mission as seen by later generations of French sociologists.

---

[25] We will use and reference Harriet Martineau's condensation of the original manuscript. This condensation received Comte's approval and currently is the most readily available translation. Martineau changed the title and added useful margin notes. Our references will be to the 1896 edition of Martineau's original 1854 edition: Auguste Comte, *The Positive Philosophy of Auguste Comte*, vol. 1, 2, and 3, trans. and cond. H. Martineau (London: George Bell and Sons, 1896; originally published in 1854).

[26] Auguste Comte, *System of Positive Polity*, vols. 1, 2, 3, and 4 (New York: Burt Franklin, 1875; originally published 1851–54).

In our review of Comte's work, we will focus primarily on his purely sociological works—that is, on those from his scientific phase. We will, of course, not ignore his more moralistic efforts, but as we will come to appreciate, they did not contribute to the emergence of sociological theory. Thus, we will examine Comte's most important early essay, "Plan of the Scientific Operations Necessary for Reorganizing Society,"[27] which was written in 1822, just before his break with Saint-Simon. In this essay are the germs of both Comte's scientific and moralistic phases. Then, and for the bulk of our examination of Comte's work, we will explore Comte's greatest treatise, *The Course of Positive Philosophy*, which was written in installments between 1830 and 1842. And finally, we will briefly examine the moralistic thoughts of Comte in his *Course of Positive Philosophy*.

Comte's Early Essays

It is sometimes difficult to separate Comte's early essays from those of Saint-Simon, since the aging master often put his name on works penned by the young Comte. Yet the 1822 essay, "Plan of the Scientific Operations Necessary for Reorganizing Society," is clearly Comte's and represents the culmination of Comte's thinking while working under Saint-Simon. This essay also anticipates, and in fact presents an outline of, the entire Comtean scheme as it was to unfold over the succeeding decades.

In this essay, Comte argued that it is necessary to create a "positive science" based on the model of other sciences. This science would ultimately rest on empirical observations, but like all science, it would seek to formulate the laws governing the organization and movement of society—an idea implicit in Montesquieu's *The Spirit of Laws*. This new science was to be termed *social physics*. Once the laws of human organization have been discovered and formulated, then they can be used to direct society. Scientists of society are thus to be social prophets, indicating the course and direction of human organization.

Comte felt that one of the most basic laws of human organization is the "law of the three stages," a notion clearly borrowed from Turgot, Condorcet, and Saint-Simon. Such stages can be described as the "theological-military," "metaphysical-judicial," and "scientific-industrial." Each stage is typified by a particular "spirit"—a notion that first appeared

---

[27] Auguste Comte, "Plan of the Scientific Operations Necessary for Reorganizing Society," reprinted in Gertrud Lenzer, ed., *Auguste Comte and Positivism: The Essential Writings* (New York: Harper Torchbooks, 1975), pp. 9–69.

with Montesquieu and was elaborated upon by Condorcet—and by temporal or structural conditions. Thus, the theological-military stage is dominated by ideas that make reference to the supernatural, while being structured around slavery and the military. The metaphysical-judicial stage, which follows from the theological and represents a transition to the scientific, is typified by ideas that make reference to the fundamental essences of phenomena and by elaborate political and legal forms. And the scientific-industrial stage is dominated by the "positive philosophy of science" and industrial patterns of social organization.

There are several points of emphasis in this law that were to be given greater emphasis in Comte's later work. First, the social world reveals both cultural and structural dimensions, with the nature of culture or idea systems being dominant—an idea that probably was taken from Condorcet. Second, idea systems, and the corresponding structural arrangements that they produce, must reach their full development before the next stage of human evolution can come into being. Thus, one stage of development creates the necessary conditions for the next. Third, there is always a period of crisis and conflict as systems move from one stage to the next, since elements of the previous stage stand in conflict to the new, emerging elements of the next stage. Fourth, movement is always a kind of oscillation, for society "does not, properly speaking, advance in a straight line."

These aspects of the law of three stages led Comte to the conviction that cultural ideas about the world are subject to the dictates of this law. All ideas about the nature of the universe must move from a theological to scientific or "positivistic" stage. Yet some ideas about different aspects of the universe move more rapidly through the three stages than others. Indeed, only when all the other sciences—first astronomy, then physics, later chemistry, and finally physiology—have successively reached the positive stage will the conditions necessary for social physics have been met. And with the development of this last great science, it will become possible to reorganize society in terms of scientific principles rather than theological or metaphysical speculations.

Comte thus felt that the age of sociology had arrived. It was to be like Newton's physics, formulating the laws of the social universe. And with the development of these laws, the stage was set for the rational and scientific reorganization of society. There is much of Saint-Simon in this advocacy, but Comte felt that Saint-Simon was too impatient in his desire to reorganize society without the proper scientific foundation. The result was Comte's *Course of Positive Philosophy* which sought to lay the necessary intellectual foundation for the science of society.

Comte's *Course of Positive Philosophy*

Comte's *Course of Positive Philosophy* is more noteworthy for its advocacy of a science of society than its substantive contribution to understanding how patterns of social organization are created, maintained, and changed. *Positive Philosophy* more nearly represents a vision of what sociology can become than a well-focused set of theoretical principles. In reviewing this great work, then, we will devote most of our attention to how Comte defined sociology and on how he thought it should be developed. Accordingly, we will divide our discussion into the following sections: (1) Comte's view of sociological theory, (2) Comte's formulation of sociological methods, (3) Comte's organization of sociology, and (4) Comte's advocacy of sociology.

Comte's View of Sociological Theory. As a descendant of the French Enlightenment, Comte was impressed, as were many of the philosophes, with the Newtonian revolution. And thus, Comte argued for a view of sociological theory that, in modern times, we would call axiomatic. All phenomena are subject to invariable natural laws and it is the task of sociologists to use their observations to uncover the laws governing the social universe, in much the same way as Newton had formulated the law of gravity. As Comte emphasized in the opening pages of *Positive Philosophy:*

> The first characteristic of Positive Philosophy is that it regards all phenomena as subject to invariable natural *Laws.* Our business is,—seeing how vain is any research into what are called *Causes,* whether first or final,— to pursue an accurate discovery of these Laws, with a view to reducing them to the smallest possible number. By speculating upon causes, we could solve no difficulty about origin and purpose. Our real business is to analyse accurately the circumstances of phenomena, and to connect them by the natural relations of succession and resemblance. The best illustration of this is in the case of the doctrine of Gravitation.[28]

There are several points of great importance in this view of sociological theory. First, sociological theory is not to be concerned with causes per se, but rather with the laws that describe the basic and fundamental relations of properties in the social world. The original vision of sociological theory, then, was more *axiomatic* than *causal process* (to use the terms of the last chapter). Currently, causal process forms of theory dominate sociology, a trend that would have dismayed Comte. Second, there is an explicit rejection of "final causes"—that is, analysis of the

---

[28] Comte, *Positive Philosophy,* vol. 1, pp. 5–6 (emphasis in original).

results of a particular phenomena for the social whole. There is a certain irony in this disavowal, since Comte's more substantive work was to help found sociological functionalism—a mode of analysis that often examines the functions or final causes of phenomena. Third, there is a clear recognition that the goal of sociological activity is to reduce the number of theoretical principles by seeking only the most abstract and only those that pertain to understanding fundamental properties of the social world—a point of emphasis which, unfortunately, has been lost in modern sociology's concern with introducing multiple and manifold variables into theoretical activity. Comte thus held a vision of sociological theory as based upon the model of the natural sciences, particularly the physics of his time. And it is for this reason that Comte preferred the term *social physics* to *sociology*.[29]

The laws of social organization and change, Comte felt, will be discovered, refined, and verified through a constant interplay between theory and empirical organization. For, as Comte observed in the opening pages of *Positive Philosophy*, "if it is true that every theory must be based upon observed facts, it is equally true that facts cannot be observed without the guidance of some theory."[30] But Comte in later pages became even more assertive and argued that what we might now term *raw empiricism* runs counter to the goals of science. For Comte saw strict empiricism as an absolute hindrance to the development of sociological theory. In a passage that sounds distinctly modern, while offering some good advice, Comte noted:

> The next great hindrance to the use of observation is the empiricism which is introduced into it by those who, in the name of impartiality, would interdict the use of any theory whatever. No other dogma could be more thoroughly irreconcilable with the spirit of the positive philosophy. . . . No real observation of any kind of phenomena is possible, except in as far as it is first directed, and finally interpreted, by some theory.[31]

---

[29] In Comte's time, the term *physics* meant to study the "nature of" phenomena. It was not merely the term for a particular branch of natural science. Hence, Comte's use of the label *social physics* had a double meaning: to study the "nature of" social phenomena and to do so along the lines of the natural sciences. Comte abandoned the term *social physics* when he realized that the same term was being used by the Belgian statistician Adolphe Quetelet. Comte was outraged that his original label for sociology had been used in ways that ran decidedly counter to his vision of theory. Ironically, sociology has become more like Quetelet's vision of social physics, with its emphasis on the normal curve and statistical manipulations, than Comte's notion of social physics as the search for the abstract laws of human organization—an unfortunate turn of events.

[30] Comte, *Positive Philosophy*, vol. 1, p. 4.

[31] Ibid., vol. 2, p. 242.

And, as he went on to conclude:

> Hence it is clear that, scientifically speaking, all isolated, empirical observation is idle, and even radically uncertain; that science can use only those observations which are connected, at least hypothetically, with some law.[32]

For Comte, then, the goal of sociology is to seek to develop abstract theoretical principles. Observations of the empirical world must be guided by such principles, with an eye to testing abstract principles against the empirical facts. Empirical observations that are conducted without this goal in mind are not useful in science. Theoretical explanation of empirical events thus involves seeing how they are connected to each other in lawlike ways. For social science "endeavors to discover . . . the general relations which connect all social phenomena: and each of them is *explained,* in the scientific sense of the word, when it has been connected with the whole of the existing situation."[33]

Comte held a somewhat ambiguous view of how such an abstract science should be "used" in the practical world of everyday affairs. He clearly intended that sociology must initially establish a firm theoretical foundation before efforts to use the laws of sociology for social engineering. In volume 1 of *Positive Philosophy,* Comte stressed:

> We must distinguish between the two classes of Natural science;—the abstract or general, which have for their object the discovery of the laws which regulate phenomena in all conceivable cases; and the concrete, particular, or descriptive, which are sometimes called Natural sciences in a restricted sense, whose function it is to apply these laws to the actual history of existing beings. The first are fundamental; and our business is with them alone; as the second are derived, and however important, they do not rise to the rank of our subjects of contemplation.[34]

In Comte's eye, sociology must not allow its scientific mission to be confounded by empirical descriptions or by an excessive concern with a desire to manipulate events. Yet, once sociology is well established as a theoretical science, its laws can be used to "modify" events in the empirical world. Indeed, such was to be the historic mission of social physics. And as Comte's later works were to testify, he took this mission seriously, and at times to extremes. But Comte's early work is filled with more reasoned arguments for using laws of social organization and change as tools for creating a variety of new social arrangements. In

---

[32] Ibid., vol. 2, p. 243.

[33] Ibid., vol. 2, p. 240 (emphasis in original).

[34] Ibid., vol. 1, p. 23.

fact, Comte stressed that the complexity of social phenomena give them more variation than either physical or biological phenomena, and hence, it would be possible to use the laws of social organization and change to modify empirical events in a variety of directions.[35]

In sum, then, Comte believed that sociology could be modeled after the natural sciences. It could seek and discover the fundamental properties and relations of the social universe, and like the other sciences, it could express these in a small number of abstract principles. Observations of empirical events could be used to generate, confirm, and modify sociology's laws. And once a well-developed set of laws had become formulated, they could be used as tools or instruments to modify the social world.

Comte's Formulation of Sociological Methods.   Comte was the first social thinker to take seriously methodological questions—that is, how are facts about the social world to be gathered and used to develop, as well as to test, theoretical principles? Comte advocated the use of four methods in the new science of social physics: (1) observation, (2) experimentation, (3) comparison, and (4) historical analysis.[36] Each of these is discussed below.

Observation.   For Comte, positivism is based upon use of the senses to observe *social facts*—a term that the next great French theorist, Émile Durkheim, was to make the center of his sociology (see Chapters 11 to 13). But much of Comte's discussion of observation involves arguments for the "subordination of Observation to the statical and dynamical laws of phenomena"[37] rather than a statement on the procedures by which unbiased observations are to be conducted. Comte simply argued that observation of empirical facts, when unguided by theory, will prove useless in the development of science. Yet Comte must be given credit for firmly establishing sociology as a science of social facts, thereby liberating thought from the debilitating realm of morals and metaphysical speculation.

Experimentation.   Comte recognized that artificial experimentation with whole societies, and other social phenomena, is impractical and often impossible. But he noted that natural experimentation frequently "takes place whenever the regular course of the phenomenon is interfered with in any determinate manner."[38] In particular, Comte thought that, much as is the case in biology, pathological events allow "the true equiva-

---

[35] See, for example, the following passages in ibid., vol. 2, pp. 217, 266, 234, 235, and 238.

[36] Ibid., vol. 2, pp. 241–57.

[37] Ibid., p. 245

[38] Ibid., p. 246.

lent of pure experimentation" in that they introduce an artificial condition and allow investigators to see normal processes reasserting themselves in the face of the pathological condition. Much as the biologist can learn about normal bodily functioning from the study of disease, so social physicists can learn about the normal processes of society from the study of pathological cases. This view of sociological experiments was to inspire later thinkers, such as Durkheim, and in many ways, it still guides the modern rationale for the study of deviance. Thus, while Comte's view of "natural experimentation" was certainly deficient in terms of the logic of the experimental method, it was nonetheless to fascinate subsequent generations of scholars.

Comparison. Just as comparative analysis in biology has proven useful, so the comparison of social forms with those of lower animals, with coexisting states, and with past systems, can generate considerable insight into the operation of these social forms. By comparing elements that are present and absent, and similar or dissimilar, knowledge about the fundamental properties of the social world can be achieved.

Historical Methods. Comte saw this procedure as a potential method, since he originally classified it as a variation of the comparative method (that is, comparing the present with the past). But his "law of the three stages" indicates the importance of a broad historical process. Comte thought that, ultimately, the laws of social dynamics could be developed only with careful observations of the historical movement of societies.

In sum, then, Comte saw four basic methods as appropriate to sociological analysis. His formulation of the methods is, of course, quite deficient by modern standards. We should recognize, however, that prior to Comte little attention had been paid to how social facts were to be collected. And thus, while the specifics of Comte's methodological proposals are not always useful, their spirit and intent were most important. Social physics was, in Comte's vision, to be a theoretical science capable of formulating and testing the laws of social organization and change. Comte's formulation of sociology's methods added increased credibility to this claim.

Comte's Organization of Sociology. Much as Saint-Simon had emphasized, Comte saw sociology as an extension of the study of "organisms" in biology to "social organs." Hence, sociology was to be the study of social *organization.* This emphasis forces the recognition that society is an "organic whole" whose components stand in relation to each other. To study these parts in isolation is to violate the essence of social organization and to compartmentalize inquiry artificially. For, as Comte emphasized, "there can be no scientific study of society, either in its conditions or its movements, if it is separated into portions, and its divisions are studied apart."[39]

Implicit in this emphasis is a mode of analysis that was later to become known as *functionalism*. As the prestige of biology grew in the 19th century, attempts at linking sociological analysis to the respected biological sciences increased. Eventually, scholars were to begin asking: What is the function of a structure for the body social? That is, what does a structure "do for" the social whole? Comte implicitly asked such questions, and even offered explicit analogies that were to encourage subsequent organismic analogizing. For example, his concern with social pathology revealing the normal operation of society is but one illustration of a biological mode of reasoning. And in his later work, Comte was to argue explicitly in biological terms when he viewed various structures as analogous to "elements, tissues, and organs" of biological organisms.[40] But in his early works, this organismic analogizing is limited to dividing social physics into "statical" and "dynamical" analysis.

This division, we suspect, represents a merger of Comte's efforts to build sociology on biology and to retain his heritage from the French Enlightenment. As a scholar who was writing in the tumultuous aftermath of the French Revolution, he was concerned with order and stability. The order of biological organisms, with their interdependent parts and processes of self-maintenance, offered to Comte a vision of how social order should be constructed. Yet the Enlightenment had emphasized "progress" and movement of social systems, holding out the vision of better things to come. It is for this reason that Comte was led to emphasize that "ideas of Order and Progress are, in Social Physics, as rigorously inseparable as the ideas of Organization and Life in Biology: from whence indeed they are, in a scientific view, evidently derived."[41] And thus, Comte divided sociology into (1) social statics (the study of social order) and (2) social dynamics (the study of social progress and change). These two aspects of Comte's sociology are explored in more detail below.

1. For Comte, social statics is the study of social structure, its elements, and their relations. He first analyzed "individuals" as elements

---

[39] Ibid., p. 225.

[40] See, in particular, his *System of Positive Polity*, vol. 2, pp. 221–76 on "The Social Organism."

[41] *Positive Philosophy*, vol. 2, p. 141.

in the analysis of social structure. Generally, Comte viewed the individual as a series of capacities and needs, some of which are innate, while others are acquired through participation in society.[42] But Comte did not view the individual as a "true social unit"; indeed, he relegated the study of the individual to biology—an unfortunate oversight since it denied the legitimacy of psychology as a distinct social science. The most basic social unit, Comte argued, is "the family." It is the most elementary unit, from which all other social units ultimately evolved:

> As every system must be composed of elements of the same nature with itself, the scientific spirit forbids us to regard society as composed of individuals. The true social unit is certainly the family,—reduced, if necessary, to the elementary couple which forms its basis. This consideration implies more than the physiological truth that families becomes tribes, and tribes become nations: so that the whole human race might be conceived of as the gradual development of a single family. . . . There is a political point of view from which also we must consider this elementary idea, inasmuch as the family presents the true germ of the various characteristics of the social organism.[43]

Comte thus took a strong sociologistic position in that social structures cannot be reduced to the properties of individuals. Rather, social structures are composed of other structures and can only be understood in terms of the properties of, and relations among, these other structures. Comte's analysis of the family then moves to descriptions of its structure, first the sexual division of labor and then the parental relation. The specifics of Comte's analysis are not important, since they are flawed and inaccurate. Far more important is the view of structure that he implied: social structures are comprised of substructures and develop from the elaboration of simpler structures.

After establishing this basic point, Comte moved to the analysis of societal social structures. His opening remarks reveal his debt to biological analysis, and the functional orientation it was to inspire:

> The main cause of the superiority of the social to the individual organism is, according to an established law, the more marked is the specialization of the various functions fulfilled by organs more and more distinct, but interconnected; so that unity of aim is more and more combined with diversity of means.[44]

---

[42] See ibid., pp. 275–81.

[43] Ibid., pp. 280–81.

[44] Ibid., p. 289.

Thus, as social systems develop, they become increasingly differentiated, and yet, like all organisms, they maintain their integration. This view of social structure led Comte to the problem that Adam Smith had originally suggested with such force: How is integration among parts maintained in the face of increasing differentiation of functions? This question was to occupy French sociology in the 19th century, culminating in Émile Durkheim's theoretical formulations (see Chapters 15, 16, and 17). As Comte emphasized:

> If the separation of social functions develops a useful spirit of detail, on the one hand, it tends on the other, to extinguish or to restrict what we may call the aggregate or general spirit. In the same way, in moral relations, while each is in close dependence on the mass, he is drawn away from it by the expansion of his special activity, constantly recalling him to his private interest, which he but very dimly perceives to be related to the public.[45]

Comte's proposed solution to this problem reveals much about how he viewed the maintenance of social structure. First, the potentially disintegrating impact of social differentiation is countered by the centralization of power in government, which will then maintain fluid coordination among system parts. Second, the actions of government must be more than "material"; they must also be "intellectual and moral."[46] Hence, human social organization is maintained by *(a)* mutual dependence of system parts on each other, *(b)* centralization of authority to coordinate exchanges of parts, and *(c)* the development of a common morality or spirit among members of a population. To the extent that differentiating systems cannot meet these conditions, pathological states are likely to occur.

In presenting this analysis, Comte felt that he had uncovered several laws of social statics, since he believed that differentiation, centralization of power, and development of a common morality are fundamentally related to the maintenance of the social order. While Comte did not carry his analysis far, he presented Durkheim with both the basic question and the broad contours of the answer.

2.   Comte appeared far more interested in social dynamics than statics, for "the dynamical view is not only the more interesting . . . , but the more marked in its philosophical character, from its being more distinguished from biology by the master-thought of continuous progress,

---

[45] Ibid., p. 293.
[46] Ibid., p. 294.

or rather of the gradual development of humanity."[47] Social dynamics studies the "laws of succession" or the patterns of change in social systems over time. It is in this context that Comte formulated the details of his law of the three stages in which idea systems, and their corresponding social structural arrangements, pass through three stages: *(a)* the theological, *(b)* the metaphysical, and *(c)* the positivistic. The basic cultural and structural features of these stages are summarized in Table 2–1:

TABLE 2–1
Comte's "Law of the Three Stages"

System	Stages		
	Theological	*Metaphysical*	*Positivistic*
Cultural (moral) system:			
a. Nature of ideas	Ideas focused on nonempirical forces, spirits, and beings in the supernatural realm.	Ideas focused on the essences of phenomena and rejection of appeals to supernatural.	Ideas developed from observation and constrained by the scientific method; rejection of speculation not based upon observation of empirical facts.
b. Spiritual leaders	Priests	Philosophers	Scientists
Structural (temporal) system:			
a. Most prominent units ...	Kinship	State	Industry
b. Basis of integration	Attachment to small groups and religious spirit.	Control by state, military, and law	Mutual dependence; coordination of functions by state; and general spirit.

Table 2–1 ignores many details that have little relevance to theory.[48] But the table communicates, in a rough fashion, Comte's view of the laws of succession. Several points of amplification on the contents of Table 2–1 should be made. First, each stage sets the conditions for the next. For example, without efforts at explanation in terms of references to the supernatural, subsequent efforts at more refined explanations would not have been possible; or without kinship systems, subsequent

---

[47] Ibid., p. 227.

[48] Most of ibid., vol. 3, is devoted to the analysis of the three stages. For a more abbreviated overview, see vol. 2, pp. 304–33.

political, legal, and military development would not have occurred, and the modern division of labor would not have been possible. Second, the course of evolution is additive: new ideas and structural arrangements are added to, and built upon, the old. For instance, kinship does not disappear, nor do references to the supernatural. They are first supplemented, and then dominated, by new social and cultural arrangements. Third, during the transition from one stage to the next, elements of the preceding stage, on the one hand, and the emerging stage, on the other, come into conflict, creating a period of anarchy and turmoil. Fourth, the metaphysical stage is a transitional stage, operating as a bridge between theological speculation and positivistic philosophy. Fifth, the nature of cultural ideas determines the kinds of social structural (temporal) arrangements, circumscribing what social arrangements are possible. And sixth, with the advent of the positivistic stage, true understanding of how society operates is possible, allowing for the manipulation of society in accordance with the laws of statics and dynamics.

While societies must eventually pass through these three stages, they do so at different rates. Probably the most important of the variable empirical conditions influencing the rate of societal succession is population size and density—an idea taken from Montesquieu and later refined by Durkheim. Thus, Comte felt that he had discovered the basic law of social dynamics in his analysis of the three stages, and coupled with the laws of statics, a positivistic science of society—that is, social physics or sociology—would allow for the reorganization of the tumultuous, transitional, and conflictual world of the early 19th century.

Comte's Advocacy of Sociology. Comte's *Positive Philosophy* can be viewed as a long and elaborate advocacy for a science of society. For most of the five volumes involve a review of the development of other sciences, with an eye toward showing how sociology represents the culmination of positivism. As the title, *Positive Philosophy*, underscores, Comte was laying a philosophical foundation and justification for all science, and then using this foundation as a means for supporting sociology as a true science. Comte's advocacy takes two related forms: (1) to view sociology as the inevitable product of the "law of the three stages" and (2) to view sociology as the "queen science," standing at the top of a hierarchy of sciences. These two interrelated forms of advocacy went a long way toward legitimating sociology in the eyes of a hostile intellectual world and should, therefore, be examined briefly.

Comte saw all idea systems as passing through the theological and metaphysical stages, and then moving into the final positivistic stage. Ideas about all phenomena must pass through these stages, with each stage setting the conditions for the next and with considerable intellectual turmoil during the transition from one stage to the next. Ideas about various phenomena, however, do not pass through these stages at the same rate, and in fact, a positivistic stage in thought about one realm of the universe must often be reached before ideas about other realms can progress to the positivistic stage. As the opening pages of *Positive Philosophy* emphasize:

> We must bear in mind that the different kinds of our knowledge have passed through the three stages of progress at different rates, and have not therefore arrived at the same time. The rate of advance depends upon the nature of knowledge in question, so distinctly that, as we shall see hereafter, this consideration constitutes an accessory to the fundamental law of progress. Any kind of knowledge reaches the positive stage in proportion to its generality, simplicity, and independence of other departments.[49]

Thus, thought about the physical universe reached the positive stage before conceptions of the organic world, since the inorganic world is simpler and since organic phenomena are built from inorganic phenomena. In Comte's view, then, astronomy was the first science to reach the positivistic stage; then came physics, next came chemistry, and after these three had reached the positivistic (scientific) stage, then thought about organic phenomena could become more positivistic. The first organic science to move from the metaphysical to positivistic stage was biology or physiology. And with biology now a positivistic doctrine, sociology could move away from the metaphysical speculations of the 17th and 18th centuries (and the residues of earlier theological thought) toward a positivistic mode of thought.

Sociology has been the last to emerge, Comte argued, because it is the most complex and because it has had to wait for the other basic sciences to reach the positivistic stage. For the time, such a line of argument represented a brilliant advocacy for a separate science of society, while at the same time it justified the lack of scientific rigor in social thought when compared to the other sciences. Moreover, while dependent upon, and derivative of, evolutionary advances in the other sciences, sociology would study phenomena that distinguish it from the lower inorganic phenomena as well as the higher organic science of biology. Although it is one of the organic sciences, sociology will be independent and study phenomena that "exhibit, in even a higher degree, the complex-

---

[49] Ibid., vol. 1, pp. 6–7.

ity, specialization, and personality which distinguish the higher phenomena of the individual life."[50]

In this argument is the notion of a "hierarchy of the sciences," with
sociology at the top of the hierarchy.[51] This notion of hierarchy represents
yet another way to legitimate sociological inquiry. For on the one hand,
it offered an explanation for why sociology was not as developed as
the other, highly respected, sciences, while on the other hand it placed
sociology in a highly favorable place (at the top of a hierarchy) in relation
to the other "positive sciences." For if sociology could be viewed as
the culmination of a long evolutionary process and as the quiescence
of the positive sciences, its legitimacy could not be questioned. Such
was Comte's goal, and while he was only marginally successful in his
efforts, he was the first to see clearly that sociology could be like the
other sciences and that it would be only a matter of time until the
old theological and metaphysical residues of earlier social thought would
be cast aside in favor of a true science of society. This advocacy, which
takes up the majority of pages in *Positive Philosophy*, rightly assures
Comte's claim to being the "founder of sociological theory."

A Note on Comte's *System of Positive Polity*

Many events converged to change the direction of Comte's thought
in his later career. The frustration over not receiving an academic appointment and the death of his first love, Clothilde de Vaux, were probably
the most significant forces that took Comte away from the search for
the laws of the social universe toward the religion of humanity. The
four volumes of *The System of Positive Polity*,[52] published between 1851
and 1854, still contain many of the old appeals to a scientific sociology,
but the real intent of the book is to reconstruct society on the basis
of a new religious spirit. In much the same way as his early mentor,
Saint-Simon, basked in the glory of a quasi-religious movement in his
late years, so now Comte proclaimed himself "The Founder of Universal
Religion" and as "The Great Priest of Humanity."

Comte's early essays anticipated both the concern for creating a unifying spirit for the maintenance of social order as well as the desire to

---

[50] Ibid., vol. 2, p. 258.

[51] The hierarchy, in descending order, is sociology, physiology, chemistry, physics,
and astronomy. Comte added mathematics at the bottom, since ultimately all sciences
are built from mathematical reasoning.

[52] Comte, *System of Positive Polity.*

reconstruct and reorganize society. But the emotional and often irrational extremes of *Positive Polity* mark it as a religious doctrine, more than a piece of science. Comte established himself as the High Priest of the new religion after the publication of *Positive Polity*, and he began an entirely new life:[53] he sent decrees to his disciples; he established churches; he advocated love as the unifying force of humanity; he sought to counsel political leaders in the manner of old theologians; and he preached to all who would listen on the virtues of the new religion. In *Positive Polity* can even be found a calendar of rituals to be performed during the year by members of the Universal Religion of Humanity.

Positive Polity does, nonetheless, contain some sociological insights. Yet we have concentrated on *Positive Philosophy* because these same insights are stated less ambiguously and without moralistic preachings from Comte, the new High Priest of Humanity.

COMTE IN RETROSPECT

For all of his advocacy of a science of society and for his insistence that sociology seek the laws of social organization, Comte himself did not develop any true sociological laws. He thought that his law of the three stages was the equivalent of Newton's law of gravitation for the understanding of social dynamics, and he implicitly argued that the proposed relationship between structural differentiation, on the one hand, and integration in terms of interdependence and unifying cultural symbols, on the other, captured the fundamental nature of social statics. Yet Comte's law of the three stages is more of an historical description than a law, and his views on social statics, while promising, are not well developed.

Comte's contribution thus resides not so much in his actual theoretical principles as in the vision of social science that his work represented. Others, such as Spencer in England and later Durkheim in France, were to build upon the suggestive leads in Comte's analysis of statics and dynamics. And most important, Comte provided an image of what sociology could be; although Comte's work was rejected in his later years, it resurfaced in the last decades of the 19th century and stimulated a burst of sociological activity. For whatever the flaws in Comte's grand scheme, he had the right vision of what a science of society should be. And while it remained for others to execute this vision, Comte

---

[53] See Coser, *Masters of Sociological Thought*, pp. 29–41, for a more detailed summary of Comte's personal life as it relates to the *System of Positive Polity.*

understood better than his contemporaries and better than many scholars today that a science of society must seek the fundamental principles by which patterns of social organization are created, maintained, and changed.

It is for this reason, then, that sociological theory first emerged with Auguste Comte. For although humans had thought about their condition for centuries, it was Comte who explicitly recognized the need for, and nature of, sociological theory. It is in this recognition that Comte's great contribution resides.

3

HERBERT SPENCER I: THE INTELLECTUAL ORIGINS OF HIS THOUGHT

SPENCER: THE FORGOTTEN GIANT

Herbert Spencer is one of sociology's most maligned early thinkers.[1] This situation is both curious and astonishing in light of the fact that Spencer was one of the dominant intellectual figures of the 19th century in both Europe and America. Why is it that Spencer has fallen into such disrepute? The main reason for Spencer's continued decline, especially at a time when Marx, Weber, Durkheim, Simmel, and other figures of the 19th and early 20th centuries have enjoyed a resurgence, results from a simple tendency: selective and prejudiced reading or opinionated nonreading. A typical contemporary commentary on Spencer might read: Herbert Spencer, the first self-conscious English sociologist, advocated a sociological perspective that supported the dominant political ideology of free trade and enterprise. He naively assumed that "society was like an organism" and developed a sociology that saw each institution as having its "function" in the "body social"—thereby propagating a conservative ideology and legitimating the status quo. What is even worse, Spencer coined the phrase "survival of the fittest" to describe the normal state of relations within and between societies—thus making it seem

---

[1] For some exceptions to this blanket tendency, see Stanislaw Andreski, "Introductory Essay," in his *Herbert Spencer: Structure, Function, and Evolution* (London: Michael Joseph, 1971) and "Introduction" in his edited version of Spencer's *Principles of Sociology* (Hamden, Conn.: Archon Books, 1909); Robert L. Carneiro, "Editor's Introduction" in his *The Evolution of Society* (Chicago: University of Chicago Press, 1967); J. D. Y. Peel, "Introduction," in his *Herbert Spencer on Social Evolution* (Chicago: University of Chicago Press, 1972); and Jay Rumney, *Herbert Spencer's Sociology* (New York: Atherton Press, 1966).

right that the elite of a society should possess privilege and that some societies should conquer others.

Even if we recognize that the above scenario is extreme, it probably corresponds to most sociologists' vague sense of Spencerian sociology. These prejudices are indeed unfortunate, for Spencer offered sociological theory some critical insights, many of which became lost and had to be rediscovered. There can be no doubt, of course, that by today's political yardstick Spencer would be conservative (although by 19th-century canons, he was a liberal). Nor is it easy to live with many of his moral preachings. Yet it would not be difficult to find similarly naive and outrageously inaccurate statements in Marx, Weber, and Durkheim. By any estimation, for example, Weber was a nationalistic supporter of German imperialism.[2] Marx's statements on primitive communism are, at best, embarrassing. Durkheim's search for the origins of religion, incest taboos, and human thought are equally painful to read.[3] As is proper, none of these figures is condemned for what they said that was wrong. Indeed, their important insights are still used to stimulate the sociological imagination. In contrast, Herbert Spencer's insights are virtually ignored because of what he said that was wrong. This tendency is indeed an intellectual tragedy, for as much as any other thinker of the last century, Spencer provided sociology with some of its basic principles of social organization.

In our analysis of Spencer's sociology, we will emphasize his enduring ideas, although it will be necessary to mention briefly those ideas for which Spencer has been condemned. One of the immediate problems in analyzing Spencer's work is its scope and volume. Spencer regarded himself as a philosopher who sought to uncover principles of the universe or cosmos. He wrote basic treatises in biology and psychology, with his work in sociology being only part of a much larger intellectual scheme. Moreover, Spencer saw himself as a moral philosopher who felt that the laws of the universe dictated certain types of social arrangements. Thus Spencer, whose original vocation was engineering, became a scientific biologist, psychologist, and sociologist who never abandoned a particular moral philosophy. And in fact, he used his insights as a scientist to buttress his moral arguments.

Our goal in these three chapters on Spencer is to understand his sociology and to see how it fits into the broader scientific and philosophic

---

[2] See, for example, Maurice Zeitlin, *Ideology and the Development of Sociological Theory* (Englewood Cliffs, N.J.: Prentice-Hall, 1968).

[3] See ibid., chap. 16.

scheme that he developed. We will begin in this chapter with a brief overview of the origins of Spencer's ideas; then, in the next chapter, we will examine the corpus of his sociological works; and finally, in the third chapter, we will delineate his models and principles, many of which can still inform current theorizing.

Spencer received only a few months of formal education outside of his family. It was Spencer's father and uncle who trained him in mathematics, engineering, and science. Indeed, Spencer's first publications were engineering articles, and it was not until 1842 that his first nonengineering article, on the "proper" sphere of government, appeared. By 1848, Spencer had abandoned engineering and assumed a full-time position on the newspaper *The Economist*. The influences on Spencer's thinking during this period are not clear, even though he wrote a somewhat self-serving autobiography where some of the influences are indicated.[4] But because so much of Spencer's training was private and because his autobiography was written so late and defensively, it is hard to denote the precise origins of Spencer's early thought. At least three general lines of influence can be isolated: (1) the political economy of 19th-century England, (2) the scientific milieu of Spencer's England, and (3) the sociology of Auguste Comte. Each of these is examined below.

THE POLITICAL ECONOMY OF 19TH-CENTURY ENGLAND

In contrast to France, where decades of political turmoil had created an overconcern for collective unity, England remained comparatively tranquil. As the first society to industrialize, England enjoyed considerable prosperity under early capitalism. Open markets and competition appeared to be an avenue for increased productivity and prosperity. It is not surprising, therefore, that social thought in England was dominated by ideological beliefs in the efficiency and moral correctness of free and unbridled competition not only in the market place but in other realms as well.[5]

In his philosophic works, Spencer advocated a laissez-faire doctrine. Individuals should be allowed to pursue their interests and to seek happi-

---

[4] Herbert Spencer, *An Autobiography* (London: Watts & Co., 1926).

[5] The major legitimating work in this context was the first volume of Adam Smith's *An Inquiry into the Nature and Causes of the Wealth of Nations* (London: Cadell and Davies, 1805).

ness as long as they do not infringe upon other's right to do so. Government should be restrained and should not regulate the pursuits of individuals. And much like Adam Smith, Spencer assumed a kind of "invisible hand of order" as emerging to maintain a society of self-seeking individuals. Most of Spencer's early essays, and his first book on *Social Statics*, represent adaptations of laissez-faire economics. But Spencer's social and economic philosophy was to be supplemented by more scientific analyses in biology.

THE SCIENTIFIC MILIEU OF SPENCER'S ENGLAND

Spencer's early training with his father and uncle was in mathematics and science. More important, his informal contacts as a free-lance intellectual were with scientists such as Huxley, Hooker, Tyndall, and even Darwin. Indeed, Spencer read less than he listened, for it is clear that he acquired an enormous breadth of knowledge by talking with the foremost scientists of his time. Biographers have frequently commented on the lack of books in Spencer's library, especially for a scholar who wrote with such insight in several different disciplines.[6] Yet, despite Spencer's reliance upon informal contacts with fellow scientists, there are several key works in biology and physics that had considerable impact on his thought.

Influences from Biology

In 1864 Spencer wrote the first volume of his *Principles of Biology*, which was used as a text at Oxford and which represented one of the most advanced treatises on biological knowledge.[7] Later, as we will see,

---

[6] For example, see Hugh Elliot, *Herbert Spencer* (New York: Henry Holt, 1917); and David Duncan, *Life and Letters of Herbert Spencer* (London: Methuen, 1908). Lewis Coser, *Masters of Sociological Thought* (New York: Harcourt Brace Jovanovich, 1977) has best summarized Spencer's relationship with his contemporaries when he notes that from informal conversations, Spencer was supplied "with scientific facts that he used so greedily as building blocks for his theories. Spencer absorbed his science to a large extent as if through osmosis, through critical discussions and interchanges with his scientific friends and associates" (p. 110).

[7] In *Principles of Biology* (New York: D. Appleton, 1864–67), Spencer formulated some original laws of biology that still stand today. For example, his formulation of the relationship among growth, size, and structure are axiomatic in biology today. Yet few biologists are aware that it was Spencer, the engineer turned scientist, who formulated the law that among regularly shaped bodies, surface area increases as the square of the linear dimensions, while volume increases as the cube of these dimensions—hence requiring new structural arrangements to support and nourish larger bodies.

Spencer sought to apply the laws of biology to "super-organic bodies,"[8] revealing the extent to which biological knowledge influenced Spencer's more purely sociological formulations. Spencer credited three sources for some of the critical insights which he was later to apply to social phenomena: (1) Thomas Malthus, (2) Von Baer, and (3) Charles Darwin.

1. Spencer was profoundly influenced by Thomas Mathus' *Essay on Population.* (Mathus, of course, was not a biologist, but his work had an influence in this sphere and, hence, is discussed in this section.) In this work, Malthus had emphasized that the geometric growth of population would create conditions favorable to conflict, starvation, pestilence, disease, and death. Indeed, Malthus argued that populations grow until "checked" by the "four horsemen": war, pestilence, famine, and disease.

Spencer reached a much less pessimistic conclusion than Malthus, for the competition and struggle that ensues from population growth would, Spencer believed, lead to the "survival of the fittest," and hence, to the elevation of society and "the races." Such a vision corresponded, of course, to Spencer's laissez-faire bias and allowed him to view free and open competition not just as good economic policy but as a fundamental "law of the organic universe."[9] In addition to these ideological uses of Malthus's ideas, the notion of competition and struggle became central to Spencer's more formal sociology. For he saw evolution of societies as the result of territorial and political conflicts. And in fact, he was one of the first sociologists to understand fully the significance of war and conflict on the internal patterns of social organization of a society.

2. Spencer was also influenced by Harvey's embryological studies as well as by Milne-Edward's work, which had borrowed from social thought the term, *the physiological division of labor.* Indeed, as Spencer so ably emphasized, biologists had often borrowed from social discourse terms that he was merely borrowing back and applying in a more refined manner to the "super-organic realm." Yet, the credit for recognizing that biological forms develop from undifferentiated, embryologic forms to highly differentiated structures, revealing a physiological division of labor was given by Spencer to Von Baer.

Von Baer's principles allowed Spencer to organize his ideas on biological, psychological, and social evolution. For as Spencer came to em-

---

[8] This is Spencer's phrase for society.

[9] See, for example, his *Autobiography;* also see the long footnote in *First Principles* (New York: A. L. Burt, 1880; originally published in 1860).

phasize, evolution is a process of development from an incoherent, undifferentiated, and homogeneous mass to a differentiated and coherent structure in which the functions of structures are well coordinated.[10] Conversely, dissolution involved movement from a coherent and differentiated state to a more homogeneous and incoherent mass. Thus, Spencer came to view the major focus of sociology as the study of the conditions under which social differentiation and de-differentiation occur.

3.   The relationship between Darwin and Spencer is reciprocal in that Spencer's early ideas about development exerted considerable influence on Darwin's formulation of the theory of evolution,[11] although Darwin's notion of "natural selection" was apparently formulated independently of Spencer's emphasis on competition and struggle. Only after *On the Origin of Species* was in press did Darwin recognize the affinity between the concepts of survival of the fittest and natural selection. Conversely, Darwin's explicit formulation of the theory of evolution was to reinforce, and give legitimacy to, Spencer's view of social evolution as the result of competition among populations, with the most organizationally "fit" conquering the less fit, and hence, increasing the level and complexity of social organization. Moreover, Darwin's ideas encouraged Spencer to view differences among "the races" and societies of the world as the result of "speciation" of isolated populations, each of which adapted to varying environmental conditions. In fact, Spencer's continuous emphasis on environmental conditions—both ecological and societal—as shaping the structure of society is the result, no doubt, of Darwin's formulations.

The theory of evolution also offered Spencer a respected intellectual tool for justifying his laissez-faire political beliefs. For both organic and super-organic bodies, he argued, it is necessary to let competition and struggle operate free of governmental regulation. To protect some segments of a population is to preserve the "less fit" and hence reduce the overall "quality of civilization."[12]

---

[10] This idea can be found in its early form in one of Spencer's early essays, "Progress: Its Law and Cause," first published in 1857 (*Westminister Review*, April 1857). Also, see Spencer's article, "The Developmental Hypothesis," *The New Leader* (1852).

[11] Indeed, Darwin explicitly acknowledges Spencer's work in the introduction to *On the Origin of Species* (London: Murry, 1890; originally published in 1859). And at one point in his life, Darwin was moved to remark that Spencer was "a dozen times his intellectual superior." For more lines of influence, see *Life and Letters of Charles Darwin* (New York: D. Appleton, 1896).

[12] It is not hard to see how these ideas were to be transformed into what became known as *Social Darwinism* in America. A more accurate term would have been *Social Spencerianism*. See Richard Hofstadter, *Social Darwinism in American Thought* (Boston: Beacon Press, 1955).

From biology, then, Spencer took three essential elements: (1) the notion that it is from competition among individuals, or collective populations, that many of the critical attributes of both individuals and society emerge; (2) the view that social evolution involves movement from undifferentiated to differentiated structures marked by interrelated functions; and (3) the recognition that differences among both individuals and social systems are the result of having to adapt to varying environmental conditions. These broad insights were supplemented by a number of discoveries in the physical sciences of Spencer's time, and together with Spencer's biologically based ideas, the "first principles" of his general "synthetic philosophy" were forged.

Physical Science Influences

From his informal education within his family and from his contacts with the most eminent scientists of his time, Spencer acquired considerable training in astronomy, geology, physics, and chemistry. In reading Spencer's many works, it is impossible not to be impressed by his knowledge of wide varieties of physical phenomena and their laws of operation. Spencer's synthetic philosophy was thus to reflect his debt to the physical sciences, particularly in regard to (1) the general mode of his analysis and (2) the specific principles of his philosophy.

1. All of Spencer's work is indebted to the post-Newtonian view of science—that is, the existence of universal laws that could explain the operation of phenomena in the world. Indeed, Spencer was to go beyond Newton and argue that there are laws that transcend all phenomena, both physical and organic. In other words, there are laws of the universe or cosmos that can be discovered and used to explain, at least in general terms, physical, organic, and super-organic (social) events. Spencer was to emphasize that each domain of reality—astronomical, geological, physical, chemical, biological, psychological, and sociological—revealed its own unique laws that pertained to the properties and forces of its delimited domain. And yet he also believed that, at the most abstract level, there are a few fundamental or "first" principles that cut across all domains of reality.

2. In seeking these first principles, Spencer relied heavily on the physics of his time. He incorporated into his synthetic philosophy notions of force, the indestructibility of matter, the persistence of motion, and other principles that were emerging in physics. We will discuss these in more detail when examining Spencer's scheme in depth, but we should

emphasize that much of the inspiration for Spencer's grand scheme came from the promise of post-Newtonian physics.

Thus, Spencer's synthetic philosophy emerged out of a synthesis of ideas and principles being developed in physics and biology. Yet, the precise way in which these ideas were used by Spencer in his sociological work was greatly influenced by his exposure to Auguste Comte's vision of a positive philosophy (see previous chapter). And hence, before we can fully appreciate Spencer's philosophy, we need to review his somewhat ambivalent and defensive reaction to Comte's work.

SPENCER'S SYNTHETIC PHILOSOPHY AND THE SOCIOLOGY OF AUGUSTE COMTE

Spencer's relation to Auguste Comte is rather unclear. In 1864, Spencer published an article entitled "Reasons for Dissenting from the Philosophy of M. Comte" in which he sought to list the points of agreement and disagreement with the great French thinker.[13] Spencer emphasized that he disagreed with Comte over the following issues: (a) that societies pass through three stages, (b) that causality is less important than relations of affinity in building social theory, (c) that government can use the laws of sociology to reconstruct society, (d) that the sciences have developed in a particular order, and (e) that psychology is merely a subdiscipline of biology.

Spencer also noted a number of points in which he was in agreement with Comte, but he stressed that many other scholars besides Comte had similarly advocated (a) that knowledge comes from experiences or observed facts and (b) that there are invariable laws in the universe. But most revealing are the few passages where Spencer explicitly acknowledged an intellectual debt to Comte. Spencer accepted Comte's term, sociology, for the science of super-organic bodies, and most important, he gave Comte begrudging credit for reintroducing the organismic analogy back into social thought. Spencer stressed, however, that Plato and Hobbes had made similar analogies and that much of his organismic thinking had been influenced by Von Baer.

---

[13] The article is conveniently reprinted in Herbert Spencer, *Reasons for Dissenting from the Philosophy of M. Comte and Other Essays* (Berkeley; Calif.: Glendessary Press, 1968). The article was written in a somewhat defensive manner in an effort to distinguish Spencer's first book, *Social Statics* (New York: D. Appleton, 1888; originally published in 1850), from Comte's use of these terms. Spencer appears to have "protested too much," perhaps seeking to hide some of his debt to the positive philosophy of Comte.

Yet one gets the impression that Spencer was working too hard at dissociating his ideas from Comte. And the fact that his most intimate intellectual companions, George Elliot and George Lewis, were well versed in Comte's philosophy argues for considerable intellectual influence from Comte's work on Spencer's initial sociological inquiries. True, Spencer would never accept Comte's collectivism, but he was to extend two critical ideas clearly evident in Comte's work: (1) social systems reveal many properties of organization in common with biological organisms, and hence, a few principles of social organization can be initially borrowed (and, of course, altered somewhat) from biology, and (2) when viewed as a "body social," a social system can be analyzed in terms of the contribution of its various organs to the maintenance of the social whole. There can be little doubt, then, that Spencer was stimulated by Comte's analogizing and implicit functionalism. But as Spencer incorporated these ideas, they were altered by his absorption of key insights from the physical and biological sciences.

WHY READ SPENCER?

When compared to other scholars, whom we will analyze in later chapters, the intellectual influences on Spencer are less clear. He did not attend a university, and hence, his mentors cannot be traced within the walls of academia. Nor did he ever hold an academic position, thereby avoiding compartmentalization in a department or particular school of thought. As a free-lance intellectual, he borrowed at will and was never constrained by the intellectual fads and foibles that sweep through academia. It is the unrestrained scope of Spencer's scheme that makes it fascinating, and perhaps it is this same feature that makes Spencer's work less appealing to present-day scholars, who tend to work within narrow intellectual traditions.

Yet, as we will explore in depth in the next chapter, Spencer offered many important insights into the structure and dynamics of social systems. And while he presented these insights in the vocabulary of the physics and biology of his time, they still have considerable relevance for sociological theorizing. Thus, as we approach the analysis of Spencer's basic works, we should be prepared to appreciate not only the scope of his work, but also the profound insights that he achieved into the nature of social systems.

4

HERBERT SPENCER II:
THE BASIC WORKS

Spencer viewed himself as a philosopher, and as such, he considered it appropriate to write both ethical and scientific treatises. His overall intellectual scheme, in both its scientific and ethical components, is termed the *synthetic philosophy*. Yet it is not difficult to distinguish Spencer's moralistic preachings from his formal scientific work, since they tend to be kept separate. In our review of Spencer's basic work, we will try to distinguish the moral and scientific elements of the synthetic philosophy, and in this way, we can appreciate Spencer as both a profound theorist and a poor philosopher.

We will focus primarily on Spencer's sociological works, although it will be necessary to address several more general philosophical statements.[1] We will begin our discussion with Spencer's first and last major works, *Social Statics* (1850) and *Principles of Ethics* (1879–1893), respectively, since these are his most extreme moral statements.[2] It is important to separate these works from the corpus of Spencer's more scientific efforts, because these moral statements are often used to condemn and obscure Spencer's better efforts. Then we will examine Spencer's *First Principles* (1862), which represents a statement of the universal laws of the cosmos. We will skip Spencer's *Principles of Biology* (1864–1867) and *Principles of Psychology* (1855), which were written before

---

[1] Spencer's complete works, except for his *Descriptive Sociology* (see later analysis), are conveniently pulled together in the following collection: *The Works of Herbert Spencer*, 21 vols. (Osnabrück: Otto Zeller, 1966). However, our references will employ the separate editions and pagination of each of his individual works.

[2] Many of the dates for the works discussed span several years, since Spencer sometimes published his works serially in several volumes (frequently after they had appeared in periodicals). Full citation will be given when discussing a particular work.

Spencer's sociological works. Although these are profound works, they do not bear directly on Spencer's sociological theorizing. Most of this section will be devoted, first of all, to Spencer's first explicitly sociological book, *The Study of Sociology* (1873), and then to the more scholarly and important *Principles of Sociology* (1876–1893).

SPENCER'S MORAL PHILOSOPHY

Social Statics and *Principles of Ethics*

In his later years, Spencer often complained that his first major work, *Social Statics*,[3] had always received too' much attention. For he saw this work as an early and flawed attempt to delineate his moral philosophy, and hence, it is not representative of his more mature thought. And yet, the basic premise of the work is repeated in one of his last works, *Principles of Ethics*.[4] Thus, despite Spencer's protests, there is considerable continuity in his moral arguments, although we should emphasize again that Spencer's more scientific statements can and should be separated from these ethical arguments.

Since Spencer's moral arguments did not change dramatically, we will concentrate on *Social Statics*. The basic argument of *Social Statics* can be stated as follows: Human happiness can only be achieved when individuals can seek to satisfy their needs and desires without infringing on the rights of others to do the same. As Spencer emphasized:

> Each member of the race . . . must not only be endowed with faculties enabling him to receive the highest enjoyment in the act of living, but must be so constituted that he may obtain full satisfaction for every desire, without diminishing the power of others to obtain like satisfaction: nay, to fulfill the purpose perfectly, must derive pleasure from seeing pleasure in others.[5]

In this early work, as well as in *Principles of Ethics*, Spencer saw this view as basic law of ethics and morality. He felt that this law was an extension of laws in the natural world, and in fact, much of his search for scientific laws represents an effort to develop a scientific justification for his moral position. Indeed, Spencer emphasized that the social

---

[3] Herbert Spencer, *Social Statics; or, The Conditions Essential to Human Happiness Specified, and the First of Them Developed* (New York: D. Appleton, 1888). This was originally published in 1850; the edition cited here is an offset print of original.

[4] Herbert Spencer, *Principles of Ethics* (New York: D. Appleton, 1892–98).

[5] Spencer, *Social Statics*, p. 448.

universe, like the physical and biological realms, reveals invariant laws. But Spencer turned this insight into an interesting moral dictum: once these laws are discovered, humans should obey them and cease trying to construct, through political legislation, social forms that violate these laws. In this way, Spencer was able to base his laissez-faire political ideas on what he saw as a sound scientific position: the laws of social organization can no more be violated than those of the physical universe, and to seek to do so will simply create, in the long run, more severe problems.[6] In contrast to Comte, then, who saw the discovery of laws as the tools for social engineering, Spencer took the opposite tack and argued that once the laws are ascertained, people should "implicitly obey them!"[7] And for Spencer, the great ethical axiom, "derived" from the laws of nature, is that humans should be as free from external regulation as is possible. Indeed, the bulk of *Social Statics* seeks to show how his moral law and the laws of laissez-faire capitalism converge and, implicitly, how they reflect biological laws of unfettered competition and struggle among species. The titles of some of the chapters best communicate Spencer's argument: "The Rights of Life and Personal Liberty," "The Right to the Use of the Earth," "The Right of Property," "The Rights of Exchange," "The Rights of Women,"[8] "The Right to Ignore the State," "The Limit of State-Duty," and so forth.

In seeking to join the laws of ethics, political economy, and biology, Spencer initiated modes of analysis that were to become prominent parts of his sociology. First, he sought to discover invariant laws and principles of social organization. Second, he began to engage in organismic analogizing, drawing comparisons between the structure of individual organisms and societies.

> Thus do we find, not only that the analogy between a society and a living creature is borne out to a degree quite unsuspected by those who commonly draw it, but also, that the same definition of life applies to both. This union of many men into one community—this increasingly mutual dependence of units which were originally independent—this gradual segregation of citizens into separate bodies, with reciprocally subservient functions—this formation of a whole, consisting of numerous essential parts—this growth of an organism, of which one portion cannot

---

[6] Ibid., pp. 54–57.

[7] Ibid., p. 56.

[8] Spencer's arguments here are highly modern and, when compared to Marx's, Weber's, or Durkheim's, are quite radical.

be injured without the rest feeling it—may all be generalized under the law of individuation. The development of society, as well as the development of man and the development of life generally, may be described as a tendency to individuate—*to become a thing.* And rightly interpreted, the manifold forms of progress going on around us, are uniformly significant of this tendency.[9]

Spencer's organismic analogizing often goes to extremes in *Social Statics*—extremes that he was to avoid in his later works. For example, he was led at one point to argue that "so completely . . . is a society organized upon the same system as an individual being, that we may almost say that there is something more than an analogy between them."[10]

Third, *Social Statics* also reveals the beginnings of Spencer's functionalism. Societies, like individuals, are viewed by Spencer as having survival needs with specialized organs emerging and persisting to meet these needs. And "social health" is defined in terms of how well these needs are being met by various specialized "social organs."

Fourth, Spencer's later emphasis on war and conflict among societies as a critical force in their development can also be observed. While decrying war as destructive, on the one hand, he argued that, on the other hand, it allows the more organized "races" to conquer the "less organized and inferior races"—thereby increasing the level and complexity of social organization. This line of argument was to be dramatically tempered in his later, scientific works, with the result that he was one of the first social thinkers to see the importance of conflict in the evolution of human societies.[11]

In sum, then, *Social Statics* and *Principles of Ethics* are greatly flawed works, representing Spencer's moral ramblings. We have examined these works first because they are often used to condemn Spencer's more scholarly efforts. While some of the major scientific points of emphasis can be seen in these moral works, and while Spencer's scientific works are sprinkled with his extreme moral position, there is, nonetheless, a distinct difference in style, tone, and insight between the ethical and scientific works. And thus, we would conclude that the worth of Spencer's thought is to be found in the more scientific works, relegating Spencer's ethics to deserved obscurity. We will, therefore, devote the balance of this chapter to understanding Spencer's sociological perspective.

---

[9] Spencer, *Social Statics*, p. 497.

[10] Ibid., p. 490.

[11] Ibid., p. 498.

SPENCER'S *FIRST PRINCIPLES*

The Basic Laws

In the 1860s, Spencer began to issue by subscription his general synthetic philosophy. The goal of this philosophy is to treat the great divisions of the universe—life, mind, and society—in terms of scientific principles. The first work in this rather encompassing scheme is *First Principles*, published in 1862.[12] It is in this book that Spencer delineated the "cardinal" or "first principles" of the universe. Drawing from the biology and physics of his time, Spencer felt that he had perceived, at the most abstract level, certain common principles that apply to all realms of the universe. Indeed, it must have been an exciting vision to feel that one had unlocked the mysteries of the physical, organic, and superorganic (societal) universe. Basically, Spencer postulated three general principles:

1. The indestructibility of matter.
2. The continuity of motion in a given direction.
3. The persistence of the force behind movement of matter in a given direction.

From these three general principles, several corollaries could be derived:

4. The transferability of force from one type of matter and motion to another.
5. The tendency of motion to pass along the line of least resistance.
6. The rhythmic nature of motion.

In enumerating these six principles, Spencer's initial purpose was to view the universe as a constant process, over time and in space, of "an unceasing redistribution of matter and motion" and a "transference of force." These processes, Spencer felt, are true of celestial bodies, chemical compounds, organic evolution, and social aggregates. Thus, the goal of his synthetic philosophy is to discover the composite laws that combine these six laws and that allow for understanding of the evolution and dissolution of all phenomena.

---

[12] Herbert Spencer, *First Principles* (New York: A. L. Burt, 1880). Originally published in 1862. The contents of this work had been anticipated in earlier essays, the most important of which are "Progress: Its Law and Cause," *Westminster Review* (April 1857) and "The Ultimate Laws of Physiology," *National Review* (October 1857); moreover, hints at these principles are sprinkled throughout the first edition of *Principles of Psychology* (New York: D. Appleton, 1880; originally published in 1855).

The Laws of Evolution and Dissolution

Commentators often fail to recognize that Spencer viewed the universe as in a constant and cyclical process of "structuring" and "de-structuring" or, in his terms, "evolution" and "dissolution." Too often, Spencer is viewed by his detractors as a strict evolutionist, when in fact he was interested in the transformations of structures, whether these transformations involve development or dissolution of phenomena.

With regard to evolution—that is, creating more differentiated and complex structures—Spencer saw aggregation of matter, the deflection of the motion contained in this matter, and the redistribution of the force of this motion as the critical variables. For example, when single-cell organisms aggregate, their motion is deflected, with the result that they differentiate into specialized organs. As this deflection occurs, the force of the motion is dissipated as it encounters resistance so that at some point the differentiated cells come into equilibrium. Similarly, when people aggregate, the retained motion that originally brought them together is deflected in various directions, creating pressures for differentiation of individuals and groups. But the force of their motion dissipates over time, with the result that their pattern of differentiation reaches an equilibrium point.

As corollaries to these principles of evolution, Spencer added that when the motion accompanying aggregation is great—that is, it is of great force—then the redistribution of this motion and differentiation of the aggregate will be extensive and the dissipation of force will take considerably longer. Thus, if one nation conquers another (a situation of high force and great motion), Spencer would predict considerable deflection of motion and consequent differentiation of the population.

Thus, evolution involves the related processes of aggregation of matter and its attendant motion as well as the force accompanying the motion of the elements that are aggregated. Under these conditions the force of the motion pushes different elements in a variety of directions, causing differentiation. But what holds the elements together as they move apart and differentiate? Spencer's answer is that evolution also involves integration of matter and the retained motion. That is, as elements of an aggregate differentiate, they become mutually dependent upon each other. Thus, as plants or animals develop separate and specialized organs, these organs provide vital substances for each other. Similarly, as people differentiate, they become mutually dependent on each other—that is, they become integrated.

When viewed in this light, much of the rather strange vocabulary in Spencer's definition of evolution can hopefully make more sense. For Spencer, evolution is "a change from a less coherent form to a more coherent form, consequent on the dissipation of motion and integration of matter."[13] But Spencer added that such change from incoherence to coherence involves a "change from a homogeneous to a heterogeneous state."[14] Whether it be the solar system, a plant, a geological form, an animal, a psychological state of mind, or a society, evolution conforms to this law.

Spencer then sought to explain why evolution involves movement from a homogeneous to a more differentiated state. And in so doing, he introduced several additional principles, which are still useful in understanding many diverse phenomena: (1) the principle of instability of the homogeneous, (2) the principle of multiplication of effects, and (3) the principle of segregation.

1. The "principle of instability of the homogeneous" argues that when a force strikes a grouping of unlinked homogeneous elements, they are inherently more unstable than when the same force hits differentiated and integrated elements. When a force hits a differentiated and integrated mass, the mutual dependence of the elements offers resistance, whereas when the elements are alike and unlinked, they will be scattered in many different directions; over time, they will become different as a result of their retained motion propelling them into diverse environments.

2. The "principle of multiplication of effects" states that as initially homogeneous parts are effected differently by a force, they become even more differentiated. The reason for this is that the retained motion pushes the parts in different directions, and as the undissipated force allows for their further elaboration and development, their differences become even more accentuated. For example, similar people who migrate (a force and motion) to new and diverse regions can become easily distinguished from each other since their initial differences are multiplied and amplified by their subsequent elaborations of biological (skin color, for example) and cultural (values, beliefs, and so on) traits as they adapt to diverse circumstances.

3. The "principle of segregation" explains how multiplication of differences can occur. Once elements become isolated from each other and must exist in somewhat varying environments, then they must make adjustments to different circumstances. As these adjustments occur, the

---

[13] Spencer, *First Principles*, p. 243.
[14] Ibid., p. 286.

elements become even more differentiated. For example, biological speciation occurs as a result of isolation and confinement of members of the same species to different ecological niches; over time, as the members of the original species adapt to their new circumstances, they eventually become distinct species. Spencer felt that the same processes occurred among and within super-organic systems. For as populations become isolated and elaborate (in terms of the principle of multiplicative effects), they must adapt to diverse environmental demands, and hence, become differentiated from each other.

Thus, for Spencer, evolution occurs because homogeneous masses are inherently unstable, and as forces push elements in different directions, their segregation in diverse environments creates differences among the elements as they adjust to different milieus. Moreover, the retained motion, as it allows segregated elements to elaborate, leads to the multiplication of differences. For Spencer, outside forces are far more disruptive to homogeneous than to heterogeneous aggregates, and once such forces can segregate the elements in an aggregate, they are likely to multiply, over time, their initial difference. Whether these processes are true of all the universe is uncertain, but the principles do seem applicable to many realms of the social universe.

As we have emphasized, Spencer also recognized that evolution and dissolution are related processes. Structures elaborate, and then they often dissolve. And while Spencer saw that the history of humankind had, in general, been one of evolution, particular populations and societies have evolved and then dissolved. At the most abstract level, Spencer viewed dissolution as occurring when the retained motion of matter and its accompanying force are completely dissipated, creating a situation in which environmental factors that have caused the dissipation of force (by providing resistance) can begin to act as a counterforce and disrupt the existing structure. Thus, only so long as a differentiated system can maintain its motion through the production of forces against the environment can it evolve. For example, should a population run out of food or cease producing a military advantage, then it is likely that environmental forces—whether predators, disease, or other militaristic societies—can begin to impinge upon this population, causing its dissolution as a distinct entity.

These principles of evolution and dissolution are, of course, somewhat obscure, and they are rather grand and cosmic in tone. Yet, as a general metaphor for understanding the institutionalization and de-institutionalization of social structures, there is much to recommend them. First, structuring and de-structuring are seen to occur in terms that can be described by invariant laws. Second, explicit variables such as *(a)* size and concentration of a population, *(b)* the the strength of forces that brought this population together, *(c)* the nature and extent of environmental resistance to such forces, *(d)* the capacity to maintain forces that can overcome environmental resistance, and *(e)* the ability to maintain interdependence in the face of differential actions, segregation, and multiplication of differences are all variables that are relevant to understanding the basic processes of differentiation, integration, malintegration, and de-differentiation in social systems. Whether in the context of organizational research, small-group experiments, historical analyses of societal development, or cross-national comparisons of contemporary societies, these variables, first seen by Spencer with great clarity, are relevant to most sociological explanations.

Yet Spencer was to move considerably beyond this general metaphor of evolution. He was to propose many specific propositions and guidelines for a science of society. For ultimately, Spencer's contribution to sociological theorizing does not reside in his abstract formulas on cosmic evolution, but in his specific analyses of societal social systems—what he called *super-organic* phenomena. This contribution can be found in two distinct works, *The Study of Sociology*, which was published in serial form in popular magazines in 1872, and the more scholarly *The Principles of Sociology*, which was published in several volumes between 1876 and 1896. The former work is primarily a methodological statement on the problems of sociology, whereas the latter is a substantive work which seeks to develop abstract principles of evolution and dissolution, and at the same time, to describe the complex interplay among the institutions of society.

SPENCER'S *THE STUDY OF SOCIOLOGY*

The Study of Sociology[15] was originally published as a series of articles in *Contemporary Review* in England and *Popular Science Monthly* in America. It represents Spencer's effort to popularize sociology and to address "various considerations which seemed needful by way of introduction to the *Principles of Sociology*, presently to be written."[16] Most of the book is a discussion of the methodological problems confronting the science of sociology. At the same time, and in less well-developed form, there are a number of substantive insights which were to form

---

[15] Herbert Spencer, *The Study of Sociology* (London: Kegan Paul, Trench, 1873).
[16] Ibid., p. iv.

the core of Spencer's *Principles of Sociology*. In our review, we will first examine Spencer's methodological discussion, and then his more theoretical analysis, even though this division does not correspond to the order of Spencer's presentation.

The Methodological Problems Confronting Sociology

The opening paragraph of chapter 4 sets the tone of Spencer's analysis.

> From the intrinsic natures of its facts, from our own natures as observers of its facts, and from the peculiar relation in which we stand toward the facts to be observed, these arise impediments in the way of Sociology greater than those of any other science.[17]

Spencer went on to emphasize that the basic sources of bias stem from the inadequacy of measuring instruments in the social sciences and from the nature of scientists who, by virtue of being members of society, observe the data from a particular vantage point. In a series of insightful chapters—far superior to any statement by any other sociologist of the 19th century—Spencer outlined in more detail what he termed *objective* and *subjective* difficulties.

Under objective difficulties, Spencer analyzed the problems associated with the "uncertainty of our data." The first problem encountered revolves around the difficulty of measuring the "subjective states" of actors, and correspondingly, of investigators' suspending their own subjective orientation when examining that of others. A second problem concerns allowing public passions, moods, and fads to determine what is investigated by the sociologists, since it is all too easy to let the popular and immediately relevant obscure from vision more fundamental problems. A third methodological problem revolves around the "cherished hypothesis" in which, regardless of its merit or importance, an investigator can be driven to pursue a particular problem while neglecting more significant problems. A fourth issue concerns the problem of personal and organizational interests influencing what is seen as scientifically important. Large-scale governmental bureaucracies, and individuals in them, will tend to seek and interpret data in ways that support their interests. A fifth problem is related to the second in that investigators often allow the most visible phenomena to occupy their attention, creating a bias in the collection of data toward the most readily accessible (not necessarily the most important) phenomena. A sixth problem stems from the fact

---

[17] Ibid., p. 72.

that any observer occupies a position in society, and hence, will tend to see the world in terms of the dictates of that position. And seventh, depending upon the point of time in the ongoing social process at which observations are made, varying results can be induced—thereby signaling that "social change cannot be judged of in its general direction by inspecting any small portion of it."[18]

Spencer's discussion is timely even today, and his advice for mitigating these "objective difficulties" is also relevant: social science must rely upon multiple sources of data, collected at different times in varying places by different investigators. Coupled with efforts by investigators to recognize their bias, their interests, and their position in society as well as their commitment to theoretically important (rather than popular) problems, these difficulties can be further mitigated. Yet, many "subjective difficulties" will persist.

There are, Spencer argued, two classes of subjective difficulty: (1) intellectual and (2) emotional. Under intellectual difficulties, Spencer returned to the first of the objective difficulties: How are investigators to put themselves into the subjective world of those whom they observe? How can we avoid representing another's "thoughts and feelings in terms of our own"?[19] For if investigators cannot suspend their own emotional states in order to understand those of others under investigation, then the data of social science will always be biased. Another subjective intellectual problem concerns the depth of analysis, for the more one investigates a phenomenon in detail, the more complicated are its elements and their causal connections. Thus, how far should investigators go before they are to be satisfied with their analysis of a particular phenomenon? At what point are the basic causal connections uncovered? Turning to emotional subjective difficulties, Spencer argued that the emotional state of an investigator can directly influence estimations of probability, importance, and relevance of events.

After reviewing these difficulties, and emphasizing that the distinction between subjective and objective is somewhat arbitrary, Spencer devoted separate chapters to the "educational bias," "bias of patriotism," "class bias," "political bias," and the "theological bias." Thus, more than any other sociologist of the 19th century, Spencer had a clear recognition of the many methodological problems confronting the science of society. And yet, as we noted earlier, this recognition did not stop Spencer from injecting his own biases into much of his sociological analysis.

---

[18] Ibid., p. 105.
[19] Ibid., p. 114.

But despite Spencer's failure to follow his own advice, his discussion of how to eliminate, or at least reduce, these sources of bias is nonetheless quite illuminating.

Spencer felt that the problems of bias could be mitigated not only by attention to one's interests, emotions, station in life, and other subjective and emotional sources of difficulty, but also by the development of "mental discipline." He believed that by studying the procedures of the more exact sciences, sociologists could learn to approach their subject matter in a disciplined and objective way. In a series of enlightening passages,[20] he argued that by studying the purely abstract sciences, such as logic and mathematics, one can become sensitized to "the necessity of relation"—that is, to the fact that phenomena are connected and reveal affinities. By examining the "abstract-concrete sciences," such as physics and chemistry, one is alerted to causality and to the complexity of causal connections. And by examining the "concrete sciences," such as geology and astronomy, one becomes alerted to the "products" of causal forces and the operation of lawlike relations. For it is always necessary, Spencer stressed, to view the context within which processes occur unfold. Thus, by approaching problems with the proper mental discipline—with a sense of relation, causality, and context—many methodological difficulties can be overcome.

The Theoretical Argument

The opening chapters of *The Study of Sociology* present a forceful argument against those who would maintain that the social realm is not like the physical and biological realms. On the contrary, Spencer argued, all realms of the universe are subject to laws. And in fact, every time people express political opinions about what legislators "should do," they are admitting implicitly that there are regularities, which can be understood, in human behavior and organization.

Given the existence of discoverable laws, Spencer stressed, the goal of sociology must be to uncover the principles of morphology (structure) and physiology (process) of all organic forms, including the super-organic (society). But, Spencer cautioned, we must not devote our energies to analyzing the historically unique, peculiar, or transitory. Rather, sociology must look for the universal and enduring properties of social organization.[21] Moreover, sociologists should not become overconcerned with

---

[20] Ibid., pp. 314–26.
[21] Ibid., pp. 58–59.

prediction of future events, since there will always be unanticipated and unknowable empirical conditions in the future which will influence the weights of variables, and hence, the outcomes of events. Much more important is the discovery of the basic relations among, and the fundamental causal forces of, phenomena.

In the early and late chapters of *The Study of Sociology*, Spencer sought to delineate, in very sketchy form, some of the principles common to organic bodies. And in so doing, he foreshadowed the more extensive analysis in *Principles of Sociology*. Spencer acknowledged[22] Comte's influence in viewing biology and sociology as parallel sciences of organic forms and in recognizing that understanding of the principles of biology is a prerequisite for discovering the principles of sociology. For as Spencer was to emphasize in all of his sociological works, there are certain common principles of structure and function in all organic bodies.

Spencer even hinted at some of these principles which were to be elaborated upon in the volumes of *Principles of Sociology*. One principle is that increases in the size of both biological and social aggregates create pressures for differentiation of functions. Another principle is that such differentiation results in the creation of distinctive regulatory, operative, and distributive processes. That is, as organic systems differentiate it becomes necessary for some units to regulate and control action, for others to produce what is necessary for system maintenance, or for still others to distribute necessary substances among the parts. A third principle is that differentiation initially involves separation of regulative centers from productive centers, and only with the increases in size and further differentiation do distinctive distributing centers emerge.

Such principles are supplemented by one of the first functional orientations in sociology. In numerous places, Spencer stressed that to uncover the principles of social organization, it is necessary to examine the special whole, to determine its needs for survival, and to assess various structures in terms of how they meet these needs.[23] While this functionalism was always to remain somewhat implicit and subordinate to Spencer's search for the principles of organization among super-organic bodies, it was to influence subsequent thinkers, particularly Durkheim (See Chapters 15 to 17).

---

[22] Ibid., p. 328.

[23] For example, Spencer was led to remark: "While . . . each society . . . presents conditions more or less special, to which the natures of citizens must adapt; there are certain conditions which, in every society, must be fulfilled to a considerable extent before it can hold together, and which must be fulfilled completely before social life can be complete." Ibid., p. 347.

In sum, then, *The Study of Sociology* is a preliminary work to Spencer's *Principles of Sociology*. It analyzes in detail the methodological problems confronting sociology; it offers guidelines for eradicating biases and for developing the proper "scientific discipline"; it hints at the utility of functional analysis; and most importantly, it begins to sketch out what Spencer thought to be the fundamental principles of social organization. For the next two decades after the publication of *The Study of Sociology*, Spencer sought to utilize the basic principles enunciated in his *First Principles* as axioms for deriving the more specific principles of super-organic bodies.

SPENCER'S *PRINCIPLES OF SOCIOLOGY*

Between 1874 and 1896, Spencer wrote in serial form his *Principles of Sociology*,[24] which is both a theoretical and descriptive work. As such, it is filled with powerful analytical statements and insightful empirical observations. In reviewing this long work, we will first discuss the general classes of variables that Spencer saw as influencing human organization and change; then we will devote most of this section to delineating Spencer's more analytical statements; and finally, we will close with a brief summary of Spencer's more interesting empirical observations on various social institutions.[25]

Critical Variables in Super-organic Evolution

In a way reminiscent of Comte, Spencer divided scientific inquiry into the study of inorganic, organic, and super-organic phenomena. Super-organic[26] sciences are those concerned with the coordinated relations among individual organisms, with the result that insect societies and human communities are both part of the super-organic realm. But Spencer quickly emphasized that human societies, by virtue of their

---

[24] Herbert Spencer, *The Principles of Sociology*, 2 vols., 8 pts. (New York: D. Appleton, 1885; originally initiated in 1874). This particular edition is the third and is printed in five separate books: subsequent references are all to this third edition. Other editions vary in volume numbering, although part numbers are consistent across various editions.

[25] Domestic institutions are examined in part 3 of volume 1; ceremonial institutions are examined in part 4 of volume 2; political in part 5; ecclesiastical in part 6; professional in part 7; and industrial in part 8.

[26] As Spencer defined it in *Principles of Sociology*, pt. 1, "Of course no absolute separation exists. If there has been Evolution, that form of it here distinguished as super-organic must have come by insensible steps out of the organic. But we may conveniently mark it off as including all those processes and products which imply the coordinated actions of many individuals."

complexity and constant transformation, are the core of the super-organic sciences. And it is thus a science, termed *sociology*, that is to dictate the basic mode of super-organic inquiry.

Such inquiry is to be evolutionary, since there can be little doubt, Spencer felt, that over the long run human patterns of social organization have followed the basic law of evolution which he had articulated in *First Principles*. Human societies have moved from an unstable, homogeneous mass to more differentiated and coherent structures. The first goal of sociology, then, is to enumerate the general classes of variables influencing the direction, speed, and nature of such evolutionary changes. Spencer termed these variables the *factors of social phenomena*, of which there are three general classes: internal conditions, external conditions, and derived conditions. Each of these factors is briefly examined below.

1.   Under internal or intrinsic conditions, Spencer listed many variables that are not relevant today in analyzing societal systems—intelligence, physical traits, and emotional states.[27] More important is the general thrust of his analysis: the attributes of actors in a system determine, at least to some extent, the properties of the system. But Spencer was quick to stress that once actors revealing certain initial attributes come together, an emergent reality is created. And once created, the properties of this emergent structure, as much as the nature of the individuals involved, will influence the subsequent course of its development.

2.   As a biologically oriented scholar, and as one who came close to articulating the theory of evolution,[28] Spencer was always concerned with the impact of environmental variables on patterns of social organization. Such external factors as climate, surface (fertility of soil, amount of land space, and so forth), configuration of surface (desert, plains, mountains, and so on), and the nature, abundance, and access to flora and fauna are all, in Spencer's vision, critical variables in sociological inquiry. Particularly among simple, homogeneous societies, which have not elaborated internal structures, are external environmental variables influential.[29]

---

[27] By today's standards, many of Spencer's statements are racist, as were those of Tylor, Morgan, Durkheim, Weber, and many others of the 19th century. Spencer's great fallacy was the result of not having genetic theory to supplement Darwin's view of evolution; thus, he was led to view populations of the world as fundamentally different in terms of intelligence and other basic attributes.

[28] See Darwin's acknowledgments in *On the Origin of Species*.

[29] It should be recalled from *First Principles* that Spencer regarded homogeneous systems as inherently unstable and particularly susceptible to environmental influence.

3. Derived conditions can be both internal and external, for as societies evolve and develop, they create internal conditions that influence their subsequent development and they become a part of each other's external environment. And with further evolution, derived factors become increasingly more important and take precedence over the attributes of individual actors and the physical environment. Under such derived conditions, Spencer felt that *(a)* the size and density of social aggregates[30] and *(b)* their relations with neighboring societies are the most important. Large and concentrated populations, as well as conflictual relations with other societies, are likely to have considerable impact on the internal structure of a society and its subsequent evolutionary development. Yet Spencer also saw such factors as cultural beliefs and material products as significant derived factors which could shape patterns of social organization.

In sum, then, Spencer opened his formal sociological analysis with a definition of sociology's basic subject matter—the super-organic and its evolution—and an overview of the general classes of variables influencing the structure and change of social systems. The remaining sections of *Principles of Sociology* then seek to analyze the super-organic realm in more detail.

The Super-organic and the Organismic Analogy

Part 2 of volume 1 of *Principles of Sociology* contains virtually all of the theoretical statements of Spencerian sociology. Employing the organismic analogy—that is, comparing organic (bodily) and super-organic (societal) organization—Spencer developed a perspective for analyzing the structure, function, and transformation of societal phenomena. Too often commentators have criticized Spencer for his use of the organismic analogy, but in fairness to Spencer, we should emphasize that he employed the analogy cautiously. The basic point of the analogy is to stress that since both organic and super-organic systems reveal organization of component parts, they should reveal certain common principles of organization. As Spencer stressed:

> Between society and anything else, the only conceivable resemblance must be due to *parallelism of principle in the arrangement of components*.[31]

---

[30] Émile Durkheim was later to incorporate these variables into his scheme. See Chapters 15 to 17.

[31] Spencer, *Principles of Sociology*, vol. 1, p. 448 (emphasis in original).

As one who saw in his *First Principles* a unity in evolutionary processes among realms of the entire universe and as one who had enumerated the principles of biology, it is not surprising that Spencer should begin his analysis of the super-organic by trying to show certain parallels between principles of societal and bodily organization. In fact, current general systems theory, living systems theory, and the cybernetic sciences all seek to do exactly what Spencer had proposed.[32] The critical question does not hinge on whether organismic analogizing is good or bad science, but whether or not Spencer's use of the organismic analogy is productive in that it achieves insight into the creation, maintenance, and change of patterns of social organization. It is on this latter criterion that we should judge Spencer's scheme.

Spencer began his analogizing by discussing the similarities in and differences between organic and super-organic systems.[33] Among important similarities, he delineated the following:[34]

1. Both society and organisms can be distinguished from inorganic matter, for both grow and develop.
2. In both society and organisms, an increase in size means an increase in complexity and differentiation.
3. In both, a progressive differentiation in structure is accompanied by a differentiation in function.
4. In both, parts of the whole are interdependent, with a change in one part affecting other parts.
5. In both, each part of the whole is also a microsociety or organism in and of itself.
6. And in both organisms and societies, the life of the whole can be destroyed, but the parts will live on for a while.

Among the critical differences between a society and an organism, Spencer emphasized the following:

1. The degree of connectedness of the parts is vastly different in organic and super-organic bodies. There is close proximity and physical contact of parts in organic bodies, whereas in super-

---

[32] Walter Buckley, *Sociology and General Systems Theory* (Englewood Cliffs, N.J.: Prentice-Hall, 1967); C. Bertalanffy, "General Systems Theory," *General Systems Yearbook* 1 (1956):1–16.

[33] Spencer, *Principles of Sociology*, vol. 1, pp. 449–62.

[34] This particular listing is taken from Jonathan H. Turner, *The Structure of Sociological Theory* (Homewood, Ill.: Dorsey Press, 1978), pp. 22–23. © 1978 by the Dorsey Press.

organic systems, there is dispersion and only occasional physical contact of elements.

2. The nature of communication among elements is vastly different in organic and super-organic systems. In organic bodies, communication occurs in terms of molecular waves passing through channels of varying degrees of coherence, whereas among humans communication occurs by virtue of the capacity to use language to communicate ideas and feelings.

3. In organic and super-organic systems, there are great differences in the respective consciousness of units. In organic bodies, only some elements in only some species reveal the capacity for conscious deliberations, whereas in human societies all individual units exhibit the capacity for conscious thought.

With these general points of comparison as his guide, Spencer then sought to enumerate in more detail some of the properties of social organization and change. This enumeration becomes exceedingly complex and is best divided into a series of related topics, which can guide our discussion. Cutting through the many chapters of part 2 in volume 1, we can isolate the following major issues: (1) properties of social growth and evolution, (2) properties of social structural elaboration, and (3) bases for classifying social systems. Each of these topic heads will organize the remaining discussion of part 2 of volume 1.

Properties of Social Growth and Evolution. As Spencer had indicated in *First Principles*, evolution involves movement from a homogeneous state to a more differentiated state with the dissipation of motion and integration of matter. Among both organic and super-organic bodies, Spencer stressed, certain common patterns of movement from undifferentiated to differentiated states can be observed.

First, growth in an organism and society involves development from initially small units to larger ones.

Second, both individual organisms and societies reveal wide variability in the size and level of differentiation.

Third, growth in both organic and super-organic bodies occurs in terms of compounding and recompounding. That is, smaller units are initially aggregated to form larger units (compounding), and then these larger units join other like units (recompounding) to form an even larger whole. In this way, organic and super-organic systems become larger and more structurally differentiated. And hence, growth in size is always accompanied by structural differentiation of those units that have been compounded. For example, small clusters of cells in a bodily organism, or a small primitive society, initially join other cells or small societies (thus, becoming compounded); then, these larger units join other units (thus, being recompounded) and form still larger and more differentiated organisms or societies; and so on for both organic and super-organic growth.

Fourth, all evolution must involve a "dissipation of motion" and "integration of matter," which means that growth and structural differentiation must be accompanied by integration. Thus, organic and societal bodies must reveal structural integration at each stage of compounding. Without such integration, recompounding is not possible. For instance, if two societies are joined, they must be integrated before they can, as a unit, become compounded with yet another society. In the processes of compounding, growth, differentiation, and integration, Spencer felt that he saw parallel mechanisms of integration in organisms and societies. For both organic and super-organic systems, integration is achieved increasingly through the dual processes of centralization and mutual dependence of unlike parts. For example, in organisms, as the nervous system and the functions of the brain become increasingly centralized and differentiated, the organs are ever more interdependent; whereas in super-organic systems, as political processes become more and more centralized and differentiated, institutions are increasingly dependent upon each other.

In this way, Spencer delineated some of the fundamental properties of societal growth. Growth is often accompanied by compounding of formerly detailed units; these detached units reveal structural differentiation; differentiation leads to integration, especially if further growth is to occur; and integration is achieved primarily through centralization of regulative functions and interdependence of parts. Whether or not these generalizations are made on the basis of organismic analogizing is less important (despite the claims of Spencer's detractors) than the fact that they do represent powerful (although incomplete) statements about fundamental properties and processes of social systems.

Properties of Structural Elaboration. Spencer argued that increases in the size of a social aggregate necessitate the elaboration of its structure. Such increases in size are the result of *(a)* internal increases in numbers of members and *(b)* joining with other social aggregates. As we saw in the last section, Spencer visualized much growth as the result of compounding and recompounding—that is, by successive joining together of previously separate social systems through treaties, conquest, expropriation, and other means. Spencer also employed the concept of compounding in another sense: to denote successive stages of internal growth and differentiation of social systems. This second usage is related to the first, since growth forces internal differentiation. For while the joining of societies causes growth, and hence necessitates internal differentiation of the system, Spencer sometimes discussed compounding of the internal system without reference to how increases in size occur. It is with this latter use of the concept of compounding that we will begin our discussion of structural elaboration as conceptualized by Spencer.

Spencer consistently made reference to primary, secondary, and tertiary compounding, and as we will see later, these three stages of differentiation are one of the major bases for his classification of social systems.[35] Primary compounding occurs when an initially homogeneous structure undergoes rudimentary structural differentiation among three great classes of functions: *(a) regulatory* functions, in which separate structures for stabilizing relations with the external environment and relations among the system's internal components can be observed, *(b) operative* or sustaining functioning, where specific structures for meeting the internal needs of the system are evident, and *(c) distributive* functions, in which particular structures for carrying vital substances and information among differentiated system parts are observable. Spencer implied that *(a)* and *(b)* are the first and most developed axes of differentiation in simple compound systems, with *(c)* being only incipient. Moreover, Spencer also emphasized that in simple compound societies, all three functional divisions within organic and superorganic systems may not be great. For example, the differentiation of regulative and operative structures may only be observable in the sexual division of labor in kinship units of a "primitive" band, with men performing leadership, hunting, and warfare activities and with women engaging in domestic work.[36]

Secondary compounding occurs, Spencer argued, when the structures involved in regulative, operative, and distributive functions undergo further differentiation. For example, internal administrative structures may become distinguished from warfare roles in the regulative system; or varieties of domestic activities, with specialized persons or groups involved in these separate activities, may become evident; and distinguishable persons or groups involved in external trade and internal commerce may become differentiated. Tertiary compounding occurs when these secondary structures each undergo further internal differentiation so that one can observe distinct structures involved in varieties of regulative, operative, and distributive processes.

---

[35] Spencer, *Principles of Sociology*, vol. 1, pp. 479–83.

[36] The accuracy of Spencer's description is not at issue here.

These distinctions among primary, secondary, and tertiary compounding will become more evident when we examine Spencer's classification of societies. For the present, we should simply emphasize that Spencer visualized structural elaboration as a process of increasing differentiation of social structures along three major axes: regulative, operative, and distributive processes.

Contained within Spencer's view of structural elaboration is a mode of functional analysis upon which we should comment. By viewing social structures with reference to regulative, operative, and distributive processes, Spencer implicitly argued that these three processes represent basic functional needs of all organic and super-organic systems. Thus, a particular structure is to be assessed in terms of its contribution to one or more of these three basic needs. But Spencer's functionalism is even more detailed, for he argued in several places that all social structures have their own internal regulative, operative, or distributive needs, regardless of which of the three functions they fulfill for the larger social whole in which they are located.[37] Furthermore, he noted that these internal needs or requisites can be visualized as four universal functions:[38] *(a)* intake of necessary materials for maintenance of the system, *(b)* operations on these materials so that they can be converted into useful commodities and distributed within the system, *(c)* the regulation of internal activity in relation to external conditions, and *(d)* the carrying away of wastes and potentially harmful materials.

Under *social functions,* Spencer also argued that structural changes are accompanied by changes in their function.[39] As a structure becomes differentiated from other structures, it assumes ever more specialized functions for the system. The result of this process is for increasingly specialized structures, performing narrow functions, to become dependent upon each other for vital materials and information. Since the specialized units cannot perform all of the processes needed for their maintenance, they become increasingly dependent upon each other for their continuance and survival. This differentiation of structures and functions, accompanied by the need for coordination of functions, forces social and bodily systems to develop high degrees of integration if they are to survive. And if such integration is achieved, then the capacity of the organism or social structure to survive in its environment is

---

[37] Spencer, *Principles of Sociology,* p. 477.

[38] This brief discussion anticipates the four requisites that Talcott Parsons was later to use in his elaborate action theory. See, for example, Talcott Parsons, *Action Theory and the Human Condition* (New York: Free Press, 1978).

[39] Spencer, *Principles of Sociology,* pp. 488–90.

increased.[40] For Spencer felt that differentiated structures could more readily adjust and adapt to a variety of environmental conditions than could homogeneous systems.[41]

These functional considerations are, in many ways, subordinate to Spencer's primary goal: to document the nature, form, and direction of structural differentiation. In so doing, he devoted considerable attention to specifying the properties of differentiation among and within regulatory, operative, and distributive systems. To appreciate the power of Spencer's analysis, then, we should minimize his more functional statements and draw attention to his discussion of the pattern of structural differentiation in social systems. To do this, we will return to Spencer's discussion of operative, regulatory, and distributive processes.

Spencer devoted the majority of his attention to analyzing the regulatory system.[42] His discussion revolves around delineating those conditions under which the regulatory system (a) becomes differentiated from operative and distributive processes and (b) becomes internally differentiated. To a very great extent, the conditions for (a) and (b) are the same and can be summarized in two general statements: (1) the more a social aggregate engages in external conflict, the more its regulatory system will develop; and (2) the more extensive are the internal operative processes within a system, the more its regulatory system will develop. Spencer also recognized the feedback processes inherent in these two conditions: once a regulatory system becomes developed in response to either internal needs for coordination or external threat, its development encourages expanded internal and external activities. For example, in a series of enlightening and contemporary passages, Spencer documented how war forces the development of a warlike governmental form; and once this form is created, it seeks out conflict with other societies, even when the original conflict under which it initially emerged has been resolved.

In general, the development of the regulatory system reveals a certain pattern. First, as it grows in size, it internally differentiates. Such differentiation is initially between separate military subsystems, which are oriented to the external environment, and internal administrative agencies, which seek to regularize operative and distributive processes. After this initial two-part differentiation, a third subsystem of the overall regulatory

---

[40] Much of Spencer's analysis here is similar to Talcott Parsons' later discussion of the process of "adaptive upgrading" that accompanies his work on evolution. See *Societies: Evolutionary and Comparative Perspectives* (Englewood Cliffs, N.J.: Prentice-Hall, 1966).

[41] Spencer had first made this generalization in *First Principles*, and later applied it to the organic realm in his *Principles of Biology* (New York: D. Appleton, 1866).

[42] Spencer, *Principles of Sociology*, vol. 1, pt. 2, pp. 519–48.

system differentiates separate monetary structures that facilitate the movement of persons and commodities within a system, and between different systems. Second, as the regulatory system grows in size and internally differentiates, it becomes increasingly centralized. And third, as the regulatory system becomes large and centralized, the volume of information necessary for regulatory activities increases and the central decision-making offices become increasingly dependent upon subordinate units for necessary information.

This pattern of development can vary somewhat, Spencer argued, depending upon whether the impetus to development comes from external conflict or internal expansion. When coming from external conflict, the regulatory system will be more militaristic and centralized. Moreover, there will be greater control over, and regulation of, internal operative and distributive processes. Yet one of the dialectics of human organization is that once operative and distributive processes become expanded under the pressures of external conflict, they increasingly begin to exert pressures for less militaristic activity and for less constrained and authoritarian centralization. Thus, for example, a nation at war will initially centralize along authoritarian lines in order to mobilize resources for the war effort, but as such mobilization expands the scope of operative and distributive processes, they develop an autonomy of their own and begin to press for greater freedom from centralized control. In this way, Spencer was able to visualize war as an important force in societal development, but at the same time, he was to see it as an impediment to development after a certain level of growth in internal system processes. And in an enlightening chapter on "social metamorphoses,"[43] Spencer argued that the dynamic underlying the overall evolution of the super-organic from homogeneous to heterogeneous states is the successive movement of societies in and out of "militant" (authoritarian) and "industrial" (less centralized) phases.

Spencer devoted considerably less space to the analysis of the operative or sustaining system and the distributive system. In his discussion of the sustaining system, he emphasized that war is often the initial impetus to growth and differentiation in operative processes. He also proposed a "law of localization," which represents an application of the principle of segregation enunciated in First Principles.[44] This law postulates that internal differentiations will tend to become concentrated in a particular

---

[43] Ibid., pp. 577–85.

[44] This law simply applied Spencer's notion that motion exerts different force on various parts of a system, propelling them in diverse directions until the force dissipates. But once a given activity is initiated, it becomes elaborated, making it more distinctive. See earlier discussion of Spencer's "laws of the cosmos."

geographical area, with the result that different towns, communities, and regions will become specialized in various activities, particularly economic tasks. Thus, there will be various types of manufacturing centers, trade centers, agricultural regions, and the like.

Probably the most insightful passages in Spencer's discussion concern the relationship between the operative and regulatory systems. On the one hand, each of these initial axes of differentiation encourages the growth and development of the other in a positive feedback cycle, while on the other hand, there is also a kind of inherent tension and dialectic between the two. For example, war expands regulatory functions; increased regulatory capacity allows for more extensive coordination of operative processes; greater operative capacity encourages expanded war efforts, and hence, expansion of the regulatory system. But, at some point in this positive feedback cycle, development of internal operative structures primarily for war making becomes counterproductive, limiting the scope and diversity of development in operative processes. And over time, and under growing pressures from the internal sector, the warlike profile of the regulatory system is reduced. Then, operative processes expand and differentiate in many different directions (in accordance with the laws of segregation and multiplication of effects), but over time, they become too divergent, poorly coordinated, and unregulated. A war can provide, Spencer thought, the needed stimulus to greater regulation and coordination of these expanded and diversified operative processes, thus setting into motion the cycle once again.

Such had been the case throughout evolutionary history, Spencer thought. But curiously, Spencer also seemed to argue that modern, industrial capitalism now made the need for war and extensive regulation by a central state obsolete. No longer would it be necessary, in Spencer's capitalistic utopia, for centralized government, operating under the pressures of war, to seek extensive regulation of operative and distributive processes. These processes were, in Spencer's utopian vision, now sufficiently developed and capable of growth, expansion, and integration without massive doses of governmental intervention. As was to be the case for Marx and other early pioneers in sociology, Spencer's initial insights are best left alone, without being diluted and distorted by infusions of ideology. For in his less ideological moments, Spencer captured one of the essential properties of system processes: the relations among growth, centralization, and decentralization.[45]

---

[45] Decentralization is relative and does not involve an absence of regulatory control, but less direct control when compared to militaristic systems.

As both regulatory and operative processes develop, Spencer argued, pressures for transportation, communication, and exchange among larger and more differentiated units increase. The result of these pressures is for new structures to emerge as part of a general expansion of distributive functions. Spencer devoted considerable attention to the historical events causing increases in transportation, roads, markets, and communication processes, and by themselves, these descriptions make for fascinating reading. At the most general level, he concluded:

> The truth we have to carry with us is that the distributing system in the social organism, as in the individual organism, has its development determined by the necessities of transfer among inter-dependent parts. Lying between the two original systems, which carry on respectively the outer dealings with surrounding existences, and the inner dealings with materials required for sustentation [sic] its structure becomes adapted to the requirements of this carrying function between the two great systems as wholes, and between the sub-divisions of each.[46]

As the regulatory and operative systems expand, thereby causing the elaboration of the distributive system, this third great system differentiates in ways that facilitate increases in (1) the speed with which material and information circulate and (2) the varieties of materials and information that are distributed. And as the capacities for rapid and varied distribution increase, then regulatory and operative processes can develop further; as the latter expand and differentiate, new pressures for rapid and varied distribution are created. Moreover, in a series of insightful remarks, Spencer noted that this positive feedback cycle involves an increase in the ratio of information to materials distributed in complex, differentiating systems.[47]

In sum, then, Spencer's view of structural elaboration emphasizes the processes of structural growth and differentiation through the joining of separate systems and through internal increases in size. As an evolutionist, Spencer took the long-range view of social development as growth, differentiation, integration, and increased adaptive capacity; then, with this new level as a base, further growth, differentiation, and integration and adaptive capacity would be possible. Spencer's view of structural elaboration is thus highly sophisticated, and while flawed in many ways, it is the equal of any other 19th-century social theorist. And as we

---

[46] Spencer, *Principles of Sociology*, p. 518.

[47] Of course, the absolute amounts of both increase, but the processing of information—credits, accounts, ideas, purchase orders, and so on—increases as a proportion of things circulated.

will examine later, there are a number of interesting models and fundamental principles contained in Spencer's view of structural elaboration. This vision also served as the basis upon which Spencer sought to classify social systems.

The Bases for Classifying Social Systems. Spencer's most famous typology is on what he termed *militant* and *industrial* societies—a typology, we feel, that has been grossly misinterpreted by commentators. Too often this typology is viewed as representing a unilinear course of evolutionary movement from traditional and militant to modern and industrial societal forms. While Spencer often addressed the evolution of societies from a primitive to modern profile, he did not rely heavily upon the militant-industrial typology in describing types or stages of evolutionary change. Rather, the militant-industrial distinction is primarily directed at capturing the difference between highly centralized authority systems where regulatory processes dominate and less centralized systems where operative processes prevail.[48] The term *industrial* does not necessarily mean "industry" in the sense of modern factories and markets. Instead, industry pertains to the degree of vitality and diversity in operative processes, whether these be those of a primitive or modern society. Thus, both the simplest and most modern societies can be militant or industrial. Spencer hoped, of course, that modern industrial capitalism would be "industrial" rather than "militaristic," but as we noted in the last section, Spencer saw societies as cycling in and out of centralized and decentralized phases. And it is this dynamic which the typology is meant to capture. In Table 4–1, we emphasize this aspect of Spencer's thought in our brief representation of the militant-industrial typology.

The distinction between militant and industrial societies emphasizes that during the course of social growth, differentiation, integration, and adaptive upgrading,[49] societies move in and out of militant (dominance of regulatory) and industrial (operative) phases. Militant phases consolidate the diversified operative structures of industrial phases. The causes

---

[48] The reason for the misinterpretation of Spencer's intent resides in the fact that the typology is introduced at several points in *Principles of Sociology.* If one reads its usage in his discussion of political and industrial (economic) institutions, it would be easy to see the typology as Spencer's version of the stages of evolution. But if one reads the more analytical statement in the early chapter on social types and constitutions in volume 1, paying particular attention to the fact that this chapter precedes the one on social metamorphoses, then our interpretation is clear. And since Spencer uses another typology for describing the long-run evolutionary trends, it seems unlikely that he would duplicate this effort with yet another typology on militant-industrial societies. See, in particular, *Principles of Sociology,* vol. 1, pt. 2, pp. 569–80.

[49] We are using Talcott Parsons's terms here because they best connote Spencer's intent. See Parsons, *Societies.*

TABLE 4–1
Spencer's Typology of Militant and Industrial Societies

Basic system processes	Militant	Industrial
1. Regulatory processes		
a. Societal goals	Defense and war.	Internal productivity and provision of services.
b. Political organization . . .	Centralized; authoritarian.	Less centralization; less direct authority on system units.
2. Operative processes		
a. Individuals	High degrees of control by state; high levels of stratification.	Freedom from extensive controls by state; less stratification.
b. Social structures	Coordinated to meet politically established goals of war and defense.	Coordinated to facilitate each structure's expansion and growth.
3. Distributive processes		
a. Flow of materials	From organizations to state; from state to individuals and other social units.	From organizations to other units and individuals.
b. Flow of information . . .	From state to individuals.	Both individuals to state and state to individuals.

of either a militant or industrial profile for a system at any given time are varied, but Spencer saw as critical *(a)* the degree of external threat from other systems and *(b)* the need to integrate dissimilar populations and cultures. The more threat from external systems, and/or the more diverse the populations of a system (an internal threat), the more likely is it to reveal a militant profile. But once external and internal "threats" have been mitigated through conquest, treaties, assimilation, and other processes, then pressures for movement to an industrial profile increase. Such is the basic dynamic underlying broad evolutionary trends from a homogeneous to heterogeneous state of social organization.

Spencer's other typology, which has received considerably less attention than the militant-industrial distinction, addresses the major stages in the evolution of societies. Whereas the militant-industrial typology seeks to capture the cyclical dynamics underlying evolutionary movement, Spencer's other typology attempts to describe the distinctive stages of long-term societal development. This typology revolves around describing the pattern and direction of societal differentiation. As such, it is concerned with the processes of compounding, leading Spencer to mark four distinctive stages of societal growth and differentiation: (1) simple, (2) compound, (3) double compound, and (4) treble compound. For stages 1, 2, and 3, Spencer provided descriptions of their structure and demographic characteristics.[50] Spencer also provided in his more detailed descriptions of various institutions a view of trebly compound (modern) societies, although in the actual presentation of the typology he assumed that readers (as members of trebly compound systems) could provide a description for themselves.[51]

In Table 4–2, we have filled in the description for all four stages and have organized the description in a somewhat more formal way than Spencer did in his narrative. But the listing of characteristics for simple (both those with leaders and those without), compound, double compound, and trebly compound in terms of regulatory, operative, and distributive and demographic dimensions captures the essence of Spencer's intent. Several points need to be emphasized. First, while certain aspects of Spencer's description are flawed, his summary of the distinctive stages is equal, or superior, to any that have been recently delineated by anthropologists and sociologists.[52] Second, this description is far superior to any developed by other anthropologists and sociologists of Spencer's time, whether the scholar be Tylor, Morgan, Maine, Weber, Marx, Durkheim, or any of many who developed evolutionary typologies.

Spencer sought to communicate with this typology what we can term *structural explanations*.[53] The basic intent of this mode of explanation is to view certain types of structures as tending to coexist. As Spencer concluded:

> The inductions arrived at . . . show that in social phenomena there is a general order of co-existence and sequence; and therefore social phenomena form the subject-matter of a science reducible, in some measure at least, to the deductive form.[54]

Thus, by reading down the columns of Table 4–2, we can see that certain structures are likely to coexist within a system. And by reading across the table, the *patterns* of change in structures with each increment

---

[50] See Spencer, *Principles of Sociology*, vol. 1. pt. 2, pp. 549–75.

[51] See ibid., vol. 1, pt. 3, and vol. 2, pts. 4–7. Moreover, Spencer's *Descriptive Sociology* provided an even more detailed account of all four stages. See later discussion of this forgotten work.

[52] See, for example, Parsons, *Societies*, and *The System of Modern Societies* (Englewood Cliffs, N.J.: Prentice-Hall, 1971); Gerhard Lenski and Jean Lenski, *Human Societies* (New York: McGraw-Hill, 1978); and Morton H. Fried, *The Evolution of Political Society* (New York: Random House, 1967).

[53] George Homans suggested this term to us.

[54] Spencer, *Principles of Sociology*, vol. 1, pt. 2, p. 597.

of societal differentiation can be observed. Moreover, as Spencer stressed, such patterns of social evolution conformed to the general law of evolution enunciated in *First Principles:*

> The many facts contemplated unite in proving that social evolution forms a part of evolution at large. Like evolving aggregates in general, societies show *integration*, both by simple increase of mass and by coalescence and re-coalescence of masses. The change from *homogeneity* to *heterogeneity* is multitudinously exemplified; up from the simple tribe, alike in all its parts, to the civilized nation, full of structural and functional unlikenesses. With progressing integration and heterogeneity goes increasing *coherence*. We see the wandering group dispersing, dividing, held together by no bonds; the tribe with parts made more coherent by subordination to a dominant man; the cluster of tribes united in a political plexus under a chief with sub-chiefs; and so on up to the civilized nation, consolidated enough to hold together for a thousand years or more. Simultaneously comes increasing *definiteness*. Social organization is at first vague; advance brings settled arrangements which grow slowly more precise; customs pass into laws which, while gaining fixity, also become more specific in their applications to varieties of actions; and all institutions, at first confusedly intermingled, slowly separate, at the same time that each within itself marks off more distinctly its component structures. Thus in all respects is fulfilled the formula of evolution. There is progress towards greater size, coherence, multiformity, and definiteness.[55]

In sum, then, Spencer provided two basic typologies for classifying societal systems. One typology—the militant-industrial distinction—is not primarily developmental or evolutionary in scope, as is too often assumed. Rather, it is a typology of cyclical phases of all societies at any particular stage of evolution. The second typology is less well known, but probably more important. It delineates the structural features and demographic profile of societies at different stages of evolution. In this typology is a series of statements on what structures tend to cluster together during societal growth and differentiation. This typology is, in many ways, the implicit guide for Spencer's structural and functional analysis of basic societal institutions, which comprises parts 3 through 7 in volumes 1 and 2 of *Principles of Sociology*. We should, therefore, close our review of *Principles of Sociology* by briefly noting some of the more interesting generalizations that emerge from Spencer's description of basic human institutions.

---

[55] Ibid., p. 596.

TABLE 4–2
Spencer's Stages of Evolution

	Simple Society	
	Headless	*Headed*
Regulatory system	Temporary leaders who emerge in response to particular problems	Permanent chief and various lieutenants
Operative system:		
a. Economic structure ..	Hunting and gathering	Pastoral; simple agriculture
b. Religious structure ...	Individualized religious worship	Beginnings of religious specialists: shaman
c. Family structure	Simple; sexual division of labor	Large, complex; sexual and political division of labor
d. Artistic-literary forms	Little art; no literature	Some art; no literature
e. Law-customs	Informal codes of conduct	Informal codes of conduct
f. Community structure	Small bands of wandering families	Small, settled groupings of families
g. Stratification	None	Chief and followers
Distributive system:		
a. Materials	Sharing within family and band	Intra- and inter-familial exchange and sharing
b. Information	Oral, personal	Oral, personal
Demographic profile:		
a. Size	Small	Larger
b. Mobility	Mobile within territory	Less mobile; frequently tied to territory

Empirical Observations on Basic Institutions

Spencer provided extensive descriptions of the structure, function, and evolutionary transformations of six basic institutions. His most prominent generalizations on each institution are summarized below.

1. Domestic Institutions.[56] Spencer saw the function of the kinship system as "the reproduction of the species." In terms of structural trans-

[56] Ibid., vol. 1, pt. 3, pp. 603–757.

Compound Society	Double Compound	Treble Compound (never formally listed)
Hierarchy of chiefs, with paramount chief, local chiefs, and varieties of lieutenants	Elaboration of political state; bureaucratized; differentiation between domestic and military administration	Modern political state
Agricultural; general and local division of labor	Agriculture; extensive division of labor	Industrial capitalism
Established ecclesiastical arrangements	Ecclesiastical hierarchy; rigid rituals and religious observance	Religious diversity in separate church structures
Large, complex; numerous sexual, age, and political divisions	Large, complex, numerous sexual, age, and political divisions	Small, simple; decrease in sexual division of labor
Artists	Artists; literary specialists; scholars	Many artistic literary specialists; scholars
Informal codes; enforced by political elites and community members	Positive law and codes; written	Elaborate legal codes; civil and criminal
Village; permanent buildings	Large towns; permanent structures	Cities, towns, and hamlets
Five or six clear ranks	Castes; rigid divisions	Classes; less rigid
Travel and trade between villages	Roads among towns; considerable travel and exchange; traders and other specialists	Roads, rail, and other nonmanual transport; many specialists
Oral, personal; at times, mediated by elites or travelers	Oral; written; edicts; oracles; teachers and other communications specialists	Oral, written, formal media structures for edicts; many communications specialists
Larger; joining of several simple societies	Large	Large
Less mobility; tied to territory; movement among villages of a defined territory	Settled; much travel among towns	Settled; growing urban concentrations; much travel; movement from rural to urban centers

formations, he saw trends toward monogamy, decreased size, equality of the sexes, and articulation of children's rights.

   2. Ceremonial Institutions.[57]   Spencer felt that ceremonies had been the first mechanisms of social control in human aggregates. But as formal political and ecclesiastical institutions evolved, the social control functions of ceremony receded. Yet during militant structural forms, the functions

[57] Ibid., vol. 2, pt. 4, pp. 3–216.

of ceremony increase as a means for symbolizing the authority hierarchy; while during industrial phases, ceremony is transformed into a concern with "politeness" as a means for facilitating interaction among strangers.

3. Political Institutions.[58] The basic function of political institutions is to control and coordinate external and internal system activity. Political institutions emerge with growth in the social aggregate, and expand in scope under (a) continued growth, (b) external conflict, and (c) the need to integrate diverse populations. Political institutions originally emerged within kinship systems, but with their structural elaboration, they become differentiated from kinship systems. During militant phases in a system, especially in compound and doubly compound societies, political centralization is accompanied by increasing class differentiation. Inequalities among classes increase; movement between classes decreases; and ceremonial activities increase as a way of symbolizing ranks. But during industrial phases, particularly in trebly compound (modern) societies, rank differentiation decreases; mobility increases; and ceremony gives way to the convention of politeness.

In the long run, political evolution involves an initial movement toward hereditary political leadership, which is legitimated by ceremonial activities and ecclesiastical beliefs and rituals. But with further differentiation toward the trebly compound stage, more representative political forms become evident. The major reason for this change is that as political structures rely upon internal taxation (as opposed to conquest and pillage), those who are taxed begin to resist political authority, and over time, they force government to become more representative.

4. Ecclesiastical Institutions.[59] Spencer stressed that the functions of religion are (a) to conserve beliefs and (b) to strengthen social bonds through ritual activities. Religion initially emerged in human societies to replace ceremonial institutions as the major social control mechanisms, and then, with the evolution of political institutions, it assumed a subordinate function to the state; although the displacement of the ecclesiastical control structure by political structures is always a conflict-ridden process. But in the end, ecclesiastical institutions come to serve legitimating functions for an expanding state. With further societal differentiation, religion becomes increasingly compartmentalized and segregated from daily activity. Moreover, ecclesiastical institutions become internally differentiated as new cults and churches appear. Thus, while the functions of religion decrease in modern societies, Spencer argued that the initial

[58] Ibid., pt. 5, pp. 229–643.

[59] Ibid., pt. 6, pp. 3–159. We should note how close this view of religious functions is to that to be developed by Émile Durkheim. See Chapter 11.

growth of ecclesiastical structures had provided the system integration which was essential for subsequent evolutionary change.

5. *Professional Institutions.*[60] Spencer noted that professional institutions become increasingly prominent in modern societies. Their major function is to provide fellowship, organization, and regulation among groups of specialists, for as the social system becomes differentiated, the needs for subgroup organization, as well as a sense of comradery among those with similar occupations increases.

6. *Industrial Institutions.*[61] As we have noted earlier, Spencer used the term *industrial*, in several different ways. In this context, he employed the term as a synonym for economic organization. His view of economic functions is that the economy provides and distributes necessary goods and services. Over the long run, the economy becomes increasingly differentiated, providing an ever-increasing volume and variety of goods and services. Spencer presented a complex feedback model in outlining economic growth: increased production forces expansion of the distributive mechanisms in a society; and as the distributive processes are altered to increase the flow of economic products, this transformation represents positive feedback to the productive sector, encouraging expanded production, which places further pressures for growth in the distributing sector; and so on. This positive feedback cycle is fed by constantly escalating consumptive desires of the population, for as people achieve one level of consumption, their needs escalate and place further demands for expansion on the productive and distributing sectors of the economy. And thus, it is out of this series of positive feedback cycles that economic growth occurs; and while such growth is facilitated or retarded by processes in other institutions, particularly political institutions, these feedback cycles represent a constant source of force and motion that fuel the evolutionary development of societies.

This brief summary of Spencer's analysis of the structure, function, and evolutionary development of basic institutions does not do justice to the sophistication of his analysis. As much as any scholar of his time, or today, Spencer saw the complex interrelationships among social structures. One reason for this sophistication in Spencer's analysis is his indepth knowledge of diverse societies, which he acquired through the efforts of his colleagues to construct descriptions of historical and contemporary societies. For throughout Spencer's work, his ideas are illustrated

---

[60] Ibid., pt. 7, pp. 179–315. Again, we should note how close this conceptualization is to Durkheim's subsequent view of "occupational" and "corporate" groups.

[61] Ibid., pt. 8, pp. 327–608.

by references to diverse societies. Such familiarity with many historical and contemporary societies came from his efforts to build a *descriptive sociology*—a fact that is often forgotten by Spencer's critics and detractors.

A NOTE ON SPENCER'S *DESCRIPTIVE SOCIOLOGY*

Spencer commissioned a series of volumes that sought to describe the characteristics of different societies.[62] These volumes were, in Spencer's vision, to contain no theory or supposition, but rather, they were to constitute the "raw data" from which theoretical inductions could be made or by which deductions from abstract theory could be tested. These descriptions became the data source for Spencer's sociological work, particularly his *Principles of Sociology.* As he noted in the "Provisional Preface" of volume 1 of *Descriptive Sociology:*

> In preparation for *The Principles of Sociology*, requiring as bases of induction large accumulations of data, fitly arranged comparison, I . . . commenced by proxy the collection and organization of facts presented by societies of different types, past and present . . . the facts collected and arranged for easy reference and convenient study of their relations, being so presented, apart from hypotheses, as to aid all students of social science in testing such conclusions as they have drawn and in drawing others.[63]

Spencer's intent was to use common categories for classifying "sociological facts" on different types of societies. And in this way, he hoped that sociology would have a sound data base for developing the laws of super-organic bodies.[64] In light of the data available to Spencer, the

[62] The full title of the work reads: *Descriptive Sociology, or Groups of Sociological Facts.* The list of volumes of *Descriptive Sociology* is as follows: 1. *English* (1873); 2. *Ancient Mexicans, Central Americans, Chibchans, Ancient Peruvians* (1874); 3. *Types of Lowest Races, Negritto, and Malayo-Polynesian Races* (1874); 4. *African Races* (1875); 5. *Asiatic Races* (1876); 6. *North and South American Races* (1878); 7. *Hebrews and Phoenicians* (1880); 8. *French* (1881); 9. *Chinese* (1910); 10. *Hellenic Greeks* (1928); 13. *Mesopotamia* (1929); 14. *African Races* (1930); and 15. *Ancient Romans* (1934). A revised edition of no. 3, edited by D. Duncan and H. Tedder, was published in 1925; a second edition of no. 6 appeared in 1885; no. 14 is a redoing by Emil Torday of no. 4. In addition to these volumes, which are in folio size, two unnumbered works appeared: Ruben Long, *The Sociology of Islam*, 2 vols. (1931–33), and John Garstang, *The Heritage of Solomon: An Historical Introduction to the Sociology of Ancient Palestine* (1934).

[63] *The English*, classified and arranged by Herbert Spencer, compiled and abstracted by James Collier (New York: D. Appleton, 1873), p. vi.

[64] The methodological premise and substance of Spencer's *Descriptive Sociology* was later adopted by the anthropologist George Murdock in his Human Area Relations Files, which, it should be emphasized, are not analytically superior to Spencer's efforts. The data for Murdock's files were obviously better than those available to Spencer and his collaborators.

volumes of *Descriptive Sociology* are remarkably detailed. What is more, the categories for describing different societies are still useful. While these categories differ slightly from volume to volume, primarily because the complexity of societies varies so much, there is an effort to maintain a consistent series of categories for classifying and arranging sociological facts. Volume 1 on *The English* can illustrate Spencer's approach.

First, facts are recorded for general classes of sociological variables. Thus, for *The English*, "facts" are recorded on the following:

1. Inorganic environment
   a. General features.
   b. Geological features.
   c. Climate.
2. Organic environment
   a. Vegetable.
   b. Animal.
3. Sociological environment
   a. Past history.
   b. Past societies from which present system formed.
   c. Present neighbors.
4. Characteristics of people
   a. Physical.
   b. Emotional.
   c. Intellectual.

It will be recalled that this initial basis of classification is consistent with Spencer's opening chapters in *Principles of Sociology*. (See his section on "Critical Variables.")

Second, the vast majority of *The English* is devoted to a description of the historical development of British society, from its earliest origins to Spencer's time, with respect to the following topic headings:

Division of labor

Regulation of labor

Domestic laws—marital

Domestic laws—filial

Political laws—criminal, civil, and
   industrial

General government

Local government

Military

Ecclesiastical

Professional

Accessory institutions

Funeral rites

Laws of intercourse

Habits and customs

Aesthetic sentiments

Moral sentiments

Religious ideas and superstitions

Knowledge

Language

Distribution

Exchange

Production

Arts

Agriculture, rearing, and so forth

Land—works

Habitations

Food

Clothing

Weapons

Implements

Aesthetic products

Supplementary materials

Third, for some volumes like *The English,* more detailed descriptions under the above headings are represented in tabular form. Thus, *The English* opens with a series of large and detailed tables, organized under the general headings "regulative" and "operative" as well as "structural" and "functional." The tables begin with the initial formation of the English peoples around A.D. 78 and documents through a series of brief statements, organized around basic topics (see above list), up to around 1850. By reading across the tables at any given time period, the reader is given a profile of the English for that period. By reading down the columns of the table, the reader can note the patterns of change of this society.

The large, oversize volumes of *Descriptive Sociology* make fascinating reading. They are, without doubt, one of the most comprehensive and detailed descriptions of human societies ever constructed, certainly surpassing that of Weber or any other comparative social scientist of the late 19th and early 20th centuries. While the descriptions are flawed by the sources of data (historical accounts and traveler's published reports), Spencer's methodology is sound. Had the volumes of *Descriptive Sociology* not lapsed into obscurity[65] and had they been updated with more accurate accounts, modern social science would, we believe, have a much firmer data base for comparative sociological analysis and for theoretical activity.

SPENCER'S WORK IN RETROSPECT

As we have emphasized, Spencer's more philosophical and moral works are best forgotten. But his sociological works, particularly *Principles of Sociology*, reveal methodological, descriptive, and theoretical power. Our primary concern in this book is on Spencer's theoretical contribution, and thus, in the next chapter, we will seek to make more explicit Spencer's abstract theoretical models and principles.

For the present, we should emphasize again that Spencer saw, as much as any scholar of his time, the fundamental relationship among increases in system size, differentiation, integration, and environmental adaptation. He also recognized the internal dynamics of systems as they cycle in and out of highly centralized and less centralized states. And with a clarity unsurpassed even today, he saw and described the basic pattern of long-run evolutionary changes in human societies. Moreover, with an unparalleled degree of sophistication, Spencer saw the need for a descriptive data base for inductive and deductive theorizing.

Thus, one of the great intellectual tragedies of 20th-century sociology is the neglect of Spencer's basic works. We hope this chapter has stimulated a renewed interest in Spencer, for his work is as deserving of our careful scrutiny as that of any other scholar of the last century.

---

[65] All of the volumes of *Descriptive Sociology* were not completed upon Spencer's death, but he left money in his will for the work to be completed by others—thus emphasizing his commitment to an empirically based science.

5

HERBERT SPENCER III:
MODELS AND PRINCIPLES

THE BASIC THEORETICAL APPROACH

Herbert Spencer devoted his life to articulating a "synthetic philosophy," and thus his sociological works are only a part of a much larger philosophical scheme. Yet there is a clear intellectual boundary to his purely sociological efforts, making it possible to delineate his basic theoretical approach in sociology. This approach begins with the "cardinal principles" of Spencer's *First Principles*.[1] The general thrust of these principles is to view evolution as a process of change from a homogeneous, incoherent, and unstable state to a more differentiated, integrated, and stable state. Spencer never waivered from this "law" and it serves as the basic theoretical premise that guides all of his sociological efforts.

When analyzing specific realms of the universe, whether psychic, biological, or sociological, Spencer would make implicit deductions from his general law of evolution to the phenomenon under investigation. Thus, when analyzing super-organic bodies, the law of evolution first enumerated in *First Principles* becomes the general axiom from which deductions to the laws of societal evolution and dissolution are made. Yet such implicit deductions are not the only theoretical tactic. Spencer also felt that comparisons between organic and super-organic phenomena could serve as a starting point for determining the kinds of derivations that are most appropriate.

Spencer's sociological analysis thus follows from his general law of evolution as mediated through comparisons between organic and super-

---

[1] Herbert Spencer, *First Principles* (New York: A. L. Burt, 1880; originally published in 1862).

organic bodies. The result of this procedure is for Spencerian sociology to be concerned with growth, differentiation, integration, and adaptation. In so doing, Spencer offered sociological theory a series of interesting theoreticial models and principles.

SPENCER'S THEORETICAL MODELS

Spencer presented two basic models of human organization. One concerned the long-run evolutionary development of human societies, while the other sought to accent the more specific dynamics of social systems. We will first present this overall evolutionary model, and then outline Spencer's more detailed models of system processes.

The Evolutionary Model

For Spencer, human evolution involves movement from simple and homogeneous societies to increasingly more differentiated and complex systems. As such, societal evolution is but one type of more general evolutionary processes in the cosmos. Societal differentiation, Spencer felt, occurs along three broad classes of functions—regulatory, operative, and distributive—and as such reveals a parallel to growth and development in organic bodies.[2] The first differentiation is between the regulatory and operative, but with growth of, and differentiation within, structures performing these functions, separate distributive structures emerge. Subsequent evolution involves growth of, and internal differentiation within, each of these three classes of structures. Thus, for example, the regulatory system of a society will initially differentiate into separate administrative (for internal affairs) and military (external relations) subsystems. And with further evolution, the military and administrative branches grow and differentiate internally, while a new type of regulatory structure, the monetary, differentiates from the military and administrative. Similarly, operative and distributive structures become increasingly differentiated from the regulatory and from each other, while becoming internally differentiated. As we saw in the previous chapter, Spencer labeled four conspicuous stages in this evolutionary process: (1) simple, (2) compound, (3) double compound, and (4) treble compound.

Simple societies are those where regulatory, operative, and distributive processes are not greatly differentiated. Compound societies are created

---

[2] This evolutionary model is best communicated in vol. 1, pt. 2 of Spencer's *Principles of Sociology* (New York: D. Appleton, 1885; originally published in 1874).

by the joining of simple societies or by internal growth. They reveal clear differentiation between regulatory and operative processes, as well as some internal differentiation within each. However, distributive structures are not clearly separated from either regulatory or operative processes. But in double compound societies, where separate regulatory and operative systems have further undergone growth and internal differentiation, a separate set of distributive processes does become clearly differentiated. And in treble compound systems, regulatory, operative, and distributive structures expand and differentiate even further.

This pattern of long-run growth and differentiation in human societies is represented in Figure 5–1. This model reproduces in diagrammatic form much of the information in Table 4–2 presented in the last chapter. But this time, the successive differentiation within and between regulatory, operative, and distributive structures is drawn in the way that Spencer visualized the process of evolution. This vision of evolution is inspired by a biological model of growth in organisms, since societal evolution involves growth and differentiation along three major functional systems that have their analogies in more complex animal organisms. Such analogizing can be viewed as a limiting constraint, but it did allow Spencer to capture many of the most salient properties of long-term societal evolution.

The Models of System Dynamics

In *First Principles*, Spencer had defined evolution as an "integration of matter and concomitant dissipation of motion; during which the matter passes from an indefinite incoherent homogeneity to a definite coherent heterogeneity; and during which the retained motion undergoes a parallel transformation."[3] Too often, this definition is seen to apply only to long-term evolution, as is diagramed in Figure 5–1 above. Yet, for Spencer, evolution is also a general term referring to the dynamics of "structuring" or "institutionalization," whether this be short or long term. This fact becomes particularly clear when it is recognized that "dissolution" is considered to be a fundamental social process.[4] Evolution and dissolution are thus the terms that Spencer used to denote the related processes of institutionalization and de-institutionalization—that is, structuring and unstructuring of social relations. Spencer offered two views of these related processes: (1) the process of institutionalization

---

[3] Spencer, *First Principles*, p. 343.

[4] See Ibid., pp. 449–67 and *Principles of Sociology*, vol. 1, pt. 2, pp. 576–87.

and (2) the cyclical phases of centralization and decentralization of institutionalized relations. Each of these is examined below.

Spencer's General Model of Institutionalization. The general "law"
of evolution provided Spencer with the metaphor for specifying the
key processes of creating and elaborating social structures. The basic
processes are *(a)* forces causing growth in system size (whether by compounding smaller units or internal creation of new units); *(b)* the differentiation of units in terms of the "laws" of segregation and multiplication
of effects (the homogeneity to heterogeneity portion of the law of evolution); *(c)* the processes whereby differentiated units become integrated
(the integration of matter and dissipation of motion portions); and *(d)*
the creation of a "coherent heterogeneity," which increases the level
of adaptation to the environment.

Thus, for Spencer, institutionalization is a process of growth in size,
differentiation, integration, and adaptation. With integration and increased adaptation, a new system is institutionalized and capable of further growth, provided that there is a "force" that can join social systems
or otherwise increase the number of units. For example, a society that
grows as the result of conquering another will tend to differentiate along
conquered and conqueror lines; it will centralize authority; it will create
relations of interdependence; and hence it will become more adapted
to its environment. The result of this integration and adaptation is an
increased capacity to conquer more societies—hence, setting into motion
another wave of growth, differentiation, integration, and adaptation. Similarly, a nonsocietal social system such as a corporation can begin growth
through mergers or expenditures of capitals, but it soon must differentiate
functions, and then integrate them through a combination of mutual
dependence of parts and centralization of authority. If such integration
is successful, it has increased the adaptive capacity of the system, and
it can grow, if some force (such as capital surplus) is available. This
vision of institutionalization is diagramed in Figure 5–2.

Figure 5–2 outlines the stages of institutionalization. As is emphasized,
the fundamental processes of growth, differentiation, integration, and
adaptive upgrading are, to some extent, conditioned *(a)* by external factors, such as the availability of natural resources, *(b)* by internal factors,
like the nature of the internal units, and *(c)* by derived factors, such
as the existence of other societies or internal values and beliefs. It is
also important to emphasize that, when viewed this way, much of the
rather strange terminology in Spencer's definition of evolution is rendered
more understandable. Some "force," whether economic capital, a new
technology, a need to gather resources, new values and beliefs, and so

FIGURE 5–1
Spencer's Model of Evolution

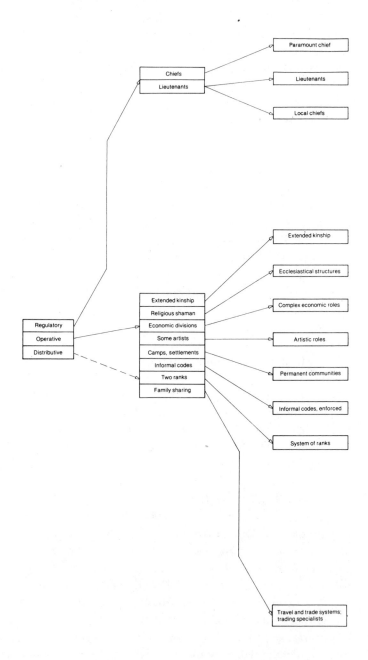

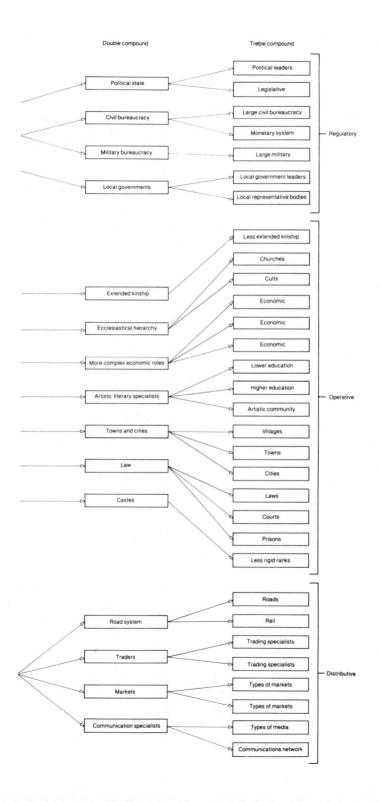

Double compound

Treble compound

Political state
— Political leaders
— Legislative

Civil bureaucracy
— Large civil bureaucracy
— Monetary system

Military bureaucracy
— Large military

Local governments
— Local government leaders
— Local representative bodies

Regulatory

Extended kinship
— Less extended kinship
— Churches
— Cults

Ecclesiastical hierarchy
— Economic
— Economic
— Economic

More complex economic roles
— Lower education
— Higher education

Artists; literary specialists
— Artistic community

Towns and cities
— Villages
— Towns
— Cities

Law
— Laws
— Courts
— Prisons

Castes
— Less rigid ranks

Operative

Road system
— Roads
— Rail

Traders
— Trading specialists
— Trading specialists

Markets
— Types of markets
— Types of markets

Communication specialists
— Types of media
— Communications network

Distributive

FIGURE 5–2
Spencer's Model of Institutionalization

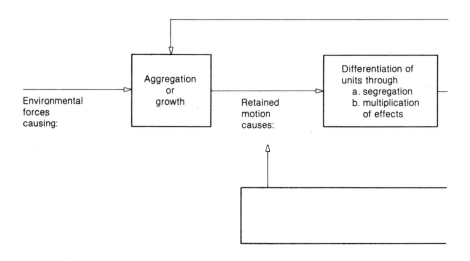

on, sets into "motion" system growth. This motion, as it acts differently on various units, sends them in different directions and "segregates" them such that their differences are "multiplied" as the retained motion allows for their elaboration in response to their distinctive environments. Yet if the system is not to explode apart, the units or "matter" must be "integrated," thereby dissipating or channeling the motion of the parts in ways that increase the "coherence" of the whole. Such coherence increases the adaptive capacity of the system.

Conversely, to the extent that integration is incomplete and/or the force that drives the system is spent and cannot be replaced, then dissolution of the system is likely. Thus, social systems grow, differentiate, integrate, and achieve some level of adaptation to the environment, but at some point their driving force is spent or units cannot become integrated, setting the system into a phase of dissolution.

The Model of System Phases. Spencer visualized that during institutionalization, social systems cycle through phases where authority becomes highly centralized, and then less centralized. As we noted in the last chapter, Spencer saw centralization as primarily a response to environmental threats and conflict or a response to extreme internal diversity. But he also recognized that the process of differentiation and integration, per se, are involved. Social systems will be centralized rapidly under conditions of external or internal threat, but regardless of these forces, they possess an inherent dialectic in that decentralized systems

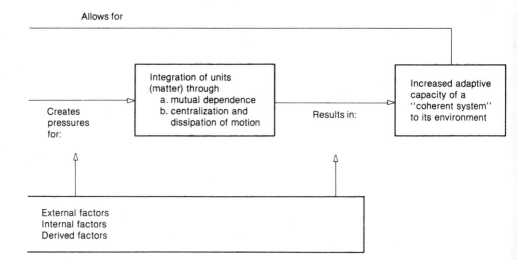

experience pressures for increased centralization, while highly centralized systems reveal pressures for less direct control by centralized authority. This cyclical process, as Spencer saw it, is modeled in Figure 5–3.

If we begin analysis of the phases at box 1, as Spencer would have intended, then the cycle is initiated with differentiation and diversification of the system and its constituent parts. Such growth leads to integrative problems, which increase with further diversifications of units (box 2), eventually creating pressures for consolidation of differentiated and diversified units. At some point, and under variable conditions, these pressures lead to centralization of authority (box 3), which results in tight control of internal operative and distributive processes by regulatory centers (box 5). Over time, such control creates stagnation by limiting the developmental options of system units (box 6), with the result that pressures for deregulation mount. At some point, under varying conditions, these pressures lead to decentralization (box 8) which sets off a new wave of differentiation and diversification (box 1).

This model supplements Spencer's general view of institutionalization (Figure 5–2) by specifying the more rhythmic cycles that occur during institutionalization. In turn, both the general mode of institutionalization and this model on the phases of institutionalization provide some insight into Spencer's view of the dynamics underlying long-term evolutionary development, as presented in Figure 5–1. While these models do not capture all of the short-term and long-term dynamics of social systems,

FIGURE 5–3
Phases of Institutionalization

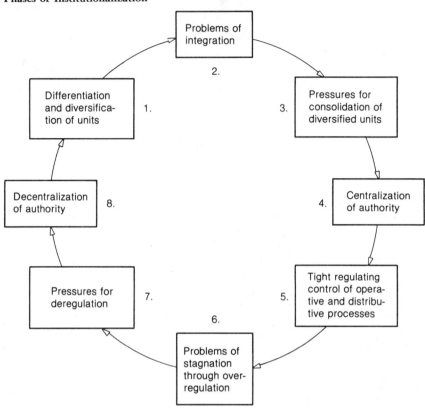

they present interesting and useful leads for further theoretical and empirical investigation. Yet, it is our view that Spencer's real theoretical contribution resides less in the models that he implicitly employed than in his formulation of a few fundamental principles of social organization.

SPENCER'S THEORETICAL PRINCIPLES

Spencer, like Comte before him, recognized that the development of sociology as a science requires the formulation of abstract principles that denote fundamental relationships among phenomena in the social, or super-organic, realm. While these principles would be connected to the universal principles of evolution, and while they would reveal some affinity to the principles of biology or organic systems, they would, nevertheless, be unique to sociology, since social systems constitute a distinctive realm in the universe. Over the course of the last chapter and in this chapter, we have alluded to these principles. Our goal in this section is to state them more formally. We will attempt to organize this more formal statement under three general headings: (1) principles of growth and differentiation, (2) principles of internal differentiation, and (3) principles of differentiation and adaptation.

Principles of System Growth and Differentiation

Spencer saw a fundamental relationship in the social universe between the size of a social aggregate and the process of structural differentiation.[5] He phrased this insight in the metaphor of "growth," with the result that differentiation in social systems is a positive function of increases in the size of a social aggregate. And with this growth metaphor, he specified additional relationships: the rate of growth and the degree of concentration of aggregate members during growth are also related to structural differentiation. Moreover, he saw that increases in system size are, to a very great extent, related to previous increases in the size and level of differentiation of an aggregate. Those aggregates that are able to integrate differentiating social units at one point in time are in a better position to increase their size and level of differentiation at a subsequent point in time. These insights into the relationship among growth, size, and differentiation in social systems can be expressed in the following propositions:

1. The larger is a social system, the greater will be its level of structural differentiation.
2. The greater is the rate of growth of a social system, the greater is its rate and degree of structural differentiation.
3. The more growth in the numbers of members in a social system is concentrated, the more likely is that growth to be accompanied by high rates of structural differentiation.
4. The more growth and differentiation at one point in time has resulted in structural integration of system units, the more likely is that system to grow and differentiate further at a subsequent point in time.

Principles 1 and 2 state what Spencer felt to be invariant relations, regardless of other conditions. Principles 3 and 4 are expressed more

---

[5] Spencer had originally arrived at this insight in his *Principles of Biology* (New York: D. Appleton, 1866).

probabilistically, since specific empirical conditions can influence the likelihood that differentiation will follow from concentration alone and previous patterns of integration. But just whether these principles represent invariant laws or probabilistic statements is probably less important than Spencer's basic insight: in the social world, growth, size, and differentiation are fundamentally related. Spencer was the first to perceive clearly this basic relationship, and it marks one of his more enduring contributions to sociological theory.

Principles of Internal System Differentiation

Spencer did more than attempt to relate structural differentiation in social systems to size, growth, population concentration, and previous patterns of integration. He also sought to understand, and express as a series of formal principles, the nature and course of structural differentiation in social systems.[6] The first of these principles concerns the sequence of differentiation among different types of structures in social systems.

5. **The more a social system has initiated the process of structural differentiation, the more likely is the initial axes of differentiation to be between regulatory and operative structures.**

6. **The more a social system has differentiated separate regulatory and operative structures, and the greater is the volume of activity in that system, the more likely are separate mediating structures involved in distributive processes to become differentiated from regulatory and operative structures.**

Once separate regulatory, operative, and distributive structures become differentiated, there are pressures for integration. Spencer saw two major mechanisms of integration:[7] *(a)* mutual dependence of diverse units on each other and *(b)* centralization of authority in the regulatory system. Hence, Spencer offered the following principle:

7. **The more differentiated are the three major axes in a social system, the greater are its integrative problems, and hence, the more likely are relations of mutual interdependence and centralized authority to develop in that system.**

For Spencer, then, differentiation in social systems occurs along three general axes, occurs in a particular order, and eventually generates pres-

---

[6] See Spencer, *Principles of Sociology*, vol. 1, pt. 2.

[7] Spencer's failure to recognize that cultural ideas are also a major integrative force led Durkheim, and others of the French tradition, to reject Spencerian sociology.

sures for integration.[8] Subsequent differentiation among either the regulatory, operative, or distributive structures also occurs, Spencer argued, in a particular pattern and sequence. The pattern of differentiation for the regulatory, operative, and distributive systems can thus be expressed as follows:

8. The greater is the degree of differentiation along the regulatory axes, the more likely is differentiation to occur initially between structures dealing with *(a)* the external environment and *(b)* internal activities, and only after the differentiation of *a* and *b* is differentiation of regulatory structures for facilitating the exchange of resources likely to occur.

9. The greater is the degree of differentiation along the operative axes, the more likely are diverse activities to become spatially separated and localized.

10. The greater is the degree of differentiation along the distributive axes, *(a)* the greater is the *rate* of movement of materials and information in the system, *(b)* the greater is the *variety* and volume of materials and information distributed in the system, and *(c)* the higher is the *ratio of information to materials* distributed in the system.[9]

These propositions are stated more abstractly than intended by Spencer who was primarily concerned with societal social systems. Yet they follow Spencer's intent, which was to stress that as the regulatory system differentiates, it initially creates separate structures for dealing with internal and external problems, such as a military and civil bureaucracy in a societal system. Later, structures evolve to facilitate the flow of materials and other vital resources, since regulation of large and complex systems is only possible with common distributive media, such as money in societal systems. These insights, expressed in principle 4 above, also apply to other types of social systems, such as organizations, communities, and perhaps large groups. Principle 9 states that differentiation, in accordance with the laws of force, motion, segregation, and multiplication of effects, tends to create ever more diverse structures, with similar activities becoming spatially concentrated into districts that are distinguishable from

---

[8] We might note that Talcott Parsons, Robert F. Bales, and Edward Shils in their *Working Papers in the Theory of Action* (Glencoe, Ill.: Free Press, 1953) reached a similar conclusion.

[9] Information does not necessarily exceed material resources; only the ratio between them decreases.

each other in terms of their type of activity. Principle 10 stresses that as distributive structures differentiate, there is greater need for increased speed and volume in the movement of materials and information, since the expansion of distributive structures is a direct response to growth in the size and complexity of operative and regulatory processes.

Spencer recognized that the nature of internal differentiation varied in terms of external and internal conditions. Systems in one kind of external environment, or with a particular composition of units, would become internally structured in ways that would distinguish them from systems in different external and internal circumstances. Spencer saw war and the diversity of races as the key external and internal variables. And if we abstract above Spencer's discussion of these variables for societal systems, the following principles become evident:

11. The greater is the degree of external environmental threat to a differentiating system, the greater is the degree of internal control exercised by the regulatory system.
12. The greater is the degree of threat to system stability posed by dissimilar units, the greater is the degree of internal control exercised by the regulatory system.
13. The greater is the degree of control by the regulatory system, the more is growth and differentiation of operative and distributive structures circumscribed by the narrow goals of the regulatory system.

Spencer recognized, however, that external and internal control create pressures for their relaxation. And with less regulatory control, internal diversity and dissimilarity increases, with the result that eventual pressures would be created favoring centralization of regulatory control. Thus, we need two final propositions to complete Spencer's analysis of internal differentiation in social systems:

14. The more operative and regulatory structures are circumscribed by centralized regulatory structures, the more likely are they, over time, to resist such control, and the more they resist, the more likely is control to decrease.
15. The less operative and distributive processes are circumscribed by centralized regulatory structures, the greater are problems of internal integration, and the more likely is the regulatory system to increase efforts at centralized control.

The Principle of Differentiation and Adaptation

Spencer felt that differentiated social structures are better able to adapt to environmental conditions.[10] As he stated in *First Principles*, homogeneous masses are unstable and vulnerable to disruption by environmental forces, whereas differentiated systems with their relations of interdependence and centralized regulatory apparatus can cope more effectively with environmental forces. Indeed, differentiated systems can act on their environment, frequently using it for their purposes. This view of differentiation and adaptation can be expressed as follows:

16. The greater is the degree of structural differentiation in a system, and the greater is its level of internal integration, the greater is its adaptive capacity.

And as emphasized in principle 4, super-organic systems that are well adapted to their environments are capable of further growth and differentiation. Well-organized systems can extract resources from the environment or they can join, absorb, or conquer other systems in their environment.

CONCLUSION

In these three chapters on Spencer, we have sought to demonstrate the power of his sociological works. For the most part, we have ignored Spencer's moral preachings, since they obscure and detract from his more sociological work.

As we turn to scholars who are more typically considered the giants of early sociology—Marx, Weber, Durkheim, and Mead—it must be emphasized that Spencer's accomplishments are equal to those of sociology's "other masters." Indeed, the models and principles presented in this chapter reveal considerable insight into the properties and processes of social systems. Had Spencer been consulted as often as Marx, Weber, Durkheim, and Mead by modern sociologists, contemporary theory would be that much further advanced. Hopefully, our sympathetic analysis of Spencer can serve as a stimulus for others to recognize the genius of one of sociology's first theorists.

---

[10] This insight he took from his *Principles of Biology*, as well as from *First Principles*.

6

KARL MARX I:
THE INTELLECTUAL
ORIGINS OF HIS THOUGHT

Karl Marx's analysis of capitalism represents one of the most striking and original achievements in the history of social thought. As we shall see in subsequent chapters, he constructed a theoretical analysis that sought to account for the origins of capitalism, its historical stability, and its eventual demise. In the process, he combined social theory and revolutionary action in a way that has never been duplicated. That his analysis is shortsighted in some respects and misbegotten in others does not detract from its evocativeness. Yet, like all scholars, Marx benefitted from the legacy of concepts and ideas that had been advanced by others.

Marx was a voracious reader, and his writings are filled with detailed analyses of the philosophers and political economists of the day. This chapter will briefly describe four of Marx's most significant intellectual debts. In the first section, Marx's reaction to the writings of G. W. F. Hegel is depicted. In the second, Marx's rejection of the ideas of Ludwig Feuerbach and the other Young Hegelians is shown. The third section portrays Marx's rejection of Adam Smith and the other capitalist political economists. In the fourth section, the influence of Friedrich Engels on Marx's thought is described.

G. W. F. HEGEL AND KARL MARX

The origin of Marx's social theory lies in his youthful reaction to the writings of George William Friedrich Hegel. In four main books, *The Phenomenology of Mind* (1807), *The Science of Logic* (1816), *The Encyclopedia of Philosophy* (1871), and *The Philosophy of Right* (1821),

114

Hegel sketched one of the most original, complex, and obscure philosophical doctrines ever devised.[1] While a student at the University of Berlin, the young Marx first came into contact with what he called the "grotesque and craggy melody" of Hegel's philosophy, and this moment marked a fundamental turning point in his life.[2] Over the next several years, Marx composed (among other works) "A Contribution to the Critique of Hegel's *Philosophy of Right*" (1843), *The Economic and Philosophical Manuscripts of 1844*, *The Holy Family* (with Friedrich Engels, 1845), and *The German Ideology* (also with Engels, 1846).[3] Paradoxically, only *The Holy Family*, the least significant of these works, was published at the time. These books and manuscripts constitute Marx's early attempts at grappling with Hegel's thought. Taken together, they reveal the process by which Marx transformed Hegel's philosophy into an empirically based social science, albeit a peculiar one, in which Hegel's idealism is decisively rejected, while Hegel's reliance on dialectical analysis is retained and applied to the material world. To appreciate Hegel's influence on Marx, we need to briefly discuss Hegel's idealist philosophy and Marx's major criticisms of it. Only then can we begin to see the continuity and discontinuity between the two men's ideas.

Hegel's Idealism

In Hegel's writing, idealism is a complex philosophical doctrine that can be only superficially sketched here. The essence of idealism consists in the denial that things in the finite world—such as trees, houses, people, or any other physical object—are ultimately real. In Hegel's words, idealism "consists in nothing else than in recognizing that the finite has no veritable being."[4] For Hegel, true reality is embodied in that which is discovered through reason. In thus emphasizing the importance of thought and reasoning, Hegel was following a philosophical

---

[1] G. W. F. Hegel, *The Science of Logic* (London: Allen & Unwin, 1969); *The Phenomenology of Mind* (New York: Macmillan, 1961); *The Encyclopedia of Philosophy* (New York: Philosophical Library, 1959); and *The Philosophy of Right* (Oxford: Clarendon Press, 1942).

[2] Karl Marx, "Discovery of Hegel (Marx to His Father)," in Robert C. Tucker, ed., *The Marx-Engels Reader* (New York: W. W. Norton, 1978), pp. 7–9.

[3] Karl Marx, "A Contribution to the Critique of Hegel's *Philosophy of Right*," in Tucker, ed., *Marx-Engels Reader* pp. 16–26 and 53–66; Karl Marx, *The Economic and Philosophical Manuscripts of 1844* (New York: International Publishers, 1964); Karl Marx and Friedrich Engels, *The Holy Family* (Moscow: Foreign Languages Publishing House, 1956); and Karl Marx and Friedrich Engels, *The German Ideology* (New York: International Publishers, 1947).

[4] Hegel, *Science of Logic*, p. 154.

tradition that originated with Plato. From this point of view, the objects perceived by the senses are not real: they are merely the phenomenal appearance of a more ultimate reality of ideas. Rather, only "logical objects," or concepts, constitute ultimate reality. As Hegel wrote, "it is *only* in thought that [an] object is truly in and for itself; in intuition or ordinary perception it is only an appearance."[5] Hegel continued by asserting that if only concepts are real, then the ultimate concept is God, and his philosophy is essentially an attempt at proving the existence of God through the application of reason. According to Hegel, previous philosophers had seen only finite things as real and had relegated the infinite (or God) to the "mere 'ideal.' " He argued that his separation is artificial and cannot show how God exists and acts through people, since it involves a logical impossibility: finite things, which must inevitably perish, remain; while the infinite, which is absolute and cannot perish, is kept separate and placed in an abstract and mentally conceived beyond. If this latter were true, Hegel argued, then God could not have come to earth in the form of Jesus, and the bread and wine of the Last Supper were merely bread and wine.

Hegel argued that there is an inherent dialectical relationship between God (the infinite) and people (the finite). The essence of the dialectic is contradiction: each concept implies its opposite or, in Hegel's terms, each concept implies its negation. Thus, after proposing that "the finite has no veritable being," Hegel immediately said, "the finite is ideal," that is, its essence lies in that which contradicts it: the infinite, God. In this way, the finite world of flesh and blood is annihilated (at least in thought) and "the infinite can pass over from the beyond to the here and now; that is, become flesh and take on earthly attire," as Jesus did a long time ago.[6] Hence, while this phrase states the issue too simply, Hegel believed that human history can be considered the autobiography of God, since it only "exists" through its negation by the infinite and the latter's manifestations in this world. Yet, as in Christianity, even as the finite world of things is destroyed, it is saved. In Hegel's words, "the finite has vanished in the infinite and what *is*, is only the *infinite,* " or everlasting life.[7] One implication of this analysis is a belief in the reality of transubstantiation. Another implication, which is also characteristic of some forms of Christianity, is a relatively passive acceptance of

[5] Ibid., p. 585 (emphasis in original).

[6] Lucio Colletti, *Marxism and Hegel* (Atlantic Highlands, N.J.: Humanities Press, 1973), p. 12. This is a good Marxist source. One of the best non-Marxist commentaries is John N. Findlay, *Hegel: A Re-Examination* (London: Allen & Unwin, 1958).

[7] Hegel, *Logic of Science*, p. 138 (emphasis in original).

the political status quo. For example, Hegel said "all that is real is rational; and all that is rational is real."[8] Statements like this were taken by many as a sanctification of the Prussian state, with its despotism, police government, Star Chamber proceedings, and censorship. Hence, the Prussian government glorified Hegel's philosophy for its own purposes and, when he died, gave him a state funeral.

Marx's Rejection of Hegel's Idealism

Marx reacted strongly against Hegel's idealism, criticizing it in a number of ways. First, and most important, he completely rejected Hegel's assertion that finite or empirical phenomena are not ultimately real. All his other criticisms follow from this basic point. Marx believed that when empirical phenomena are only understood as thoughts, then people's more significant practical problems are ignored. Neither material objects nor relationships can be changed by merely thinking about them.[9] The puerile quality of Hegel's point is evident, Marx suggested, in a simple example: if people are alienated such that they have no control over their lives or the material things produced by their labor, they cannot end their alienation by changing their perception of reality (or by praying, for that matter).[10] Rather, people must change the social structure in which they live; that is, they must make a revolution in this world rather than waiting for the next. Marx believed that life in this world posed a variety of very practical problems that people could only solve in practical ways, and human reason is of little use unless it is applied to the problems that exist in the finite world.

Second, according to Marx, Hegel's emphasis on the ultimate reality of thought led him to misperceive some of the essential characteristics of human beings. For example, Marx charged that while Hegel correctly "grasps labor as the essence of man," "the only labor which [he] knows and recognizes is abstractly mental labor."[11] Yet people have physical needs, Marx noted, such as for food, clothing, and shelter, which can only be satisfied by productive activity in the finite world. Hence, for Marx, the most significant labor is productive activity rather than mental

---

[8] Quoted in Friedrich Engels, "Ludwig Feuerbach and the End of Classical German Philosophy," in Karl Marx and Friedrich Engels, *Selected Works*, vol. 3 (Moscow: Progress Publishers, 1970), p. 337.

[9] See Marx, *Manuscripts of 1844*, p. 176, where he writes that in Hegel, physical "entities, objects, [only] appear as thought entities."

[10] Ibid., p. 175.

[11] Ibid., p. 177.

activity. Similarly, Marx said that Hegel's belief in the unreality of finite things led him to a position in which people are regarded as nonobjective, spiritual beings. But Marx asserted that people are "natural beings," that is, they have physical needs that can only be satisfied in this world.

> As a natural, corporeal, sensuous, objective being [a person] is a suffering, conditioned and limited creature, like animals and plants. That is to say, the objects of his instincts exist outside him, as objects independent of him; yet these objects are objects that he needs—essential objects, indispensable to the manifestation and confirmation of his essential powers. To say that man is a corporeal, living, real, sensuous, objective being full of natural vigor is to say that he has real, sensuous, objects as the objects of his being or of his life, or that he can only express his life in real sensuous objects.[12]

Marx's third criticism is also an outgrowth of the first in that he rejected the religious motif that pervades Hegel's work. As noted above, Hegel denied reality to the finite world in order to prove the existence of God, albeit a Christian God. But Marx believed that when "reason" is applied to such impractical problems, people are prevented from recognizing that they are exploited and that they have an interest in changing the status quo in this world. For Marx, the next world was a religious fantasy, not worth worrying about. Thus Marx was particularly vitriolic, yet strangely poetic, in his denunciation of the religious implications of Hegel's philosophy.

> Religion is the sigh of the oppressed creature, the sentiment of a heartless world, and the soul of soulless conditions. It is the opium of the people. The abolition of religion as the illusory happiness of men, is a demand for their real happiness. The call to abandon their illusions about their conditions is a call to abandon a condition which requires illusions. The criticism of religion is, therefore, the embryonic criticism of this vale of tears of which religion is the halo.[13]

Marx believed that one of the main functions of religion is to blind people so they cannot realistically evaluate their true situation and interests. Religion does this by emphasizing that compensation for misery and exploitation on earth will come in the next world.

Marx's fourth criticism of Hegel is that idealism is politically conservative rather than revolutionary. It creates the illusion of a community of people rather than the reality of a society riddled with opposing inter-

---

[12] Ibid., p. 181.

[13] Marx, "A Contribution to the Critique of Hegel's *Philosophy of Right*," p. 54.

ests. This illusion results in part from Hegel's assertion that the state, a practical and physical entity, emerges out of the Spirit, or thought. In this way, Hegel imbued the state with a sacred quality. As Marx noted, Hegel "does not say 'with the will of the monarch lies the final decision' but 'the final decision of the will is—the monarch.' "[14] When the state is sacred, then history can be seen as part of an overall divine plan that is not only reasonable but necessary. It is for this reason that Marx interpreted Hegel's philosophy as politically conservative.

Marx's Acceptance of Hegel's Dialectical Method

Despite his complete rejection of idealism, Marx saw a significant tool in Hegel's use of the dialectic. But in Hegel's hands, the entire analysis is couched in terms of a mystical theology. Thus, as Marx noted in *Capital*, Hegel's dialectic "is standing on its head. It must be turned right side up again, if you would discover the rational kernal within the mystical shell."[15] As we will show in Chapter 6, the process by which Marx turned the dialectic "right side up" involved its application to the finite world where people make history by producing their sustenance from the environment. Rather than being concerned with the existence of God, Marx emphasized that the focus must be on concrete societies (seen as social systems) and with actual people who have conflicting interests.

The significance of turning Hegel "on his head" is that, for Marx, no product of human thought or action can be final; there can be no absolute truth which, when discovered, needs only be memorized. From this point of view, science can only increase knowledge, it cannot discover absolute knowledge. Moreover, there can be no end to human history, at least in the sense of attaining an unchanging utopia, a perfect society. Such social structures can only exist in the imagination. Rather, every society is only a transitory stage in an endless course of human development. This development occurs as conflict is systematically generated out of people's opposing interests. While each stage of history is necessary and, hence, justified in terms of the conditions in which it originated, progress occurs as the old society inevitably loses its reason for being. In Marx's work, the dialectical method means that nothing can be final or absolute or sacred: everything is transitory and conflict is everywhere.

---

[14] Quoted in Sidney Hook, *From Hegel to Marx* (Ann Arbor: University of Michigan Press, 1962), p. 23.

[15] Karl Marx, *Capital*, vol. 1. (New York: International Publishers, 1967), p. 20.

LUDWIG FEUERBACH AND KARL MARX

During the 1830s and early 1840s, Marx belonged to a group of alienated philosophers and other intellectuals, all of whom were disciples or students of Hegel. These Young Hegelians, as they are called, produced a tremendous volume of writing in which they tried to cope with the intellectual edifice built by the master. Apart from Marx, the major figures in the group were such men as David Strauss, Bruno Bauer, Max Stirner, and Ludwig Feuerbach.[16] Among them, the most important influence on Marx's intellectual development was unquestionably Feuerbach.

The Young Hegelians and Marx's Thought

Like Hegel, the Young Hegelians dealt with the nature of reality and the relationship between religious belief and reality. However, since religion legitimated oppressive political conditions, the Young Hegelians rejected the political conservatism that seemed inherent to Hegel's thought. They reacted in this way partly because of the social conditions in which they lived, since during most of the 19th-century Prussia was perhaps the most repressive nation in Europe. And, in Prussia, religion was seen as one of the chief pillars of the state. The Young Hegelians believed that the church's emphasis on the sanctity of tradition, authority, and the renunciation of worldly pleasures helped to prop up an oppressive governmental apparatus. But since political agitation was not possible (without being arrested or expatriated), the Young Hegelians sought to criticize the state indirectly by investigating the sacred texts, doctrines, and practices of Christianity.

For example, in 1835, David Strauss published *The Life of Jesus Critically Examined*, in which he tried to show that the Gospels are not accurate historical narratives.[17] This book prompted great controversy, since if the life of Jesus as portrayed in the Gospels is not to be believed, then the authority of the church is seemingly undermined. Shortly thereafter, Bruno Bauer published a series of articles in which he denied the historical existence of Jesus altogether and tried to explain the Gospels as works of pure fiction.[18] By debunking the nature and logic of Christian tenets (and, hence, the church) in this way, the Young

---

[16] See Hook, *Hegel to Marx*, for a good exposition of the Young Hegelians' writings.

[17] David Strauss, *The Life of Jesus Critically Examined* (London: Swan Sonneschein, 1902).

[18] On Bauer, see Hook, *Hegel to Marx*.

Hegelians hoped also to impugn the authority of the state. However, the Prussian government quickly recognized the seditious implications of these works, and as a result, Bauer was dismissed from his university post, while the other Young Hegelians suffered varying degrees of surveillance and political harassment.

Nonetheless, despite their political stance, all these men were still Hegelian in orientation, and this fact eventually led to Marx's split with them. For example, in *The Ego and His Own: The Case of the Individual Against Authority* (1844), Max Stirner argued that there is nothing objective outside the individual.[19] According to Stirner, social institutions, such as the church, are oppressive to the individual's spirit. Like a true Hegelian, Stirner then asserted that reality is not based upon people's sense perceptions. As in Hegel, reality is created by the imagination and will of each person and, as a corollary, there is no objective reality apart from the ego. Thus, according to Stirner, individuals should avoid participating in the society as much as possible and, in this way, they can avoid being oppressed by authority. With this argument, Stirner anticipated the development of anarchist thought some years later. Marx, however, believed that Stirner's position was politically futile, since social institutions must be controlled rather than ignored.

As will be seen in our discussion of *The German Ideology* in Chapter 7, Marx believed that the Young Hegelians were intellectual mountebanks, and he wrote hundreds of pages of vituperation against them. For example, he and Engels made fun of Stirner, Bauer, and others by calling them "The Holy Family," and referring to them as "Saint Max" and "Saint Bruno."[20] More generally, Marx developed four main criticisms of the Young Hegelians, all of which can be seen as variations on his criticisms of Hegel. First, their writings treated the development of theology independently of the actual activities of the church and other social institutions that were pervaded by theological ideas. Such an emphasis ignored the fact that the development of ideas never proceeds apart from human practices. Second, the Young Hegelians were essentially idealists in that the origin of religious as well as other kinds of thought was to be found in the Spirit; but for Marx, religion and all other ideas emerge from people's actual social relationships and in their need to survive. Third, the Young Hegelians' writings were fatalistic in that the historical process was seen as automatic and inexorable, either

---

[19] Max Stirner, *The Ego and His Own: The Case of the Individual Against Authority* (New York: Libertarian Book Club, 1963).

[20] See Marx and Engels, *Holy Family*, and the latter portions of *German Ideology*.

because it was directed by the Spirit or because it was directed by individuals (such as the Prussian king) who were somehow connected with the Spirit. For Marx, while history has direction and continuity, it can also be shaped by human action. Fourth, and most fundamentally, the Young Hegelians foolishly believed that by changing ideas they could change human behavior. Therefore, they fought a war against the state, using words as the primary weapons. Wars must be fought with guns, Marx believed, and those who do not recognize this elementary fact are very unrealistic. There is one exception to his indictment of the Young Hegelians, however. The only member of the group whom Marx did not vilify, even though the two men disagreed strongly, was Ludwig Feuerbach.

Feuerbach and Marx's Thought

Like the other Young Hegelians, Feuerbach was also interested in the religious implications of Hegel's philosophy, but unlike the other Young Hegelians, Feuerbach fundamentally altered the direction of Marx's thought. This occurred, first, in terms of Marx's critique of Hegel and, second, in the development of Marx's peculiar but highly effective version of social theory.

In his book *The Essence of Christianity* (1841), Feuerbach undercut both Hegel's and the Young Hegelians' writings by arguing that religious beliefs arise out of people's unconscious deification of themselves.[21] According to Feuerbach, human beings have taken all that they believe is good in themselves and simply projected these characteristics onto God. He showed how the "mysteries" of Christianity—the mysteries of the Creation, the suffering God, the Holy Trinity, the Immaculate Conception, the Resurrection, and the like—all represent human ideals. Thus, Feuerbach argued that theology is simply a mythical vision of human aspirations and that "what man praises and approves, that is God to him; what he blames [and] condemns is the non-divine."[22] The true essence of religion, Feuerbach believed, was to be found in anthropology not theology, for "religion is man's earliest . . . form of self-knowledge."[23]

With this analysis, Feuerbach emerged as the leader of the Young Hegelians for several reasons. First, while most Young Hegelians were

---

[21]Ludwig Feuerbach, *The Essence of Christianity* (New York: Harper Torchbooks, 1957).

[22] Quoted in Hook, *Hegel to Marx*, p. 246.

[23] Feuerbach, *Essence of Christianity*, p. 13.

content to analyze and critique Christian theology, Feuerbach decisively rejected any analysis that treated theology as existing independently of empirical activities. Second, while many Young Hegelians still accepted the idea that God necessarily directed human affairs, Feuerbach argued that an abstract and amorphous Spirit cannot be the guiding force in history, since people are simply worshipping projections of their own characteristics and desires. Third, while the other Young Hegelians continued to be mired in idealism, Feuerbach was a materialist in the sense that he believed people's consciousness of the world is the product of their brains and, hence, of physical matter. To Marx and others, this position seemed clearsighted after the obfuscations and puerile logic of Hegel, Strauss, Bauer, and Stirner.

Feuerbach's argument had yet another consequence for Marx. In Feuerbach's work, Marx found the key to criticizing Hegel and, ultimately, to developing a social theory designed to promote revolutionary action. Marx realized that Feuerbach's analysis of religion as an expression of human desires could be generalized to people's relationships to other social institutions (especially the state) and, in fact, to any situation in which human beings are ruled by their own creations. Thus, following Feuerbach, Marx reversed Hegel's argument, which asserted that the state emerges from the spirit, by arguing that the modern state emerged out of capitalist social relationships (which he called "civil society").[24] This argument has important implications, for if the state is the product of human action, then it can be changed by human action. Marx's mature social theory follows from this fundamental insight.

ADAM SMITH AND KARL MARX

By the late 18th-century, England had already become a relatively industrialized and commercial nation. As such, it constituted the first fully capitalist society, with the result that scholars attempted to account for the origins of capitalism, its nature, and its future development. Along with Marx, such men as Adam Smith, David Ricardo, and many others developed a new mode of analysis—called *political economy*— and sought to understand the characteristics of industrial capitalism. After being introduced to the study of political economy by Friedrich Engels and others, Marx began to deal with the topics characteristic of the new discipline. For example, in *The Economic and Philosophical Manuscripts of 1844*, he analyzed (among other things) the origin of

---

[24] Marx, "Hegel's *Philosophy of Right.*"

the value of commodities, the origin of profit, the role of land in a capitalist economy, and the accumulation of capital. However, his most detailed analyses and criticisms did not occur until the 1850s in his notebooks (subsequently published as the *Grundrisse*, or "outlines") and in *The Contribution to a Critique of Political Economy*.[25] From these efforts Marx's great work, *Capital*, was eventually to emerge.

Political Economy and Marx's Thought

Marx's detailed analyses of various political economists are less important today than his more general criticisms of their works. In his opinion, the literature in political economy displayed two fundamental defects. First, capitalist social relations were assumed to reflect "irrefutable natural laws of society." As a result of this emphasis, basic types of social relations, such as exchange, exploitation, and alienation, were all assumed (at least by implication) to be historically immutable. Second, the political economists analyzed each part of society separately, as if it had no connection with anything else.[26] For example, even strictly economic categories such as production, exchange, distribution, and consumption were generally treated as if they were separate and unconnected phenomena. But Marx had learned from Hegel (and Feuerbach) that history has a dialectical pattern to it. As a result, Marx saw capitalism as a historically unique pattern of social relationships that would inevitably be supplanted in the future. Thus, he set himself the task of developing a scientific analysis of capitalist society which could account for both its pattern of development and its eventual demise.

While Marx regarded most political economists as simply bourgeois ideologues, he believed that Adam Smith and David Ricardo were the two most objective and insightful observers of the economics of capitalism. In the course of analyzing their work, many of Marx's fundamental insights into the dynamics of capitalism emerged. For illustrative purposes, we focus here on Smith's work.

Adam Smith and Marx's Thought

Adam Smith was a moral philosopher as well as a political economist. In his first book, *The Theory of Moral Sentiments*, originally published

---

[25] Karl Marx, *Grundrisse* (New York: Vintage Books, 1973).

[26] Karl Marx, "Introduction," *A Contribution to the Critique of Political Economy* (New York: International Publishers, 1970), pp. 188–217.

in 1759, Smith argued that there is a natural order to the world, including both its physical and social aspects, that was created by God and carefully balanced so as to benefit all species.[27] Hence, Smith emphasized the beneficent qualities of the natural order and the general inadequacy of human institutions that tried to change or alter this order. His subsequent book, *An Inquiry into the Nature and Causes of the Wealth of Nations*, published in 1776, represented Smith's attempt at applying the principles of naturalism to the problems of political economy.[28]

The Wealth of Nations deals with three main issues. First, Smith wanted to discover the "laws of the market" holding society together. In dealing with this issue, Smith hoped to show both the way in which commodities acquired value and why this value included profit for the capitalist. Second, Smith wanted to understand the laws of evolution characteristic of capitalist society. Third, like most work in political economy (at least according to Marx), *The Wealth of Nations* is a thoroughgoing defense of capitalist society, a defense that Marx was to find inadequate. Each of these facets of Smith's work is briefly analyzed below.

Laws of the Market. Smith's attempt at showing how the economic "laws of the market" hold society together begins with the assertion that people act out of self-interest when they produce commodities for other members of the society to purchase. For "it is not from the benevolence of the butcher, brewer, or the baker, that we expect our dinner but from their regard to their own interest. We address ourselves, not to their humanity, but to their self-love, and never talk to them of our own necessities but of their advantages."[29] And the advantage accrued to the butchers, bakers, and other capitalists is profit. Indeed, in Smith's view, the exchange of commodities for profit becomes a fundamental characteristic of human society whenever the division of labor and private property develop beyond a certain point. However, Marx believed that Smith was guilty of trying to make patterns of interaction that were characteristic of capitalist social relationships valid for all times and places. As an alternative, Marx envisioned a modern society without exchange relationships, since he felt that they are inherently exploitative. Nonetheless, for Smith the origin of value and profit resided in the process of commodity exchange, and by distinguishing between the "use value"

---

[27] Adam Smith, *The Theory of Moral Sentiments* (Oxford: Clarendon Press, 1976).
[28] Adam Smith, *An Inquiry into the Nature and Causes of the Wealth of Nations* (Oxford: Clarendon Press, 1976).
[29] Ibid., pp. 26–27.

and the "exchange value" of commodities, Smith achieved an insight that was later to guide Marx's thought.[30]

Smith went on to formulate a version of the labor theory of value in which the amount of labor time going into a product is the source of its value—a thesis that Marx would take over some 90 years later. But if labor is the source of value, then Smith could not account for the origin of profit, since those who profit generally contribute very little labor to the creation of the product. They merely invest money and reap a return on it. Thus, while *The Wealth of Nations* displays much vacillation and confusion, Smith ultimately dropped the labor theory of value and simply argued that profit was added on to the costs of production by the capitalists. As we shall see in the next chapter, Marx was able to adopt the labor theory of value and still account for the origin of profit by distinguishing between the workers' labor and their labor power (or capacity to work).

By arguing that profit is merely part of the cost of production, Smith created a potential problem: the "natural price" of a commodity is difficult to determine, since nothing prevents capitalists from constantly and arbitrarily raising prices. His solution was to argue that competition operates to prevent avaricious persons from pushing prices too high, for those capitalists who try to raise prices unduly (and Smith was very aware that they constantly try to do just that) will inevitably find other enterprising persons underselling them, thereby forcing prices back down. Similarly, those capitalists who attempt to keep wages too low will find that they have no workers because others offer them higher wages. In this way, then, both profits and wages are more or less automatically regulated—as if by an "invisible hand." And, paradoxically, people's selfish motives promote social harmony through the natural operation of the market, even though that goal is not their objective. In Smith's words, "by directing that industry in such a manner as its produce may be of the greatest value, he intends only his own gain . . . he is in this, as in many other cases, led by an invisible hand to promote an end which was no part of his intention."[31]

The final step in Smith's analysis is to argue that these laws of the market also insure that the proper quantities of products are produced. For example, if the public prefers to own coats rather than tables, then a greater number of the former will be produced, and since the profit involved in making tables will fall as a result, capitalists (and workers)

[30] Ibid., pp. 44–45.

[31] Ibid., p. 73.

will turn to the manufacture of coats. Thus, natural mechanisms inherent to the market govern the allocation of resources in the society and, hence, the production of goods. And once again, this process occurs as a result of people acting in terms of their own self-interest.

Laws of Evolution. During the latter portion of the 18th century and well into the 19th, many political economists speculated that as capitalism advanced, the rate of profit on investment would fall. However, Smith had a rather optimistic view of the process of history, and he did not believe this calamity would occur. To Smith, in addition to being self-regulating, society seemed to be improving because of the operation of two relatively simple laws of evolution. The first can be called the "law of capital accumulation." Smith saw that capitalists continuously try to accumulate their savings or profits, invest them, accumulate even more savings or profits, and invest them again. The latent consequence of this activity is that it increases both production and employment. Thus, from Smith's point of view, selfish motives can be seen once again to redound to the public good, since the expansion of production and employment benefits everyone in some way. (Smith did not worry about whether savings would be invested; that was to become a problem for later economists.)

Yet, if accumulation is to continue and production expand, more and more workers are required. And when the supply of workers is exhausted, then profits will fall, and hence, the rate of accumulation will also fall—just as many feared. Smith dealt with this problem by formulating a "law of population," his second law of evolution. Basically, this hypothesis asserts that when wages are high, the number of workers will increase; and when wages are low, the number of workers will decrease. He meant this statement literally, in terms of people living and dying, not their periodic ventures into or out of the labor market. Mortality rates, especially among children, were extraordinarily high in those days; it was not uncommon for a woman to have a dozen or more children and have only one or two survive. Yet it was still possible for a higher standard of living to effect decisively people's ability to feed, clothe, and protect their children. As a result, Smith argued, higher wages would allow for greater numbers of children to survive and become workers themselves. Lower wages, of course, would have the reverse effect. Thus, Smith believed that the advance of capitalism would be accompanied by an increase in population and that this increase would, in turn, allow capital accumulation to continue. Therefore, according to Smith, the rate of profit will not fall and capitalist society will constantly improve itself, all because of the natural forces, unencumbered by rules and regulations established by the state. While he recognized that an expanding population would always act to deflate wages, as long as capital accumulation continued, wages had to remain above the level of subsistence. Of course, Smith's argument in Marx's view assumes that capitalist social relations are somehow irrefutable "natural laws" of the social universe.

The Defense of Capitalism. As enunciated by Adam Smith, the logical implication of *The Wealth of Nations* is fairly simple: leave the market alone. From Smith's point of view, this stricture meant that the natural regulation of the market would occur as consumers' purchasing practices forced business to cater to their needs. Such a process could only occur, Smith believed, if business was not protected by the government and did not form monopolies. Hence, he opposed all efforts at protecting business advantage. However, Smith's analysis quickly became an ideological justification for preventing government regulation in some important areas. Moreover, since any act of government could be seen as interfering with the natural operation of the market, *The Wealth of Nations* was used to oppose humanitarian legislation designed to protect workers from the many abuses that were already apparent in Smith's time.

For Marx, this result was to show the inherent weakness in classical political economy, for there is nothing "natural" about the operation of the market, or any other social relationship. The market could not be left alone without the use of governmental power, which was impossible because the capitalists, like all ruling classes, controlled the government. Hence, Marx argued that theory must take into account the interconnections among the parts of society, with special attention to the way in which political power is used to justify and enforce exploitative social relationships. The capitalists, again like all ruling classes, also controlled the dissemination of ideas, which suggested to Marx why they were able to use *The Wealth of Nations* for their own ideological purposes. Hence, in the development of his own theory, Marx emphasized the importance (and the difficulty) of stimulating an awareness in the working classes of their true interests.

FRIEDRICH ENGELS AND KARL MARX

Friedrich Engels and Karl Marx were friends and collaborators for more than 40 years. When possible, they saw each other every day; at other times, they corresponded about every other day. Despite Marx's sometimes churlish temperament, the two men never broke off their relationship. As is well known, Engels provided Marx with his major source of income for many years. And after Marx's death in 1883, Engels spent the remaining 12 years of his own life disseminating Marx's theoretical and political legacy. Most commentators see Engels's role in the development of Marx's theory, apart from these last years, as secondary; with regard to their joint works, especially *The German Ideology* and *The Communist Manifesto*, this appears to be an accurate assessment (see Chapter 7).[32] Yet two of Engels' works, "Outlines of a Critique of Political Economy" (1844) and his much-neglected classic, *The Condition of the Working Class in England in 1844* (1845),[33] fundamentally influenced the development of Marx's thought at a time when he was still searching for a way of understanding and changing the world.

Engels' Critique of Political Economy and Marx's Thought

Engels's short and angry essay, "Outlines of a Critique of Political Economy," appeared in the same journal as did Marx's critique of Hegel's philosophy. In this essay, which is characterized by the excessively acerbic prose of a young man, Engels indicted both the science of political economy and the existence of private property. He began by noting caustically that political economy ought to be called "private economy," since it existed only to defend the private control of the means of production. He continued (although in a quite disorganized way) by stridently attacking the institution of private property. According to Engels, a modern industrial society based on the private ownership of property is inevitably inhumane, inefficient, and alienating. In the process of his attack, Engels also suggested (albeit vaguely) that, despite these faults, capitalism is historically necessary in order for a communist society to emerge in the future.

From Engels' point of view, capitalism is inhumane for two reasons. First, people do not and cannot trust each other. When private property exists in an industrial context, Engels wrote, trade and competition are the center of life. And since everyone seeks to buy cheap and sell dear, people must distrust and try to exploit each other. In Engels' words,

---

[32] Engels, "Ludwig Feuerbach," p. 361.

[33] Friedrich Engels, "Outlines of a Critique of Political Economy," in *Marx, Manuscripts of 1844*, pp. 197–228; and Friedrich Engels, *The Condition of the Working Class in England* (Stanford, Calif.: Stanford University Press, 1968). The current translation omits the year 1844 from the title of Engels' book; yet, he always wished to emphasize the historical nature of his analysis and rejected attempts at "universalizing" the book by dropping the year from the title. See Steven Marcus, *Engels, Manchester and the Working Class* (New York: Vintage Books, 1975), p. xii.

"trade is legalized fraud."[34] The second reason capitalism is inhumane is that competition generates an increased division of labor, one of the major manifestations of which is the factory system. As we shall see below, Engels regarded factory work and the urban life-style accompanying it as one of the most inhumane and oppressive forms of social organization in history. Yet as he saw it during the 1840s, the factory system was becoming more pervasive, and as a result, capitalist society was being divided into two groups, those who owned the means of production and those who did not.

Engels argued that capitalism is inefficient because those who dominate it can neither understand nor control the recurrent and steadily worsening economic crises that afflict every nation. Capitalist society is, therefore, beset by a curious paradox: while its productive power is incredibly great, overproduction periodically results in misery and starvation for the masses: "The economist has never been able to explain this mad situation," Engels wrote.[35] Moreover, he believed that people living under capitalism are inevitably alienated because they have no sense of community with one another. In the competitive environment that is characteristic of capitalism, each person's interests are always opposed to every other person's. As a result, "private property isolates everyone in his own crude solitariness," with the consequence that people's lives have little meaning and carry no intrinsic rewards.[36] Underlying this entire argument, however, is Engels' belief that the rise of capitalism is historically necessary in order to make a communist society possible, for only now are people "placed in a position from which we can go beyond the economics of private property" and end the "unnatural" separation of individuals from each other and from their work.[37]

Prior to 1844, the still youthful Marx was relatively unfamiliar with political economy. It was Engels' essay that, as much as any other event, introduced Marx to the topic and made him recognize its importance in developing a theory of society.[38] Thus, after reading the essay, Marx began an intensive study of political economy that was to last for more than 20 years. Ultimately, Marx indicted the science of political economy for essentially the same reason as had Engels: it defended capitalist society. In addition, all the main ideas noted above subsequently appeared in a more sophisticated fashion in Marx's theory.

---

[34] Engles, "Political Economy," p. 202.
[35] Ibid., p. 217.
[36] Ibid., p. 213.
[37] Ibid., pp. 199 and 212.
[38] David McClellan, *Friedrich Engels* (New York: Penguin Books, 1978).

Engels' Analysis of the Working Class and Marx's Thought

In order to continue his business training at the textile mills in which his father was part-owner, Engels left his native Germany for Manchester, England, in 1842. At that time, Manchester was the greatest industrial city in the most industrialized nation in the world; to many observers, it was the epitome of the new kind of society that was forming as a result of the industrial revolution. Engels spent two years in Manchester, leading something of a double life, since he not only learned the textile business but also gathered the materials for his book. During this period, nearly all his leisure time was spent walking through Manchester and the surrounding towns, talking to and drinking with working-class people, and reading the many governmental reports and other descriptions of living conditions in Manchester. The result was the first urban ethnography, and a damning indictment of the English ruling class.

Engels' analysis of *The Condition of the Working Class in England in 1844* can be divided into three parts. First, he sketched an idyllic rural society that existed prior to industrialization and briefly suggested the factors that had destroyed that society. Second, he described the conditons of working-class life in Manchester. And third, he indicated the attitudes of the bourgeosie toward the proletariat and concluded that a violent revolution is inevitable.

Peasant Life Prior to Industrialization. Like many other observers, Engels saw that the industrial revolution had utterly transformed Western society. And also like other observers, he believed that feudal society had been better for people in many ways. As a result, he described the feudal past in a very idyllic manner. While he has been justifiably criticized for idealizing the past, it is not altogether clear how (in the middle of the nineteenth century) he could have obtained a sound or accurate portrayal of feudal society.[39] Thus, *The Condition of The Working Class* begins with a description of simple, God-fearing peasants who lived in a stable and patriarchal society where "children grew up in idyllic simplicity and in happy intimacy with their playmates." Engels saw feudal life as "comfortable and peaceful," and believed that most peasants generally had a higher standard of living in the past than did factory workers in 1844.

> They were not forced to work excessive hours; they themselves fixed the length of their working day and still earned enough for their needs. They had time for healthy work in their gardens or smallholdings and such

---

[39] See Marcus, *Engels.*

labor was in itself a recreation. They could also join their neighbors in various sports such as bowls and football and this too kept them in good physical condition. Most of them were strong, well-built people, whose physique was virtually equal to that of neighboring agricultural workers. Children grew up in the open air of the countryside, and if they were old enough to help their parents work, this was only an occasional employment and there was no question of an eight- or twelve-hour day.[40]

At the same time, Engels argued, these peasants were "spiritually dead" because they were ignorant, concerned only with their "petty private interests," and contented with their "plantlike existence."[41]

While this depiction of life prior to industrialization is clearly not accurate, it does identify some of the themes that Engels used in his indictment of capitalist society: people are forced to work excessive hours; they are in chronic ill health; and child labor is pervasive. In addition, this sketch of feudal life also implied the historical inevitability of a communist revolution; for according to Engels, industrialization not only shattered forever this idyllic life-style, it also forced people to become aware of their subordination, exploitation, and alienation. As we shall see, Marx and Engels believed this recognition is the first necessary step to a communist revolution. Thus, Engels' portrayal of the atrocities characteristic of urban life in the 1840s should be seen in light of his optimistic vision of the historical development of a revolutionary proletariat capable of seizing the world for itself. All of Marx's subsequent work was imbued with this vision, which he and Engels shared and tried to actualize in the political arena.

Having described peasant life prior to industrialization, Engels noted the four interrelated factors that went into making the modern working class that he observed in Manchester. First, the use of water- and steam power in the productive process meant that, for the first time in human history, muscle power was not the primary motive force in producing goods. Second, the massive introduction of modern machinery into the productive process signaled not only that machines rather than poeple set the pace of work, but also that more goods were being produced than ever before. Third, the intensification of the division of labor meant that the number of tasks in the productive process increased while the requirements for each task were simplified. And fourth, the tendency in modern society for concentration of both work and ownership caused not only the rise of the factory system but also a division of society

---

[40] Engels, *Condition of the Working Class*, p. 10.
[41] Ibid., pp. 11–12.

into owners and producers. According to Engels, and he was not alone, these factors were the "great levers" of the industrial revolution that have been used to "heave the world out of joint."[42] In *Capital*, Marx was to take these same ideas and place them in a theoretical context which, in his mind, allowed him to demonstrate why a proletarian revolution was inevitable.

Working-Class Life in Manchester. The world Engels saw was indeed "out of joint." His description began with a portrayal of the neighborhoods in which working-class people were forced to live. Manchester was a city that had grown from a town of 24,000 people in 1773 to a metropolitan area of more than 400,000 persons in 1840. Yet throughout this period, it had no effective city government, little police protection, and no sewage system. Engels observed that middle-class people and the owners of the factories and mills lived apart and provided themselves with city services, police protection, and sewage disposal. In contrast, the working classes were forced to live with pigs in the slums available to them. When Engels said that human beings lived with pigs (and, unavoidably, like pigs) he meant it literally.

Since there were no modern sewage facilities in Manchester, people had to use public privies. In some parts of the city, over two hundred people were served by a single receptical. In a city without government, there were few provisions for cleaning the streets or removing debris. Engels described the result in some detail; for example, in one courtyard, "right at the entrance where the covered passage ends, is a privy without a door. This privy is so dirty that the inhabitants can only enter or leave the court by wading through puddles of stale urine and excrement."[43] Thus, in *The Condition of the Working Class*, Engels portrayed a situation in which thousands of men, women, and children were living in their own bodily wastes. And if it can be imagined, the situtation was even worse for those thousands of people living in cellars, below the waterline. As Steven Marcus has observed, "that substance [their bodily waste] was also a virtual objectification of their social condition, their place in society: that was what they were."[44]

Engels continued by describing the neighborhoods where pigs and people lived together:

> Heaps of refuse, offal and sickening filth are everywhere interspread with pools of stagnant liquid. The atmosphere is polluted by the stench and

---

[42] Ibid., pp. 27–29.
[43] Ibid., p. 58.
[44] Marcus, *Engels*, pp. 184–85.

is darkened by the thick smoke of a dozen factory chimneys. A horde of ragged women and children swarm about the streets and they are just as dirty as the pigs which wallow happily on the heaps of garbage and in the pools of filth. In short, the horrid little slum affords as hateful and repulsive a spectacle as the worst courts to be found on the banks of the Irk [river]. The inhabitants live in dilapidated cottages, and windows of which are broken and patched with oilskin. The doors and the door posts are broken and rotten. The creatures who inhabit these dwellings and even their dark, wet cellars, and who live confined amidst all this filth and foul air—which cannot be dissipated because of the surrounding lofty buildings—must surely have sunk to the lowest level of humanity.[45]

It is not hard to conclude, as many did, that a society in which people have gone back to living like animals has something terribly, deeply wrong with it. And yet, as noted above, for many observers, Manchester epitomized a new and better kind of world, an industrial world.[46]

The Bourgeoisie, the Proletariat, and Revolution. Engels concluded *The Condition of the Working Class* by describing the attitudes of the bourgeoisie toward the proletariat. In Engles's prose they are portrayed as debased persons who know nothing except greed and see all human ties as having a "cash nexus." He used the following vignette to illustrate these traits.

One day I walked with one of these middle-class gentlemen into Manchester. I spoke to him about the disgraceful unhealthy slums and drew his attention to the disgusting conditon of that part of the town in which the factory workers lived. I declared that I had never seen so badly built a town in my life. He listened patiently and at the corner of the street at which we parted company he remarked: "And yet there is a great deal of money made here. Good morning, Sir."[47]

Yet the proletarians were not incapable of responding to their condition in life. While much self-destructive behavior always occurs among oppressed people (as with the use of drugs, alcohol, and the like), Engels noted that Manchester was "the mainspring of all working class movements" in England.[48] And he described the long history of working-class efforts at organizing themselves in opposition to the factory owners, for only by acting together rather than competing with one another could they effectively oppose the capitalists. More generally, however,

[45] Engels, *Condition of the Working Class*, p. 71.
[46] Ibid., p. 50.
[47] Ibid., p. 312.
[48] Ibid., p. 50.

Engels aruged that the proletarians' true interest was in establishing a noncompetitive society, which meant the abolition of the private owner- ship of the means of production (although this last point was not made explicitly).

> Every day it becomes clearer to the workers how they are affected by competition. They appreciate even more clearly than the middle classes that it is competition among the capitalists that leads to those commercial crises which cause such dire suffering among the workers. Trade unionists realize that commercial crises must be abolished, and they will soon dis- cover *how* to do it.[49]

The Condition of the Working Class ends with Engels' prophecy of a violent proletarian revolution. While this "revolution must come," Engels believed, he had not shown why, since his work accounts for neither how capitalist society functions nor why it would inevitably be destroyed.[50] He had not, in short, developed a theory to explain what he had observed. But at a time when Marx was searching for the underly- ing dynamics of society, Engels had demonstrated the significance of the proletariat. Furthermore, Engels had recognized (although the point is not made very clearly) that the evils of capitalism were a necessary prelude to a communist revolution. Yet it was Marx, rather than Engels, who developed a set of theoretical concepts and propositions that would purport to show why a revolution would occur in capitalist societies. And it is in developing these theoretical arguments that Marx was to contribute to the emergence of sociological theory.

---

[49] Ibid., p. 249 (emphasis in original).
[50] Ibid., p. 335.

KARL MARX II:
THE BASIC WORKS

Karl Marx wanted to formulate a theoretical justification for revolutionary conflict.[1] Unlike other theorists, he believed that science and politics are linked; in his terms, theory always implies action. Thus, success in theory building represented an important step toward Marx's revolutionary goal: collective control of the society so that, in a cooperative context, people can be free to develop their potential as human beings. Marx's social theory is an attempt at showing that such collective control is not only possible, it is inevitable. He thought he had explained why social structures giving advantages to one group become historically obsolete and are replaced by structures giving advantages to other groups.[2] The pattern of history, Marx thought, would lead inevitably to a communist society in which "the free development of each is the condition for the free development of all."[3] We will illustrate these aspects of Marx's thought by examining his three most important works: *The German Ideology*, *The Communist Manifesto*, and *Capital*.

THE GERMAN IDEOLOGY

The German Ideology was completed in 1846, when Marx was 28 and his co-author, Friedrich Engels, was 26 years old.[4] Much of the

---

[1] Two short biographies of Marx are Isiah Berlin, *Karl Marx: His Life and Environment* (New York: Oxford University Press, 1963), and David McLellan, *Karl Marx: His Life and Thought* (New York: Harper Colophon, 1973).

[2] The phrase is from Arthur Stinchcombe, *Constructing Social Theories* (New York: Harcourt, Brace, and World, 1968), p. 93.

[3] Karl Marx, "The Communist Manifesto," as reprinted in Dirk Struik, ed., *The Birth of the Communist Manifesto* (New York: International Publishers, 1971), p. 112.

[4] Karl Marx and Friedrich Engels, *The German Ideology*, trans. R. Pascal (New York: International Publishers, 1947), p. 3. Unless otherwise indicated, we shall use this translation throughout.

rather lengthy book is given over to heavy-handed and satirical polemics against various Young Hegelians, who are of little historical importance today. The publisher declined to accept the manuscript at the time, perhaps for political reasons (since Marx was already well known as a political radical and had been expelled from both Germany and France) or perhaps because of the arcane writing style. In any case, Marx later recalled, the manuscript was "abandoned to the gnawing criticism of the mice . . . since we had achieved our main purpose—self-clarification."[5] Since part 1 of *The German Ideology* is the only theoretically significant portion of the book, it is the only section dealt with here.[6]

The Attack on the Young Hegelians

Marx opened *The German Ideology* with a bitter attack on the Young Hegelians, whom he described at one point as engaging in "theoretical bubble blowing."[7] For the Hegelians, Marx observed, great conflicts, struggles, and revolutions take place only in the realm of thought, for no buildings are destroyed and no one is injured or dies. Thus, despite their excessive verbiage, Marx believed that the Young Hegelians had merely criticized the essentially religious nature of Hegel's work and substituted their own negative religious canons. "It is an interesting event we are dealing with," he said caustically, "the putrescence of the absolute spirit."[8]

Marx's rejection of German philosophy as it was then practiced was total. Like all idealists, the Young Hegelians saw people's relationships, their opportunities, and their limitations as merely products of the mind and consciousness, and the Young Hegelians' solution to the problems of the world was merely to demand a change in people's consciousness. Yet this demand only amounts to asserting that people should interpret reality in another way, which is to say they should accept their lot in life by means of another interpretation. For this reason, Marx called

---

[5] Karl Marx, "Preface," *A Contribution to the Critique of Political Economy* (New York: International Publishers, 1970), p. 22.

[6] It is generally assumed that Engels's contribution to part 1 is not significant for two reasons. First, the text appears to be an elaboration of the famous "Theses on Feuerbach" which Marx originally outlined for himself in 1845. Second, Engels stated repeatedly that Marx had already developed his materialist conception of history prior to the beginning of their collaboration. Therefore, in what follows we shall generally refer only to Marx.

[7] Marx and Engels, *German Ideology*, p. 3.

[8] Ibid.

them the "staunchest conservatives," since they supported the status quo and would change nothing in this world, only the phrases used to describe it.

The Empirical Basis of Social Theory

As an alternative to the "idealistic humbug" of the Young Hegelians, Marx offered three premises that were to guide his own theoretical formulations.

First, social theory must be grounded in "the existence of living human individuals" who must survive, often in a relatively hostile physical environment.[9] Marx's second premise is that people distinguish themselves from other animals because they manipulate and alter their environment in order to obtain need-satisfaction. Unlike other animals, people "begin to produce their means of subsistence, a step which is conditioned by their physical organization."[10] This idea implies that people are "conscious," that is, they are self-reflective and rational. By implication, then, individuals can reflect on themselves and their situation, and as a result, they are capable of assessing their positions in society and acting in terms of their own interests.

This line of reasoning suggested to Marx a third premise: consciousness arises out of human existence. This argument is directly opposed to German idealism in which ideas about morality, religion, and all other forms of consciousness are considered to have an existence independent of human beings. In contrast, Marx asserted that people produce their ideas and conceptions of the world in light of the social structures in which they are born, raised, and live, and that people's interpretations are based on material facts. Further, as social structures evolve, the contents of people's consciousness change historically.[11]

In breaking with the idealists in this way, however, Marx did not wish to support a simpleminded materialist philosophy. For Marx, mind is not a passive receptacle. It is active, and it can respond to, and act upon, the material world.[12]

These premises imply a methodological point of view which emphasizes that human beings and their activities are at the center of all theoretical work, not in some metaphysical sense, but in the sense that

---

[9] Ibid., p. 7.

[10] Ibid., p. 8.

[11] Ibid., p. 14.

[12] Sidney Hook, *From Hegel to Marx* (Ann Arbor: University of Michigan Press, 1962), pp. 275–76.

people's material conditions determine their thoughts and actions.[13] By rejecting speculation in favor of "real life," Marx's work constitutes a fundamental epistemological break with idealism. In effect, Marx "stood Hegel on his head" by giving philosophy a scientific basis.

The Organization of Production

Based on these methodological and ontological premises, Marx then tried to orient analysis toward "the real process of production" by focusing on the way people have actually organized themselves throughout history—both socially and in relationship to the physical environment. Marx began this line of argument by emphasizing that there are three essential characteristics that all societies have in common. These characteristics (Marx called them "moments") do not refer to evolutionary stages of development, but rather, to conditions that have "existed simultaneously since the dawn of history and the first men, and they still assert themselves in history today."[14]

The first characteristic of all societies is that people must produce sustenance from their physical environment in order to live and thereby "make history." As Marx observed, human "life involves before anything else eating and drinking, a habitation, clothing, and many other [material] things." Such need-satisfaction is only possible through the production of goods, that is, interaction with the environment in some socially organized manner.

The second characteristic of all societies is that people are always creating new needs. The process of need-creation not only involves the desire for improved food, clothing, and shelter, but also for the various amenities of life. The reason behind need-creation is that production (work) always involves the use of tools or instruments of various sorts, which are periodically improved. Thus, the processes of production and consumption feed back upon each other in a cumulative manner, such that as one set of needs is satisfied, new ones emerge—a situation that encourages people to create new instruments of production that satisfy these new needs.[15]

The third characteristic of all societies is that production, including

---

[13] Marx and Engels, *German Ideology*, p. 15.

[14] Ibid., p. 18.

[15] See the posthumously published "Introduction" to Karl Marx, *A Contribution to the Critique of Political Economy* (New York: International Publishers, 1970), pp. 188–217. Because production and consumption are so closely interrelated, Marx says that each is "simultaneously" the other, see pp. 195–99.

human reproduction, occurs in a cooperative context; that is, people divide up the tasks that need to be done. Marx emphasized that in most societies people's work is forced upon them, and as a result, most people are exploited for the benefit of a few. Moreover, the connections among people fostered by the division of labor (that is, the patterns of exploitation) are continually taking on new forms.

One frequent consequence of the division of labor, Marx asserted, is alienation. For when the division of labor is based upon private property, and Marx thought this to be true in all societies, there is always competition among people and, hence, an inevitable conflict between individual interests and communal interests. Because this conflict is always resolved in favor of individual interests, people are alienated; that is, they cannot control either their own activities or the products they produce. Rather, what they produce goes to benefit those who own the means of production. Thus, paradoxically, alienated people produce that which enslaves them: private property. In this exploitive context, alienation takes the form of a fantastic reversal, in which people feel themselves to be freely active, or human, only in their animal-like functions—such as eating, drinking, and procreating—while in their peculiarly human tasks, the most important of which is their work, they no longer feel human because they control neither the process nor the result. Thus, Marx concluded, in capitalism "what is animal becomes human and what is human becomes animal."[16]

Only after considering the characteristics described above did Marx believe it appropriate to examine consciousness. He made two points, each designed to distinguish his own position from others. First, he emphasized the importance of consciousness in human life, since it is the way in which people are distinguished from animals. In an amazingly modern passage, Marx argued that human language is practical consciousness, for it is the vehicle by which people become social beings. Without language, self-reflection would be impossible. Without the ability to analyze and act upon their needs and interests, people would be unable to alter their environment.[17] This emphasis on the practical impact of consciousness distinguishes Marx's brand of materialism from utilitarian philosophy. Utilitarianism is materialist in that consciousness is seen as a relatively passive phenomenon: people merely react to external stimuli. However, the utilitarians asserted that all living things try to preserve themselves, and further, the pursuit of self-interest is the clearest manifes-

---

[16] Karl Marx, *The Economic and Philosophical Manuscripts of 1844* (New York: International Publishers, 1964), p. 113.

[17] Marx and Engels, *German Ideology*, p. 19.

tation of this tendency. Thus, utilitarianism embodies the philosophical apotheosis of self-interest. Marx believed that under these conditions the rule of "live and let live" became "exploit or be exploited," and a whole set of harmful, that is to say competitive, social relationships appeared.[18] Marx's second point regarding consciousness is expressed in the phrase he used as the subtitle for this section of *The German Ideology:* "concerning the production of consciousness." He asserted bluntly that consciousness is a social product. Rather than originating from some external reality, as Hegel would have it, Marx said that consciousness results from people's practical efforts at obtaining sustenance, creating needs, and working together.

The Stages of History

Based upon the analysis above, Marx sketched the "real basis of ideology" in terms of the stages of history since the Middle Ages. The exposition in *The German Ideology* is an early example of what has come to be called *dialectical materialsm*, although Marx never used that term. Hence, we begin this section by identifying the essential characteristics of Marx's dialectical analysis as it is applied to history, particularly his description of the historical transition from feudal society to capitalist society.

Dialectical materialism is Marx's way of explaining how social structures giving advantages to one group become historically obsolete and are replaced by structures giving advantages to other groups. It is Marx's method for studying the patterns of history. The historical mechanisms underlying Marx's dialectical analysis are the emergence of opposing interests within a population and class conflict based on that opposition. While the analysis is sketchy in *The German Ideology*, the way history can be interpreted dialectically can be outlined in the following manner.

Within any social system a way of producing things exists, both in terms of what is produced and the social organization of production. Marx called this aspect of the society the "productive forces."[19] In all

---

[18] See theses 9 and 10 of the "Theses on Feuerbach," and Hook, *Hegel to Marx*, p. 299.

[19] Sometimes, Marx defines the forces of production narrowly, so that the term only refers to the instruments used in the productive process. Sometimes, however, he defines the forces of production broadly, so that the term refers to both the instruments used in production and the social organization that accompanies their use. By social organization is meant not only the organization of work, but also family life, law, politics, and all other institutions. This kind of tactic occurs with many of Marx's key concepts. See Bertell Ollman, *Alienation: Marx's Concept of Man in Capitalist Society* (New York: Oxford University Press, 1976), pp. 3–69.

societies, the productive forces are established and maintained in terms of property relations. Those few who own the means of production are the dominant class, while those who do not are the subordinate class. However, over time, new ways of producing things are devised, whether based on advances in technology, changes in the way production is organized, or both. Such new forces of production better satisfy old needs and also stimulate new ones. These new forces of production are in the hands of a new class, and they exist in contradiction to (that is, in opposition to) existing property relations and forms of intercourse. In the long run, the tension between these opposing classes erupts into revolutionary conflict, as Marx illustrated in his analysis of the transition from feudalism to capitalism.

During the Middle Ages there arose two great divisions in society. The first was between town and country. Marx believed, and he was wrong on this point, that towns arose anew in the Middle Ages as freed serfs fled the domination of the nobility. These people had little property at first—skills and the tools of their trade, perhaps. But the development of towns signifies the separation of capital from landed property. The second great division, Marx argued, occurred within the towns themselves, with the formation of guilds. He insisted, and he appears to have been correct, that guilds were designed to curb competition as well as to regulate and control labor; that is, they protected property in its new urban form. The "serfs, persecuted by their lords in the country, came separately into the towns, where they found an organized community, against which they were powerless, in which they had to subject themselves to the station assigned to them by the demand for their labour and the interest of their organized competitors."[20] These workers remained an unorganized rabble who were forced to compete with one another for jobs in an urban context where they could not provide for their own needs without employment by guild members or nascent capitalists.

According to Marx, "the next extension of the division of labor was the separation of production and commerce" such that a special class of merchants was formed.[21] As a consequence, communication and contact among towns assumed greater importance as buying and selling increased in volume. Towns began to interact with each other; began to specialize in producing particular products; and gradually, the traditional barriers to trade were broken down. Over time, with the gradual

---

[20] Marx and Engels, *German Ideology*, p. 45.
[21] Ibid., p. 47.

ascendence of capital as the dominant form of property, the bourgeois class arose.

The bourgeoisie was formed as individual merchants and producers in the different towns recognized their common interests and began to act in concert. Concomitantly, the process of transforming landed property into industrial or commercial capital continued, although not without a great deal of conflict. The process by which serfs were transformed into proletarians was neither smooth nor easy. In Marx's view, the nascent capitalists' productive forces (both the tools used and the social organization of production) existed very precariously in most places. Only the extension of trade and communication assured the permanence of the newly acquired productive forces. As this occurred, individuals found their conditions of existence predestined such that their position in the division of labor and their personal destiny was assigned to them by their class membership.[22]

Manufacturing, the next stage in the transformation of Western society, arose as one consequence of the division of labor between towns and the development of commerce. The concentration of population in urban areas, the availability of mobile capital in the form of cash, and the existence of advanced machines combined to allow manufacturing to develop. Textiles were the first major manufacturing industry, Marx claimed, and there is some basis for this judgment. The employment of unskilled workers in textiles and other new manufacturing entities "became a refuge of the peasants from the guilds." As a result, the thousands of vagabonds created by the demise of the feudal system were gradually absorbed by these emerging industries.[23] The rise of manufacturing had great political significance as well, Marx believed, because trade had to be protected and labor regulated so that people could acquire the newly available amenities (and profit could be made). The guilds could perform neither of these tasks, and hence, they declined in all areas where manufacturing took hold.

Inevitably, "big industry" arose and completed the transformation of society. According to Marx, big industry was based on the existence of a completely dependent proletarian class, a world market, worldwide communication, mobile capital which circulates freely and rapidly, and the modern state which operates to protect private property. In this context, Marx dwelt again on the importance of the state under capitalism, asserting that in an environment where "pure private property"

---

[22] Ibid., p. 49.
[23] Ibid., p. 51.

exists—that is, where there are no communal ties among people because landed property has been converted into cash and other forms of capital— the state has been purchased by the owners of property in order to protect their investment. He meant this literally, claiming that the existence of the state "has become wholly dependent on the commercial credit which the owners of property, the bourgeois, extend to it."[24]

In Marx's analysis, industrialization has two interrelated consequences. The first is the alienation of labor, since with industrialization all "natural relationships" with other people, based on personal and patriarchal ties, are transformed into "money relationships."[25] This occurs as industry makes use of both the "automatic system," by which machines are linked with new forms of power such as steam. As a result, human beings become dependent on the machines at which they toil and must adjust their needs (both biological and social) to those of the machines they are tending. In addition, the necessity for a large and concentrated labor pool means that people are forced to live in the miasmatic atmosphere of large cities, of which Manchester was only one example. Thus, modern life is paradoxical, for in an enviroment characterized by the greatest productive forces in history, labor only sustains people's lives by stunting them, by preventing them from recognizing or developing their peculiarly human abilities. Work is no longer an expression of human creativity or impulse, because people are now just like animals: they work constantly in an environment they cannot control in order to barely subsist.

The second consequence of industrialization follows from the first and is interrelated with it. A revolutionary class is created—the proletariat—"which in all nations has the same interest and with which nationality is already dead; a class which is really rid of all the old world and at the same time stands pitted against it."[26] In *The German Ideology*, however, Marx did not suggest the conditions under which the proletarians might be able to unite, as that analysis first appeared in the *Manifesto*, written two years later. Nonetheless, he believed that life in capitalist society was so intolerable and incapable of amelioration that "individuals must appropriate the existing totality of productive forces, not only to

---

[24] Ibid. p. 59.

[25] Marx used the term *natural* in several different ways. Sometimes he meant that which occurs in nature without interference by humans. Sometimes he meant relationships that are determined by "natural predispositions" (ibid. p. 20), such as physical strength. Sometimes he meant relationships that reflect human dependence on the physical environment, such as landed property (p. 63). Sometimes he meant capitalist social relationships. However, "civilized" (that is, cooperative) social relationships are never described as "natural" by Marx.

[26] Ibid., p. 57.

achieve self-activity, but also, merely to safeguard their very existence."[27]

Thus, Marx's description of the transition from feudalism to capitalism emphasized the dialectic between the new and old. And as is also evident, the emergence of capitalism created new pressures for social transformation. Eventually, Marx hoped, capitalism would be displaced by communism. Yet at this stage in his thinking, Marx believed that it would be unwise to predict the nature of the society to come after a communist revolution. We can, nevertheless, offer a few observations based on hints found in the final section of *The German Ideology*. First, in Marx's eyes, communism represents a systematic effort by people to transform collectively their relations with one another so that they can act cooperatively rather than individualistically. Second, the communist revolution will bring with it both the abolition of private property and the end of alienation. Up until the present, people have been alienated because their work and all other aspects of their lives were determined by external forces over which they had no control. But under communism, the community or proletarians "puts the conditions of the free development and movement of individuals under their control—conditions which were previously abandoned to chance and had won an independent existence over against the separate individuals."[28]

In *The German Ideology*, then, Marx made his final break with Hegel and the Young Hegelians, and laid the foundation for a theory of society that links thought and action. The focus of Marx's social theory is conscious people who manipulate and alter the physical environment, not only in order to produce sustenance for themselves but also to express their unique human qualities. Because people do these things, they have a history, the direction of which can be understood by the participants. True understanding of history can only occur when people's actual social relationships are examined, and when they are examined, it will be discovered that most people are and always have been alienated. Alienation occurs in all societies because the division of labor is based on the private possession of the means of production. In such a context, people always have opposing interests and must compete with one another in order to survive. Over the long run, this process insures that a few will benefit while most are exploited—a fact that is especially characteristic of capitalist society. Marx concluded *The German Ideology* by briefly sketching the historical transformation from feudalism to capitalism and tentatively suggesting some of the characteristics of the communist society to come.

---

[27] Ibid., p. 66.
[28] Ibid., p. 75.

Yet *The German Ideology* did not raise a most crucial issue: how are the oppressed proletarians to become aware of their true interests and seize control of the society for the benefit of all. This and other problems of revolutionary action are dealt with in *The Communist Manifesto*.

THE COMMUNIST MANIFESTO

In 1847 Marx and Engels joined the Communist League, an organization of radical European emigrants. They soon came to dominate the league; and under their influence, its aim became the overthrow of bourgeois society and the establishment of a new society without classes and without private property. Marx and Engels were asked to compose a manifesto that would publicly state the Communist League's doctrines. Accordingly, Engels wrote an initial draft in catechism form, entitled "Principles of Communism," and sent it to Marx.[29] During the early days of 1848, Marx completely rewrote the draft, and although the final version incorporated many of Engels's ideas, the document that was printed in February of that year was strikingly different and original.

The *Manifesto* opens with a menancing phrase that immediately reveals its revolutionary intent. "A spector is haunting Europe—the spector of Communism. All the Powers of old Europe have entered into a holy alliance to exorcise this spector." In a political context where opposition parties of all political persuasions were being called communists, Marx wrote, it was time for the communists themselves to "meet this nursery tale of the spector of Communism with a Manifesto of the party itself."[30] The remainder of the *Manifesto* is organized into four sections, which are summarized below.

Bourgeois and Proletarians

Marx began his analysis with the assertion that "the history of all hitherto existing society is the history of class struggles," because he believed that those who own the means of production always oppress those who do not. Thus, in his view, bourgeois society has merely substituted new forms of oppression and, hence, struggle, in place of the old feudal forms. However, Marx argued, the distinctive feature of bour-

---

[29] Engels's "Principles of Communism" is reprinted in Struik, ed., *Birth of the Manifesto*.

[30] We are using the standard translation by Samuel Moore, as reprinted in Struik, ed., *Birth of the Manifesto*. This will be referred to as *Communist Manifesto*.

geois society is that it has simplified class antagonism, since the "society as a whole is splitting up more and more into two great hostile camps, into two great classes directly facing each other: Bourgeoisie and Proletariat."[31]

Although the nature of classes and the pervasiveness of class struggle are the first essential ideas in the *Manifesto*, Marx never fully explained what he meant by the concept of class, and he used the term in a very cavalier manner.[32] However, the key to Marx's use of class (and to his version of dialectical materialism) lies in the idea of opposition, for Marx always saw classes as opposed to one another. Regardless of their number or composition, the members of different classes are enemies because they have opposing interests and experiences.

Marx believed that a person's position in the social structure implies quite specific interests and experiences that are different from those of others, and he placed individuals into opposing classes on this basis. For example, if the position of an aggregate of people in society makes starvation a constant problem and if these people cannot control their activities or express their human creativity, then they are clearly in subordinate positions in relationship to others. In their alienation they have an interest in changing the status quo, whether they are aware of it or not. On the other hand, if the position of an aggregate of people in society is such that their needs are satisfied (or perhaps even satiated), and if they can both control their own activities and express their human creativity, then such persons are clearly in superordinate positions and have an interest in preserving the status quo. However, according to Marx, the oppressors are also alienated because their relationship to other people and to the means of production is competitive rather than cooperative. For Marx, then, the existence of classes means that people have opposing interests and experiences, based on their positions in society. In bourgeois society Marx saw these differences as coalescing so that society was increasingly divided into two classes, although he clearly recognized that all social structures are very diverse and complex.

However, the concept of class also implies more than the fact that aggregates of people are enemies because they have opposing interests and experiences. Ultimately, it implies class struggle, as people attempt to resolve the historically developed contradictions. The prerequisite for class struggle is the development of class consciousness such that members

---

[31] Marx, *Communist Manifesto*, p. 89.

[32] For an analysis of the various ways Marx used the concept of class see Bertell Ollman, "Marx's Use of 'Class,' " *American Journal of Sociology* 73 (March 1968):573–80.

of an aggregate become aware of *(a)* themselves as a group, *(b)* their historical destiny, and *(c)* their need to seize power in the name of the future of mankind. One of Marx's purposes in writing the *Manifesto* was to stimulate the development of class consciousness, that is, the transformation of the proletariat from a class "in itself" to a class "for iteself." In the *Manifesto*, he predicted that such a transformation is ultimately inevitable and sketched both the revolutionary rise of the bourgeoisie out of feudalism and the rise of the proletariat out of capitalism. As in *The German Ideology*, the analysis is an example of Marx's version of dialectical materialism.

He began by asserting that "from the serfs of the Middle Ages sprang the chartered burghers of the earliest towns. From these burgesses the first elements of the bourgeoisie were developed."[33] Such changes were not historical accidents but the inevitable result of people acting in terms of their own interests. The European discovery of America, along with the rise of trade and exchange, were new and powerful productive forces facing a feudal nobility that had exhausted itself by constant warfare. Further, as it was increasingly exposed to other cultures, the nobility had become consumptively oriented with the result that they enclosed the land in order to raise cash crops using new methods of production. As this process occurred, the serfs were forced to the cities, where over time a merchant class arose.

At first, the merchants existed to serve the needs of the nobility. But eventually, money rather than land became the key to power in Western Europe, for only by worldwide exchange with cash as a lubricant could the nobility obtain the commodities necessary to satisfy their consumptive needs.

Marx then described the truly revolutionary nature of the capitalist mode of production. As a result of the industrial revolution, the bourgeoisie "has accomplished wonders far surpassing Egyptian pyramids, Roman aqueducts, and gothic cathedrals; it has conducted expeditions that put into the shade all former Exoduses of nations and crusades."[34] However in order for the bourgeoisie to exist, Marx predicted, they must constantly revolutionize the instruments of production and thereby create new needs that can be filled by manufactured products. As this process occurs the bourgeoisie also seizes political power in each country, so that "the executive of the modern state is but a committee for managing the common affairs of the whole bourgeoisie."[35]

---

[33] Marx, *Communist Manifesto*, p. 90.

[34] Ibid., p. 92.

[35] Ibid., p. 91.

Inevitably, then, the implementation of new forces of production creates new social relationships among people, which is to say new forms of exploitation. Thus, rather than the communal and patriarchal ties existing between lord and serf, under capitalism there is "no other nexus between man and man than naked self-interest, than callous 'cash payment.' " Having described the great historical changes accompanying the rise of capitalism, Marx then made two of his most famous predictions concerning the ultimate demise of the capitalist system.

The first prediction is that capitalism is inherently unstable because of its recurrent industrial cycles and its downfall is inevitable as a result. Capitalism, Marx wrote, is characterized by "an absurdity—the epidemic of overproduction." According to Marx, the essential problem of 19th-century capitalism was that its industrial cycles, epitomized by recurrent commercial crises, were weathered only by the destruction of products, more thorough exploitation of old markets, and the continued conquest of new markets. But such tactics clearly could not succeed over the long run because capitalists continually undercut each other. Thus, Marx argued, as industrialization advances, the productive forces become no longer capable of operating efficiently in a competitive context where people try to maximize profits by pursuing their individual self-interest.

Marx's second prediction was that "the modern working class, the proletarians," would become increasingly impoverished and alienated under capitalism. Because they could no longer be self-supporting, the proletarians had become "a class of laborers who live only so long as they find work, and who find work only so long as their labor increases capital."[36] Thus, in an industrial context characterized by the extensive use of machinery owned and controlled by others, proletarians have no control over their daily lives or the products of their activities. Each person becomes, in effect, a necessary but low priced appendage to a machine. In this situation, Marx said, even women and children are thrown into the maelstrom. Thus, under capitalism, human beings are simply instruments of labor whose only worth is the cost of keeping them minimally fed, clothed, and housed. Confronted with their own misery, Marx predicted, the proletarians would ultimately become class conscious and overthrow the entire system.

The rise of the proletariat as a class for itself proceeds with great difficulty, however, primarily because individual proletarians are forced to compete among themselves. For example, some are allowed to work in the capitalists' factories while others are not. Within the factories,

---

[36] Ibid., p. 96.

a few are allowed to work at somewhat better-paying or easier jobs while others labor at lower-paying and more-difficult jobs. After work, proletarians with too-little money still compete with each other for the inadequate food, clothing, and shelter that is available. Under these competitive conditions, it is difficult to create class consciousness among people. Nonetheless, individuals and aggregates of workers have periodically rebelled since the beginnings of capitalism, although they often directed their attacks against the instruments of production rather than the capitalists. And at times, when they did organize, the proletarians were often co-opted into serving the interests of the bourgeoisie.[37] However, with the development of large-scale industry, the proletariat constantly increases in size. Like many other observers of 19th-century society (such as Fourier and Saint Simon), Marx predicted that the number of working-class people would continually increase as elements of the lower-middle class—artisans, shopkeepers, and peasants—were gradually absorbed into it. Furthermore, Marx believed that even those persons in professions such as medicine, law, science, and art would increasingly become mere wage laborers. He thought that all the skills of the past are being swept aside by modern industry, which creates but two great classes.

The revolutionary development of the proletariat would, Marx argued, be aided by the fact that it was increasingly urban, and hence, its members were better able to communicate with one another. Further, they were becoming better educated and politically sophisticated, partly because the bourgeoisie constantly dragged them into the political arena. And although the proletarians' efforts at organizing against the bourgeoisie were often smashed, Marx believed that they were destined to rise up again, "stronger, firmer, mightier." All of these factors would further the development of class consciousness among the proletariat, Marx asserted.

Proletarians and Communists

As Marx expressed it, the major goal of the communists could be simply stated: the abolition of private property. After all, he noted, under capitalism nine tenths of the population has no property anyway. As might be imagined, the bourgeois were especially critical of this position. But Marx felt that just as the French Revolution abolished feudal forms

---

[37] See Karl Marx, "The Class Struggles in France," in Marx and Engels, *Selected Works*, vol. 1 (Moscow: Progress Publishers, 1969), pp. 186–299. In this series of essays Marx shows how the proletarians actively participated in subjecting other classes to the rule of the bourgeoisie.

of private property in favor of bourgeois forms, so the communist revolution would abolish bourgeois control over capital—without substituting a new form of private ownership. Marx emphasized, however, that the abolition of the personal property of the petty artisan or the small peasant was not at issue. Rather, the communists wished to abolish bourgeois "capital, i.e., that kind of property which exploits wage labor and which cannot increase except upon condition of begetting a new supply of wage labor for fresh exploitation."[38]

For Marx, the means of production ought to be "a collective product" controlled by the "united action of all members of the society." This is not possible in bourgeois society, with its emphasis on "free" competition and its apotheosis of private property. Marx believed that collective control of the society is only possible under communism, where "accumulated labor is but a means to widen, to enrich, to promote the existence of the laborer." Thus, the communists aim at abolishing bourgeois individuality, bourgeois independence, and bourgeois freedom in the name of the individuality, independence, and freedom of the vast majority of people.

The first step in the working-class revolution, Marx argued, is for the proletariat to seize control of the state. Once attaining political supremacy, the proletariat will then wrest "all capital from the bourgeoisie," "centralize all instruments of production in the hands of the state," and "increase the total of productive forces as rapidly as possible." Furthermore, the following measures would also be taken in most countries.[39]

1. Abolition of private ownership of land.
2. A heavy progressive income tax.
3. Abolition of all rights of inheritance.
4. Confiscation of the property of emigrants and rebels.
5. Centralization of credit and banking in the hands of the state.
6. Centralization of communication and transportation in the hands of the state.
7. State ownership of factories and all other instruments of production.
8. Equal liability of all to labor.
9. Combination of agricultural and manufacturing industries so as to abolish the distinction between town and country.
10. Free public education for all children and the abolition of child labor.

[38] Marx, *Communist Manifesto*, pp. 104–5.
[39] Ibid., p. 111. Marx took these measures largely from Engels's draft.

Marx knew that the measures he was advocating could only be implemented arbitrarily, and he forecast a period of temporary communist despotism. In his "Critique of the Gotha Program," written many years later, he would label this transition period as the "revolutionary dictatorship of the proletariat."[40] Ultimately, however, Marx's apocalyptic vision of the future was one in which people would be free, self-governing, and cooperative. They would no longer be mutilated by a division of labor over which they had no control. It is a splendid vision—not that of the sorcerer, but of the sorcerer's apprentice.

Socialist and Communist Literature

The *Manifesto* now turns to attacking political literature of the day. Marx recognized that in all periods of turmoil and change, there is inevitably a desire by some to return to times past or to invent fantastic utopias as the way to solve humankind's ills. Marx believed that such dreams are, at best, a waste of time and, at worst, a vicious plot on the part of reactionaries. Thus, the third section of the *Manifesto* is a brief critique of socialist literature as it then existed. He classified this literature as (1) reactionary socialism (including here feudal socialism, petty-bourgeois socialism, and German "true" socialism), (2) conservative or bourgeois socialism, and (3) critical-utopian socialism. Each of these is discussed briefly below.

Reactionary Socialism. Because the bourgeoisie supplanted the feudal nobility as the ruling class in society, the remaining representatives of the aristocracy attempted revenge by trying to persuade the proletarians that life had been better under their rule. Marx characterized this pernicious literature as "half lamentation, half lampoon; half echo of the past, half menace of the future," and said their efforts are misbegotten primarily because the mode of exploitation is different in an industrial context and a return to the past is not possible.

Petty-bourgeois socialism is also ahistorical and reactionary. While

---

[40] Karl Marx, "Critique of the Gotha Program," in Marx and Engels, *Selected Works*, vol. 3, pp. 9–30. While his vision of an inevitable future never changed, Marx altered his political tactics over the years in light of experience and changing conditions. In particular, the *Manifesto* implies that a small elite will seize power in the name of the proletarians and retain it while educating them. With the formation of the International Workingmen's Association in 1864 Marx argued that education of the workers and mass action were the vital first steps. See McLellan, *Karl Marx*, or Berlin, *Karl Marx;* see also Karl Marx, "The Civil War in France," in Marx and Engels, *Selected Works*, vol. 2, pp. 178–242. Nonetheless, despite his humane vision, Marx's thought has very authoritarian implications; see Robert A. Nisbet, *The Social Philosophers* (New York: Thomas Y. Crowell, 1973), pp. 249–318.

its adherents have dissected capitalist society with great acuity, they also have little to offer but a ridiculous return to the past: a situation in which corporate guilds exist in manufacturing and patriarchal relations dominate agriculture. Because they manage to be both reactionary and utopian, which is difficult, this form of socialism always ends "in a miserable fit of the blues." Marx had previously criticized German or "true" socialism in *The German Ideology*. In the *Manifesto*, he merely emphasized once again (with typically acerbic prose) that the Germans wrote "philosophical nonsense" about the "interest of human nature, of Man in General, who belongs to no class, has no reality, who exists only in the misty realm of philosophical fantasy."[41]

Conservative or Bourgeois Socialism. In Marx's estimation, bourgeois socialists, such as Proudhon, wanted to ameliorate the miserable conditions characteristic of proletarian life without abolishing the system itself. Today he might call such persons liberals. In any case, Marx believed this goal was impossible to achieve, for what Proudhon and others did not understand was that the bourgeoisie cannot exist without the proletariat and all the abuses inflicted on it.

Critical-Utopian Socialism. Utopian socialism is represented by the early communist systems devised by Saint-Simon, Fourier, Owen, and others. While these writers had many critical insights into the nature of society, Marx believed their efforts were historically premature because the full development of the proletariat had not yet occurred, and hence, they were unable to see the material conditions necessary for its emancipation. As a result, they tried to construct a new society independent of the flux of history. For the utopian socialists, the proletarians were merely the most suffering section of society rather than a revolutionary class destined to abolish the existence of all classes.

Communist and Other Opposition Parties

In the final section of the *Manifesto*, Marx described the relationship between the communist party, representing the most advanced segment of the working class, and other opposition parties of the time. Basically, in all nations the communists are supportive of all efforts to oppose the existing order of things, for Marx believed that the process of opposition would eventually "instill into the working class the clearest possible recognition of the hostile antagonism between the bourgeoisie and the

---

[41] Marx, *Communist Manifesto*, p. 117.

proletariat."[42] In this regard, communists would always emphasize the practical and theoretical importance of private property as the means of exploitation in capitalist society.

Marx, the revolutionary, concludes the *Manifesto* with a final thundering assault on the bourgeoisie:

> The communists disdain to conceal their views and aims. They openly declare that their ends can be attained only by the forcible overthrow of all existing social conditions. Let the ruling classes tremble at a Communist revolution. The proletarians have nothing to lose but their chains. They have a world to win. WORKING MEN OF ALL COUNTRIES, UNITE![43]

As Isaiah Berlin has commented, the power of the *Manifesto's* opening and closing statements has never been equaled anywhere.[44] If Marx had written nothing else, this document would have ensured his lasting fame as a revolutionary. Fortunately, as we will examine in the next chapter, there is also a series of important theoretical statements in this boisterous work.

CAPITAL

As it was originally conceived, Marx's scientific analysis of capitalism was to comprise several massive volumes, but in the end only the first was finished during his lifetime.[45] Originally publishing it in 1867, Marx spent a considerable amount of time prior to his death in 1883 editing and reediting it for subsequent editions and translations. Thus, even though he anticipated additional volumes, it is fair to assume that he believed it could stand alone as an independent work. As Engels observed in the preface to the first English edition of *Capital*, "this first book is in a great measure a whole in itself, and has for twenty years ranked as an independent work."[46] More than 100 years later, it is still the

---

[42] Ibid., p. 125.

[43] Ibid.

[44] Berlin, *Karl Marx*, p. 167.

[45] Using Marx's rough drafts as a basis, Engels published volumes 2 and 3 of *Capital* after Marx's death. See Karl Marx, *Capital: The Process of Circulation of Capital* and *Capital: The Process of Capitalist Production as a Whole* (New York: International Publishers, 1967). Marx also left behind a draft of what has been presumed to be a fourth volume of *Capital*. However, it comprises three volumes by itself and was published by Karl Kautsky beginning in 1905 under the title *Theories of Surplus Value* (New York: International Publishers, 1952). Finally, Marx also left his notes for *Capital*. Written in the years 1857–58, they have only recently been translated and published under the title *Grundrisse* (New York: Vintage Books, 1973).

[46] Friedrich Engels, "Preface to the First English Edition," in Karl Marx, *Capital: A Critical Analysis of Capitalist Production*, vol. 1 (New York: International Publishers, 1967), p. 5.

case that the first volume is regarded as the single best example of Marx's scientific analysis of capitalism.

In *The German Ideology* Marx attacked the Young Hegelians because they avoided an empirical examination of social life, and it is in *Capital* that he demonstrated the intent of this criticism by engaging in his own analysis of the workings of capitalist society.[47] Using England (and copious amounts of British government data) as his primary example, Marx sought to show that the most important characteristic of the capitalist mode of production is the constant drive to accumulate capital through the use of alienated and exploited labor. As a result of the need to accumulate capital, Marx argued, the processes of production are incessantly revolutionized, and over the long run, the instability and degradation of people characteristic of capitalist society will lead to its complete transformation. Thus, in contrast to the *Manifesto*, which is a call to arms, *Capital* is a scholarly attempt at showing why such a transformation of capitalist society will inevitably occur. As such, *Capital* is much more than a narrow work of economics; it is an analysis of capitalist social structure and its inevitable transformation.

This explication of *Capital* is divided into five sections. First, Marx began by sketching the labor theory of value. All the analyses that follow are based on this initial idea. The second section comprises Marx's description of the process of exchange and the development of capital. The third section contains his analysis of surplus value and shows why it is the source of capitalist social relations. The fourth section sketches Marx's explanation of capital accumulation and its consequences for the eventual downfall of capitalism. And the final section explicates Marx's analysis of the origins of capitalism, which he called primitive accumulation.

The Labor Theory of Value

The labor theory of value is sketched in the opening chapter of *Capital*. While Marx approached this issue from what appears to be a strictly economic vantage point—the nature and value of commodities—his discussion turns out to have considerably broader implications. A commodity is "an object outside of us, a thing that by its properties satisfies human wants of some sort or another."[48] For purposes of his analysis, both

---

[47] Karl Marx, *Capital: A Critical Analysis of Capitalist Production*, vol. 1 (New York: International Publishers, 1967), p. 10. This edition uses the standard translation by Samuel Moore and Edward Aveling. Unless otherwise indicated, we shall use it throughout. In all quotations the original spelling will be retained.

[48] *Capital*, p. 35.

the origin of people's wants and the manner in which commodities satisfy them are irrelevant. Rather, the more important question is: what makes a commodity valuable? In the answer to this question lies the key to Marx's analysis of capitalist society.

There are two analytically different sources of value inherent in all commodities, each of which can be treated independently of the other. One source of value resides in the "use value" of commodities—that is, in the fact that they are produced in order to be consumed. For example, people use paper to write on, autos for transportation, and so forth. Clearly some things that have value, such as air and water, are not produced but are there for the taking (at least they were in the 19th century). In referring to use values in capitalist society, Marx was primarily interested in those items manufactured by people. Commodities having use value are qualitatively different from one another; for example, a coat cannot be compared to a table. As a result, when thinking of use values the amount of labor that has gone into appropriating them is irrelevant.

Another source of value can be found in the "exchange value" of commodities. As we shall see, Marx believed that an emphasis on the exchange value of commodities is peculiar to capitalist social relations and that it comprises capitalism's greatest strength and weakness. Because the exchange of commodities occurs independently of their use, Marx argued that exchange value must exist independently of use value. Yet commodities had to have some basis for comparison in order for exchange to take place. Thus, Marx decided that the only way that they could be compared to one another was in terms of the labor time required to produce them. Essentially, then, the labor theory of value states that the value of commodities is determined by the labor time necessary to produce them. Marx phrased the labor theory of value in the following way:

> That which determines the magnitude of the value of any article is the amount of labour socially necessary, or the labour-time socially necessary for its production. Each individual commodity, in this connexion, is to be considered, as an average sample of its class. Commodities, therefore, in which equal quantities of labour are embodied, or which can be produced in the same time, have the same value. The value of one commodity is to the value of any other, as the labour-time necessary for the production of the one is to that necessary for the production of the other. "As values, all commodities are only definite masses of congealed labor-time."[49]

---

[49] Ibid., pp. 39–40.

Marx supplemented the labor theory of value in five ways. First, different kinds of "useful labour" are not comparable. For example, the tasks involved in producing a coat are qualitatively different than those involved in producing linen. All that is comparable is the expenditure of human labour power in the form of brains, nerves, and muscles. Thus, the magnitude of exchange value is determined by the quantity of labor as indicated by its duration in terms of hours, days, or weeks. Marx called this quantity "simple average labour."

Second, although different skills exist among workers, Marx recognized that "skilled labour counts only as simple labour intensified, or rather, as multiplied simple labour."[50] Thus, in order to simplify the analysis, he assumed that all labor is unskilled. In practice, he asserted, people make a similar assumption in their everyday lives.

Third, the value of a commodity differs according to the technology available. With mechanization, the labor time necessary to produce a piece of cloth is greatly reduced (and so, by the way, is the value of the cloth—at least according to Marx). During the initial stages of his analysis, Marx wished to hold technology constant. Thus, he asserted that the value of a commodity is determined by the labor time socially necessary to produce an article under the normal conditions of production existing at the time.

Fourth, and this point will become very important later on, under capitalism labor itself is a commodity which has exchange value. The production of commodities requires expenditure of energy—brains, nerves, muscles, and so on—that must be replenished. Because other people must work to provide each person with sufficient food, clothing, shelter, and the various amenities of life that are deemed necessary in any society, labor is a commodity just like linen and coats. Thus, "the value of labor power is determined as in the case of every other commodity, by the labor time necessary for the production, and consequently, the reproduction, of this special article."[51]

Fifth, an important implication of the labor theory of value is the development of what Marx called the "fetishism of commodities." The fetishism of commodities occurs when people come to believe that the products they produce have human attributes which make them capable of interacting with and exploiting people. Marx thought that such beliefs are only possible when commodities are produced by alienated labor for purposes of exchange. In capitalist society, the fetishism of commodi-

---

[50] Ibid., p. 44.
[51] Ibid., p. 170.

ties manifests itself in two different ways. (1) Machines (as a reified form of capital) are seen as exploiting workers, which is something only other people can do. Thus, products that were designed and built by people, and can be used or discarded at will, not only come to be seen as having human attributes but even as independent participants in human social relationships. (2) When machines are seen to exploit workers, the social ties among people are hidden such that their ability to understand or alter the way they live is impaired. In this context, Marx wrote, "there is a definite social relation between men, that assumes, in their eyes, the fantastic form of a relation between things."[52]

In later chapters of *Capital*, Marx illustrated what he meant by the fetishism of commodities by showing that machines set the pace and style of work rather than laborers and by showing that machines "need" the night work of laborers so that they may be in continuous operation. Of course, as we shall see, hidden behind the machines stand capitalists, who are the real villains.

Marx concluded his chapter on the labor theory of value by briefly alluding to an alternative form of society that would not be characterized by the fetishism of commodities. In passages reminiscent of *The German Ideology* and *The Communist Manifesto*, he described a "community of free individuals, carrying on their work with the means of production in common, in which the labour-power of all the different individuals is consciously applied as the combined labour-power of the community."[53] Such a communist society would be cooperative rather than competitive and, as a result, would be characterized by the production of commodities as use values rather than as exchange values. From the point of view of people oriented to the production of use values, commodities are "social" in the sense that they belong to everyone. However, in a cooperative community where neither exchange nor alienation exists, some principle for distributing the means of subsistence must be found, and Marx said that the basis for distributing goods in a communist society is "from each according to his ability, to each according to his needs."[54]

The Process of Exchange and the Development of Capital

Historically, commodities with differing use values were exchanged directly by bartering, but over time, some commodities began to be

---

[52] Ibid., p. 72.

[53] Ibid., p. 78.

[54] Ibid., pp. 78–79. The quotation is from the "Critique of the Gotha Program," p. 19.

produced specifically to be bartered and the volume of trade increased so that exchange became a normal act. In such a context a universal measure of value and price was necessary, with the result that money, either in the form of gold or backed by it, became that measure. Money became, in effect, a symbol of the human labor embodied in commodities.

According to Marx, the process of exchange initially involves the metamorphosis of commodities into money and back again into commodities, which he represented by the following formula.

$$\text{Commodity}\text{———}\text{Money}\text{———}\text{Commodity}$$
$$\text{or}$$
$$C\text{———}M\text{———}C$$

In the process of commodity circulation shown above, money lubricates the exchange. However, Marx was more interested in the development of capital, since in modern society it is the possession of capital (whether in the form of money or machines) that allows some persons to exploit others. The basic formula for capital is precisely the reverse of that presented above. Rather than $C\text{———}M\text{———}C$, it is $M\text{———}C\text{———}M$. In the latter case, one's object is to use money to purchase a commodity and then sell it for money. As Marx noted, the formula for capital "commences with money and ends with money. Its leading motive, and the goal that attracts it, is therefore mere exchange value."[55] But this process is ludicrous, Marx observed, since one ends up with the same amount of money at the end as at the beginning, and there is no point to the exchange. Thus, the capitalist transaction is really $M\text{———}C\text{———}M'$, where M' is larger than M. In other words, one "buys cheap and sells dear." Marx called the increment that results "surplus value" (or profit).

The significance of surplus value in capitalism can be suggested with the following example. A tailor has $1,000 and purchases linen from a weaver. The tailor then employs other tailors who make suits out of the linen. The suits sell for a total of $2,000. After deducting the amount paid to employees, say $500, the tailor makes $500. This $500 is profit, or surplus value. What differentiates this type of transaction from others is that capitalists have no intention of consuming the products they purchase, since use values are of little interest to them. Marx writes that "the restless never-ending process of profit-making alone is what [the capitalist] aims at."[56] In this way, capitalists continually throw their money into circulation in a constant effort to increase its supply.

---

[55] Ibid., p. 149.
[56] Ibid.

Surplus Value

The Source of Surplus Value. In discovering the origin of surplus value, Marx had to resolve a key problem. We should recall here his assertion that labor is the source of value—whether of linen, suits, or any other commodity. How then does capital increase, as indicated by the appearance of surplus value? Marx considered several alternatives: among them, buying commodities above or below their value and speculation. However, he quickly dismissed these arguments. Since Marx believed that the source of all value is labor, he had to show how labor creates surplus value for the capitalists. He finally decided that paying people in the form of wages hides the true exchange that is taking place, since wages make all labor appear to be paid labor. For example, a person is paid three shillings for 12-hours' work, and thus, from a superficial point of view, it appears reasonable to refer to the "value of labour" as three shillings. But this formulation is misleading because the source of surplus value is not evident. For example, if a worker takes leather worth six shillings and makes one pair of boots each day, then (adding three shillings in wages) the value of the boots is nine shillings and there is no profit for the capitalist. But since capitalists clearly do make a profit, Marx had to account for its origin.

Marx believed he could show where surplus value came from by distinguishing between "labor" and "labor power." Labor is the work people actually do when they are employed by capitalists, whereas labor power is the capacity to work that the capitalist purchases from the worker. As Marx puts it, "by labour-power or capacity for labour is to be understood the aggregate of those mental and physical capabilities existing in a human being, which he exercises whenever he produces a use-value of any description."[57] Labor power is a commodity just like any other, and in fact, it is all the workers have to sell. Marx noted that the laborer, "instead of being in the position to sell commodities in which his labour is incorporated, [is] obliged to offer for sale as a commodity that very labour-power, which exists only in his living self."[58] Furthermore, in a capitalist society the proletarians can only sell their labor power to capitalists, who own the means of production. The two meet, presumably on an equal basis, one to sell labor power and the other to buy it.

The value, or selling price, of labor power is "determined, as in the case of any other commodity, by the labour-time necessary for the pro-

---

[57] Ibid., p. 167.
[58] Ibid., pp. 168–69.

duction, and consequently also the reproduction, of this special article."[59] Thus, labor power is, at least for the capitalist, a mass of congealed labor time—as represented by the cost of food, clothing, shelter, and all the other things necessary to keep the workers returning to the market-place with their peculiar commodity. Since workers must also reproduce new generations of workers, the cost of maintaining wives and children must be included—although, as will be seen below, capitalists have use for them also.

The key to the production of surplus value, then, resides in the fact that proletarians are forced to work longer than is necessary to obtain subsistence, and the capitalists keep for themselves the excess value created by the laborers. This is possible, Marx believed, precisely because the capitalists have purchased labor power rather than labor. For example, Marx speculated, it cost three shillings, on the average, to support workers and their families. Without at least that amount of money, the workers' labor power, or their capacity to work, would deteriorate (through sickness and death), and they would be unable to return to the marketplace. So the capitalists purchase labor power for three shillings. Marx further speculated that it took, on the average, six hours of labor to produce commodities valued at three shillings. So the capitalists, having purchased the workers' labor power rather than their labor, simply make them work for 12 hours. In that time, the workers produce commodities worth six shillings. The capitalists, who have not worked, pay the agreed-upon three shillings to the proletarians and keep the other three for themselves. This situation seemed unfair to Marx, and it is this inequity that he found to be the key to capitalist exploitation, class warfare, and eventually communism.

Having discovered the source of surplus value in labor power, Marx wished to be able to calculate its rate. In order to do so, and to understand the examples that follow, two definitions are necessary. First, Marx defined "constant capital" as "that part of capital which is represented by the means of production, by the raw material, auxiliary material, the instruments of labor, and does not undergo any quantitative alteration of value" in the production process.[60] For example, in the textile industry the constant capital (or means of production) would include the cost of raw cotton, spindles and looms, buildings, and all other materials necessary to turn cotton into linen. In the productive process, the value of all these items is transformed into the finished product—in this case,

---

[59] Ibid., p. 170.
[60] Ibid., p. 209.

linen. Second, "variable capital" is that portion of the means of production "represented by labour power, [that] does, in the process of production, undergo an alteration of value. It both reproduces the equivalent of its own value, and also produces an excess, a surplus value."[61] In calculating surplus value, constant capital is ignored since, as noted above, its value is simply transferred in altered form to the product. The rate of surplus value, then, is simply a ratio of surplus value over variable capital, or:

$$\frac{s}{v}$$

Marx thus provided a very precise definition of exploitation, since "the rate of surplus value is therefore an exact expression for the degree of exploitation of labour-power by capital, or of the labourer by the capitalist."[62] More broadly, in *Capital* exploitation is not simply a form of economic injustice, although it originates from a view of the economy based on the labor theory of value. The social classes that result from the acquisition of surplus value by one segment of society are also precisely defined. Those classes accruing surplus value, administering the government, passing laws, and regulating morals are the capitalists (or bourgeoisie), while those classes being exploited are the workers, or the proletarians.

In order to obtain the greatest imaginable benefits for themselves, capitalists attempt to exploit workers as much as possible. Their efforts can be conceptualized and measured in terms of the rate of surplus value, as denoted by the ratio given above. For example, we can recall that Marx speculated it took three shillings per day to support workers and their families, and by making people work 12 hours per day, the capitalists were able to pocket three shillings per day for themselves, for each worker in their employ. In this case, the rate of surplus value was calculated by Marx as follows:

$$\frac{s}{v} = \frac{3}{3} = 1.0$$

However, this rate can be changed in favor of the capitalists by increasing the numerator and decreasing the denominator. By increasing s, which Marx now called "absolute surplus value," the capitalists benefit. They do this by lengthening the working day. By decreasing v, which

---

[61] Ibid.
[62] Ibid., p. 218.

Marx now called "relative surplus value," the capitalists also benefit. They do this by making labor more productive. Each of these concepts is explained below.

Absolute Surplus Value. As noted above, the essential idea in the capitalists continuing efforts at increasing surplus value is to keep laborers working longer than is necessary to sustain them and to pay them no more than is necessary to keep them returning to the labor market. Absolute surplus value is increased by lengthening the working day.[63] Marx used an example dealing with the production of cotton to show how the capitalists obtain absolute surplus value from laborers.

	Hypothetical Costs per Worker
Constant capital (spindles, machines, etc.)	12 shillings/day
Constant capital (raw cotton)	12 " "
Variable capital (labor power)	3 " "
Total daily costs to capitalists	27 shillings/day
Value of finished cotton produced by each worker in 12 hours	30 shillings/day
Minus costs	27 " "
Surplus value created by each worker	3 shillings/day

Because the length of the working day was an important source of surplus value for the capitalists, it was also an arena of conflict throughout the 19th century. Thus, Marx spent a considerable amount of space documenting the manner in which the early capitalists forced laborers to work as many hours as possible.[64] However, the significance of these remarkable pages of *Capital* is that they are probably the first systematic use of historical and governmental data in social scientific research. Further, despite their anecdotal quality (by today's standards), Marx's data are clearly correct: they show the extent to which capitalists sought to extend the working day and keep the proletarians in an utterly depraved condition. In general, Marx believed that the drive to extend the working day so as to obtain as much absolute surplus value as possible is characteristic of capitalism and that the proletariat is helpless to resist.

Relative Surplus Value. Marx called the surplus value that is produced by lengthening the working day absolute surplus value. The surplus value produced by curtailing necessary labor time, and hence, increasing the productiveness of labor, was called relative surplus value.

The productiveness of labor can be increased in two interrelated ways. The first is by altering the organization of the productive process and

---

[63] Ibid., p. 193.

[64] Ibid., pp. 231–312.

the second is by the application of advanced forms of technology to the productive process. In either case, by increasing the workers' productivity (so that more is produced in the same or less time), the capitalists can cheapen the prices of their commodities, and yet still increase their profit—at least temporarily. From the capitalists' point of view, the fact that the degree of exploitation of the proletarians has increased is irrelevant. Similarly, the possible long-term consequences of this practice are ignored because of the capitalists all-consuming need for increased profit.

Marx illustrated how relative surplus value is increased with the following hypothetical example.

At one level of technology, one pair of boots can be produced by each worker per day.

	Shillings
Constant capital	6
Variable capital	3
Total costs	9
Value of finished boots	11
Minus cost	9
Surplus value	2

With increasing technology, two pairs of boots can be produced by each worker per day.

	Shillings
Constant capital	12
Variable capital	3
Total costs	15
Value of each pair of boots	10
Value of two pair of boots	20
Minus costs	15
Surplus value	5

Thus, with the implementation of advanced forms of technology, capitalists can produce more boots or any other item, undersell their competitors, and still realize greater profit (that is, surplus value). In this example, Marx assumed that capitalists actually compete with one another, a viable assumption in the 19th century.

By discovering the advantages of increasing productivity, Marx thought he had uncovered the hidden dynamic of capitalism that would lead inexorably to increasing exploitation, increasing industrial crises, and ultimately to the overthrow of the capitalist system itself. His rationale is that the capitalist's increased profits are short-lived, since other capitalists immediately copy any innovation, and thus, the extra surplus value generated by increasing productivity disappears "so soon as the new method of productivity has become general, and has consequently caused the difference between the individual value of the cheapened commodity and its social value to vanish."[65] In terms of the example cited above, other capitalists soon learn to produce two boots per day and change their system of production accordingly, with the result that the innovator's advantage is obviated. However, over time, someone else figures out how to produce three boots per day and begins to do so, realizing greater relative surplus value for a time. Soon, however, other capitalists copy the new system of production and again eliminate the innovator's initial advantage. This process continues inexorably, as capitalists are constantly motivated to increase productivity. The ultimate result, Marx predicted, would be the sort of chaos originally depicted in *The Communist Manifesto*.

Since the reorganization of the productive process and the introduction of machines into the workplace where important sources of surplus value for the capitalists, they were also the locus of much conflict during the 19th century. For such changes meant that the proletarians had to either work harder or in a more dehumanizing environment. As in his analysis of absolute surplus value, Marx spent much time empirically documenting the capitalists' efforts at increasing relative surplus value.[66] By using historical and governmental data, Marx was again able to show how productivity had steadily increased through greater exploitation of the proletarians.

The Accumulation of Capital

Marx's discussion of surplus value was a systematic attempt at showing the dynamics of capitalist exploitation. His description of the process of capital accumulation expands on this analysis by dealing with two interrelated issues stemming from the nature of surplus value. The first, which he called *simple reproduction*, focuses on the way capitalist social relations are continuously recreated by wage laborers. The second issue, which Marx called the "conversion of surplus value into capital," focuses on the way in which surplus value is used to accumulate capital. As we shall see, the result of capital accumulation is a contradiction in

---

[65] Ibid., p. 319.
[66] Ibid., pp. 336–507.

capitalist society so great that its transformation to "a higher form of society" ultimately becomes inevitable.

Simple Reproduction. Simple reproduction occurs as workers continuously produce products that become translated into surplus value for capitalists and wages for themselves. Proletarians use their wages in two ways, both of which contribute to the stability of the capitalist system. First, because capitalists own the means of production and the commodities produced with them, as proletarians purchase the necessities of life they must give their wages back to the capitalists. The capitalists, of course, use that money all over again to make still more money for themselves. Second, after minimally satisfying their needs, workers return to the marketplace ready to sell their labor power and ready once again to augment capital by creating surplus value. Over time, then, capitalist society is continuously renewed, since proletarians produce not only commodities, not only their own wages, and not only surplus value, but also capitalist social relations: with alienated workers on one side as wage labor and capitalists on the other side exploiting wage labor.

The Conversion of Surplus Value into Capital. Capitalists consume at least part of the surplus value they obtain from proletarians. The remainder is reinvested in such a way that the reproduction of capital occurs on a progressively increasing scale, with the result, as Marx observed, that "the circle in which simple reproduction moves, alters its form and . . . changes into a spiral."[67]

Marx predicted that the conversion of surplus value into capital, which he called capital accumulation, would have three interrelated consequences for the future of capitalism. His first prediction was that proletarians will be separated from owning or controlling private property and even their own labor. This situation occurs because capitalists consume first their own capital and then the unpaid labor of others. Yet, paradoxically, the laborers have not been defrauded—at least according to capitalist rules of the game—for as we saw above, the capitalists merely pay laborers for the value of their commodity, labor power. And since proletarians have only labor power to sell, they have little choice but to participate according to the capitalists' rules.

Marx's second prediction regarding the consequences of the conversion of surplus value into capital is that proletarians will become increasingly impoverished and an industrial reserve army of poor people would be created. He labeled this process the *general law of capital accumulation*, and he believed that it would occur as capitalists increasingly used ma-

---

[67] Ibid., p. 581.

chines in the factories in order to make labor more productive and, hence, lower the price of goods. As laborers become more productive, fewer of them are needed and their labor power can be purchased at a lower price. Thus, Marx predicted not only that proletarians will continuously reproduce their relations with the capitalists, but also that they will produce the means by which they are rendered into a superfluous population that is forced to work anywhere, anytime, for any available wages. However, Marx believed that under these extreme conditions proletarians will become increasingly class conscious.

Marx's third prediction about the consequences of capital accumulation is that the rate of profit will inevitably fall, bring on industrial crises of even greater severity, and eventually an impoverished proletariat will overthrow what had become a chaotic capitalist system in favor of a more humane and cooperative one. The logic of Marx's analysis can be understood when it is recalled that labor power is the source of surplus value. As the proportion of surplus value invested in machines (constant capital) goes up in comparison to the amount invested in labor power (variable capital), profits fall. In those areas where profits become unacceptably low, even though large quantities of goods are being produced, production has to slow down or cease altogether, throwing more people out of work. Marx argued that as industrial cycles repeatedly occur, they will become ever more serious, and he predicted that the logic of capitalist development will produce the conditions necessary for its overthrow: an industrial base along with an impoverished and class-conscious proletariat. Ultimately, these dispossessed people will usher in a classless society in which production occurs for the common good.

The Origins of Capitalism

Marx's analysis of capitalism presupposes that it is an ongoing social system. Thus, in the final pages of *Capital* he once again sketched the origins of capitalism, which he now called the process of *primitive accumulation*. We should recall that capitalist social relations only occur under quite specific circumstances, that is, the owners of money (the means of production) who desire to increase their holdings confront free laborers who have no way of obtaining sustenance other than by selling their labor power. Thus, in order to understand the origins of capitalist social relations, Marx had to account for the rise of both the proletariat and the bourgeoisie. Typically, and by way of anticipating our remarks about Max Weber in Chapters 9 to 11, Marx opted for a structural explanation of the origins of capitalism, as opposed to Weber's emphasis on such cultural factors as religious beliefs and values.

According to Marx, the modern proletariat arose because self-supporting peasants were driven from the land (and from the guilds) and transformed into rootless and dependent urban dwellers. This process began in England during the 15th and 16th centuries and then spread throughout Western Europe.

Using England as his example, Marx argued that this process involved, first, the clearing of the old estates by breaking up feudal retainers, robbing peasants of the use of common lands, and abolishing peasants' rights of land tenure under circumstances that he described as "reckless terrorism." Second, Marx argued that one of the major effects of the Protestant Reformation was "the spoilation of the church's property" by its conversion into private property—illegally, of course. Third, the widespread theft of state land and its conversion into privately owned property ensured that nowhere in England could peasants continue to live as they had during medieval times. In all three cases (although this analysis is clearly too simplistic), the methods used were far from idyllic, but they were effective, and they resulted in the rise of capitalist agriculture capable of supplying the needs of a "free" proletariat. Further, given that they had nowhere to go, thousands of displaced peasants became beggars, robbers, and vagabonds. Hence, throughout Western Europe beginning in the 16th century there was "bloody legislation against vagabondage" with severe sanctions against those who would not work for the nascent capitalists who were then emerging.

For Marx, the emergence of the capitalist farmer and the industrial capitalist occurred concomitantly with the rise of the modern proletariat. Beginning in the 15th century, those who owned or controlled land typically had guarantees of long tenure, could employ newly "freed" workers at very low wages, and benefitted from a rise in the price of farm products of all sorts. In addition, they were able to increase farm production, despite the smaller number of people working the land, through the use of improved methods and equipment, which increased cooperation among workers in the farming process and concentrated land ownership in fewer hands. Thus, primitive accumulation of capital could occur.

Marx felt that the genesis of industrial capitalism developed as the result of a variety of interrelated events. First, he emphasized, usury and commerce had existed throughout antiquity—despite laws against such activity—and laid a basis for the primitive accumulation of capital to occur. Second, the exploration and exploitation of the new world brought great wealth into the hands of just a few people. In this regard,

Marx pointed especially to the discovery of gold and silver, along with the existence of native populations that could be exploited. Finally, Marx noted the emergence of a system of public credit and its expansion into an international credit system. On this basis, he claimed, capitalism emerged in Western Europe.

SUMMARY AND CONCLUSION

In *The German Ideology*, Marx developed a philosophy of science that emphasized the importance of studying people's actual social relationships as they evolve through history. On this basis, he quickly concluded that capitalist society is inherently exploitative because individuals privately own the means of production. In such a context, Marx believed, competition rather than cooperation is inevitable, and people cannot realize their full potential as human beings.

Similarly, in *The Communist Manifesto*, Marx tried to stimulate a proletarian revolt by describing this same situation in highly polemical terms. However, in the *Manifesto* the political significance of the proletariat is given a theoretical basis for the first time. The new world order that Marx prophesized is seen as an inevitable result of people acting in terms of their own best interests. Despite Marx's own rather authoritarian temperament, his professed goal (which he transformed into a historical inevitability) was to create a society in which people act together for the common good. As he put it in the *Manifesto* "we shall have an association in which the free development of each is the condition for the free development of all."

Capital represents the culmination of Marx's thought, for in it he takes these ideas and places them in a scientific context. Based on the labor theory of value, Marx was able to show (at least to his satisfaction) how capitalist society maintains itself by the exploitation of the proletariat and why it cannot continue to operate in this fashion. The logic of Marx's analysis leads to the conclusion that an industrial society based on private ownership of the means of production and the exchange of commodities cannot endure, for the only measure of exchange value is labor and the only beneficiaries are capitalists. On this basis, he predicted that the destruction of capitalism would usher in a new and more humane society based upon the communal possession of the means of production and the use value of commodities.

While the specifics of Marx's analysis are clearly incorrect, both Marxist and non-Marxist sociologists still find a great deal that is useful in his work. In Chapter 8 we will extract from Marx's writing the models and principles that form his more enduring theoretical legacy.

8

KARL MARX III:
MODELS AND PRINCIPLES

Among the early pioneers of sociological theory, Karl Marx was to prove the most enduring and influential. Comte and Spencer were to fade, and are probably read very little today. But Marx's work endures and is still the center of intellectual controversy the world over. One source of this controversy is the political thrust of Marx's work, making it a seedbed for ideological debate. For our purposes, however, Marx's theoretical contribution is most important; but as we will emphasize, Marx's efforts as a social theorist are tied to political action, creating a mixture of science and action that continues to stimulate debate.

In this chapter, our goal is to make more explicit the strictly theoretical contribution of Marx. In the last chapter, we have reviewed Marx's basic works, and now we will (a) summarize the key elements in his theoretical approach, (b) indicate how these elements are combined into formal models, and (c) extract the more abstract principles to be found in Marx's work. It is in these areas of inquiry, we feel, that Marx's enduring intellectual contribution resides, for Marx as a social theorist provided modern theory with a number of critical conceptual elements, several suggestive models, and some important principles on the nature of social organization and change.

THE BASIC THEORETICAL APPROACH

Marx's approach to the study of capitalist society is fundamentally different from that of many other social theorists of his time. Unlike Comte and Spencer, he was not interested in formally stating abstract and universal laws of social organization. Rather, Marx was both a revolutionary and a social scientist who sought to establish a theoretical justification for the revolutionary overthrow of capitalist society. His goal was nothing less than the complete transformation of capitalist social relations so that people could collectively control their society and, hence, their destiny. If people can be organized cooperatively rather than competitively, he argued, they will be free to develop their potential as human beings.

Marx's vision thus exemplifies a humanist philosophy of the highest order. Although his own social relationships were often marred by bitter invective, Marx's work points toward a society where the dignity and innate worth of human beings would be respected and where people's efforts at self-realization would be encouraged. Yet in this regard, he was little different from the many other utopian thinkers of the 18th and 19th centuries. What gives Marx's work its power and evocativeness is not his utopian statements, but rather his analytical approach to the study of social systems.

Marx's basic approach can be divided into three interrelated parts: (1) a view of the nature of theory as historically specific rather than abstract, (2) an emphasis on combining theory and action, and (3) a reliance on what has come to be called dialectical materialism as the mode of analysis. After each of these essential elements is explained, they are drawn together by means of a brief example.

The Historical Specificity of Marx's Theory

Marx was interested in understanding capitalism, and thereby hastening its demise. Hence, unlike many of the early classical theorists, he did not seek to develop abstract laws about the nature of society after the fashion of the natural or physical sciences. Rather, all of Marx's predictions and propositions are historically specific: they apply only to capitalist society as it existed in Europe during the 19th century. Thus, for example, neither his "general law of capitalist accumulation" nor his prediction of increasing impoverishment of the proletariat is intended to be trans-historical or abstract in the sense that it could be applied to any society in diverse historical epochs.

Part of the reason for Marx's emphasis on the historical specificity of theory undoubtedly lies in his reaction to German idealism as seen in the works of Hegel and the Young Hegelians. They were unable to comprehend, he felt, the social processes (and, hence, the human misery) characteristic of 19th-century capitalism, primarily because they focused on ideas about history rather than on actual historical events. Furthermore, and unlike many of the social theorists who came after him, Marx never worked and probably would not have wanted to work in an academic environment. Yet, such a detached environment can stimulate a concern for developing highly formal and abstract laws based on the observation of events in the real world. It was in such an academic environment that sociology was to develop and prosper in the years following Marx. But for Marx, theoretical detachment was the last of his concerns; his goal was to link theoretical ideas to political and social action.

The historically specific character of Marx's work thus makes its status as a generalizing science unclear. On the one hand, his propositions about the nature of capitalism resist formalization. Abstract and universal statements or laws are simply not "Marxist"; indeed, the vision of Comte and Spencer for a science of society, similar to that in the natural sciences, is abhorrent to Marxists.

But, on the other hand, Marxists often refer to his "scientific" analysis of capitalism. This apparent contradiction is resolved by further understanding Marx's view of the relationship between theory and action.

The Combination of Theory and Action

Because he sought to provide a theoretical explanation for a communist revolution, Marx's approach combines theory and action in a way that many modern observers do not accept. As a result, when Marxists and non-Marxists write about a "scientific finding," they are each referring to something entirely different. And it is little wonder, therefore, that they talk past one another or engage in acrimonious debate.

Non-Marxists generally try, although not always successfully, to separate science and scientific analysis from political values and activity. As we observed in Chapter 1, theory is comprised of abstract assertions about the properties of the real world and is tested by observation. From this perspective (which is shared to varying degrees by all non-Marxist sociologists), the underlying value in social science is that of truth, as it is revealed by the use of observations of events to test and/or generate theoretical principles. Thus, social scientific questions refer to what patterns of social organization are actually like, not to what they should or could be like. And therefore, an approach such as Marx's, which sees theory and action as combined, cannot be scientific—at least from a non-Marxist point of view. And the assertion that Marxism is a scientific political doctrine will typically be seen as a contradiction in terms by modern, non-Marxists.

Marx would not have accepted this argument. When he asserted in

The German Ideology that theory ought to be empirically based, he only meant that analysis must begin with people's material needs and the practical problems they face in everyday life. Based on such observations, he went on to emphasize the crucial importance of "practical-critical activity" (or *praxis*), that is, action informed by thought. For Marx, theory and action are to be combined. And thus, when Marx argued that philosophers have only interpreted the world, when the point is to change it, he had a methodological as well as a substantive point in mind. As Richard Appelbaum has noted, Marx's approach is distinguished from that of all other social theorists because "the theory itself is changed as the [social] circumstances are altered through theoretically informed political practice."[1] As a result, the epistemological status of Marx's work is left unclear. On the one hand, the combination of theory and knowledge as well as thought and action means that it cannot be scientific in the normal sense: usually scientists seek knowledge, not action (at least ideally). But, on the other hand, from Marx's perspective, scientific questions about what society should be like are not only possible, they are required, since theoretical activity must have a revolutionary goal. From this angle of vision, then, the truth or falseness of a theory is decided not merely by observation but by what it leads people to do—or leave undone—as they attempt to satisfy their needs. No other social theorist has constructed an intellectual edifice as original, or as politically powerful.

Dialectical Materialism in Marx's Work

Marx wished to understand the pattern of history in order to show why capitalism could not survive. And as we saw in Chapter 5, Hegel's dialectic was the perfect tool for this task. However, rather than dealing with an amorphous world of ideas as the Young Hegelians had done, Marx's version of dialectical materialism allows for an explanation of why it is that a social structure giving advantages to one group (the feudal aristocracy) became historically obsolete and was replaced by a social structure giving advantages to another group (capitalists). On this basis, he predicted with great confidence that a similar pattern would repeat itself in such a way that capitalism would be replaced by communism. In Marx's version of dialectical materialism, the historical mechanisms by which this movement proceeds are the emergence of opposing

---

[1] Richard P. Appelbaum, "Marx's Theory of the Falling Rate of Profit: Towards a Dialectical Analysis of Structural Social Change," *American Sociological Review* 43 (February 1978):73.

interests and class conflict based on that opposition. However, these two essential ideas must be placed within a more general theoretical context, which is left largely implicit in Marx's work.

First, as noted in Chapter 5, all societies are social systems composed of interrelated parts. In Marx's work, this point of emphasis signals that all social relations imply their opposites. For example, in the *Manifesto* he noted that it is tautologous to speak of wage laborers without also referring to capitalists, since one cannot exist without the other. Similarly, the presence of exchange relationships in capitalism implies the existence of surplus value, exploitation, and ultimately revolution. Second, social change is inherent in all societies, as people make history by satisfying their needs. Marx's work thus provides a theory of endogenous social change; that is, the most fundamental source of change comes from within the society rather than outside of it. And hence, not only do all social relations imply their opposites, they also contain their own inherent "contradictions" which will generate or cause their opposites to develop. For example, according to Marx, feudalism contained within itself the social relations that eventually became capitalism.

Third, social change has a recognizable direction. For example, just as a flower is inherent in the nature of a seed, so the historical development of a more complex social structure, such as capitalism, is inherent in the nature of a less complex one, such as feudalism. As Robert Nisbet has commented, Marx was a child of the Enlightenment and he believed in the inevitability of human progress.[2] And no less than Condorcet, Turgot, Hegel, Saint-Simon, or Comte, Marx had a vision of progress toward a utopian endpoint. For Marx, this endpoint is the communist society. Yet, Marx knew that history is not imposed on people and that it does not proceed in a strictly linear direction, and thus a fourth point should be emphasized. Because people act to control their destiny and protect their interests, the direction of history is decisively shaped by predictable patterns of opposition and class conflict which develop within every society. For example, given a knowledge of property relations in capitalism, the differing interests of the proletarians and the capitalists are predictable, as is the generation of class conflict (under certain conditions that can be specified). Once again, then, a communist revolution is a predictable historical event that is ushered in by acting people who recognize and try to protect their interests.

---

[2] Robert A. Nisbet, *Social Change and History* (New York: Oxford University Press, 1969).

Marx's Approach: An Example

The three elements of Marx's approach discussed so far can be conveniently illustrated with an example drawn from *Capital:* the theory of the falling rate of profit.[3] We should recall Marx's prediction that capitalists' rate of profit would fall as their investment in machines increased in proportion to their investment in labor power, with the overthrow of capitalism as the eventual result. This hypothesis can be presented in terms of a mathematical equation, a tactic that Marx often used in *Capital:* [4]

$$P = S/(C + V)$$

where P = profit, S = absolute surplus value, C = constant capital (machines), and V = variable capital (labor power). Following Marx, Appelbaum shows that this equation can be algebraically decomposed so that:

$$P = S'(1 - Q)$$

where $S' = S/V$ and $Q = C/(C + V)$. It follows, then, that as Q approaches 1, the quantity $(1 - Q)$ approaches 0, and the overall rate of profit falls.

As Appelbaum notes, these equations appear to be much like those of any science: they represent in mathematical terms the empirical relationship among profit, surplus value, constant capital, and variable capital. They therefore form an abstract and formal statement that could, at least in principle, be falsified. But this sort of testable hypothesis is not Marx's intent, for as we have emphasized, Marx was writing about 19th-century capitalist society in which class struggle was the means by which the dialectic worked itself out. In this context, each of the elements determining the rate of profit constitutes an arena for class struggle and, hence, an area in which theoretically informed political activity can alter both the direction of history and the theory used to explain it.

Thus, in order to understand the conditions under which profit will

---

[3] This entire section has been freely adapted from Richard P. Appelbaum's outstanding article cited above.

[4] Marx's most extensive presentation of the law of the falling rate of profit is in *Capital: The Process of Capitalist Production as a Whole*, vol. 3 (New York: International Publishers, 1967), pp. 211–66.

fall in capitalist society, we must learn the outcomes of struggles over the rate of surplus value, the use of machines (constant capital) in the manufacturing process, and the cost of labor power (variable capital). But the results of these struggles cannot be known in advance, although the historical and, hence, theoretical parameters within which solutions will be worked out are clear. For example, as we saw in the last chapter, the struggle over surplus value occurs first over the length of the working day. Capitalists obtain absolute surplus value by forcing proletarians to work longer than necessary to obtain their subsistence. Marx's exhaustive documentation of the struggle over the working day is designed to illustrate its political and theoretical import. While he knew, based upon his theoretical analysis, that capitalists would constantly try to increase their exploitation and proletarians would try to resist, he could not predict the outcome in any specific instance. As a result, the value of S in the equations above is unknown, although not because it cannot be observed. Rather, it is unknown because it is the result of continuously recurring "practical-critical activity." Similarly, capitalists and proletarians also struggled over the introduction of machinery into the manufacturing process. When it occurred, fewer proletarians became more productive (generally at lower wages) and relative surplus value increased—at least for a time. The result of this struggle effected the value of constant capital (C) in the equations shown above. But once again, while Marx believed he could explain the general direction in which this struggle would be resolved, its outcome was not predictable in any particular instance. Finally, the wages paid to proletarians (variable capital, or V in the equations) constituted another area of struggle. Laborers' success depended on their degree of organization, militancy, internationalization, and a host of other factors—most of which were not economic—so that the outcome was not predictable here either.

Thus, Marx's analysis of the falling rate of profit was not scientific in the sense we ordinarily think of science, and it was not intended to be. In Marx's work, equations provide the appearance of quantitative precision, abstractness, and universality, but this is not their intent. Rather, Marx tried to provide a set of theoretical guidelines for political behavior, and these guidelines are continually modified in light of subsequent historical events. In this way, he constructed a "scientific" political doctrine that cannot be refuted. His approach embodies a vision of science in which history provides the context, human action is built into the theory, and the dialectic of progress unfolds inexorably as human beings attempt to realize their interests.

MARX'S THEORETICAL MODELS

Marx's approach can be translated into two different models of social organization. The first version, which we call Marx's *elaborated model*, retains the essential characteristics of his analysis in order to apply it to modern conditions. In this form, it is a perfectly reasonable and plausible way of understanding the nature of social structures today, assessing where they are going, and suggesting appropriate political action that might someday lead to a communist revolution. The second version, which we call Marx's *restricted model*, is quite different because its historical and revolutionary elements have been eliminated. In this form, it is a useful heuristic device for understanding certain aspects of social structures in general, whether these be societal social systems or some other type of social unit. In addition, it leads to a number of abstract and trans-historical statements about patterns of social organization. Marxists and many Marxian oriented sociologists tend to use some variation of the elaborated model, while non-Marxist sociologists generally see the restricted model as most useful.

Marx's Elaborated Model

Marx never abandoned the basic approach first developed in *The German Ideology*. Indeed, both the *Communist Manifesto* and *Capital* represent, although in different ways, applications of the peculiar philosophy of science that was first presented in 1846. Thus, the three books dealt with here contain within them a model of the generation of social stratification, conflict, and change in capitalist societies. Figure 8–1 depicts an abstract version of this model.

As shown in our explication of *The German Ideology*, Marx believed that stable patterns of social organization are based upon productive activity, a division of labor, and the satisfaction of human needs. All his other works reaffirm this insight. The cornerstone of all social life is productive activity, that is, interaction with the environment must occur in some organized manner or no society can exist for long. As a result, all social institutions (such as law, kinship, and so on) develop in light of this fundamental fact. It should be emphasized that the issue here, from Marx's point of view, is not that economic activity determines behavior in other spheres but, rather, that all social action is conditioned by the forms of productive activity existing in a society. In such a context, the division of labor facilitates both productivity and need-satisfaction—although, as we shall see, the division of labor

FIGURE 8–1
Marx's Elaborated Model of the Generation of Stratification, Conflict, and Change of Social Structures

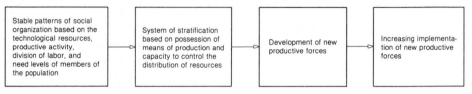

is always organized so as to benefit those who control the means of production. According to Marx, human needs are rank-ordered such that the basic material needs of food, clothing, and shelter must first be satisfied, followed by a panoply of psychological needs: to be in control of one's environment, to express creativity and originality, and to develop diverse skills and abilities. However, the relationship among all these factors is very complex, as Marx recognized, because people compare themselves to others and also assess what sorts of commodities are available to them. Their needs also change over time in light of the social structures within which they live. Thus, human nature varies depending upon historical circumstances.

Marx asserted, and there is some merit to his assertion, that a system of stratification emerges in all societies based on the control over the means of production. This fact implies, of course, that those persons who benefit from the existing means of production have an interest in maintaining the status quo. Control over the means of production can occur in a variety of contexts, not all of which Marx foresaw: for example, under capitalism the private possession of property is deemed important while in communist societies the state possesses property. In either case, the group controlling the means of production (the capitalists or the communist party) is the dominant class in the society, since its members determine the way commodities, services, and other benefits are distributed.[5] Further, the dominant class acts to legitimize its benefits by promulgating and supporting values among the masses that, directly or indirectly, support its position. Sometimes the dominant class also controls the military and imposes its will in that manner.

Marx believed that the members of the dominant class will also act to increase their benefits, which is a fateful step because over the long run such acts lead to the development of new ways of producing things.

---

[5] On the communist party as the dominant class possessing the means of production, see Milovan Djilas, *The New Class* (New York: Praeger, 1965).

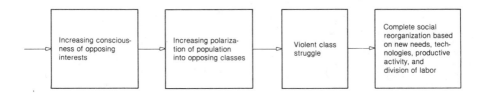

These new productive forces can be based on advances in technology, changes in the way production is organized, or both. Thus, Marx's endogenous theory of social change follows from his belief that the origin of these new productive forces is inherent in any society, largely because of people's desire to produce more and better goods for themselves. He asserted that only with the rise of industrialization has it been possible to realistically think about producing commodities for the common good of all. However, this goal has not been realized in any country, and as a result, Marxists can still show that the masses who do not control the means of production have an interest in overthrowing the status quo in the name of all humankind.

Marx emphasized that under specifiable conditions, people will become aware of their true interests. Further, theoretically informed leaders can help polarize a society and, again under specifiable conditions, induce class struggle. Many Marxists believe, probably rightly, that class struggle of the sort they desire inevitably will be violent. As announced in the *Manifesto* in 1848, the ultimate goal is the overthrow of the existing order of things in favor of a more humane society. The resulting social reorganization would thus be based upon new ways of producing things, a new division of labor, and new needs. The result would be a radically different and stable society. It should be remembered that the sequence of events depicted in Figure 8–1 represents, according to Marx, the result of free human action as it occurs in light of people's recognition of their interests and their theoretical acumen.

There are four aspects of this elaborated model that must be noted. First, Marx relied exclusively on structural variables. The influence of patterns of culture (for example, religious beliefs and values) is omitted. Marx believed that such phenomena were relatively unimportant in stimulating social change, although they were useful in preventing the members of subordinate classes from recognizing their true interests. Second, while Marx's view of human nature is fairly flexible in that people's needs and desires change as historical circumstances change, he does

FIGURE 8–2
Marx's Restricted Model of the Generation of Stratification, Conflict, and Change of Social Structures

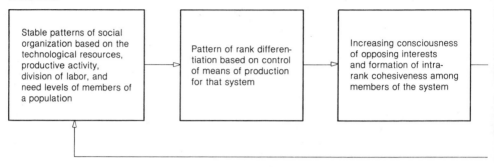

see one overarching characteristic: people are acquisitive creatures who, when they are in dominant positions, are unable to restrain their avariciousness. Third, Marx's elaborated model of stratification, conflict, and change is one that does not occur very often in history, since what is meant by social reorganization is the total transformation of whole societies, comparable to that which occurred as feudalism gave way to capitalism over a period of several hundred years. Marx, in fact, said at one point that there have been only three great epochs in human history, which he called the ancient, feudal, and bourgeois,[6] with his version of communism being the fourth and last epoch. Finally, although the elaborated model presented in Figure 8–1 is abstract and could therefore be applied to any modern society, it still implies the combination of theory and action that is characteristic of Marx's approach and embodies the principles of dialectical materialism outlined above.

From a Marxist perspective, this elaborated model is very useful for both theoretical and political purposes. For example, it allows one to argue that the productive forces characteristic of capitalism have not completely developed as of yet, and hence, the great revolution is still to come. Or, similarly, patterns of opposition and conflict in a society can be interpreted in light of a larger historical and evolutionary purpose. Thus, as presented here, Marx's elaborated model does not suggest refutable propositions, and is not intended to, since political victories or defeats are simply seen as episodes in an ongoing class struggle. But it does provide theoretical guidelines for the interpretation of political events,

---

[6] See Karl Marx, "Preface," *A Contribution to the Critique of Political Economy* (New York: International Publishers, 1970).

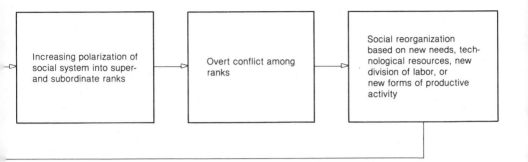

which is what Marx intended. However, as indicated above, non-Marxist sociologists generally reject this view of theory. Thus, when they wish to study the processes in which Marx was interested—stratification, conflict, and change—a more theoretically restricted model is usually preferred.

Marx's Restricted Model

Figure 8–2 depicts what we call Marx's restricted model of the generation of stratification, conflict, and change. It encapsulates those processes that occur and recur without emphasizing the global transformation that Marx foresaw, the combination of theory and action, or the principles of dialectical materialism. Thus, Figure 8–2 begins with Marx's emphasis on the fact that stable patterns of social organization in any social system, whether an entire society or smaller social unit, are based upon some level of technology, a form of productive activity, a division of labor, and an established level of needs. These forces create a pattern of rank differentiation among members of the system which is organized around control over the means of production. Whether such control is concentrated among few persons or within a small group, a large group, or among the members of several groups is quite variable, but it generally produces tangible benefits in terms of the unequal distribution of scarce resources.[7] Thus, Marx was probably correct in his argument that those who control the means of production generally comprise the most powerful class in a society and receive the greatest rewards as a result. But

---

[7] See Gerhard Lenski, *Power and Privilege* (New York: McGraw-Hill, 1966).

Marx's insight for societal social systems also applies to other types of systems, such as groups, organizations, communities, and the like. Thus, there is always some degree of rank differentiation among the members of a population in terms of their control of the means of production, whether this be industrial factories, task activities in small groups, or organizational resources in a bureaucracy. And while Marx was interested in the distribution of power and material well-being in societal systems, his insights are, to some degree, relevant for understanding the distribution of other resources, such as prestige and approval, in other types of social systems.

Under certain conditions, which need to be specified, low- and high-ranking members of a social system may become aware of their opposing interests; polarization can occur, struggles may ensue, and some degree of social reorganization can occur. This situation may lead to a new level of stability based on changes in the social structure or upon increased repression (since the subordinate group does not always win).

Four aspects of this restricted model need to be noted. First, virtually all the linkages in the model imply testable and refutable theoretical principles (some of which will be identified in the next section). Thus, while the restricted model builds on Marx's insight as to which social processes in a society are the most important, it implies a theoretical approach that is decisively non-Marxist in orientation. Second, because the restricted model has no historical implications, the feedback loop suggests that processes of stratification, conflict, and change periodically recur—which, in fact, appears to be the case in most social systems. Third, like the elaborated model presented above, Marx's restricted model deals only with certain structural variables. As a result, many important factors are omitted. For example, the model does not take into account the fact that class struggles generally occur within an ongoing normative framework. Thus, a more complete depiction of the process of stratification, conflict, and change would have to make clear the impact of a variety of additional cultural, structural, and psychological variables. Fourth, as presented in Figure 8–2, the restricted model is, at least in principle, applicable to many kinds of social systems in addition to societies. Thus, for example, a corporation, a labor union, and a university are all susceptible to the "Marxist" analysis suggested by the restricted model, for it serves as a heuristic guide to some of the most important processes that occur in all social systems. It is for these reasons that non-Marxist sociologists who are interested in the generation of stratification, conflict, and change find the model to be a useful theoretical tool.

MARX'S THEORETICAL PRINCIPLES

When Marx's work is cast into models, whether elaborated or restricted, his emphasis on the way in which the organization of production influences social structure can be seen with great clarity. However, by recasting his ideas in terms of abstract theoretical principles, we can convey the complexity of his analysis more fully. We should emphasize that this presentation incorporates a non-Marxist view of science. The reason for such an emphasis can be seen when a few of Marx's predictions about the future of capitalism are considered: (1) the greater the development of capitalism, then the more it will divide into two opposing classes; (2) the greater the development of capitalism, then the more alienated and impoverished the proletariat will become; (3) the greater the development of capitalism, then the lower the rate of profit and the more severe the resulting industrial crises; and (4) the greater the frequency and severity of industrial crises, then the greater the likelihood of a communist revolution. Even when they are phrased as statements of covariance, it is apparent that Marx's predictions (and these are only a few of them) are not theoretical principles of the sort desired by non-Marxist sociologists. Rather, they are historical prophecies, and with the benefit of hindsight, it is relatively easy to see that they did not come true—even if they did seem reasonable from Marx's point of view.

However, there are a number of important abstract principles implicit in Marx's work that can still inform non-Marxist sociological theorizing. These principles can be sketched most easily by dividing them into two groups: (1) those dealing with the organizational properties of social systems and (2) those dealing with the properties of inequality and change in social systems. It should be noted that although Marx's writings abound with suggestive leads and ideas, we have tried to retain only those elements that appear to be both essential in his work and useful to non-Marxist social theorists.

Principles of Social Organization

The German Ideology, the *Manifesto*, and *Capital* all contain, to varying degrees, a set of fundamental ideas about the nature of social organization. Despite the varied contexts in which Marx presents these ideas, they imply a question that virtually all social theorists ask themselves: How is it that patterns of social organization emerge, persist, and change over time? Or, as Marx phrased it in *The German Ideology:* How is it possible for human societies to have a history? His answer to this question can be seen in the five interrelated principles presented below.

1. The greater is the level of technological resources available to members of a population, the greater is their productive activity; and conversely, the greater is the productive activity of a population, the more likely is the level of technology to increase, setting into motion increased productivity.

2. The greater is the level of productive activity among members of a population, the more likely is that population to reveal high levels of social differentiation; and conversely, the greater is the level of social differentiation, the more likely is productivity to increase, setting into motion pressures for increased differentiation.

3. The greater are the levels of productivity and social differentiation in a system, the greater is the capacity of that system to support a larger population; and by implication, the larger is the population, the greater are the pressures for increased productivity and social differentiation.

4. The larger is the population and the greater is the degree of social differentiation, the more is integration among members of that population achieved, at least in the short run, through the rank differentiation and concentration of power.

5. The greater are the levels of rank differentiation and concentration of power, the more likely are belief and normative systems to be controlled by those with power and used to legitimize the inequalities in the distribution of scarce resources that are associated with rank differentiation.

These five principles emphasize Marx's conviction that levels of technology, productivity, social differentiation, population size, rank differentiation, concentration of power, and the exploitive use of beliefs and norms are fundamentally related. We have phrased Marx's ideas more neutrally in order that the insights they offer into the nature of social organization can be divorced from Marx's polemics.

Marx argued that members of social systems use technological resources to facilitate their productivity and that increased productivity encourages the related phenomena of social differentiation and population growth. In this portion of Marx's view of social organization, there is little that goes beyond Spencer and others in the 18th and early 19th centuries who recognized that social differentiation is a function of population density and technological advances. The unique part of Marx's view is his analysis of how integration in differentiated systems is achieved. Whereas Comte, and French thinkers in general, emphasized the importance of such cultural forces as a "collective spirit," "universal consensus," "collective consciousness," and other somewhat vague references to common values and beliefs to account for system integration, and whereas Spencer and other utilitarians stressed the "invisible hand of order" associated with exchange activities in markets, Marx argued that rank differentiation, concentration of power, and manipulation of idea systems by those in power are the means by which populous and differentiated social systems are maintained. But as he was also to emphasize, this basis of organization contains the seeds for its transformation, since inequality inexorably sets into motion forces for conflict and change.

Principles of Inequality and Change in Social Systems

Marx focused on how inequalities generated in capitalist societal systems will lead to conflict and change. Our goal, however, is to liberate Marxian principles from their historical specificity and to state them at a sufficiently high level of abstraction so that they have relevance for more than societal systems. For Marx, the key question is how a system of rank differentiation in which those with power use beliefs and the normative structure to perpetuate permanent inequalities in resource distribution inexorably generates the potential for conflict and change in the system. Marx was able to visualize the genesis of conflict and change with the recognition that those who hold different shares of a system's resources have a conflict of interest: that is, those with resources have an interest in preserving their privilege, while those with fewer resources have an interest in taking them from the privileged. Since power is the most critical resource—because it can be used to secure other resources—the unequal distribution of power will signal the greatest conflict of interests. Marx's ideas can be expressed in the following propositions:

6.   The more unequal is the distribution of scarce resources in a system, the greater will be the conflict of interest between dominant and subordinate segments in that system.

    6a.   The more those with power use this power to consolidate their control over other resources, the more unequal is the distribution of scarce resources in a system.

> 6*b*. The more those with power seek to limit the upward mobility of those in lower ranks, the more unequal is the distribution of scarce resources in a system.

These propositions follow, of course, from Marx's assumption that a conflict of interest is inherent in inequality and that those in advantageous positions will seek to increase their privilege at the expense of those in lower-rank positions. (We might add that these assumptions may be highly questionable, and yet, they are at the core of Marx's theory of social organization and change.)

Marx's next theoretical task is thus quite straightforward: to document the conditions under which awareness of interests causes subordinates to begin questioning the legitimacy of an existing pattern of inequality in resource distribution. These conditions are summarized in the following propositions:

> 7. The more subordinate segments become aware of their true collective interests, the more likely are they to question the legitimacy of the unequal distribution of scarce resources.
>
> > 7*a*. The more social changes wrought by dominant segments disrupt existing relations among subordinates, the more likely are the latter to become aware of their true collective interests.
> >
> > 7*b*. The more practices of dominant segments create alienative dispositions among subordinates, the more likely are the latter to become aware of their true collective interests.
> >
> > 7*c*. The more members of subordinate segments can communicate their grievances to each other, the more likely are they to become aware of their true collective interests.
> >
> > > 7c1. The greater is the spatial concentration of members of subordinate groups, the more likely are they to communicate their grievances.
> > >
> > > 7c2. The more subordinates have access to educational media, the more diverse are the means of their communication and the more likely are they to communicate their grievances.
> >
> > 7*d*. The more subordinate segments can develop unifying systems of beliefs, the more likely are they to become aware of their true collective interests.

7d1. The greater is the capacity to recruit or generate ideological spokespersons, the more likely is ideological unification.

7d2. The less is the ability of dominant groups to regulate the socialization processes and communication networks in a system, the more likely is ideological unification.

Marx's great insight is that the concentration of power results in actions (specified in the elements of principle 7) on the part of those with power that result in subordinates developing awareness of their interests. For as those with power seek to consolidate their position, they often disrupt the routines of subordinates, while creating alienative dispositions. Or, as they seek to organize subordinates so as to increase their productivity (and hence the resources of those with power), they create conditions favoring communication among subordinates and awareness of their common interests. Although Marx visualized these processes as occurring at the societal level, as the bourgeoisie used their power to exploit the proletariat in the interest of greater productivity and profit, his insights are, we feel, applicable to a broader range of social units and to any historical period. What principles 7a, b, c, and d underscore is the inherent tension built into the unequal distribution of resources, especially power, and the tendency of concentrated power to be used in ways that create sources of counterpower.

However in order for these counter sources of power to become effective, an awareness of common interests, Marx felt, must be translated into organization among subordinates. In capitalist systems, Marx saw this process as one in which the proletariat went from a class "of itself" to one organized "for itself." But Marx's insight applies, we would argue, to more than social classes in societal social systems. The process of organization among subordinates who are aware of their interests is both trans-historical and applicable to any social unit revealing inequalities in power. The following proposition specifies some of the conditions that Marx felt to be important in translating an awareness of interests and a questioning of legitimacy into organizational forms designed to pursue conflict:

8. The more subordinate segments of a system are aware of their collective interests, the greater is their questioning of the legitimacy in the distribution of scarce resources, and the more likely are they to organize and initiate overt conflict against dominant segments of a system.

8*a*. The more the deprivations of subordinates move from an absolute to a relative basis, the more likely are they to organize and initiate conflict.

8*b*. The less the ability of dominant groups to make manifest their collective interests, the more likely are subordinate groups to organize and initiate conflict.

8*c*. The greater the ability of subordinate groups to develop a leadership structure, the more likely are they to organize and initiate conflict.

In these propositions, Marx summarized some of the conditions leading to those forms of organization among subordinates that, in turn, will result in overt conflict. The first key question in addressing this issue is why an awareness of conflicting interests and a questioning of legitimacy of the system would lead to organization and the initiation of conflict. Seemingly, awareness would have to be accompanied by intense emotions if people are to run the risks of opposing those holding power. Presumably Marx's proposition on alienation would indicate one source of emotional arousal, because for Marx, alienation goes against human beings' basic needs. Further, ideological spokespersons would, as Marx's own career and works testify, arouse emotions through their prose and polemics. But the key variable in the Marxian scheme is "relative deprivation." The emotions aroused by alienation and ideological spokespersons are necessary but insufficient conditions for taking the risks of organizing and initiating conflict against those with power. Only when these conditions are accompanied by rapidly escalating perceptions of deprivation by subordinates is the level of emotional arousal sufficient to prompt organization and open conflict with superordinates. Such organization, however, is not likely to be successful unless dominant groups fail to organize around their interests and unless leaders among the subordinates can emerge to mobilize and channel aroused emotional energies.

Thus, while Marx assumed that conflict is inevitable, his theory of its origins was elaborate, setting down a series of necessary and sufficient conditions for the occurrence of conflict. It is in these propositions that Marx's great contribution to a theory of conflict resides, for his subsequent propositions appear to be simple translations of his dialectical assumptions into statements of covariance, without the careful documentation of the necessary and sufficient conditions that would cause these conflict processes to occur.

In his next propositions, Marx attempted to account for the degree of violence in the conflict between organized subordinates and superordinates. The key variable here is polarization, a somewhat vague concept denoting the increasing partitioning of a system into two conflicting organizations:

9. The more subordinate segments are unified by a common belief and the more developed their political leadership structure, the more the dominant and subjugated segments of a social system will become polarized.

10. The more polarized the dominant and subjugated, the more violent will be the ensuing conflict.

In contrast to his previous propositions, propositions 9 and 10 do not specify any conditions under which polarization will occur, nor do they indicate when polarized groups will engage in violent conflict. Marx just assumed that such would be the case as the dialectic mechanically unfolds. Presumably, highly organized subordinates in a state of emotional arousal will engage in violent conflict. But as only a cursory review of actual events underscores, such a state often results in just the opposite: less violent conflicts with a considerable degree of negotiation and compromise. This fact points to the Marxian scheme's failure to specify the conditions under which polarization first occurs and then leads to violent conflict. For it is not just coincidental that, at this point in his scheme, Marx's predictions about class revolutions in capitalistic societies begin to go wrong. Thus, the Marxian legacy points rather dramatically to a needed area of theoretical and empirical research: Under what conditions is conflict likely to be violent? And more specifically, under what conditions is conflict involving highly organized and mobilized subordinates likely to be violent and under what conditions are less combative forms of conflict likely to occur?

The final proposition in the Marxian inventory also appears to follow more from a philosophical commitment to the dialectic than carefully reasoned conclusions:

11. The more violent the conflict, the greater will be the structural change of the system and the redistribution of scarce resources.

This proposition reveals Marx's faith in the success of the revolution as well as his assertion that new sets of super-subordinate relations of power would be established by these successful revolutionaries. As such, the proposition is ideology rephrased in the language of theory, especially since no conditional statements are offered on just when violent conflict leads to change and redistribution and just when it does not. Had Marx not assumed conflicts to become polarized and violent, then he would have paid more attention to the degrees of violence and nonviolence in the conflict process, and this in turn, would have alerted him to the variable outcomes of conflict for social systems. In fact, as suggestive as Marx's propositions are, the entire scheme suffers from a failure to specify clearly the interaction among variables. For example, the schema begs questions like: What kinds or types of inequality create what types of conflict of interest? What types of awareness and questioning actually lead to what degrees of overt violence and to what types of ideological unification and political leadership, producing what types of polarization leading to what types of violent conflict causing what types of structural change? It is to answering these questions in Marx's theory that contemporary social theorists have begun to address their efforts.

These considerations lead us to the recognition that Marx's insights, like those of all theorists, into the fundamental properties of social systems are incomplete. However, he clearly saw, more than any scholar of his century, how differentiation, inequality, concentrations of power, organized resistance to power, and conflict are fundamentally related. Propositions 5, 6, 7, and 8 represent important sociological principles and mark Marx's enduring contribution to sociological theory. While Marxist social theorists would not accept as appropriate or legitimate our recasting of Marx's ideas into theoretical principles, this procedure is, at least for non-Marxists, the only way to highlight the strengths and weaknesses of Marx's ideas.

Marx is read today because, like a number of sociology's first theorists, his ideas are considered to capture the essence of certain critical properties in social systems. And although Marx's polemics and political views represent another source of fascination, his purely theoretical contribution to a non-Marxist view of science has often been lost amidst the concern with linking theory and action. And thus, our efforts in this chapter have been devoted to making explicit Marx's purely theoretical ideas and to showing that they are applicable to a wide variety of social systems. For it is our conviction that Marx's theoretical principles are too significant to be buried in political polemics or to be maintained as the exclusive property of Marxist's sociologists. His ideas can serve both Marxist's and non-Marxist's views of science, but in order to serve the latter they have had to be transformed into a series of theoretical principles. And it is these principles that represent Marx's enduring contribution to a non-Marxist view of social science.

PART II

The Maturing Tradition
in Europe

9

MAX WEBER I:
THE INTELLECTUAL
ORIGINS
OF HIS THOUGHT

While Max Weber is generally regarded as one of the great classical theorists, the exact lines of influence of his theoretical contributions are sometimes difficult to ascertain. Part of the reason for this lack of precision is the breadth of Weber's work. Indeed, some have argued that no sociologist before or since has displayed Weber's intellectual range or sophistication. He analyzed the historical significance of the Protestant Reformation, the characteristics of Indian and Chinese social structure and religion, the genesis of modern legal systems, the nature of modern bureaucracies, the types of political domination, the origin of the city in the West, and many other topics. As a result of this breadth of concern with a variety of substantive topics, his influence on the development of modern sociological theory remains unclear. For the scope of Weber's empirical concerns suggests that he was not primarily interested in development of abstract laws of human behavior and organization. Nonetheless, this set of chapters will show that despite his rather limited theoretical goals, Weber's works have contributed enormously to sociological theory.

The origins of Weber's sociology lie in his reaction to intellectual trends in Germany at the turn of the century. This chapter focuses on four of the most important influences on his thought. First, and perhaps most significantly, Weber rejected both Marx and Marxism as too simplistic and inherently nonscientific. Second, Weber rejected as nonproductive the long-standing debate over the nature of the social sciences that dominated late 19th-century German thought. This debate,

193

called the *methodenstreit* (or "methodological controversy"), involved two competing schools of thought whose attitudes toward the practice of social science were quite at odds with one another: the classical or theoretical economists and the historical economists. The third major influence on Weber's thought was Wilhelm Dilthey, who emphasized the importance of understanding the subjective meanings people attach to their behavior. In a somewhat altered form, this idea became one of the cornerstones of Weber's thought. Fourth, Weber took many of the methodological precepts developed by Heinrich Rickert for use in the study of history and altered them in such a way as to facilitate his own brand of sociology. As will be seen in Chapter 10, the result of these four influences was an original form of sociological analysis.

KARL MARX AND MAX WEBER

Despite the fact that Marx is rarely cited in Weber's works, it is clear that he carried on a "silent dialogue" with the dead revolutionary. Hans Gerth and C. Wright Mills, in fact, have carried this idea so far as to argue that Weber's writings should be seen as an effort at "rounding out," or supplementing, Marx's interpretation of the rise and fall of capitalist society.[1] While this point of view ignores the fundamental differences between Marx and Weber, many modern scholars have agreed with Gerth and Mills. Hence, it is worth noting some of the points of similarity between the two men, prior to emphasizing their essential differences.

First, in *The Protestant Ethic and the Spirit of Capitalism*, Weber showed the relationship between the cultural values associated with the Protestant Reformation and the rise of the culture of capitalism in the West, but he explicitly did not deny the importance of the material factors that Marx had previously identified.[2] In fact, apart from the importance of Puritanism, Marx and Weber generally agreed on the structural factors involved in the rise of modern society. Second, both Marx and Weber can be seen as "systems theorists" in the sense that their conceptual schemes represent an attempt at mapping the connections among the situational and environmental contexts in which people act. Third, both scholars recognized the extent to which individuals'

---

[1] Hans Gerth and C. Wright Mills, "Introduction," in *From Max Weber: Essays in Sociology* (New York: Oxford University Press, 1946), pp. 3–76.

[2] Max Weber, *The Protestant Ethic and the Spirit of Capitalism* (New York: Scribner's, 1958).

freedom of action is limited in modern societies, although each did so in a somewhat different way: in Marx's work people are alienated because they do not control the means of production, while in Weber's work individuals often find themselves in an "iron cage" constructed by increasingly omnipresent and powerful bureaucracies. Fourth, despite the constraints just noted, both Marx and Weber observed the importance of human decision-making in shaping history. For Marx, who was always a hopeful utopian and revolutionary, action will usher in a new era of freedom for all people; for Weber, who was less hopeful about the future, individuals have a wider range of choices in modern societies than was possible in the traditional communities of the past. Finally, as will be seen in Chapter 11, there is some complementarity in the theoretical principles that can be extrapolated from Marx's and Weber's work.

Nonetheless, despite these areas of similarity, Weber's work was different than Marx's in origin, purpose, and style. Marx combined revolution and theory in order to explain what he saw as the pattern of history. Weber helped to establish an academically based sociology committed to the objective observation and understanding of historical processes, which he regarded as inherently unpredictable. These differences in orientation cannot be reconciled without obliterating the distinctiveness of each man's work. Hence, rather than "rounding out" Marx, it is clear that Weber had an overriding interest in refuting Marxist thought as it existed at the turn of the 20th century. For example, in the *Protestant Ethic*, Weber went out of his way to note that his findings flatly contradicted those postulated by "historical materialism" and he wondered at the naiveté of those Marxists who espoused such doctrines.[3] More generally, Weber disagreed with Marx and the Marxists (the two are not the same) on three interrelated and fundamental topics: (1) the nature of science, (2) the inevitability of history, and (3) economic determinism.

The Nature of Science

As seen in Chapter 5, Marx combined science and revolution in such a way that theories are verified by action, by what they lead people to do (or not do) based on their material interests. Weber, on the other hand, saw science as the search for truth and argued that knowledge is verified by observation. In making observations, research must be "value free" in the sense that concepts are clearly defined, agreed upon rules

---

[3] Ibid., pp. 55, 75, 90–92, 183, 266, 277.

of evidence are followed, and logical inferences made. For only in this way could there be an objective science of sociology.[4]

While recognizing that Marxists are often motivated by moral outrage at the conditions under which most people are forced to live, Weber asserted that ethical positions are not scientifically demonstrable, no matter how laudable they might be. Further, by combining science and revolution in order to justify their view of the future, Weber asserted that Marxists inevitably confuse "what is" and "what ought to be," with the result that their ethical motives are undermined.[5] Such confusion should be eliminated as much as possible, Weber insisted, by making social science value free through an exclusive emphasis on "what is." Nonetheless, Weber recognized that social scientists' values inevitably intrude into social inquiry, since they influence the topics that are considered important for research. But this fact, Weber argued, does not preclude the possibility that the process of research can and should be value free. Thus, while Weber believed that science cannot tell people how to live or how to organize themselves, it can provide them with the sort of information necessary to make such decisions. On this basis, Weber sought to understand the origin and characteristics of modern societies by developing a set of concepts that could be used in understanding social action.

The Inevitability of History

Marx posited the existence of historical laws of development, with the result that he saw feudalism as leading inevitably to capitalism and the latter leading inexorably to a more humane communist society. Against this position, Weber argued that there are no laws of historical development and that capitalism arose in the West as a result of a series of historical accidents.

As will be shown in Chapters 10 and 11, Weber's sociology is oriented to understanding how modern Western societies could have arisen when and where they did. Essentially he argued that a number of historical processes occurred together which resulted in the rise of modern capitalism in the West. Among these processes were the following: industrialization, the rise of a free labor force, the development of logical accounting

---

[4] Max Weber, "Science as a Vocation," in Gerth and Mills, eds., *From Max Weber*, pp. 129–58.

[5] Guenther Roth, "[Weber's] Historical Relationship to Marxism," in Reinhard Bendix and Guenther Roth, eds., *Scholarship and Partisanship: Essays on Max Weber* (Berkeley: University of California Press, 1971), pp. 227–52.

methods, the rise of free markets, the development of modern forms of law, the increasing use of paper instruments of ownership (such as stock certificates), and the rise of what Weber called the "spirit of capitalism.[6] As will be seen, he believed the last factor to be the most significant. Further, Weber argued that none of these phenomena could have been predicted in advance; rather, they were all dependent on chance. Thus from his point of view, societies are always perpetually balanced between the opposing forces of determinism and chance. For the course of history is often altered by unforeseen political struggles, wars, ecological calamities, or the charisma of single individuals.

Economic Determinism

By the beginning of the 20th century, many Marxists were arguing that certain economic arrangements, especially the private ownership of the means of production, inevitably caused specific political forms as well as other social structures to develop. While this crude form of economic determinism distorts Marx's analysis and eliminates its subtlety, it had the advantage of allowing for quick and easy (not to mention nasty) assessments of modern capitalist societies. Weber attempted to refute this rather congealed form of Marx's analysis in two somewhat different ways. First, in the *Protestant Ethic* he showed the importance of religious ideas in shaping the behavior of the Puritans and, by extrapolation, all Western people. Second, in *Economy and Society*, he showed the extent to which systems of domination are maintained because they are viewed as legitimate by citizens—a commitment that generally overwhelms the socioeconomic divisions that always exist.[7] In Weber's words, "it is one of the delusions rooted in the modern overestimation of the 'economic factor' . . . to believe that national solidarity cannot survive the tensions of antagonistic economic interests, or even to assume that political solidarity is *merely* a reflection of the economic substructure."[8]

THE *METHODENSTREIT* AND MAX WEBER

The methodological controversy that dominated German academic life in the latter half of the 19th century can only be understood in

---

[6] Max Weber, *General Economic History* (New York: Collier Books, 1961), pp. 207–76.

[7] Max Weber, *Economy and Society* (New York: Bedminster Press, 1968).

[8] Max Weber, quoted in Roth, "[Weber's] Historical Relationship to Marxism," p. 234 (emphasis in original).

light of two interrelated factors. First, in Germany there tended to be a rather rigid division between the natural sciences and the cultural disciplines such that only natural phenomena—such as those studied in physics, chemistry, biology, and the like—were seen as amenable to theoretical (that is, scientific) analysis. Based on the philosophy of Immanuel Kant (and Hegel, but to a much lesser extent), it was believed that the social and cultural realms, the world of the "spirit," could not be analyzed in scientific terms. Hence, studies of natural and social phenomena developed in much different directions in Germany.[9]

Second, since the early work of Adam Smith and David Ricardo, non-Marxist economic theory became stagnant, with the result that economists had great difficulty in trying to explain the workings of actual industrial economies as they existed in the 19th century. Now, there were two main ways of dealing with the problem. One way was to develop better theory, while another was to eschew science altogether and to concentrate on depicting the historical development of particular economic systems. The members of the "historical school" of economics chose the latter course, a position that fitted comfortably with the dominant German intellectual tradition. Nonetheless, there remained a number of scholars (although they were a very small minority in German academic circles) who chose to develop non-Marxist economic theory. For the most part, these "theoretical economists" were non-Germans who came from a positivistic background roughly similar to Durkheim's.

The major figures in the German historical school were individuals who are generally not remembered today, largely because their writings have not proven to be of enduring significance. Wilhelm Roscher, Bruno Hildebrand, and Karl Knies, all of whom were contemporaries of Marx, are generally credited with founding the movement during the middle portion of the 19th century. Later, such men as Lujo Brentano and Gustav Schmoller added to and modified this perspective. While there were inevitably some differences in the way each of these scholars approached the study of economics and, by extrapolation, social science in general, they shared a number of basic criticisms of theoretical economics as well as a relatively common methodological approach to their subject matter.

On the other side of the conflict were the members of the theoretical school, many of whom remain well-known figures in the history of economic thought, largely because their writings furthered the development

---

[9] See Talcott Parsons, *The Structure of Social Action* (Glencoe, Ill.: Free Press, 1948), pp. 473–86.

of the discipline as a science. Among these scholars are Leon Walras, W. S. Jevons, Eugen Böhm-Bawark, and Karl Menger. However, Menger is by far the most important because he discovered the theory of marginal utility, an idea that went a long way toward solving the theoretical dilemmas that had plagued economics throughout the latter half of the 19th century. Since the *methodenstreit* is primarily remembered in terms of the acrimonious and often vicious debate between Menger and Schmoller that occurred during the 1870s, we shall refer to them as the representative of each school of thought.

Methodological Issues Dividing Historical and Theoretical Economics

There were four very fundamental issues over which the historical school and the theoretical school disagreed, all of them stemming from the divergence between economic theory and economic reality noted previously.[10] The first involved the importance of deduction versus induction. Schmoller and the historical economists charged that the theoreticians' use of deductive methods was faulty, chiefly because their theories could not explain reality. Hence as an alternative, the historical economists emphasized the importance of observing and describing people's concrete patterns of action (often down to the smallest details), and they spent many years compiling such data. Unlike some of the other historians, for whom description quickly became an end in itself, Schmoller asserted that the long-run result of this descriptive work would be the discovery of economic laws through the use of inductive methods. He believed that the resulting propositions would better describe reality because they would take the complexity of people's actual behavior into account. Alternatively, Menger and the theoretical economists charged (correctly, as it turned out) that the historians were so immersed in data that no laws would ever result. Further, Menger said that the more realistic response to the inadequacies of economic theory is to develop better theories, which was precisely what he and others were doing at that time.

The second issue dividing the two schools had to do with the universality versus relativity of findings. Schmoller and the historical economists

---

[10] The following paragraphs have benefitted from Thomas Burger, *Max Weber's Theory of Concept Formation: History, Laws, and Ideal Types* (Durham, N.C.: Duke University Press, 1976), pp. 140–50; Joseph Schumpeter, *Economic Doctrine and Method* (New York: Oxford University Press, 1954), pp. 152–201; and Charles Gide and Charles Rist, *A History of Economic Doctrine* (Boston: D. C. Heath, 1948), pp. 383–409.

asserted that the theoreticians' emphasis on the universal applicability of economic laws was absurd. Rather, from the historians' point of view, their empirical research had shown that economic development occurs in evolutionary stages that are unique to each society, which implies that it is possible to understand a society's present stage of economic advancement only by ascertaining previous stages. Menger and the theoreticians responded by observing that theory, whether in the social sciences or the natural sciences, is oriented toward that which is common rather than that which is unique. Hence, economic theories can (at least in principle) explain certain aspects of human behavior that are common to all societies but, admittedly, not every element of social action can be explained theoretically. On this basis, Menger argued that there is a place for both theory and history in economics and the other social sciences.

The third issue of debate in the *methodenstreit* had to do with the degree of rationality versus nonrationality in human behavior. Schmoller and the historical economists believed that the theoretical economists' view of economic man as rational and motivated only by narrow self-interest was unrealistic. They went on to assert that there is a unity to all of social life in the sense that people act out of a multiplicity of motives which are not always rational. Thus, in order to obtain a comprehensive view of social reality, historical research often went far beyond the narrow confines of economic action, dealing with the interrelationships among economic, political, legal, religious, and other social phenomena. While there is a sense in which Schmoller was right here, Menger simply replied that economic theory deals with only one side of human behavior (that is, people's attempts at material need satisfaction) and the other social sciences must focus on other aspects of social action. Over the long run, Menger believed, the result would be a comprehensive understanding of human behavior.

Finally, the fourth issue separating the two schools had to do with economics as an ethical discipline versus economics as a science. Schmoller and other member of the historical school unquestionably saw economics as an ethical discipline that could help solve many of the problems facing German society, with the result that their scholarly writings often had an avowedly political intent. This attitude was partly a consequence of the long-standing German division between the natural sciences and the cultural disciplines, and partly a consequence of the fact that Schmoller and many of the others held important university and governmental positions. In opposition, Menger charged that Schmoller's political value judgments were hopelessly confused with his scholarly analyses, to the detriment of both. In science, Menger said, the two must be kept separate.

Weber's Response to the Methodenstreit

In economics, the *methodenstreit* eventually dissipated, although more by the force of theoretical developments than the rhetoric of the participants. However, on several occasions Weber appears to have used the arguments raised in the controversy as a baseline from which to develop his own methodological orientation.[11]

In regard to the first issue, the importance of inductive versus deductive methods, Weber tried to bridge the gap between the two schools so as to create a historically based social science. With the historical economists, Weber argued that if the social sciences imitated the natural sciences by seeking to discover general laws of social behavior, then not very much useful knowledge would be produced. His reasoning was that any social science oriented toward the development of timelessly valid laws would, of necessity, emphasize those patterns of action that are common from one society to another, with the result that idiographic events would inevitably be omitted from consideration. Yet it is often the case that unique phenomena, such as the Protestant Reformation, are the most significant factors influencing the development of a culture. Hence, a science seeking to understand the structure of social action in any society must necessarily focus on precisely those factors that are not amenable to lawlike formulations. Put differently, Weber argued that the social sciences had to make use of historical materials. Nonetheless, with the theoretical economists Weber asserted that the development of abstract concepts was absolutely necessary in order to guide empirical research. As will be seen in the next chapter, Weber's goal was an objective (that is, scientific) comprehension of modern Western society, and for that reason he needed to develop a set of clear and precise concepts, which he called ideal types, that could be used in understanding historical processes.

Weber's response to the second issue dividing the two schools follows from the first: that is, a historically based social science cannot be univer-

---

[11] For Weber's views on Menger and the theoretical economists, see his " 'Objectivity' in Social Science and Social Policy," in *The Methodology of the Social Sciences* (Glencoe, Ill.: Free Press, 1949), and "Marginal Utility Theory and the So-Called Fundamental Law of Psychophysics," *Social Science Quarterly* 56 (June 1975). For Weber's views on the historical economists, see his *Roscher and Knies: The Logical Problems of Historical Economics* (New York: Free Press, 1975).

sally applicable; rather, findings are always relative to a particular culture and society. One implication of this point of view is that while Weber tried to understand the origins of modern Western society, his findings may not have any relevance for the process of modernization in the Third World today, because those societies are operating in a rather different historical context. However, it should be emphasized here that Weber strongly disagreed with the historical economists' evolutionary interpretations. Rather, he believed that economic development does not occur in evolutionary stages, since unpredictable events, such as wars, ecological changes, charismatic leaders, and myriads of other phenomena, alter the course of history.

The third issue in the *methodenstreit* was to become essential to Weber's sociology, for the protagonists inadvertently identified one of the fundamental characteristics of modern Western society: the tension between rational and nonrational action. Thus, Menger's argument that rational economic behavior needs to be conceptually distinguished from other modes of action seemed reasonable to Weber because he had observed that action in the marketplace is characterized by an emphasis on logic and knowledge which is often absent in other arenas. Yet at the same time, Schmoller's emphasis on the unity of social life and people's multiplicity of motives, some of which are based on values other than logic, also seemed reasonable. Hence, Weber tried to conceptually summarize the "types of social action" so as to systematically distinguish modern Western societies from the traditional ones that had preceded them and to show the wider range of behavioral choices which are available to occidental people.[12]

Weber's reaction to the fourth issue in the methodological controversy was similar to his response to Marx and the Marxists; that is, Weber asserted that Menger was absolutely correct: the social sciences must be value free. While Schmoller and the other historical economists were generally political liberals with whom Weber was in sympathy, he believed there can be no scientific justification for any ethical or political point of view. However, Weber argued that objective scientific analyses can provide people with the knowledge necessary to make intelligent ethical decisions based on their values.

WILHELM DILTHEY AND MAX WEBER

The origin of Weber's response to the *methodenstreit* can be found in the works of Wilhelm Dilthey and Heinrich Rickert. Essentially,

---

[12] Weber, *Economy and Society*, pp. 24–26.

Weber built his sociology with the methodological tools they provided, although he went beyond each of them in a number of fundamental ways. Neither Rickert nor Dilthey is very well known in the English-speaking world, primarily because the problems they addressed are peculiar to the German intellectual scene during the late 19th century. Given the traditional idealist separation of the worlds of nature and human activity, the establishment of the social sciences *as sciences* was an extremely vexing problem.

Dilthey's Methodology of the Social Sciences

Essentially, Dilthey argued that while both the sphere of human behavior and the sphere of nature can be studied scientifically, it must be recognized that the subject matter of each and the kind of knowledge that each produces are different. He then went on to explore some of the implications of this argument.[13]

The logic of Dilthey's analysis can be seen in three steps. First, and most obviously, the two sciences have different subject matters. The natural sciences are oriented toward the explanation of physical or natural events, while the social sciences are oriented toward the explanation of human action. Second, and as a result of the first, researchers in each field obtain quite different forms of knowledge. In the natural sciences, knowledge is external in the sense that physical phenomena are affected by one another in ways that can be seen and explained in terms of timelessly valid laws. In the social sciences, however, knowledge is of necessity internal in the sense that each person has an "inner nature" that must be comprehended in some way in order to explain events. Third, as a result, researchers in the two spheres must have altogether different orientations to their subject matter. In the natural sciences, it is enough to observe events and relationships. For example, an object falling through space can be explained in terms of the force of gravity, and this explanation is true regardless of the cultural background of different researchers who may concern themselves with this topic. In the social sciences, however, scholars must go beyond mere observation and seek some sort of intuitive understanding *(verstehen)* of each person's inner nature in order to adequately explain events and

---

[13] While most of Dilthey's works remain untranslated, see his *Meaning and History: W. Dilthey's Thoughts on History and Society* (London: Allen & Unwin, 1961). See also, H. A. Hodges, *Wilhelm Dilthey: An Introduction* (London: Trubner, 1944); and H. Stuart Hughes, *Consciousness and Society: The Reorientation of German Social Thought, 1890–1930* (New York: Vintage, 1958), pp. 183–200. Our sketch of Dilthey's thought is adapted from Hughes's discussion.

relationships. Further, the explanations offered may well vary depending on the cultural background of the different researchers.

For Dilthey, then, the means by which observers obtain an understanding of each person's inner nature is the key to the scientific knowledge of human action. In this light he tried to classify the various fields devoted to the study of social behavior in terms of their typical mode of analysis. The first type of analysis consists of descriptions of reality, of events that have occurred, and this is the field of history. Unlike Rickert, Dilthey does not appear to have been very concerned with whether historical descriptions are accurate or objective. The second way of discussing human action consists of value judgments made in light of historical events, and this is the field of ethics or politics. The third way of dealing with social behavior consists of formulating abstractions from history, and this is the field of the social sciences. This last mode of analysis is the most important for understanding action, Dilthey asserted, because abstractions provide the conceptual tools without which it would be impossible to comprehend behavior. However, he was unable to face the implications of this insight, for Dilthey went on to argue that the systematic development of abstract concepts would not be of much long-term use in understanding people's inner states and he opted instead for the necessity of relying on intuition (what he called the "fantasy of the artist") in comprehending social action. Such intuitive understanding occurs when, in some unexplainable and imperfect way, observers reexperience in their own consciousness the experiences of others. The result of this emphasis on the manner in which one mind becomes aware of another was that Dilthey's point of view led ultimately to a dead end. In the long run, as Weber realized, an excessive reliance on the researcher's subjective impressions cannot lead to an objective social science.

Weber's Response to Dilthey's Work

From Weber's point of view, Dilthey's methodological orientation was useful in three ways.[14] First, Dilthey was correct in noting that the social sciences can obtain a quite different form of knowledge than the natural sciences. Second, social scientific statements are different from and, Weber added, must be kept separate from value judgments

---

[14] While Weber never wrote a formal commentary on Dilthey's work, his writings suggest an easy familiarity with Dilthey's teachings, see Hughes, *Consciousness and Society*, p. 309. For Weber's analysis of *verstehen* and its relationship to ideal types, see *Economy and Society*, pp. 8–20.

of any sort. And third, the key to social scientific knowledge is understanding *(verstehen)* the subjective meanings people attach to their actions.

However, Weber believed that the major problem in Dilthey's work lies in his emphasis on understanding each person's inner nature, as if an objective social science could be founded on some sort of mystical and intuitive reexperiencing of others' desires and thoughts. Hence, Weber developed a rather different way of emphasizing the importance of *verstehen*, one that proved to be a great deal more successful than Dilthey's. Essentially, Weber argued, while social action can only be understood when "it is placed in an intelligible and more inclusive context of meaning," the key to such understanding resides in the development of a set of abstract concepts (ideal types) which classify the dimensions of social action and reflect the norms that are appropriate in different spheres. By focusing his work in this way, Weber emphasized the importance of understanding individual behavior while, at the same time, he was able to assess the significance of historical events (such as the Reformation) in an objective and scientific manner.

HEINRICH RICKERT AND MAX WEBER

Like Dilthey, Rickert was concerned with the problems created by the disjunction between the world of nature and the world of human activity that had been created by idealist philosophy. However, the two men had somewhat different solutions in mind. As seen above, Dilthey's work addressed the problem of the dissimilar subject matter characterizing the natural and social sciences, emphasizing that the different forms of knowledge in each sphere require distinct methodological orientations on the part of researchers. Rickert, however, had a more narrow interest; he tried to show that history could be an objective scientific discipline because the knowledge it produced was based on a valid principle of concept selection. Like Dilthey, Rickert was not entirely successful in his task, largely because he misperceived the nature of science and drifted into metaphysical speculation.[15] Nonetheless, Rickert's writings constituted an important influence on Max Weber's work, for Weber, who was much more practical than Rickert, adapted some of Rickert's methodological principles for his own more general purposes.

---

[15] Heinrich Rickert's works remain untranslated. This account draws on H. H. Bruun, *Science, Values, and Politics in Max Weber's Methodology* (Copenhagen: Muunksgaard, 1972), pp. 84–99; Burger, *Weber's Theory of Concept Formation*, pp. 3–56; and Hughes, *Consciousness and Society*, pp. 190–91.

Rickert on the Objectivity of History

Rickert began his attempt at demonstrating that history can be an objective science by dealing with a number of relatively noncontroversial epistemological issues. He argued that empirical reality is infinite in space and time which, for him, meant that reality can, in principle, be divided into an infinite number of objects for study and these objects can, in turn, be dissected into an unlimited number of parts. An important implication of this fact is that reality can never be completely known because there will always be some other way of looking at it. The practical problem, then, becomes how people can know anything at all about the world around them, and Rickert's answer was that by formulating concepts human beings select out those aspects of reality that are important to them. Thus, concepts are the means by which we know the world, for without them people could not distinguish among its significant parts. In light of this necessity, Rickert came to the peculiar conclusion that the essence of science centered around the problem of concept formation. From this point of view, a discipline can be regarded as a science if it uses a principle of concept selection that everyone agrees produces objective knowledge. Not surprisingly, Rickert said there are two valid principles of concept selection—those used in the natural sciences and history—and, in this way he tried to show that history is a scientific discipline.

In the natural sciences, Rickert noted, concepts are designed to identify the common traits of the empirical objects to which they refer. This tactic allows concepts to become more and more abstract and, hence, to be fitted into a theory that summarizes empirical regularities (for example, the movements of the planets and their effects on one another through the force of gravity). The result is a set of general concepts that can, at least in principle, be used in a single all-embracing law of nature. On this basis, Rickert concluded that the principle of concept selection used in the natural sciences is valid because it succeeds in identifying regular and recurrent features of the physical environment.

In history, however, Rickert argued that scholars' interests are altogether different, which means the principle of concept selection must be different as well. In order to chronicle the events of the past and their significance for the present, historians must focus on their uniqueness. With this purpose in mind, historical concepts are formulated so as to identify those aspects of the past that make them distinctive and different from one another (for example, traditional society or the spirit of capitalism). Thus, historians produce concepts, which Rickert called "historical individuals," that summarize a complex set of events in terms of their historical significance (that is, their uniqueness). On this basis, Rickert concluded that the principle of concept selection used in history is valid because it allows observers to understand how particular societies developed their specific characteristics. This result would be impossible if the historians imitated the natural sciences and conceptualized only those aspects of the past that were common to all societies. Hence despite these differences in concept formation, according to Rickert, history is a science.

Rickert next confronted the problem of how scholars select topics for study, and it is at this point that his emphasis on concept formation as the essence of science trapped him in a nonproductive philosophical argument. Essentially, Rickert asserted, the researchers' choice of topics is made in terms of "value-relevance." That is, some events are seen as worth conceptualizing based on the scientists' interpretation of what the members of a society value. However, this emphasis on value-relevance implies a subjective rather than an objective conception of knowledge, since scientists are inevitably forced to rely on their own values in determining what topics are worth knowing about, or conceptualizing. Now Rickert tried to avoid this implication by postulating that a kind of "normal consciousness" characterizes all human beings. On this basis, he argued, there are areas of concern shared by all members of every society, for example, religion, law, the state, customs, the physical world, language, literature, art, and the economy. But this postulate is inherently metaphysical (and typically idealist), since it assumes that values have an existence independently of human beings.

Ultimately, as with Dilthey, Rickert's analysis led to a dead end, for he failed to recognize that concept formation is only one essential aspect of science and, partly as a result, found himself entangled in idealism. Nonetheless, Rickert's work provided a fundamental baseline from which Weber could establish sociology as a science.

Weber's Response to Rickert

Weber was intimately familiar with Rickert's writings, as is indicated by acknowledgments of Rickert in his early methodological essays.[16] However, these citations do not indicate the extent to which Weber adapted some of Rickert's ideas for his own rather different purposes. While it cannot be known for sure, it is probable that Weber's preoccupation with refuting Marxism and solving the dilemma created by the *methodenstreit* allowed him to recognize what Rickert had failed to see:

---

[16] See Weber, "Objectivity," p. 50; and *Roscher and Knies*, pp. 211–18.

the essence of science involves not only a coherent conceptual scheme but also, and just as importantly, the use of logical and systematic procedures in the interpretation of observations. Hence, even though the social sciences have different goals because they must deal with quite different data than the natural sciences (Dilthey's "inner nature" of human beings), what unites the two as sciences is their procedural similarity. It is this insight that pervades all of Weber's writings and constitutes the basis for his response to Rickert. The manner in which Weber adapted portions of Rickert's work can be sketched in the following way.

First, there is little doubt that Weber simply accepted Rickert's argument that reality is infinite and human beings can have knowledge only in terms of the concepts used to select out significant aspects of the world for examination.[17] Second, unlike Rickert, Weber recognized that it did not matter why a scholar chooses one topic over another for study, since the only practical basis for such a choice can be one's ultimate values. What matters, Weber argued, is that the research process is objective, and this goal is achieved only when the data are clearly conceptualized and systematically analyzed.[18] Third, Weber adapted Rickert's notion of "historical individuals" for his more general purposes, that is, Weber sought to understand the origin of modern Western society, and in order to do this he needed to develop a set of concepts that captured the distinctiveness of historical processes. However, rather than historical individuals, Weber called his concepts "ideal types," a phrase that seemed to convey more clearly what he meant: concepts that are logically perfect in the sense that they summarize a "conceptually pure type of rational action."[19] With these and other methodological tools, Weber was able to study modern societies in what he felt was an objective and scientific manner.

MAX WEBER'S THEORETICAL SYNTHESIS

In adapting some of the conceptual tools provided by Dilthey and Rickert, Weber was able to forge a response to Marx and the

---

[17] See Weber, "Objectivity," pp. 78–79.

[18] See Weber, "Science as a Vocation;" and Weber, "Critical Studies in the Logic of the Cultural Sciences," in his *Methodology of the Social Sciences*, pp. 113–88.

[19] See Weber, *Economy and Society*, pp. 18–20, and "Objectivity," pp. 87–112. Rickert's term *historical individuals* appears in Weber's essays in *Roscher and Knies* and (once) in the *Protestant Ethic*, p. 47. However, Weber appears to have adopted the term *ideal type* from George Jellinek; see Bendix and Roth, *Scholarship and Partisanship*, pp. 160–64.

methodenstreit that constitutes a continuing legacy to sociology. As we shall see in the next chapter, Weber's methodology of the social sciences began with a consideration of the problem of objectivity in the social sciences, which he resolved by emphasizing the overriding importance of value-free sociology. No scientific analysis can include ethical values within it and be regarded as objective. The second methodological problem Weber confronted was that of how to treat social and historical data, which he resolved by emphasizing the importance of understanding social action in terms of ideal types. Because these concepts are formulated as rational models, they allow actual historical processes to be dealt with in an objective manner. The way in which Weber went about this task can be seen in his substantive works. Since he did not have modern means of gathering or analyzing data available to him, Weber was forced to construct "logical experiments" designed to show that sociological analyses could be done using scientific procedures. Thus, the next chapter depicts how Weber demonstrated the manner in which cultural values circumscribe and direct social action in the *Protestant Ethic*. Similarly, in *Economy and Society*, Weber provided subsequent researchers with a system of concepts that has proven to be of enormous use in understanding the nature of modern societies. Chapter 10 illustrates the way Weber did this by focusing on his analysis of stratification and domination in Western societies.

10

MAX WEBER II:
THE BASIC WORKS

In one of his last writings, Max Weber defined the fledgling discipline of sociology in the following way.

> Sociology . . . is a science concerning itself with the interpretive understanding of social action and thereby with a causal explanation of its course and consequences. We shall speak of "action" insofar as the acting individual attaches a subjective meaning to his behavior—be it overt or covert, omission or acquiescence. Action is "social" insofar as its subjective meaning takes account of the behavior of others and is thereby oriented in its course.[1]

Weber believed that this definition would allow him to achieve two interrelated goals that, taken together, signify an altogether original approach to the study of social organization. First, he wanted to obtain a social scientific understanding of the origin and unique characteristics of modern Western civilization. Second, Weber wanted to construct a system of abstract concepts that would be useful in describing and, hence, understanding, modern societies. Without a set of clear and precise concepts, Weber argued, systematic social scientific research would be impossible. The result was an "analytical ordering of reality," or a series of conceptual models of the modern world.

Weber's work can be divided into two periods. In the ten years prior to 1898, his writings were primarily historical in nature, dealing with such topics as the history of trading companies in the Middle Ages,

---

[1] Max Weber, *Economy and Society*, trans. and ed. Guenther Roth and Claus Wittich (New York: Bedminster Press, 1968), p. 4.

the relationship between Roman agrarian history and the development of law, and the characteristics of rural peasants in eastern Germany. While the works of this first period reveal traces of Weber's mature thought, they are less interesting sociologically and, hence, have not been translated.[2]

Between the years 1898 and 1902, Weber suffered a complete mental breakdown and did not write.[3] But in the years following his recovery (1903–1920), Weber produced a massive volume of work that constitutes a decisive turning point in the development of sociological thought. His writings during this period can be divided into three areas, which correspond to the three divisions in this chapter. The first section of the chapter explains Weber's methodological point of view, for it is impossible to appreciate fully his substantive writings without an understanding of his overall theoretical strategy. The second section of the chapter explicates Weber's work on religion. And the third section of the chapter describes Weber's analysis of social stratification in modern societies in the context of his more general political sociology.

WEBER'S METHODOLOGY OF THE SOCIAL SCIENCES

In 1904, Weber opened one of his first and most important essays on methodological issues in the social sciences by posing a fundamental question: "In what sense are there 'objectively valid truths' in those disciplines concerned with social and cultural phenomena?"[4] All of his subsequent writings can be seen as an application of his answer to this simple question. Indeed, Weber's goal was to show how objective research is logically possible in academic disciplines that deal with subjectively meaningful phenomena. His ingenious solution is presented here in two parts. First, Weber's presentation of the problem of values in sociological analysis is shown, and second, his solution to this problem is described.

---

[2] For information on these early studies, see Roth's "Introduction," in Weber, *Economy and Society;* or Reinhard Bendix, *Max Weber: An Intellectual Portrait* (Garden City, N.Y.: Doubleday, 1962).

[3] The best biography of Max Weber is that by his wife; see Marianne Weber, *Max Weber: A Biography,* trans. Harry Zohn (New York: John Wiley, 1975). For a psychoanalytic interpretation of Weber's life and work, see Arthur Mitzman, *The Iron Cage: An Historical Interpretation of Max Weber* (New York: Alfred A. Knopf, 1970).

[4] Max Weber, " 'Objectivity' in Social Science and Social Policy," in Weber, *The Methodology of the Social Sciences,* trans. Edward A. Shils and Henry A. Finch (Glencoe, Ill.: Free Press, 1949), p. 51.

The Problem of Values

During Weber's time, the problem of values in social scientific research was important because many observers did not believe that an objective social science was possible and opted, instead, for a kind of moral philosophy in which political, religious, and other sorts of beliefs are infused into analyses of social organization. The problem of values remains a serious one even today, for the way in which this dilemma is solved still fundamentally determines whether the social sciences can discover "objectively valid truths." Weber confronted the problem of values in two ways. First, he asserted that sociological inquiry must be "value free" in the sense that researchers' values or material interests should not affect the process of scientific analysis. Second, he argued that researchers' values inevitably serve as the underlying basis for sociological inquiry because they direct attention to certain problems and theoretical strategies rather than others.

Value-Free Sociology. According to Weber, sociology must be value free because there is no other way of producing scientific understanding of social processes. It is this fundamental concern with attaining objective and verifiable knowledge that links all the sciences, natural and social. Value-free analyses are only possible, Weber argued, if sociologists use a "rational method" in which the research process is systematic; that is, the research process must assure that *(a)* empirical data are categorized in terms of clearly formulated concepts, *(b)* proper rules of evidence are employed, and *(c)* only logical inferences are made. In his words, "all scientific work presupposes that the rules of logic and method are valid."[5]

This simple argument has a number of implications that need to be mentioned. In Weber's view, sociology cannot be a moral science; that is, it cannot identify scientifically "proper" norms, values, or modes of action.[6] A value-free sociology is thus not compatible with a moral or political position because the research process must be logical (or rational) rather than evaluative. According to Weber, people can only decide what they ought to do and how they ought to live in terms of their basic values, and such beliefs always exist independently of scientific findings. Unlike many of his predecessors, then, Weber explicitly distinguished between "what ought to be" and "what is."

---

[5] Max Weber, "Science as a Vocation," in *From Max Weber; Essays in Sociology,* trans. Hans Gerth and C. Wright Mills (New York: Oxford University Press, 1946), p. 143.

[6] Weber, "Objectivity," p. 57.

Another implication of Weber's argument for a value-free sociology is that, as a science of society, the new discipline helps to contribute to an ongoing historical process in which magic and other irrational beliefs that are used to explain events in traditional societies become less and less acceptable to people. Weber referred to this development as the process of "rationalization," and it is a dominant theme in all his work. He believed that social life is becoming increasingly "rationalized" in the sense that people tend to lead relatively methodical lives. Sociology participates in the process of rationalization to the extent that it produces objective knowledge about social and historical phenomena, with the result that sociology can help people make decisions by providing them with accurate information.

A final underlying element in Weber's argument for a value-free sociology asserts that objective knowledge of social processes is useful and worthwhile. For Weber, "what is yielded by scientific work is important in the sense that it is 'worth being known.' "[7] But, once again, he emphasized that people can only make a determination of "worthiness" in light of their ultimate values. For example, in the industrialized West, people have come to value mastery over the environment. Partly as a result, they also have come to value scientific knowledge, for its application leads to increasing control over the environment. But since a desire to master the environment is not a cultural universal, the belief that scientific knowledge is worth knowing also varies from one culture to another. Inevitably, then, evaluative elements are intrinsic to the research process even in a value-free science, and the way in which Weber integrated values into scientific research is the topic to which we now turn.

Values as Guides for Research. After proposing that the research process should be value free, Weber faced the practical problems of (1) how to select a topic for social scientific research and (2) how to determine the goals of social scientific research. His solution to the first problem is very explicit and has come to be recognized as characteristic of all sociological inquiry. There can be no scientific justification for considering one problem rather than another. Instead, it is always the case that scientists' religious values, material interests, or other biases lead them to specific areas of research.

Weber's solution to the second problem has proven to be very controversial for (as will be seen in the next chapter) it constitutes one of the most fundamental divisions in the practice of sociological research today. Unlike nearly all the other classical sociologists (except Marx,

---

[7] Weber, "Science as a Vocation," p. 143.

whose orientation is altogether different), Weber rejected the search for general laws in favor of historical theories that provide an "interpretive understanding of social action and . . . a causal explanation of its course and consequences." Weber took this position not for scientific reasons but for evaluative ones. He perceived that any system of abstract and timeless laws must focus on events that are typical and recurrent, as in the natural sciences. A search for universal laws necessarily excludes from consideration important and unique historical events. Weber summarized his position in the following way:

> For the knowledge of historical phenomena in their concreteness, the most general laws, because they are most devoid of content are also the least valuable. The more comprehensive the validity,—or scope—of a term, the more it leads us away from the richness of reality since in order to include the common elements of the largest possible number of phenomena, it must necessarily be as abstract as possible and hence devoid of content. In the [social] sciences, the knowledge of the universal or general is never valuable in itself.[8]

In effect, then, Weber was most interested in focusing on the "big empirical questions," such as why capitalism originated in the West rather than somewhere else, and he knew that an emphasis on the development of general theories would not allow for a direct examination of such issues.

Weber's Solution to the Problem of Values: The Construction of Ideal Types

Weber argued that sociology is inherently different from the natural sciences because its essential task is "the interpretive understanding of social action and thereby . . . a causal explanation of its course and consequences." "Understanding" is the usual translation of the German word *verstehen*, and there has been considerable controversy as to the theoretical and methodological implications of this term.[9] However, Weber's argument can be presented in a reasonably straightforward manner, for he believed that only the use of ideal types could lead to an "interpre-

---

[8] Weber, "Objectivity," p. 80.

[9] See Theodore Abel, "The Operation Called *Verstehen*," *American Journal of Sociology* 54 (November 1948):211–18; Peter A. Munch, "Empirical Science and Max Weber's *Verstehende Soziologie*," *American Sociological Review* 22 (February 1957):26–32; Murray L. Wax, "On Misunderstanding *Verstehen*: A Reply to Abel," *Sociology and Social Research* 51 (April 1967):322–33; and Theodore Abel, "A Reply to Professor Wax," *Sociology and Social Research* 51 (April 1967):334–36.

tive understanding of social action," and hence, to a "causal explanation" of historical events.

Weber argued that social action exists only "insofar as the acting individual attaches a subjective meaning to his behavior." Sociological analysis, therefore, must ultimately refer to individual action rather than to collective social phenomena because such entities as a "state" do not think or act; only people act. Yet, as he emphasized, it is generally the case that concepts referring to structural or collective phenomena are necessary in order to understand individual social action. However, such concepts "must be treated as *solely* the resultants and modes of organization of the particular acts of individual persons, since these alone can be treated as agents in a course of subjectively understandable action."[10] Weber's emphasis on the need for conceptualizing individual action led him to reject functional analysis, as epitomized in his time by "the method of the so-called 'organic' school of sociology." He argued that in functional analysis concepts tend to be reified such that the "needs" of the social system become the focus of attention rather than individual action. Moreover, Weber felt that functional analysis is inevitably oriented toward the development of general theories similar to those in the natural sciences, an emphasis that can never result in an understanding of the subjective meaning individuals attach to behavior. It is this concern with subjective meaning, or *verstehen*, that forced Weber to rely on ideal types as a mode of sociological analysis.

As shown in Chapter 9, Wilhelm Dilthey first proposed the concept of *verstehen* as central to the social scientific task. However, in Weber's hands the concept became considerably less mystical and intuitive, and more oriented to the necessity of systematic sociological research. Weber's comments on the importance of *verstehen* in sociology are quite brief, focusing on two kinds of understanding. First, there is "direct observational understanding of the subjective meaning of a given act."[11] Such observational understanding implies that extensive knowledge of the broader social context within which an individual's action takes place is not necessary. For example, Weber noted that observations of certain facial expressions or verbal exclamations are immediately understood as representing anger. Thus, intrinsic to observational understanding is a certain intuitive knowledge of, or empathetic identification with, other people. However, Weber's definition of sociology as a science focusing

---

[10] Weber, *Economy and Society*, p. 13–14. (In all quotations, the italicized words and phrases appear in Weber's original.)

[11] Ibid., pp. 8 and 58 (note 7).

on the "interpretive understanding of social action" clearly suggests that he intended this kind of understanding as a limiting case; in a science, "interpretive" must mean that evidence other than intuition is necessary.

Hence, Weber also referred to a second kind of *verstehen:* "explanatory understanding," that is, "rational understanding of motivation, which consists in placing the act in an intelligible and more inclusive context of meaning."[12] For example, Weber noted that an outbreak of anger can be understood more clearly when it is known that an insult preceded it. Nonetheless, even in this example, understanding seems to involve some intuitive knowledge of how people normally respond in certain situations. But Weber emphasized that while one's intuitive insight may well be right, its correctness must be shown logically and then verified by comparison with concrete events. Thus, Weber argued that any attempt at explanatory understanding in the social sciences is at first "only a peculiarly plausible hypothesis," or hunch. In science, the verification of such a hunch presupposes that the concepts used to refer to concrete events are precisely defined, that clear rules of evidence are followed in regard to data analysis, and that inferences based on the evidence are logical. Only in this way is it possible to achieve "rational understanding of [people's] motivation."

During Weber's time, however, accurate verification of social scientific hypotheses was only possible in a few cases, such as in controlled psychological experiments. Although he participated in several early survey research projects, modern statistical procedures were not available to describe "mass phenomena," with the result that hypotheses were not seen as verifiable using such techniques. Thus, a new way of doing research had to be invented which, for Weber, turned out to be ideal types.[13]

While there has been some confusion because of his use of the word *ideal*, Weber explicitly stated that he did not intend for these concepts to have a normative connotation. Rather, they were designed "to be perfect on logical grounds," most of the time by summarizing a "conceptually pure type of rational action." Weber used ideal types in different ways and for somewhat different purposes, and unfortunately, he did not make any clear or explicit distinction among them, with the result

---

[12] Ibid., pp. 8–10.

[13] Weber's approval of, and participation in, research projects designed to obtain quantitative data show clearly that he was amenable to the use of such information as one means of "explanatory understanding." See Paul F. Lazarsfeld and Anthony R. Oberschall, "Max Weber and Empirical Social Research," *American Sociological Review* 30 (April 1965):185–99.

that scholars have often complained about the inconsistent way in which he used his conceptual tools.[14] Yet despite some areas of inconsistency, we can distinguish two kinds of ideal types in Weber's work. The first can be called the *historical ideal type* and the second can be termed the *classificatory ideal type*. While Weber did not use these labels, they provide a convenient way of organizing the discussion below.

Historical Ideal Types.   These are reconstructions of past events, or ideas, in which some aspects are accentuated such that they are logically (or *rationally*, to use Weber's word) integrated and complete. By conceptualizing historical events in this way, it is possible to systematically compare them to the ideal type and, by observing deviations from the rational model, arrive at causal judgments. This strategy enabled Weber to place historical processes, such as the Protestant Reformation, in "an intelligible and more inclusive context of meaning" and thereby understand their significance for the development of the modern world.

In 1904 Weber noted that the historical ideal type "has the significance of a purely ideal *limiting* concept with which the real situation or action is *compared* and surveyed for the explication of certain of its significant components."[15] On this particular point there was great continuity in Weber's thought, for in part 1 of *Economy and Society* (written around 1919) he made a similar observation:

> The construction of a purely rational course of action . . . serves the sociologist as a type (ideal type) which has the merit of clear understandability and lack of ambiguity. By comparison with this it is possible to understand the ways in which actual action is influenced by irrational factors of all sorts, such as affects and errors, in that they account for the deviation from the line of conduct which would be expected on the hypothesis that the action [is] purely rational.[16]

Classificatory Ideal Types.   During the years between 1904 and 1920, however, Weber apparently became increasingly aware of the need for an inventory of concepts that would serve as a means for more precisely describing the fundamental social processes occurring in all societies. As a result of this awareness, part 1 of *Economy and Society* is spent simply enumerating a system of abstract concepts that could be used in understanding the process of social action. We have labeled these concepts classificatory ideal types, and they constitute the conceptual

---

[14] See Thomas Burger, *Max Weber's Theory of Concept Formation: History, Laws, and Ideal Types* (Durham, N.C.: Duke University Press, 1976), pp. 130–34.

[15] Weber, "Objectivity," p. 93.

[16] Weber, *Economy and Society*, p. 6.

core of the discipline of sociology as Weber ultimately perceived it. While Weber's death prevented completion of his system of core concepts, his intent can be illustrated by examining his conceptualization of the types of social action.[17]

According to Weber, people's actions may be classified in four analytically distinct ways.[18] The first is "instrumentally rational" (or *zweckrational*) action, which occurs as a person systematically takes into account the actual and potential behavior of others and uses this knowledge as " 'conditions' or 'means' for the attainment of the actor's own rationally pursued or calculated ends;" that is, instrumentally rational action exists when means and ends are systematically taken into account based on knowledge, especially (but not necessarily) scientific knowledge.

The second type of action is "value rational" (or *wertrational*) action, which is behavior undertaken for its own sake, in light of one's basic values, and independently of chances for success. Weber noted that "value rational action always involves 'commands' or 'demands' which, in the actor's opinion, are binding."

The third type of action is "traditional," which is behavior "determined by ingrained habituation." Weber's point here was that in a social context where beliefs and values are second nature and patterns of social action have been stable and repetitive for many years, people generally do not have a wide range of choices. Rather, they generally respond in a normal fashion to those situations that have become familiar to them over the centuries. In a sense, they become creatures of a shared normative structure that binds them together into a stable and cohesive group. In such societies, people are very resistant to changing their long established ways of living, which are often sanctified in religious terms. As a result, individuals often continue in the old ways even when some aspect of the situation has changed.

The fourth type of social action is "affectual," which is behavior determined by a person's emotions within a given situation. This last

---

[17] As an aside, it should be recognized that *Economy and Society* was left in a highly disorganized state at Weber's premature death in 1920, and what he intended to do with the fragments that were eventually placed together under that title is not altogether clear. Part 1 is actually the last section Weber wrote, apparently between 1918 and 1920, while part 2 appears to have been written several years earlier, between 1910 and 1914. Titled simply "Conceptual Exposition," part 1 is essentially an unfinished catalogue of the meaning Weber attached to each of his key concepts. As such, it is quite different in style and tone from the earlier, more lengthy, and more historically oriented part 2. There is some indication that Weber intended to rewrite what he had previously written in terms of the system of concepts he had recently developed.

[18] Weber, *Economy and Society*, pp. 24–26.

mode of social action is clearly a residual category that Weber acknowledged but did not explore in any detail.

These "types" of action classify social behavior by visualizing its four "pure forms." While Weber knew that actual empirical situations would not correspond perfectly with these types, by conceptualizing the "ideal types" of action he had a common reference point for comparing actual empirical cases. With the common reference point, different empirical cases could be compared since there was a common point of reference—the ideal type. This strategy is represented in Figure 10–1. Ideal types thus represent for Weber a quasi-experimental method. The "ideal" serves as the functional equivalent of the "control group" in an experiment. Variations or deviations from the ideal are seen as the result of causal forces (or a "stimulus" in a real laboratory experiment), and effort is then undertaken to find these causes. It is in this sense that Weber could achieve two goals: (1) to analytically and logically accentuate the

FIGURE 10–1
The Ideal Type Methodology

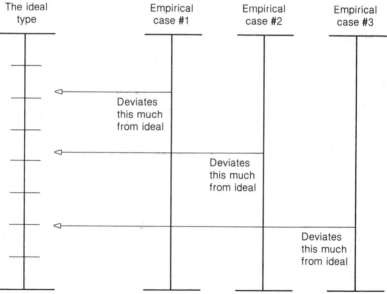

By recording actual deviations from each empirical case from the ideal, the cases are compared to each other using a common reference point. Then, by asking what causes the deviations, or differences among the three cases, the causes of empirical events in each case can be isolated, and compared.

elements of social action and (2) to discover the causes of unique variations in specific empirical cases. For example, by noting the extent to
which actual empirical cases compare to "instrumental rational" action,
the causes of conformity to, or deviation from, this ideal can be assessed.
In this way, the unique aspects of empirical cases can be emphasized,
and yet, systematically and logically analyzed.

WEBER'S STUDY OF RELIGION

The Protestant Ethic and the Spirit of Capitalism is Weber's most
famous and in some ways his most important study.[19] Published in two
parts in 1905 and 1906, it was one of his first works to be translated
into English, and even more significantly, it was the first application
of his mature methodological orientation (the essay on "objectivity"
was written in 1904). As a result, the Protestant Ethic is neither a historical analysis nor a politically committed interpretation of history. Rather,
it is part of an exercise in historical hypothesis testing in which Weber
constructed a logical experiment using ideal types as conceptual tools.

In retrospect, it can be seen that Weber had three interrelated purposes in writing the Protestant Ethic. First, he wanted to refute those
forms of Marxist analysis that were prevalent at the turn of the century.
Second, he wished to understand why the culture of capitalism emerged
in the West. As such, Weber's work is not only an explanation of how
the modern world, dominated by instrumental rationality, came into
being, but also a demonstration that an objective, value-free sociology
can deal with historical topics. Third, Weber also wanted to demonstrate
that cultural values and other ideas or beliefs circumscribe social action,
primarily by directing people's interests in certain directions.

While the Protestant Ethic is by far the most important of Weber's
studies in the sociology of religion, it is nonetheless only a small portion
of a much larger intellectual enterprise that he pursued intermittently
for about 15 years. In this grandiose "imaginary experiment," Weber
tried to account not only for the confluence of events that were associated
with the rise of capitalism in the West, but also to explain, logically,
why capitalism was not likely to have developed in any other section
of the world: that is, "why did not the scientific, the artistic, the political,
and the economic development [of China, India, and other areas] enter

---

[19] Max Weber, The Protestant Ethic and The Spirit of Capitalism, trans. Talcott
Parsons (New York: Scribner's, 1958).

upon that path of rationalization which is peculiar to the occident?"[20] Thus, the *Protestant Ethic* is the first portion of a two-stage experiment. The second element in Weber's experiment is contained in a series of book-length studies on *The Religion of China* (1913), *The Religion of India* (1916–17), and *Ancient Judaism* (1917).[21]

Before reviewing either the *Protestant Ethic* or Weber's other work on religion, we should make explicit the implicit research design of these works. In so doing, we will see another sense in which Weber constructed "quasi-experimental designs" for understanding the causes of historical events. Weber's basic question is: Why did industrialization initially occur in the West and not in other parts of the world? Such a question directs attention to the "cause" of industrialization. To isolate this cause, Weber constructed the "quasi-experimental design" diagramed in Figure 10–2.

In Figure 10–2 steps 1 through 5 approximate the stages of a laboratory situation as it must be adapted to historical analysis. The West represents the experimental group in that something stimulated industrialization, whereas China and India represent the control groups since they did not industrialize, even though they were as advanced as the West in terms of technologies and other social forms. The stimulus that caused industrialization in the West was the religious beliefs associated with Protestantism (see step 3 of Figure 10–2), and it is for this reason that Weber wrote *The Protestant Ethic and the Spirit of Capitalism*.

The Protestant Ethic and the Spirit of Capitalism

Weber opened the *Protestant Ethic* with what was a commonplace observation at the end of the 19th century: occupational statistics in those nations of mixed religious composition invariably show that those in higher socioeconomic positions are overwhelmingly Protestant. This relationship is especially true, Weber wrote, "wherever capitalism . . .

[20] Weber, "Author's Introduction," in *Protestant Ethic*, p. 25. It is important to recognize that Weber wrote this introduction in 1920 for the German edition of his *Collected Essays in the Sociology of Religion*. Thus, it is an overall view of Weber's work in the sociology of religion and not merely an introduction to the *Protestant Ethic*. Scribner's more recent 1976 edition of the book does not make this fact clear, mainly because they chose to omit the translator's preface, by Talcott Parsons.

[21] Max Weber, *The Religion of China*, trans. Hans Gerth, (Glencoe, Ill.: Free Press, 1951); Max Weber, *The Religion of India*, trans. Hans Gerth and Don Martindale (Glencoe, Ill.: Free Press, 1958); Max Weber, *Ancient Judaism*, trans. Hans Gerth and Don Martindale (Glencoe, Ill.: Free Press, 1952). In addition, part 2 of *Economy and Society* contains a book-length study, "Religious Groups *(The Sociology of Religion)*," that is also available in paperback under the title *The Sociology of Religion*, trans. Ephraim Fischoff (Boston: Beacon Press, 1963).

FIGURE 10-2
Weber's Quasi-Experimental Design in the Study of Religion

Group	Step 1 Find two "matched" societies in terms of their minimal conditions.	Step 2 Do historical research on their properties before stimulus introduced.	Step 3 Examine the impact of the key stimulus, religious beliefs.	Step 4 Use historical evidence to assess the properties of other stimulus.	Step 5 Differences between Europe and China are viewed as caused by religious beliefs.
Quasi-experimental group	Western Europe	Descriptions of Europe (using historical ideal types).	Experiences stimulus with emergence of Protestantism.	Industrial revolution.	Western Europe is changed.
Quasi-control group	China	Descriptions of China (using historical ideal types).	Experiences no stimulus.	No industrial revolution.	China is much the same as before.
Quasi-control group	India	Descriptions of India (using historical ideal types).	Experiences no stimulus.	No industrial revolution.	India is much the same as before.

has had a free hand."[22] Many observers in economics, literature, and history had commented on this phenomena before Weber, and he cited a number of them.[23] Hence in the *Protestant Ethic*, Weber was not trying to prove that a relationship between Protestantism and economic success in capitalist societies existed, since he took its existence as given. In his words, "it is not new that the existence of this relationship is maintained. . . . Our task here is to explain the relation."[24]

In order to show that Protestantism was related to the origin of the "spirit of capitalism" in the West, Weber began with a sketch of what he meant by the latter term. Like many of Weber's key concepts, the notion of the spirit of capitalism is a historical ideal type in that it is a conceptual accentuation of certain aspects of the real world which he used as a tool for understanding actual historical processes.[25] Although he did not state what he meant very clearly, an omission that helped contribute to the tremendous controversy over the *Protestant Ethic's* thesis, Weber's concept of the spirit of capitalism appears to have the following components.[26]

First, work is valued as an end in itself. Weber was fascinated by the fact that a person's "duty in a calling [or occupation] is what is most characteristic of the social ethic of capitalistic culture, and is in a sense the fundamental basis of it."

Second, in capitalist society, acquisitiveness, trade, and profit are taken not only as evidence of occupational success but also as indicators of personal virtue. In Weber's words, "the earning of money within the modern economic order is, so long as it is done legally, [seen as] the result and the expression of virtue and proficiency in a calling."

Third, a methodically organized life governed by reason is valued not only as a means to a long-term goal, economic success, but also as an inherently proper and even righteous state of being.

---

[22] Weber, *Protestant Ethic*, p. 35.

[23] Ibid., pp. 43–45 and 191 (note 23). See also Reinhard Bendix, "The Protestant Ethic—Revisited," in Bendix and Guenther Roth, eds., *Scholarship and Partisanship: Essays on Max Weber* (Berkeley: University of California Press, 1971), pp. 299–310.

[24] Weber, *Portestant Ethic*, p. 191.

[25] Weber hints at his ideal type strategy but does not bother to explain it in the initial paragraphs of chapter 2 of the *Protestant Ethic*, (p. 47). He refers to the need to develop a "historical individual," that is, "a complex of elements associated in historical reality which we unite into a conceptual whole from the standpoint of their cultural significance." This phrasing apparently comes from his methodological essays that have been published under the title, *Roscher and Knies: The Logical Problems of Historical Economics* trans. Guy Oakes (New York: Free Press, 1975). As noted in Chapter 9, Weber eventually abandoned use of "historical individual" in favor of "ideal type."

[26] Weber, *Protestant Ethic*, p. 53–54.

Fourth, embodied in the righteous pursuit of economic success is a belief that immediate happiness and pleasure should be forgone in favor of future satisfaction. As Weber noted, "the *summum bonum* of this ethic, the earning of more and more money, combined with the strict avoidance of all spontaneous enjoyment of life, is above all completely devoid of an eudaemonistic, not to say hedonistic, admixture." In sum, then, these values—the goodness of work, success as personal rectitude, the use of reason to guide one's life, and delayed gratification—reflect some of the most important cultural values in the West, since they constitute perceptions of appropriate behavior that are shared by all.[27]

Weber emphasized, however, that the widespread application of such values to everyday life is historically unique and of relatively recent origin. Hence, he distinguished the modern culture of capitalism from both its premodern form, which he called *adventurer capitalism*, and from the traditional values characteristic of the late Middle Ages. By adventurer capitalism, Weber referred to those acquisitive individuals throughout history who have sought to make money ruthlessly and saw themselves "bound to no ethical norms whatever. . . . Capitalistic acquisition as an adventure has been at home in all types of economic society which have known trade with the use of money."[28] However, the activities of adventurer capitalists have rarely received social approval and never embodied dominant conceptions of appropriate behavior. More often, their avariciousness, especially when directed toward outsiders, has been merely tolerated because it was deemed necessary to the community. Weber believed that the effect of adventurer capitalists on the development of the modern culture of capitalism was minimal, even though such persons clearly flourished as the new ethos became more and more widespread.

According to Weber, the greatest barrier to the rise of the culture of capitalism in the West was the inertial force of traditional values. To varying degrees, European societies prior to the 17th century were dominated by what Weber later called "traditional modes of action." For example, religion rather than science was used as the primary means of verifying knowledge (as in Galileo's forced recantment of his findings regarding the movement of the planets). Bureaucracies composed of

---

[27] Some current observers believe that the salience of these values is declining, see Christopher Lasch, *The Culture of Narcissim* (New York: W. W. Norton, 1979), pp. 52–55.

[28] Weber, *Protestant Ethic*, pp. 57–58; see also Max Weber, "Anticritical Last Word on the *Spirit of Capitalism*," trans. Wallace A. Davis, *American Journal of Sociology* 83 (March 1978):1127.

technical experts were unknown. Patterns of commerce and most other forms of daily life were dominated by status rather than class considerations; that is, people acted in terms of their membership in religious and ethnic groups rather than in light of simple market factors. Finally, legal adjudication did not involve the equal application to all individuals of clear legal codes. In short, the choice between instrumentally rational action and value rationalization did not exist.

But over time, the power of tradition was broken and capitalism emerged in Western Europe. In his *General Economic History* written some years later, Weber identified the major historical factors that he believed, taken together, caused the development of capitalism in Western Europe rather than elsewhere: (1) the process of industrialization through which muscle power was supplanted by new forms of energy, (2) the rise of a free labor force whose members had to work in commercial enterprises or starve, (3) the increasing use of rational accounting methods in industrial undertakings, (4) the rise of a free market unencumbered by irrational restrictions, (5) the gradual imposition and legitimation of a system of calculable law, (6) the increasing commercialization of economic life through the use of stock certificates and other paper instruments, and (7) the rise of the spirit of capitalism. While all these developments were to varying degrees unique to the West, in the *General Economic History* Weber still regarded the last factor as the most decisive one.[29] Thus, in attempting to understand the origin of the economic differences between Protestants and Catholics, Weber's point was not to deny the fundamental significance of these historical factors, but merely to show the nature and significance of the culture of capitalism and its logical relationship to the Protestant ethic.

To Weber, the cultural values of traditional society were destroyed by Puritanism, although this was not the intent of those who adopted the Reformed faiths and could not have been predicted in advance. In the *Protestant Ethic*, Weber focused mainly on Calvinism, with much shorter discussions of Pietism, Methodism, and Baptism appended to the main analysis. His general theoretical strategy was to describe Calvinist doctrines by quoting extensively from the writings of various theologians, then to impute the psychological consequences those doctrines had on people who accepted them, and finally, to show how they resulted in specific (and historically new) ways of living. In Weber's words, he

---

[29] Max Weber, *General Economic History*, trans. Frank Knight (New York: Collier Books, 1961), pp. 207–70. In the *Protestant Ethic* (p. 61), Weber does mention the fundamental importance of free workers who are compelled to sell their labor on the market without restriction.

was interested in ascertaining "those psychological sanctions which, originating in religious belief and the practice of religion, gave a direction to practical conduct and held the individual to it."[30] In this way, he believed he could give a powerful example of the manner in which cultural phenomena influence social action and, at the same time, rebut the vulgar Marxists who thought economic factors were the sole causal agents in historical change.

Based on an analysis of Calvinist writings, such as the *Westminster Confession of 1647*, which he quoted extensively, Weber interpreted Calvinist doctrines as having four consequences for those who accepted its tenets.

First, because the Calvinist doctrine of Predestination led people to believe that God, for incomprehensible reasons, had divided the human population into two groups, the saved and the damned, a key problem for all individuals was to determine the group to which they belonged. Second, because people could not know with certainty whether they were saved and because salvation could not be guaranteed either by magical sacraments administered by a priest (as in Catholicism) or by a mystical union with God (as in Lutheranism), they inevitably felt a great inner loneliness and isolation. Third, while a change in one's relative state of grace was seen as impossible, people inevitably began to look for signs they were among the elect. In general, Calvinists believed that two clues could be used as evidence: (1) the first was faith, and everyone had an absolute duty to consider themselves chosen and to combat all doubts as temptations of the devil, and (2) the second clue taken as a sign of salvation was intense worldly activity, for in this way the self-confidence necessary to alleviate religious doubts could be generated. Fourth, all believers were expected to lead methodical and ascetic lives such that they were unencumbered by irrational emotions, superstitions, or desires of the flesh. As Weber put it, the good Calvinist was expected to "methodically supervise his own state of grace in his own conduct, and thus to penetrate it with asceticism," with the result that each person engaged in "a rational planning of the whole of one's life in accordance with God's will."[31] The significance of this last doctrine is that in Calvinist communities worldly asceticism was not restricted to monks and other "religious virtuosi" (to use Weber's word) but required of everyone as they conducted their everyday lives in their mundane occupations, or callings.

---

[30] Weber, *Protestant Ethic*, p. 97.
[31] Ibid., p. 153.

In order to show the relationship between the worldly asceticism fostered by the Protestant sects and the rise of the spirit of capitalism, Weber chose to focus on the Puritan minister's guidelines for everyday behavior, as contained in their pastoral writings. The clergy's teachings, which were set forth in such books as Richard Baxter's *Christian Directory*, tend to reflect the major pastoral problems they encountered. As such, their writings provide an idealized vision of everyday life in the Puritan communities. While it must be recognized that social action does not always conform to cultural ideals, such values do provide a general direction for people's actions. Most people try, even if imperfectly, to adhere to those standards of appropriate behavior that are dominant in their community, and the Puritans were no exceptions. Further, the use of this sort of data suggests the broad way in which Weber interpreted the idea of "explanatory understanding" *(verstehen):* since people's own explanations of their actions often involve contradictory motives that are difficult to reconcile, he was perfectly willing to use an indirect means of ascertaining the subjective meaning of social action among the Puritans.

Based on Weber's analysis, it appears that the Puritan communities were dominated by three interrelated dictums that, while a direct outgrowth of Puritan theology, eventuated over the long run in a rather utilitarian (and relatively nonreligious) culture of capitalism.

The first of these pronouncements is that God demands rational labor in a calling. As Weber noted, Puritan pastoral literature is characterized "by the continually repeated, often almost passionate preaching of hard, continuous bodily or mental labour."[32] From this point of view, there can be no relaxation, no relief from toil, for labor is an exercise in ascetic virtue, and rational, methodical behavior in a calling is taken as a sign of grace. Hence, from the Puritan's standpoint, "waste of time is . . . the first and in principle the deadliest of sins," since "every hour lost is lost to labour for the glory of God." As Weber observed, this dictum not only provides an ethical justification for the modern division of labor in which occupational tasks are divided up rationally, but reserves its highest accolades for those sober, middle-class individuals who best exemplify the methodical nature of worldly asceticism. As an aside, it should be noted that members of this stratum became the primary carriers of Puritan religious beliefs precisely because they garnered immense economic, social, and political power as a result. In gen-

---

[32] Ibid., p. 158.

eral, Weber emphasized that those who are able to define and sanctify standards of appropriate behavior also benefit materially.[33]

The second directive that dominated the Puritan believers also follows from Puritan theology and states that the enjoyment of those aspects of social life that do not have clear religious value is forbidden. Thus, from the point of view of the Puritan ministers, secular literature, the theatre, and nearly all other forms of leisure time activity were at best irrelevant and at worst superstitious. As a result, they tried to inculcate in their parishioners an extraordinarily serious approach to life, for people should direct their attention toward the practical problems dominating everyday life and subject them to rational solutions.

The third guideline that permeated the daily lives of the Puritans specifies that people have a duty to use their possessions for socially beneficial purposes that redound to the glory of God. Thus, the pursuit of wealth for its own sake was regarded as sinful, for it could lead to enjoyment, idleness, and "temptations of the flesh." From this point of view, those who acquire wealth through God's grace and hard work are mere trustees who have an obligation to use it responsibly.

Even allowing for the usual amount of human imperfection, Weber argued that the accumulation of capital and the rise of the modern bourgeoisie were the inevitable result of whole communities sharing values dictating hard work, limited enjoyment and consumption, and the practical use of money. Hence, capitalism emerged. Weber's causal argument is diagramed in Figure 10–3. Over time, of course, Puritan ideals gave way under the secularizing influence of wealth because people began to enjoy their material possessions. Thus, while the religious roots of the spirit of capitalism inevitably died out, Puritanism bequeathed to modern people "an amazingly good, we may even say a pharisaically good, conscience in the acquisition of money." The predominance of such a value throughout an entire epoch is absolutely historically unique.

But in the concluding paragraphs of the essay, Weber allowed himself some personal and rather pessimistic observations. He argued that one of the most significant legacies of the Protestant Reformation is that in modern society "the idea of duty in one's calling prowls about in our lives like the ghost of dead religious beliefs," with the result that while "the Puritan wanted to work in a calling; we are forced to do so." Further, because modern people are inexorably tied to the technical and economic conditions of industrial production, our culture has become "an iron cage" from which there appears to be no escape and for which

---

[33] See Weber, *Economy and Society*, pp. 439–517.

FIGURE 10–3
Weber's Causal Argument for the Emergence of Capitalism

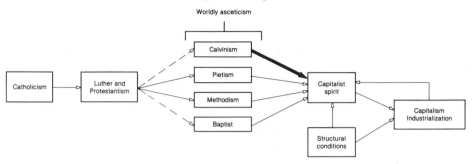

there is no longer a religious justification. This recognition leads to Weber's last, sad lament: "specialists without spirit, sensualists without heart;
this nullity imagines that it has attained a level of civilization never
before achieved."[34]

Weber's Comparative Studies of Religion and Capitalism

During the years following the publication of the *Protestant Ethic*
considerable controversy and misunderstanding developed over Weber's
thesis, and he participated in the debate over it by making several attempts at refuting his critics.[35] In addition, he apparently began to see
the need for some further studies of the relationship between religious
belief and social structure in order to show why it was not very likely
that capitalism as an economic system could have emerged anywhere
else in the world. Weber's most important works in this regard are
The Religion of China (1913) and *The Religion of India* (1917), which
represent a continuation of the logical experiment begun some years
earlier.

Both of these extended essays are similar in format in that Weber
began by assessing those characteristics of Chinese and Indian social
structure that either inhibited or, under the right circumstances, could
have contributed to the development of capitalism in that part of the

---

[34] Weber, *Protestant Ethic*, pp. 180–83.

[35] See Weber, "Anticritical Last Word," as well as the many explanatory footnotes
in the *Protestant Ethic*. Most of these footnotes were added around 1920. The controversy
over the Protestant ethic thesis has continued up to the present; see Robert L. Green,
ed., *Protestantism and Capitalism: The Weber Thesis and Its Critics* (Boston: D. C.
Heath, 1959); and S. N. Eisenstadt, ed., *The Protestant Ethic and Modernization* (New
York: Basic Books, 1968).

world (see Figure 10–2 for Weber's implicit experimental design). For purposes of illustration, all the examples used here come from *The Religion of China*. Thus, in China during the period when capitalism arose in the West, a number of positive factors existed that could have led to a similar development in the Orient. First, there was a great deal of internal commerce and trade with other nations. Second, due to the establishment and maintenance (for more than 1,200 years) of nation-wide competitive examinations, there was an unusual degree of equality of opportunity in the process of status attainment. Third, the society was generally stable and peaceful, although Weber was clearly too accepting of the myth of the "unchanging China." Fourth, China had many large urban centers, and geographical mobility was a relatively common occurrence. Fifth, there were relatively few formal restrictions on economic activity. Finally, there were a number of technological developments in China that were more advanced than those in Europe at the same time (the use of gunpowder, knowledge of astronomy, book printing, and so forth). As Weber noted, all of these factors could have aided in the development of a Chinese version of modern capitalism.

However, he emphasized that Chinese society also displayed a number of characteristics that clearly inhibited the widespread development of any form of capitalism in that part of the world. First, while possessing an abundance of precious metals, especially silver, an adequate monetary system had never developed in China. Second, because of the early unification and centralization of the Chinese empire, the cities never became autonomous political units, with the result that the development of local capitalistic enterprises was inhibited. Third, Chinese society was characterized by the use of "substantive ethical law" rather than rational and calculable legal procedure. As a result, legal judgments were made in terms of the particular characteristics of the participants and sacred tradition rather than in terms of the equal imposition of common standards. Finally, the Chinese bureaucracy was made up of classically learned persons rather than trained experts. Thus, the examinations regulating status attainment "tested whether the candidate's mind was thoroughly steeped in literature and whether or not he possessed the ways of thought suitable to a cultured man."[36] Hence, the idea of the trained expert was foreign to the Chinese experience.

In sum, according to Weber, all of these characteristics of Chinese social structure inhibited the development of an oriental form of modern capitalism. Nonetheless, the positive examples noted above do suggest

---

[36] Weber, *Religion of China*, p. 121.

that such a development was not impossible. And yet Weber argued that the rise of capitalism as an economic system was quite unlikely in either China or India, for he found no evidence of patterns of religious beliefs that could be compatible with any facsimile of the spirit of capitalism in either of these societies. And he believed that without the transformative power of religion, the rise of a new cultural ethos was not very likely. In China prior to this century the religion of the dominant classes, the bureaucrats, was Confucianism. Weber characterized Confucianism by the fact that it had no concept of sin, but only faults resulting from deficient education. Further, Confucianism had no metaphysic, with the result that there was no concern with the origin of the world or with the possibility of an afterlife and, hence, no tension between sacred and secular law. According to Weber, Confucianism was a rational religion concerned with events in this world, but with a peculiarly individualistic emphasis. Good confucians were less interested in the state of society than with their own propriety, as indicated by their development as educated persons and by their pious relations with others (especially their parents). In Weber's words, the educated Chinese person "controls all his activities, physical gestures, and movements as well, with politeness and with grace in accordance with the status mores and the commands of 'propriety.' "[37] Rather than salvation in the next world, the Confucian accepted this world as given and merely desired to behave prudently.

And thus, on this basis, Weber asserted that Confucianism was not very likely to result in the development of an oriental form of the culture of capitalism. He came to the same conclusion four years later in his study, *The Religion of India.* Thus, by means of these comparative studies, Weber showed not only why Protestantism was associated with the rise of the culture of capitalism in the West but also why no other religion could have stimulated a similar development in any other part of the world.

In conclusion then, beginning from a relatively simple empirical fact—income differences between Protestants and Catholics in 19th-century Europe—Weber asserted that even after taking into account the unique occurrence of a number of important phenomena (free labor, rational law, political independence of cities, early industrialization, and so on), the most important factor accounting for the rise of capitalism as an economic system was the spread of a new cultural ethos, which he called the spirit of capitalism. This ethos was the inadvertent consequence of Puritan religious beliefs that over the long run produced behavior (among

[37] Ibid., p. 156.

both believers and nonbelievers) that was uniquely compatible with other historical developments occurring during that period. Over time, of course, the religious origin of modern values and action have disappeared from view, leaving a secular legacy of beliefs in the innate goodness of work, acquisitiveness, the methodical organization of one's life, and delayed gratification. However, Weber believed that without the canalizing influence of Puritan religious beliefs, modern society would be fundamentally different than it is today. In his words, "it was the power of religious influence, not alone, but more than anything else, which created the differences of which we are conscious today."[38]

SOCIAL STRATIFICATION IN MODERN SOCIETY

It will be recalled that Max Weber's sociology can be seen as having two interrelated goals. First, he wished to provide a scientific account of the origin and characteristics of modern Western society. In this chapter the *Protestant Ethic* has been used to illustrate one way Weber achieved this goal: by suggesting how the Puritans' beliefs were transformed into more general cultural values that continue to dominate the structure of social action in the West, he was able to show the religious origins of modern life. Weber's second goal was the development of a system of concepts, what we have called classificatory ideal types, that could be used for understanding social processes in industrial societies. While Weber's attempt at an "analytical ordering of reality" is flawed in some respects, his work in this area has endured because much of his writing is characterized by unusual theoretical insight and prescience. One of the best examples of Weber's conceptual inventory is his analysis of social stratification, especially when it is seen as an aspect of his more general political sociology (or "sociology of domination," as it is also called).

While *Economy and Society* contains two somewhat overlapping sections on social stratification, the full title of the more well-known essay, "The Distribution of Power within the Political Community: Class, Status, and Party," is suggestive of his overall intent: to show how the structure of inequality in modern societies is interrelated with the nature of domination in such nations.[39] Following Weber's lead, this section is divided into two parts. First, the general theoretical perspective underlying his assertion that social stratification is a manifestation of power

---

[38] Weber, *Protestant Ethic*, p. 89.
[39] Weber, *Economy and Society*, pp. 284–306 and 901–38.

within the political community is explained. Second, his analysis of the structure of classes and status groups is explicated in some detail.

The Distribution of Power within the Political Community

Although Weber is somewhat ambiguous, the term *political community* appears to refer to the modern nation states within which classes and status groups compete for access to goods and services. For the moment, classes can be defined as being composed of those persons having similar economic positions in a society, while status groups are made up of individuals possessing similar levels of prestige. As we shall see, such competition among classes and status groups implies the existence of what Weber called a "rational-legal system of domination." Yet Weber was also interested in the more general problem of understanding the nature of power and authority in all societies, and his sociology of domination is an attempt at developing a set of classificatory ideal types that could be used in logical experiments similar to those undertaken in the *Protestant Ethic*. An outline of Weber's political sociology is presented here in three steps: (1) what Weber meant by power and domination is noted, (2) his classification of the three types of domination is sketched, and (3) his depiction of the modern political community in which rational-legal authority is the mode of domination is briefly explained. On this basis, Weber's analysis of classes and status groups can be more clearly understood, since the system of domination provides the political context in which stratification occurs.

Power and Domination. Weber defined power as the ability of people to obtain their goals even against the resistance of others.[40] Power, then, involves the coercion of some persons by others, and in all societies some individuals seek power for themselves or their group. However, Weber was interested in those manifestations of power, which he called domination or authority *(Herrschaft)*, that are most typical of social organizatons.[41] In Weber's scheme, systems of domination are defined by two interrelated elements that together provide the basis for his classification of the types of authority. The first element characterizing every system of domination is beliefs about the legitimacy of authority: that is, the use of power is legitimate when leaders assert their right to com-

---

[40] Ibid., p. 926.

[41] There has been considerable controversy over the proper translation of the German *Herrschaft*, with Parsons translating it as "authority" and many others as "domination." Both are correct. See Guenther Roth's long explanatory note on this topic in Weber, *Economy and Society*, pp. 61–62.

mand and citizens believe they have a duty to obey.[42] Those who exercise power always attempt to establish a belief in the legitimacy of their domination, Weber said, because such a commitment obviates the need for using force, and therefore, leads to long-term stability. Those who are subjected to power choose to accept its legitimacy, either because its use corresponds to their interests or because its use reflects accepted values, or both. The second element intrinsic to any system of domination is an administrative apparatus: that is, society-wide authority relationships require a staff that can enforce commands and in other ways serve as a link between leaders and masses.[43]

The Three Types of Domination. In Weber's scheme, the forms of domination are ideal types that permit classification of a society in terms of its resemblance to one of them, although in actuality any society will display aspects of all three.

The first type is called *charismatic domination.* The term *charisma* has a religious origin and means literally "gift of grace," implying that a person is endowed with divine powers.[44] However, in practice Weber did not restrict his use of charisma to manifestations of divinity but often used the concept to refer to those extraordinary individuals who somehow identify themselves with the central facts or problems of people's lives and who, by the force of their personality, are able to communicate their inspiration to others and lead them in new directions. Thus, persons in other than religious roles can sometimes be considered charismatic: for example, politicians, soldiers, or artists.[45]

In Weber's view, charismatic leadership emerges during times of crisis, when established ways of doing things seem inappropriate, outmoded, or inadequate to the problems confronting people. The essence of charismatic domination, then, involves people's renunciation of the past in favor of a new direction based on the master's inspiration. As Weber put it, every charismatic leader implicitly or explicitly argues that "it is written . . . but I say unto you . . ." Thus, the basis for the legitimacy of charismatic domination lies in both the leader's demonstration of extraordinary insight and accomplishment, and in the followers' acceptance of the master. It is irrelevant, from Weber's point of view, whether a charismatic leader turns out to be a charlatan or a hero; rather, what

---

[42] Weber, *Economy and Society*, p. 946.

[43] Ibid., pp. 956–58.

[44] Ibid., p. 241.

[45] See Edward Shils, "Charisma, Order, and Status," *American Sociological Review* 30 (April 1965): 199–213; and Reinhard Bendix, "Charismatic Leadership," in Bendix and Roth, eds., *Scholarship and Partisanship*, pp. 170–87.

is important is that the masses are inspired to freely follow the master. Toward that end, the charismatic leader's administrative staff usually consists (at least initially) only of a band of faithful disciples who serve the master's immediate personal and political needs.

While charismatic leadership is often a vehicle for social change, Weber felt that it is generally unstable over extended periods for two reasons. (1) Its legitimacy is dependent on the leader's claim to special insight and accomplishment; if success eludes the leader for long and crises are not resolved satisfactorily, then it is likely the masses will reject the charismatic figure and his or her authority will disappear. (2) Over the long run, every regime led by a charismatic leader faces the "problem of routinization," which involves both finding a successor to the leader and handling the day-to-day decisions that must be made. Weber noted that the problem of succession can be resolved in a variety of ways: for example, by simply searching for a new charismatic leader, by the leader's designation of a successor, or by the disciples' designation of a successor. The decision-making problem can be resolved either by the development of a full-fledged administrative staff or the takeover of an already existing organization. However, in both cases, the inevitable result is the transformation of the relationship between the charismatic leader and his or her followers from one based on beliefs in the master's extraordinary qualities to one based on tradition or law. These new bases of legitimation represent the other two types of domination in Weber's ideal type, as is explored below.

The second type of domination is that based on *tradition*. In Weber's words, "authority will be called traditional if legitimacy is claimed for it and believed in by virtue of the sanctity of age-old rules and powers."[46] In traditional systems of domination, leaders usually obtain their positions and justify their power in light of custom; and they issue commands in terms of those areas of discretion that tradition leaves open to them. Conversely, the masses obey edicts in recognition of the ruler's rightful place and out of personal loyalty. Thus, Weber's analysis of traditional authority suggests how traditional types of social action are generalized into normative systems of domination.

Weber distinguished between two forms of traditional authority, which he called *patriarchalism* and *patrimonialism*. Patriarchalism is a type of domination that occurs in households and other small groups where the use of an organizational apparatus to enforce commands is not necessary. Patrimonialism is a form of traditional domination that occurs in

---

[46] Weber, *Economy and Society*, p. 226.

larger social systems which require an administrative staff to execute edicts. This staff is composed of personal retainers who are exclusively loyal to the ruler. Weber observed that in addition to its grounding in custom, the officials' loyalty is based either on their dependence on the ruler for their positions and remuneration or on their pledge of fealty to the leader. In either case, the essence of traditional authority when coupled with an administrative staff (patrimonialism) is expressed by the following characteristics:

1. Officials attain positions based on custom and loyalty to the leader
2. Obedience is owed only to the person issuing commands rather than to enacted rules and
3. There is no separation of one's office and private affairs because the members of the staff either appropriate the means of production themselves or are granted them by the ruler.[47]

These elements of traditional authority typically reflect cultural values and patterns of social action that have been stable for many years. As such, they distinguish those societies in which custom guides action from those guided by instrumental and value rational orientations. Thus, it should not be surprising that in *Economy and Society* Weber described traditional modes of domination as inhibiting the development of capitalism, primarily because rules are not rationally established, officials have too wide a range for personal arbitrariness, and they are not technically trained.[48] Capitalism and, to some extent, industrialization require an emphasis on logic, procedure, and knowledge. Furthermore, as we shall see, modern systems of stratification are not possible in social structures in which statuses and roles are circumscribed by tradition.

The third type of authority is that based on law, or *rational-legal domination*. As Weber phrased it, "legal domination [exists] by virtue of statute. . . . The basic conception is: that any legal norm can be created or changed by a procedurally correct enactment."[49] Thus, legal domination is based on a belief in procedure; that is, laws are seen as legitimate by the people when they are enforced in what is defined as the proper way. Similarly, the leaders who promulgate laws are seen as having the right to act when they have obtained their positions in what is perceived as the procedurally correct ways (through election or appointment, for example). Weber called the administrative apparatus in a ra-

---

[47] Ibid., pp. 226–36.
[48] Ibid., pp. 237–41.
[49] Weber, quoted in Bendix, *Intellectual Portrait*, pp. 418–19.

tional-legal system a bureaucracy and observed that it is oriented to the creation and enforcement of rules in the public interest. Essentially, Weber argued, dominant Western cultural values emphasizing hard work, success, and a methodical (or rational) life-style are reflected in the system of authority characteristic of modern political communities—a fact that can be seen in the nature of the state, its administrative apparatus, and its political processes.

The Modern Political Community. For Weber, the modern political community, or nation-state, is defined in terms that reflect its style of domination.[50] (1) The state regulates social action in a contiguous territory. (2) The use of the army and other forms of force to regulate social action is the exclusive property of the government. (3) Citizens share a common cultural background, what Weber called a "community of memories," epitomized by elements of the spirit of capitalism. (4) Legitimacy is based on the creation and enforcement of written regulations and procedures in the context of a centralized administrative apparatus, a bureaucracy.

It is in this context, then, that Weber defined the modern state as based on the monopoly of physical coercion, a monopoly made legitimate by a system of laws binding on both the rulers and the ruled. Furthermore, it is in this setting that the bureaucracy, as the archetypal example of instrumentally rational action, is the primary means of governmental administration and the focus of conflict as the members of classes and status groups vie to control it.

While many people condemn bureaucracies as inefficient, rigid, and incompetent, Weber argued that, in industrial societies, the bureaucratic mode of administration is the only means of attaining efficient, flexible, and competent regulation under the rule of law. In its logically pure form (that is, as an ideal type), a bureaucratic apparatus has a set of unique characteristics that clearly set it apart from the form of administration typical of a traditional society.[51]

1. Employment and promotion are based on technical training and experience, with the result that administration is based on knowledge rather than custom.

---

[50] Weber, *Economy and Society*, pp. 904–10. It should be recognized that Weber's analysis of the modern state only refers to Western societies, and its relevance for nations that industrialized later, such as Japan, or industrialized in a totalitarian context is not clear; see Eisenstadt, ed., *Protestant Ethic and Modernization*.

[51] Ibid., pp. 217–20; Weber also noted the dysfunctional aspects of bureaucratic forms of administration (see pp. 990–94). See also Reinhard Bendix, "Bureaucracy," in Bendix and Roth, eds., *Scholarship and Partisanship*, pp. 129–55.

2. The rights and duties of officials are explicitly described in written regulations that have been properly enacted, with the result that staff members owe their primary allegiance to the system of rules governing their behavior rather than to the capriciousness of superiors.

3. Officials receive contractually fixed salaries and do not own either their positions or the means of production, with the result that administrative duties are separated from private affairs.

According to Weber, bureaucratic administration in a rational-legal system is realized to the extent that staff members "succeed in eliminating from official business love, hatred, and all purely personal, irrational, and emotional elements."[52] While Weber recognized that no actual bureaucracy operates in this way, his ideal type expresses a fundamental value characteristic of modern societies: political administration should be impersonal, objective, and based on knowledge; for only in this way can the rule of law be realized. Further, he emphasized that while these characteristics and values seem commonplace to most people today, they are historically new; they arose only in the West and have come to be the dominant form of authority only in the last few hundred years. Finally, Weber's definition of bureaucracy points toward a fundamental arena of conflict in modern societies: who is to make laws and who is to administer them through their control of the bureaucratic apparatus?

Within the context of a rational-legal system of authority, political parties are the forms in which classes and status groups struggle for power. As Weber put it, "a political party . . . exists for the purpose of fighting for domination" in order to advance the class or status interests of the group it represents, but it does so under the aegis of statutory regulation.[53] In general, the point of the struggle is to direct the bureaucratic staff via the creation of law, for in this way the material and ideal interests of classes and status groups are served. For example, those who own income-producing property in the United States act to make sure that their economic interests are codified into law; this is why income from stock dividends and other kinds of investments is taxed at a much lower rate than is income from ordinary wages, thereby allowing owners of capital to keep a higher proportion of their income. Similarly, people at all class and status levels act to protect their interests, and the needs of those who do not organize and compete are ignored. The political process in Western societies, then, reflects those basic cultural values

---

[52] Weber, *Economy and Society*, p. 975.
[53] Ibid., p. 951.

whose origin Weber discovered in the *Protestant Ethic:* economic and social success are highly valued; they are achieved through competition under the law; and the process is rational in the sense of being pursued into a methodical manner. Weber's analysis of classes and status groups shows in a different way how the structure of inequality in modern societies also mirrors these values.

Classes and Status Groups in Modern Societies

In his analysis of the structure of inequality in modern societies, Weber was attempting an elaborate mapping operation in order to provide observers with an inventory of concepts reflecting the complexity of stratification processes. At the core of his scheme are the two classificatory ideal types noted above—social classes and status groups—and the following discussion is organized in terms of this analytical distinction.

Social Classes. According to Weber, a class consists of those persons who have a similar ability to obtain positions in society, procure goods and services for themselves, and enjoy them via an appropriate life-style.[54] Hence, in Weber's terminology, classes are statistical aggregates rather than groups (although he recognized that people with similar economic characteristics can occasionally organize themselves into groups). As such, the process by which people obtain positions, purchase goods and services, and enjoy them is characterized by an individualistic rather than a group orientation. For example, even though investors trying to make money on the stock market may have some common interests, may share certain kinds of information with one another, and may even join together to prevent outsiders from participating, they each act individually in seeking profits or in experiencing losses. Further, in the process of seeking profits, their behavior is typically characterized by an instrumentally rational orientation—that is, action is based on a systematic calculation of means and ends based on knowledge (even if such knowledge is imperfect).

In Weber's analysis, classes are essentially economic phenomena that can only exist in a legally regulated money market where income and profit are the desired goals. In such a context, people's membership in a class can be determined very objectively, based upon their power to dispose of goods or skills for the sake of income. And income, of course, can be exchanged for goods or services, or for education, which can qualify a person for an occupational position. For this reason Weber felt that one's "class situation is, in this sense, ultimately [a] market

---

[54] Ibid., pp. 302 and 927.

situation."[55] Two of the most important characteristics of a money market are that, in its logically pure form, it is impersonal and objective. For example, in the purchase of stock, a person's ethnicity, religion, or family background are all irrelevant, since all that matters (or is supposed to matter) are such objective factors as one's cash and credit rating. Similarly, a person's class situation is also objectively determined, with the result that people can be ranked in terms of their common economic characteristics and life chances.

A key problem, of course, involves the basis on which people are to be identified as having similar amounts of economic power and placed together in classes. At least one commentator has charged that the Weberian analysis is not very useful because it allows for the possibility of an infinite number of classes.[56] His argument is based on the idea that since no two people will have exactly the same positions, goods, and life-styles, they cannot have either similar economic interests or similar amounts of economic power—ergo, the number of possible classes is infinite. But this interpretation is incorrect, for Weber argued explicitly that while people are never exactly alike it is still possible to conceptually delineate "the class structure of the advanced societies" in a way that is both helpful to observers and subjectively meaningful to the participants, and he provided sociologists with a conceptual map that is still used today. Like Marx, Weber began by distinguishing between those who have property and those who do not. As he put it, " 'property' and 'lack of property' are . . . the basic categories of all class situations." For the possession or nonpossession of income-producing property (or capital) allows for fundamentally different styles of life, and as we shall see, differences in lifestyle are the key to status distinctions in modern societies.

Considering first those who own income-producing property, Weber argued that they are differentiated according to the use to which their possessions are put. "The propertied, for instance, may belong to the class of rentiers or to the class of entrepreneurs."[57] In Weber's terminology, *rentiers* are those who live primarily off fixed incomes from investments or trust funds; for example, stock dividends or interest from tax-free municipal bonds. In Weber's time the German Junkers were rentiers, since these old families controlled much of the land and received their

---

[55] Ibid., p. 928.

[56] Anthony Giddens, *The Class Structure of the Advanced Societies.* (New York: Harper & Row, 1973), p. 78.

[57] Weber, *Economy and Society*, pp. 303 and 928. On Weber's analysis of the German *Junkers*, see Bendix, *Intellectual Portrait*, pp. 85–87.

incomes from peasants or tenant farmers who actually worked it. As a result of their possession of capital, the Junkers were able to lead a less overtly acquisitive life-style than most Germans; yet they had a great deal of economic power and social honor. According to Weber, *entrepreneurs* are those persons, such as merchants, shipowners, and bankers, who own and operate businesses. Weber called them a commercial or entrepreneurial class because they actually work their property for the economic gain it produces, with the result that in absolute terms the members of the entrepreneurial class often have more economic power, but less social honor, than rentiers.

This distinction between the uses to which capital-producing property is put allowed Weber to differentiate between those who work as an avocation and those who work because they must; that is, it reflects fundamental differences in life-style. These variations in life-style, Weber believed, reflect differences in values that serve to demarcate rentiers and entrepreneurs as distinct status groups. Thus, in most societies there exist privileged status groups, such as rentiers, the members of which "consider almost any kind of overt participation in economic acquisition as absolutely stigmatizing," despite its potential economic advantages.[58] Thus, Weber argued, even though economic (or class) oriented action is individualistic and dominated by instrumentally rational action, values that are noneconomic in origin always impinge themselves on behavior.

This same point can be made in another way as well. Weber asserted that the possession of capital by both rentiers and entrepreneurs, despite their differences, provides them with great economic and political power, and sharply distinguishes them from those who do not own such property.[59] Both rentiers and entrepreneurs are able to monopolize the purchase of expensive consumer items; both can and do pursue monopolistic sales and pricing policies, whether legally or not; to some extent, both can and do control opportunities for others to acquire wealth and property; and finally, both rentiers and entrepreneurs monopolize costly status privileges, such as education, that provide young people with future contacts and skills. In these terms, then, rentiers and entrepreneurs can be seen to have (roughly) similar levels of power and, in part because they are always a very small proportion of the population, they are often able to act together to protect their life-styles. The distribution of property, in short, tends to prevent nonowners from competing for highly

---

[58] Weber, *Economy and Society*, p. 937.
[59] Ibid., pp. 303 and 927.

valued goods and perpetuates the system of stratification from one generation to another.

In constructing his conceptual map of the class structure, Weber
next considered those who do not own income-producing property. Despite the fact that they do not own the means of production, such
persons are not without economically and politically important resources;
and they can be meaningfully differentiated into a number of classes.
The main criteria that Weber used in making class distinctions among
the unpropertied are the worth of their services and the level of their
skills, since both factors are important indicators of people's ability to
obtain positions, purchase goods, and enjoy them. In Weber's classificatory scheme, the "middle classes" are composed of those individuals
who today would be called white-collar workers because the skills they
sell do not involve manual labor: public officials, such as politicians and
administrators; managers of businesses; members of the professions, such
as doctors and lawyers; teachers and intellectuals; and specialists of various
sorts, such as technicians, low-level white-collar employees, and civil
servants.[60] Because their skills are in relatively high demand in industrial
societies, these persons generally have more economic and political power
than those who work with their hands. According to Weber, the less-
privileged propertyless classes are composed of people who today would
be called blue-collar workers because their skills primarily involve manual
labor. Without much explanation, Weber said that such persons can
be divided into three levels: skilled, semiskilled, and unskilled workers.

By means of these classificatory ideal types, Weber provided a description of a modern complex class structure in which the key factors distinguishing one class from another are the uses to which property are put
by those who own it and the worth of the skills and services offered
by those who do not own it. These factors combine in the marketplace
to produce identifiable aggregates, or classes, the members of which
have a similar ability to obtain positions, purchase goods, and enjoy
them via appropriate life-styles.

The final topic of importance in Weber's analysis of social class is
the possibility of group formation and unified political action on the
part of the propertyless classes. Weber felt that this phenomenon is
relatively rare in history because those who are propertyless generally
fail to recognize their common interests. As a result, action based on
a similar class situation is often restricted to inchoate and relatively
brief mass reactions. Nonetheless, throughout history perceived differ-

---

[60] Ibid., p. 304.

ences in life chances have periodically led to class struggles, although in most of these cases the point of conflict focused on rather narrow economic issues, such as wages or prices, rather than the nature of the political system that perpetuates their class situation.[61] While Weber only briefly alluded to the conditions under which the members of the propertyless classes might challenge the existing political order, he did identify some of the same variables that Marx had: (1) large numbers of persons must perceive themselves to be in the same class situation; (2) they must be ecologically concentrated, as in urban areas; (3) clearly understood goals must be articulated by an intelligentsia (here, Weber suggested that people must be shown that the causes and consequences of their class situation result from the structure of the political system itself); and (4) the opponents must be clearly identified. The reason for this last criterion is that, historically, the most bitter class struggles occurred only between the workers and the representatives of the proper-tied classes. As Weber put it, "it is not the rentier, the shareholder, and the banker who suffer the ill will of the worker, but almost exclusively the manufacturer and the business executive who are the direct opponents of workers in wage conflicts." Yet it is precisely the owners of capital who are the workers' real opponents in industrial conflicts.

Status Groups. In Weber's work, social status refers to the evaluations people make of one another, and a status group is comprised of those individuals who share "a specific, positive or negative, social estimation of honor."[62] Essentially, Weber used the concepts of "status" and "status group" to distinguish the sphere of prestige evaluation from that of monetary calculation. Although the two are highly interrelated, the analytical distinction is designed to emphasize the fact that people's actions cannot be understood in economic terms alone, rather, their values often play an important role in channeling action in specific directions. Thus, as in the *Protestant Ethic,* Weber's analysis of social stratification also showed how cultural phenomena circumscribe social action and, in so doing, refuted the Marxist emphasis on economic factors as the primary causal agents in history.

The decisive difference between class and status can be summarized in the following way. On the one hand, because the income from a person's job provides the ability to purchase goods and enjoy them, class membership is objectively determined based upon a simple monetary calculation. On the other hand, because status and honor are based on

---

[61] Ibid., pp. 305 and 930–31.
[62] Ibid., pp. 305–6 and 932.

the personal evaluations people make of one another, one's membership in a status group is always subjectively determined. Hence, status-oriented behavior is illustrative of value-rational action; that is, action based on some value or values held for their own sake. Thus, rather than behaving in terms of their economic interests, status-oriented action involves people acting as members of a group with whom they share a specific style of life and level of social honor. In Weber's words, "in contrast to classes, *Stände* (status groups) are normally groups. They are, however, of an amorphous kind"[63] For example, corporate executives dining together during the lunch hour rather than with the blue-collar subordinates are engaged in value-rational action, since they are acting rationally in terms of their values, or ideas of honor, and they are expressing their common life-style. In principle, prestige or honor can be attributed based on virtually any quality that is both valued and shared by an aggregate of people.

It is important to recognize that status groups exist at all levels, and that they generally correspond to the social classes identified above. Thus, skilled blue-collar people (say, unionized construction workers) are as much a status group as corporate executives, and the differences between the two groups, expressed by a lack of commensality (an unwillingness to eat with one another), suggest both the defining quality of status groups and the link between class and status: prestige or honor results from a specific style of life that is expected of all those who would belong to the group. Thus, despite the fact that the two concepts refer to analytically distinct phenomena, in practice classes and status groups tend to coalesce such that the ranks within each hierarchy parallel each other and people tend to be at the same level on each.

With some prescience, Weber noted that individuals develop styles of living in light of their parental background and upbringing, formal education, and occupational experiences—factors that have been subsequently shown to be fundamental to the process of status attainment.[64] On these bases, people at all levels tend to associate with others whom they perceive as having similar life-styles and they frequently try to prevent the entry of outsiders into the group. For despite their amorphous qualities, the members of status groups are both aware of their situation and active in maintaining it. The mechanism by which this is accomplished is inherently based on a subjective judgment, but it is consciously used and powerful in its consequences: social discrimination.[65]

---

[63] Ibid., p. 932.

[64] Ibid., p. 306.

[65] Reinhard Bendix, "Inequality and Social Structure: A Comparison of Marx and Weber," *American Sociological Review* 39 (April 1974):153.

Essentially, Weber argued, status "always rests on distance and exclusiveness" in the sense that members of a status group actively express and protect their life-styles in a number of specific ways: (1) they extend hospitality only to social equals, (2) they restrict potential marriage partners to social equals (connubium), (3) they practice unique social conventions and activities, and (4) they try to monopolize "privileged modes of acquisition."[66] This last tactic is important, for those in common status positions act politically in order to close off social and economic opportunities to outsiders in order to protect their capital or occupational investments. For example, because particular skills (say, in doctoring or carpentry) acquired over time necessarily limit the possibility for acquiring other skills, competing individuals "become interested in curbing competition" and preventing the free operation of the market. So they join together and, in spite of continued competition among themselves, attempt to close off opportunities for outsiders by influencing the creation and administration of law. Such attempts at occupational closure are everrecurring at all status levels, and they are "the source of property in land as well as of all guild [or union] monopolies."[67] The result is that "privileged modes of acquisition" are retained, people's life-styles are protected, and the system of strata is maintained.

As a final point in the analysis of status groups, Weber argued that the attempt by members of status groups to discriminate against others in order to protect their style of life can have extreme consequences, for the segregation of status groups can evolve into castes in which positions are closed by legal and religious sanctions. However, he believed that caste distinctions usually develop only when based on underlying ethnic or racial differences, as has occurred in the United States. But Weber emphasized that patterns of ethnic segregation do not inevitably, or even normally, produce caste relations. The latter are always dependent on unique historical events.[68]

CONCLUSION

The originality of Max Weber's sociology lies in its dual rejection of both Marxism and theory that is modeled after the natural sciences. In 1904, Weber asserted that his aim was "to understand the uniqueness

---

[66] Weber, *Economy and Society*, pp. 306 and 935.

[67] Ibid., pp. 342–43.

[68] Ibid., p. 933. On the importance of ethnicity in Weber's work, see Michael Hechter, "The Political Economy of Ethnic Change," *American Journal of Sociology* 79 (March 1974):1151–78; and "Response to Cohen: Max Weber on Ethnicity and Ethnic Change," *American Journal of Sociology* 81 (March 1976): 1162–69.

of the reality in which we move," and he never deviated from this goal. Because of his twin emphases on understanding social action in terms of the subjective meanings people attach to their behavior and conceptualizing patterns of interaction in terms of ideal types, Weber succeeded in conveying an understanding of the modern world to an extent that has probably not been surpassed by any subsequent sociologist.

However, in the next chapter we turn to a consideration of some of the abstract theoretical models and principles that can be extracted from his work. While this effort reflects a theoretical orientation that Weber rejected, this rejection was probably shortsighted. For subsequent theoretical work has shown that certain important aspects of human behavior and organization can be understood when sociologists pursue the construction of general theories. It is to be hoped that the research strategy adopted here is seen as a useful addition to Weber's approach to the study of social organization rather than a rejection of it. It will also allow Weber's work to endure beyond the specific times and places that he so fervently wished to "understand."

11

MAX WEBER III:
MODELS AND PRINCIPLES

THE BASIC THEORETICAL APPROACH

Max Weber's approach to the study of social organization must be looked at in light of his goals: (1) a social scientific understanding of the origin and nature of modern society and (2) the development of conceptual tools, such as ideal types, that would facilitate such understanding. In order to achieve these two goals, and thereby to establish sociology as an academic discipline, Weber developed a methodological approach that was unique among the classical social theorists. While it is an old stereotype that Weber's methodological writings are relatively unconnected to his substantive works,[1] his portrait of the origin and nature of modern society is consistent with his methodological vision.

As we have emphasized in the previous chapter, this vision has three main elements. First, Weber argued that the research process in sociology must be value free, for all sciences share a single goal: the search for truth through the use of rational methods, clear concepts, and logical inferences. Thus, he believed that there is no place in the social sciences for ethically or politically committed interpretations of historical events. Second, Weber recognized that in both the natural and social sciences, researchers' value orientations inevitably guide the selection of topics

---

[1] For example, see Stephen Warner, "The Role of Religious Ideas and the Use of Models in Max Weber's Comparative Studies of Non-Capitalist Societies," *Journal of Economic History* 30 (March 1970):88; and Thomas Burger, *Max Weber's Theory of Concept Formation: History, Laws, and Ideal Types* (Durham, N.C.: Duke University Press, 1976), p. 119.

for study.[2] Hence, while there can be no scientific justification for his specific concern with the significance of the Protestant ethic or his more general concern with understanding the nature of the modern world, these topics were deemed important in European intellectual circles during Weber's time, and he simply tried to contribute to an ongoing debate. That his work still incites controversy today is a testament to the continuing importance of Weber's choice of topics. Third, and perhaps most important, Weber felt that it is necessary to understand social phenomena at "the level of meaning" and that it is best to employ ideal types in order to obtain such understanding. This strategy not only allowed him to bridge the gap between the cultural disciplines and the natural sciences as they existed in Germany; it also allowed him to justify sociology as a scientific enterprise.

These elements of Weber's approach make his work unique and give it enormous descriptive power. Indeed, as much as any sociologist of his time, Weber was able to isolate the key processes underlying the historical events of the last few centuries. Yet his work also presents some theoretical limitations. The most significant of these is the historical specificity of his models and principles. While this specificity has great descriptive merit, it often becomes difficult to translate Weber's ideas into abstract models and principles that transcend a particular historical period and location. It is nevertheless useful to attempt this translation of Weber's empirical and analytical work into more abstract models and principles, for in making the attempt, we can more fully appreciate the nature of Weberian sociology.

WEBER'S THEORETICAL MODELS

The most difficult problem in trying to extract models from Weber's work revolves around liberating his ideas from their historical context. Some would, of course, consider such an effort to be inappropriate; indeed, this kind of exercise violates the very essence of Weber's sociology. But our focus in this chapter is not on Weber's strategy, but on what his works can offer to sociology as a purely theoretical enterprise.

We believe that Weberian sociology consists of two types of abstract models. One type deals with articulating the basic dimensions of the social universe. The other concerns isolating the properties of social

---

[2] The controversy over values has not abated. See William Goode, "The Place of Values in Social Analysis," in his *Explorations in Social Theory* (New York: Oxford University Press, 1973), pp. 33–63.

change, especially as social systems move from undifferentiated to differentiated states.

Basic Dimensions of the Social Universe

In all of Weber's work, he employed, at least implicitly, a vision of the social universe that consists of three analytically separable dimensions: (1) culture, (2) patterns of social action, and (3) psychological orientations (see Figure 11–1). Cultural values and beliefs, patterned ways of acting in the world, and psychological states are all reciprocally related.[3] *The Protestant Ethic and the Spirit of Capitalism* is perhaps the best illustration of this model, for as was emphasized in the last chapter, the

FIGURE 11–1
Weber's Model of the Basic Dimensions of the Social Universe

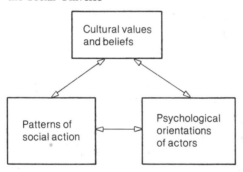

Protestant Ethic is an attempt at understanding what Weber called the "spirit of capitalism." It will be recalled that the components of the spirit of capitalism include an emphasis on work as an end in itself, an emphasis on the legitimacy of acquisition and profit, an emphasis on living a methodical life-style in order to obtain economic success, and a belief that immediate happiness and pleasure should be foregone in expectation of greater satisfaction in the future (that is, in the next world). Stripped of their religious connection, all of these phenomena have become fundamental Western cultural values; that is, they embody shared beliefs about right and wrong, appropriate and inappropriate behavior. The *Protestant Ethic* is, therefore, a book about culture and

---

[3] In this and other ways, Weber contributed to the development of Talcott Parsons' sociology; see the latter's *The Social System* (Glencoe, Ill.: Free Press, 1951), and his subsequent writings.

seeks the origin of the values dominating modern life. And Weber's answer, of course, is that these values are the secular result of certain peculiar religious movements that began in the 17th century.

But the book is about much more than cultural phenomena. Indeed, Weber was no more an idealist than Marx. Since the Puritan's religious beliefs plainly did not become dominant cultural values by themselves, Weber had to take into account the extent to which both patterns of social action and people's psychological orientations are reciprocally related to the cultural values that he was analyzing. Thus, he argued that the religious beliefs characteristic of the Reformed faiths fundamentally influenced patterns of social action among people—not only among the Puritans but also among those who came into contact with the underlying beliefs of these faiths. Given the rise of industrialization along with a number of other vitally important historical events, none of which Weber bothered to state explicitly in the *Protestant Ethic* but of which he was clearly aware, Puritan values spread in part because people found them to be congenial to their own secular ambitions as they developed during a time of great change. Hence, as people adopted new beliefs and values they altered their daily lives and, conversely, as individuals began living in new ways (often because they were forced to) they changed their fundamental beliefs and values. Thus, historically new patterns of social action reinforced the new values that had arisen.

Weber, however, concentrated on the Puritans themselves, describing the psychological consequences their beliefs must have had for their daily lives. Because of their uncertainty and isolation, people looked for signs, and found them in the ability to work hard and maintain their faith. Hence, the Puritan's psychological needs led them to historically new and unique patterns of social action characterized not only by hard work (for medieval peasants certainly worked as hard) but also by a methodical pursuit of worldly goods. The inevitable result was the secularization of Puritan religious values and their transformation into what has come to be called the spirit of capitalism. Hence, it is possible to extrapolate from Weber's analysis a set of generic factors—culture, patterns of social action, and psychological orientations—that are taken today as the fundamental features of social organization in social scientific analyses.

Weber's model of the most general components of social organization has proven to be of tremendous significance in the development of sociology. For example, virtually all introductory sociology textbooks (which we will use here as a rough indicator of the state of the field) now contain a series of chapters, usually located at the beginning, titled something like "culture," "social structure" or "society," and "personality and socialization." The reason for this practice is that these topics provide an essential conceptual orientation to the discipline of sociology. Weber's model, then, serves as a heuristic device rather than a dynamic analysis of the process of interaction. It can, however, lead to such an analysis—which is all Weber intended. Thus, the model is an essential first step in the construction of a set of concepts that would be useful in describing and, hence, in understanding modern societies.

Weber's Models of Social Change

Weberian sociology is oriented toward understanding the properties and direction of social change, especially during the process of industrialization in the West. As such, it is purely descriptive, since it is concerned with the historical events of the past few hundred years, and as a consequence, it is not easy to develop models from Weber's work that transcend this historical epoch. Yet we can at least make Weber's models somewhat more abstract, although we must admit that they are still tied to a limited range of empirical events. In this attempt at making Weber's models more abstract, we have developed two different types of models: (1) a model of evolution and (2) a model of internal system dynamics.

Weber's Evolutionary Model. Although Weber generally eschewed evolutionary analyses of history, his description of the finality with which the nature of authority in Western societies changed from traditional to rational-legal implies just such an interpretation. The key dynamic of this change revolves around problems of integration created by disjunctions among (and within) cultural values and beliefs, patterns of action, and psychological orientations. Under a variety of unpredictable empirical conditions, such disjunctions create "crises" in those systems where a significant segment of the population questions the existing leadership and the basis of leadership. Such crises, Weber implicitly argued, are escalated when inequality in the system increases. When power, wealth, and prestige are highly correlated, when rewards are distributed inequally, and when rates of upward mobility are low, then those in subordinate positions begin to recognize the conflict of interest between them and elites. If charismatic leaders can mobilize the sentiments of subordinates, then change in the system can occur. But charismatic authority presents its own problems of coordination and control, with the result that new charismatic leaders may emerge. But eventually, charisma is routinized through the creation of rational-legal authority.

This general vision of evolutionary change can be diagramed in several different ways. One way is presented in Figure 11–2. In this model the similarities and differences between Marx and Weber are highlighted. In Figure 11–2, the movement of social systems from traditional to rational-legal authority is seen as related to inequality and charisma. The arrows connecting the boxes emphasize that there is a sequence, or direction, to change. The arrows from the bottom emphasize that unique historical events will influence the rate of movement from one stage to another. The feedback arrows on the top stress that, under particular circumstances, a social system may cycle at a given stage. For example, one charismatic leader may create, and be unable to resolve, integrative problems that push the system back to traditional authority. But, despite the fact that a system may cycle at a given stage, or temporarily regress to a previous stage, Weber implied that a worldwide movement to forms of rational-legal authority was inevitable over the long run. It is this feature of Weber's argument that makes his thought evolutionary.

Weber's Model of Internal System Dynamics. The cycling of systems at a given stage of evolution underscores the fact that integrative problems—typically associated with disjunctions among cultural values, action patterns, and psychological orientations—can create processes for change. Figure 11–3 diagrams how Weber visualized internal system dynamics as societies attempt to resolve integrative problems. It also suggests a somewhat different way of interpreting his analysis of the process of social change.

Weber argued that the struggle for power is a continuous process in every society. For example, in traditional societies rulers attempt to enlarge their areas of discretion and power at the expense of administra-

FIGURE 11–2
Weber's Evolutionary Model of Social Change

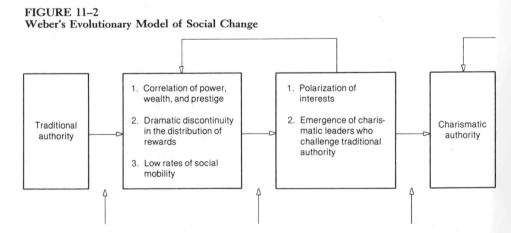

tive officials and notables. They do so by various methods: for example, the use of military force, economic coercion, co-optation, and political alliances. In all cases, they continue to justify their action in terms of those customs that have been handed down over generations. Conversely, officials and notables attempt to increase their power at the expense of the rulers, and they use many of the same tactics. While this pattern can remain stable for many years, the gradual development of structural disjunctions—as signified by incongruity among values and beliefs, patterns of action, and psychological orientations—is not uncommon. As indicated in Figure 11–3, it is during the crises emerging from such mal-integration that charismatic leaders are most likely to emerge and attempt to change the course of history. If such leaders are ineffective, the crises may continue and even escalate, with the result that leaders will eventually lose their following as the population turns to some other charismatic figure for solutions. But if the charismatic leaders are effective in resolving crises, then the process of routinization occurs as their authority is implemented over time. The inevitable result is the transformation of charismatic authority into either a traditional or rational-legal form of domination. In this context, Weber argued, the development of rational-legal authority makes a reoccurrence of traditional domination less likely. What is more likely is that social systems characterized by rational-legal forms of authority will resolve integrative crises in such a way that patterns of social action reflect either instrumental or value-rational orientations. However, the choice between these two alternatives is not inevitable, since Weber emphasized the importance of chance in human history. Hence, Figure 11–3 builds in the possibility (even

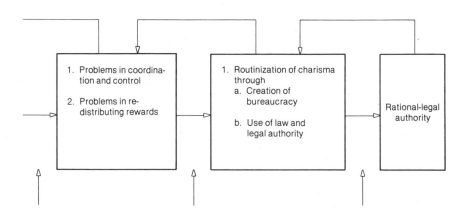

FIGURE 11-3
Weber's Model of Internal System Dynamics

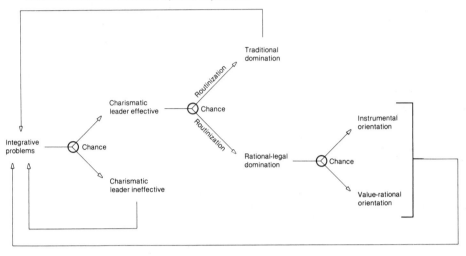

if unlikely) that a society can resolve integrative problems by returning to a form of traditional authority.

In sum, when Weber's ideas are translated into more abstract models, they can seem rather pedestrian, primarily because the empirical content that made them so rich has been extracted. Yet Figures 11-2 and 11-3 underscore the fact that, at times, Weber's empirical descriptions can be translated into abstract models that can provide theoretical leads. But it would still be difficult to visualize Weber's models as equal to those developed by Marx, Spencer, or Pareto. We should emphasize, of course, that such models were not Weber's goal. But in a book on the development of sociological theory, defined as an interrelated set of timelessly valid propositions, we have been compelled to see if interesting abstract models exist in Weber's work.

WEBER'S THEORETICAL PRINCIPLES

While Weber's historical approach is clearly useful for describing the origin and nature of modern Western societies, his rejection of general theory in sociology was shortsighted. By stating explicitly how the generic elements of social organization are interrelated, sociologists have an additional and a very powerful means for understanding the structure of social action. Further, an emphasis on the formulation of theoretical principles makes it easier to test theories than when Weber's approach is followed. Hence, we need to examine Weber's major works to see if any abstract theoretical principles exist. That is, did Weber implicitly formulate a set of timelessly valid propositions? As might be expected from his basic approach, our answer is that very few such statements can be gleaned from his works. Nonetheless, the small number of principles that we have extrapolated from Weber's writings are here divided into three groups: (1) those dealing with charismatic leadership and authority, (2) those dealing with social stratification, and (3) those dealing with the likelihood of revolutionary action by dispossessed people.

Principles of Charismatic Leadership and Authority

As indicated in Figure 11–3, Weber emphasized the role of chance in human affairs and was not really interested in making judgments about their future direction. However, his analysis of charisma implicitly contains a set of theoretical principles dealing with the origins of charismatic leadership and the consequences of charismatic authority. These propositions are summarized here.

1. The lower is the level of integration in a social system, the more likely are incumbents in that system to articulate their grievances, and hence, the more likely are they to be receptive to the influence of charismatic leaders.
2. The less effective is a charismatic leader in resolving the grievances of incumbents in a system, the more likely are integrative problems to escalate, and hence, the more likely is a leader's authority to decrease; and conversely, the more effective is a charismatic leader in resolving the grievances of incumbents in a system, the more likely are integrative problems to decrease, and hence, the more likely is a charismatic leader's authority to endure.
3. The more effective a charismatic leader is in resolving system incumbents' grievances, the more likely is that leader to change the existing social structural arrangements as well as the cultural values and psychological orientations of system incumbents.
4. The longer is the duration of charismatic authority, the more likely are decision-making tasks to be transferred to an administrative staff, and hence, the more likely is the relationship between the leader and system incumbents to be transformed from one based upon charisma into one based upon law or tradition.

Weber argued that charismatic leaders are often catalysts for social change, and this first set of principles attempts to rephrase his argument as abstract theoretical statements. Thus, Proposition 1 identifies the most important factor stimulating the emergence of charismatic leaders: low levels of integration in a system—as signified again by an incompatibility among the values and beliefs people hold, their patterns of action, their psychological orientations, or any combination of these factors. When integration declines, such incongruities come to be defined as problems and translated into grievances that must be resolved. And it is often the case that charismatic leaders are the only persons who seem able to provide solutions. The actual effectiveness of the leaders' solutions is, of course, critical, since those leaders who appear to be less effective tend to lose authority, as in Proposition 2. However, those charismatic leaders who are effective often serve as historical catalysts, leading people in new directions (Proposition 3). For example, one of the great virtues of *The Protestant Ethic and the Spirit of Capitalism* is its implicit demonstration of the manner in which the leaders of the reformed faiths were able to combine people's spiritual concerns (for certitude of life after death) with their material concerns (for economic success in this world). The juxtaposition of these two needs in the context of the large number of other historical changes accounts for the transformative impact of the Protestant ethic during the 17th and 18th centuries.

Finally, one of Weber's greatest insights was his recognition that charismatic authority is inherently unstable; it must be routinized through the development of an administrative staff that can make and enforce decisions. Hence, as specified in Proposition 4, the longer is the duration of charismatic authority, then the more such tasks are delegated to an administrative staff—whether it be some form of patrimonial hierarchy or a modern bureaucracy.

Principles of Stratification

As with all his works, Weber's essays on social stratification represent an attempt to describe the characteristics of modern Western societies. However, despite the brilliance of this description, only two abstract principles are readily extracted from the corpus of this work.

5. **The more status differences are based on ascriptive criteria and the more salient such criteria are, then the greater is the range of discrimination against those having different life-styles.**
6. **The lower is the rate of technological change in a system, the**

> more stable is the stratification system and the higher is the
> level of social integration; and conversely, the higher is the rate
> of technological change in the system, then the less stable is
> the stratification system and the lower is the level of social
> integration.

In all societies, Weber said, people act to protect their way of life
from the encroachments of others who are regarded as socially inferior.
He noted that some of the more common strategies people use involve
restrictions on hospitality offered to others, restrictions on potential marriage partners among the young, the practice of unique social customers,
and the monopolization of property. But more generally, as specified
in Proposition 5, Weber's analysis implies that when ascriptive criteria,
such as race or religion, become the basis for status attainment in a
society, then the range of discrimination against those with different
life-styles becomes much broader. For example, sometimes the result
can be relatively rigid, or castelike, divisions among the population.

Weber was also concerned with the effect of technological change
on society. For example, it has been emphasized that the culture of
capitalism originated during a time of great historical change. One of
the most significant changes occurring during that period was the development of increasing knowledge of how to manipulate the environment
to satisfy human needs. An important result of such technological changes
was the complete transformation of the system of stratification from
one based on the possession of land to one based on the possession of
capital. At the same time, of course, the cultural basis on which Western
societies were integrated was also completely transformed. Weber believed that this joint development was no accident. His argument has
been expressed here in Proposition 6 which summarizes more abstractly
the relationships implied by Weber's analysis. Thus, in general, low
rates of technological change result in a stable stratification system and
a high level of social integration, while high rates of technological change
have the opposite effect.

Principles of Conflict and Change

Like all his works, Weber's essays on social stratification are an attempt
at refuting Marxist thought. Yet Weber evidently felt compelled to
recognize Marx's assertions about the conditions under which those without property will view the distribution of resources within a society as
illegitimate and will attempt to change the system and the distribution

of scarce resources. Hence, Weber's first two principles of revolution essentially repeat Marx's assertions.

7. The continuity in patterns of social organization is a positive function of the degree of legitimacy given to political authority, and the degree of legitimacy of political authority is a negative function of the following:

    7a. The degree of correlation of status, classes, and power, with the degree of correlation being a negative function of rationality in, and complexity of, patterns of organization.

    7b. The degree of discontinuity in social hierarchies, with the degree of discontinuity being a negative function of rationality in, and complexity of, patterns of social organization.

    7c. The degree to which upward mobility for lower-ranking units is blocked, with the degree of blockage being a negative function of rationality in, and complexity of, patterns of social organization.

8. The degree of change in patterns of social organization is a positive function of conflict, and the degree of conflict is a positive function of the following:

    8a. The degree of polarization of status, class, and power groups, with the degree of polarization being a positive function of 7a, 7b, and 7c.

    8b. The availability of charismatic leaders who oppose the existing distribution of power.

CONCLUSION

In conclusion, when the purpose of sociological theory is seen as the development of abstract principles that have wide empirical applicability, then Weber clearly did not contribute a great deal of theoretical development in sociology. Because he pursued his basic approach with great consistency, Weber's work does not lead to very many of the sort of propositions in which we are most interested. This is one reason why it is normally difficult to place Weber in any of the dominant theoretical schools today, such as symbolic interactionism, conflict theory, or functionalism (see Chapter 25). Nonetheless, Weber is still regarded as one of the most important of the classical sociologists. We believe there are three main reasons for this attribution, only the first of which has been dealt with in these chapters. First, during a time when the origins and nature of modern industrial society were the fundamental issues facing intellectuals in all disciplines, Weber achieved his goals brilliantly. Perhaps no other sociologist has conveyed the uniqueness of modern Western society more insightfully than Max Weber. Second, the logic of Weber's approach and many of his key concepts have been taken over by subsequent empirically oriented sociologists. For example, much of the current work in social stratification, such as the literature on status attainment and status inconsistency, is essentially Weberian in both approach and in terms of the key concepts used. Finally, and this is a very controversial issue, while Weber did not pursue abstract sociological theory, he fundamentally influenced the single most important modern American theorist: Talcott Parsons. Essentially, Weber's research strategy was taken over and adapted by Parsons for his own, rather different, theoretical purposes. In these ways, then, Max Weber decisively contributed to the development of modern sociology.

12

GEORG SIMMEL I:
THE INTELLECTUAL ORIGINS
OF HIS THOUGHT

A NOTE ON SIMMEL AND WEBER

Georg Simmel's sociological writings span the same three decades, 1890 to 1920, as those of his German colleague and friend, Max Weber. However, despite the fact that both men worked in a similar social and cultural environment, their respective orientations to the sociological task were rather dissimilar, in part because each man was trained differently and, hence, responded to somewhat different influences.

Weber was trained in the law and in economics, with the result that he was forced to react to the *methodenstreit* (the German methodological controversy, see Chapter 9). As we have seen, Weber used the works of Dilthey and Rickert to fashion a unique sociology that eschewed the development of abstract laws, because he believed that such theoretical statements could not get at the significance of those historical phenomena in which he was most interested. In contrast, Simmel was a philosopher as well as a sociologist; his published works include books and articles on such diverse figures as the philosophers Arthur Schopenhauer, Friedrich Nietzsche, and Immanuel Kant; the writer, Johann Goethe; and the painter, Rembrandt. In addition, Simmel also considered morals, ethics, aesthetics, and many other topics from a philosophical vantage point. As might be expected, then, his brand of sociology is also unique, and quite different from Weber's. After an early dalliance with Herbert Spencer and some elements of Social Darwinism, Simmel's mature works reflect his adaptation of some of Kant's philosophical doctrines to the study of human society. Essentially, Simmel contended that the social processes in which human beings engage constitute orga-

260

nized and stable structures, that these patterns of social organization affect action in systematic ways, and that their consequences can be both observed and predicted independently of the specific objectives of the actors involved. Thus, unlike Max Weber, Simmel held that sociology should be oriented to the development of "timelessly valid laws" of social organization, a point of view that followed from his Kantian orientation.

However, Simmel and Weber were alike in at least one respect, for both felt compelled to react to the ideological and theoretical challenge posed by Marxism as it existed at the turn of the century. While this interest is more central to Weber's sociology than to Simmel's, the latter's analysis is a sociologically sophisticated rejection of Marx and Marxism.

HERBERT SPENCER, SOCIAL DARWINISM, AND SIMMEL'S THOUGHT

Like most of the classical social theorists, Simmel wished to understand the nature of the modern industrial societies. And the title of his first sociological treatise, *Social Differentiation*, published in 1890, suggests immediately the fundamental change that he saw: modern societies are much more differentiated than those of the past.[1] Like Herbert Spencer (see Chapter 4), Simmel saw this change in evolutionary terms and as an indication of human progress. Indeed he labeled it an "upward development." Further, just as Spencer often used organismic analogies to illustrate his argument, so did Simmel. For example, in *Social Differentiation* he argued that just as a more complex organism can save energy in relation to the environment and use that energy to perform more difficult and complex tasks, so can a more highly differentiated society.[2] Like Spencer, Simmel never confused biological analogies with social facts, partly because his arguments are also illustrated with many other kinds of analogies and examples. While some of Simmel's later works do not reveal much systematic concern with either the problem of evolution or the historical transition to industrialization, they display a lasting interest in understanding the structure of modern, differentiated societies and in showing how people's participation in complex social systems affects their behavior.

---

[1] Georg Simmel, *Ueber Sociale Differenzierung* (Leipzig: Duncker und Humblot, 1890). While most of this book remains untranslated, two chapters, "Differentiation and the Principle of Saving Energy" and "The Intersection of Social Spheres," do appear in *Georg Simmel: Sociologist and European*, trans. Peter Laurence (New York: Barnes & Noble, 1976).

[2] Simmel, "Differentiation and the Principle of Energy Saving."

The evolutionary discussion in *Social Differentiation* also shows a less attractive side to the young Simmel, since he embraced some of the more questionable aspects of the Social Darwinism that were current during the late 19th century. For example, he insisted "on the hereditary character of the criminal inclination," and even protested "against the preservation of the weak, who will transmit their inferiority to future generations."[3] However, Simmel's mature writings betray no trace of such views. In fact, while he generally did not comment on political events in a partisan manner, his analyses of the poor, of women, and of working people all suggest a sympathetic understanding of their plight.[4] In all these cases, Simmel's discussion reflects his more general attempt at focusing on the consequences of social differentiation in modern societies. His emphasis on demonstrating the manner in which social structures influence interaction among human beings independently of their specific purposes is one result of his neo-Kantian orientation.

IMMANUEL KANT AND SIMMEL'S THOUGHT

Immanuel Kant did not finish his most significant work until the age of 51. But that book, *The Critique of Pure Reason*, published in 1781, stimulated a revolution in philosophy.[5] Among other results, it led eventually to Hegel's denial that material phenomena are real (see Chapter 6). However, Hegel is hardly read today, except by Marxists, while Kant's influence has endured. In this section we will begin by sketching Kant's basic ideas and then briefly discuss the way in which Simmel adapted them for use in sociology.

Kant's Basic Ideas

In a short discourse on the nature of philosophy, Simmel remarked that individual philosophers often raise what appears to be a general

---

[3] Paul Honigsheim, "The Time and Thought of the Young Simmel," pp. 167–75 in Kurt Wolff, ed., *Essays on Sociology, Philosophy and Aesthetics by Georg Simmel et al.* (New York: Harper Torchbooks, 1965), p. 170.

[4] See Georg Simmel, "The Poor," in *Georg Simmel on Individuality and Social Forms* (Chicago: University of Chicago Press, 1971), pp. 150–78. On working people and women, see Georg Simmel, *Conflict and the Web of Group Affiliations* (Glencoe, Ill.: Free Press, 1955). See also Lewis A. Coser, "Georg Simmel's Neglected Contributions to the Sociology of Women." *Signs* 2 (Summer 1977):869–76.

[5] Immanuel Kant, *The Critique of Pure Reason* (London, Macmillan, 1929). Like Hegel, Kant is extraordinarily difficult to read and understand. For purposes of this brief discussion of his work we are following the interpretation offered in Will Durant, *The Story of Philosophy* (New York: Simon & Schuster, 1926). For a more complete analysis, see T. E. Wilkerson, *Kant's Critique of Pure Reason: A Commentary for Students* (Oxford: Oxford University Press, 1976).

problem, but they state the issue so that its solution conforms to their preconceptions.[6] Simmel undoubtedly had Kant in mind when stating this little aphorism, for Kant's *Critique of Pure Reason* is an investigation of the knowledge potential of "pure reason" that exists apart from the mundane and disorganized sense impressions which human beings experience. In phrasing the problem in this way, Kant's definition of "pure reason" is crucial. By this term he meant knowledge that exists independently of, or prior to, sense experience, which implies that "pure reason" is knowledge inherent to the structure of the mind. After defining the issue in this way, Kant was able to conclude that all human conceptions of the external world are products of the activity of the mind, which shapes the unformed and chaotic succession of sense impressions into a conceptual unity that can be understood in terms of scientific laws.[7]

While previous philosophers, such as John Locke and David Hume, had assumed that material phenomena are inherently organized and that human beings' sensations of objects and events in the world merely reflect that organization, Kant held that neither supposition is true. Rather, he asserted that the sensations people have are intrinsically chaotic, reflecting nothing more than the endless succession of sights, smells, sounds, odors, and other stimuli that, in and of themselves, are disorganized and meaningless. Kant claimed that the mind transforms this chaos of sense impressions into meaningful perceptions through a process he called the *transcendental aesthetic*. Simmel summarized this part of Kant's philosophy by observing that human sensations are "given forms and connections which are not inherent in them but which are imposed on them by the knowing mind as such."[8] This transformation of disorganized sensations into organized perceptions is accomplished by two fundamental "categories," or forms—space and time—which are inherent parts of the mind. In Kant's view, space and time are not things perceived but modes of perceiving that exist prior to, or independently of, our knowledge of the world; they are elements of "pure reason." Only by using these categories are human beings able to transform the chaotic sensations that they receive from the external world into systematic perceptions. The laws of mathematics are the best examples of both the a priori nature of space and time and the way in which the mind changes disorder into order. Thus, it has always been and always will be true that the shortest distance between two points is a straight line.

---

[6] Georg Simmel, "The Nature of Philosophy," in Wolff, ed., *Essays by Georg Simmel*, pp. 282–310.

[7] Simmel, "The Nature of Philosophy."

[8] Ibid., pp. 290–99.

Mathematical laws such as this are absolute and necessary to human perception of events and objects in the external world, for they allow people to orient themselves to the material phenomena making up the world.

Yet merely being able to perceive objects and events is not enough, for people's perceptions are not spontaneously organized either. Rather, like sensations, perceptions are experienced as confused sequences of observations. Thus, Kant emphasized that "pure reason" aims at the establishment of higher forms of knowledge: general truths that are independent of experience. These are the laws of science; truths that are abstract and absolute. Hence, in a process that Kant called *transcendental logic*, the mind transforms perceptual knowledge into conceptual knowledge—for example, the transformation of the observation of a falling apple into the law of gravity or (on a different level) the transformation of observations of action during conflict into laws stating the consequences of social conflict for human behavior. Kant claimed that the mind uses a set of a priori "categories," or forms, by which to arrange perceptions. For example, the ideas of cause, unity, reciprocal relations, necessity, and contingency are modes of conceptualizing empirical processes that are inherent to the mind; like space and time, they are elements of "pure reason." In Simmel's words, it is only through the activity of the mind that human perceptions "become what we call nature: a meaningful, intelligible coherence in which the diversity of things appears as a principled unity, knitted together by laws."[9] In this regard, Kant also insisted that the manner in which observations are conceptualized always depends on the purposes of the mind. For example, consider a system of thought, such as Darwin's theory of evolution or Marx's theory of revolution. Kant said that these means of conceptualizing empirical data (perceptions) reveal the purposeful activity of the mind, for in neither case are the objects or events in the world prearranged in the manner conceptualized by the theory. Thus, over the long run, scientific knowledge is one result of the existence of pure reason as an intrinsic characteristic of human beings.

In this context, it is important to remember that, unlike Hegel, Kant never denied the existence of the material world; he merely averred that human knowledge of external phenomena occurs through the forms imposed on it by the active mind. Put differently, the empirical world is an orderly place because the categories of thought organize our sensations, organize our perceptions, and organize our conceptions to produce

---

[9] Ibid.

systematic scientific knowledge. Nonetheless, while Kant contended that such knowledge is absolute, he also indicated that it is limited to the field of actual experience. Therefore, he believed that it is impossible to know what objects and events are "ultimately like" apart from the receptivity of human senses. One of the most important implications of this point of view is that attempts at discovering the nature of ultimate reality, either through religion or science, are impossible. In Kant's phrase, "understanding can never go beyond the limits of sensibility."[10]

Simmel's Adaptation of Kant's Ideas

The link between Kant and Simmel is most clearly explained in the latter's essay "How Is Society Possible?," which was originally appended to the first chapter of his *Sociology: Studies in the Forms of Sociation.*[11] According to Simmel, the basic question in Kant's philosophy is "how is nature possible?" That is, how is human knowledge of nature (the external world) possible? As we have seen, Kant answered this query by positing the existence of certain a priori categories that observers use to shape the chaotic sensations they receive into conceptual knowledge. This point of view means that when the elements of nature are conceptualized in some manner, their unity is entirely dependent on the purposes of the observer.

In contrast, the unity of society is both experienced by the participants and observed by sociologists. In Simmel's words, "the unity of society needs no observer. It is directly realized by its own elements [human beings] because these elements are themselves conscious and synthesizing units."[12] Thus, as people conduct their daily lives, they are absorbed in innumerable specific relationships with one another—economic, political, social, and familial, for example—and these connections give them an amorphous sense of their unity, a feeling that they are part of an ongoing and stable social structure. To Max Weber, the fact that people experience and attribute meaning to the social structures in which they participate indicates that neither the methods nor the goals of the natural sciences are appropriate for the social sciences. So he formulated a version of sociology oriented toward the scientific understanding of historical processes.

---

[10] Quoted in Durant, *Story of Philosophy*, p. 298.

[11] Georg Simmel, "How Is Society Possible?" in Wolff, ed., *Essays by Georg Simmel et al*, pp. 337–56.

[12] Ibid., p. 338.

Simmel, however, took a different view—one that has had lasting consequences for the emergence of sociological theory. Based on his study of Kant, Simmel argued that social structures (which he called *forms of interaction*) systematically influence people's behavior prior to and independently of an actor's specific purposes. And Simmel used this argument to show that theoretical principles of social action can be adduced, despite the complications inherent in the fact that human beings' own experiences are the objects of study. As he put it, the entire contents of *Sociology: Studies in the Forms of Sociation* constitute an inquiry "into the processes—those which, ultimately, reside in individuals—that condition the existence of individuals in society."[13] More generally, as we will show in the next chapter, Simmel's sociology is oriented toward identifying those basic social forms—conflict, group affiliation, exchange, size, inequality, and space—that influence social action regardless of the intentions of the participants. Because these forms constitute the structure (or, as Kant would say, the "categories") within which people seek to realize their goals, knowledge of the manner in which they affect social behavior can lead to theory. In this sense, then, Simmelian sociology is thoroughly Kantian in orientation. It is perhaps this philosophical underpinning that allowed Simmel to see some of the major pitfalls in Marx's work.

KARL MARX AND SIMMEL'S THOUGHT

Although the extent to which Simmel was familiar with Marx's writings is unknown, it must have been considerable. For Simmel's sociology constitutes a complete repudiation of the substance of Marx's major work, *Capital*, as well as a rejection of his basic revolutionary goal: the establishment of a cooperative society where people would be free to develop their human potential.[14] It will be recalled from Chapter 7 that *Capital* is an attempt at demonstrating that the value of commodities (including human beings) results from the labor power necessary to produce them; Marx called this the labor theory of value. In the *Philosophy of Money* (1907), Simmel rejected the labor theory of value by arguing more generally that people in all societies place value on items in light of their relative desirability and scarcity.[15] By following Kant rather than Hegel, Simmel believed that he could better account for the value that individuals attribute to commodities in different societies (capitalist as

---

[13] Ibid., p. 340.

[14] Karl Marx, *Capital* (New York: International Publishers, 1967).

[15] Georg Simmel, *The Philosophy of Money* (Boston: Routledge & Kegan Paul, 1978).

well as socialist) by showing how cultural and structural phenomena systematically influence what is both scarce and desired. In this way, then, he undercut the theoretical basis for Marx's analysis. However, it should be remembered that Marx has a rather different definition of science, and theory, than did Simmel, or any other classical social theorist.

Simmel rejected Marx's argument in a second way as well, by focusing on the importance of money as a medium of exchange. In *Capital*, Marx tried to show that one of the necessary consequences of capitalism is people's alienation from one another and from the commodities that they produce. In this regard, he emphasized the fact that actors have no control over those activities that distinguish them, as human beings, from other animals. Simmel approached the problem of alienation by simply recognizing that in any highly differentiated society people are inevitably going to be alienated. Indeed, Simmel saw as more fundamental the decline in personal and emotional contact among humans than the lack of control by people of their own activities. Apparently he believed that in most societies, most individuals lack control over their daily lives. However, having recognized the inevitability of alienation, Simmel went on to argue that the dominance of money as a medium of exchange in modern social systems helps to lower alienation; a fact that Marx, writing some 40 years earlier, had failed to see. While some of the positive consequences of money are identified here, a much fuller analysis of *The Philosophy of Money* is presented in the next chapter of this book. In opposition to Marx, Simmel argued that the widespread use of money allows exchanges between people who are spatially separated from one another, thereby creating multiple social ties and lowering the level of alienation. In addition, he suggested that the generalized acceptance of money in exchanges increases social solidarity because it signifies a relatively high degree of trust in the stability and future of the society. Finally, Simmel concluded that the dominance of money allows individuals to pursue a wider diversity of activities than is possible in barter or mixed economies, and hence, it gives them vastly increased options for self-expression. The result of this last factor, of course, is that people have greater control over their daily lives in money economies. As an aside, Simmel's explanation of the consequences of money in modern societies is a good example of the way in which social processes "condition the existence of individuals in society" independently of their specific purposes. In this case, the specific ways that money is used are less important, sociologically, than its effects on the general nature and form of human relationships in systems where money is the modal medium of social exchange.

Finally, Simmel also discussed Marx's formulation of the problem of alienation in his essay on the functions of social conflict. In that context, he reasoned that individuals probably have the best chance of developing their full human capacities in a competitive rather than a cooperative society.

> Once the narrow and naive solidarity of primitive social conditions yielded to decentralization (which was bound to have been the immediate result of the quantitative enlargement of the group), man's effort toward man, his adaptation to the other, seems possible only at the price of competition, that is, of the simultaneous fight *against* a fellowman *for* a third one— *against* whom, for that matter, he may well compete in some other relationship *for* the former. Given the breadth and individualization of society, many kinds of interest, which eventually hold the group together throughout its members, seem to come alive and stay alive only when the urgency and requirements of the competitive struggle force them upon the individual.[16]

Simmel did not deny, of course, that competition can have "poisonous, divisive, destructive effects;" rather he simply noted that these liabilities must be evaluated in light of the positive consequences of competition. Like money, Simmel claimed that competition gives people more freedom to satisfy their needs, and in this sense, a society that is competitively organized probably has less-alienated citizens. In addition, as indicated in the quotation, Simmel believed that competition is a form of conflict which promotes social solidarity in differentiated social systems because people establish ties with one another that involve a relatively constant "concentration on the will and feeling of fellowmen"—an argument that also implies a lessening of alienation. Finally, Simmel indicated that competition is an important means of creating values in society, a process that occurs as human beings produce objective values (commodities, for example) for purposes of exchange; in this way, they attain satisfaction of their own subjective needs and desires. This argument not only suggests that competitive societies display less alienation than do noncompetitive ones, it also implies that Marx's revolutionary goal— a cooperative society—is impractical in modern, industrialized, highly differentiated social systems. On this basis, Simmel rejected socialist and communist experiments inspired by Marxist thought. For he believed that they are attempts at institutionalizing, indeed enforcing, cooperative relationships among people in order to prevent the waste of energy and inequalities that inevitably occur in a competitive environment. However,

---

[16] Simmel, *Conflict.*

Simmel insisted that even though such results seem positive, they can only be "brought about through a central [political] directive which from the start organizes all [people] for their mutual interpenetration and supplementation."[17] And Simmel implied that an end to alienation will not and cannot occur in such an authoritarian social context. Thus, while Simmel's works do not represent a long-term debate "with the ghost of Marx," as was the case for Weber, Simmel addressed the same issues as Marx and other early theorists—issues such as the properties of social differentiation, inequality, power, conflict, cooperation, and the procedures for understanding the nature of the social world. This fact can best be appreciated by examining some of Georg Simmel's most basic works.

---

[17] Ibid., pp. 72–73.

13

GEORG SIMMEL II: THE BASIC WORKS

Simmel's writings do not constitute a fully articulated theoretical system, in part because of the disparate subjects he chose to explore.[1] In addition to the breadth of his interests, Simmel also had a tendency to deal with the same topics over and over again, each time revising and updating his thinking on the issue at hand. Simmel's investigations can thus be described as a series of prologues which are designed to justify the existence of sociology as an academic discipline. In this effort, Simmel succeeded brilliantly, and in order to illustrate his contribution to the development of sociological theory, this chapter considers four of his most significant studies. First, Simmel's methodological approach to the analysis of society is explained. Then, his sketch of the significance of people's "web of group affiliations" in modern societies is described.[2] Next, Simmel's explanation of the functions of social conflict is explicated.[3] And finally, his investigation into the importance of social exchange is reviewed.[4]

---

[1] Georg Simmel, *Sociology: Studies in the Forms of Sociation* (1908). This book, Simmel's major sociological work, still has not been completely translated, and what has been done appears in many different places. See note 21.

[2] Georg Simmel, "The Web of Group Affiliations," *Conflict and the Web of Group Affiliations,* trans. Reinhard Bendix (Glencoe, Ill.: Free Press, 1955), pp. 125–95. The original title of this essay was "The Intersection of Social Circles."

[3] Georg Simmel, "Conflict," *Conflict and the Web of Group Affiliations,* trans. Kurt Wolff, pp. 14–124. There is a long literature on this essay; see Lewis A. Coser, *The Functions of Social Conflict* (Glencoe, Ill.: Free Press, 1956); and Jonathan H. Turner, *The Structure of Sociological Theory,* rev. ed. (Homewood, Ill.: Dorsey Press, 1978), pp. 121–42. © 1978 by The Dorsey Press.

[4] Georg Simmel, *The Philosophy of Money,* trans. Tom Bottomore and David Frisby (Boston: Routledge & Kegan Paul, 1978).

SIMMEL'S METHODOLOGICAL APPROACH TO THE STUDY OF SOCIETY

In an essay titled "The Problem of Sociology," Simmel concluded as early as 1894 that an exploration of the basic and generic forms of interaction offered the only viable subject matter for the nascent discipline of sociology.[5] In chapter 1 of *Sociology: Studies in the Forms of Sociation*, written in 1908, he reformulated and reaffirmed his thoughts on this issue.[6] In 1918, he revised his thinking again in one of his last works, *Fundamental Problems in Sociology*.[7] In what follows, we rely mostly on this final brief sketch, since it represents his most mature statement.

Simmel began his book on the *Fundamental Problems of Sociology* by lamenting the fact that "the first difficulty which arises if one wants to make a tenable statement about the science of sociology is that its claim to be a science is not undisputed." In Germany after the turn of the century there were many scholars who still denied that sociology constituted a legitimate science, and in order to retain their power within the university system, they wanted to prevent its establishment as an academic field. Partly for these reasons, it was proposed that sociology should be merely a label to refer to all the social sciences dealing with specific content areas—such as economics, political science, and linguistics. This tactic was a ruse, of course, for Simmel (and many others) recognized that the existing disciplines had already divided up the study of human life and nothing would be "gained by throwing their sum total into a pot and sticking a new label on it: 'sociology.' "[8] In order to combat this strategy and to justify sociology as an academic field of study, Simmel argued that it was necessary for the new discipline to develop a unique and "unambiguous content [or subject matter], dominated by one, methodologically certain, problem idea."[9] However, we

---

[5] The translation appeared the following year. See Georg Simmel, "The Problem of Sociology," *Annals of the American Academy of Political and Social Science* 6 (1895):412–23.

[6] Georg Simmel, "The Problem of Sociology," in *Essays on Sociology, Philosophy and Aesthetics by Georg Simmel et al.* trans. Kurt Wolff (New York: Harper Torchbooks, 1959), pp. 310–36. This is chapter 1 of Simmel's, *Sociology: Studies in the Forms of Sociation.*

[7] Simmel, *Fundamental Problems of Sociology*, appears as part 1 of *The Sociology of Georg Simmel*, trans. Kurt Wolff (Glencoe, Ill.: Free Press, 1950):3–86.

[8] Ibid., p. 4.

[9] This remark is from the "Preface" to *Sociology: Studies in the Forms of Sociation;* it is quoted in Kurt Wolff's "Introduction" to *The Sociology of Georg Simmel*, p. xxvi.

shall see that while he succeeded splendidly in identifying a conceptually significant subject for sociology, there is nonetheless an important area of weakness inherent in his analysis. Simmel's discussion is organized around three questions: What is society? How should sociology study society? What are the problem areas of sociology?

What Is Society?

Simmel's answer to this question is very simple: "Society" exists when "interaction among human beings" occurs with enough frequency and intensity so that people mutually affect one another and organize themselves into groups or other social units. Thus, Simmel used the term *society* rather loosely to refer to any pattern of social organization in which he was interested. As he put it, society refers to relatively "permanent interactions only. More specifically, the interactions we have in mind when we talk about 'society' are crystallized as definable, consistent structures such as the state and the family, the guild and the church, social classes and organizations based on common interests."[10]

The significance of defining society in this way lies in the recognition that patterns of social organization are constructed from basic processes of interaction. Hence, interaction, per se, becomes a significant area of study. Sociology, in his words, is founded on "the recognition that man in his whole nature and in all his manifestations is determined by the circumstances of living in interaction with other men."[11] Thus, as an academic discipline, "sociology asks what happens to men and by what rules do they behave, not insofar as they unfold their understandable individual existences in their totalities, but insofar as they form groups and are determined by their group existence because of interaction."[12] With this statement, Simmel gave sociology a unique and unambiguous subject matter: the basic forms of social interaction.

How Should Sociology Study Society?

Simmel's answer to this question is again very simple: sociologists should begin their study of society by distinguishing between form and content. Simmel's use of these particular terms has often been misunderstood by subsequent scholars, mainly because their Kantian origin has

---

[10] Simmel, *Fundamental Problems*, p. 9.

[11] Ibid., p. 12.

[12] Ibid., p. 11.

been ignored.[13] What must be remembered in order to understand these terms is that Simmel's writings are pervaded by analogies, with the distinction between form and content being drawn from an analogy to geometry. Geometry investigates the spatial forms of material objects; while these spatial forms clearly have material contents of various sorts, the process of abstraction in geometry involves ignoring their specific contents in favor of an emphasis on the common features, or forms, of the objects under examination. Simmel simply applied this geometric distinction between form and content to the study of society in order to suggest how sociology can investigate social processes independently of their content. The distinction between the forms and contents of interaction offers the only "possibility for a special science of society" because it is a means of focusing on the basic processes by which people establish social relations and social structures, while ignoring for analytical purposes the contents (goals and purposes) of social relations.

Thus, forms of interaction refer to the modes "of interaction among individuals through which, or in the shape of which, that content attains social reality."[14] Simmel claimed that attention to social forms leads sociology to goals that are fundamentally different from those of the other social scientific disciplines, especially in the Germany of his time. For example, sociology tries to discover the laws influencing small group interaction rather than describing particular families or marriages; it attempts to uncover the principles of formal and impersonal interaction rather than examining specific bureaucratic organizations; it seeks to understand the nature and consequences of class struggle rather than portraying a particular strike or some specific conflict. By focusing on the properties of interaction rather than its purposes, Simmel believed that sociology can discover the underlying processes of social reality.[15] For while social structures may reveal diverse contents, they may have similar forms:

> Social groups which are the most diverse imaginable in purpose and general significance, may nevertheless show identical forms of behavior toward one another on the part of individual members. We find superiority and subordination, competition, division of labor, formation of parties, repre-

---

[13] The most well-known criticisms of Simmel's presumably excessive "formalism" are by Theodore Abel, *Systematic Sociology in Germany* (New York: Octagon Press, 1965); and Pitirim Sorokin, *Contemporary Sociological Theories* (New York: Harper & Bros., 1928). The best defense of Simmel against this spurious charge is that by F. H. Tenbruck, "Formal Sociology," pp. 61–69 in Wolff, ed., *Essays by Georg Simmel et al.*

[14] Simmel, "Problem of Sociology," p. 315.
[15] Simmel, *Fundamental Problems*, p. 18.

sentation, inner solidarity coupled with exclusiveness toward the outside, and innumerable similar features in the state, in a religious community, in a band of conspirators, in an economic association, in an art school, in the family. However diverse the interests are that give rise to these sociations, the *forms* in which the interests are realized may yet be identical.[16]

On this basis, then, Simmel believed that it is possible to develop "timelessly valid laws" about social interaction. For example, the process of competition or other forms of conflict can be examined in many different social contexts at different points in time: within and among political parties, within and among different religious groups, within and among businesses, among artists, and even among family members. The result can be some theoretical insight into how the process of competition (as a form of conflict) affects the participants apart from their specific purposes of goals. Thus, even though the terminology has changed over the years, Simmel's distinction between form and content constitutes one of his most important contributions to the emergence of sociological theory. However, the next task Simmel faced was the identification of the most basic forms of interaction; in his words, sociology must delineate its specific problem areas. Yet Simmel's inability to complete this task represents the most significant flaw in his methodological work.

What Are the Problem Areas of Sociology?

Unlike his responses to the questions posed above, Simmel's answer to this query has not proven to be of enduring significance for the development of sociological theory. In his initial attempts at conceptualizing the basic social forms with which sociology ought to be concerned, Simmel referred to "a difficulty in methodology." For the present, he felt, the sociological viewpoint can only be conveyed by means of examples, since only later would it be possible "to grasp it by methods that are fully conceptualized and are sure guides to research."[17]

Both the title and the organization of Simmel's *Fundamental Problems of Sociology* (1918) suggest that the major impetus for writing this last little book was his recognition that the "difficulty in methodology" remained unresolved. Unfortunately, this final effort at developing systematic procedures for identifying the generic properties of the social world studied by sociology was not very successful either. In this book, Simmel

---

[16] Ibid., p. 22 (emphasis in original).
[17] Simmel, "Problem of Sociology," pp. 323–24.

identified three areas that he said constitute the fundamental problems of sociology. First, there is the sociological study of historical life and development, which he called *general sociology.* Second, there is the sociological study of the forms of interaction independently of history, which he called *pure, or formal, sociology.* And third, there is the sociological study of the epistemological and metaphysical aspects of society, which he called *philosophical sociology.* In *Fundamental Problems,* which has only four chapters, Simmel devoted a separate chapter to each of these problem areas.

General Sociology. Simmel began by noting that "general sociology" is concerned with the study "of the whole of historical life insofar as it is formed societally," that is, through interaction. However, the process of historical development can be interpreted in a number of different ways, and Simmel believed that it is necessary to distinguish the sociological from the nonsociological approach. For example, he indicated that Durkheim saw historical development "as a process proceeding from organic commonness to mechanical simultaneousness," while Comte saw it as occurring through three distinct stages: theological, metaphysical, and positive.[18] While both of these claims are reasonable, Simmel remarked, neither of them constitutes a justification for the existence of sociology. Rather, the historical development of those observable social structures studied by the existing disciplines (politics, economics, religion, law, language, and others) must be subjected to a sociological analysis by distinguishing between social forms and social contents. For example, when the history of religious communities and labor unions is studied, it is possible to show that the members of both are characterized by patterns of self-sacrifice and devotion to ideals. These similarities can, in principle, be summarized by abstract laws.

What Simmel was apparently arguing, although this is not entirely clear, is that studies of the contents of interaction can yield valid theoretical insights only when attention is paid to the more generic properties of the social structures in which people participate. However, Simmel's chapter on general sociology, which deals with the problem of the development of individuality in society, proceeds in ways that are, at best, very confusing.[19] Thus, the overall result is that readers are left wondering just what the subject matter of general sociology is and how it relates to the other problem areas.

---

[18] Simmel, *Fundamental Problems,* p. 19–20. In general, Simmel does not cite his sources. On these two pages, however, his references are relatively clear, even though neither Durkheim nor Comte is mentioned by name.

[19] Ibid., pp. 26–39.

Pure, or Formal, Sociology. For Simmel, "pure, or formal, sociology" consists of the investigation of "the societal forms themselves." Thus, when "society is conceived as interaction among individuals, the description of this interaction is the task of the science of society in its strictest and most essential sense."[20] However, Simmel's problem was to isolate and identify fundamental forms of interaction. In his earlier work he had attempted to do this by focusing on a number of less-observable but highly significant social forms which can be divided (roughly) into two general categories, although Simmel did not use these labels: (1) generic social processes, such as differentiation, conflict, and exchange, and (2) structural role relationships, such as the role of the stranger in society. Nearly all of Simmel's substantive work consists of studies of these less observable social forms. For example, a partial listing of the table of contents of *Sociology: Studies in the Forms of Sociation,* reveals that the following topics are considered.[21]

1. The quantitative determinateness of the group.
2. Superordination and subordination.
3. Conflict.
4. The secret and the secret society.
5. Note on adornment.
6. The intersection of social circles (the web of group affiliations).
7. The poor.
8. The self-preservation of the group.
9. Note on faithfulness and gratitude.
10. Note on the stranger.
11. The enlargement of the group and the development of the individual.
12. Note on nobility.

Yet, Simmel's description of pure, or formal, sociology suffers from a fundamental defect:[22] it does not remedy the "methodological difficulty" referred to above. For in *Fundamental Problems,* Simmel failed to develop

---

[20] Ibid., p. 22.

[21] Items 1, 2, 4, 5, and 9 are available in *The Sociology of Georg Simmel.* Items 3 and 6 are in *Conflict and the Web of Group Affiliations.* Item 10 is in *Essays by Georg Simmel.* Item 8 is in the *American Journal of Sociology* 3 (March 1900):577–603. Items 7, 11, and 12 are in *Georg Simmel on Individuality and Social Forms,* trans. Donald Levine (Chicago: University of Chicago Press, 1971). The remaining chapters, about one fourth of the book, are still untranslated. They deal with such topics as social psychology, hereditary office holding, the spatial organization of society, and the relationship between psychological and sociological phenomena.

[22] Simmel, *Fundamental Problems,* pp. 40–57.

a precise method for either identifying the most basic forms of interaction or analyzing their systematic variation.

Philosophical Sociology. Simmel's "philosophical sociology" is an attempt to recognize the importance of philosophical issues in the development of sociology as an academic discipline. As he put it, the modern scientific attitude toward the nature of empirical facts suggests a "complex of questions concerning the fact 'society.'" These questions are philosophical, and they center on epistemology and metaphysics. The epistemological problem has to do with one of the main cognitive presuppositions underlying sociological research: Is society the purpose of human existence, or is it merely a means for individual ends?[23] Simmel's explanatory chapter on philosophical sociology deals with this question by studying the relationship between the individual and society in the 18th and 19th centuries.[24] However, as with the other chapters in *Fundamental Problems*, this material is so confusing as to be of little use. Apparently, Simmel wanted to argue that questions about the purpose of society or the reasons for individual existence cannot be answered in scientific terms, but even this reasonable conclusion is uncertain.[25] Ultimately, then, Simmel's vision of philosophical sociology has simply been ignored, mainly because his analysis is both superficial and unclear.

In the end, Simmel had to confess that he had failed to lay a complete methodological foundation for the new discipline. This failure stems from Simmel's uncertainty about his ability to isolate truly basic or generic structures and processes. Thus, both *Sociology* and *Fundamental Problems* contain disclaimers suggesting that his analysis of specific topics—such as the significance of group affiliations, the functions of social conflict, and the process of social exchange—can only demonstrate the potential utility of an analysis of social forms.[26] We turn now to an examination of Simmel's three most important studies in formal and pure sociology.

"THE WEB OF GROUP AFFILIATIONS"

"The Web of Group Affiliations" is essentially a sociological analysis of the way in which patterns of group participation are altered with social differentiation and the consequences of such alterations for people's

---

[23] This same issue was dealt with ten years earlier in Georg Simmel, "Note on the Problem: How Is Society Possible?" in Wolff, ed., *Essays by Georg Simmel et al*, pp. 337–56.

[24] Simmel, *Fundamental Problems*, pp. 58–86.

[25] Ibid., p. 25.

[26] Ibid., p. 18.

everyday behavior. Simmel first dealt with this topic in his *Social Differentiation* (1890).[27] However, this early version is not very useful, and the text explicated here is taken from *Sociology: Studies in the Forms of Sociation* (1908). Like all the classical sociologists, Simmel saw a general historical tendency toward increasing social differentiation in modern industrialized societies. But rather than tracing this development either chronologically or in terms of increased functional specialization, he focused on the nature and significance of group memberships. In this way, he was able to identify a unique social form.

The Web of Group Affiliations as a Social Form

It will be recalled that social forms refer to the modes of interaction through which people attain their purposes or goals. In "The Web of Group Affiliations," Simmel was interested in the extent to which changes in the network of social structures making up society affect people. Indeed, in Simmel's eye, the number of groups a person belongs to and the basis on which they are formed influences interaction apart from the interests that the groups are intended to satisfy.

One of the most important variables influencing the number of groups to which people belong, as well as the basis of their attachment to groups, is the degree of social differentiation; in an undifferentiated society, people are simply unable to come into contact with others who have unique attributes and experiences, since the accident of birth forces people to interact and establish ties within a homogeneous group. But in a more differentiated society, humans are able to choose among a variety of groups and interact with others in terms of "similarity of talents, inclinations, activities," and other factors over which they have some control.[28] The remainder of "The Web of Group Affiliations" is an attempt at showing how structural changes that have occurred with increasing social differentiation have resulted in the increasing potential for role conflict as people express their individuality and freedom through their choice of group affiliation. In this way, Simmel demonstrated how a sociological analysis can reveal what happens to people "insofar as they form groups and are determined by their group existence because of interaction."

---

[27] See Georg Simmel, "The Intersection of Social Spheres," in *Georg Simmel: Sociologist and European*, trans. Peter Laurence (New York: Barnes & Noble, 1976), pp. 95–110.

[28] Simmel, "Web of Group Affiliations," pp. 127–28.

Structural Changes Accompanying Social Differentiation

Simmel observed that the process of social differentiation has produced two fundamental changes in the way people interact with one another in society. The first is that group formation based on what he called *organic* criteria has been replaced by group formation based on *rational* criteria. That is, when group affiliation has an organic basis, external phenomena over which individuals have no control are the grounds for participating in a group. Examples of such factors, which are generally determined by birth, are people's family, place of residence (city), ethnicity, and sometimes age and sex. Alternatively, when affiliation is rational, groups are formed on the basis of conscious reflection and planning, with the result that individual choice is the primary grounds for joining them. For example, Simmel noted that English trade unions originally "tended toward local exclusiveness" and were closed to workers who came from other cities or regions.[29] But over time workers ended their dependence on local relationships, and the unions became nationally organized in terms of workers' trades. Simmel summarized the change he saw in the basis of group information in the following way.

> Criteria derived from knowledge came to serve as the basis of social differentiation and group formation. Up to the Renaissance, social differentiation and group-formation had been based either on criteria of self-interest . . . or emotion (religious), or a mixture of both (familial). Now, intellectual and rational interests came to form groups, whose members were gathered from many other social groups. This is a striking example of the general trend, that the formation of groups, which has occurred more recently, often bears a rational character, and that the substantive purpose of these groups is the result of conscious reflection and intelligent planning. Thus, secondary groups, because of their rational formation, give the appearance of being determined by a purpose, since their affairs revolve around intellectually articulated interests.[30]

The second structural change accompanying social differentiation is that there has been a very large increase in the number of groups with which people can affiliate. Thus, when group participation is based on organic criteria, people generally belong only to a small number of primary groups, such as their family, church, and city. From Simmel's point of view, the most important sociological characteristics of these groups are

---

[29] Ibid., p. 129.
[30] Ibid., p. 137.

that individuals have no choice in participation, that everyone belongs to the same groups, and that in most respects people are seen as members of a group rather than as unique persons. This means that in many important ways, every individual is like every other.

However, when group affiliation is based on rational criteria, individuals can belong to a multiplicity of groups. For example, Simmel observed that modern people are affiliated with their family of origin, family of procreation, and their spouse's family. Each of these groups can be quite different in terms of socioeconomic status, ethnicity, or place of residence. In addition, everyone may also belong to other kinds of groups, such as occupational groups of various sorts, purely social groups, and a virtually unlimited number of special-interest groups. Further, they may also identify themselves as members of a social class and a military reserve unit. Finally, they may see themselves as citizens of cities, states, regions, and nations. Not surprisingly, Simmel concludes:

> This is a great variety of groups. Some of these groups are integrated. Others are, however, so arranged that one group appears as the original focus of an individual's affiliation, from which he then turns toward affiliation with other, quite different groups on the basis of his special qualities, which distinguish him from other members of his primary group.[31]

Put differently, group affiliations in differentiated societies are characterized by a superstructure of secondary groups that develops over and above primary group membership. From Simmel's point of view, the most important sociological characteristics of these secondary groups are that individuals choose to affiliate, that everyone belongs to different groups, and that people are often treated as individuals having unique attributes and experiences. This means that, in many important respects, every person is different from every other.

The Consequences of Social Differentiation

Simmel believed that the expansion of people's web of group affiliations, coupled with the fundamental change in the basis of group formation, have important consequences for those who live in modern societies. The most obvious result is that there is a greatly increased potential for role conflict: "As the individual leaves his established position within *one* primary group, he comes to stand at a point at which many groups 'intersect.' " The result is that "external and internal conflicts arise

---

[31] Ibid., p. 138.

through the multiplicity of group affiliations, which threaten the individual with psychological tensions or even a schizophrenic break."[32] However, Simmel insisted that while role conflict can have adverse psychological consequences, such need not be the case, since most people are able to balance their obligations to competing groups by keeping their activities spatially and temporally separated.

In addition, Simmel argued, that in modern and highly differentiated societies each person develops a specific personality (what he called "a core of inner unity") comprised of those attributes and experiences that make each human being a unique individual who is not irrevocably tied to a primary group. Two indicators of this process are: (1) people in modern societies do not have the same pattern of group affiliations and (2), individuals can occupy positions of different ranks in the various groups to which they belong. Neither phenomenon would have been observed in, for example, the Middle Ages, where the group absorbed the whole person. Thus, "the mere fact of multiple group affiliations [has] enabled the person to achieve for himself an individualized situation in which the groups [have] to be oriented towards the individual."[33] In this way, then, people become aware of their own uniqueness. Such awareness is a real step toward increasing personal freedom, a phenomenon that also appears with an expansion of the web of group affiliations. As he noted, "the narrowly circumscribed and strict custom of earlier conditions was one in which the social group as a whole . . . regulated the conduct of the individual in the most varied ways."[34] Such regulation is not possible in differentiated societies, Simmel observed, because people step out of their primary groups by joining or forming many different secondary groups.

CONFLICT

Simmel's essay on conflict is a demonstration of its positive functions within and between groups. While his initial adumbration of "The Sociology of Conflict," appeared in 1903, the basis for our commentary is a much revised version that was included as a chapter in *Sociology: Studies in the Forms of Sociation* (1908).[35] Simmel began the latter essay by remarking that while the social "significance of conflict has in principle

---

[32] Ibid., p. 141 (emphasis in original).

[33] Ibid., p. 151; see also, pp. 139 and 149.

[34] Ibid., p. 165.

[35] Georg Simmel, "The Sociology of Conflict," *American Journal of Sociology* 9 (1903–4):490–525, 672–89, and 798–811.

never been disputed," it is most commonly seen as a purely destructive factor in people's relationships, one that should be prevented from occurring if possible. He believed that this orientation toward the negative effects of social conflict stems from an emphasis on exploring the contents of interaction; people observe the destructive consequences of conflict on other individuals (both physically and psychologically) and assume that it must have a similar effect on collectivities. But in Simmel's view, this emphasis is shortsighted because it fails to recognize that conflict often serves as a means of maintaining or increasing integration within groups. In his words, "it is a way of achieving some kind of unity." For example, people's ability to express their hostilities toward one another can give them a sense of control over their destiny and thereby serve to increase social solidarity within a group.

Conflict as a Social Form

Human beings, Simmel observed, have an "*a priori* fighting instinct;" that is, they have an easily aroused sense of hostility toward others. While this "fighting instinct" is probably the ultimate cause of social conflict, Simmel emphasized that humans are distinguished from other species by the fact that, in general, conflicts are means to goals rather than merely instinctual reactions to external stimuli. This fact, which is a fundamental principle in Simmel's discussion, means that conflict is a vehicle by which individuals achieve their purposes in innumerable social contexts, such as marriage, work, play, politics, and religion. As such, conflict reveals certain common properties in all contexts, and hence, it can be viewed as a basic social form.

Moreover, conflict is nearly always combined with cooperation: people agree on norms that regulate when, where, and how to fight with one another; and this is true in marriage, business, games, war, and theological disputes. As Simmel wrote, "there probably exists no social unit in which convergent and divergent currents among its members are not inseparably interwoven. An absolutely centripetal and harmonious group . . . not only is empirically unreal, it could show no real life process."[36] The importance of this fusion of conflict and cooperation can be seen most clearly in those instances where a cooperative element appears to be lacking, for example, interaction between muggers and their victims or when conflict is engendered exclusively by the lust to fight. However, Simmel believed that these examples are clearly limiting cases, for if

---

[36] Simmel, "Conflict," in *Conflict and the Web of Group Affiliations*, p. 15.

"there is any consideration, any limit to violence, there already exists a socializing factor, even though only as the qualification of violence."[37] This is why he emphasized the fact that social conflict is usually a means to a goal; its "superior purpose" implies that people can change or modify their tactics depending on the situation.

In his essay on conflict, then, Simmel sketched some of the alternative forms of conflict, the way in which they are combined with regulatory norms, and the significance this form of interaction has for the groups to which people belong. In order to carry out this task, he first examined how conflict within groups affects the reciprocal relations of the parties involved, and then he turned to the consequences that conflict with an outgroup has for social relations within a group. The following sections deal with each of these topics.

Conflict within Groups

Simmel's investigation of the sociological significance of conflict within groups revolves around three forms: (1) conflicts in which the opposing parties possess common personal qualities, (2) conflicts in which the opposing parties perceive each other as a threat to the existence of the group, and (3) conflicts in which the opposing parties recognize and accept each other as legitimate opponents.

Common Personal Qualities and Conflict.[38] Simmel noted here that "people who have many common features often do one another worse or 'wronger' wrong than complete strangers do," mainly because they have so few differences that even the slightest conflict is magnified in its significance. As examples, he referred to conflict in "intimate relations," such as marriages, and to the relationship between renegades and their former colleagues. In both cases, the solidarity of the group is based on the parties possessing many common (or complementary) characteristics. As a result, people are involved with one another as whole persons and even small antagonisms between them can be highly inflammatory, regardless of the content of the disagreements. Thus, when conflict does occur, the resulting battle is sometimes so intense that previous areas of agreement are forgotten. Most of the time, Simmel observed, opponents develop implicit or explicit norms that serve to keep conflicts within manageable bounds. However, when emotions run high or when the participants see the conflict as transcending their

---

[37] Ibid., p. 26.
[38] Ibid., pp. 43–48.

individual interests, then the fight may become violent. At that point, he suggested, the very existence of those who differ may be taken as a threat to the group.

Conflict as a Threat to the Group.[39] In this case, conflict occurs among opponents who have common membership in a group. Simmel argued that this type of conflict should be treated as a distinct form because when a group is divided into conflicting elements, the antagonistic parties "hate each other not only on the concrete ground which produced the conflict but also on the sociological ground of hatred for the enemy of the group itself." Such antagonism is especially intense and can easily become violent, Simmel argued, since each party identifies itself as representing the group and sees the other as a mortal enemy of the collective.

Conflicts among Recognized and Accepted Opponents. Simmel distinguished two forms of conflicts where the opposing parties are recognized and accepted. When conflict is "direct," the opposing parties act squarely against one another in order to obtain their goals.[40] When conflict is "indirect," the opponents only interact with a third party in order to obtain their goals. Simmel referred to this latter form of conflict as "competition."[41] Yet, both of these forms share certain distinguishing characteristics that differentiate them from the forms of conflict noted above: opponents are seen to have a right to strive for the same goal; conflict is pursued mercilessly and yet in a nonviolent manner; personal antagonisms and feelings of hostility are often excluded from the conflict; and the opponents either develop agreements among themselves or accept the imposition of overriding norms that regulate the conflict.

The purest examples of direct conflict are antagonistic games and conflicts over causes. In the playing of games "one *unites* [precisely] in order to fight, and one fights under the mutually recognized control of norms and rules."[42] Similarly, in the case of conflicts over causes, such as legal battles, the opponents' essential unity is again the underlying basis for interaction, since in order to fight in court, agreed-upon normative procedures must always be followed. Thus, even as parties confront one another, they affirm their agreement on larger principles. The analysis of direct conflict within groups was, however, of less interest to Simmel,

---

[39] Ibid., pp. 48–50.
[40] Ibid., pp. 34–43.
[41] Ibid., pp. 57–86.
[42] Ibid., p. 35 (emphasis in original).

with the result that he did not devote much space to it. Rather, he emphasized the sociological importance of competition, since this form of fighting most clearly illustrates how conflict can have positive social consequences. For by proceeding indirectly, competition functions as a vital source of social solidarity within a group.

While recognizing the destructive and even shameful aspects of competition that Marx and other observers had pointed to, Simmel argued that even after all its negative aspects are taken into account, competition has positive consequences for the group because it forces people to establish ties with one another, thereby increasing social solidarity within the group. Because competition between parties proceeds by the opponents trying to win over a third party, each of them is implicated in a web of affiliations that functions to connect them with one another.[43]

With some exceptions, Simmel noted that the process of competition is restricted, because unregulated conflict can too easily become violent and lead to the destruction of the group itself.[44] Hence, all collectivities that allow competition usually regulate it in some fashion, either through inter-individual restrictions, in which regulatory norms are simply agreed upon by the participants, or through super-individual restrictions, in which laws and other normative principles are imposed on the competitors.[45] Indeed, the existence of competition often stimulates normative regulation, thereby providing a basis of social integration.

Finally, it will be recalled from the previous chapter that Simmel recognized that there are instances where groups or societies try to eliminate competition in the name of a higher principle. For instance, in socialist or communist societies, competition is suspended in favor of an emphasis on organizing individual efforts in such a way as to (a) eliminate the wasted energy that accompanies conflict and (b) provide for the common good. Nonetheless, Simmel appears to have regarded a competitive environment as more useful than a noncompetitive one in modern, highly differentiated societies, not only in economic terms but also in most other arenas of social life. He believed that such an environment provides an outlet for people's "fighting instincts" that redounds to the common good as well as a stimulus for regulatory agreements that also contribute to the common good.

---

[43] Ibid., p. 62.

[44] Simmel recognized that within families and, to some extent, within religious groups, the interests of the groups often dictate that members refrain from competing with one another. Ibid., pp. 68–70.

[45] Ibid., p. 76.

Conflict between Groups

In the final section of his essay, Simmel examined the consequences that conflict between groups has "for the inner structure of each party itself."[46] Put differently, he was concerned with understanding the effect that conflict has on social relationships within each respective party to the conflict. In order to make his point, Simmel identified the following consequences of conflict between groups: (1) it increases the degree of centralization of authority within each group, (2) it increases the degree of social solidarity within each group and, at the same time, decreases the level of tolerance for deviance and dissent, and (3) it increases likelihood of coalitions among groups having similar opponents. Each of these consequences is examined below.

Conflict and Centralization.[47] Just as fighters must psychologically "pull themselves together," Simmel observed, so must a group when it is engaged in conflict with another group. There is a "need for centralization, for the tight pulling together of all elements, which alone guarantees their use, without loss of energy and time, for whatever the requirements of the moment may be." This necessity is greatest during war, which "needs a centralistic intensification of the group form." In addition, Simmel noted, the development and maintenance of a centralized group is often "guaranteed best by despotism," and he argued that a centralized and despotic regime is more likely to wage war precisely because people's accumulated energies (or "hostile impulses") need some means of expression. Finally, Simmel remarked that centralized groups generally prefer to engage in conflict with groups that are also centralized. For despite the conflict-producing consequences of fighting a tightly organized opponent, conflict with such an opponent can be more easily resolved, not only because the boundaries separating each side are clearly demarcated but also because each party "can supply a representative with whom one can negotiate with full certainty." For example, in conflicts between workers and employers or between nations, Simmel argued, it is often "better" if each side is organized so that conflict resolution can proceed in a systematic manner.

Conflict, Solidarity, and Intolerance.[48] Simmel argued that conflict often increases social solidarity within each of the opposing groups. As he phrased it, a "tightening of the relations among [the party's] members and the intensification of its unity, in consciousness and in action, occur."

---

[46] Ibid., p. 87.
[47] Ibid., pp. 88–91.
[48] Ibid., pp. 91–98 and 17–19.

This is especially true, Simmel claimed, during wars or other types of violent conflicts. Moreover, increasing intolerance also accompanies rising solidarity, for while antagonistic members can often coexist during peacetime without harm to the group, this luxury is not possible during war. As a result, "groups in any sort of war situation are not tolerant" of deviance and dissent, since they often see themselves as fighting for the existence of the group itself and demand total loyalty from members. Thus, in general, conflict between groups means that members must become solidary with one another, and those who cannot are often either expelled or punished. As a result of their intolerance toward deviance and dissent, Simmel remarked, groups in conflict often become smaller, as those who would compromise are silenced or cast out. This tendency can make an ongoing conflict more difficult to resolve, since "groups, and especially minorities, which live in conflict and persecution, often reject approaches or tolerance from the other side." The acceptance of such overtures would mean that "the closed nature of their opposition without which they cannot fight on would be blurred." Finally, Simmel suggested that the internal solidarity of many groups is dependent on their continued conflict with other parties and that their complete victory over an opponent can result in a lessening of internal social solidarity.

Conflict, Coalitions, and Group Formation.[49]   Under certain conditions, Simmel wrote, conflict between groups can lead to the formation of coalitions and, ultimately, to new, solidary groups where none had existed before. In his words, "each element in a plurality may have its own opponent, but because this opponent is the same for all elements, they all unite—and in this case, they may, prior to that, not have had anything to do with each other." Sometimes such combinations are only for a single purpose and the allies' solidarity declines immediately at the conclusion of the conflict. However, Simmel argued, when coalitions are engaged in wars or other types of violent conflicts and when their members become highly interdependent on one another over a long period, then more cohesive social relations are likely to ensue. This phenomenon is even more pronounced when a coalition is subjected to an ongoing or relatively permanent threat. As Simmel wrote, "the synthetic strength of a common opposition may be determined, not [only] by the number of shared points of interest, but [also] by the duration and intensity of the unification. In this case, it is especially favorable to the unification if instead of an actual fight with an enemy, there is a permanent *threat* by him."

---

[49] Ibid., pp. 98–107.

In summary, then, Simmel's inquiry into the functions of social conflict outlines some of the conditions under which conflict within and between groups can promote social solidarity. In this analysis, Simmel maintained his emphasis on conflict as a form of interaction; in this way, he sought to justify sociology as an academic discipline with a unique subject matter. Similarly, Simmel also explored another basic social form that, like conflict, contains admixtures of competition and cooperation. This form is the process of social exchange, which is examined in his *The Philosophy of Money.*

THE PHILOSOPHY OF MONEY

Simmel's *The Philosophy of Money* is a study of the social consequences of exchange relationships among human beings, with special emphasis on those forms of exchange in which money is used as an abstract measure of value. Like all his work, *The Philosophy of Money* is an attempt at exposing how the forms of interaction affect the basic nature of social relations independently of their specific content. While Simmel had first considered this issue as early as 1889 in an untranslated article titled "The Psychology of Money," the final formulation of his ideas did not appear until the second edition of *The Philosophy of Money* was published in 1907.[50] Unlike the works reviewed above, *The Philosophy of Money* is both a sociological and philosophical treatise, and as such it presents problems of analysis. For sociologists, the philosophical portions are generally useful to the extent they provide a set of assumptions from which theoretical propositions are derived. Conversely, the sociological portions are interesting to philosophers to the degree that they illustrate a deeper ontology. It is this "middle ground" between philosophy and sociology that makes *The Philosophy of Money* both more ambiguous and more ambitious than most of Simmel's other writings.[51] In our explication of this book, we will initially place Simmel's ideas into a specifically sociological context by showing how social exchange constitutes a form of interaction and then describe how he translated certain philosophical assumptions into a number of interesting theoretical insights.

---

[50] Georg Simmel, "Psychologie des Geldes," *Jahrbücher für Gesetzgebung, Verwaltung und Volkswirtschaft* 23 (1889):1251–64.

[51] It is often forgotten that Simmel was a philosopher as well as a sociologist. As noted in Chapter 12, he wrote books and articles on the works of Kant, Goethe, Schopenhauer, and Nietzsche; and considered more general philosophical issues and problems as well.

Exchange as a Social Form

The Philosophy of Money represents Simmel's effort to isolate another basic social form. Not all interaction is exchange, but exchange is still a universal form of interaction.[52] In analyzing social exchange, Simmel concentrated on "economic exchange" in general and on money exchanges in particular. While not all economic exchanges involve the use of money, historically money has come into increasing use as a medium of exchange. This historical trend, Simmel emphasized, reflects the impact of such evolutionary processes as social differentiation, growth, and rationalization. But it does much more: money is also a major cause and force behind these evolutionary processes. Thus, the sociological portions of *The Philosophy of Money* are devoted to analyzing the transforming effects on social life of the ever-increasing use of money in social relations.

In seeking to analyze social evolution in terms of an exchange perspective, Simmel was able to develop a number of philosophical assumptions and link these to a sociological analysis of the modern world. For, much like his friend and intellectual defender, Max Weber, Simmel was interested in understanding not just the forms of modern life, but also their historical origins.[53] But unlike Weber, Simmel did not engage in detailed historical analyses, nor was he interested in constructing elaborate taxonomies. Rather, his works always sought to link certain philosophical views about humans and the social universe to understanding the properties of a particular social form. Thus, before explicating Simmel's specific analysis of money and exchange, it is necessary to place his analysis in philosophical context.

Simmel's Assumptions about Human Nature

In *The Philosophy of Money*, Simmel presented a vision of human nature that is implicit but less visible in his sociological works. He began by asserting that people are teleological beings; that is, they act on the environment in the pursuit of anticipated goals. In the essay on conflict, Simmel emphasized that it was just this fact that makes human conflict different from that occurring among other animals. In *The Philosophy of Money*, Simmel took the more general position that while people's

---

[52] Simmel, *Philosophy of Money*, p. 82.

[53] Simmel was excluded from senior academic positions for much of his career, and his work was often attacked. Weber was one of his most consistent defenders and apparently helped Simmel maintain at least a marginal intellectual standing in Germany.

goals will vary, depending on their biological impulses and social needs, all action reflects the human ability to manipulate the environment in an attempt to realize their goals. In so doing, individuals use a variety of "tools," but not just in the obvious material sense. Rather, people use more subtle, symbolic tools, such as language and money, to achieve their goals. In general, Simmel argued that the more tools people possess, the greater is their capacity to manipulate the environment and the more the actor can causally influence the flow of events. Moreover, the use of tools allows for the connecting of many events, as is the case when money is used to buy a good (the money, in turn, pays the salary of the seller, becomes profit for the manufacturer, and is transformed into wages for the worker, and so on). Thus, for Simmel all action reveals the properties presented in Figure 13–1:

FIGURE 13–1
Simmel's Assumptions about Social Action

Impulse →Establishment→Selection and→Manipulation→Consummation
of   use of tools   of   and
goals   environment   satisfaction

Money, Simmel asserted, is the ultimate social tool because it is generalized; that is, people can use it in so many ways to manipulate the environment in order to obtain their goals. This fact means that money can potentially connect many events and persons who would not otherwise be related. In an indirect way, then, the use of money allows a vast increase in the number of groups to which individuals may belong, and it is thus a prime force behind social differentiation.

A related assumption is that humans have the capacity to divide their world into an (1) internal, subjective state and (2) an external, objective state. This division only occurs when impulses are not immediately satisfied—that is, when the environment presents barriers and obstacles. When such barriers exist, humans separate their subjective experiences from the objects of the environment which are the source of need or impulse satisfaction. For as Simmel emphasized:

> We desire objects only if they are not immediately given to us for our use and enjoyment; that is, to the extent that they resist our desire. The content of our desire becomes an object as soon as it is opposed to us, not only in the sense of being impervious to us, but also in terms of its distance as something not enjoyed.[54]

---

[54] Simmel, *Philosophy of Money*, p. 66.

It is from this subject-object division that "value" inheres. In contrast to Marx, Simmel stressed that the value of an object does not exist in the "labor power" required to produce it, but in the extent to which it is both desired and unattainable—that is, value resides in the process of seeking objects that are scarce and distant. Value is thus tied to humans' basic capacity to distinguish a subjective from objective world and in the relative difficulty in securing objects. Patterns of social organization, Simmel emphasized, perform much of this subject-object separation: they present barriers and obstacles, they create demands for some objects, and they determine how objects will circulate. And the economic production of goods and their sale in a market is only a special case of the more general process of subject-object division among humans. For long before there were money, markets, and productive corporations, there were humans who desired objects that were not easily obtainable. Thus, whether in the economic marketplace or the more general arena of life, value is a positive function of the extent in which an object of desire is difficult to obtain.[55]

Money, as Simmel was to show, greatly increases the creation and acceleration of value, because it provides a common yardstick for a quick calculation of values (that is, "how much" is this or that commodity or service "worth"). Moreover, as a "tool" it greatly facilitates the acquisition of objects, and as money circulates and is used at each juncture to calculate values, all objects in the environment become assessed in terms of their monetary value. Unlike Marx, Simmel did not see this as a perverse process, but as a natural reflection of humans' innate capacity and need to create values in the objects of their environment.

Yet another assumption about human nature is to be found in Simmel's discussion of "world view."[56] People naturally seek stability and order in their world, he argued. They seek to know the place of objects and of their relationship to these objects. For example, Simmel observed that humans develop totems and religious rituals to regularize their relations to the supernatural; similarly, the development of money as a standardized measurement of value is but another manifestation of this tendency for humans to seek order and stability in their view of the world. For by developing money, objects can be readily compared in terms of their respective value and humans can, therefore, develop a "sense of order" about their environment.

In sum, then, the development of money is for Simmel an expression

[55] Ibid., pp. 80–98.
[56] Ibid., pp. 102–10.

and extension of basic human nature. Money is a "tool" in teleological acts; it is a way to express the value inherent in humans' capacity for subject-object division; and it is a means for attaining stability and order in people's world view. All of these innate tendencies are the driving force behind much human action, and it is for this reason that exchange is such a basic form of social interaction. For exchange is nothing more than the sacrificing of one object of value for the attainment of another. Money greatly facilitates this process because it provides a common reference point for calculating the values of objects that are exchanged.

Money in Social Exchange

For Simmel, social exchange involves the following elements:[57]

1. The desire for a valued object that one does not have.
2. The possession of the valued object by an identifiable other.
3. The offer of an object of value to secure from another the desired object.
4. The acceptance of this offer by the possessor of the valued object.

Contained in this portrayal of social exchange are several additional prints that Simmel emphasized. First, value is idiosyncratic and is, ultimately, tied to an individual's impulses and needs. Of course, what is defined as valuable is typically circumscribed by cultural and social patterns, but how valuable an object is will be a positive function of (a) the intensity of a person's needs and (b) the scarcity of the object. Second, much exchange involves efforts to manipulate situations so that the intensity of needs for an object are concealed and the availability of an object is made to seem less than what it actually is. Inherent in exchange, therefore, is a basic tension which can often erupt into other social forms, such as conflict. Third, to possess an object is to lessen its value and to increase the value of objects that one does not possess. Fourth, exchanges will only occur if both parties perceive that the object given is less valuable than the one received.[58] Fifth, collective units as well as individuals participate in exchange relations, and hence, are also subject to the four processes listed above. Sixth, the more liquid the

---

[57] Ibid., pp. 85–88.

[58] Surprisingly, Simmel did not explore in any great detail the consequences of unbalanced exchanges, where people are forced to give up a more valuable object for a less valuable one. Simmel simply assumed that at the time of exchange, one party felt that an increase in value had occurred. Retrospectively, a redefinition may occur, but the exchange would not occur if at the moment people did not perceive that they had received more value than they had given up.

resources of an actor in an exchange—that is, the more resources can be used in many types of exchanges—the greater will be that actor's options and power. For if an actor is not bound to exchange with any other, and can readily withdraw resources and exchange them with another, then that actor has considerable power to manipulate any exchange.

Economic exchange involving money is only a special case of this more general social form. But it is a very special case. For when money becomes the predominate means for establishing value in social relationships, the properties and dynamics of social relations are transformed. This process of displacing other criteria of value, such as logic, ethics, and aesthetics, with a monetary criterion is precisely the long-term evolutionary trend in societies. This trend is, as we mentioned earlier, both a cause and effect of money as the medium of exchange. Money emerged to facilitate exchanges and to realize even more completely humans' basic needs. But once established, the use of money has the power to transform the structure of social relations in society. It is in seeking to understand how money has this power to alter social relations that Simmel's *The Philosophy of Money* becomes distinctly sociological.

Money and Its Consequences for Social Relations

In much of Simmel's work, there is an implicit functionalism. Simmel often asked: What are the consequences, or functions, of a social form for the larger social whole? As we saw earlier, this functionalism is most evident in Simmel's analysis of conflict, but it is also to be found in Simmel's analysis of money. For Simmel asked two related questions in tracing the consequences of money for social patterns: (1) What are the consequences of money for the structure of society as a whole? (2) What are the consequences of money for individuals?

In answering these two questions, Simmel added to his lifelong preoccupation with several issues that pervade his work. We should mention these in order to place into context his specific analysis of the consequences of money for society and the individual. One prominent theme in all of Simmel's work is the dialectic between individual attachments to, and freedom from, groups. On the one hand, Simmel praised social relations that allow individuals freedom to choose their options, while on the other hand he was dismayed over the alienation from, and lack of personal integration of, individuals into the collective fibre of society. This theme is tied to another prominent concern in Simmel's work: the growing rationalization of society, or as he phrased the matter, the "objectification" of social life. As social relations lose their traditional and religious content, they become mediated by impersonal standards—law, intellect, logic, and money. The application of these standards increases individual freedom and social justice, but it also makes life less emotional and involving. It reduces relations to rational calculations, devoid of the emotional bonds that come with attachments to religious symbols and long-standing traditions. It is in the context of these two themes that Simmel's analysis of the "functions" of money for individuals and the social whole must be viewed.

Money and the Social Whole. Much like Weber, but in a less systematic way, Simmel was concerned with the historical trend toward rationalization, or objectification, of social relations. In general, humans tend to symbolize their relations with both each other and the natural environment. In the past, this was done with religious totems and then with laws. More recently, Simmel believed, people have come to express their relationships to physical items and to each other in monetary terms, with the result that they have lost intimate and direct contact with others as well as with the objects in their environment. Thus, money represents the ultimate objective symbolization of social relations, because unlike material items, it has no intrinsic value. It merely represents values, and it is used to express the value of one object in relation to another. While initial forms of money, such as coins of valuable metals and stones that could be converted into jewelry, possessed intrinsic value, the evolutionary trend is toward the use of paper money and credit which merely express values in exchanges. As paper money and credit come to dominate, social relations in society are profoundly altered, in at least the following ways.

1. The use of money enables actors to make quick calculations of respective values.[59] People do not have to bargain and haggle over the standards to be used in establishing the respective values of objects—whether commodities or labor. As a result, the "velocity" of exchanges dramatically increases. People move through social relations more quickly and at a faster pace.

2. Since money increases the rate of social interaction and exchange, it also increases values. As was mentioned earlier, Simmel felt that people do not engage in exchanges unless they perceive that they will get more than they give up. Hence, the greater is the rate of exchange, the greater will be peoples' accumulation of value, that is, the more they will perceive that their needs and desires can be realized.[60]

---

[59] Simmel, *Philosophy of Money*, p. 143; pp. 488–512.
[60] Ibid., p. 292.

3. The use of money as a liquid and nonspecific resource allows for much greater continuity in social relations. It prevents gaps from developing in social relations, as is often the case when people only have hard goods, such as food products or jewelry, to exchange in social relations. Money gives people options to exchange almost anything, since respective values can be readily calculated. As a result, there is greater continuity in social relations, since all individuals can potentially engage in exchanges with each other.[61]

4. In a related vein, money also allows for the creation of multiple social ties. With money, people join groups other than those established at birth and thereby establish relations with many more others than is possible with a more restrictive medium of exchange.[62]

5. Money also allows for greatly protracted exchanges among human beings located at great distances. As long as interaction involves exchange of concrete objects, there are limits to how distant people can be from each other and how many actors can participate in a sequence of exchanges. But with money, these limitations are removed. Nations can engage in exchanges; individuals who never see each other—such as a factory worker and consumers of goods produced in the factory—can be indirectly connected in an exchange sequence (since some of the payment for a good or commodity will, ultimately, be translated into wages for the worker). Thus, money greatly extends the scope of social organization; it allows for organization beyond face-to-face contact or beyond the simple barter of goods. With money, more and more people can become connected through direct and indirect linkages.[63]

6. Money also promotes social solidarity in the sense that it represents a "trust;" that is, if people take money for goods or services, they believe that it can be used at a future date to buy other goods or services. This implicit trust in the capacity of money to meet future needs reinforces people's "faith in" and "commitment to" society.[64]

7. In a related line of argument, money increases the power of central authority, for the use of money requires that there be social stability and that a central authority guarantee the worth of money.[65] As exchange relations come to rely upon government to maintain the stability of money, government acquires power. Moreover, with money, it becomes

---

[61] Ibid., p. 124.
[62] Ibid., p. 307.
[63] Ibid., pp. 180–86.
[64] Ibid., pp. 177–78.
[65] Ibid., pp. 171–84.

much easier for central government to tax people.[66] As long as only property could be taxed, there were limitations on the effectiveness of taxation by a remote central government, since knowledge of property held would be incomplete and since extracting property, such as land, is not easily converted into values that can be used to increase the power of central government (how can, for example, property effectively buy labor services in the army or administrative staff of government). As a liquid resource, however, tax money can be used to buy those services and goods necessary for effective central authority.

8. The creation of a tax on money also promotes a new basis of social solidarity. Since all social strata and other collectivities are subject to a monetary taxation system, they have at least one common interest: control and regulation of taxes imposed by central government. This common interest laces diverse interests together vis-à-vis the taxing powers of government.

9. The use of money often extends into virtually all spheres of interaction. As an efficient means for comparing values, it replaces other, less-efficient ways to calculate value. Yet as money begins to penetrate all social relations, resistance to its influence in areas of "personal value" increases. Efforts to maintain the "personal element" in transactions escalate, and norms about when it is inappropriate to use money become established. For example, traditions of paying a "bride price" vanish; using money to "buy influence" is considered much more offensive than personal persuasion; "paying a price" as punishment for certain crimes decreases; and so on.[67]

10. At the same time as these efforts to create spheres where the use of money declines, there is a general "quantification" and "objectification" of social relations.[68] Interactions become quantified as their value is expressed in terms of money. As a result, moral constraints on what is possible decrease, since "anything is possible" if one just has the money. Money thus increases *anomie*, to borrow Durkheim's term. It releases people from the constraints of tradition and moral authority; it creates a system in which it is difficult to restrain individual aspirations and desires. Deviance and "pathology" are, therefore, more likely in systems where money becomes the prevalent medium of interaction.[69]

Money and the Individual. For Simmel, the extensive use of money in social interaction has a number of consequences for individuals. Most

---

[66] Ibid., p. 317.

[67] Ibid., pp. 369–87.

[68] Ibid., p. 393.

[69] Ibid., p. 404.

of these reflect the inherent tension between individual freedom from constraint, on the one hand, and alienation and detachment from social groups, on the other hand. For money gives people new choices and options, but it also depersonalizes their social milieu. It is in this light that Simmel isolated the following consequences of money for individuals:

1.   As a "tool," money is nonspecific and thus gives people an opportunity to pursue many diverse and varied activities. For unlike less-liquid forms of expressing value, money does not determine how it can be used. Hence, individuals in a society that uses money as its principal medium of exchange enjoy considerably more freedom of choice than is possible in a society that does not use money.[70]

2.   In a similar vein, money gives people many options for self-expression. For to the degree that individuals seek to express themselves in terms of the objects of their possession, money allows unlimited means for self-expression. As a result, the use of money for self-expression leads to, and indeed encourages, diversity in a population that is no longer constrained in the pursuit of their needs (except, of course, by the amount of money they have).[71]

3.   Yet, at the same time, money creates a distance between one's sense of self and the objects of self-expression. With money, objects are easily acquired and discarded, and hence, long-term attachments to objects do not develop.[72]

4.   As noted earlier, money allows a person to enter many different types of social relations. One can, for example, buy such relationships by paying membership dues in organizations or by spending money on various activities which assure contacts with particular types of people. Hence, money encourages a multiplicity of social relations and group memberships. At the same time, however, money discourages intimate attachments. It increases the multiplicity of involvements, but it atomizes and compartmentalizes an individual's activities and often keeps them from emotional involvement in each of their segregated activities. This trend is, Simmel felt, best personified by the division of labor that is made possible by money wages but that also compartmentalizes individuals, often alienating them from others and their work.[73]

5.   Money also makes it less necessary to know people personally, since their money "speaks" for them. In systems without money, social relations are mediated by intimate knowledge of others and adjustments

---

[70] Ibid., p. 307.
[71] Ibid., pp. 326–27.
[72] Ibid., p. 297.
[73] Ibid., p. 454.

among people are made in terms of the particular characteristics of each individual. But as money begins to mediate interaction, the need to know another, personally, is correspondingly reduced.

Thus, in Simmel's analysis of consequences, money is a mixed blessing for both the individual and society. It allows for greater freedom and provides new and multiple ways for connecting individuals. But, it also isolates, atomizes, and even alienates individuals from the persons and objects in their social milieu. Money thus alters the nature of social relations among individuals in society, and thus, an analysis of its consequences is decidedly a sociological topic. And the consequences of money as the medium of exchange allowed Simmel to address more philosophical issues on the nature of humans and their patterns of social organization.

SIMMEL IN RETROSPECT

Reviewing Georg Simmel's basic works is difficult for at least two reasons. First, Simmel tended to argue by example and illustration, thereby obscuring the more analytical points being made. Second, Simmel typically moved from topic to topic, providing fascinating insights and yet never integrating his ideas into a coherent and unified view. Nevertheless, despite these shortcomings, Simmel's emphasis on the forms of interaction led him to seek basic laws of human organization. These laws tend to be expressed implicitly and are often buried in illustrations and examples, but there can be little doubt that in Simmel's diverse works there are important theoretical principles. It is to extracting and articulating these principles that the next chapter is devoted.

GEORG SIMMEL III:
MODELS AND PRINCIPLES

THE BASIC THEORETICAL APPROACH

Georg Simmel's major theoretical contribution to sociology resides in his concern with the basic forms of interaction. By seeking to look behind differences in the "contents" of diverse social relations and by attempting to uncover their more generic forms, he was able to show that seemingly different situations reveal basic similarities. Such similarities, he implicitly argued, can be expressed as abstract models and/or laws.

Thus, while Simmel did not employ the vocabulary of abstract theory, his many essays on different topics reveal a commitment to formulating abstract statements about basic forms of human relationships. However, a superficial reading of Simmel might initially lead us to the opposite conclusion, for his works tend to focus on a wide variety of empirical topics, and even when he explored a particular type of social relation, such as conflict and exchange, he tended to argue by example. He would, for instance, talk about conflicts among individuals and wars among nation-states in virtually the same passage. Such tendencies give his work an inductive and descriptive flair, but a more careful reading indicates that he clearly held a "covering law" or deductive view of theory in sociology. For example, if conflict between such diverse entities as two individuals and two nations reveals certain common forms, then diverse empirical situations can be understood in terms of the same abstract law or principle.

Simmel's work is often difficult to read and understand as he jumps from topic to topic, from the micro to the macro, and from the historical past to what were contemporary situations in his times. Yet if we keep in mind that this seeming lack of focus represents an effort to use abstract models and principles to explain many diverse empirical cases, then much of the confusion surrounding Simmel's work recedes. His goal is similar to that of all theorists: to explain many empirical events with a few highly abstract models and principles. Indeed, unlike others who were influenced by the German tradition, such as Karl Marx and Max Weber, his explanations are committed to transcending historical epochs and specific empirical events.

In Simmel's view, sociology could be a unique discipline, primarily because it sought to abstract above the contents of social life. Therefore, in this last chapter on Simmel, we should attempt to make more explicit the implicit theoretical models and principles that guide his theoretical efforts. To realize this goal, we will concentrate on the theoretical models and principles that Simmel developed with respect to several related issues:

1. Like most theorists of the 19th and early 20th centuries, Simmel was preoccupied with the process of social differentiation. But unlike Weber, or even Durkheim, he was not so much interested in the historical causes of differentiation as in understanding the reciprocal relationship between social differentiation and patterns of cooperative and conflictual interaction.

2. One such pattern of interaction revolves around the reciprocal relationship between social differentiation, on the one hand, and the changing criteria by which humans form social relations, on the other. In particular he was concerned with the relationship among (a) the reliance on rationality and calculation, (b) the decline of ascription, (c) the use of money, and (d) the way in which a, b, and c are connected to social differentiation.

3. A related issue in Simmel's theoretical efforts is understanding the reciprocal relationship between social differentiation and alterations in the number, volume, rate, and scope of interpersonal ties as well as patterns of group membership.

4. Yet another issue is "individuality." Throughout Simmel's work is found a pervasive concern for "individuality" or "individualization" of people. By these terms, we mean that Simmel was concerned with the growth of personal freedom and autonomy in differentiated societies. At the same time, however, he was also alarmed over the isolation and detachment of individuals from collective involvement in modern society.

5. In all of these concerns is an implicit emphasis on patterns of social integration. For in all of Simmel's major works, questions such as, how individuals are attached to each other and to groups, or how individuals and collective units develop regulatory agreements, prevail.

This theme in Simmel's works is best underscored by the analysis of how conflict promotes social integration.

SIMMEL'S THEORETICAL MODELS

In each of the three basic substantive works examined in the last chapter,[1] Simmel appears to have employed a somewhat distinctive model. Yet the models reveal considerable similarity in that they all address the issues listed above. They all deal with the implications of differentiation for patterns of interaction, and they all address the varying bases of integration associated with different interactive forms. The differences and similarities among the implicit models are outlined in Figures 14–1, 14–2, and 14–3.

FIGURE 14–1
Model 1: Simmel's Image of Group Affiliations

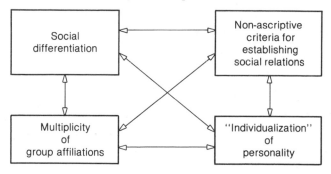

In model 1, Simmel's view of the interrelations among (1) social differentiation, (2) nonascriptive criteria for establishing social relations, (3) multiplicity of group affiliations, and (4) "individualization" of personality are diagramed. Social differentiation encourages the development of nonascriptive bases for establishing social relations, and conversely, the use of nonascriptive criteria results in greater freedom to establish diverse types of social relations—thereby escalating social differentiation. Without the constraints of ascription, and especially with trends toward social differentiation, people begin to form multiple group affiliations which, in turn, further entrenches the use of nonascriptive criteria for establishing social relations. All of these processes lead to growing "individuality" of personality in that people have much freedom of choice.

---

[1] Georg Simmel, *The Philosophy of Money*, trans. Don Bottomore and David Frisby (Boston: Routledge & Kegan Paul, 1978); and *Conflict and the Web of Group Affiliations*, trans. Kurt Wolff and Reinhard Bendix (Glencoe, Ill.: The Free Press, 1955).

FIGURE 14–2
Model 2: Simmel's Image of Social Exchange

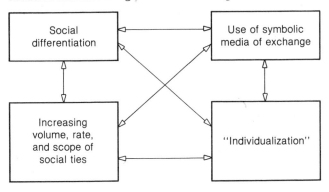

Such individuality, however, discourages long-term commitments to, and involvement with, other individuals and collectivities.

In model 2, Simmel's implicit conceptualization in *The Philosophy of Money* is outlined. Social differentiation, the use of symbolic media of exchange, such as money, and the increasing volume, rate, and scope of social relationships are all viewed as interrelated. These processes further individualization by decreasing peoples' attachments to material objects and social groups. For now, individuals are freed to use symbolic media to engage in wide varieties of short-term relations.

In model 3, Simmel's general model of conflict is presented. While "hostile impulses" are, in Simmel's view, a cause of conflict, the differentiation of populations into diverse structural units gives these "impulses" a vehicle for expression. As is emphasized in the model, social differentiation and conflict often operate to increase the degree of organization of the parties to a conflict. Organization of parties to a conflict also encourages regulation of the conflict through the establishment of regula-

FIGURE 14–3
Model 3: Simmel's Image of Social Conflict

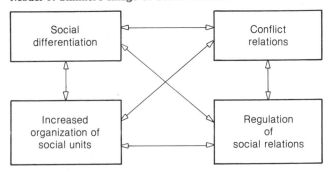

tory agreements and/or the acceptance of control by external authority. The creation of such regulatory arrangements encourages further social differentiation, while institutionalizing conflicts among differentiated and organized social units.

These three models are, of course, highly abstract and present only an image of the general classes of variables, and their interrelations, that Simmel saw as important in understanding the basic forms of interaction. When translated into propositions, these conceptual images take on greater clarity and offer more potential for explaining specific forms of interaction.

SIMMEL'S THEORETICAL PRINCIPLES

Principles of Social Exchange

In *The Philosophy of Money*, Simmel developed a set of theoretical principles of social exchange. Unfortunately, even though this work anticipated contemporary exchange theory, it does not appear to have exerted any great influence on modern theory (primarily because it remained untranslated until recently). The key insight in *The Philosophy of Money* is that the use of different criteria for assessing value has an enormous impact on the form of social relations. Thus, as money replaces barter and other criteria for determining values, social relations are fundamentally changed. But they are transformed in accordance with some basic principles of social exchange, which are never codified by Simmel but which can be extracted from his more discursive argument. These principles are summarized below.

The Attraction Principle.

1. The more actors perceive as valuable each other's respective resources, the more likely is an exchange relationship to develop among these actors.

The Value Principle.

2. The greater is the intensity of an actor's needs for a resource of a given type, and the less available is that resource, the greater is the value of that resource to the actor.

The Power Principles.

3. The more an actor perceives as valuable the resources of another actor, the greater is the power of the latter over the former.

4. The more "liquid" are an actor's resources, the greater will be the exchange options and alternatives, and hence, the greater will be the power of that actor in social exchanges.

The Tension Principle.

5. The more actors in a social exchange manipulate the situation in an effort to misrepresent their needs for a resource and/or conceal the availability of resources, the greater is the level of tension in that exchange and the greater is the potential for conflict.

In these five principles can be found the underlying dynamics of social interaction, as visualized by Simmel. Principle 1 states that interaction occurs because actors value each other's resources, and in accordance with principle 2, value is a dual function of *(a)* actors' needs for resources and *(b)* the scarcity of resources. Principles 3 and 4 underscore the fact that power is a part of the exchange process. Actors who have resources that others value are in a position to extract compliance from those seeking these resources (principle 3), while actors who have liquid or generalized resources, such as money, will be more likely to have power, since liquid resources can be more readily exchanged with alternative actors. Principle 5 states that as actors seek to manipulate situations in order to conceal the availability of resources and their needs for resources, tensions are created, and these tensions can result in conflict.

While these propositions summarize the underlying exchange perspective in Simmel's work, his actual analysis in *The Philosophy of Money* is devoted to summarizing the consequences of a generalized and symbolic media of exchange on social relations and the individual. Thus, Simmel was primarily concerned with the dual questions of how the use of symbolic media of exchange affect *(a)* the form of interaction in a social system and *(b)* the properties of actors in the system.

The first of these two issues can be summarized in the following propositions:

6. The greater is the degree of differentiation in a social system, the greater will be the use of generalized and symbolic media of social exchange, and vice versa.

7. The greater is the use of generalized and symbolic media of exchange in a social system, the greater will be:
   7a. The volume of exchange relations.
   7b. The rate of social exchange.
   7c. The scope of social exchange.
   7d. The accumulation of value in social exchange.

> 7e. The continuity of interaction and exchange.
> 7f. The multiplicity of social ties and exchanges.
> 7g. The differentiation of power to regulate social relations and exchanges.

With respect to the position and properties of actors, Simmel's analysis yields the following propositions:

> 8. The greater is the use of generalized and symbolic media of exchange in a social system, the greater will be:
>> 8a. The options of individuals.
>> 8b. The diversity of individuals.
>
> and the less will be:
>> 8c. The attachment of individuals to objects, others, and groups.

While stated at a somewhat higher level of abstraction than intended by Simmel, these propositions summarize his observations on the consequences of money for social life. His observations on money, however, apply anytime objective and symbolic measures of value are used in exchange relations. And when stated somewhat more abstractly, the purely theoretical implications of Simmel's argument become more evident. The above propositions, we feel, provide a set of interesting theoretical leads for sociologists.

Principles of Social Conflict

Simmel's propositions on conflict can be divided into three groups: (1) those on the conditions affecting the degree of violence in a conflict, (2) those on the consequences of conflict for the overall social system in which the conflict occurs, and (3) those on the consequences of conflict for the units engaged in conflict.

Simmel's propositions on the degree of violence in a conflict can be summarized in the following way:

> 9. The greater is the degree of emotional involvement of parties to a conflict, the more likely is the conflict to be violent.
>> 9a. The greater is the respective solidarity among members of conflicting parties, the greater is the degree of their emotional involvement.
>> 9b. The greater is the previous harmony between members of conflicting parties, the greater is the degree of their emotional involvement.
> 10. The more a conflict is perceived by members of conflict groups

to transcend individual aims and interests, the more likely is the conflict to be violent.

11.   The more conflict is perceived as a means to an end, the less likely is the conflict to be violent.

Simmel's propositions on the consequences of conflict focus on less-violent conflict, since he viewed high degrees of violence to be less frequent than regulated competition. Moreover, most of his propositions concern the integrative consequences of conflict for the larger social system, as is emphasized by the following proposition:

12.   The less violent and more frequent is the conflict among social units in a differentiated social system, the more likely is the conflict to:

   12a.   Allow units to release hostilities before they accumulate to extremely high levels.

   12b.   Encourage the creation of norms to regulate the conflict.

   12c.   Encourage the development of authority and judiciary systems to regulate the conflict.

Similarly, when analyzing the consequences of conflict for the respective parties to a conflict, Simmel stressed the integrative consequences of conflict, especially violent conflict. Thus, in Simmel's eye, violent conflict may have disintegrative consequences for the social whole, but it can promote integration within the parties to the conflict, as is evident in the following propositions:

13.   The more violent are intergroup hostilities and the more frequent is conflict among groups, the less likely are group boundaries to disappear.

14.   The more violent is the conflict, the more likely is centralization of power in the conflict groups.

15.   The more violent is the conflict, the greater will be the internal solidarity of conflict groups, especially if:

   15a.   The conflict group is small.

   15b.   The conflict group represents a minority position.

   15c.   The conflict group is engaged in self-defense.

16.   The more violent and the more prolonged is the conflict between groups, the more likely is the formation of coalitions among previously unrelated groups in a system.

17.   The more prolonged is the threat of violent conflict between groups, the more enduring are the coalitions of each of the conflict parties.

Principles of Group Affiliation

"The Web of Group Affiliations" presents a number of interesting propositions on the consequences of social differentiation for social relations and individuals. Yet, despite the number of examples in this essay, the argument boils down to relatively few propositions when stated more abstractly. The most important of these abstract principles are listed below:

18.   The greater is the degree of social differentiation, the less likely are group affiliations to be concentric[2] and the more likely they are to be multiple and across diverse groups.[3]

---

[3] "Multiple and across diverse groups" can be diagrammed as follows:

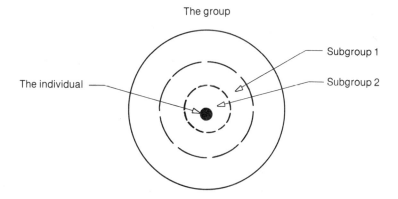

[2] "Concentric" is defined as relations occurring within successive subgroups of a larger collectivity. Diagrammatically, such relations would reveal the following form:

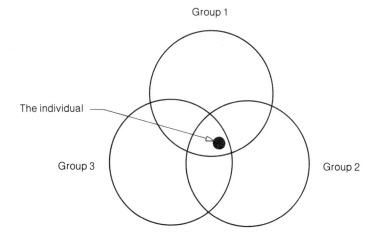

19. The more group affiliations cut across diverse groups, the greater is:
    19a. The distinctiveness of individual personality.
    19b. The freedom of individuals.
    19c. The potential for role-conflict.

SIMMEL'S LEGACY

The theoretical models and principles presented in this chapter offer only a partial glimpse at how Simmel viewed the social world. His many diverse works each add an element to these models and principles, and yet, they do not alter the basic thrust of Simmelian theory. For in models 1, 2, and 3, as well as in the abstract principles that we have listed, the core of Simmel's theoretical contribution is summarized.

In these principles are a number of critical insights that have had to be rediscovered in modern theory. Equally significant is Simmel's strategic advocacy: the search for the laws governing the underlying properties or forms of social relations. This advocacy, we feel, is still good advice for contemporary sociology.

ÉMILE DURKHEIM I:
THE INTELLECTUAL ORIGINS
OF HIS THOUGHT

INTRODUCTION

In the latter half of the 19th century, the French tradition in sociology reemerged. Saint-Simon's and Comte's vision was rekindled as Émile Durkheim began to pull together diverse lines of thought from both the 18th and 19th centuries and to codify a particular mode of sociological analysis. In our review of the origins of Durkheim's thought, we will focus on two 18th-century thinkers in the French tradition—Charles Montesquieu and Jean-Jacques Rousseau—and two 19th-century figures—Auguste Comte and Alexis de Tocqueville. We will also discuss Durkheim's reaction against Herbert Spencer and Karl Marx. Durkheimian sociology, then, represents a curious blend of ideas stimulated by the work of Montesquieu, Rousseau, Comte, Spencer, Marx, and Tocqueville.

CHARLES MONTESQUIEU

As we saw in our analysis of Comte's work, Montesquieu marks the beginning of a French intellectual line that comes to a climax with Durkheim. To appreciate many of Durkheim's concepts, points of emphasis, and methodological approach, then, we must return to Montesquieu—one of the giant intellects of the 18th century.

Montesquieu as the First Social Scientist

Montesquieu introduced an entirely new approach to the study of society. If we look at any number of scholars whose thought was prominent in Montesquieu's time, we can immediately observe dramatic differences between their approach to the study of society and Montesquieu's.

Many scholars of the 18th century were philosophers who were primarily concerned with the question: What is the ultimate origin of society? Their answer to this question was more philosophical than sociological and tended to be given in two parts. First, humans reveal a certain "nature" and they once existed in a "natural state" before the first society was created. Theory about society thus began with speculations about "the state of nature"—whether this state be warlike (Hobbes), peaceful (Locke), or idyllic (Rousseau). Secondly, by necessity or circumstance humans in the state of nature formed a "social contract" and thereby created "society." People agreed to subordinate themselves to government, law, general values and beliefs, and a variety of contracts.

In contrast to these philosophical doctrines, Montesquieu emphasized that humans have never existed without society. They are the product of society, and thus, speculation about the "natural state" of humans did not for Montesquieu represent an analysis of the facts of human life. In contrast, Montesquieu was an empiricist; he was concerned with facts rather than speculation about the essence of humans and the ultimate origins of their society. In many ways, he was attracted to the procedures employed by Newton in physics: observe the facts of the universe, and from these, make statements about their basic properties and the lawlike relations. While it was left to Comte in the following century to trumpet the new science of "social physics," it was Montesquieu who was the first to see that a science of society, molded after the physical sciences, was possible.

Durkheim saw Montesquieu as positing that society is a "thing" or "fact" in the same sense that physical matter constitutes a thing or fact. Montesquieu was the first to recognize, Durkheim believed, that "morals, manners, customs" and the "spirit of a nation" are subject to scientific investigation. From this initial insight, it is a short step to recognizing, as Comte was to do, that a discipline called sociology can study society. Durkheim gave explicit credit to Montesquieu for recognizing that a:

> discipline may be called a science only if it has a definite field to explore. Science is concerned with things, realities. . . . Before social science could begin to exist, it had to be assigned a subject matter.[1]

---

[1] Émile Durkheim, *Montesquieu and Rousseau* (Ann Arbor: University of Michigan Press, 1960), p. 3.

Montesquieu never completely carried through on his view that society could be studied in the same manner as the phenomena of other sciences, but his classic book, *The Spirit of Laws*, represents one of the first sociological works with a distinctly scientific tone. While Montesquieu had become initially famous for other works, it is *The Spirit* that had the most direct influence on Durkheim.[2] Indeed, Durkheim's Latin thesis was on *The Spirit of Laws* and was published a year before his famous French thesis, *The Division of Labor in Society*.[3] From *The Spirit*, Durkheim was to take both methodological and substantive ideas, as is emphasized in the following review of Montesquieu's work and its influence on Durkheim.

Montesquieu's View of "Laws"

The opening lines of *The Spirit of Laws* reads:

> Laws, in their most general signification, are the necessary relations arising from the nature of things. In this sense all beings have their laws: the Deity His laws, the material world its laws, the intelligences superior to man their laws, the beasts their laws, man his laws.[4]

There is an ambiguity in this passage that is never clarified, for Montesquieu used the term *law* in two distinct senses: (1) law as a "commandment" or "rule" created by humans to regulate their conduct and (2) law as a scientific statement of the relations among properties of the universe in its physical, biological, and social manifestations. The first is a substantive conception of law—that of the jurist and political scientist. The second is a conception of scientific laws that explain the regularities among properties of the natural world. Durkheim was to incorporate implicitly this distinction in his own work. On the one hand, his first great work on *The Division of Labor in Society*[5] is about law, for variations in laws and the penalties for their violation were used by Durkheim as

---

[2] Montesquieu's major works include: *The Persian Letters* (New York: Meridian Books, 1901; originally published in 1721); and *Considerations on the Grandeur and Decadence of the Romans* (New York: Free Press, 1965; originally published in 1734). In many ways, these two early books represented a data source for the more systematic analysis in *The Spirit of Laws*, 2 vols. (London: The Colonial Press, 1900; originally published in 1748).

[3] In academic circles of Durkheim's time, two doctoral dissertations were required—one in French and another in Latin. The Latin thesis on Montesquieu was published in 1892 and the French thesis on the division of labor was published in 1893.

[4] Montesquieu, *Spirit of Laws*, p. 1.

[5] Émile Durkheim, *The Division of Labor in Society* (Glencoe, Ill.: Free Press, 1947; originally published in 1893).

concrete indicators of social integration. On the other hand, *The Division of Labor* also involved a search for the scientific laws that explain the nature of social integration in human societies.[6]

Montesquieu also revealed in implicit "hierarchy of laws"—an idea that may have suggested to Comte the hierarchy of the sciences (see Chapter 2). For Montesquieu, "lower order" phenomena, such as physical matter, cannot deviate from the scientific laws that govern their operation, but higher order beings with intelligence can violate and transgress laws, giving the scientific laws of society a probabilistic rather than absolute character. This idea of probabilistic relations among social phenomena was also adopted by Durkheim who was to view statistical "rates" as "social facts" in many of his works.[7]

Montesquieu's Typology of Governments

To search for the scientific laws of the social world, Montesquieu argued that classification and typology are necessary. The enormous diversity of social patterns can easily obscure the common properties of phenomena unless the underlying type is exposed. The first 13 books of *The Spirit* are thus devoted to Montesquieu's famous typology of governmental forms: (1) republic, (2) monarchy, and (3) despotism. Both methodological and substantive facets of Montesquieu's typology were to influence Durkheim. On the methodological side, Durkheim saw as significant the way in which Montesquieu went about constructing his typology. Durkheim stressed the more strictly methodological technique of using "number, arrangement, and cohesion of their component parts" for classifying social structures.[8] In many ways, Durkheim was reading into Montesquieu on this matter, since Montesquieu was never very explicit. Yet Durkheim's lifelong advocacy of typology and of using the number, arrangement, and cohesion of parts as the basis for constructing typologies was apparently inspired by Montesquieu's typology of government.

Another methodological technique that Durkheim appeared to borrow from Montesquieu is the notion that laws enacted by governments will reflect not only the "nature" (that is structural form) of government, but also its "principle" (underlying values and beliefs). Moreover, laws will reflect the other institutions that the nature and principle of govern-

---

[6] Durkheim, *Montesquieu and Rousseau.*

[7] Émile Durkheim, *Suicide* (Glencoe, Ill.: Free Press, 1951; originally published in 1897).

[8] Durkheim, *Montesquieu and Rousseau*, p. 26.

ment influence.[9] Law is thus a good indicator of the culture and structure of society. This premise was to become the central methodological tenet of Durkheim's first major work on the division of labor.

On the substantive side, Montesquieu's view of government as composed of two inseparable elements, nature and principle, probably influenced Durkheim more than he acknowledged. For Montesquieu, each government's nature or structure is a reflection of *(a)* who holds power and *(b)* how power is exercised. Each government also reveals a principle, leading to the classification of governments in terms of structural units and cultural beliefs. For a republic, the underlying principle is "virtue" in which people have respect for law and for the welfare of the group; for a monarchy, the guiding principle is respect for rank, authority, and hierarchy; and for despotism, the principle is fear. The specifics of Montesquieu's political sociology are less important than the general insight they illustrate: social structures are held together by a corresponding system of values and beliefs that individuals have internalized. Moreover, as Montesquieu emphasized, when a government's nature and principle are not in harmony—or more generally, when social structures and cultural beliefs are in contradiction—social change is inevitable. These are theoretical issues with which Durkheim was to wrestle for his entire intellectual career. Yet one finds scarce notice in Durkheim's thesis of Montesquieu's profound insight into this aspect of social reality.

Another substantive issue, for which Montesquieu is most famous, is the "balance of powers" thesis. The basic argument is that a separation or division of powers among elements of government is essential to a stable government. Power must be its own corrective, for only counterpower can limit the abuse of power. Thus, Montesquieu saw the two branches of the legislature (one for the nobility, the other for commoners) as they interact with each other and with the monarch as providing checks and balances on each other.[10] The judiciary, the third element of government, was not considered by Montesquieu to be an independent source of power—as it became in the American governmental system. Several points of emphasis in this analysis no doubt influenced Durkheim. First, Montesquieu's distrust of mass democracy in which the general population directly influences political decisions was to be retained in

---

[9] Ibid., p. 1.

[10] If one computes these balances, they consistently work out in favor of the nobility and against the common person. The nobility and commoners unite to check the monarch, while the nobility and monarch check the commoners. But the monarch cannot, as an elevated figure, unite with the commoners. Montesquieu's aristocratic bias is clearly evident.

Durkheim's analysis of industrial societies. In Durkheim's eye, representation is always to be mediated in order to avoid instability in political decisions. Second, Durkheim shared Montesquieu's distrust of a single center of power. Montesquieu feared despotism, while Durkheim distrusted the monolithic and bureaucratized state, but both recognized that in order to avoid the dangers of highly centralized power, counterpower must be created.

The Causes and Functions of Governments

In addition to the notion of social types and scientific laws, the most conspicuous portions of Durkheim's Latin thesis are those on the "causes" and "functions" of government—a distinction that became central to Durkheimian sociology.

Montesquieu's *The Spirit* is often a confused work; and his analysis of "causes" has frequently been misunderstood by commentators. After the typology of governments in the first 13 books of *The Spirit*, Montesquieu suddenly launched into a causal analysis that could appear to undermine his emphasis on the importance of "the principle" in shaping the "nature," or structure, of government. For suddenly, in books 14 through 25, a variety of physical and moral causes of governmental forms are enumerated. Climates, soil fertility, manners, morals, commerce, money, population size, and religion are introduced one after another as causes of governmental and social forms.

The confusion that is often registered in this abrupt discussion of causes can be mitigated by the recognition of Montesquieu's underlying assumptions. First, these causes do not work directly on governmental forms. Each, in its own way, affects people's behavior, temperament, and disposition in ways that create a "general spirit of the nation"—an idea that was not far from Durkheim's conceptualization of the "collective conscience" and "collective representations" or Comte's similar notions. Thus, "physical causes," such as climate, soil and population size, as well as "moral causes," such as commerce, morals, manner and customs, all operate to constrain how people act, behave, and think. Out of the collective life constrained and shaped by these causes comes the "spirit of a nation," which is a set of implicit ideas that bind people to one another and give them a sense of their common purpose.[11]

Once it is recognized that these causes do not operate directly on

---

[11] This line of argument is derived from Louis Althuser, *Politics and History* (Paris: Universities of Paris, 1959).

the "nature" or structure of government, a second point of clarification is possible. The underlying "principle" of government is linked to the "general spirit" that emerges from the actions and thoughts of people as they are constrained by the list of "causes." Montesquieu was not clear of ambiguity on this issue, but this interpretation is the most consistent with how Durkheim probably viewed Montesquieu's argument. Yet curiously, despite the similarity of their views on the importance of collective ideas or "spirits" on social relations, Durkheim did not give Montesquieu much credit for this aspect of his sociology.

Durkheim did give Montesquieu explicit credit, however, for recognizing that a society must assume a "definite form" as a result of its "particular situation" and that this form stems from "efficient causes." In particular, he indicated that Montesquieu's view of ecological and population variables was to stimulate his concern with "material density" and how it influences "moral density." Durkheim recognized that to view social structures and ideas as the result of identifiable causes marks a dramatic breakthrough in social thought, especially since many social thinkers of the time were often locked into discussions of human nature and the "origins" of the first social contract.

Durkheim was, however, highly critical of Montesquieu's causal analysis in one respect: he saw Montesquieu as arguing in terms of "final causes." That is, the ends served by a structure such as law cause it to emerge and persist. As Durkheim stressed:

> Anyone who limits his inquiry to the final cause of social phenomena, loses sight of their origins and is untrue to science. This is what would happen to sociology if we followed Montesquieu's method.[12]

Durkheim recognized that Montesquieu was one of the first scholars to argue for what is now termed *cultural relativism*. Social structures must be assessed, not in relation to some absolute, ethnocentric, or moralistic standard, but in their own terms and in view of the particular context in which they are found. For example, Montesquieu could view slavery not so much as a moral evil but as a viable institution in certain types of societies in particular historical periods. Implicit in this kind of argument is the notion of "function": a structure must be assessed in terms of its functions for the social whole; if a social pattern, even one like slavery, promotes the persistence and integration of a society, then it cannot be said, a priori, to be an evil or good pattern. Durkheim felt that Montesquieu too easily saw the results of structures—that is,

---

[12] Durkheim, *Montesquieu and Rousseau*, p. 44.

integration—as their cause, with the result that Montesquieu's functional and causal analysis frequently became confused. Yet Montesquieu may have suggested to Durkheim a critical distinction between causal and functional analysis.

In sum, Durkheim gave Montesquieu credit for many insights that became a part of his sociology. The social world can be studied as a "thing"; it is best to develop typologies; it is necessary to examine the number, arrangement, and relations among parts in developing these typologies; it is important to view law as an indicator of broader social and cultural forces; and it is wise to employ both causal and functional analysis.

Yet, despite Durkheim's praise of Montesquieu, it is interesting to note what he did not acknowledge in Montesquieu's work: the view that laws, like those of physics, can be formulated for the social realm (Durkheim in the thesis gave Comte credit for this insight);[13] the recognition that social morphology and cultural symbols are interconnected; the position that causes of morphological structures are mediated through, and mitigated by, cultural ideas; the notion that causes, and the laws that express relations among events, are probabilistic in nature; and the view that power in social relations must be checked by counterpower. Yet there can be little doubt that these ideas became an integral part of Durkheim's thinking, and thus, much of Montesquieu's theoretical legacy was to live in Durkheimian sociology.[14]

JEAN-JACQUES ROUSSEAU

Writing his major works in the decade following the 1748 publication of Montesquieu's *The Spirit of Laws*, Jean-Jacques Rousseau produced a philosophical doctrine that contains none of Montesquieu's sense for social science, but much of his sense for the nature of social order.[15]

---

[13] As Durkheim noted: "No further progress could be made until it was recognized that the laws of societies are no different from those governing the rest of nature and that the method by which they are discovered is identical with that of the other sciences. This was Auguste Comte's contribution." (Ibid., pp. 63–64.)

[14] For further commentary on Montesquieu's work, see Althuser, *Politics and History*, pp. 13–108; Raymond Aron, *Main Currents in Sociological Thought I* (Garden City, N.Y.: Doubleday Anchor, 1968), pp. 13–72; W. Stark, *Montesquieu: Pioneer of the Sociology of Knowledge* (Toronto: University of Toronto Press, 1961); and Thomas L. Pangle, *Montesquieu's Philosophy of Liberalism; A Commentary on "The Spirit of Laws"* (Chicago: University of Chicago Press, 1973).

[15] Jean-Jacques Rousseau, *The Social Contract and Discourses*, translated by G. D. H. Cole (New York: E. P. Dutton, 1950). This book is a compilation of Rousseau's various *Discourses* and *The Social Contract*—his most important works—which were written separately between 1750 and 1762. It is *The Social Contract* that Durkheim was to analyze and it is this that appears, along with his Latin thesis on Montesquieu, in Durkheim, *Montesquieu and Rousseau*, pp. 65–138.

While not greatly admired in his time, Rousseau's ideas were, by the beginning of the 19th century, to be viewed in a highly favorable light. Indeed, in retrospect, Rousseau was to be considered the leading figure of the Enlightenment, surpassing Hobbes, Locke, Voltaire, and certainly Montesquieu. It is not surprising, therefore, that Durkheim read with interest Rousseau's philosophical doctrine and extracted many ideas.

Rousseau's Doctrine

Rousseau's doctrine was a unique combination of Christian notions of the Fall that came with Original Sin and Voltaire's belief in the progress of humans.[16] Rousseau first postulated a presocietal "state of nature" in which individuals were dependent upon nature and had only simple physical needs, for "man's"[17] desires "do not go beyond his physical needs; in all the universe the only desirable things he knows are food, a female, and rest." In the "state of nature," humans had little contact or dependence upon each other; and they had only crude "sensations" that reflected their direct experiences with the physical environment.

It was from this natural state that the great "fall" came. The discovery of agriculture, the development of metallurgy, and other events created a new and distinct entity: society. People formed social relations; they discovered private property; they appropriated property; they competed; those with property exploited others; they began to feel emotions of jealousy and envy; they began to fight and make war; and in other ways they created the modern world. Rousseau felt that this world not only deviates from humans' natural state, but it makes their return to this state impossible.

As an emergent reality that destroys the natural state, modern society poses a series of problems that make life agonizing misery. In particular, humans feel no limit to their desires and passions; self-interest dominates; and one human exploits another. For Rousseau society is corrupt and evil, destroying not only the natural controls on passions and self-interest but also the liberty from exploitation by one's fellows that typified the natural state.

Rousseau's solution to this evil was as original as it was naive, and yet it was to exert considerable influence on Durkheim. His solution was to eliminate self-interest and inequality by creating a situation in

---

[16] J. H. Broome, *Rousseau: A Study of His Thought* (New York: Barnes & Noble, 1963), p 14.

[17] Rousseau's phraseology uses the term *the natural state of man* which is here retained.

which human beings have the same relation to society as they once had to nature. That is, people should be free from each other and yet equally subject to society. In Rousseau's view, only the political state could assure individual freedom and liberty, and only when individuals totally subordinate their interest to what he termed the *general will* could inequality, exploitation, and self-interest be eliminated. For if all individuals must subjugate themselves equally to the general will and the state, then they are equal. And if the state can assure individual freedom and maintain equal dependence of individuals on the general will, then the basic elements of nature are re-created: freedom, liberty, and equal dependence on an external force (society instead of nature).

What is the "general will"? And how is it to be created? Rousseau was never terribly clear on just what constitutes the general will, but it appears to have referred to an emergent set of values and beliefs embodying "individual wills." The general will can be created and maintained, Rousseau asserted, only by several means: (1) the elimination of other-world religions, such as Christianity, and their replacement by a "civil religion" with the general will as the supreme being; (2) the elimination of family socialization and its replacement by common socialization of all the young into the general will (presumably through schools); and (3) the creation of a powerful state that embodies the general will and the corresponding elimination of groups, organizations, and other "minor associations" that deflect the power of general will and generate pockets of self-interest and potential dissensus among people.[18]

Rousseau and Durkheim

Society as an Emergent Reality. In Durkheim's courses, he gave Rousseau credit for the insight that society constitutes a moral reality, *sui generis*, that can be distinguished from individual morality.[19] While Montesquieu had achieved a similar recognition, Rousseau phrased the matter in a way the Durkheim was to emulate on frequent occasions. For Rousseau as well as Durkheim, society is "a moral entity having specific qualities [separate] from those of the individual beings who com-

---

[18] For more detailed analyses of Rousseau's doctrines, see Broome, *Rousseau;* Ernst Cassirer, *The Question of Jean-Jacques Rousseau* (Bloomington: Indiana University Press, 1963); Ronald Grimsley, *The Philosophy of Rousseau* (London: Oxford University Press, 1973); John Charuet, *The Social Problem in the Philosophy of Rousseau* (Cambridge: Cambridge University Press, 1974); and David Cameron, *The Social Thought of Rousseau and Burke: A Comparative Study* (Toronto: University of Toronto Press, 1973).

[19] Durkheim's essay on Rousseau in *Montesquieu and Rousseau,* was drafted from a course that he taught at Bordeaux. It was published posthumously in 1918.

pose it, somewhat as chemical compounds have properties that they owe to none of their elements."[20]

Thus, Durkheim took from Rousseau the view of society as an emergent and moral entity, much like emergent physical phenomena. And like Rousseau, Durkheim also abhorred a society in which competition and exchange dominate over a common morality. Indeed, for Durkheim, society was not possible without a moral component guiding exchanges among individuals.

Social Pathology. Durkheim viewed Rousseau's discussion of the natural state as a "methodological device" that could be used to highlight the pathologies of contemporary society and to provide guidelines for the remaking of society. While many others in the 18th and 19th centuries had also emphasized the ills of the social world, Durkheim appeared to be drawn to three central conditions emphasized by Rousseau. Durkheim was to term these (1) *egoism*, (2) *anomie*, and (3) *the forced division of labor*, but his debt to Rousseau is clear. For Durkheim, egoism is a situation where self-interest and self-concern take precedence over commitment to the larger collectivity. Anomie is a state of deregulation such that the collective no longer controls people's desires and passions. The forced division of labor is a condition where one class can use its privilege to exploit another and to force people into certain roles. Indeed, the inheritance of privilege and the use of privilege by one class to exploit another was repugnant to Durkheim. Like Rousseau, Durkheim felt that inequalities should be based upon "natural" differences that spring from "a difference of age, health, physical strength, and mental and spiritual qualities."[21]

Thus, Durkheim was highly sympathetic to Rousseau's conception of what ailed society: people force others to do their bidding; they are deregulated; and they are unattached to a larger purpose. And hence, the social order must be structured in ways that mitigate these pathologies.

The Problem of Order. Durkheim thus accepted the dilemma of modern society as Rousseau saw it. How is it possible to maintain individual freedom and liberty, without also releasing people's desires and encouraging rampant self-interest while, at the same time, creating a strong and cohesive social order that does not aggravate inequality and oppression?

---

[20] Durkheim, *Montesquieu and Rousseau*, p. 82. Durkheim took this quote from Rousseau.

[21] Ibid., p. 86.

For Rousseau, this question could be answered with a strong political state that assured individual freedom and a general will that emulated nature. Like Rousseau, Durkheim believed that the state was the only force which would guarantee individual freedom and liberty, but he altered Rousseau's notion of society as the equivalent of the physical environment in the state of nature. For Durkheim, society and the constraints that it imposes must be viewed as natural, with the result that people must be taught to accept the constraints and barriers of society in the same way that they accept the limitations of their biological makeup and the physical environment. Only in this way could both egoism and anomie be held in check. For Durkheim, constraint by the moral force of society is in the natural order of things.

Like Rousseau, Durkheim was also to argue for a view of society as "sacred" and for the transfer of the same sentiments toward civil and secular society that people traditionally had maintained towards the gods which, Durkheim would come to emphasize, are only symbolizations of society.[22] Moreover, like Rousseau, Durkheim was to stress the need for a moral education outside of the family in which children could be taught in schools to understand and accept the importance of commitment to the morality of the collective.

Such commitment could be achieved, Durkheim was to argue, through a unified "collective conscience" or set of "collective representations" which could regulate people's desires and passions. Such a view represented a reworking of Rousseau's view of absolute commitment to the general will. Yet, in sharp contrast to Rousseau, Durkheim came to believe that only through attachment to cohesive subgroups, or what Rousseau had called "minor associations," could egoism be mitigated. Such groups, Durkheim felt, could attach individuals to the remote collective conscience and give them an immediate community of others. Moreover, like Montesquieu, Durkheim distrusted an all-powerful state, and hence, he came to view these subgroups as a political counterbalance to the powers of the state.

Thus, Durkheim borrowed many ideas from Rousseau. Some of his most central concepts about social pathologies—anomie, egoism, and the forced division of labor—owed much to Rousseau's work. His vision

---

[22] Many of the specifics of Durkheim's ideas about religion as the symbolization of society were borrowed from Roberton Smith. See Steven Lukes, *Émile Durkheim: His Life and Work: A Historical and Critical Study* (London: Allen Lane, 1973), p. 450. For a further documentation of the influences on Durkheim's sociology of religion, see Robert Alun Jones and Mariah Evans, "The Critical Moment in Durkheim's Sociology of Religion" (Paper read at the American Sociological Association, September 1978).

of society as integrated by a strong state and by a set of common values and beliefs also reflected Rousseau's vision of how to eliminate these pathologies. His desire to use schools to provide moral education for the young and to rekindle the spirit of commitment to secular society that people once had toward the sacred was also inspired by Rousseau.

Yet Durkheim could never accept Rousseau's trust of the state. For Durkheim, the state could not be too powerful; its power must be checked and balanced. And people must be free to associate and to join groupings that encourage diversity based upon common experiences and that create centers of counterpower to mitigate the state's power. Durkheim thus internalized Rousseau's vision of an integrated society in which individual freedom and liberty prevail. And he accepted the challenge of proposing ways to achieve that society. But he could never abide by Rousseau's vision of an all-powerful state and almost oppressive general will.[23]

Rousseau's impact on Durkheim was, no doubt, profound, but the extremes of Rousseau's philosophy are mitigated in Durkheim's work. Montesquieu's emphasis on the balancing of power with counterpower, and his emphasis on empirical facts rather than moral precepts, represented one tempering influence on Durkheim. Still another mitigating influence came from Auguste Comte, whose work consolidated many intellectual trends into a clear program for a science of society that could be used to create the "good society."

AUGUSTE COMTE

It is difficult to know how much of the French intellectual tradition of the 18th century came to Durkheim through Auguste Comte, since Durkheim did not always acknowledge his debt to the titular founder of sociology. This difficulty is compounded by the fact that, like Durkheim's work, Comte's intellectual scheme represents a synthesis of ideas from Montesquieu, Rousseau, Turgot, Condorcet, Saint-Simon[24] and others in the French lineage. Yet, it is clear that many of the specific features of Durkheimian sociology owed much to Comte's grand vision for the science of society. Since we have reviewed Comte's thought in Chapter 2, we will only focus on specific aspects of Comte's intellectual scheme that appear to have exerted the most influence on Durkheim.

---

[23] For a discussion of Durkheim's differences with Rousseau, see Lukes, *Émile Durkheim*, chap. 14.

[24] Many have noted how much Comte took from his teacher, Saint-Simon. Yet, we can argue that Saint-Simon's more scientific concerns reached Durkheim via Comte's reinterpretation. Saint-Simon's utopian socialism was rejected by Durkheim.

The Science of Positivism

Comte must have reinforced for Durkheim Montesquieu's insistence that "facts" and "data," rather than philosophical speculation, should guide the science of society. Borrowing Comte's vision of a science of "social facts," Durkheim agreed with Comte in the latter's view that the laws of human organization could be discovered. These laws, as Montesquieu had stressed, will not be as "rigid" or "deterministic" as in sciences lower in the "hierarchy of sciences," but they will be the equivalent of those laws in physics, chemistry, and biology in that they will allow for the understanding of phenomena. Thus, Comte cemented in Durkheim's mind the dictum that the search for sociological laws must be guided by empirical facts, and conversely, the gathering of facts must be directed by theoretical principles.

The Methodological Tenets of Postivism

To collect facts requires a methodology, and Comte was the first to make explicit the variety of methodological approaches that could guide the new science of society. As he indicated, four procedures are acceptable: (1) "observation" of the social world by the use of human senses (best done, he emphasized, when guided by theory), (2) "experimentation," especially as allowed by social pathologies, (3) "historical" observation in which regular patterns of change in the nature of society—especially in the nature of its ideas—can be seen, and (4) "comparison" in which (a) human and animal societies, (b) coexisting human societies, and (c) different elements of the same society are compared with an eye toward isolating the effects of specific variables. Durkheim was to employ all of these methods in his sociology, and hence, there can be little doubt that Comte's methodological approach influenced Durkheim's methodology.

Another methodological aspect of Comte's thought revolved around the organic analogy. Comte, as we saw in Chapter 2, often viewed society as like a biological organism, with the result that a part, such as the family or the state, could be understood in terms of what it did for or contributed to the "body social." Montesquieu had made a similar point, although it was Comte who first drew the clear analogy between the social and biological organisms. The functional method developed by Durkheim thus owed much to Comte's biological analogy. Indeed, as Durkheim was to emphasize, complete understanding of social facts is not possible without assessing their functions for maintaining the integration of the social whole.[25]

Much less prominent in Comte's than Montesquieu's scheme was the emphasis on typology. Yet, Comte recognized that the construction of somewhat "idealized" types of social phenomena could help in sociological analysis. While many intermediate cases would not conform to these extreme types, their deviations from the types could allow for their comparison against a common yardstick, that is, the idealized type.[26] In his early work, Durkheim was to develop typologies of societies, and thus, we can assume that Montesquieu's emphasis on types, as reinforced by Comte's emphasis on the use of types as an analytical device for comparison, must have shaped Durkheim's approach. For throughout his career, Durkheim was to insist that classification of phenomena in terms of their "morphology" or structure must precede either causal or functional analysis.

Social Statics and Dynamics

Durkheim was also influenced by the substance of Comte's scheme. As can be recalled from Chapter 2, Comte divided sociology into "statics" and "dynamics"—a distinction that Durkheim was implicitly to maintain. Moreover, the specific concepts that Comte used to understand statics and dynamics were adopted by Durkheim.

With regard to "social statics," Durkheim shared Comte's concern with social solidarity and with the impact of the division of labor on this solidarity. In particular, Durkheim was to ask the same question as Comte: How can *consensus universalis*, or what Durkheim was to term the *collective conscience*, be a basis for social integration with growing specialization of functions in society? How can consensus over ideas, beliefs, and values be maintained at the same time that people are differentiated and pulled apart by their occupational specialization? *The Division of Labor*, Durkheim's first major work, addressed these questions, and while Rousseau in the 18th century and a host of others in the 19th century, had also tried to answer these same issues, Durkheim's approach owed more to Comte than any other thinker.[27]

---

[25] For a more complete analysis of Comte's organicism and its impact on Durkheim's functionalism, see Jonathan H. Turner and Alexandra Maryanski, *Functionalism: An Intellectual Portrait* (Menlo Park, Calif.: Benjamin/Cummings, 1979).

[26] This approach obviously anticipated by a half century Max Weber's ideal-type method.

[27] Durkheim, *Division of Labor.*

With respect to "social dynamics," Comte held an evolutionary vision of human progress. Societies, especially their ideas, are moving in a direction—from theological, through metaphysical, to positivistic modes of thought. Durkheim was to adopt this specific view of the evolution of ideas from a religious to a positivistic basis late in his career in his work on religion. But more fundamentally, he retained the evolutionary approach to studying social change held by Comte and a host of other thinkers. Societies were seen by Durkheim as moving from simple to complex patterns of social structure and, correspondingly, from religious to secular systems of ideas. Almost everything that Durkheim was to examine was couched in these evolutionary terms which, to a very great extent, were adopted from Comte.

Science and Social Progress

Like his teacher and collaborator, Saint-Simon, Comte saw the development of sociology as a means to creating a better society. Although Durkheim's sense of pathology about the modern world probably owes more to Rousseau than to either Saint-Simon or Comte, Durkheim accepted their hope for a society based upon the application of sociological laws. Durkheim was much less extreme than either Saint-Simon or Comte, who tended to make a religion out of science and to advocate unattainable utopias, but he retained Comte's view that a science of society could be used to facilitate social progress. Indeed, Durkheim never abandoned his dream that a just and integrated social order could be created by applying the laws of sociology.

In sum, then, Durkheim's debt to Rousseau was mitigated by his exposure to Comte. Durkheim's view of science as reliant upon data and as generating laws of human organization came as much from Comte as any other thinker, as did his adoption of explicit methodological techniques. Durkheim's substantive view of society similarly reflected Comte's emphasis: a concern for social integration of differentiated units and for determining how ideas (values, beliefs, and norms) are involved in such integration. And Comte's insistence that science be used to promote the betterment of the human condition translated Rousseau's passionate and moralistic assessment of social ills into a more rational concern with constructing an integrated society employing sociological principles.

ALEXIS DE TOCQUEVILLE

In 1835, Alexis de Tocqueville, a young member of an elite family, published the first two volumes of a book based on his observations of

American society. Almost immediately, *Democracy in America* was a success, propelling Tocqueville into a lifelong position of intellectual and political prominence in France. The third and fourth volumes of *Democracy in America* appeared in 1840,[28] and after a short political career culminating in his abbreviated appointment as foreign minister for France, Tocqueville retired to write what he defined as his major work, *The Old Regime and the French Revolution*, which appeared in 1857.[29] His death in 1859 cut short the completion of *The Old Regime*, but the completed volumes of *Democracy in America* and the first part of *The Old Regime* established Tocqueville as the leading political thinker in France, one who carried the tradition of Montesquieu into the 19th century and one whom Durkheim read carefully.

Tocqueville probably never read Comte, but his effort to emulate Montesquieu's method of analysis must have had considerable influence on Durkheim. Indeed, it is from Tocqueville's analysis of democracy in America that Durkheim was to get many of the ideas that were to mitigate the extremes of Rousseau's political solutions to social pathologies.

Tocqueville's *Democracy in America*

Tocqueville saw the long-term trend toward democracy as the key to understanding the modern world. In *Democracy in America*, the young Tocqueville attempted to discover why individual freedom and liberty were being preserved in the United States, and implicitly, why French efforts toward democracy had experienced trouble (a theme more explicitly developed in *The Old Regime and the French Revolution*). In this effort, Tocqueville isolated two trends that typified democracies:

1. *The trend toward a leveling of social status.* While economic and political ranks are preserved, democratic societies bestow equal social status on their members—creating, in Tocqueville's eye—an increasingly homogeneous mass.
2. *The trend toward centralization of power.* Democratic governments tend to create large and centralized administrative bureaucracies and to concentrate power increasingly in the hands of legislative bodies.

---

[28] Alexis de Tocqueville, *Democracy in America*, (New York: Alfred A. Knopf, 1945; originally published in 1835 and 1840).

[29] Alexis de Tocqueville, *The Old Regime and the French Revolution* (Garden City, N.Y.: Doubleday, 1955; originally published in 1857).

Tocqueville saw a number of potential dangers in these two trends. First, as differences among people are leveled, the only avenue for social recognition becomes ceaseless material acquisition motivated by blind ambition. Tocqueville felt that traditional status and honor distinctions had kept ambition and status-striving in check, but as these are released and as the old hereditary basis bestowing honor is destroyed, the individual is atomized and freed of constraint—a condition that is reminiscent of Rousseau's analysis and which was, no doubt, to stimulate Durkheim's conceptualization of egoism and anomie.

Second, the centralization of administrative power can become so great as to result in despotism which then undermines individual freedom and liberty. Moreover, centralized governments tend to rely on external war and to suppress internal dissent in an effort to promote further consolidation of power.

Third, the centralization of decision-making in the legislative branch can make government too responsive to the immediate, short-lived, and unreasoned sentiments of the social mass. Under these conditions, government becomes unstable as it is pulled one way, and then another, by public sentiment.

Montesquieu's influence is clearly evident in these concerns. But unlike Montesquieu, Tocqueville saw another side of democracy, a side where individual liberty and freedom could be preserved even with the centralization of power, and where people's ambitions and atomization could be held in check even as the old system of honor and prestige recedes. The democratic pattern in America, Tocqueville believed, provided an illustration of conditions that could promote this other side of democracy.

As a student of Montesquieu, it is not surprising that Tocqueville's analysis of democracy in America made references to historical causes, placing emphasis on geography, unique historical circumstances, the system of laws (in particular, the constitution), and most importantly, the "customs, manners, and beliefs" of the American people. Out of these "causes," Tocqueville delineated several conditions that mitigate the concentration of political power and the overatomization of individuals:

1. The system of checks and balances in government, with power in the federal government divided into three branches.
2. The federalist system in which state and local governments, with their own divisions of powers, check each other's power as well as that of the federal government.
3. A free and independent press.

4. A strong commitment of the people to use and rely upon local institutions.
5. The freedom to form and use political and civil associations to achieve individual and collective goals.
6. A powerful system of values and beliefs stressing individual freedom and liberty.

The power and subtlety of Tocqueville's description of America cannot be captured with a short list like that above. Yet, this list probably best communicates what Durkheim was to pull out of Tocqueville's work. Rousseau and Tocqueville had both highlighted the ills of the modern world—unregulated passions and rampant self-interest—but Rousseau's solution to these problems was too extreme for the liberal Durkheim, whereas Tocqueville's analysis of America provided a view of a modern and differentiated social structure where freedom, liberty, and individualism could be maintained without severe pathologies or without recourse to a dictatorial state.

Durkheim and Tocqueville

Durkheim was to view modern social structure as integrated when (a) differentiated functions are well coordinated, (b) individuals are attached to collective organizations, (c) individual's freedom is preserved by a central state, (d) this central state sets broad collective goals and personifies common values, and (e) the state's broad powers are checked and balanced by countersources of power.

It is not hard to find these themes in Tocqueville's work. In particular, Durkheim was to find appealing the idea of "civil and political" associations. These associations can provide people with a basis for attachment and identification, and they also serve as a mechanism for mediating between their members and the state. Durkheim was to term these associations *occupational* or *corporate* groups, and there can be little doubt that he took much from Tocqueville's analysis of voluntary civil and political associations. Moreover, in adopting Montesquieu's emphasis on customs, manners, and beliefs that promote strong commitments to freedom and liberty, without also promoting atomization, Durkheim recognized in Tocqueville's work the importance of general values and beliefs (Rousseau's "general will" and Comte's "consensus universalis" and "general spirit") for promoting integration among the diversified groupings of modern societies. For even if these values and beliefs emphasized individual freedom and liberty, they can be used to unite people by stressing a collective respect for the rights of the individual.

Thus, Tocqueville gave to Durkheim a sense for some of the general conditions that could mitigate the pathologies of modern societies. These conditions were to become a part of Durkheim's practical program as well as his more strictly theoretical analysis.

HERBERT SPENCER

Montesquieu, Rousseau, Comte, and Tocqueville represent the French intellectual heritage from which Durkheim took many of his most important concepts.[30] His criticism of these thinkers is not severe, and we can sense that Durkheim never reacted against their thought. He took what was useful and ignored obvious weaknesses. Such is not the case with Herbert Spencer, for throughout Durkheim's career, Spencer was singled out for very special criticism.

Durkheim and Spencerian Utilitarianism

Durkheim was to react vehemently against any view of social order that ignored the importance of collective values and beliefs. Utilitarian doctrines in general, and Herbert Spencer's utilitarianism in particular, stress the importance of competition, and exchange in creating a social order held together by contracts among people pursuing their self-interest. Durkheim was not to ignore the importance of competition, exchange, and contract, but he was to see blind self-interest as a social pathology. A society could not be held together by self-interest and legal contracts alone; there must be a "moral" component or an underlying system of collective values and beliefs guiding people's interactions in the pursuit of "collective" goals or interests.

Durkheim was thus highly critical of Spencer's sociology which, as we saw in Chapter 3, coined such phrases as "survival of the fittest" and which saw society as laced together by contracts negotiated out of the competition and exchange of self-interested actors. Indeed, Durkheim's works are so filled with references to the inadequacies of Spen-

---

[30] This is not to deny the influence of specific teachers and less-well-known scholars. But we think that the degree to which Durkheim took from the giants of French thought has been underemphasized in commentaries. There is too much similarity in the combined legacy of Montesquieu, Rousseau, Comte, and Tocqueville, on the one hand, and Durkheim's thought on the other, for the impact of these prominent social thinkers to be ignored.

cerian sociology that we might view Durkheimian sociology as a lifelong reaction, perhaps overreaction, against Spencer.[31]

Durkheim and Spencerian Organicism

As we noted in Chapter 3, Spencer wore two intellectual hats: (1) the staunch individualist and utilitarian and (2) the organicist who saw society as like an organism. As we saw, it was Spencer who took Comte's organic analogy and converted it into an explicit functionalism: system parts function to meet explicit needs of the "body social." Durkheim clearly derived considerable inspiration from this mode of analysis, since one of his major methodological tenets is to stress the importance of assessing the functions of social phenomena, whether the division of labor, religious cults, legal systems, or punishments for deviance. We might even go so far as to speculate that, had Spencer not formulated functionalism, it is unlikely that Durkheim would have adopted this mode of sociological analysis.

Durkheim and Spencerian Evolutionism

As we observed in Chapter 3, Spencer had an evolutionary view of societies as moving from a "simple" to a "treble compound" group. While clearly deficient in many respects, Spencer's description was attuned, far more than Comte's, to the explicitly structural and cultural aspects of social evolution. Comte's evolutionism had been vague, with references to the movement of systems of thought and the view of the social organicism as embracing all of humanity. In contrast, Spencer's analysis was far more sociological and attuned to explicit variables that could distinguish types of societies from one another and that could provide a view of the dimensions along which evolutionary change could be described. Thus, it is difficult to imagine that Durkheim was unimpressed with Spencer's analysis of the broad contours of social evolution.[32] Indeed, Durkheim's first major work was to explore social evolution from simple primitive to complex industrial societies—a task that had initially occupied Spencer in volume 1 of his *Principles of Sociology*.

---

[31] For a more detailed analysis of Durkheim and Spencer, see Turner and Maryanski, *Functionalism*, chap. 1.

[32] Recent commentaries, surprisingly those by British scholars, have tended to underemphasize Spencer's impact on Durkheim. While all commentaries note the positive reaction of Durkheim to the German organicist Albert Schaffle, they fail to note that Schaffle was simply adopting Spencer's ideas.

KARL MARX

Durkheim analyzed social and communist doctrines in his courses, especially in a course on the history of social thought. He was often critical, as can be seen in posthumously published essays taken from course lectures.[33] Yet, there is some evidence that Durkheim wanted to devote a full course to Karl Marx's thought, but apparently, he never found the time. Durkheim was thus aware of Marx, but was generally dismayed by socialism's "working-class bias" and by the emphasis on revolution and conflict. Durkheim felt that the problems of alienation, exploitation, and class antagonism are problems of all sectors of society and that revolution causes more pathology than it resolves. Yet in his first work, Durkheim discussed the forced division of labor, the value theory of labor, and the problems of exploitation—points of emphasis that are highly reminiscent of Marx's conceptualization.

On balance, however, Marx's influence was negative. Durkheim reacted against Marx's insistence that integration in capitalist societies could not be achieved because of its "internal contradictions." What for Marx was the "normal" conflict-generating forms of capitalism were for Durkheim "abnormal forms" which could be eliminated without internal revolution. Indeed, French sociology in the aftermath of the French Revolution and the lesser revolution of 1848, was decidedly conservative and did not consider revolutionary conflict as a productive and constructive way to bring about desired change. Thus while Marx's influence on Durkheim is evident, it is not profound. Unlike Weber, for whom the "ghost of Marx" was ever present, Durkheim considered Marx's thought, reacted against Marx's ideas in his first works, and eventually rejected and ignored Marx in later works.

ANTICIPATING DURKHEIMIAN SOCIOLOGY

A scholar's ideas are the product of multiple influences, some obvious and others more subtle. A number of biographical examinations of Durkheims work have examined the more subtle influences, and thus, we have not sought to duplicate these efforts. Rather, we have explored the more apparent sources of Durkheim's distinctive intellectual style. Surprisingly, much less has been said about these more obvious sources of Durkheim's ideas. Indeed, by simply looking at the key elements of Durkheim's thought, and then by examining the major figures of Dur-

---

[33] See, for example, Durkheim *Socialism and Saint-Simon* (Yellow Springs, Ohio: Antioch Press, 1959; originally published in 1928).

kheim's intellectual milieu, the source of his basic concepts and concerns becomes startlingly clear.

The influence of various scholars on Durkheim's sociology is evident at different points in his career, a fact that will become clear in the next chapter. By way of anticipating this discussion, we close this chapter with a brief listing of the elements of Durkheim's sociology. All of these elements derive from the scholars discussed in this chapter, but Durkheim was to combine them in ingenious ways, creating a distinctive sociological perspective. Durkheimian sociology can be seen as *(a)* a series of methodological tenets, *(b)* a theory-building strategy, *(c)* a set of substantive topics, and *(d)* a host of practical concerns. Each of these is briefly summarized in an effort to anticipate the detailed analysis of the next chapter.

Methodological Tenets. From Montesquieu and Comte, Durkheim came to view a science of society as possible only if social and moral phenomena are considered as a distinct reality. Moreover, a science of the social world must be like that of the physical and biological worlds; it must be based upon data or facts. Montesquieu had initially emphasized this point, but it was Comte who provided the articulation of methods to be employed by the "science of society." Historical, comparative, experimental, and observational techniques must all be used to discover the social facts that can build a theory of society.

Theoretical Strategy. Again, it was from Montesquieu and Comte that Durkheim received the vision that sociological laws can be discovered. In particular, it was from Montesquieu that causal analysis came to be an integral part of Durkheim's approach. Theory should seek the general causes of phenomena, for only in this way can the abstract laws of social organization be uncovered. Yet without a corresponding, but nonetheless separate, analysis of the functions served by social phenomena, these laws will remain hidden—a point of emphasis that was implicit in Montesquieu's and Comte's work and that became explicit in Herbert Spencer's sociology. Thus for Durkheim, the laws of sociology will come from the causal and functional analysis of social facts.

Substantive Interests. For Durkheim the basic theoretical question was: What forces hold society together? At a substantive level, this question involved the examination of *(a)* social structures, *(b)* symbolic components, such as values, beliefs, and norms, and *(c)* the complex relations between *(a)* and *(b)*. From Montesquieu, Tocqueville, and Spencer, Durkheim acquired a sense for social structure and from Montesquieu's spirit of a nation, Rousseau's general will, and Comte's consensus universalis, he came to understand the significance of cultural symbols for integrating social structures. The specific topics of most concern to Durkheim—religion, education, government, the division of labor, intermediate groups, and collective representations—come from all the scholars discussed in this chapter and from specific intellectual and academic concerns of Durkheim's time. But it is the emphasis on symbolic and structural integration that connected Durkheim's examination of specific topics—a fact that will become increasingly clear in the next chapter.

Practical Concerns. Like Rousseau and Comte, Durkheim wanted to create a well-integrated society. Such a goal could only be achieved by recognizing the pathologies of the social order that were first articulated with a moral passion in Rousseau's work and then reinforced in Tocqueville's more dispassionate analysis of American democracy. As Durkheim came to view the matter, the solution to these pathologies involved the creation of a system of constraining ideas (Comte, Rousseau, and Montesquieu), integration in intermediate subgroups (Tocqueville), coordination of differentiated functions through exchange and contract (Comte and Spencer), and the creation of a central state that provides overall coordination, while maintaining individual freedom (Rousseau, Tocqueville, and Comte).

In sum, then, these methodological, theoretical, substantive, and practical concerns mark the critical elements of Durkheim's sociology. It is now our task to explore the specific works that can yield further insight into Durkheim's thought.

16

ÉMILE DURKHEIM II:
THE BASIC WORKS

INTRODUCTION

The sociological legacy of Rousseau, Comte, Spencer, and Tocqueville lives in the works of Émile Durkheim. For much of Durkheim's sociology synthesizes their ideas in an effort to answer the basic questions: How is society possible? What forces allow for collective organization among individuals? While Durkheim was to teach courses in such diverse areas as family and kinship, education, the history of socialism, religion, and the division of labor, his primary theoretical concern was understanding the forces that maintain and change patterns of social organization.

While all commentators agree that Durkheim was concerned with social order—indeed, many think that he was overconcerned—there is considerable disagreement as to whether or not his theoretical perspective changed between the publication of his first and last major works. Some scholars, such as Anthony Giddens, argue that all of the basic questions and elements of Durkheim's approach are clearly evident in his first important work, *The Division of Labor in Society* (published in 1893), and that subsequent writings represent merely extensions and elaborations.[1] Others, such as Talcott Parsons, stress that during the course of his career Durkheim increasingly came to stress the importance of idea systems, and their internalization by individuals, as the basic process underlying social order.[2] Our analysis of Durkheim's major works will

---

[1] Anthony Giddens, *Capitalism and Modern Theory: An Analysis of the Writings of Marx, Durkheim, and Max Weber* (Cambridge: Cambridge University Press, 1971); and Anthony Giddens, ed. and trans., *Émile Durkheim: Selected Writings* (Cambridge: Cambridge University Press, 1972).

[2] Talcott Parsons, *The Structure of Social Action* (New York: McGraw-Hill, 1937).

lend support to both positions. Giddens is certainly correct in noting that Durkheim's collective work represents an elaboration of ideas first presented in *The Division of Labor*, but Parsons is also correct, at least to some degree, in his view that Durkheim became increasingly interested in social-psychological issues, especially with how social structures and idea systems influence individual thought processes.[3]

Out goal in this chapter, therefore, is to communicate both the continuity and the shifting areas of inquiry that can be found in Durkheim's work. We will not examine all of Durkheim's written work—a task that is beyond our reach.[4] But we will examine in detail Durkheim's four major works: *The Division of Labor in Society* (1893), *The Rules of the Sociological Method* (1895), *Suicide* (1897), and *The Elementary Forms of Religious Life* (1913). While these four works can offer a fairly comprehensive overview of Durkheim's intellectual concerns, we will supplement our discussion with reference to a variety of other written works and posthumously published lectures.

THE DIVISION OF LABOR IN SOCIETY

Durkheim's first major work was the published version of his French doctorate thesis, *The Division of Labor in Society*.[5] The original subtitle of this thesis was "A Study of the Organization of Advanced Societies."[6] On the surface, the book is about the causes, profile, and functions of the division of labor in modern societies, but as we will explore in this and the next chapter, the book presents a more general theory of social organization—one that can still inform sociological theorists.[7] In our review of this classic work, we will pursue a number of issues that Durkheim stressed: (1) social solidarity, (2) the collective conscience, (3) social morphology, (4) mechanical and organic solidarity, (5) social deviation, (6) social functions, (7) the causes of change, and (8) social pathology.

[3] Steven Lukes, *Émile Durkheim, His Life and Work: A Historical and Critical Study* (London: Allen Lane, 1973), p. 66.

[4] For the most complete bibliography of Durkheim's published works, see Ibid., pp. 561–590. See also Robert A. Nisbet, *The Sociology of Émile Durkheim* (New York: Oxford University Press, 1974), pp. 30–41, for an annotated bibliography of the most important works that form the core of Durkheim's theoretical system.

[5] Émile Durkheim, *The Division of Labor in Society* (Glencoe, Ill.: Free Press, 1947; originally published in 1893).

[6] See Lukes, *Émile Durkheim*, chap. 7, for a detailed discussion.

[7] Our review of Durkheim's *The Division of Labor in Society* underemphasizes the social evolutionism contained in this work, since we think that too much concern is placed on the model of social change and not enough on the implicit theory of social organization.

Social Solidarity

The Division of Labor is about the shifting basis of social solidarity as societies evolve from an undifferentiated and simple[8] to a complex and differentiated profile.[9] Today, this topic would be termed *social integration*, since concern is with how units of a social system are coordinated. For Durkheim, the question of social solidarity or integration turns on several related issues: (1) How are individuals made to feel part of a larger social collective? (2) How are their desires and wants constrained in ways that allow them to participate in the collective? (3) How are individuals' and other social units' activities coordinated and adjusted to each other? These questions, we should emphasize, not only dominated *The Division of Labor*, but they guided all of Durkheim's subsequent substantive works.

As is evident, these questions take us into the basic problem of social order: How are patterns of social orgnaization created, maintained, and changed? It is little wonder, therefore, that Durkheim's analysis of social solidarity contains a more general theory of social organization, as we will explore in the next chapter. For the present, it is necessary to delineate some of the concepts and ideas that Durkheim developed to provide an answer to the problem of order. One of the most important of these is "the collective conscience."

The "Collective Conscience"

Throughout his career, Durkheim was vitally concerned with "morality" or "moral facts." While he often was somewhat vague on what constituted a moral fact, we can interpret the concept of morality to embody what sociologists now call *culture*. That is, Durkheim was concerned with the systems of symbols, particularly the norms, values, and beliefs that humans create and use to organize their activities.

It should be remembered that Durkheim had to assert the legitimacy of the scientific study of moral phenomenon, since other academic disciplines such as law, ethics, religion, philosophy, and psychology all laid claim to symbols as their subject matter. And thus, Durkheim was to insist that:

---

[8] Durkheim described such simple societies as based on mechanical solidarity. *Mechanical* was a term intended to connote an image of society as a body where cohesion is imposed upon like elements: "the social molecules . . . could operate in harmony in so far as they do not operate independently."

[9] Such societies were seen as based upon organic solidarity. *Organic* was intended to be an analogy to an organism in which "society becomes more capable of operating in harmony, in so far as each of its elements operates more independently."

> Moral facts are phenomena like others; they consist of rules of action recognizable by certain distinctive characteristics. It must, then, be possible to observe them, describe them, classify them, and look for laws explaining them.[10]

We should emphasize, however, that Durkheim in his early work often used the concept of moral facts to denote structural patterns (groups, organizations, and so on) as well as systems of symbols (values, beliefs, laws, norms). Yet, in *The Division of Labor*, we can find clear indications that he wanted to separate analytically the purely structural from symbolic aspects of social reality. This isolation of cultural or symbolic phenomena can best be seen in Durkheim's formulation of another somewhat ambiguous concept that suffers in translation: the "collective conscience." Durkheim was later to drop extensive use of this term in favor of "collective representations" which, unfortunately, adds little clarification. But we can begin to understand Durkheim's meaning with the formal definition provided in *The Division of Labor:*

> The totality of beliefs and sentiments common to average citizens of the same society forms a determinate system which has its own life; one may call it the *collective* or *common conscience.*[11]

Durkheim went on to indicate that while the terms *collective* and *common* are "not without ambiguity," they suggest that societies reveal a reality independent of "the particular conditions in which individuals are placed." Moreover, people are born into the collective conscience, and it comes to regulate their perceptions and behaviors. What Durkheim was denoting with the concept of collective conscience, then, is the fact that social systems evidence systems of ideas, such as values, beliefs, and norms constrain the thoughts and actions of individuals.

In the course of his analysis of the collective conscience, he conceptualized its varying states in terms of four variables: (1) volume, (2) intensity, (3) determinateness, and (4) religious versus secular content.[12] *Volume* denotes the degree to which the values, beliefs, rules of the collective conscience are shared by the members of a society; *intensity* indicates the extent to which the collective conscience has power to guide a person's

---

[10] Durkheim, *Division of Labor*, p. 32. This idea owes its inspiration to Comte. As Durkheim noted in his Latin thesis on Montesquieu: "No further progress could be made until it was recognized that the laws of societies are no different from those governing the rest of nature. . . . This was Auguste Comte's contribution." (Émile Durkheim, *Montesquieu and Rousseau* [Ann Arbor: University of Michigan Press, 1960; originally published in 1892], pp. 63–64.)

[11] Durkheim, *Division of Labor*, pp. 79–80 (emphasis in original).

[12] Ibid., p. 152 for 1, 2, 3, and throughout book for 4. For interesting secondary discussions, see Lukes, *Émile Durkheim*, and Giddens, ed., *Selected Writings.*

thoughts and actions; *determinateness* denotes the degree of clarity in the components of the collective conscience; and *content* pertains to the ratio of religious to purely secular symbolism in the collective conscience.

Social Morphology

Borrowing from Montesquieu, Durkheim saw social structure, or as he termed it *morphology*, as involving an assessment of the "nature," "number," "arrangement," and "interrelations" among parts, whether these parts be individuals or corporate units such as groups and organizations. Their nature is usually assessed in terms of such variables as size and functions (economic, political, familial, and so on). Arrangement concerns the distribution of parts in relationship to each other; interrelations deals with the modes of communication, movement, and mutual obligations among parts.

Although Durkheim's entire intellectual career involved an effort to demonstrate the impact of social structures on the collective conscience as well as on individual cognitions and behavior, he never made explicit use of these variables—that is, nature, number, arrangement, and interrelations—for analyzing social structures. In his more methodological statements, he argued for the appropriateness of viewing social morphology in terms of nature, size, number, arrangement, and interrelations of specific parts. Yet, his actual analysis of social structures in his major substantive works left these more formal properties of structure implicit.[13]

Mechanical and Organic Solidarity

Following the methodology borrowed from Montesquieu and Spencer, Durkheim developed a typology of societes in terms of their basis of solidarity. One type is termed *mechanical* and the other *organic*.[14] As will be shown below, each of these types rests on different principles of social integration, involving different morphologies, different systems of symbols, and different relations between social and symbol structures.

---

[13] The concern for "social morphology" was, no doubt, an adaptation of Comte's idea of social statics, as these were influenced by the German organicist, Albert Schaffle, with whom Durkheim had been highly impressed. See Lukes, *Émile Durkheim*, pp. 86–95.

[14] Such typologizing was typical in the 19th century. As we saw in Chapter 4, Spencer had distinguished societal types, but more influential was Toennies's distinction between *Gemeinschaft* and *Gesselleschaft*. Durkheim spent a year in Germany as a student in 1885–86, and while Toennies's famous work was not yet published, his typology was well known and influenced Durkheim's conceptualization of mechanical and organic solidarity.

Durkheim's distinction between mechanical and organic is both a descriptive typology of traditional and modern societies, as well as a theoretical statement about the changing forms of social integration that emerge with increasing differentiation of social structure.

At a descriptive level, mechanical solidarity is based upon a strong collective conscience regulating the thought and actions of individuals located within structural units that are all alike. In terms of the four variables by which Durkheim conceptualized the collective conscience, it is high in volume, intensity, determinateness, and religious content. Legal codes, which in Durkheim's view are the best empirical indicator of solidarity are repressive and sanctions are punitive. The reason for such repressiveness is that deviation from the dictates of the collective conscience is viewed as a crime against all members of the society and the gods. The morphology or structure of mechanical societies reveals independent kinship units that organize relatively small numbers of people who share strong commitments to their particular collective conscience. The interrelations among kin units are minimal, with each kin unit being like the others and autonomously meeting the needs of its members. Not surprisingly, then, individual freedom, choice, and autonomy are low in mechanical societies. People are dominated by the collective conscience and their actions are constrained by its dictates and by the constraints of cohesive kin units.

In contrast, organically structured societies are typified by large populations, distributed in specialized roles in many diverse structural units. Organic societies reveal high degrees of interdependence among individuals and corporate units, with exchange, legal contracts, and norms regulating these interrelations. The collective conscience becomes "enfeebled" and "more abstract," providing highly general and secular value premises for the exchanges, contracts, and norms regulating the interdependencies among specialized social units. This alteration is reflected in legal codes that become less punitive and more "restitutive," specifying nonpunitive ways to redress violations of normative arrangements and to reintegrate violators back into the network of interdependencies that typify organic societies. In such societies, individual freedom is great, and in fact, the secular and highly abstract collective conscience becomes dominated by values stressing respect for the personal dignity of the individual.

This descriptive contrast between mechanical and organic societies is summarized in Table 16–1.[15]

---

[15] This table is similar to one developed by Lukes, *Émile Durkheim*, p. 151, but differs in many important respects.

TABLE 16–1
Descriptive Summary of Mechanical and Organic Solidarity

Morphological features	Mechanical solidarity	Organic solidarity
1. Size	Small	Large
2. Number of parts	Few	Many
3. Nature of parts	Kinship-based	Diverse: dominated by economic and governmental content
4. Arrangement	Independent, autonomous	Interrelated, mutually interdependent
5. Nature of interrelations	Bound to common conscience and punitive law	Bound together by exchange, contract, norms, and restitutive law
Collective conscience		
1. Volume	High	Low
2. Intensity	High	Low
3. Determinateness	High	Low
4. Content	Religious, stressing commitment and conformity to dictates of sacred powers	Secular, emphasizing individuality

At the more theoretical level, Durkheim's distinction between mechanical and organic solidarity posits a fundamental relationship in the social world among "structural differentiation," "value-generalization," and "normative specification." As societies, or perhaps any social system (group, organization, community), reveal structural differentiation, values become more abstract.[16] The collective conscience

> . . . changes its nature as societies become more voluminous. Because these societies are spread over a vaster surface, the common conscience is itself obliged to rise above all local diversities, to dominate more space, and consequently to become more abstract. For not many general things can be common to all these diverse environments.[17]

Yet as basic values lose their capacity to regulate the specific actions of large numbers of differentiated units, then normative regulations arise to compensate for the inability of general values to specify what people should do and how individuals as well as corporate units should interact.

> If society no longer imposes upon everybody certain uniform practices, it takes greater care to define and regulate the special relations between

---

[16] Durkheim, *Division of Labor*, p. 171.
[17] Ibid., p. 287.

different social functions and this activity is not smaller because it is different.[18]

It is certain that organized societies are not possible without a developed system of rules which predetermine the functions of each organ. In so far as labor is divided, there arises a multitude of occupational moralities and laws.[19]

Thus, in his seemingly static comparison of mechanical and organic societies, Durkheim was actually proposing lawlike relationships among structural and symbolic elements of social systems.

Social Change

Durkheim's view of social change revolves around an analysis of the causes and consequences of increases in the division of labor:

The division of labor varies in direct ratio with the volume and density of societies, and, if it progresses in a continuous manner in the course of social development, it is because societies become regularly denser and generally more voluminous.[20]

Some translation of terms is necessary if this *proposition*, as Durkheim called it, is to be understood. *Volume* refers to population size and concentration; *density*, pertains to the increased interaction arising out of escalated volume. Thus, the division of labor arises out of increases in the concentration of populations whose members increasingly come into contact. Durkheim also termed the increased rates of interaction among those thrust into contact *dynamic* and *moral* density. Durkheim then analyzed those factors that increase the volume and density of a population. Ecological boundaries (rivers, mountains, and so on), migration, urbanization, and population growth all operate directly to increase volume and thus indirectly to increase the likelihood of dynamic density (increased contact and interaction). Technological innovations, such as new modes of communication and transportation, directly increase rates of contact and interaction among individuals. But all of these direct and indirect influences are merely lists of empirical conditions influencing the primary explanatory variable, dynamic or moral density.

How, then, does dynamic density cause the division of labor? Dynamic density increases competition among individuals who, if they are to survive the "struggle," must assume specialized roles and then establish

---

[18] Ibid., p. 205.
[19] Ibid., p. 302.
[20] Ibid., p. 262.

exchange relations with each other. The division of labor is thus the mechanism by which competition is mitigated.

> Thus, Darwin says that in a small area, opened to immigration, and where, consequently, the conflict of individuals must be acute, there is always to be seen a very great diversity in the species inhabiting it. . . .
>
> Men submit to the same law. In the same city, different occupations can co-exist without being obliged mutually to destroy one another, for they pursue different objects.[21]

However, Durkheim emphasized that competition drives individuals apart unless there is some "force" keeping them together.[22] Echoing Comte, Durkheim emphasized that this force is a common conscience that attaches individuals to the society and its values at the same time that they compete with each other.[23] Thus, the causes of the division of labor are dynamic density and competition which force differentiation of specialized roles. Indeed, these conditions "*necessitate* a greater division of labor."[24]

Social Functions

As we observed in the discussion of Spencer's sociology in Chapter 4, it was Spencer who clearly formulated the notions of structure and function, with functions being assessed in terms of the needs of the social organism being met by a structure. Durkheim appears to have borrowed these ideas and, indeed, opened *The Division of Labor* with an assessment of its functions.[25] The function of the division of labor is to promote social solidarity, or societal integration. Such functional analysis, Durkheim argued, must be kept separate from causal analysis. It will be recalled from the previous chapter that Durkheim was highly critical of Montesquieu's analysis in terms of "final causes" or functions. And thus, in his first major work, Durkheim attempted to keep his functional and causal analyses separated.

We might now ask a more fundamental question: Why did Durkheim engage in functional analysis? That is, why did he feel it necessary to determine the consequences for society of the division of labor? In his

---

[21] Ibid., pp. 266–67.

[22] Ibid., p. 270.

[23] Ibid., pp. 275–76.

[24] Ibid., p. 262 (emphasis in original).

[25] For a more detailed analysis of Durkheim's debt to Spencer and of his contribution to functionalism, see Jonathan H. Turner and Alexandra Maryanski, *Functionalism: An Intellectual Portrait* (Menlo Park, Calif.: Benjamin/Cummings, 1979).

Latin thesis, Durkheim had been highly critical of Montesquieu for not separating his scientific observations from his personal feelings about what society should be. However, Durkheim was more sympathetic to Comte, who explicitly argued that the science of society could be used to create a better society. It was thus in the French tradition—Montesquieu, Rousseau, Saint-Simon, and Comte—to seek a better society. Beginning with Comte and culminating with Durkheim, then, scholars felt that an understanding of the laws of society could be used to create a new and better society.

Yet Durkheim wanted to keep the science of sociology separated from such disciplines as moral philosophy and ethics. He had utter contempt for what he saw as the idle speculation and moral imperialism of these and related disciplines. Rather, he had a vision of sociology as like the applied side of biology—that is, sociologists could be the "physicians of society."

The concept of function was central to this vision, especially in conjunction with the related notions of societal types. By assessing what a structure "does for" a society of a particular type or at a specific stage of evolution, one is in a position to determine what is "normal" and "abnormal" for that society—a point that Comte had first made in his advocacy of the experimental method as it could be used in sociology. The concept of function allowed Durkheim to judge whether a structure, such as the division of labor, is functioning "normally" for a particular type of society. And hence, to the degree that the division of labor fails to promote societal integration or social solidarity in a society, Durkheim viewed that society as in a "pathological" state and in need of alterations to restore "normality" to the "body social." It is these considerations that led Durkheim to analyze "abnormal forms" of the division of labor at the close of this first major work, since abnormality of structures can only be determined in reference to their "normal functions."

Pathology and Abnormal Forms

Durkheim opened his discussion of abnormal forms with the following statement:

> Up to now, we have studied the division of labor only as a normal phenomenon, but, like all social facts, and, more generally, all biological facts, it presents pathological forms which must be analyzed. Though normally the division of labor produces social solidarity, it sometimes happens that it has different, and even contrary results.[26]

---

[26] Durkheim, *Division of Labor*, p. 353.

Durkheim isolated three abnormal forms: (1) the anomic division of labor, and (2) the forced division of labor, and (3) the inadequately coordinated division of labor. In discussing these abnormal forms, he drew considerable inspiration from his French predecessors, particularly Rousseau and Tocqueville, while carrying on a silent dialogue with Marx and other socialists. Thus, Durkheim's analysis of abnormal forms represents his effort to address issues that had been discussed and debated for several previous generations of intellectuals. Indeed, the isolation of the individual, the detachment of people from society, their sense of alienation, their exploitation by the powerful, and related issues had been hotly debated in both intellectual and lay circles. Yet, while Durkheim's selection of topics is not unique, his conclusions and their theoretical implications are highly original.

The Anomic Division of Labor. The concept of anomie (or anomy) was not well developed in *The Division of Labor*. It was only later, in the 1897 work *Suicide*, that this concept became theoretically significant. Durkheim's discussion in *The Division of Labor* is explicitly directed at Comte who had noted the essence of the basic dilemma confronting organic social systems. As Comte had stated:

> From the moral point of view, while each individual is thus made closely dependent on the mass, he is naturally drawn away from it by the nature of his special activity, constantly reminding him of his private interests, which he only very dimly perceives to be related to the public.[27]

For Durkheim, this dilemma was expressed in terms of maintaining individuals' commitment to a common set of values and beliefs, while at the same time allowing them to pursue their specialized interests. At this stage in Durkheim's thinking, anomie represented insufficient normative regulation of individuals' activities, with the result that they do not feel attached to the collectivity.

Anomie is inevitable when the transformation of societies from a mechanical to organic basis of social solidarity is rapid and causes the "generalization" or "enfeeblement" of values. With value-generalization, individuals' attachment to, and regulation by, these values is lessened. The results of this anomic situation are diverse. One result is that individuals feel alienated, since their only attachment is to the monotony and crushing schedule dictated by the machines of the industrial age. Another is the escalated frustrations and the sense of deprivation, manifested by increased incidence of revolt, that comes in a state of underregulation.

Unlike Marx, however, Durkheim did not consider these consequences

---

[27] Quoted in Lukes, *Émile Durkheim*, p. 141.

inevitable. He rejected the notion that there are inherent contradictions in capitalism, for "if, in certain cases, organic solidarity is not all it should be . . . [it is] because all the conditions for the existence of organic solidarity have not been realized."[28] Nor would he accept Comte's or Rousseau's solution to anomie: the establishment of a strong and somewhat dictatorial central organ, the state. And Spencer's solution, which amounted to a new invocation of Adam Smith's invisible hand of order, was also unacceptable.

Yet in the first edition of The Division of Labor, Durkheim's own solution is vague, since the "solution" to anomie involves reintegration of individuals into the collective life by virtue of their interdependence with other specialists and the common goals that all members of a society ultimately pursue.[29] In many ways, this line of argument substitutes for Adam Smith's invisible hand of order the "invisible power of the collective" without specifying how this integration into the collective is to occur.

Durkheim recognized the inadequacy of this solution to the problem of anomie. Moreover, his more detailed analysis of anomie in Suicide (1897) must have further underscored the limitations of his analysis in The Division of Labor. Thus, the second edition of The Division of Labor, published in 1902, contained a long preface that sought to specify the mechanism by which anomie is to be curbed. This mechanism is the "occupational" or "corporate" group.[30]

Durkheim recognized that industrialism, urbanization, occupational specialization, and the growth of the bureaucratized state all operate to lessen the functions of family, religion, region, and neighborhood as mechanisms promoting the integration of individuals into the societal collectivity. And with the generalization and enfeeblement of the collective conscience, coupled with the potential isolation of individuals in an occupational specialty, Durkheim saw that new structures would have to evolve in order to avoid anomie. These structures promote social solidarity in several ways: (1) they organize occupational specialties into a collective; (2) they bridge the widening gap between the remote state and the specific needs and desires of the individual; and (3) they provide a functional alternative to the old loyalties generated by religion, regionalism, and kinship. These new intermediate structures are not only occupational but also political and moral groupings that lace together specialized occupations, counterbalance the power of the state, and provide specific

28 Durkheim, Division of Labor, pp. 364–65.

29 Ibid., pp. 372–73.

30 Ibid., pp. 1–31.

interpretations for the more abstract values and beliefs of "the collective conscience."

As is evident, Durkheim had taken the idea of "occupational groups" from Tocqueville's analysis of intermediate organizations in America (see Chapter 5). But he extended the concept considerably, and in so doing, he posited a conception of how a society should be economically, politically, and morally organized.[31] Economically, occupational groups would bring together related occupational specialties into an organization that could set working hours and wage levels and that could bargain with management of corporations and government.

Politically, the occupational group would become a kind of political party whose representatives would participate in government. Like most French scholars in the post-Revolutionary era, Durkheim distrusted mass democracy, since short-term individual passions and moods can render the state helpless in setting and reaching long range goals. He also distrusted an all-powerful and bureaucratized state, because its remote structure is too insensitive and cumbersome to deal with the specific needs and problems of diverse individuals. Moreover, Durkheim saw that unchecked state power inevitably leads to abuses—an emphasis that comes close to Montesquieu's idea of a balance of powers in government. Thus, the power of the state must be checked by intermediate groups which channel public sentiment to the state and which administer the policies of the state for a particular constituency.[32]

Morally, occupational groups are to provide many of the recreational, educational, and social functions formerly performed by family, neighborhood, and church. By bringing together people who, because they belong to related occupations, are likely to have common experiences, occupational groups can provide a place where people feel integrated into the society and where the psychological tensions and monotony of their specialized jobs can be mitigated. Moreover, these groups can make the generalized values and beliefs of the entire society relevant to the life experiences of each individual. Through the vehicle of occupational groups, then, an entire society of specialists can be reattached to the collective conscience.[33]

---

[31] We are supplementing Durkheim's discussion of occupational groups with additional works; see Émile Durkheim, *Professional Ethics and Civic Morals* (London: Routledge & Kegan Paul, 1957), and his *Socialism and Saint-Simon* (Yellow Springs, Ohio: Antioch Press, 1958).

[32] "Preface to the Second Edition," in Durkheim, *Division of Labor*, p. 28.

[33] Durkheim rarely addressed Marx directly; though he wanted to devote a special course to Marx's ideas in addition to his course on Saint-Simon and socialism, he never got around to doing this. Yet, much as with Weber, one suspects that Durkheim's discussion of "abnormal forms" represented a "silent dialogue" with Marx.

Inequality and the Forced Division of Labor. Borrowing heavily from Rousseau, Saint-Simon, and Comte, but reacting to Marx, Durkheim saw inequalities based upon ascription and inheritance of privilege as "abnormal." He advocated an inheritance tax that would eliminate the passing of wealth, and indeed, he felt that in the normal course of things, this would come about. But unlike Marx, he had no distaste for the accumulation of capital and privilege, as long as it was earned and not inherited.

What Durkheim desired was for the division of labor and inequalities in privilege to correspond to differences in people's ability. For Durkheim, it was abnormal in organic societies for wealth to be inherited and for this inherited privilege to be used by one class to oppress and exploit another. Such a situation represents a "forced division of labor" and it is in the context of analyzing this abnormality that Durkheim examined explicitly Marxian ideas: (1) the value theory of labor and exploitation and (2) the domination of one class by another. Each of these is briefly examined below.

1. Durkheim felt that the price that one pays for a good or service should be proportional to the "useful labor which it contains."[34] To the degree that this is not so, he argued, an abnormal condition prevails. What is necessary, and inevitable in the long run, is for buyers and sellers to be "placed in conditions externally equal"[35] in which the price charged for a good or service corresponds to the "socially useful labor" in it and where no seller or buyer enjoys an advantage or monopoly that would allow prices to exceed socially useful labor.

2. Durkheim recognized that as long as there is inherited privilege, especially wealth, one class can exploit and dominate another. Durkheim felt that the elimination of inheritance was inevitable, since people could no longer be duped by a strong collective conscience into accepting privilege and exploitation (a position that parallels Marx's notion of "false consciousness"). For as religious and family bonds decrease in salience, and as individuals are liberated from mechanical solidarity, people can liberate themselves from the beliefs that have often been used to legitimate exploitation.

Durkheim was certainly naive in his assumption that these aspects of the forced division of labor would, like Marx's state, "wither away." What Durkheim saw as normal was a situation that sounds reminiscent of Spencer's and the utilitarian's vision.[36]

---

[34] Durkheim, *Division of Labor*, p. 382.

[35] Ibid., p. 383.

[36] Ibid., p. 377.

Lack of Coordination. Durkheim termed the lack of coordination *another abnormal form* and did not devote much space to its analysis.[37] At times, Durkheim noted, specialization of tasks is not accompanied by sufficient coordination, creating a situation where energy is wasted and individuals feel poorly integrated into the collective flow of life. In Durkheim's view, specialization must be "continuous," where functions are highly coordinated and where individuals are laced together through their mutual interdependence. Such a state, Durkheim argued, would be achieved as the natural and normal processes creating organic solidarity become dominant in modern society.

On this note, *The Division of Labor* ends. As we will examine in more detail in the next chapter, this book represents not only a descriptive account of social evolution and of the operation of modern societies, but also a set of theoretical principles dealing with the nature of human social organization. Durkheim's next major work, published two years after *The Division of Labor*, sought to make assumptions and methodological guidelines implicit in *The Division of Labor* more explicit. *The Rules of the Sociological Method* (1895), as we will come to see, represents a methodological interlude in Durkheim's efforts to understand how and why patterns of social organization are created, maintained, and changed.

THE RULES OF THE SOCIOLOGICAL METHOD

The Rules of the Sociological Method is both a philosophical treatise and set of guidelines for conducting sociological inquiry.[38] Durkheim appears to have written the book for at least three reasons.[39] First, he sought intellectual justification for his approach to studying the social world, especially as evidenced in *The Division of Labor*. Second, he wanted to persuade a hostile academic community as to the legitimacy of sociology as a distinctive science. And third, because he wanted to found a school of scholars, he needed a manifesto to attract and guide potential converts to the science of sociology. The chapter titles of *The Rules* best communicate Durkheim's intent: (1) "What Is a Social Fact?" (2) "Rules for the Observation of Social Facts," (3) "Rules for Distinguishing between the Normal and the Pathological," (4) "Rules for the Classification of Social Types," (5) "Rules for the Explanation of Social

---

[37] Ibid., pp. 389–95.

[38] Émile Durkheim, *The Rules of the Sociological Method* (New York: Free Press, 1938; originally published in 1895).

[39] Lukes, *Émile Durkheim*, chap. 10.

Facts," (6) "Rules Relative to Establishing Sociological Proofs." Each of these is examined below.

What Is a Social Fact?

As we have already observed, Durkheim was engaged in a battle to establish the legitimacy of sociology. In *The Division of Labor*, he had proclaimed "moral facts" to be sociology's subject matter, but in *The Rules*, he changed his terminology to that employed earlier by Comte and argued that "social facts" are the distinctive subject matter of sociology. For Durkheim, a social fact "consists of ways of acting, thinking, and feeling, external to the individual, and endowed with power of coercion, by which they control him."[40]

In this definition, Durkheim lumped behaviors, thoughts, and emotions together as the subject matter of sociology. The morphological and symbolic structures in which individuals participate are thus to be the focus of sociology, but social facts are, by virtue of transcending any single individual, "external" and "constraining." They are external in two senses. (1) Individuals are born into an established set of structures and an existing system of values, beliefs, and norms. Hence, these structural and symbolic "facts" are initially external to individuals; and as people learn to play roles in social structures, to abide by norms, and to accept basic values, they feel and sense "something" outside of them. (2) Even when humans actively and collaboratively create social structures, values, beliefs, and norms, their "nature is not different," for once created they become an emergent reality that is external to any single individual.

This externality is accompanied by a sense of constraint and coercion. The structures, norms, values, and beliefs of the social world compel certain actions, thoughts, and dispositions. They impose limits, and when deviations occur, sanctions are applied to the deviants. Moreover, social facts are "internalized" in that people want and desire to be a part of social structures and to accept the norms, values, and beliefs of the collective. In the 1895 edition of *The Rules*, this point had been underemphasized, and thus in the second edition Durkheim noted that:

> Institutions may impose themselves upon us, but we cling to them; they compel us, and we love them.[41]

> [Social facts] dominate us and impose beliefs and practices upon us. But

---

[40] Durkheim, *The Rules*, p. 3.
[41] Ibid., footnote 5.

they rule us from within, for they are in every case an integral part of ourself.[42]

Durkheim thus asserted that when individuals come into collaboration, a new reality consisting of social and symbolic structures emerges. This emergent reality cannot be reduced to individual psychology, because it is external to, and constraining on, any single individual. And yet, like all social facts, it is registered on the individual and often "rules the individual from within." Having established that sociology has a distinct subject matter—social facts—the rest of the book is devoted to explicating rules for studying and explaining social facts.

Rules for Observing Social Facts

Durkheim offered several guidelines for observing social facts: (1) Personal biases and preconceptions must be eliminated. (2) The phenomena under study must be clearly defined. (3) An empirical indicator of the phenomenon under study must be found, as was the case for "law" in *The Division of Labor*. (4) And in a manner reminiscent of Montesquieu, social facts must be considered as "things." Social facts are things in two different, although related, ways. First, when a phenomenon is viewed as a thing, it is possible to assume "a particular mental attitude" toward it. We can search for the properties and characteristics of a thing and we can draw verifiable conclusions about its nature. Such a position was highly controversial in Durkheim's time, since moral phenomena—values, ideas, morals—were often not considered as proper topics of scientific inquiry, and when they were, they were seen as a subarea in the study of individual psychology. Second, Durkheim said that phenomena such as morality, values, beliefs, and dogmas constitute a distinctive metaphysical reality, not reducible to individual psychology. And hence they can be approached with the same scientific methods as any material phenomenon in the universe.[43]

Rules for Distinguishing between the Normal and the Pathological

Throughout his career, Durkheim never wavered from Comte's position that science is to be used to serve human ends:

---

[42] Ibid., "Preface to the Second Edition," p. 7.

[43] Many commentators, such as Giddens, *Capitalism and Modern Theory*, and Lukes, *Émile Durkheim*, emphasize that Durkheim was not making a metaphysical statement. We think he was making both a metaphysical and methodological statement.

> Why strive for knowledge of reality if this knowledge cannot serve us in life? To this we can make reply that, by revealing the causes of phenomena, science furnishes the means of producing them.[44]

To use scientific knowledge to implement social conditions requires a knowledge of what is "normal" and "pathological." Otherwise, one would not know what social facts to create and implement, or one might actually create a pathological condition. To determine normality, the best procedure, Durkheim argued, is to discover what is most frequent and typical of societies of a given type, or at a given stage of evolution. That which deviates significantly from this average is pathological.

Such a position allowed Durkheim to make some startling conclusions for his time. In regard to deviance, for example, a particular rate of crime and some other form of deviance could be normal for certain types of societies. It is only when rates of deviance exceed what is typical of a certain societal type that abnormality is present.

Rules for the Classification of Social Types

Durkheim's evolutionary perspective, coupled with his strategy for diagnosing normality and pathology in social systems, made inevitable a concern with social classification. While specific systems reveal considerable variability, it is possible to group them into general types on the basis of (a) the "nature" and "number" of their parts and (b) the "mode of combination" of parts.

In this way, Durkheim believed, societies that reveal superficial differences can be seen as belonging to a particular class or type. Moreover, by ignoring the distracting complexities of a society's "content" and "uniqueness," it is possible to establish the stage of evolutionary development of a society.

Rules for the Explanation of Social Facts

Durkheim emphasized again a point that he made in *The Division of Labor:*

> When the explanation of social phenomena is undertaken, we must seek separately the efficient cause which produces it and the function it fulfills.[45]

---

[44] Durkheim, *The Rules*, p. 48.
[45] Ibid., p. 95.

Causal analysis involves searching for antecedent conditions that produce a given effect. Functional analysis is concerned with determining the consequences of a social fact (regardless of its cause) for the social whole or larger context in which it is located. Complete sociological explanation involves both causal and functional explanations, as Durkheim had sought to illustrate in *The Division of Labor.*

Rules for Establishing Sociological Proofs

Durkheim advocated two basic procedures for establishing "sociological proofs"—proofs being documentation that causal, and by implication, functional, explanations are correct. One procedure involves comparing two or more societies of a given type (as determined by the rules for classification) in order to see if one fact, which is present in one but not the other(s), leads to differences in these otherwise similar societies.

The second procedure is the method of concomitant variation. If two social facts are correlated and one is assumed to cause the other, and if all alternative facts that might also be considered to be causative cannot eliminate the correlation, then it can be asserted that a causal explanation has been "proven." But if an established correlation, and presumed causal relation, can be explained away by the operation of another social fact, then the established explanation has been disproven and the new social fact can, until similarly disproven, be considered "proven." The essence of Durkheim's method of concomitant variation, then, was similar in intent to modern multivariate analyses: to assert a relation among variables, controlling for the impact of other variables.[46]

The Rules marks a turning point in Durkheim's intellectual career. It was written after his thesis on the division of labor, and while he was pondering the question of suicide in his lectures. Yet, it was written before his first public course on religion.[47] Durkheim had clearly established his guiding theoretical interests: the nature of social organization and its relationship to values, beliefs, and other symbolic systems. He had developed a clear methodology: asking causal and functional questions within a broad comparative, historical, and evolutionary framework. He had begun to win respect in intellectual and academic circles for the fact that social organization represents an emergent reality, sui generis, and that it is the proper subject matter for a discipline called sociology.

---

[46] Durkheim made other assertions: A social fact can only have only one cause and this cause must be another social fact (as opposed to individual or psychological).

[47] Lukes, *Émile Durkheim,* p. 227.

His next work appears to have been an effort to demonstrate the utility of his methodological and ontological advocacy. For he sought to understand sociologically a phenomenon that, at the time, was considered to be uniquely psychological: suicide. It is in this work that Durkheim attempted to demonstrate the power of sociological investigation of seemingly psychological phenomena, employing social facts as explanatory variables. But far more important than the specifics of suicide, we believe, is the fact Durkheim extended concepts introduced in *The Division of Labor*, and in so doing, he presented additional theoretical principles on why patterns of social organization are created, maintained, and changed.

SUICIDE

In *Suicide*, Durkheim self-consciously appeared to follow the "rules" of his sociological method.[48] He was interested in studying only a social fact, and hence, he did not study individual suicides but the general pervasiveness of suicide in a population—that is, a society's aggregate tendency toward suicide. In this way, suicide could be considered as a social rather than individual fact and it could be approached as a "thing." Suicide is clearly defined as "all causes of death resulting directly or indirectly from a positive or negative act of the victim himself which he knows will produce this result."[49] The statistical rate of suicide is then used as the indicator of this social fact.[50] Suicide is classified into four types: egoistic, altruistic, anomic, and fatalistic. The cause of these types is specified in terms of the degree and nature of individual integration into the social collective. And a variant of modern correlational techniques is employed to demonstrate or "prove" that other hypothesized causes of suicide are spurious and that integration into social and symbolic structures is the key explanatory variable.

The statistical manipulations in *Suicide* are important because they represent the first systematic effort to apply correlational and contingency techniques to causal explanation. Our concern, however, is with the theoretical implications of this work, and hence, the following summary will focus on theoretical rather than statistical issues.

---

[48] Émile Durkheim, *Suicide: A Study in Sociology* (Glencoe, Ill.: Free Press, 1951; originally published in 1897).

[49] Ibid., p. 44.

[50] Ibid., p. 48. It should be emphasized that suicide had been subject to extensive statistical analysis during Durkheim's time, and thus, Durkheim was able to borrow the data compiled by others.

Types of Suicide

Durkheim isolated four types of suicide in terms of varying causes. We should emphasize that, despite Durkheim's statistical footwork, isolating types in terms of causes, and then explaining these types in terms of the causes used to classify them, is a suspicious, if not spurious, way to go about understanding the social world. But these flaws aside, Durkheim's analysis clarified notions of social integration that are somewhat vague in *The Division of Labor*. Basically, Durkheim argued that suicides can be classified in terms of the nature of an individual's integration into the social fabric. There are, in Durkheim's eye, two types of integration:

1. *Attachment* to social groups and their goals. Such attachment involves the maintenance of interpersonal ties and the perception that one is a part of a larger collectivity.
2. *Regulation* by the collective conscience (values, beliefs, and general norms) of social groupings. Such regulation limits individual aspirations and needs, keeping them in check.

In distinguishing these two bases of integration, Durkheim was explicitly recognizing the different "functions" of the morphological and symbolic elements of the social world. Interpersonal ties that bind individuals to the collective operate to keep them from becoming too "egoistic"— a concept borrowed from Tocqueville and widely discussed in Durkheim's time. Unless individuals can be attached to a larger collective and its goals, they become egoistic or self-centered in ways that are highly destructive to their psychological well-being. In contrast, the regulation of individuals' aspirations, which are potentially infinite, operates to prevent anomie (or anomy). Without symbolic constraints, individual aspirations, as Rousseau[51] and Tocqueville had emphasized, escalate and create perpetual misery for individuals who pursue goals that constantly recede as they are approached. It is these two varying bases of individual integration into society, then, that form the basis for Durkheim's classification of four types of suicide—egoistic, altruistic, anomic, and fatalistic. Each of these is briefly discussed below.

Egoistic Suicide. When a person's ties to groups and collectivities are weakened, then there is the potential for excessive individualism and, hence, egoistic suicide. Durkheim stated this relation as a clear

---

[51] As Rousseau noted: "The more one has, the more one wants." This view of humans, we should note, is very similar to that of Marx.

proposition: "Suicide varies inversely with the degree of integration of social groups of which the individual forms a part."[52] And as a result:

> The more weakened the groups to which he belongs, the less he depends on them, the more he consequently depends only on himself and recognizes no other rules of conduct than what are founded on private interest. If we agree to call this state egoism, in which the individual ego asserts itself to excess in the face of the social ego and at its expense, we may call egoistic the special type of suicide springing from excessive individualism.[53]

Altruistic Suicide. If the degree of individual integration into the group is visualized as a variable continuum, ranging from egoism on the one pole to a complete fusion of the individual with the collective at the other pole, then the essence of Durkheim's next form of suicide can be captured. Altruistic suicide is the result of individuals being so attached to the group that, for the good of the group, they commit suicide. In such a situation, individuals count for little; it is the group that is paramount, with individuals subordinating their interest to those of the group. Durkheim distinguished three types of altruistic suicide.

1. *Obligatory altruistic suicide*—where individuals are obliged, under certain circumstances, to commit suicide.
2. *Optional altruistic suicide*—where individuals are not obligated to commit suicide, but where it is the custom for them to do so under certain conditions.
3. *Acute altruistic suicide*—where the individual "kills himself purely for the joy of sacrifice, because, even with no particular reason, renunciation in itself is considered praiseworthy."[54]

In sum, then, egoistic and altruistic suicides result from either overintegration or underintegration into the collective. Altruistic suicide tends to occur in traditional systems—what Durkheim termed *mechanical* in *The Division of Labor*—and egoistic suicide is more frequent in modern, organic systems which reveal high degrees of individual autonomy. But at the more abstract level, Durkheim is positing a critical dimension of individual and societal integration: the maintenance of interpersonal bonds within coherent group structures.

Anomic Suicide. In *The Division of Labor*, Durkheim's conceptualization of anomie was somewhat vague. In many ways he incorporated both anomie (deregulation by symbols) and egoism (detachment from

---

[52] Durkheim, *Suicide*, p. 209.
[53] Ibid.
[54] Ibid., p. 223.

structural relations in groups) into the original definition of anomie. But in *Suicide*, Durkheim clarified this ambiguity in that anomic suicide came to be viewed narrowly as the result of deregulation of individuals' desires and passions. Although both egoistic and anomic suicide "spring from society's insufficient presence in individuals,"[55] the nature of the disjuncture or deficiency between the individual and society differs.

> In egoistic suicide it is deficient in truly collective activity, thus depriving the latter of object and meaning. In anomic suicide, society's influence is lacking in the basically individual passions, thus leaving them without a check-rein.[56]

Fatalistic Suicide. Durkheim discussed this form of suicide in a short footnote. Just as altruism is the polar opposite of egoism, so fatalism is the opposite of anomie. Fatalistic suicide is the result of "excessive regulation, that of persons with futures pitilessly blocked and passions violently choked by oppressive discipline."[57] Thus, when individuals are overregulated by norms, beliefs, and values in their social relations, and when they have no individual freedom, discretion, or autonomy in their social relations, then they are potential victims of fatalistic suicide.

Suicide and Social Integration

These types of suicide reveal a great deal about Durkheim's conception of humans and the social order. With respect to human nature, the study of suicide allows us a glimpse at how Durkheim conceived of humans. Reading between the lines in *Suicide*, the following features of human nature are posited.[58]

1. Humans can potentially reveal unlimited desires and passions which must be regulated and held in check.
2. Yet total regulation of passions and desires creates a situation where life loses all meaning.
3. Humans need interpersonal attachments and a sense that these attachments connect them to collective purposes.
4. Yet excessive attachment can undermine personal autonomy to the point where life loses meaning for the individual.

These implicit notions of human nature, it should be emphasized, involve a vision of the "normal" way in which individuals are integrated

---

[55] Ibid., p. 258.

[56] Ibid.

[57] Ibid., p. 276 in footnote.

[58] See also Lukes, *Émile Durkheim*, chap., 9 for a similar, but different, discussion.

into the morphological and symbolic structures of society. Indeed, Durkheim was unable to even address the question of human nature without also talking about the social order. For Durkheim, the social order is maintained only to the degree that individuals are attached to, and regulated by, patterns of collective organization. This fact was to lead Durkheim in his later career to explore in more detail an essentially social-psychological question: In what ways do individuals become attached to society and willing to be regulated by its symbolic elements?

Suicide and Deviance

Durkheim made an effort to see if other forms of deviance, such as homicide and crime, are related to suicide rates, but the details of his correlations are not as important as the implications of his analysis for a general theory of deviance. As he had in *The Division of Labor*, Durkheim recognized that a society of a certain type will reveal a "typical" or "average" level of deviance, whether suicide or some other form. However, when rates of suicide, or deviance in general, exceed certain average levels for a societal type, then a "pathological" condition prevails.

Durkheim's great contribution was to recognize that deviance is caused by the same forces that maintain conformity in social systems. Moreover, he specified the key variables in understanding both conformity and deviance: (1) the degree of group attachment and (2) the degree of value and normative regulation. Thus, excessive or insufficient attachment and regulation will cause varying forms of deviance in a social system. Moreover, the more a system reveals moderate degrees of regulation and attachment, the less likely are pathological rates of deviance and the greater the social integration of individuals into the system.

Thus, Durkheim's analysis in *Suicide* is much more than a statistical analysis of a narrowly defined topic. It is also a venture into understanding how social organization is possible. This fact becomes particularly evident near the end of the book where Durkheim proposes his solution to the high rates of suicide and other forms of deviance that typify modern or "organically" structured societies.

Suicide and the Social Organization of Organic Societies[59]

At the end of *Suicide*, Durkheim abandoned his cross-sectional statistical analysis and returned to the evolutionary perspective contained in

---

[59] Durkheim dropped the term *organic societies*, but we have retained the term here to emphasize the continuity between *Suicide* and *The Division of Labor*.

The Division of Labor. During social change, as societies move from one basis of social solidarity, deregulation (anomie) and detachment (egoism) of the individual from society can occur, especially if this transition is rapid. Deregulation and detachment create not only high rates of deviance, but also problems in maintaining the social order. If these problems are to be avoided and if social "normality" is to be restored, new structures that provide attachment and regulation of individuals to society must be created.

In a series of enlightening pages, Durkheim analyzed the inability of traditional social structures to provide this new basis of social integration. The family is an insufficiently encompassing social structure; religious structures are similarly too limited in their scope and too oriented to the sacred; and government is too bureaucratized and hence remote from the individual. For Durkheim, the implications of these facts are that modern social structures require intermediate groups to replace the declining influence of family and religion and to mediate between the individual and state as well as to check the growing power of the state. The "occupational group" was seen by Durkheim as the only potential structural unit that could regulate and attach individuals to society.

Thus, it is in *Suicide* that the ideas that were later to be placed into the 1902 "Preface to the Second Edition" of *The Division of Labor* find their first forceful expression. And while suicide is, on the surface, a social-psychological study,[60] the problem of order remains the central focus of the book. The analysis of suicide allowed Durkheim to explore further the concept of social integration, and it is for this reason that *Suicide* represents both an application of the method advocated in *The Rules* and a clarification of substantive ideas contained in *The Division of Labor.*

THE ELEMENTARY FORMS OF RELIGIOUS LIFE

Although Durkheim turned to the study of religion in his last major work, it had been an important interest for a long time; indeed, from 1895 on, he had taught courses on religion.[61] Durkheim pursued the study of religion over most of his career because it allowed him to gain insight into the basic theoretical problem that guided all of his work: the nature of social organization. In *The Division of Labor*, he had argued that in mechanical societies the collective conscience is religious

---

[60] Durkheim would, of course, not admit to this label.

[61] Émile Durkheim, *The Elementary Forms of Religious Life* (Glencoe, Ill.: Free Press, 1947; originally published in 1912).

in content and that it integrates the individual into the collective. But he had recognized that in organic systems, the collective conscience becomes "enfeebled" and religion as a pervasive influence recedes. The potential pathologies that can occur with the transition from mechanical to organic solidarity—particularly anomie—became increasingly evident to Durkheim. Indeed, the naive optimism that these pathologies would "spontaneously" wither away became increasingly untenable, and as is evident in *Suicide*, Durkheim began to ponder how to create a social system in which individuals are both regulated by a general set of values and attached to concrete groups. As Durkheim came to view the matter, these concerns revolved around the more general problem of "morality."

Durkheim never wrote what was to be the culmination of his life's work: a book on morality. But in many ways, his study of religion represents the beginning of his formal work on morality. While he had lectured on morality in his courses on education[62] and had written several articles on morality,[63] he saw in religion a chance to study how interaction among individuals leads to the creation of symbolic systems that *(a)* lace together individual actions into collective units, *(b)* regulate and control individual desires, and *(c)* attach individuals to both the symbolic and structural (morphological) facets of the social world. In the face of anomie and egoism, Durkheim thought that an understanding of religious morality in primitive social systems would throw light on how such morality could be created in modern, differentiated systems. Thus, we could retitle *The Elementary Forms of Religious Life* "the fundamental forms of moral integration" and be close to Durkheim's major purpose in examining religion in primitive societies, particularly the Arunta Aborigines of Australia.[64]

In the course of writing what was his longest work, however, Durkheim introduced many other intellectual issues that had come to occupy his attention over the years. Thus, *Elementary Forms* is more than a study

---

[62] The work on "moral education" will be examined later in this chapter in a discussion of Durkheim's more general concern with "morality."

[63] See, for example, Émile Durkheim, "The Determination of Moral Facts," *Sociology and Philosophy*, trans. D. F. Poccock, (New York: Free Press, 1974). This article was originally published in 1906.

[64] Baldwin Spencer and F. J. Gillian, *The Native Tribes of Central Australia* (London: Macmillan, 1899), presented the first collection of "accounts" of these primitive peoples, which was, in itself, fascinating to urbane Europeans. Sigmund Freud, in *Totem and Taboo* (London: Penguin, 1938; originally published in 1913); and the anthropologists, Bronislaw Malinowski, in *The Family among the Australian Aborigines* (New York: Schocken, 1963, originally published in 1913), and A. R. Radcliffe-Brown, in "Three Tribes of Western Australia" *Journal of Royal Anthropological Institute of Great Britain and Ireland 43* (1913), were all preparing works on the Aborigines of Australia at the same time as Durkheim was writing *The Elementary Forms of Religious Life*.

of social integration; it is also an excursion into human evolution, the sociology of knowledge, functional and causal analysis, the origin and basis of thought and mental categories, the process of internalization of beliefs and values, and many other issues. Between the long descriptive passages on tribal life among the Australian tribes, a myriad of ideas burst forth and give evidence of the wide-ranging concerns of Durkheim's intellect.

Elementary Forms is thus a long, complex, and, unlike his earlier works, less coherently organized book. This fact requires that the analysis be divided into a number of separate topics. After a brief overview of the argument in *Elementary Forms*, we will examine in more detail some of its implications.

The Elementary Forms of Religious Life: An Overview

By studying the elementary forms of religion among the most primitive[65] peoples, it should be possible, Durkheim felt, to understand the essence of religious phenomena, without the distracting complexities and sociocultural overlays of modern social systems.[66] As dictated in *The Rules*, a clear definition of the phenomenon under study was first necessary. Thus, Durkheim defined religion as:

> A unified system of beliefs and practices relative to sacred things, that is to say, things set apart and forbidden—beliefs and practices which unite into one single moral community called a Church, all those who adhere to them.[67]

Durkheim believed that religiosity first emerged among humans when they would occasionally assemble in a larger mass. Out of the mutual stimulation and "effervescence" that comes from animated interaction, people came to perceive a force, or "mana," that seemed superior to them. The mutual stimulation of primitive peoples thus made them

---

[65] Obviously Durkheim was wrong on this account, but this was one of his assumptions.

[66] It should be noted that this strategy was the exact opposite of that employed by Max Weber, who examined the most complex systems of religion with his "ideal type" methodology.

[67] Durkheim, *Elementary Forms*, p. 47. Durkheim's earlier definition of religious phenomena emphasized the sacred, beliefs and ritual, but did not stress the morphological units of community and church. For example, an early definition read: "Religious phenomena consist of obligatory beliefs united with divine practices which relate to the objects given in the beliefs." (Quoted in Lukes, *Émile Durkheim*, p. 241.) His exposure to the compilation in Spencer and Gillian, *Native Tribes*, apparently alerted him to these morphological features.

"feel" an "external" and "constraining" force above and beyond them.[68] This force seemed to be embued with special significance and with a sense that it was not part of this world. It was, then, the first notion of a "sacred" realm that is distinct from the routine or "secular" world of daily activities. The distinction between sacred and secular was thus one of the first sets of mental categories possessed by humans in their evolutionary development.

As humans came to form more permanent groupings or clans, the force that emerges out of their interaction needed to be more concretely represented.[69] Such representation came with "totems," which are animals and plants that symbolize the force of mana. In this way, the sacred forces could be given concrete representation and groups of people organized into "cults" could develop "ritual" activities directed toward the totem, and indirectly, toward the sacred force that they collectively sensed.

Thus, the basic elements of religion are "beliefs in the sacred," organization of people into "cults" that engage in "rituals" or "rites" toward "totems" that represent the forces of the sacred realm. What the primitives did not recognize, Durkheim argued, is that in worshiping totems, they are worshiping society. Totemic cults are nothing but the material symbolization of a force that is created by their interaction and collective organization into clans.

As people first became organized into clans and associated totemic cults, and as they perceived a sacred realm that influenced events in the secular world, their first categories of thought were also formed. Notions of causality could emerge only after people perceived that sacred forces determine events in the secular world. And notions of time and space could only exist after the organization of clans and their totemic cults. According to Durkheim, the basic categories of human thought— cause, time, space, and so on—first emerged after people developed religion. And thus in an ultimate sense, science and all forms of thought have emerged from religion—a line of argument, we might note, that is reminiscent of Comte's "law of the three stages." Prior to religion, humans experienced only physical sensations[70] from their physical envi-

---

[68] Durkheim clearly borrowed the ideas of crowd behavior developed by Gustave LeBon and Gabriel Tarde, even though the latter was his lifelong intellectual enemy.

[69] Durkheim, in both *The Division of Labor* and *The Rules,* had stressed that the segmental clan was the most elementary society. The presocietal "mass" out of which the clan emerges was termed by Durkheim *the horde.*

[70] As can be recalled, Durkheim takes this idea from Rousseau and his description of the "natural state of man."

ronment, but with religion, their mental life became structured by categories—the cornerstone of all thought, including scientific thought and
reasoning. In looking back on *Elementary Forms* a year after its publication, Durkheim was still moved to conclude:

> The most essential notions of the human mind, notions of time, of space,
> of genus and species, of force and causality, of personality, those in a
> word, which the philosophers have labelled categories and which dominate
> the whole logical thought, have been elaborated in the very womb of
> religion. It is from religion that science has taken them.[71]

For Durkheim the cause of religion was the interaction among people
created by their organization into the simplest form of society, the clan.
The functions of religion are *(a)* to regulate human needs and actions
through beliefs about the sacred and *(b)* to attach people, through ritual
activities ("rites") in cults, to the collective. Because they are internalized,
religious beliefs generate needs for people to belong to cults and participate in rituals. And as people participate in rituals, they reaffirm these
internalized beliefs, and hence, reinforce their regulation by, and attachment to, the dictates of the clan. Moreover, the molding of such basic
mental categories as cause, time, and space by religious beliefs and cults
functions to give people a common view of the world, thus facilitating
their interaction and organization.

Some Implications of *Elementary Forms*

Practical Concerns. Durkheim's analysis of pathologies in *Suicide*
had, along with other essays, forced the recognition that a more active
program for avoiding egoism and anomie might be necessary to create
a normal "organic" society. Religion, he thought, offered a key to understanding how this could be done. But early in his career, he had rejected
the idea that religion could ever again assume major integrative functions.
The modern world was too secular and individualistic for the subordination of individuals to gods. He had also rejected, to a much lesser degree,
Saint-Simon's and Comte's wish to create a secular religion of humanity
based upon science and reason. While the functions of religion and
the basic elements of religion needed to be maintained, Durkheim had
difficulty accepting Comte's ideal of positivism which, as Robert Nisbet
notes, was "Catholicism minus Christianity." For Comte, the Grand

---

[71] Quoted in Lukes, *Émile Durkheim*, p. 445 (taken from *L' Année Sociologique*
12). This line of thought is simply Comte's idea of the movement of thought from
the theological through metaphysical to positivistic.

Being was society, and the church was the hierarchy of the sciences, and the rites were the sacred canons of the positive method.[72] And yet, neither could Durkheim accept Max Weber's pessimistic view of a secular, rational world filled with disenchantment and lacking in commitments to a higher purpose.

The "solution" that is implied in *Elementary Forms*, and advocated elsewhere in various essays, is for the re-creation in secular form of the basic elements of religion: the feeling of the sacred, beliefs and values about the sacred, common rituals directed toward the sacred, and cult structures in which these rituals and beliefs are reaffirmed. Since society is the source and object of religious activity, the goal must be to make explicit this need to "worship" society. Occupational groups and the state would become the church and cults; nationalistic beliefs would become quasi sacred and would provide underlying symbols; and activities in occupational groups, when seen as furthering the collective goals of the nation, would assume the functions of religious ritual in *(a)* mobilization of individual commitment, *(b)* reaffirming beliefs and values, and *(c)* integrating individuals into the collective.

Theoretical Concerns. Contained in these practical concerns are a number of important theoretical issues. First, integration of social structures presupposes a system of values and beliefs that reflects and symbolizes the structure of the collective. Second, these values and beliefs require periodic actions—rituals—explicitly directed at reaffirming them as well as the social structures that they represent or symbolize. Third, large collectivities, such as a nation, require subgroups in which values and beliefs can be affirmed by ritual activities among a more immediate community of individuals. And fourth, to the degree that values and beliefs do not correspond to actual structural arrangements and to the extent that substructures for the performance of actions that reaffirm these values and beliefs are not present, then a societal social system will experience integrative problems.

It can be seen, then, Durkheim's practical concerns follow from certain theoretical principles that he had tentatively put forth in *The Division of Labor*. The study of religion seemingly provided Durkheim with a new source of data to affirm the utility of his first insights into the social order. There are, however, some noticeable shifts in emphasis, the most important is the recognition that the "conscience collective" cannot be totally "enfeebled"; it must be general but also strong and relevant to the specific organization of a social system. Yet despite these

---

[72] Nisbet, *Émile Durkheim*, p. 159.

refinements, *Elementary Forms* affirms the conclusion contained in the "Preface" to the Second Edition" of *The Division of Labor*.

The most interesting aspect of the analysis is perhaps the social psychological emphasis of *Elementary Forms*. While Durkheim, in courses and essays, had begun to feel comfortable with inquiry into the social psychological dynamics of social and symbolic structures, these concerns are brought together in this last major book.

Social Psychological Concerns. *Elementary Forms* contains the explicit recognition that morality—that is values, beliefs, and norms—can only operate to integrate the social order if they become part of an individual's psychological structure. Statements in *Elementary Forms* mitigate the rather hard line taken in the first edition of *The Rules* where social facts are seen as external and constraining things. With the second edition of *The Rules*, Durkheim felt more secure in verbalizing the obvious fact of internalization of values, beliefs, and other symbolic components of society into the human psyche. And in *Elementary Forms*, he revealed even fewer reservations:

> For the collective force is not entirely outside of us; it does not act upon us wholly from without; but rather, since society cannot exist except in and through individual consciousnesses, this force must also penetrate us and organize itself within us, it thus becomes an integral part of our being.[73]

Durkheim hastened to add in a footnote, however, that although society is an "integral part of our being" it cannot ever be seen as reducible to individuals.

Another social psychological concern in *Elementary Forms* is the issue of human thought processes. For Durkheim, thought occurs in terms of categories that structure experience for individuals.

> At the roots of all our judgments there are a certain number of essential ideas which dominate all our intellectual life; they are what philosophers since Aristotle have called the categories of the understanding: ideas of space, class, number, cause, substance, personality, etc. They correspond to the most universal properties of things. They are like the solid frame which encloses all thought.[74]

Durkheim had sought in *Elementary Forms* to reject the philosophical positions of David Hume and Immanuel Kant. Hume, the staunch empiricist, had argued that thought is simply the transfer of experiences to

---

[73] Durkheim, *Elementary Forms*, p. 209.

[74] Ibid., p. 9.

the mind and that categories of thought are merely the codification of repetitive experiences. In contrast to Hume, Kant had argued that categories and mind are inseparable—the essence of mind is categorization. Categories are innate and not structured from experience. Durkheim rejected both of these positions; and in their place, he wanted to insert the notion that categories of thought—indeed, all thinking and reflective mental activity—are imposed upon individuals by the structure and morality of society. Indeed, this imposition of society becomes a critical condition not just for the creation of mind and thought but also for the preservation of society.[75] Thus, Durkheim believed that the basic categories of thought, such as cause, time, and space, are social products in that the structure of society determines them in the same way that values and beliefs also structure human "will" or motivations. For example, the idea of a sacred force, or "mana," beyond individuals became, in the course of human evolution, related to ideas of causality as rituals and beliefs came to concern the effects of sacred acts in the secular world. Similarly, the idea of time emerged among humans as they developed calendrical rituals and tied them to solar and lunar rhythms. And the conception of space was shaped by the structure of villages, so that if the aboriginal village is organized in a circle, the world will be seen as circular and concentric in nature. These provocative insights were at times taken to excessive extremes in other essays, especially in the essay written with his nephew and student, Marcel Mauss, on "primitive classification."[76] Here, mental categories are seen to be exact representations of social structural divisions and arrangements. Moreover, Durkheim and Mauss appeared to have selectively reported data from primitive societies to support their excessive claims.[77]

A SCIENCE OR "MORALITY"

As early as *The Division of Labor*, Durkheim defined sociology as the science of "moral facts," and he always wanted to write a book on morality. In light of this fact, perhaps we should close our analysis of Durkheim by extracting from his various works what would have been the core ideas of this uncompleted work.[78]

---

[75] Ibid., pp. 17–18.

[76] Emile Durkheim and Marcel Mauss, *Primitive Classification* trans. Rodney Needham (Chicago: University of Chicago Press, 1963; originally published in 1903).

[77] See introduction to translation for documentation of this fact.

[78] See, in particular, Émile Durkheim, *Moral Education: A Study in the Theory and Application of the Sociology of Education*, trans. E. K. Wilson and H. Schnurer,

What is Morality?

In only two places did Durkheim provide a detailed discussion of morality.[79] For Durkheim, morality consisted of several elements, (1) rules, (2) attachment to groups, and (3) voluntary constraint, each of which is examined briefly below:

Rules. Morality is ultimately a system of rules for guiding the actions of people. Yet many rules are not moral because they lack two additional elements.

1. *Authority.* Moral rules are invested with authority—that is people feel they ought to obey them and they want to abide by them. Moral rules are a "system of commandments."
2. *Desirability.* Moral rules also specify the "desirable" ends toward which a collectivity of people should direct their energies. They are more than rules of convenience; they carry conceptions of the good and desirable, and must, therefore, be distinguished from strictly utilitarian norms.

Attachment to Groups. Moral rules attach people to groups. Moral rules are the product of interactions in groups, and as they emerge, they bind people to groups and make them feel a part of a network of relations that transcends their individual being.

Durkheim termed these two facets of morality *the spirit of discipline.* Morality provides a spirit of self-control and a commitment to the collective. In terms of the concepts developed in *Suicide*, morality eliminates anomie and egoism, because it regulates desires and attaches people to the collective. But true morality in a modern society must do something else: it must allow people to recognize that the constraints and restraints that it imposes upon them are in the "natural order of things."

Voluntary Constraint. Modern morality must allow people to recognize that unlimited desires (anomie) and excessive individualism (egoism) are pathological states. These states violate the nature of human society and can only be corrected by morality. In simple societies, morality seems to operate automatically, but "the more societies become complex, the more difficult [it becomes] for morality to operate as a purely auto-

---

(Glencoe, Ill.: Free Press, 1961; originally published in 1922). This work is a compilation of lectures given in 1902–1903. This course was repeated in 1906–1907, and had been given in somewhat different form early in Durkheim's teaching career.

[79] One is in Durkheim, *Moral Education*: the other is in an article, published in 1906, on "The Determination of Moral Facts." (Reprinted in Èmile Durkheim, *Sociology and Philosophy* [New York: Free Press, 1974] from papers originally collected and translated in 1924).

matic mechanism."[80] And thus, morality must be constantly implemented and altered to changing conditions. But individuals must also come to see that such alteration is necessary and essential, since to fail in establishing a morality and to allow people to feel free of its power is to invite the agonies of anomie and egoism.

Durkheim then resumed an argument first made by Rousseau (see Chapter 15): morality must be seen as a natural constraint in the same way that the physical world constrains individuals' options and actions. So it is with morality; humans can no more rid themselves of its constraint than they can eliminate the physical and biological world on which their lives depend. In light of this situation, then, the only recourse is to use a science of morality, just as we use the physical and biological sciences, to understand how morality works.[81]

Thus, Durkheim never abandoned his original notion, first given forceful expression in *The Division of Labor*, that sociology is the science of "moral facts." But Durkheim's conception of morality had become considerably more refined, in several senses:

1. Morality is a certain type of rule that must be distinguished from *(a)* the morphological aspects of society and *(b)* other, nonmoral, types of normative rules.
2. Morality is, therefore, a system of rules that reflects certain underlying value premises about the desirable.
3. Morality is not only external and constraining; it is also internal. It calls people to obey from within. For while morality "surpasses us it is within us, since it can only exist by and through us."[82]

By the end of Durkheim's career, the study of morality involved a clear separation among types of norms and rules: those vested with value premises and those that simply mediate and regularize interactions. Moreover, an understanding of these types of rules could only come by visualizing their relationship to the morphological aspects of society—nature, size, number, and relations of parts—and to the process by which internalization of symbols occurs. Durkheim had thus begun to develop a clear conception of the complex relations among normative systems, social structures, and personality processes of individuals.

---

[80] Durkheim, *Moral Education*, p. 52.
[81] Ibid., pp. 119–20.
[82] Durkheim, "Determination of Moral Facts," p. 55.

The Unfinished Work on Morality

What would Durkheim have said in his last work—the book on morality—if he had lived to write it? Durkheim's work on *Moral Education,* when viewed in the context of his published books, can perhaps provide some hints about the direction of his thought. For *Moral Education* offers a view of how a new secular morality can be instilled.

For a new, secular morality to be effective, the source of all morality must be recognized: society. This means that moral rules must be linked to the goals of the broader society. But they must be made specific to individuals through their participation in occupational groups. And the commitment to the common morality must be learned in schools where the teacher operates as the functional equivalent of the priest. As such, the teacher gives young students an understanding of, coupled with a reverence for, the nature of the society and the need to have a moraltiy that regulates passions and provides attachments to groupings organized to pursue societal goals. Such educational socialization must assure that the common morality is a part of students' motivational needs (their "will" in Durkheim's language), their cognitive orientations ("categories of mind"), and their self-control processes ("self-mastery").

A modern society that cannot meet these general conditions, Durkheim would have argued in this unwritten work, is a society that will be rife with pathologies revolving around *(a)* the failure to limit individual passions, desires, and aspirations; and *(b)* the failure to attach individuals to groups with higher purposes and common goals.

Durkheim must have felt that the implicit theory of social organization contained in this line of argument had allowed him to realize Comte's dream of a "science of society" that could create "the good society." As we will come to see in the next chapter, however, Durkheim's specific proposals were often simplistic, if not somewhat reactionary. But at the same time, there is the germ of a theory of human organization. This theory can best be appreciated when the strictly theoretical implications of Durkheim's work are examined alone.

17

ÉMILE DURKHEIM III: MODELS AND PRINCIPLES

THE BASIC THEORETICAL APPROACH

To appreciate the kinds of theoretical models and principles that Durkheim developed it is necessary to review the basic elements of his approach. We can view this approach as revealing six distinctive features: (1) the stress on the development of scientific laws, (2) the concern with emergent social and culture structures, (3) the emphasis on evolutionary patterns, (4) the search for causal relations, (5) the assessment of functions; and (6) the analysis of social pathologies. It is in the context of these distinctive features that Durkheim presented modern sociological theory with models and principles.

The Search for Scientific Laws

From the inspiration first provided by Montesquieu and then reinforced by Comte, Durkheim never wavered from his commitment to discovering the laws of human organization. On only rare occasions did Durkheim explicitly state laws as formal propositions, but he was one of the first social scientists to attempt to develop theoretical statements about the basic properties of social and cultural structures.

Although Durkheim appeared to retain Montesquieu's and Comte's view that the "laws" of society will be probabilistic, he also seemed to have a vision that the fundamental properties of the social world could be stated as laws similar to those in the physics of Newton or the biology of Darwin. In the tradition of Comte and Spencer, then, Durkheim sought to develop statements that expressed the lawful relations of social structure.

Durkheim's "Structuralism"

Long before the anthropologist Claude Lévi-Strauss or the structural linguist Noam Chomsky were to label a school of thought *structuralism*, Durkheim argued for a science of social structure. Moral and social facts constitute a distinctive, emergent reality. When individuals interact, a new reality emerges, and the properties of this reality are not reducible to those individuals. This reality consists of the relations among individuals and other social units, and thus, a "science of society" must seek to understand the processes that create, maintain, and change the emergent properties of social relations.

While Durkheim was always interested in how emergent social and cultural realities are reflected in the activities of individuals, all of his theoretical models and principles focus on the nature of social and cultural structures, rather than on individuals. True, Durkheim emphasized that cultural values, beliefs, and norms are internalized by individuals and become a part of their sense of self and their mechanisms for self-control, and there can be little doubt that late in his career Durkheim also came to stress that "mental categories" reflect, or mirror, social and cultural arrangements. But in his theories, Durkheim took human personality as a "given," as something that psychologists study. And while he recognized that social psychology would be a useful interstitial discipline, it must await a well developed set of principles on the properties of social structure.

Durkheim's Evolutionism

Durkheim never abandoned the evolutionary perspective first revealed in *The Division of Labor*, for he always viewed societies as moving from simple to complex forms. The task of sociological theorizing, Durkheim felt, is to trace the general cause of this societal movement and to articulate the theoretical principles explaining changes in the basis of social solidarity or integration that occur with social evolution. Thus, Durkheim's models and theories of the social order are almost always placed within an evolutionary framework.

Durkheim's evolutionism often led him into dangerous intellectual territory. In the spirit of Rousseau and other "social contract" thinkers, he was often to search for the origins of social phenomena. Yet while

Durkheim's analysis of societal origins is often absurd,[1] his sense for the empirical changes accompanying social evolution is generally insightful:

1. Cultural ideas become increasingly differentiated into separable systems of values, beliefs, and norms.
2. Cultural ideas become increasingly secular and rational.
3. Specific institutions become increasingly differentiated from the religio-kinship basis of primitive societies.
4. The economy and a bureaucratized central government increase in scope and influence.
5. Kinship and religion recede in scope and influence.
6. Rates of deviance increase and bring about greater efforts at restitution.
7. Law becomes a major integrative mechanism.
8. Education becomes a major socializing influence.
9. Community life becomes more "voluminous" with urbanization.
10. Inequalities based on ascription tend to decrease, with a trend toward greater correspondence between talent and inequality (although Durkheim clearly underemphasized the perpetuation of ascriptive privilege in modern societies).
11. Democracy becomes the dominant political and social form.
12. Voluntary political and civil organizations increasingly come to replace kinship, region, religion, and community as major centers of affiliation.

These observations, which are sprinkled throughout Durkheim's work, reveal a keen sense for the empirical nature of social change in the present world. While they do not have the systematic character or analytical depth evident in Max Weber's work, they are testimony to Durkheim's sense of the cultural and structural transformations accompanying social evolution. And, unlike Weber, Durkheim used this knowledge of empirical events to develop abstract theoretical principles about the nature of social organization in both simple and differentiated social systems (these will be discussed later in this chapter).

Durkheim's Causal Analysis

From Montesquieu, Durkheim retained the emphasis on causality. To understand a "social fact" it is necessary to determine its cause

---

[1] See, for example, Émile Durkheim, *Incest: The Nature and Origin of the Taboo* (New York: Lyle Stuart, 1963; originally published in 1913). This essay more than any other, reveals Durkheim's tendency to engage in wild speculation on the "origins" of society.

which, as he always stressed, must be another social fact. For Durkheim, then, theoretical explanation that does not address causality—that is, the effects of antecedent conditions on a given phenomenon—is not a complete explanation.[2] There can be little doubt, then, that Durkheim was a pioneer in causal modeling. His explanations of social phenomena often involved causal models that trace the patterns of influence among social phenomena. Yet despite his efforts at conducting sound causal modeling, Durkheim's functionalism frequently obscured his causal models. For even though Durkheim stressed early in his career the importance of not arguing in terms of "final causes," he continually confused causal and functional approaches to explanation.

Durkheim's Functionalism

In Durkheim's view, causal explanation would be incomplete without a functional analysis. He believed that while the functional and causal explanations must be kept separated, complete understanding of social phenomena could only come with both. Thus, on the one hand, the antecedent events leading to the emergence of a social fact, such as the division of labor, religious ritual, or type of criminal sanction, must first be determined (causal analysis), but then the functions of this fact for maintaining the integration or solidarity of the social whole must also be analyzed.

Durkheim's insistence that phenomena be assessed in terms of what they "do for" and "contribute to" the "body social" stemmed from his desire to be the sociological counterpart of the physician—a vision of the sociologist's role that he absorbed from Comte. By knowing the "functions" of a social fact for the integration of the social whole, then it is possible to determine if this fact is "normal" or "pathological." For Durkheim, functional analysis gives the sociologist a means for isolating "social pathologies" and for recommending "treatments" for ridding the "body social" of the pathology.

Durkheim's View of "Social Pathology"

What is normal and pathological in a society could, in Durkheim's view, only be assessed in relation to "societal types." A given type of society will have a series of general structural and cultural arrangements that are normal for that type. Although wide variations in the way these

---

[2] Here again we can observe Montesquieu's insistence on developing types and on seeking the causes of general types or classes of events.

general arrangements are manifested in specific empirical systems will be evident, the general profile of institutions and cultural systems will tend to be similar for societies of a given type. Implicit in this line of argument is the notion that "normality" can be defined not only in terms of modal social facts, but also with respect to the degree that a structure or cultural component promotes social solidarity.

It is the concept of "solidarity" that moves Durkheim's analysis into the grey area of moral philosophizing. Since Durkheim tended to equate integration and solidarity with normality, the "good society" for Durkheim is an "integrated society." What, then, was solidarity and integration? As he emphasized in *The Division of Labor,* the basis of solidarity varied from one societal type to another. Thus, for a modern, organic society, one definition of "goodness" applied, while for a mechanical society, yet another definition pertained. In organic or modern societies, integration (or goodness) involved *(a)* coordination of parts, *(b)* individual freedom and liberty, *(c)* democratic government, *(d)* a high correlation between talent and inequality, *(e)* pluralistic centers of power, *(f)* individual commitment to collective values and goals, and *(g)* individual attachment to groups. It is difficult to view these conditions as normal; rather, they represent Durkheim's hopes and dreams about what a modern society should be.

Social pathologies in organic systems thus become those conditions that deviate from Durkheim's concept of the "good society." Anomie, egoism, the forced division of labor, and poor coordination of functions were quite typical, if not modal, in the societies of Durkheim's time (and for that matter, in the present), but they were considered by Durkheim to be pathologies because they do not promote the type of social solidarity and integration that he considered "good." And it is this concern with the good society and social pathologies that makes a more formal statement of Durkheim's theoretical models and principles somewhat ambiguous.

DURKHEIM'S THEORETICAL MODELS

Durkheim's Overall Model of Social Reality

As we have emphasized in Chapter 1 and elsewhere, a model is an analytical accentuation of what are considered to be the critical elements, and the interrelations among these elements, for some specific domain of reality. A causal model denotes the causal interrelations among elements, accentuating how sets of antecedent conditions bring about certain results. Almost all of Durkheim's models are causal, owing to his concern with evolution, origins, and history. Thus, Durkheim constructed implicit causal models for a variety of phenomena: the division of labor, suicide rates, religion, incest taboos, and cognitive categories. Underlying these specific models can be discerned a more general view of the key causal relations in the social world. This more general model is summarized in Figure 17–1.

FIGURE 17–1
Durkheim's Overall Model of Social Organization

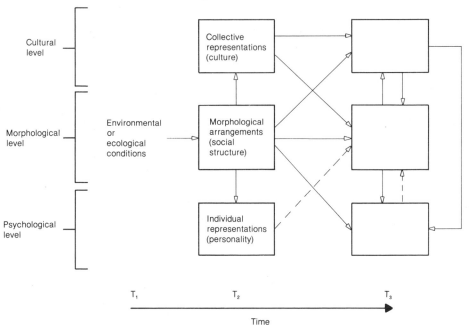

Early in his career, Durkheim did not clearly distinguish among the cultural, social structural, and psychological dimensions of the social world. His primary concern was with separating "moral facts" (culture and structure) from individual psychology. By the end of his career, however, he saw that personality, social-structural, and symbolic elements constitute distinctive levels of reality and that it is important to understand properties of each level, as well as the relations among these levels. However, Durkheim never abandoned his insistence that the cultural and morphological levels represent a distinctive reality that could not be reduced to, or understood in terms of, psychological processes. Thus, in Figure 17–1, a dotted line is drawn for causes emanating from the psychological level. Yet, in almost all of his discussions, psychological variables "sneak" into the analysis, usually as dependent variables, but sometimes as implicit independent variables.

All of Durkheim's models reveal a time dimension. He rarely engaged in cross-sectional analysis. Typically, there are three broad time periods in his models, as is represented by T_1, T_2, and T_3 in Figure 17–1. While T_1 is sometimes omitted, most of Durkheim's models begin with ecological (population density and arrangement), demographic (population size), or environmental (resources, other societies) variables. These variables are seen to influence morphological arrangements or patterns of association and interaction among people at T_2. In turn, morphological arrangements create symbolic representations—ideas, beliefs, values, and norms—that reflect patterns of interaction. And implicitly, individual personality components—cognitive orientations, motivational needs, and self-control processes—are shaped by the morphological arrangements of people.

At T_3, the relations of morphological, cultural, and psychological elements become reciprocal. Once values, beliefs, and norms emerge, they shape subsequent structural arrangements, as well as having a dynamic of their own in determining subsequent cultural symbols. Morphological variables continue to shape subsequent cultural and psychological states, as well as determining the nature of structural conditions at T_3. Thus, by T_3, Durkheim viewed the social world as involving a series of reciprocal relations among structural and cultural variables. Buy psychological states remained dependent variables and thus they only reflect structural and symbolic conditions.

The interconnections among the three levels of social reality presented at T_3 of Figure 17–1 are now so much a part of the sociological perspective that we may not recognize what a revolutionary insight they represented in the 1890s and early 1900s.[3] The giants of this period—Weber, Mead, Freud, and Durkheim—were all grappling with the connections represented at T_3, and while each offered his own unique perspective, they all had a similar insight: at the most general analytical level, social reality can be divided into constituent psychological, structural, and symbolic properties and this reality can only be understood by exploring the relations within and among these emergent properties.

---

[3] As an illustration of this point, it is a rare introductory text that does not begin with separate discussions of culture, social organization, and personality.

Durkheim's Specific Causal Models

In contrast to the more general model with which Durkheim approached the analysis of the social world, his more specific models are so mired in evolutionism, especially in the notions of origins and function that they have little utility today. We can best illustrate some of the problems of Durkheim's specific models by examining in more detail two of his most famous models: (1) on the emergence of the division of labor and (2) on the origins of religion.

The Division of Labor. In this work,[4] Durkheim viewed societies as moving from a simple, homogeneous form (mechanical) to a more complex, differentiated form (organic). In this discussion, Durkheim presented a model of social evolution that is illustrated in Figure 17–2.

As Figure 17–2 illustrates, Durkheim saw migration, population growth, and ecological concentration as causing increased "material density" which, in turn, caused increased "moral" or "dynamic" density—that is, escalated social contact and interaction. Such interaction could be further heightened by varied means of communication and transportation, as is illustrated in the model. The increased rates of interaction characteristic of a larger population within a confined ecological space cause increased competition or "struggle" among individuals. Such competition allows those who have the most resources and talents to maintain their present positions and assume high-rank positions, while the "less fit" seek alternative specialties so as to mitigate the competition. Out of this competition and differentiation comes the division of labor which, when "normal," results in organic solidarity.

The major problem with the model is the implicit argument by "final causes." The function of the division of labor is to promote social solidarity, and Durkheim implied that the need for social solidarity causes the struggle to be resolved by the division of labor. Yet Durkheim never specified precisely how the needs met by the division of labor (that is, social solidarity) cause it to emerge. Without clear specification of this causal connection, the model becomes an illegitimate teleology in which the end-state (social solidarity) causes the very thing (the division of labor) that brings about this end-state. The model is also circular or tautological in that cause and effect become difficult to separate: the division of labor causes social solidarity, while the need for social solidarity

---

[4] Émile Durkheim, *The Division of Labor in Society* (Glencoe, Ill.: Free Press, 1947; originally published in 1893).

FIGURE 17–2
Durkheim's Causal Model of the Division of Labor

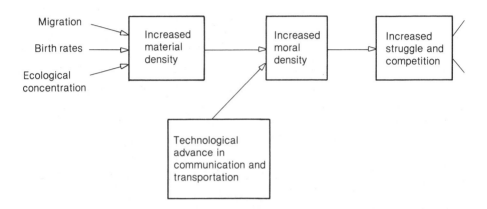

causes the division of labor. In such an argument, just what causes what becomes unclear.

The model in Figure 17–2 thus contains some suggestive ideas, particularly the notion that material density causes moral density, that moral density causes competition, that competition causes differentiation, and that differentiation causes new mechanisms of integration. But on the other hand, without specifying the conditions under which *(a)* moral density causes competition, *(b)* competition causes differentiation, and *(c)* differentiation causes new integrative processes, the model is vague. As we will come to appreciate, these relationships among size, interaction rates, competition, differentiation, and integration are better suited to axiomatic theory as abstract principles from which deductions to specific empirical systems are made. And as deductions to empirical systems are preformed, some of the needed specifications of conditions under which propositions hold true can be made. As a causal model, these relationships are too indeterminate to be useful.

The Elementary Forms of Religion. In Durkheim's last major work,

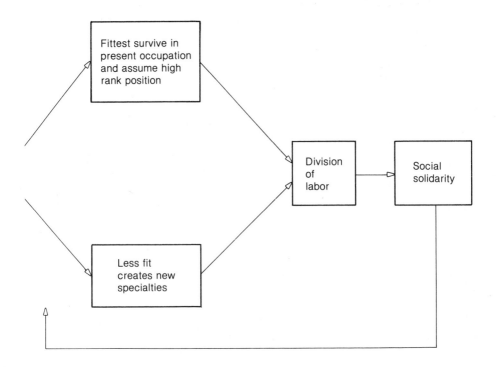

The Elementary Forms of Religious Life,[5] he developed a similar evolutionary model, although it was directed at the origins of the first religions rather than at the movement of religion from simple to complex forms. Figure 17–3 presents this causal model.

Durkheim's model is a statement of both the origins and functions of religion. With respect to origins, Durkheim had an image of "primitive" peoples periodically migrating and concentrating themselves in temporary gatherings. Once gathered, increased interaction escalates collective emotions which produce a sense that there is "something" external and constraining in individuals. This sense of constraint is given more articulate expression as a sacred force or "mana." This causal sequence occurs, Durkheim maintained, each time "primitives" gather in their periodic festivals. But once they come to form more permanent groupings, called clans, the force of mana is given more concrete expres-

[5] Èmile Durkheim, *The Elementary Forms of Religious Life* (London: Allen & Unwin, 1915; originally published in 1912).

FIGURE 17-3
Durkheim's Model of Religious Evolution

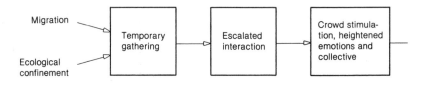

sion as a sacred totem. The creation of totems, and beliefs about as well as rituals toward the totem, promotes clan solidarity.

This model is substantively inaccurate, as are all of Durkheim's intellectual expeditions into the origins of society. For example, clans were not the first kinship structure and many "primitives" do not worship totems. These errors can be attributed to Durkheim's reliance upon Australian Aborigine kinship and religious organization which, in many ways, deviate from modal patterns among hunting and gathering peoples. Aside from these factual errors, the same problems evident in the model of the division of labor resurface. First, the conditions under which any causal connection holds true are not specified. Second, the functions of religious totems (social solidarity) promote their creation. And additionally, a psychological need—the "primitive need" to make concrete and symbolize "mana"—is invoked to explain why totems emerge.

In light of these problems, it must be concluded that the model does not present any useful information in its causal format. But as a statement of relationships among rates of interaction, structural arrangements, emotional arousal, and symbolic representation, Durkheim's statements can be organized into a series of propositions. Durkheim's critical insight is that highly concentrated interactions increase collective sentiments that mobilize actors' actions and that small social structures tend to develop symbols to represent their collective sentiments. Properly

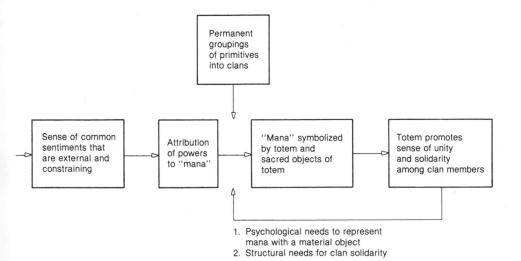

1. Psychological needs to represent mana with a material object
2. Structural needs for clan solidarity

phrased, this insight could be tested. Thus, as causal statements, Durkheim's analysis has little to offer, but as a series of propositions on fundamental relationships between patterns of interaction and social structure, on the one hand, and cultural symbols, on the other, Durkheim's ideas are more theoretically interesting.

In sum, then, Durkheim's models of the division of labor and religion do not offer much to contemporary sociological theory. They are too abstract, too tied to naive evolutionism, and too confused by notions of function. But as we have suggested, they seem to offer more to sociological theory as abstract statements of relations among basic properties of the social world.

DURKHEIM'S THEORETICAL PRINCIPLES

Durkheim rarely stated his arguments as propositions or theoretical principles. Ordinarily, it is not difficult to pull from a discursive context a thinker's propositional statements, but in the case of Durkheim, such an exercise presents a number of problems. Durkheim's theoretical statements are often couched in functional terms: x structure functions to meet y need. A statement of this kind is difficult to translate into a theoretical principle of the form: x varies with y. This problem is compounded by Durkheim's implicit and explicit mingling or moral statements about what should be and what is. Durkheim frequently defined actual events and structures as abnormal and pathological in terms of his moral yardstick and then postulated an almost utopian state as normal. Under these conditions, it is difficult to determine those relationships that he felt are basic to the nature of the social world, and therefore, worthy of statement as an abstract principle.

Yet if we accept these limitations and recognize that they force some degree of inference, we can develop a series of abstract principles that summarize Durkheim's thought. Since Durkheim employed an evolutionary framework, his theoretical principles always concern the concomitants of increasing social differentiation. His basic theoretical question appears to have been: What is the basis of social organization within a differentiating social system?

We have, of course, phrased this question more abstractly than Durkheim may have intended, but this is exactly what must be done if Durkheim's genuis is to be fully appreciated. We must pull away from the subtle nuances, pay less attention to the burning (but now less-relevant) issues of his time, abandon much of his vocabulary and translate his terms into modern jargon,[6] and seek a consistently high level of abstraction in order to present the full explanatory power of Durkheim's ideas.

Our discussion of Durkheim's theoretical principles will be organized into four sections: (1) principles of social system differentiation, (2) principles of system integration, (3) principles of deviance, and (4) principles of system mal-integration. It is in these principles that Durkheim's theoretical contribution resides, and the degree to which these principles are considered insightful will determine the extent to which we can still learn from Durkheim's work.

Principles of System Differentiation

In *The Division of Labor*,[7] Durkheim isolated a series of variables that he felt influence differentiation and specialization in society. His basic idea is that increased "moral density"—that is, contact and interaction among people—escalates competition for resources, forcing social differentiation. This conceptualization is too enveloped in Darwinian

---

[6] Contrary to many, we feel that jargon is essential, since it gives precision to terms. Only those who have abandoned sociology as a science could advocate the abandonment of precise concepts—that is, jargon.

[7] Durkheim, *Division of Labor*.

and Spencerian cannotations to be useful. But if we abandon his harsh vocabulary and ask what is the postulated relationship among such variables as size, interaction, competition, on the one hand, and system differentiation, on the other, then a more powerful set of theoretical statements becomes evident.

1. The greater is the concentration of a population, the greater is the degree the social contact among its members, and hence, the greater is the rate of interaction among members of that population.

While this may not seem a startling revelation, it is nonetheless a basic principle of social organization.[8] Durkheim's analysis in *The Division of Labor* added several additional propositions that specified some of the conditions increasing likelihood of concentration of a population.

1a. The greater is the size of a population, the more likely is it to be concentrated.

1b. The more pronounced are the ecological barriers confronting a population, the more likely is it to be concentrated.

Durkheim saw a relationship between social interaction and competition for resources in a system. While he phrased the matter in terms of a "struggle for existence," a more muted terminology can better communicate a second Durkheimian principle.

2. The greater are the rates of interaction among a concentrated population, the greater is the level of competition over scarce resources among members of that population.

2a. The greater is the number and diversity of communication channels available to members of a population, the more likely are these members to interact and, hence, compete.

2b. The more available and the greater is the variety of transportation facilities in a system, the more likely are members of this system to interact and hence, compete.

Durkheim thus saw competition over resources as increasing with interaction. While this is no doubt true (since competition is a form of interaction and cannot occur without interaction), there is a whole series of

---

[8] It should be remembered that good theory simplifies and denotes the basic and fundamental relations among properties of the universe. It does not seek the esoteric, the subtle empirical nuance, or extreme case.

conditions that influence the intensity and violence of competition. Durkheim did not specify these conditions, but as we saw in Chapter 8, Marx presented a number of conditions that could provide further specification. Durkheim's key insight, we believe, does not reside in his analysis of the specific conditions associated with competition, but rather in his recognition that rates of interaction and competition are related to social differentiation.

> 3. **The greater is the competition for resources among members of a population in a social system, the more likely are they to become socially differentiated.**

This proposition is stated more probabilistically than either principles 1 or 2, because Durkheim felt that differentiation would only occur under certain conditions. For without the operation of conditions listed below, competition would lead to dispersion of the population.

>> 3a. **The more bounded is a population, the more likely is competition over scarce resources to result in social differentiation.**
>>> 3a1. **The more pronounced are geographical or ecological boundaries, the more bounded is a population.**
>>> 3a2. **The more politically organized is a system, the more bounded is a population.**
>> 3b. **The more symbolically unified is a population, the more likely is competition over scarce resources to result in social differentiation.**

Thus, for Durkheim, there must be a "force" preventing competition over scarce resources from dispersing the members of a population. Geopolitical boundaries and a common culture (values, beliefs, language) represent two general forces that keep a population intact. Competition, therefore, leads to social differentiation when actors cannot readily leave the system.

These three principles, and their qualifying propositions, present the essence of Durkheim's theory of social differentiation. (We might note that it is similar to several more modern formulations.[9]) In these principles, Durkheim was positing a fundamental set of relationships among population concentration, interaction, competition, and differentiation. These principles represented for Durkheim a realization of Montesquieu's

---

[9] See, for example, Peter M. Blau, *Exchange and Power in Social Life* (New York: John Wiley, 1966).

and Comte's dream of sociological laws and indeed, they might be considered some of sociology's "first principles."[10]

This theory is further developed in Durkheim's next series of propositions on differentiation and integration. For as he recognized more than any other scholar of his time, increasing system differentiation creates integrative problems and requires altered bases of integration.

Principles of System Integration

For Durkheim, social system integration, or as he phrased it, *social solidarity*, can be defined only by references to what he saw as "abnormal." Anomie, egoism, poor coordination, and the forced division of labor all represented to Durkheim instances of mal-integration. Thus, "normal" integration would represent the converse of these conditions, allowing us to formulate the following definition: integration occurs when individual passions are regulated by cultural symbols, where individuals are attached to the social collective, where actions are regulated and coordinated by norms, and where inequalities are considered legitimate.[11]

For Durkheim, differentiating systems face a dilemma, first given forceful expression by Comte: the compartmentalization of actors into specialized roles also partitions them from each other, driving them apart and decreasing their common sentiments. In *The Division of Labor*, Durkheim recognized that differentiation is accompanied by the growing abstractness, enfeeblement, or generalization of the collective conscience. Or, in terms of the specific variables he used to describe the collective conscience, values and beliefs become less voluminous, less intense, less determinate, and less religious. For only through increasing generality of the collective conscience could actors in specialized and secularized roles hold common values and beliefs. If values and beliefs are too specific, too rigid, too intense, and too sacred they cannot be relevant to the diversity of actors' secular experiences and orientations in differentiated roles, nor can they allow for the flexibility that comes with the division

---

[10] We might also include Spencer here, since these principles come from his inspiration as much as from either Comte or Montesquieu, although Durkheim would never had admitted to this influence.

[11] This last element of the definition is altered somewhat from Durkheim's own formulation, since we have tried to capture what he defined as integration, per se. His discussion of "the forced division of labor" was geared to modern societies, and he did not seem to consider inequalities in traditional societies that are not based upon natural talent as "abnormal." And his main argument for why the forced division of labor would not persist was that people would not accept it as legitimate in the modern age. Thus, his meaning appears to be that, when inequalities are not legitimated, they come to be "forced," or to appear "forced."

of labor in society. Hence, moral imperatives become more abstract and general. Durkheim thus saw a fundamental relationship between system differentiation and the generalization of cultural values and beliefs, as is summarized below:

4. **The greater is the degree of system differentiation in a social system, the more generalized are the values, beliefs, and other evaluational symbols in that system.**

The term *generalized* in this proposition is used to summarize Durkheim's view of the collective conscience becoming less determinate, voluminous, and intense. Such a process of value generalization presents differentiating systems with an integrative problem: What is to provide for unity in the face of the generalization of evaluational symbols and high levels of role specialization? In answering this question, Durkheim often inserted what he thought should occur, but even with his moralistic bias, he saw certain fundamental integrative tendencies in differentiated systems. These can be summarized by a series of additional principles.

5. **The greater is the degree of differentiation and value-generalization in a social system, the more likely is normative specification of evaluational premises for relations within and between social units in that system.**

Durkheim recognized that social integration in organic societies depends upon the development among social units of functional interrelations regulated by "contract," and upon regularization of behaviors within social units through concrete norms. In reacting to Spencer and the utilitarians, Durkheim emphasized that there is always a "moral component" or "noncontractual" basis of contract and that norms are more than utilitarian and instrumental "conveniences." They are tied, or at least he hoped that they were, to general values and beliefs, giving actors a common set of premises and assumptions. Principle 5 extracts the essence of Durkheim's argument from its moralistic trappings and argues that there is a fundamental relationship in the social world among structural differentiation, value generalization, and normative specification.

6. **The greater is the degree of differentiation and value-generalization in a social system, the more likely are subgroups to form around similar or related role activities in that system.**

Durkheim's discussion of occupational groups was, in many ways, an expression of his hopes and desires. At a more abstract level, however, he appears to have captured the essence of an important structural principle: as roles become differentiated and specialized and as common value premises generalize, clusters and networks of positions—or, in the terms of principle 6, subgroups—form among those engaged in similar activities. Such subgroup formation reinforces the process of normative specification delineated in princple 5.

7.   The greater is the degree of differentiation and value-generalization in a social system, the more likely is coordination of activity to be centralized in that system.

From Rousseau, Durkheim appears to have absorbed the idea that the "state" could personify the "collective conscience" and coordinate activities in pursuit of collective goals and purposes. If we seek a more abstract principle to translate Durkheim's somewhat moralistic vision, it can be seen that in any system experiencing differentiation and value generalization, there is increased probabilities for not only normative specification (principle 5) and subgroup formation (principle 6), but also centralization of authority. Yet Durkheim also distrusted centralized authority which went unchecked by counterauthority—an idea that he had taken from Montesquieu and Tocqueville. It is not clear that centralized authority automatically engenders counterauthority, but if we are to be true to Durkheim's argument, this process must be stated as a general principle. Durkheim felt that subgroups in a differentiating system with centralized authority are likely to become sources of power which check and balance the power of the central authority. Thus, we can formulate the following principle.

8.   The greater is the degree of centralized authority in a differentiated social system revealing subgroups, the more likely are subgroups to become centers of counterauthority mitigating the centralized authority of that system

Durkheim did not see such counterauthority as likely in less differentiated systems, but as systems differentiate and "naturally" tend to form subgroups around specialized roles and functions (principle 6), then there is a strong likelihood that these groups will resist the arbitrary use of power by the centralized authority, thereby creating a "balance of powers" in a system.

9.   The greater is the degree of differentiation and value-generalization in a social system, the more likely is the distribution of scarce resources to correspond to the unequal distribution of talents among members of that system.

This is a highly questionable Durkheimian principle. What defines talent? Is it innate intelligence, training, or cunning? And why would those who have resources at one point in time not pass them on to designated others, creating an ascriptive system in which talent and rewards become poorly correlated. Yet despite these problems with the proposition, there is a slight tendency in highly differentiated systems for resources to be distributed in accordance with the ability of actors to contribute to the system. But this is not a strong tendency and is weakened by ascriptive processes. Thus, principle 9, more than principles 1 through 8, reflects Durkheim's hope for the future rather than a clear assessment of structural tendencies.

10. **The greater is the degree of differentiation and value-generalization in a social system, the more likely are sanctions against deviance to be restitutive than punitive in that system.**

Durkheim incorrectly overestimated the degree of punishment in mechanical (primitive) social systems and he underestimated the punitive sanctions in modern systems. Yet he may have been correct in his view that the ratio of restitutive to punitive sanctions increases with differentiation and value generalization. Since differentiated systems have less-immediate value premises to offend and since they require coordination of parts, Durkheim may be correct in his view that there is a fundamental relationship in social systems among differentiation, value generalization, and restitutive sanctions.

Principles 4 through 10 summarize Durkheim's vision of the basis of integration in differentiating systems. These principles were developed by Durkheim for understanding whole societies, but we suspect that they apply to any differentiating social system, whether a group, organization, or community. While these principles are not without ambiguities, we believe that they can still inform modern sociological theorizing and provide a promising place from which to begin further work.

Principles of Deviance

Durkheim's analysis of suicide is much more than a discussion of suicide rates; it is also an exploration into the structural and cultural sources of deviance in general. The basic issue in Durkheim's discussion of suicide is the question: What is the nature of individual integration into social systems? His answer is that there are two bases of individual integration: (1) regulation of individual desires and passions by values, beliefs, and norms and (2) attachment of individuals to collective units of organization. Regulation and attachment must be balanced so that there is not too much or too little of either. If the balance is disturbed, then suicide-prone individuals are likely to commit suicide, thereby raising the rate of suicide in society.

If we abstract above suicide, which is only one type of deviance, we have a perspective for visualizing its general characteristics. Since anomie, or deregulation, and egoism, or detachment, are Durkheim's primary concern in *Suicide* and elsewhere in his work, we will focus on these two conditions and their relation to deviance in general.[12] In so doing, it will become evident that Durkheim saw deviance as intimately connected to the principles of differentiation already presented. Durkheim viewed increases in the rates of deviance as "normal" in differentiating systems, but under certain conditions, the rates increase to a point where a pathological condition prevails. If we ignore this distinction between normal and abnormal rates (for no objective criterion exists for determining what is normal and abnormal in social systems), and focus on his statements about the conditions increasing rates of deviance in general, then the following two principles are evident in Durkheim's work:

11. The greater is the degree of structural differentiation and value-generalization without a corresponding degree of normative specification in a social system, the greater is the level of anomie, and hence, the greater is the rate of deviance in that system.

12. The greater is the degree of structural differentiation and value-generalization without a corresponding degree of subgroup formation in a social system, the greater is the level of egoism, and hence, the greater is the rate of deviance in that system.

These two principles summarize Durkheim's view that deregulation of individual passions (anomie) and detachment of people from collective goals and purposes of groups (egoism) are related to basic processes of social differentiation. When the inevitable process of value generalization in differentiating systems is not accompanied by the processes denoted in principle 5 (normative specification) and in principle 6 (subgroup formation), then anomie and egoism are likely. And with either or both of these states, rates of deviance are likely to increase. Thus, Durkheim was arguing that there is a fundamental relationship in social systems among structural differentiation, value-generalization, and subgroup for-

---

[12] Èmile Durkheim, *Suicide: A Study in Sociology (Glencoe, Ill.: Free Press, 1951; originally published in 1897).*

mation, on the one hand, and rates of deviance, on the other. Such an insight was truly revolutionary for Durkheim's time, and it can, no doubt, still inform contemporary theorizing on deviation in social systems.

Principles of System Mal-integration

As we have emphasized, Durkheim's view of social pathology represented a moral view of the world: that which deviated from Durkheim's conception of normality was seen as pathological. A scientific theory of the social world, we believe, should try to keep such moralistic evaluations out of the analysis. Yet much of Durkheim's view of the world concerns mal-integration in social systems, and despite the moral connotations of his analysis, he presented a number of principles that might be useful to modern theory.

In many respects, Durkheim's statements on mal-integration are the converse of principles of 4 through 10 on the conditions of integration, or they are extensions of those on deviance. In this view, mal-integration of a social system can occur when (1) anomie (deregulation) and egoism (detachment) are great, (2) coordination of functions is not achieved, and (3) inequalities in the distribution of resources create tensions between those with and without resources.

13. The greater is the differentiation and value-generalization in a social system, and the less the degree of normative specification, then the greater is the level of anomie, and hence, the more likely are individuals to be poorly integrated into that system.

14. The greater is the differentiation and value-generalization in a social system, and the less the formation of subgroups, then the greater is the level of egoism, and hence, the more likely are individuals to be poorly integrated into that system.

15. The greater is the differentiation and value-generalization in a social system, and the less the normative specification of relations among social units, then the less is the coordination of units, and hence, the less integrated is that system.

16. The greater is the differentiation and generalization of values in a social system, and the less the centralization of authority, then the less is the coordination of units, and hence, the less integrated is that system.

17. The greater is the differentiation, value-generalization, and centralization of authority in a social system, and the less the

countervailing power of subgroups, then the greater is the level of tensions between those with and those without power, and hence, the less integrated is that system.

18. The greater is the differentiation and value-generalization in a social system, the less the correlation perceived to exist between the distribution of scarce resources and talents, then the greater is the level of tensions between those with and without resources, and hence, the less integrated is that system.

Pinciples 13 and 14 above concern individual integration into the system; principles 15 and 16 deal with coordination among system units, whether individuals or corporate units, and principles 17 and 18 deal with the mal-integrative impact of tensions between those with, and those without, scarce resources, including power. These last two propositions are as close to Marx as Durkheim comes, for despite his acceptance of Rousseau's abhorrence of inherited inequalities, Durkheim was always more concerned with the dual issues of individual integration into the social system and coordination among differentiated system parts than he was with social inequality.

Yet, principles 13 through 18 provide interesting theoretical leads as to those forces that are involved in either the change or the breakdown of social systems. Of particular importance is the fact that these principles employ the same variables that are contained in those principles explaining social order and integration. Thus, the same variables explain both order, disorder, and change in social systems. In this way, it can be seen that principles 1 through 18 provide clear evidence that Durkheim took the task of sociological theorizing seriously.[13] For indeed, these principles address the basic question posed in Chapter 1: Under what conditions are patterns of social organization created, maintained, or changed?

---

[13] See, for example, the recent and excellent commentaries by: Robert A. Nisbet, *The Sociology of Emile Durkheim* (New York: Oxford University Press, 1974); Steven Lukes, *Émile Durkheim, His Life and Work: A Historical and Critical Study* (London: Allen Lane, 1973); Ernest Wallwork, *Durkheim, Morality and Milieu* (Cambridge, Mass.: Harvard University Press, 1972); and Dominick La Capra, *Emile Durkheim; Sociologist and Philosopher* (Ithaca, N.Y.: Cornell University Press, 1972).

18

VILFREDO PARETO I: THE INTELLECTUAL ORIGINS OF HIS THOUGHT

Vilfredo Pareto represents a curious anomaly in 19th- and early 20th-century thought.[1] Pareto understood that the internal dynamics of social systems revolve around the nature of economic production, the distribution of political power, patterns of inequality, and systems of beliefs. Nonetheless, despite his insight into the relations among these elements, Pareto's work is often ignored by contemporary theorists and is relegated to chapters in books on the history of social thought.[2]

Part of the reason for the neglect of Pareto resides in his awkward, and somewhat ambiguous, use of terms and concepts. For example, concepts such as "sentiments," "residues," and "derivations" do not appeal to the modern sociologist. Moreover, Pareto employed the much misunderstood concept of "equilibrium" in his analysis—signaling to many uncritical thinkers that Pareto's scheme is "functional," conservative, and supportive of the status quo.[3] These kinds of prejudices against a

---

[1] This chapter and the next two chapters are coauthored with Charles Powers of the University of California at Riverside.

[2] And yet, some of the first modern social theorists, such as Talcott Parsons, George Homans, and some of their contemporaries, were influenced in the 1940s and 1950s by Pareto's thought. Barbara Heyl, "The Harvard 'Pareto Circle,' " *Journal of the History of the Behavioral Sciences*, 4 (October 1968): 316–34.

[3] As will become clear, Pareto's theory of social systems is more dynamic than most critics realize. Nor was Pareto as conservative as is often assumed. Pareto fell into disfavor with many for his attacks on Marxism. However, he also opposed colonialism, militarization, stationary elites, and ideological doctrines of all sorts. For a brief but accurate characterization of Pareto's politics and personality se S. E. Finer, "Pareto and Pluto-Democracy: The Retreat to Galapagos," *American Political Science Review* 62 (June 1968): 440–50.

careful reading of Pareto's work are indeed unfortunate. For once we penetrate Pareto's vocabulary and seek to understand his vision of the structure and dynamics of social systems, we can come to appreciate fully the power of Pareto's analysis. In these three chapters on Pareto, then, we will attempt to clarify his thought and to demonstrate its relevance to current sociological theorizing.

In reviewing the origins of Pareto's thought, we will begin with his exposure to broad intellectual currents of the 19th century and then focus on the more specific scholars who directly shaped the course of his thinking. In this way, we will see why Pareto chose to use what appear to be awkward and confusing terms. More importantly, we will also appreciate how he was able to achieve considerable insight into the nature of social systems.

19th CENTURY INTELLECTUAL CURRENTS AND PARETO'S THOUGHT

In seeking to unravel the intellectual milieu in which Pareto's economic, political, and sociological analysis developed, we begin with the recognition that Pareto was a child of the Newtonian revolution and the view of science that it presented. At the same time, he was greatly influenced by three dominant schools of thought, utilitarianism, positivism, and historicism, as well as the Italian intellectual tradition.[4] The influence on Pareto of each of these intellectual currents is briefly examined below.

Pareto and the Newtonian Revolution

Pareto was formally trained as a mathematician and civil engineer, and as a result, he was greatly influenced by the promise of Newtonian physics: through observation of the empirical world, the basic and fundamental properties of this world can be isolated and their lawlike relations can be discovered. Throughout his varied intellectual career, whether as an engineer, social polemist, academic economist, or sociologist, Pareto

---

[4] A brief but interesting review of the intellectual milieu in which Pareto was raised is provided in Vincent Tarascio, *Pareto's Methodological Approach to Economics* (Chapel Hill: University of North Carolina Press, 1966), chap. 1. Brief comments interspersed throughout Pareto's work indicate the comparative importance of a variety of intellectual influences.

never waivered from the position that his "sole interest is the quest for social uniformities, social laws."[5]

From Pareto's view, then, the ultimate goal of all reflection on the social world is the development of universal laws. And thus, meta-theoretical speculation, philosophical schemes, and concrete empirical observations are useful only to the extent that they help to develop abstract laws of the social universe. Unbridled philosophical speculation, Pareto maintained, can remove discourse from the actual properties of the world, while the mindless accumulation of empirical facts can impede the process of abstraction that is so essential to the development of universal laws. Hence, social theory will emerge when facts and philosophy are harnessed to the goals of all science: the discovery of uniformities and the articulation of laws that make these uniformities understandable.[6]

Positivism and Pareto's Thought

As we observed in Chapter 2 on Auguste Comte, the Newtonian vision fostered the development of positivism in the social sciences. Yet, while Pareto read and admired Comte's work, he rejected many of the points of emphasis contained in positivist doctrines: that analogies to the biological realm are useful, that social systems reveal stages of progress and evolution, that structures can be analyzed in terms of their functions, and that the laws of sociology could be used to reconstruct society.[7]

Rather, he accepted only aspects of the Newtonian vision as they had been reformulated by Comte and other positivists. That is, the general principles of the social realm can be discovered through the direct observation of social facts, through experimentation, through comparisons of different types of societies, and through the analysis of historical records. Thus, Pareto absorbed from positivism the view that diverse methods of empirical inquiry can be used to uncover the laws governing the operation of empirical regularities in the social world.

---

[5] Vilfredo Pareto, *The Mind and Society* (New York: Harcourt, Brace, 1935). This was originally titled *Treatise on General Sociology* and published in 1916. Hereafter, this will be referred to as *Treatise*, s86, for example, with s denoting the paragraph numbers that Pareto employed.

[6] Vilfredo Pareto, *Manual of Political Economy* (New York: August M. Kelley, 1971; originally published in 1906, significantly revised in 1909, and translated into English from the revised version), chap. 1, pp. 47–50; and *Treatise* ss 2, 102, and 144.

[7] Preto, *Treatise*, ss 217, 287–88, 827–28.

Utilitarianism and Pareto's Thought

As we observed in our discussion of Herbert Spencer, utilitarian thinkers of the last century, inspired by Adam Smith, tended toward an atomis-
tic view of humans and an evolutionary view of society in which order
and progress ensue from people's pursuit of individual self-interest. Out
of such pursuits, individuals find their place or niche in society, with
the character of society being determined by the qualities of its members.
From this perspective a science of society must be based on the study
of individuals. As such, rationality and pursuit of happiness are thought
by utilitarians to be the major forces motivating human behavior, and
like the principle of attraction in astronomy, they are seen to occupy a
place of central theoretical importance.

In his early works, Pareto accepted the utilitarian position that unim-
paired and free-market conditions lead to the optimum collective good,
but by the middle of his career, he became aware that government
intervention, corporate monopolies, and labor unions all violate precepts
of classical economics and make policy decisions based on the assumption
of free-market operations invalid. After spending years trying to justify
laissez-faire and free-trade policies as the best possible economic system,
Pareto eventually came to realize that those who try to "discover" what
form of society is "best" simply disguise their own sentiments in the
cloak of pseudo "scientific" investigation.[8]

In reacting to what he perceived to be the failings of utilitarianism,
Pareto brought into clearer focus properties essential to understanding
patterns of social organization: power, interest, and ideological rationalization. Yet, while Pareto was rejecting much of the substance of utilitarian
doctrines, he retained elements of the utilitarian mode of analysis. In
particular, notions of "cycles," "supply and demand," and "equilibrium"
were to become a prominent part of Pareto's sociological system.

Historicism and Pareto's Thought

Historicists of the 19th century tended to view a given society as
the product of unique events rather than as a manifestation of certain
lawlike relations among properties of the social world. Even more analytical historicists, such as Hegel and Marx, tended to confine their notions
of "social laws" to specific historical epochs, rejecting the idea that there
are universal laws applicable to all times and places. In discussing this

---

[8] Pareto, *Manual*, pp. 268–69.

tradition, Pareto saw as unfortunate the unwillingness of historicists to broaden their vision and to adopt the Newtonian premise.[9]

Yet at the same time, Pareto's positivism led him to view historical events as a major source of data, especially since he was most interested in the rhythmic and cyclic dynamics of social systems over time. Thus, Pareto remained sympathetic to historical inquiry—indeed his work is filled with historical illustrations—but he rejected what he saw as the atheoretical bias of most historicists.

A Note on the Italian Tradition and Pareto's Thought

The established schools of thought that influenced Pareto were, to a very great extent, tied to a particular country: positivism to France, utilitarianism to England and Scotland, and historicism to Germany. In contrast to predominant modes of thinking in these nations, social thought in Italy was more eclectic, drawing inspiration from many diverse sources.

Yet Italy did reveal some unique intellectual traditions, most notably the concern with social power and its use. While German scholars, such as Max Weber, were also concerned with power, the work of Niccolò Machiavelli set the tone of much Italian scholarship. Indeed, Pareto felt that criticisms of Machiavelli's *The Prince* had been unjust, for Machiavelli had described not so much his personal ideas as a paramount reality of the social world: the use of power to create more power.[10] Another trend of thought in Italian intellectual circles concerned the way values and beliefs are used to control and manipulate populations. For example, the work of Giambattista Vico on the importance of cycles in belief systems exerted considerable influence on Pareto.

Thus, to the extent it was distinctive, the Italian intellectual tradition focused on two related issues: the use of power and the impact of cyclical changes of beliefs on social arrangements. Both of these issues were to become prominent in Pareto's sociology.

SPECIFIC LINES OF INFLUENCE ON PARETO'S THOUGHT

Working within the broad intellectual traditions of Pareto's time were a number of scholars from whose Pareto borrowed key assumptions and

---

[9] Pareto, *Treatise*, 1790. See also Vilfredo Pareto, "Introduction à Marx" (originally published in 1893) in *Marxisme et Économie Pure* (Geneva: Librarie Droz, 1966).

[10] Niccolò Machiavelli, *The Prince* (New York: Heritage Press, 1954; originally published in 1532).

concepts. In order to fully appreciate the genesis of Pareto's social theories, then, it is critical to review the influence of several immediate intellectual predecessors as well as some of his contemporaries.

Auguste Comte and Pareto. While rejecting Comte's organismic analogy, his concern for normalcy and social planning, and his moralistic pronouncements, Pareto accepted—indeed he embraced—Comte's concern with "social facts" and his proposed methodology. Moreover, he adopted Comte's definition of social facts as widespread patterns of observable behavior and the patterns of beliefs guiding such behavior.

Adam Smith and Pareto. Although Pareto was eventually to reject Smith's advocacy of free and open competition, Pareto did embrace Smith's insights on the laws of supply and demand. And in fact, Pareto was to advance the science of economics significantly in his formulation of structural equations to describe the dynamics of supply, demand, and other economic forces. Moreover, the equilibrium processes implied in Smith's economic analysis were to be adopted and altered in a way that would allow for the analysis of sociopolitical phenomena. In particular, Pareto took the notion from Smith's *The Wealth of Nations* that the social world can be viewed as a system of interdependent properties, tending toward equilibrium points, but also subject to change with alterations in the value of any one property.[11]

Maffeo Pantaleoni, Leon Walrus, and Pareto. Even after publication of *The Wealth of Nations*, economics remained a largely discursive and inexact discipline. The role that Maffeo Pantaleoni played in creating a science of economics is seldom recognized, but in his *Pure Economics*, Pantaleoni attempted to formalize verbal propositions on the relationships among such major economic concepts as cost, supply, demand, interest, wages, rent, profit, utility, and value.[12] Pareto read Pantaleoni's book in 1891 and was charged with excitement by the prospects that it offered for the development of scientific economics. Within a short time, Pareto established correspondence with Pantaleoni and directed his effort away from political commentary to the development of mathematical equations corresponding to Pantaleoni's propositions.

Pantaleoni suggested that Pareto reread the works of Leon Walrus who had articulated a theory of marginal utility and who had developed a general theory of equilibrium which characterized economic activity

---

[11] Adam Smith, *An Inquiry into the Nature and Causes of the Wealth of Nations* (New York: Random House, 1937; originally published in 1776–84).

[12] Maffeo Pantaleoni, *Pure Economics* (London: Macmillan, 1898; originally published 1889).

as the result of understandable competitive market adjustments and responses to events occurring within a unified socioeconomic system. Walrus had sought to develop his equilibrium model into a general framework for the scientific study of economics, complete with equations specifying relationships among aspects of the economic system. When Walrus retired from his professorial chair in political economy at the University of Lausanne, he followed Pantaleoni's recommendation and requested that Pareto replace him.[13] In his new position, Pareto was to spend several years clarifying and formalizing Walrus' economic equilibrium theory, and from his efforts to found mathematical economics.

Equally important, as Pareto worked with the idea of equilibrium, he soon came to realize the limitations of the concept when it included purely economic variables. Thus, Pareto's exposure to economics gave him a profound appreciation for the analytical power of formal equilibrium models, but at the same time, he came to recognize their limitations. This recognition led Pareto to examine more carefully the sociological works of Herbert Spencer, the dominant utilitarian social thinker of the 19th century.

Herbert Spencer and Pareto. Following publication of several of his works in economics, Pareto attracted considerable attention, and yet, he became increasingly disillusioned with two shortcomings of economic analysis: (1) many important factors that are known to vary are assumed to be constant in economic models and (2) the analysis of human motivation in economic models tends to be simplistic. Spencer's early treatment of these two subjects encouraged Pareto to broaden his equilibrium theory, changing it fundamentally in the process.[14]

First, Pareto found Spencer's essays on the interdependent nature of social systems appealing, and thus, he concluded that sociological and economic phenomena which are part of the same system must be studied by the same methods of analysis and treated within a common theoretical framework. Indeed, Pareto came to emphasize that studying social and economic phenomena separately merely serves to obscure the most fascinating theoretical questions about the nature of their interdependence. Second, Spencer's early work was credited by Pareto for the critical insight that much human behavior is nonlogical, and therefore, not subject to economic models assuming the rationality of behavior.

---

[13] Arthur Livingston, "Bibliographical Note," in Pareto's *Mind and Society.*

[14] Pareto was particularly impressed with Herbert Spencer, *The Classification of the Sciences* (New York: D. Appleton, 1864). Pareto was less impressed with Spencer's other works, although he seems to have read them with interest.

Karl Marx and Pareto. There was a natural affinity between Marx's and Pareto's analysis of social systems. Both Marx and Pareto recognized the importance of economic interests, both saw the connection between economic and political processes, both realized the significance of cultural symbols in legitimating social conditions, and both saw inequality in the distribution of resources as a driving force behind social change. Indeed, Pareto gave much credit to Marx for demonstrating the connections among economic interests, political power, cultural beliefs, and patterns of inequality.

Yet Pareto disagreed with the specifics of Marx's analysis of capitalism. He regarded Marx's belief in the intrinsic value of labor as a vestige of outmoded economic theory. The importance of surplus value in Marx's analysis led Pareto to the conclusion that Marx built a misguided theoretical edifice upon false assumptions. Moreover, Pareto regarded Marx's analysis of the expansion and collapse of capitalism as flawed. In Pareto's eye, Marx maintained that consumption is the driving force behind capitalist expansion (money begets money through the circulation of commodities). In contrast, Pareto argued that high levels of consumption are associated with capital depletion and economic downturn. But even more fundamental is Pareto's criticism of Marx's tendency to infuse his theory with ideology and to make his doctrine a religious faith—a criticism similar to that leveled against Comte's "religion of humanity." But, despite these sources of disagreement, Marx reinforced Pareto's critical insight that societies constitute systems and that the key properties of such systems are economic interests, power, inequality, and cultural symbols.[15]

Georges Sorel and Pareto. As a Marxist who became increasingly disillusioned with the communist party, Georges Sorel provided some of the most penetrating attacks on the self-serving tendencies of elites who seek to use power to create additional power, and hence, to increase their capacity to exploit others. For whatever their ideological position, Sorel argued, the leaders of political parties are driven by the paramount interest to preserve their privileged position. Sorel's analysis supported Pareto's insights on the "circulation of elites" and encouraged Pareto to continue refining the theory for which he is best known.[16] Coupled

---

[15] Pareto, "Introduction à Marx."

[16] Many people credit the theory of circulating elites to Gaetano Mosca, who published on the subject before Pareto. However, similarities between their theories seem to have been the result of independent interpretation of history. To the extent that Pareto's theory was modified in response to the work of others, an intellectual debt may exist, since Pareto was greatly impressed with Sorel's work. Sorel's work most often cited by

with his observation that history is the "graveyard of elites," and his reinterpretation of Marx, Pareto came to recognize that elites come into power, exploit others, create conditions for their own downfall, and are then replaced by others who initiate the cycle again.

PARETO'S SYNTHESIS: A PREVIEW

As is evident, Pareto worked within a number of intellectual traditions and was influenced by diverse scholars. It is this eclecticism that gives Pareto's thought its originality and vitality, but it is also what makes his work difficult to capture as a whole. Yet, in closing this chapter and in anticipating the next, we should review the general themes to be found in all of Pareto's diverse works.

During the course of his career, Pareto never abandoned the Newtonian vision of science, especially as it had been interpreted by Auguste Comte and French positivism. The goal of science is to discover the abstract principles that express the fundamental relations among properties of the social universe. In attempting to realize this goal, Pareto's thought was shaped by economic modes of analysis: the social world is to be viewed as a system, with equilibrium tendencies; the social scientist should first seek to identify key structural properties of the system; then, underlying relations among, and dynamics of, these properties should be articulated; and finally, these relations and dynamics should be formally stated as an abstract model or as a series of principles. Of particular importance in understanding Pareto's theoretical strategy is his emphasis on mutal dependence among system elements, and his corresponding de-emphasis of one-way causality in theoretical models and principles.

Methodologically, Pareto accepted Comte's advocacy of the use of diverse methods, particularly the historical method—a point of emphasis inspired, no doubt, by German historicism. And he followed the French tradition in his insistence that aggregate data, rather than individual cases, be used as a means for discovering regularities in the social world. Once these regularities are observed, they must then be used to generate, or to test, more abstract models and principles. Pareto thus emphasized that methodoligical procedures and theory-building activities are intimately connected.

At the substantive level, Pareto took ideas and foci from many scholars,

Pareto is "The Decomposition of Marxism" (originally published in 1908), reprinted in Irving Louis Horowitz, ed., *Radicalism and the Revolt Against Reason: The Social Theories of Georges Sorel* (New York: Humanities Press, 1961).

but over the course of his career, he became increasingly concerned with the distribution of power, the nature of economic interests, the circulation of political and economic elites, the consequences of inequality on economic and political processes, and the significance of symbols for all of these processes. Such are the basic properties of social systems in Pareto's view, and hence, the major theoretical goal is to discover the relations among, and dynamics of, these basic properties. Pareto sought to realize this goal in a long and varied intellectual career, punctuated by a number of critical works. It is to understanding these works in light of Pareto's theoretical, methodological, and substantive orientation that the next chapter is dedicated.

19

VILFREDO PARETO II:
THE BASIC WORKS

Pareto's works reflect his long and varied career. During the course of his life, he was a practicing engineer who wrote a baccalaural dissertation on molecular mechanics, a political and social commentator who published nearly 200 articles, an academic who made major breakthroughs in economics and political science, and finally, a retired academic who wrote a major treatise on sociology. Thus in approaching Pareto's work, we are faced with the immediate problem of selecting the most sociologically important pieces. This task of selection is particularly difficult in light of the fact that each varied stage in Pareto's career provided him with certain key concepts that were to become an integral part of his culminating work in sociology.

Thus, we should initially apporach Pareto's work by analyzing how various nonsociological works set the conceptual stage for his purely sociological efforts. We will, therefore, discuss Pareto's work as the product of four distinct stages: (1) the engineering, (2) the commentary, (3) the academic, and finally, (4) the sociological.

PARETO'S EARLY WORK IN ENGINEERING, 1865–1880

Pareto's dissertation for the School of Applied Engineering in Turin, Italy, examines a theoretical topic, the "Fundamental Principles of the Theory of Elasticity in Solid Bodies and Research Concerning Integration of the Differential Equations Defining Their Equilibrium."[1] The details

---

[1] Vilfredo Pareto, "Principi Fondamentali della Toeria della Elasticità de' Corpi Solidi e Richerche sulla Integrazione della Equazioni differenziali che ne Definiscono l'Equilibrio" (1869), in *Scritti Teorici* (Milan: Malfasi, 1952), pp. 593–639.

of Pareto's analysis are obviously less important than the general approach that he employed. Pareto began by emphasizing the limitations of molecular mechanics—limitations that he was later to view as relevant to sociological inquiry. Since change is inherent in molecular particles, since it is impossible to know precisely which combination of infinite possible arrangements among atoms will bond, and since uncontrolled and extraneous influences will affect such bonding, theory and research should follow certain guidelines:[2]

1. Theory should not be concerned with the final or end states of phenomena.
2. Theory and research should concentrate on aggregate data rather than on the movement of individual elements.
3. Theory should seek to discover general principles on the underlying processes of phenomena rather than attempt to model each and every specific empirical outcome.
4. Variable and uncontrollable extraneous factors cannot be a part of theory and should be given less emphasis than the principles stating the general processes underlying phenomena.

Coupled with this concern over the discovery of general principles, Pareto introduced the concept of equilibrium to his analysis. For Pareto, equilibrium is a state of balance among system elements. This balance will reflect the operation of general laws, and if specific empirical conditions alter the values of the elements, change in the system of elements will occur. Such change, however, will occur in accordance with the general laws of the equilibriate phenomena. Pareto never abandoned his commitment to the concept of equilibrium, and hence, we should stress how he employed this often misunderstood concept:[3]

1. Phenomena organize themselves into systems of relations.
2. The generic properties of such phenomena can be isolated and their relations can be described.
3. Change in the values of one component will, in accordance with certain laws, produce changes in the values of other elements.
4. The same laws that allow for understanding of why a stable equilibrium exists for a time can also be used to understand disequilibrium and equilibrium movement.

Pareto's training and work in engineering and mathematics thus allowed him to see the futility of trying to describe or model all the

<hr />

[2] Ibid., pp. 595–97.

[3] Ibid., pp. 600–612.

varieties of empirical forces operating on phenomena. Rather, science should search for abstract principles on the fundamental properties, relations, and processes of phenomena. In this search, the concept of equilibrium is particularly useful. Such were Pareto's intellectual commitments as he turned to social commentary.

PARETO'S COMMENTARIES, 1880–1893

Pareto's training as an engineer and scientist gave him a strategy for analyzing phenomena, but he did not possess a clear idea about the basic elements of the social world, nor did he appear to have a sense for key social processes. This sense for what is important in social systems came during Pareto's commentary phase. Between 1880 and 1893, he wrote nearly 200 articles on the political, economic, and social events of his time.[4] Initially an advocate of free markets and open competition in the economic sphere, he deplored the efforts of economic interests and government to reduce competition. And he sought to expose the "false ideologies" used to justify privilege.

Gradually, Pareto began to recognize some of the limitations of his laissez-faire advocacy. But more importantly, he began to isolate certain properties and processes of social systems as essential to understanding the structure and dynamics of those systems. This new focus to his thought would remain incomplete for many years, but by the early 1890s Pareto had come to recognize the importance of the following processes:[5]

1. Economic interests operate to consolidate their position by exerting influence on political elites to intervene on their behalf.
2. Political elites seek to consolidate their power by transferring wealth from the nonelite classes to the elite classes.
3. Economic and political elites create ideologies to legitimate their activities, while attempting to give some benefits to nonelites in order to maintain their allegiance.
4. At some point, elites lose their vitality and capacity to control nonelites, setting into motion processes that lead to their demise and the ascendance of new elites who initiate another cycle of self-interested action and manipulation of nonelites.

---

[4] For example, "The Parliamentary Regime in Italy" in Vilfredo Pareto, *The Ruling Class in Italy Before 1900* (New York: S. F. Vanni, 1950; originally published in 1893); Vilfredo Pareto, *La Liberté Economique et les Evénements d'Italie* (New York: Burt Franklin, 1968, originally published in 1898 as a compilation of previously published materials).

[5] Pareto, "Parliamentary Regime," and *Liberté Economique*, pp. 32–37 and 47–48.

These general lines of thought were to remain somewhat dormant in the 1890s. Yet it is clear that Pareto never abandoned his recognition that economic interests, political and economic elites, the distribution and dispositions of nonelites, and the use of ideology are among the critical variables in understanding social systems. But as Pareto left his commentary phase and moved into a more purely academic setting, he began to sharpen his analytical skills first in economics, then in politics, and finally, in sociology.

PARETO'S ACADEMIC WORKS, 1893–1907

After reading Matteo Pantaleoni's *Pure Economics* in 1891, Pareto become convinced that social science was possible and that economics would be its cutting edge. Drawing on his view of equilibrium developed in his engineering phase, as it became reinforced by Leon Walrus's equilibrium theory (see previous chapter), Pareto set out to formalize economics. But as he did so, he apparently had a broader vision that involved applying the same analytical approach to political phenomena.

Pareto's early economic work attracted Walrus's attention, with the result that upon Walrus's retirement, Pareto replaced him in the professorial chair of political economy at the University of Lausanne, Switzerland. And thus began Pareto's academic phase.[6] During this stage in his career, Pareto wrote two great works in economics, *Course in Political Economy* (1896–1897)[7] and *Manual of Political Economy* (1906–1909).[8] In the decade between publication of these works, Pareto began to extend his analysis to noneconomic phenomena. The result was his *The Rise and Fall of the Elites* (1901),[9] the work for which Pareto is perhaps best known, and his *The Socialist Systems* (1902–1903).[10] Written between the first and last revisions of his purely economic work, these books sensitized Pareto to the complex interconnections among social, eco-

---

[6] Arthur Livingston, "Bibliographical Note," in Vilfredo Pareto, *The Mind and Society* (New York: Harcourt, Brace, 1935).

[7] Vilfredo Pareto, *Corso di Economia Politica* (Turin: Boringhieri, 1961; originally published (1896–97).

[8] Vilfredo Pareto, *Manual of Political Economy* (New York: August M. Kelley, 1971). *Manual* was first published in 1906 and was revised in 1909; the English translation is based upon the revised version of *Manual*.

[9] Vilfredo Pareto, *The Rise and Fall of the Elites; An Application of Theoretical Sociology*, introduced by Hans Zetterberg (Totowa, N.J.: Bedminster Press, 1968; originally published in 1901).

[10] Vilfredo Pareto, *Les Systèmes Socialistes* (Geneva: Librairie Drox, 1965; originally published 1902–1903).

nomic, political, and ideological phenomena. And by his retirement from academia in 1907, Pareto had become convinced that:

> Human society is the subject of many researches. Some of them constitute specialized disciplines: law, political economy, political history, the history of religions, and the like. Others have not yet been distinguished by special names. To the synthesis of them all, which aims at studying society in general, we may give the name of *sociology*.[11]

To appreciate how Pareto came to this conclusion and why he chose to analyze social systems in his own distinctive way, we need to summarize the substance, style, and strategy evident in Pareto's academic stage. Hence, we will first analyze the two great economic works and then those dealing with political phenomena, for it is out of these works that Pareto's sociology was to emerge after his retirement from academia.

Course in Political Economy and Manual of Political Economy

Course in Political Economy is, in many ways, a defense of classical economics, and ideological biases are evident.[12] The basic contribution of *Course* is its application of the equilibrium concept to major economic functions—production, capital formation and movement, and economic cycles. In particular, Pareto demonstrated considerable methodological sophistication in *Course*, employing formal equations as well as occasionally using longitudinal and cross-cultural data.

Far more important from a sociological perspective is *Manual of Political Economy*, in which Pareto rejected his past polemics and sought to sharpen his analytical edge. The result is a classic in economics in which a theory of maximum efficiency is developed, indifference curves are introduced, and a refined statement on the equilibrium dynamics of supply and demand is presented. Drawing renewed inspiration from his early engineering works, Pareto reasserted that theory must seek general principles by isolating generic properties of systems from the mass of empirical data and, then, attempt to specify the conditions under which these principles hold true.[13] The concept of equilbrium is also expanded to admit political, social, and cultural variables.[14]

Pareto did not argue, as some have maintained, that all existing struc-

---

[11] Vilfredo Pareto, *Treatise on General Sociology*, s 1 (see note 5 in preceding chapter for explanation of mode of citation).

[12] Pareto, *Corso*.

[13] Pareto, *Manual*, especially chap. 1.

[14] Ibid., especially chap. 3.

tural features are the products of equilibrium. For example, features of exchange are often set by government regulation (e.g., price controls) or are fixed by other obstacles and are not products of an equilibriated balance between those "tastes" and "obstacles" that would otherwise set conditions of exchange. Nor did Pareto maintain that existing structural features constitute the best possible structural arrangements. No equilibrium can be thought of as the "best" possible state unless one assumes a large number of givens, which are in reality likely to change. Changing conditions promote equilibrium movement and the resulting system may be an improvement over the old.

Further refinements in the concept of equilibrium are evident, as Pareto outlined two kinds of equilibrium movements. "Stable equilibrium" occurs when a change in one component of a system stimulates modifications within the system that tend to minimize or reverse the original change. For example, an increase in consumer demand can lead to price increases that dampen demand. "Unstable equilibrium," a temporary condition in Pareto's eye, occurs when change in one component of a system results in modifications within the system that tend to add to the initial change. For instance, increasing demand can lead to an increase in the number of competing suppliers, changes in economy of scale, or technological innovations, each of which can result in lower prices and stimulate still greater demand. It is important to recognize that stable and unstable states are both types of equilibria and are understandable in terms of balances among those social, cultural, and political variables that influence the weights of variables composing the economic system. To mistake Pareto's discussions of stable periods (which he generally refers to simply as *equilibria*) for his entire equilibrium perspective is an error that should be avoided.[15]

Thus, Pareto saw that the economic system can be analyzed in much the same way as he had once studied molecular mass: (1) generic components of systems can be identified and (2) a few abstract principles can account for the nature of interdependence among these elements. But now, the concept of equilibrium was extended in ways that draw attention to the fact that mutual dependence of parts creates a situation where change in one direction produces pressures in the opposite direction, with the result that equilibrium phenomena reveal cyclical patterns. Thus, in contradiction to the evolutionary theories of his time, Pareto saw economic and social systems as equilibriated systems that reveal

---

[15] Ibid., pp. 142–43.

cyclical patterns of organization. This metaphor was to be the hallmark of Pareto's sociological theory.

The Rise and Fall of the Elites

The original title of this work was "An Application of Sociological Theory"—a clear indication of the direction in Pareto's thinking. In this work, Pareto sought to identify the major features of society that fluctuate cyclically, to describe the movement of these cycles in equilibrium terms, and to indicate ways in which the structural features and general form of society emerge from the equilibria being described. *The Rise and Fall of the Elites* is an initial statement of the theory of circulation of elites for which Pareto was to become well known. Undulating features of society discussed in *The Rise and Fall of the Elites* are circulation of political elites, business cycles, and fluctuations in popular sentiment (for example, as reflected in religious or ideological commitment). Pareto skillfully demonstrated how power, interests, ideology, and inequality emerge from these cycles and characterize societies. But what is frequently forgotten in commentaries on this work is that Pareto intended the theory of circulation of elites to be but a single aspect of his more general sociological theory of society and to serve only as a provisional statement and model that could be used in specifying other aspects of his sociological theory.

The basic argument in *Rise and Fall* can be stated as follows:[16]

1. Cyclical changes in the *sentiments*—that is values, beliefs, and world view—of economic and political elites and nonelites are prominent features of social systems.
2. At any point in time, political processes are dominated by elites who, in terms of their underlying sentiments, are either *lions* or *foxes*. Lions are individuals who are strong willed, direct, and conservative. They favor adherence to tradition and established ways. On the other hand, foxes are cunning, devious, innovative, and experimental.
3. At any given time, economic processes are dominated by elites who, in terms of their underlying sentiments, are either *rentiers* or *speculators*. Rentiers are conservative and not prone to innovation, whereas speculators are innovative and entrepreneurial.
4. Since elites tend to recruit others like themselves, excluding those

---

[16] Pareto, *Rise and Fall of Elites*, for instance, pp. 30–31, 36, 40–41, 59–60, and 68–71.

who violate their sentiments, political and economic elites tend to become homogeneous.

5. Homogeneous elites lack variety and vitality which make them vulnerable to infiltration or overthrow by their opposites. Therefore, lions and rentiers are eventually replaced by foxes and speculators, and vice versa.

6. The rate of replacement in this perpetual cycle is a dual function of (a) how soon in the cycle elites resort to the use of force to maintain their position and (b) how exploitive of nonelites they become.

7. As nonelites become alienated by exploitive activities, their alienation eventually creates pressures that exceed the capacity of elites to use force, thereby resulting in the replacement of one type of elite by another type.

8. The cycles of elites are positively correlated with each other and with economic conditions, with the result that lions and rentiers tend to ascend to elite positions together during times of economic contraction, whereas foxes and speculators tend to ascend to elite positions during times of economic growth and prosperity.

9. Accompanying, and roughly corresponding to, these political and economic cycles, are cycles in ideological beliefs between conservative and liberal tenets.

In these arguments, we can see Pareto's more sociological imagination beginning to assert itself, even though he was still primarily concerned with formal economic models. But the concepts of equilibrium and cyclical change have now been extended to embrace sociological variables: elites, mobility, underlying values or sentiments, and more clearly articulated ideologies. While Pareto had recognized the importance of these variables in his commentaries, they are now part of a more formal equilibrium model of human organization—a model that only matured after Pareto's excursion into formal economics.

The Socialist Systems

In *The Socialist Systems* Pareto demonstrated similarities between two "socialist" camps wishing government patronage and protection— bourgeoisie and union labor. But this book is more important for signaling a shift in emphasis than for its substantive, theoretical, and methodological contribution. For Pareto indicated unequivocally his view that most human action is nonlogical and that people seek to devleop ex post facto rationalizations to justify their conduct.[17] Any effort to explain human behavior in terms of rationality will, therefore, be incorrect. Thus, a science other than economics, which all too often assumes rationality, will be required if human behavior and organization are to be understood.

In *Socialist Systems*, high priority is given to cultural beliefs and ideology as basic properties of social systems, and Pareto's insights on this subject are an important feature of the *Treatise*. Pareto saw people reacting to events as they are filtered through the prism of their beliefs. Moreover, he saw beliefs as cycling between two poles, one revolving around "faith" and the other around "scepticism." The term *faith* denotes the fact that during some periods beliefs emphasize adherence to tradition and the status quo, whereas during other periods, beliefs stress an attempt to assess events logically, even though such "logical assessments" are always an illusion.[18]

One cannot, Pareto argued, understand the nature of a social system unless an assessment of beliefs is made. Of particular importance is determining not only the direction of beliefs, whether toward faith or scepticism, but also their location in the cycle between these two poles.[19] Moreover, in *Treatise* Pareto specifies an inherent dialectic in belief systems, with the dominance of beliefs based on faith setting into motion changes toward those based on scepticism, and vice versa. Thus, as blind conformity to tradition creates tensions between people's beliefs and their actual experiences, they become disillusioned with these beliefs and seek those that "rationally fit" their actual circumstances. But as beliefs become dominated by pseudo logic, several tensions may be generated. When beliefs are constantly altered to meet changing circumstances people begin to seek certainty and fixity in their beliefs, thereby setting into motion pressures for beliefs based on faith. Moreover, pseudo-logical beliefs sometimes have less social utility than beliefs based on faith, and hence, there may be pressure to return to old ways.[20]

Thus, by the end of *The Socialist Systems*, beliefs are as prominent as economic and political variables in Pareto's emerging analytical system. And like the circulation of economic and political elites, beliefs reveal a cyclical pattern which is, to some extent, connected to economic and political cycles. With Pareto's retirement from academia in 1907, the

---

[17] Pareto, *Socialist Systems*, vol. 1, pp. 15, and 178, and vol. 2, p. 110; *Treatise*, s 1710.

[18] Pareto, *Socialist Systems*, volume 1, pp. 30–34.

[19] Ibid., vol. 2, p. 419.

[20] Pareto, *Treatise*, ss 1678–83.

stage was set for his most ambitious work, a theory of human social organization.

PARETO'S SOCIOLOGICAL STAGE, 1907–1923

During his career, Pareto had come to view economic and political events as only parts of more general social processes. And thus, after semiretiring from Lausanne in 1907 (Pareto continued to teach a sociology course until 1916), "the lone thinker of Céligny" began to work on a purely sociological analysis of social phenomena. This work was to be the climax of his career, pulling together his early commitment to the Newtonian vision, his commentaries on the importance of economic, political, and ideological variables, and his more formal analysis of equilibrium processes in the economic and political spheres. This climactic work has the title, *The Mind and Society*, although its original title, *Treatise on General Sociology*, more accurately communicates its contents. As Pareto indicated, the purpose of his *Treatise on General Sociology* is "to discover the form that society assumes in virtue [*sic*] of the forces acting upon it."[21]

The *Treatise* is divided into four volumes, each with its own distinctive emphasis. Volumes 1, 2, and 3 are, in many ways, preliminary and lay the groundwork for sociology. Volume 1 is devoted to establishing the nonrational basis of human behavior and organization. Volume 2 develops his famous concepts of "sentiments" and "residues." And volume 3 posits a theory of "derivations." Much of the confusion over Pareto's work revolves around these rather unconventional terms, but as we see, volume 4 on the "general form of society" employs these concepts in a way that renders their meaning less ambiguous. In our discussion of the *Treatise*, then, we will briefly examine volumes 1, 2, and 3, and then, devote most of our attention to volume 4 where Pareto finally, at the age of 65, pulled together some of the diverse strands of his theoretical perspective.[22]

Treatise on General Sociology: Volume 1

The basic argument of volume 1 can be summarized as follows: most human action is not rational and is guided by "sentiments" rather than logic. Pareto had frequently employed the term *sentiments* in his previous

---

[21] Ibid., footnote to s 1687.

[22] Most of volume 4 appears to have been written during 1913.

work, but had never given the concept rigorous definition. Unfortunately, even in his culminating work, Pareto failed to provide a formal definition, but from the context of his works, we can sense the phenomena that Pareto sought to denote with this concept. Pareto wished to stress that humans hold, often unconsciously, basic values that serve to guide their conduct. By virtue of socialization and other experiences, humans acquire basic standards of judgment and evaluation which shape their thoughts, perceptions, and actions.[23]

The two most important types of sentiments are values emphasizing the importance of (1) *group persistence* and (2) new *combinations*. With these terms, Pareto sought to communicate that people's basic value standards cohere around two types of issues. Some values emphasize group persistence, or the importance of tradition and the preservation of current social arrangements. The content of values can vary enormously; they can be religious or secular in context, and they can manifest themselves in many different ways. But the critical point is that humans always carry with them basic values of group persistence. Other values stress new combinations, or the appropriateness of innovation, and "combinazioni" in the Italian sense of persuasiveness and guile. Again, the content, degree of secular-religious emphasis, and specific manifestations can vary, but humans always carry with them value standards favoring change and innovation.[24]

Since these two basic value standards are somewhat contradictory, Pareto emphasized that one or the other tends to dominate the members of a society at a given point in time. But the value standards of a population tend to oscillate between dominance of value standards emphasizing "group persistence" and new "combinations." Beliefs in what Pareto had labeled *scepticism* and *faith* in his earlier work are not movements between logical and nonlogical thought and action. Rather, all thought, perception, and action are nonlogical and guided by unconscious value standards or sentiments. Beliefs based on faith are merely overt manifestations of value standards emphasizing group persistence, whereas beliefs in scepticism are reflective of underlying sentiments for new combinations.[25]

Treatise on General Sociology: Volume 2

Pareto felt that many of the forces influencing human behavior, such as instincts and value standards, cannot be directly measured. Thus, to

---

[23] Pareto, *Manual*, p. 39, and *Treatise*, ss 888 ff.

[24] Pareto *Treatise*, ss 157 and 113.

[25] Pareto *Treatise*, ss 304, 1806–47, and 2048–50.

discover the operation of these forces, it is necessary to concentrate observations on their residual by-product—behavior. In this way Pareto introduced the concept of "residues," by which he meant observable behaviors that serve as empirical indicators of those unmeasurable influences on human action.

It is of the utmost importance to understand Pareto's use of the terms *sentiment* and *residue*. Sentiments are underlying value orientations, while residues are the behaviors that actors emit in accordance with their orientations. Pareto's meaning has been the subject of some misunderstanding because he often refers to sentiments as residues.

> Returning to the matter of our modes of expression, we must further note that since sentiments are manifest by residues we shall often, for the sake of brevity, use the word "residues" as including the sentiments that they manifest. So we shall say, simply, that residues are among the elements which determine social equilibrium.[26]

What Pareto did, then, was to use behaviors as empirical indicators of value orientations. This is not unlike the approaches employed by other sociologists. Pareto regarded the distinction between sentiments and residues as important. Therefore, *sentiment* will be used whenever sentiments were the object of Pareto's intent, even if they are referred to as residues in the Paretan passages under consideration.

Pareto's classification of generic types of residues is no less confusing, since he viewed six classes of residues as reflecting both innate instincts and deeply internalized value standards (sentiments). In Pareto's view, all human behavior represents one of six instinctive drives. The discovery of phosphorus, for example, occurred when an alchemist mixed urine and sand in an attempt to synthesize gold. This experiment was motivated by the human instinct for "combination" rather than scientific deduction. Instincts are constant. However, societies differ in the extent to which collective sentiments impede, legitimize, or give rise to behavioral expression of instincts. Thus behavioral expressions, or residues, reflect underlying patterns of sentiment and influence the form of society. Pareto's delineation of six basic types, or "classes," of residues reveals the following form:[27]

Class I: "Combinations," or behaviors involving innovation and experimentation.

Class II: "Group persistence," or behaviors involving adherence to tradition and the status quo.

---

[26] Ibid., s 1690.
[27] Ibid., ss 885–99 and 992.

Class III: "Activity," or behaviors revealing expressiveness and emotion.

Class IV: "Sociality," or behaviors seeking to generate or maintain group affiliation and membership.

Class V: "Integrity," or behaviors attempting to assert independence and self-esteem.

Class VI: "Sex," or behaviors reflecting biological sex drives.

These six classes of residues reflect instincts for combination, group persistence, activity, sociality, integrity, and sex. But since Pareto assumed that instincts are a constant, while sentiments vary enormously, variations in behavior will ultimately reflect differences in value standards. For values will channel instincts such as sex and activity, while at the same time, values will determine which class of residues, such as combinations versus group persistence, will dominate action at any given time. Thus, Pareto's list of sentiment-residue types accomplished several analytical tasks: (1) It allowed him to view human action as directed along six major axes and thus gave him an exhaustive system of categories for classifying behaviors. (2) It allowed him to classify different populations in terms of varying configurations among the six types of value standards. In this way, then, Pareto felt he had captured both the constancy and variability of human action and organization.[28]

In examining Pareto's actual use of the six classes of residues, several themes are evident. First, the distribution, content, and intensity of residues vary across individuals, groups, classes, occupations and other sociological categories. Second, the more homogeneous a population, the greater will be the similarity in distribution, content, and intensity of their sentiments.[29] Third, an individual's personality or character can be assessed in terms of enduring patterns of sentiments as they shape and guide basic instincts.[30] Fourth, the residues of combinations and group persistence are the most important because many of the dynamics of social systems must be viewed as a result of shifts in the ratio between sentiments for group persistence and combinations.[31] Sex is of interest

---

[28] Ibid., ss 1716–25.

[29] Ibid., ss 1041–47.

[30] Ibid., s 2232. This is an important assumption which underlies all of Pareto's contentions about circulation. If personality were extremely flexible, elites could adapt to changing requirements of their situations. Instead, Pareto maintains that classes of elites find themselves with insufficient diversity (in terms of personality traits) to meet exigencies effectively, and nonelites who are strong in the traits generally missing among elites are able to ascend in class.

[31] Ibid., ss 1721, 2342, and 2413.

as an empirical indicator of combinations and group persistences. Pareto hypothesized that literary and other forms of sexual expression are more likely to be tolerated in times in which sentiments of combinations are strong than times in which sentiments of group persistence are strong.

When we cut through Pareto's awkward terminology and his effort to simultaneously classify instincts, sentiments, and overt behavior with a typology of six classes of residues, a rather simple analytical and empirical point is being emphasized: Human behavior is motivated in basic directions; each line of potential action is circumscribed by corresponding value standards; overt behavior will thus reflect the way in which values have channeled instinctual drives; some classes of residues—behavior shaped by the ratio of values for combinations and group persistence— are more important than others for understanding social system dynamics.

Treatise on General Sociology: Volume 3

In his commentary phase, Pareto had come to recognize that humans seek to rationalize and justify their conduct. The products of these efforts are what Pareto termed *derivations,* by which he meant the rationalizations that are constructed to legitimate a particular line of conduct. As such, derivations rarely reflect actual intentions or the real situation, but rather, they represent efforts to throw into an acceptable light narrow and often destructive interests.[32] Furthermore, if one derivation is discovered to be false, others can easily be created to justify the same behavior. For example, when colonial powers felt, at the turn of the century, "civilizing" local inhabitants was no longer an appropriate justification for pillaging China, they then contented themselves with pillaging in order to protect "vital interests."[33]

Since derivations are reconstituted at will, without any necessary change in sentiments or interests, they must be analyzed cautiously. As long as their content is not taken literally, derivations can provide clues as to which interests in a society are most active, and hence, most involved in justifying their conduct. Moreover, they can provide an indicator as to which sentiments prevail at a given time in a particular society. Again, as long as the accuracy of derivations is not assumed, the general profile of derivations—that is, their emphasis and the nature of their appeal—can provide a rough indicator of underlying value standards,

---

[32] Ibid., s 1400.
[33] Ibid., s 1462.

since people and groups are likely to attempt to legitimate their actions by appealing to basic and underlying value premises.[34]

Pareto also saw derivations as critical to understanding social system dynamics. The cyclical fluctuations in sentiment that are so important in Pareto's model result, in part, from an inherent contradiction between the usefulness of derivations and their correspondence with reality. People want derivations that allow them to do things that might otherwise be questionable, but they also want derivations that seem to be consistent with the real world. For example, shifts in beliefs from those based on "faith" to those on "scepticism" occur as people search for beliefs that are both useful and in apparent correspondence with their perceptions of reality. But there is an inherent dialectic in people's efforts to justify their actions: the more they seek rational accounts, the greater likelihood they will see contradictions, and hence, be driven to rely upon faith and tradition. Conversely, the more people rely on blind faith, the greater it contradicts actual conditions, and thus, the more they will seek to rationalize their accounts of their actions:

> Hence those perpetually recurrent swings of the pendulum, which have been observable for so many centuries, between scepticism and faith, materialism and idealism, logico-experimental science and metaphysics. And so it is, considering for the moment only one or two of such oscillations, that in a little more than a hundred years, and, specifically, from the close of the eighteenth to the beginning of the twentieth century, one witnesses a wave of Voltairean scepticism, and then Rousseau's humanitarianism as a sequel to it; then a religion of Revolution, and then a return to Christianity; then scepticism once more—Positivism; and finally, in our time, the first stages of a new fluctuation in a mystico-nationalist direction.[35]

By the end of volume 3, Pareto had performed the preliminary work for his general treatise, but he had not developed, to any great degree, his general analysis of social systems. He had, nevertheless, confirmed in his mind that most human behavior is nonlogical, that people construct symbolic edifices or derivations to justify their conduct, that human action is ultimately guided by value standards or sentiments which are reflected in their behavior or residues, and that politics, economics, and value standards reveal both cyclical and equilibrium tendencies. With these initial insights, Pareto then began volume 4 of his *Treatise*.

---

[34] Ibid., s 1522.
[35] Ibid., ss 1680–81.

Treatise on General Sociology: Volume 4

One can sense Pareto's frustration over the time that he devoted to volumes 1, 2, and 3 which, in his mind, were only preliminary works. As an aging scholar, Pareto appeared to recognize that he had spent too much time on the early volumes and that only a little time would be left to realize the goal of this last volume on the "general form of society." Perhaps, because he was hurried, impatient, and frustrated, this volume lacks complete clarity, and yet, it is sociologically the most important.

The General Argument. As we have seen, Pareto had isolated certain basic properties as essential to the understanding of social systems. Moreover, he had come to visualize these properties as existing in a dynamic equilibrium, with discernible cycles evident among economic productivity, political power, value standards, and inequality. These terms are slightly more abstract than those sometimes used by Pareto, and are employed in hopes of more clearly reflecting Pareto's meaning. (1) Pareto believed that the level of prosperity and the nature of productive efforts in a system determine the character of exploitive mechanisms and, therefore, the nature of class "interests" of elites and nonelites. Prosperity and productivity are thought to result in dominance of speculators, and the proliferation of diverse commercial interests and hidden exploitation. In less prosperous times, rentiers dominate, economic interests are less diverse, and exploitation is more overt. (2) Lions and foxes have their own respective styles of political control. Lions tend to rule through centralized mechanisms and employ force to gain compliance, while foxes tend to rule through decentralized mechanisms and rely on co-optation to gain compliance. Elites have the greatest amount of power when they are most "heterogeneous." (3) Residues and derivations reflect changes in underlying sentiments, or value standards. (4) Although the distribution of wealth is relatively stable in every society, political and economic trends result in some redistribution. Inequality is greatest when elites are most homogeneous.

To comprehend the "form of society," therefore, it is necessary to discover several classes of facts. First, the distribution of political power, the level of economic productivity, the nature of sentiments as reflected in beliefs, and the level of inequality between elites and nonelites must be assessed. Second, the relations among these phenomena must be determined. For example, do changes in economic productivity signal changes in political elites? How far behind economic and political changes do beliefs lag? How have economic and political changes influenced inequality and how are beliefs used to legitimate such inequalities? Third, since inequality, political power, productivity, and beliefs reveal cyclical patterns, the associations among their respective cycles must be assessed.

Thus, the "general form of society" will reflect cyclical relations among the distribution of power, the level of productivity, the nature of beliefs, and patterns of inequality. To some extent, the cycles for each of these basic properties of social systems are accelerated or retarded by particular environmental circumstances.[36] For example, the level of natural resources, the existence of hostilities with neighboring societies, the nature of technology, and other highly variable conditions determine the nature and speed of cycles between lions and foxes, speculators and rentiers, beliefs based upon faith and scepticism, and high and low degrees of inequality and social mobility. Yet, Pareto emphasized that the cycles of political power, economic productivity, beliefs, and inequality all contain their own internal dynamics.[37] Regardless of environmental influences, the ascendance of foxes eventually creates conditions favorable to their demise and replacement by lions; the expansion of productivity and ascendance of speculators sets into motion forces that decrease productivity and that assure the dominance of rentiers; the existence of beliefs based on faith (as they reflect sentiments of "group persistence") creates conditions favorable to a change in sentiments (to new "combinations,") and beliefs based on scepticism; and increases in inequality accumulate to a point where pressures for more equality become manifest.

Not only do cycles in these basic properties of social systems reveal their own internal dynamic, each cycle sets constraints on the others. Thus, the cycling of political elites sets constraints for economic productivity, and vice versa; the nature of beliefs, and underlying sentiments, imposes barriers to the distribution of power and economic productivity, and vice versa; and the level of inequality influences the distribution of power, the level of productivity, the nature of beliefs, and vice versa. As much as external environmental conditions, then, each property of a social system, and its cyclical dynamic, represents a most important internal environment for the other properties.[38]

Although each cycle sets limits on the variability of the others, Pareto saw some system properties as more of a force behind change than

---

[36] Ibid., ss 2060 and 2289.
[37] Ibid., s 2336.
[38] Ibid., ss 2097 and 2205–7.

others. Borrowing a page from Adam Smith and Karl Marx, Pareto implicitly viewed economic productivity and the distribution of political power as more important in understanding the ultimate source of change than either beliefs or patterns of inequality.[39] Just whether economic or political forces are more important in causing a shift in system equilibrium is, Pareto felt, the result of specific environmental influences.

Thus, Pareto's general approach to analyzing social systems adopts the view that certain basic properties of systems can be isolated, that they exist in dynamic equilibrium, that they reveal cyclical phases and complex relations among these phases, and that these phases interact with particular environmental conditions. To appreciate the sophistication of his approach, we need to examine in more detail Pareto's discussion of power, productivity, beliefs, and inequality. As we do so, we can see how Pareto implemented the general analytical approach that we have just outlined.

Economic Interests, Productivity, and the Form of Society. Pareto recognized that economic productivity reveals cycles between periods of expansion and contraction. During periods of expansion, several related trends are evident: increases in the gross national product; decentralization of economic control; increase in the size of the economic elite and its dominance by speculators; corporate growth through innovation; and capital depletion accompanied by inflation.[40] Such trends for expansion set into motion, Pareto argued, conditions that favor economic contraction. Some of these conditions are purely economic, as when capital depletion, especially when fueled by inflation, make less capital available for economic investment and expansion.[41] Other conditions are political, as when expanded economic productivity creates so many diverse economic units, that integrative problems escalate to the point where they force centralization. Still other conditions are social, as when increases in the number of economic units and expansion of patronage increase avenues of exploitation and inequality to a point where alienation and resistance of nonelites forces political centralization and greater governmental control of all societal processes coupled with more conservative economic policy. Lagging behind these conditions are cultural pressures, as when the dominance of beliefs in scepticism, which support expanded, diverse, and innovative economic activity, discourage saving and, hence,

---

[39] Ibid., s 2299.
[40] Pareto, *Manual*, chap. 9.
[41] Pareto, *Treatise*, ss 2225–8, and "Parliamentary Regime."

deter capital accumulation or create such ambiguity and uncertainty that people develop more traditional orientations and beliefs, which tend to support political centralization and less economic diversity.[42]

The result of these economic, political, social, and cultural conditions is to set into motion decreases in economic productivity. Such decreases initiate trends toward a declining gross national product, centralization of economic control; a decline in size of the economic elite, increasing dominance of the economic elite by rentiers; and capital accumulation as well as a declining rate of inflation. In turn, decreases in productivity eventually create economic, political, social, and cultural conditions encouraging economic growth. Beliefs in faith encourage saving; capital accumulates to a point facilitating substantial investment; political centralization creates pressures for less authoritarian control; and people begin to demand the upward social mobility that economic growth can create.[43]

Political Power, the Circulation of Elites, and the Form of Society. Pareto felt that political processes reveal the same cyclical fluctuations as economic processes. In the political realm, the distribution of power moves through phases of centralization and decentralization which correspond, respectively, to phases of economic contraction and expansion.[44] During periods of political decentralization, the following trends become evident: the creation of a large ruling class composed of foxes; rule by consent and the use of patronage, and co-optation to gain compliance; and social mobility into elite classes from nonelite classes.[45]

As with economic cycles, processes of political decentralization create conditions favorable to centralization. A decentralized political system that encourages diversity and rules by co-optation eventually has difficulty controlling and coordinating system elements, with the result that consolidation, centralization, and the use of force become increasingly necessary to maintain order. A decentralized political system also encourages expanded economic productivity, resulting in increasing demands placed on government by a diversifying economic sector. Over time a decentralized political system encourages beliefs in scepticism, impairing the ease with which governments can rule. And a decentralized political system generates economic conditions favorable to exploitation and increased inequality, with the result that centralized force rather than ideological

---

[42] Pareto, *Treatise*, ss 2215–21 and 2585.

[43] Ibid., s 2318.

[44] Vilfredo Pareto, *Trasformazione della Democrazia* (Rome: Guanda, 1946; originally published in 1921), pp. 47, 60; and *Treatise*, s 2216.

[45] Pareto, *Treatise*, ss 2257–59 and 2274–77; and *Trasformazione*, pp. 47 ff.

manipulation and co-optation become necessary to control alienated and frustrated nonelites.

As these pressures mount, centralization is initiated, and as centralization of power occurs, several related trends are evident: a small ruling class emerges, dominated by lions; a strong police and military force develops; and upward social mobility of nonelites decreases. But as these trends come to dominate, they foster political economic, social, and cultural conditions that set into motion the process of decentralization. The use of force, per se, eventually creates resistance and resentment, which causes pressures for decentralization of power. Moreover, centralized power reduces social mobility and thereby escalates resentments among the population, who seek opportunities for upward social mobility. Centralized power tends to inhibit, Pareto argued, economic growth and productivity, with the result that economic interests begin to exert pressure for less control. Over time, centralized power encourages beliefs in faith, which legitimate political authority but which eventually foster contradictions between people's beliefs and actual circumstances. And so, with the accumulation of these political, social, economic, and cultural pressures, the trend toward centralization is reversed and a phase of decentralization is initiated.[46]

Sentiments, Beliefs, and the Form of Society.   Pareto came to the conclusion that the sentiments of group persistence and new combinations—or, tradition versus innovation—are in balance, with one or the other dominating at a given point in time. One can discover the cyclical shifts in these basic values by observing residues (behavior), and derivations (ideology). In particular, changing sentiments can be noted by observing a shift in beliefs from those based on faith, or adherence to tradition and maintenance of the status quo, to those predicated on scepticism or a questioning of actions and construction of ad hoc and pseudo-logical explanations.[47]

These shifts in beliefs tend to lag behind economic and political cycles, since people's ideas resist change.[48] Only after structural conditions are at considerable variance with people's values, beliefs, and ideological explanations are pressures for change in sentiments, and hence, beliefs and ideologies, initiated. As values change, they then begin to reinforce and legitimate changes in economic and political cycles, thereby accelerat-

[46] Pareto, *Rise and Fall of Elites: Treatise*, ss 2178–79, 2227–28, 2484–88, and 2546–53; and *Trasformazione*, pp. 47–48 and 87–90.

[47] Pareto, *Treatise*, ss 2339–54.

[48] Ibid., s 2225.

ing the rate of change in these cycles. But once economic, social, and political conditions swing about and move in a new direction, beliefs are increasingly at variance with the new structural conditions, and after a lag, they also swing in a new direction and accelerate the rate of change in these structural conditions.

After a slight lag, beliefs in faith follow the shift toward political centralization, reduced social mobility, and decreased economic productivity. Then, when the cycle reverses itself toward decentralization, increased mobility, and expanded productivity, beliefs begin to change toward a profile of scepticism. Such changes in beliefs, Pareto emphasized, are only observable manifestations of a shift in the balance of underlying sentiments or value standards, primarily those concerned with new combinations and group persistence.

Patterns of Inequality and the Form of Society. Pareto implicitly recognized two different aspects of inequality. One concerned the degree of inequality in the distribution of scarce resources and the other dealt with the upward structural mobility of individuals from nonelite to elite positions. Of particular importance in understanding this distinction is Pareto's conviction that resource inequality and upward mobility reveal different cycles.

Upward mobility corresponds to increases in productivity, and decreases in centralization.[49] Thus, rates of mobility follow general economic and political cycles. In contrast, inequality in resource distribution reveals a more complicated cyclical pattern. In general, this form of inequality reveals a double cycle for any single cycle of economic expansion-contraction and political centralization-decentralization. The reason for this is that inequality is greatest when there is homogeneity of political and economic elites. When foxes and speculators dominate, high rates of inequality exist because there are more potential exploiters of nonelites, because elites are innovative in their search for new avenues of exploitation, and because claims of large numbers of people to patronage and protection become institutionalized. When lions and rentiers dominate, there are fewer exploiters but they have the consolidated power to hoard resources and to use coercion to back up their hoarding of resources.[50]

---

[49] Pareto, *Manual*, p. 316, and *Treatise*, ss 2308–9.

[50] Pareto, *Rise and Fall of Elites*, pp. 69–71; *Manual*, pp. 287–300; and *Treatise*, ss 2310, 2416, 2546–53, and 2607–11. The contention that distribution of wealth remains relatively stable in any society has come to be known as Pareto's "law of income distribution." However, it is clear from Pareto's discussions and examples that the distribution of resources does vacillate somewhat; that resistance to the redistribution grows, eventually influencing a reversal; and that cycles of inequality are generic properties of social systems.

Thus, in seeking to understand how patterns of inequality influence the general form of society, we need to recognize Pareto's distinction between mobility and resource distribution. And we must recall that these reveal different cyclical patterns. As mobility increases with expanded productivity and decentralization of power, the influx of new personnel increases the rate of productivity and decentralization. But after a period, the elite population becomes increasingly homogeneous, since foxes prefer to recruit foxes into political roles and speculators tend to recruit speculators into economic roles. As their homogeneity increases, they become less flexible and less capable of controlling either economic, political, or social events—thus, setting into motion processes of economic contraction, political centralization, and reduced upward mobility. But with such contraction and centralization, people become resentful of their reduced opportunities and they begin to exert pressures for mobility, and along with pressures from the economic sector, decentralization of power, expanded productivity, and mobility begin to increase.

During this general cycle, the degree of resource inequality, Pareto felt, will have reached two peaks, one when foxes and speculators are homogeneous and the other when lions and rentiers are dominant. And the maximum degree of equality will have been reached twice, once when foxes and speculators are increasing but not yet ascendant and once when lions and rentiers are consolidating their position but do not yet dominate. Thus, the maximum degree of equality occurs with maximum levels of heterogeneity in elites.

The Form of Society: Pareto's View. Unlike most other sociologists of his time, and since his time, Pareto employed the concepts of equilibrium and cycles in his sociological analysis. With these concepts he was able to stress the interdependent nature of four basic system properties: power, productivity, cultural values and beliefs, and inequality. Moreover, in contrast to the more unilinear schemes of Marx, Weber, and Durkheim, but in concert with Spencer's discussion of militant and industrial cycles, Pareto saw social systems as cycling between states of centralization, productive contraction, cultural conservatism, and immobility, on the one hand, and decentralization, productive expansion, cultural liberalism, and mobility, on the other. And it is in these cycles, Pareto felt, that the universal laws of human organization are to be found. For whatever the "stage" of evolution of a society, and whatever the specifics of its environment, it will still be subject to the laws of equilibrium and patterned, cyclical change.

Had Pareto lived longer, or had he begun his explicitly sociological work earlier in his career, he probably would have articulated these laws. Pareto's ultimate concern for the discovery of general laws of social systems is clear as early as 1893[51] and is clearly articulated in *Treatise:*

> Social facts are the elements of our study. Our first effort will be to classify them for the purpose of attaining the one and only objective we have in view: the discovery, namely, of uniformities (laws) in the relations between them. When we have so classified kindred facts, a certain number of uniformities will come to the surface by induction; and after going a good distance along that primarily inductive path, we shall turn to another where more ample room will be found for deduction. So we shall verify the uniformities to which induction has carried us, give them a less empirical, more theoretical form, and see just what their implications are, just what picture they give of society.[52]

Pareto continued to use the inductive method throughout *Treatise*, but in a series of articles written shortly before his death, sought to articulate his theory in more abstract and straightforward terms.[53] Unfortunately, by the time Pareto began this process he was over 70 years old and ill, and left much to be done. As it stands now, these laws are implicit in his discussion and must be pulled from discursive context. Yet, we should seek to do Pareto justice and articulate the more abstract models and principles which, from his earliest days as an engineer, he felt inhered in the nature of phenomena. This is the goal of our next and last chapter on Pareto.

---

[51] Pareto, "Parliamentary Regime," pp. 11–12.

[52] Pareto, *Treatise,* s 144.

[53] See, for example, Pareto, *Trasformazione*, p. 47.

20

VILFREDO PARETO III: MODELS AND PRINCIPLES

In his last work, *Transformation of Democracy*, one senses Pareto's recognition that he had been insufficiently abstract in his sociological work.[1] *Transformation* is a refreshing work, in which Pareto clearly articulates many of the insights developed in *Treatise* and employs the concept of centralization to present a more sophisticated treatment of power than is apparent in *Treatise*. Although Pareto was unable to complete the process of presenting his theory in abstract form and organizing it into a coherent deductive theory, this was the direction in which he was working upon his death. In effect, he was returning to his vision of Newtonian physics.

In this chapter, we will seek to realize Pareto's Newtonian vision and phrase his arguments more abstractly. For much of the present-day difficulty in reading Pareto, we think, stems from what Pareto himself belatedly realized: his work is too mired in historical and empirical specifics. Our goal in this chapter, then, is to liberate Pareto's ideas from their empirical context, to rephrase his concepts in more contemporary terms, and to articulate more formally and abstractly Pareto's basic models and principles.

THE BASIC THEORETICAL APPROACH

Pareto always maintained that social science should seek to emulate physics in its search for abstract principles that can account for the relations among basic properties of the social universe. Unfortunately,

---

[1] Vilfredo Pareto, *Trasformazione della Democrazia* (Rome: Guanda, 1946; originally published in 1921).

his definitions of basic properties are consistently obscure; his models of social phenomena are never stated with the same precision and clarity as his economic models; and as his last written words testify, his principles are not formally stated, nor are they couched at a sufficient level of abstraction. Yet, despite these failings, we can state the essentials of his theoretical approach in a way that will allow us to realize Pareto's original goal.

Throughout his career, Pareto followed his early training in engineering by insisting that the individual could not be the unit of sociological analysis. Rather, only aggregated phenomena could be a useful topic of inquiry, since the specific qualities of individuals are too idiosyncratic and variable for sociological inquiry. At best, sociologists would have to deal with averages, tendencies, and affinities among aggregated individuals.

This view led Pareto to the concept of social systems in which certain fundamental properties of collectivities could be isolated from more unique and idiosyncratic properties of individuals and broad environmental conditions. Theories about human organization must be about these fundamental properties rather than specific environmental conditions or individual qualities. As a system, these properties would be viewed as mutually interdependent, with a change in one creating pressures for change in other elements. To describe such system interconnections and their alterations, two concepts would be critical: equilibrium and cycles. Thus, to understand Pareto's sociology, we need to highlight his conceptualization of (1) basic social system properties, (2) the nature of their interdependence and equilibrium, and (3) the cyclical pattern of their change.

Basic System Properties. As Pareto's thought matured, he came to view the most important properties of social systems as (1) the distribution of power, (2) the degree of system productivity, (3) the profile of values and beliefs, (4) the degree of resource inequality, and (5) the level of social mobility. We have phrased these ideas more abstractly than in the last chapter, a tactic that the mature Pareto would appreciate. A formal definition of each system property is offered below:

1. *The distribution of power* in a social system concerns *(a)* the degree of centralization of decision-making positions and *(b)* the way in which incumbents in these positions exert power. Power is defined as the capacity to regulate and control other system units and its variable states can be described as follows:

(a). *Centralization-decentralization:* Centralized power refers to systems in which there are few decision-making positions and in which these positions are arranged in a hierarchy of authority. Decentralized power describes a situation where there are numerous decision-making positions in a system, with considerably less hierarchy than in centralized systems.

(b). *Force-co-optation:* Force denotes the use of coercion to achieve compliance with decisions by those in positions of power. Co-optation refers to the use by those in power of various forms of manipulation, chiefly the development of extensive patronage systems, which make the goals of diverse actors interdependent, to achieve compliance with decisions. Heterogeneous elites capable of employing both force and co-optive techniques to gain compliance are more powerful than elites who tend to rely almost exclusively on one or the other.[2]

2. *Degree of productivity* denotes the fact that all social systems create and distribute products and services for system maintenance. Productivity can vary in terms of whether or not positions revolving around creation and distribution of goods and services are expanding or contracting and whether or not the total amount of goods and services is increasing or decreasing.[3]

3. *The profile of values and beliefs* refers to the symbolic components of social systems. The incumbents in social systems can be typified as having unconscious value standards which guide their thoughts, perceptions, and actions. The basic value standards are reflected

---

[2] This terminology was adopted by Pareto in an effort to more abstractly articulate and more fully capture ideas contained in his theory of "circulation of elites" (for example *Transformation*, pp. 47–48). We believe this reflects a late and therefore infrequently recognized, though very important, development in Pareto's work, as he sought to focus on structural properties rather than personality traits. "Lions," as personality types, tend to rely on centralized power and the use of force to gain compliance. "Foxes," as personality types, tend to rely on decentralized power and the use of co-optation to gain compliance. Personality plays an important role in Pareto's description of phenomenon, but his ultimate concern seems to rest with structural properties.

[3] Pareto sometimes refers to "interests," sometimes to "prosperity," and sometimes to traits of economic elites in his discussions of economic cycles. A basic point is that mechanisms of exploitation, and the interests that correspond to them, are qualitatively different during periods of expansion than they are during periods of contraction. Elite types are identified by involvement with one kind of exploitive mechanism or the other, and the nature of their corresponding economic interests. It is, therefore, consistent with Pareto's descriptions to focus on productivity as the primary feature characterizing economies.

in conscious beliefs that incumbents in social systems use to interpret their situation. Values vary between standards favoring continuation of the status quo, on the one hand, and innovation, on the other hand. Beliefs therefore vary between those advocating traditionalism and those emphasizing liberalism. When discussing values and beliefs together, we can conveniently label them cultural directives.[4]

4. *The degree of resource inequality* denotes the extent to which those things that are considered valuable are distributed unequally to different incumbents.

5. *The level of social mobility* refers to the degree of movement of system incumbents from nonelite to elite positions, defined as either power, symbolic, or material resources.

In delineating these basic properties, Pareto was emphasizing that the structure, form, and dynamics of social systems will be a function of the variable states of, and interconnections among, power, productivity, values and beliefs, resource distribution, and mobility. In other words, when individual actors become aggregated, they form a social system which, at the most abstract level, can be typified in terms of the basic properties listed above.

Equilibrium and the Interrelations among System Properties. Basic components of social systems are mutually connected and can, in Pareto's view, be conceptualized as being in equilibrium. The concept of equilibrium emphasizes three aspects of social systems. First, an initial change in one property of a system will activate pressures from the other properties tending to bring it back into line. But second, if the initial changes are of sufficient magnitude, secondary changes in the other properties will occur and the system will reach a new equilibrium point. And third, the mutual interrelations of system properties that stand in equilibrium make the concept of one-way causality comparatively unimportant in theoretical analysis, since the connections of system properties are mutual and the source of change can vary depending upon particular empirical conditions. What the concept of equilibrium stresses is that system parts mutually react to alterations in their respective states.[5]

Cyclical Patterns of Change. Descriptions of evolutionary develop-

---

[4] Use of the term *cultural directives* emphasizing "traditionalism" or "liberalism" is simply a rephrasing, in more contemporary language, of what Pareto termed *sentiments* emphasizing "group persistence" (accompanied by "derivations" or beliefs emphasizing faith and adherence to traditional ways) or *sentiments* emphasizing "combinations" (accompanied by derivations or beliefs emphasizing scepticism and innovativeness).

[5] Refer to the previous chapter.

ment, Pareto felt, will tend to be mere historical accounts of how societies have grown and developed. Far more important than changes in size, territory, technologies, and other variables that influence historical events are the regular patterns of oscillation in the basic properties of social systems.[6] It is these patterns, rather than the unique and particular events of history, that are to be the topic of theorizing. In the historical and empirical record on human societies, Pareto argued, cyclical patterns of change can be discerned. Inherent in these cycles are the notions of (1) interdependence and (2) dialectic tendencies.

1. Because system properties are interconnected, alterations in one part will, if sufficiently great, force alterations in others. And because parts are connected, change tends to reveal patterns of parallel movement in all basic properties of social systems. Modifications in power and productivity are particularly likely to stimulate changes in other system properties.

2. Changes among system properties create the conditions for their reversal in the opposite direction. And as the conditions for reversal are realized for one system property, interdependence of properties assures that other properties will also begin to reverse themselves. Thus, social systems oscillate as their interconnected properties create conditions that not only inhibit further movement in a particular direction, but also increase the likelihood of movement in an opposite direction.

PARETO'S THEORETICAL MODEL

Since Pareto de-emphasized one-way causality and stressed, instead, mutual interdependence, his model of human organization does not resemble a flow diagram. Rather, his emphasis on equilibrium and cyclical dynamics results in a model that delineates the oscillations of basic system properties—power, productivity, beliefs, inequality, and mobility—over time. Emphasis is on the dynamics of, and relations among, the cyclical oscillations of these properties. We have represented Pareto's model of social organization in Figure 20–1.[7]

---

[6] Pareto, *Transformation*, pp. 57–60. Cyclical patterns of change result from equilibria among social forces. The character of the political system is, for example, determined by a balance among pressures encouraging centralization and pressures encouraging decentralization within the system. As those pressures change the balance among them is reestablished at a different point and structural features of the system are modified.

[7] Pareto did not expect all cycles to be graphically even or of the same magnitude or duration, and he maintained that every major cycle is composed of a series of lesser cycles. In these respects, the graphic representation simplifies Pareto's predictions in order to maximize clarity.

428

FIGURE 20–1
Pareto's Model of Social Organization

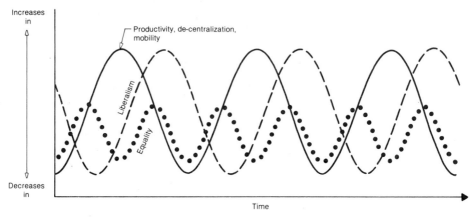

As the model indicates, Pareto saw decentralization of power, expanded productivity, and increased upward mobility as cycling together. Just whether political decentralization or expanded productivity initiates the cycle is dependent upon the particular environmental and internal conditions of a concrete empirical system. But once initiated, decentralization, productivity, and upward mobility will all increase. Lagging somewhat behind these increases are values, standards, and beliefs which require some alterations in people's existential and empirical situation before they begin to shift toward a more liberal profile, emphasizing innovation and experimentation. Yet, as the juxtaposition of the cycles delineates, once values and beliefs begin to change, the shared slope of the other cycles increases, indicating that alterations in cultural patterns accelerate decentralization, productivity, and mobility. For as long as beliefs remain traditional, they impede structural alterations, but once they also shift, they act as a stimulus to the other cycles.

The double cycle of resource inequality in Figure 20–1 emphasizes that inequality is greatest when the decentralization-centralization and expanded-contracted productivity cycles are at their maximum. Thus, the greatest inequality in resource distribution is evident at the height of either the decentralization and productivity cycle or the centralization and contracted productivity cycle. Equality reaches its maximum at the midpoints of these cycles toward either greater productivity-decentralization or lessened productivity and centralization.

As the figure underscores, decentralization, productivity, and upward mobility increase until quasi-dialectical forces set into motion their decline. This decline is accelerated when values and beliefs, which lag somewhat behind, also begin to shift toward a traditional profile, emphasizing faith, orthodoxy, preference for the past, or other traditionalist tenets. Once these slopes reach their bottom point, then quasi-dialectical forces reverse the trend and a new wave of expanded productivity, decentralization, upward mobility, and liberalism is initiated.

As we emphasized in the last chapter, the specific profile of the slopes and curves for Figure 20–1 are influenced by specific environmental conditions as they affect the generation of opposing structural tendencies. What is important in Pareto's view is the relationship among the curves, regardless of their specific slopes. For the relationships, Pareto felt, are far less variable, since the fact of mutual interdependence ties the slope of one system property to the others.

The utility of this model is that it allows for the portrayal of social systems in terms of where they are located on a given cycle. Moreover, since the cycles vary together in the pattern portrayed in Figure 20–1, determination of the direction of a cycle and the point along that cycle of one system property, such as productivity, would allow for an understanding of the points and direction of other system properties. Such a model thus has not only descriptive value, but some degree of predictive value as to the future trends in a system at a particular point in the cycle.

Yet despite the ingenuity of this model, it lacks a specification of why system properties cycle in a particular pattern. Indeed, Pareto was vitally concerned with why properties cycle and why they reveal certain patterns of oscillation. And when seeking to answer why the patterns in Figure 20–1 should be evident in all social systems, Pareto implicitly formulated a number of interesting theoretical propositions, or principles.

PARETO'S THEORETICAL PRINCIPLES

In articulating Pareto's implicit principles, we need to develop two types of propositions. (1) Those that specify the generation of opposite tendencies inherent in each system property and which, therefore, answer the question: Why should system properties oscillate in a cyclical pattern? (2) Those that denote the relations among system properties and answer the question: Why do the cycles of system properties reveal certain invariant relations?

Principles of Oscillation of System Properties

Political Oscillation. Pareto emphasized that the distribution of political power oscillates between centralized and decentralized extremes. The key dynamic behind these shifts in political organization is the problem of integration and control. Pareto viewed two basic options for political control, co-optation and force, with each creating its own problems of coordination and control of system units. Control by ideological manipulation, interlocking interests, and informal administrative liaison allows for great diversity in a system, but it creates, over time, severe problems of coordination and regulation of diverse units. The result is for these problems to escalate to a point requiring more consolidation of control and decision-making prerogatives. But such efforts are often resisted, with the consequence that the threat or actual use of force becomes necessary as attempts to control diverse units intensify. But centralized control, maintained by force, creates resistance and organized opposition that, over time, are sufficient to force decentralization. These basic opposing processes inhering in the distribution of power can be summarized as follows:

1. The greater is the degree of decentralized decision-making in a system, the greater is the use of co-optation as a means of social control.
2. The more continued is the use of co-optation as a means of social control in a system, the greater are the number and diversity of control activities and the more coordination and control rest upon voluntary compliance.
3. The greater are the number and diversity of control activities and the more coordination and control rest upon voluntary compliance in decentralized systems, the more likely are problems of coordination and control to increase.
4. The more problematic coordination and control become in decentralized systems, the more likely are efforts at consolidation and centralization of power to increase.
5. The greater is the degree of centralization of power, the more likely is force, or the threat of force, to be used as a means of social control.
6. The greater and more prolonged is the use of force as a means of social control in a system, the more likely, over the long run, are system units to resist centralized power and to initiate pressures for the decentralization of power.

The Oscillation of Productivity. Pareto dealt primarily with economic productivity in societal social systems, but his ideas may have relevance to productivity in all types of social systems. For in all systems, whether a small group, complex organization, or community, incumbents engage in behaviors that produce materials or services which maintain the system or help it to realize goals. In this process, capital—whether material or human labor services—is expended, or invested. It is this relationship between activities of system members and the investment of capital that Pareto saw as crucial in understanding the oscillation of productivity. This relationship can be expressed in the following principles:

7. The greater is capital investment, the greater is the level of productivity in a social system.
8. The more rapid is the rate of increase in productivity in a social system, the greater is the relative investment in facilities producing consumer goods and services as opposed to investment in capital-producing facilities.
9. The greater is the relative commitment of resources to production of consumer goods and services, the more likely is capital depletion.
10. The greater is the rate of capital depletion in a system, the more likely are investment and productivity to decline.
11. The greater are decreases in investment and productivity in a system, the greater is the long-term accumulation of capital.
12. The greater is the accumulation of capital in a system, the more likely is the level of investment in new and diverse productive facilities to increase.

The Oscillation of Values and Beliefs. Pareto recognized that beliefs represent applications of values to concrete situations. Beliefs thus reveal considerable variability, whereas values tend to emphasize the appropriateness of innovation or conformity to established patterns. Such basic values can be revealed in many different kinds of beliefs—religious, secular, nationalistic, for example—which will be tailored to the specific circumstances of a population. Beliefs reflecting values emphasizing innovation, Pareto stressed, present people with many behavioral options and tend to remove behavioral constraints and restrictions. But over time, such beliefs create a situation where ambiguity over how to behave escalates and pressures for more certainty and fixity of beliefs and norms begin to increase. Thus, values emphasizing innovation, and their attending "liberal" beliefs, eventually create conditions favoring a shift in "sentiment" to values stressing conformity and attending beliefs that emphasize "traditionalism." This dialectical relationship between liberalism and traditionalism can be expressed in the following principles:

13. The more cultural values, and attending beliefs, are "liberal" in profile, the more diverse and less constraining are cultural directives (and attending beliefs).
14. The more diverse and less constraining are cultural directives (and attending beliefs), the greater is the level, over time, of ambiguity in—and conflict among—them, and the more equivocal and less utilitarian they become as guides for behavior.
15. The greater is the level of ambiguity in, and conflict among, cultural directives (and attending beliefs), the more likely are efforts at creating coherence among cultural directives to be initiated.
16. The more efforts at creating coherence among cultural directives persist, the more likely are cultural values, and attending beliefs, to assume a "traditional" profile.
17. The more values, and attending beliefs, are traditional in profile, the more likely are cultural directives, over time, to come into conflict with actual experiences and structural conditions.
18. The more traditional cultural directives come into conflict with actual experiences and structural conditions, the more likely are efforts at creating consistency between existential conditions and cultural directives to be initiated.
19. The more efforts at creating consistency persist, the more likely are cultural values, and attending beliefs, to assume a "liberal" profile.

Principles of Relations among System Properties

While patterns of resource inequality and upward mobility—the other two properties of social systems not discussed in the previous section—reveal a cyclical profile, Pareto did not discuss their internal dialectics. Rather, he saw inequality and mobility as forces that responded to, and resulted from, the dialectics of power, productivity, and cultural directives. Thus, inequality and mobility could, in Pareto's eye, only be understood by examining their mutual relations to power, productivity, and cultural directives.

Resource Inequality. As Pareto emphasized, and as is evident in Figure 20–1, inequality reaches a maximum when political and economic cycles are at their peaks. When decentralization of power and expanded productivity are near their maximum point before the inevitable reversal, and when cultural directives are at their maximum rate of movement to a liberal profile, inequality is great, since there are many potential exploiters, numerous avenues of exploitation, and ready cultural legitimation for virtually any kind of political or economic activity. When centralization and decreased productivity are at their maximum, and when cultural directives are at their highest rate of acceleration toward a traditional profile, then inequality is great, since a few elites, using coercive force and positively sanctioned by traditional beliefs, can expropriate and hoard resources.

In either case, Pareto argued, high levels of inequality create alienative dispositions among nonelites. As they escalate, such dispositions can become a powerful force for change in the distribution of power, the nature of productivity, and the content of cultural symbols. For once alienation reaches a peak level, people become willing to organize and resist their exploiters, whether a centralized and decentralized elite, and they become capable of unmasking beliefs used to legitimate their exploitation. People develop beliefs, or derivations, that justify their behaving in accordance with their own economic interests and cultural directives. When nonelites come to view their interests as conflicting with elite interests, they reject ideologies that legitimize privilege and develop ideologies that legitimize assault upon privilege. The result is for exploited nonelites to initiate changes toward more resource equality. Thus, when the system is centralized, they exert pressures toward decentralization, expanded productivity, and liberal cultural directives in an attempt to throw off the shackles of coercive repression; and when the system is decentralized, they exert pressure for centralization, reduced productivity, and traditionalism in an effort to shed their many and diverse exploiters. These basic relations that Pareto saw among inequality, power, productivity, and cultural directives can be expressed in the following principles:

20. The greater is the level of production and decentralization in a system, and the greater is the rate of movement of cultural directives toward a liberal profile, then the greater are the number of exploiters and avenues for co-optive exploitation in that system.

21. The greater the number of exploiters and avenues of exploitation in a decentralized system, then the more likely are inequities to increase and the greater is the level of alienation among nonelites in that system.

22. The greater is the level of alienation of nonelites in a system, the more likely are they to become aware of inequalities, to resist exploitation, and to debunk cultural beliefs.

23. The greater are the efforts of nonelites to resist exploitation by decentralized elites, the more likely are elites to begin centralizing power and using coercive force.

24. The more power becomes centralized in a predominantly decentralized system and the more productivity becomes contracted in a previously expanding economic system, then the greater are the number of avenues of exploitation abolished, the more equitable becomes distribution of rewards, and the more likely are cultural directives to become traditional in profile.

25. The greater is the degree of centralization and decrease in productivity in a system, and the greater is the rate of movement of cultural directives toward a traditional profile, then the greater is the level of exploitation through appropriation of resources by a few elites.

26. In predominantly centralized systems, the greater is the level of exploitation by centralized elites, the more likely are inequalities to increase, the greater is the level of alienation of nonelites, and the more likely are nonelites to become aware of inequalities, to resist exploitation, and to debunk cultural beliefs.

27. The greater are the efforts of nonelites to resist exploitation by a centralized elite, the more likely are elites to become decentralized, the more likely are co-optive means of exploitation to be initiated, and the more likely are beliefs to shift toward a liberal profile.

28. The more decentralized a predominantly centralized system becomes, and the greater the rate of economic expansion and diversification in a previously contracted economy, the less exploitive-power centralized elites have and the more equitable the distribution of resources.

Upward Mobility. Pareto emphasized that elites in the political and productive sectors of a social system tend to recruit selectively. During times of traditionalism, productive contraction, and political centralization, little mobility into elite ranks occurs, but what mobility there is tends to involve the recruitment of conservative and tradition-bound personnel who are not adverse to the use of force. The lack of recruitment creates frustration among nonelites who perceive a reduction in their opportunities. Moreover, the selective recruitment of personnel into elite positions decreases the capacity of elites to deal flexibly with situations, with the result that order and control must increasingly be maintained by force. The use of force, coupled with decreased opportunities, merely escalates the alienation and resistance of nonelites, eventually leading to decentralization of power, expanded productivity, and liberalization of beliefs. During this new phase, extensive recruitment of personnel to the increasing number and diversity of elite positions occurs, thus increasing the available opportunities of nonelites. But such recruitment also tends to be selective, with the result that, over time, resources are shifted away from the productive sector of the economy and new elites have little capacity or inclination in the use of force to maintain order and control. In the face of mounting integrative problems, a renewed trend toward traditionalism, centralization, and decreased productivity becomes apparent. As production decreases, elites have fewer resources for co-optation, thus further decreasing mobility. Moreover, at just the point that productivity and decentralization peak and begin to decline, liberal beliefs are at their highest rate of increase (see slopes in Figure 20–1), thus raising people's expectations at just the time that opportunities for mobility are decreasing. Such a situation of relative deprivation increases the pressures from nonelites for system reorganization.

These relations among mobility processes, productivity, power, inequality, and cultural directives can be summarized with the following principles:

29. The greater is the level of productivity and decentralization in a system, the greater is the level of upward mobility and the larger is the elite population in that system.

30. The greater is the rate of upward mobility in a decentralized system, the more recruitment is selective, and hence, the more elites become homogeneous and "liberal" in their values and beliefs.

31. The more homogeneous and liberal is the elite population in a decentralized system, the less able is it to deal with escalating integrative problems in a decentralized system and the less able is it to select its recruits, and hence, the more heterogeneous the elite becomes.

32. The greater are integrative problems in a decentralized system, the greater are the pressures for centralization of power, decreased productivity, and traditional cultural directives.

32a. The greater is the gap between declining productivity and opportunities, on the one hand, and increasingly liberal cultural directives, on the other, the greater are the integrative problems of a system.

32b. The more decreased productivity reduces the resources available for co-optation, the greater are the integrative problems of a system.

32c. The more inequalities have increased alienative dispositions among nonelites, the greater are the integrative problems of a system.

32.d. The greater is the diversification of production and distribution of power, the less able are elites to use force effectively, and hence, the greater are the integrative problems of a system.

33. The more pressures for centralization of power, productive contraction, and traditionalism are successful, the less is the rate of upward mobility and the less available are opportunities for nonelites.

34. The less are the opportunities of nonelites, and the greater is the use of force by elites, the greater are the alienative dispositions of nonelites and the greater is their frustration over the lack of opportunity, and hence, the greater are the pressures for decentralization, expanded productivity, and liberal cultural directives.

Productivity, the Distribution of Power, and Cultural Directives. While power, productivity, and cultural directives reveal their own quasi-dialectical processes, they are also mutually interdependent—a fact that Pareto's notion of equilibrium emphasizes. Each property of a system represents a force influencing the cycle of the others. These relationships can be expressed in the following principles.

35. The greater is the level of production in a system, the greater is the number and diversity of productive units and, hence, the greater are the pressures for decentralization of power and liberal cultural directives, and vice versa.

36. The greater is the level of political decentralization, the greater is the reliance on co-optation as a means of social control, and hence, the greater are the pressures for liberal beliefs and expanded productivity as a means of co-optation, and vice versa.

37. The more liberal the beliefs, the less people save and accumu-

late capital, and hence, the more rapidly investment leads to depletion of available capital and economic contraction.

38. The more decentralized and productive a system, the greater are its integrative problems, and hence, the more likely are pressures for centralization, reduced productivity, and traditional cultural a directives as means of social control.

39. The more a system is centralized, restricted in its productivity, and traditional in its cultural directives, the greater are pressures for either, or both, decentralization and expanded productivity.

These propositions emphasize that productivity, power, and cultural directives are interconnected. But they also stress Pareto's view that power and productivity are more likely to cause shifts in system equilibrium and to initiate cyclical changes than cultural factors. Values and beliefs tend to lag behind these structural changes, but once cultural directives shift, they accelerate structural changes in the organization of production and the distribution of power (as well as inequality and mobility). Just whether production or power is the prime mover in a system will be determined by the empirical specifics of a particular system.

PARETO'S THEORETICAL LEGACY

Pareto's theoretical efforts would appear to offer both some interesting theory-building leads as well as some conceptual deadends. His general view of equilibrium and cycles has been given, we feel, insufficient attention in sociological theory. Many social phenomena do reveal interrelated cyclical patterns. Moreover, Pareto's recognition that social phenomena—particularly power, productivity, and cultural directives—reveal internal dynamics producing oscillation, as well as mutual constraints, is a point of emphasis that is worth pursuing. And Pareto's insistence that theoretical models and principles focus on the more generic and universal properties of social systems, rather than on their empirical specifics and historical idiosyncracies, is good advice for social theorists, especially since this advice is often unheeded.

Pareto is probably less useful if we maintain his vocabulary and if we follow too closely his economic vision of social processes. For behind all of Pareto's work, and his analysis of the basic properties of social systems, is an image of "the business cycle of Western capitalism." This image is too restrictive to serve as a basis for general social theory, and in fact, it is not completely isomorphic with economic processes in even capitalist societies (to say nothing of socialist and communist systems). It is problematic, for example, if the distribution of power, productivity, cultural systems, inequalities, and mobility reveal clear cyclical patterns that resemble those of the business cycle. Strict adherence to this notion would be unwise. In particular, Pareto's analysis of productivity in social systems is too constrained by the business-cycle image (see propositions 7 to 12) to bear much relation to actual properties of empirical systems.

Yet Pareto's other propositions can alert contemporary theorists to what may be some basic processes in social systems. The relationship among political decentralization, centralization, and social integration (propositions 1 to 6) is certainly worthy of further inquiry. The hypothesized relations among power, productivity, and cultural directives (propositions 13 to 19 and 36 to 39) may indeed offer some interesting theoretical leads. The relations among centralization-decentralization, force, co-optation, and resource inequality is also worthy of further thought and investigation (propositions 20 to 27). The relations among power, productivity, and mobility (propositions 30 to 35) is a topic that needs to be more thoroughly integrated into sociological theory.

In sum, Pareto's scheme is the victim of his vocabulary and overuse of models describing fluctuations in capitalist economies. Yet, the isolation of power, productivity, cultural symbols, mobility, and resource inequality as the basic properties of social systems is worthy of our careful evaluation. And the implicit articulation of fundamental relations within, and among, these properties provides a series of important theoretical leads for modern sociology.

PART III

The Emerging
Tradition in America

GEORGE HERBERT MEAD I: THE INTELLECTUAL ORIGINS OF HIS THOUGHT

At the same time that Europeans were developing some basic principles on macro processes, American scholars were discovering some of the fundamental principles of interaction. While Weber, Simmel, Durkheim, and others had seen the importance of interpersonal dynamics and social psychological processes, they failed to develop concepts and propositions in these areas that greatly advanced sociological theory. But in America, a number of thinkers had begun to unlock some of the mysteries of the micro-social world. These efforts culminated in the work of the American philosopher, George Herbert Mead, who synthesized diverse lines of thought into a unified view of "mind, self, and society."

To appreciate Mead's contribution, we will review the sources of his ideas, and in so doing, we will summarize the key concepts of other important scholars. For it is in Mead's ability to pull together different lines of thought that his contribution resides. Indeed, Mead did not consider his synthesizing unique or original.[1] And yet, it is this synthesis of others' ideas that marks an important turning point in sociological theory.

MEAD'S SYNTHESIS OF SCHOOLS OF THOUGHT

As a philosopher, Mead was attuned to basic philosophical issues and to currents in many diverse intellectual arenas. His broader philosophical

---

[1] Lewis A Coser, *Masters of Sociological Thought* (New York: Harcourt Brace Jovanovich, 1977), p. 347.

scheme reflects this fact, but equally significant, his social psychology also pulls together the general metaphors contained within four dominant intellectual perspectives of his time: (1) utilitarianism, (2) Darwinism, (3) pragmatism, and (4) behaviorism.[2] Just how each of these influenced Mead is examined below.

Utilitarianism

In England during the 18th and 19th centuries, the economic doctrine that became known as utilitarianism dominated social thought. Mead had clearly read such prominent thinkers as Adam Smith, David Ricardo, John Stuart Mill, Jeremy Bentham, and to the extent that he can be classified as a utilitarian, Thomas Malthus. And few, including Mead, in the 19th century could ignore either the psychological or sociological doctrines of the staunch utilitarian, Herbert Spencer.[3] While perhaps these had the least influence on his dominant intellectual positions, Mead absorbed several key ideas from utilitarian doctrines.

First, utilitarians saw human action as self-interested actors who seek to maximize their "utility" or benefit in free and openly competitive marketplaces. While this idea was expressed somewhat differently by various advocates of utilitarianism, Mead appears to have found useful the emphasis *(a)* on actors as seeking rewards, *(b)* on actors as attempting to adjust to a competitive situation, and *(c)* on actors as goal-directed and instrumental in their behaviors. Later versions of utilitarianism stressed "pleasure" and "pain" principles which captured the essence of the behaviorism that was to emerge in Mead's time and to influence greatly his scheme.

Second, utilitarians often tended to emphasize—indeed to overemphasize—the rationality of self-seeking actors. From a utilitarian perspective actors are rational in that they gather all relevant information, weigh alternative lines of conduct, and select an alternative that will maximize utilities, benefits, or pleasures. Mead never came to accept this overly rational view of human action, but his view of the human "mind" as a process of reflective thought in which alternatives are covertly designated, weighed, and rehearsed was, no doubt, partially inspired by the utilitarian position.

Thus, while utilitarianism was the least influential perspective on

---

[2] See also, Jonathan H. Turner, *The Structure of Sociological Theory*, rev. ed. (Homewood, Ill.: Dorsey Press, 1978), pp. 312–15. © 1978 by The Dorsey Press.

[3] See Chapter 3.

Mead, his theoretical scheme was to correspond to several central points of emphasis in utilitarianism. Mead probably borrowed these points both directly and indirectly, since utilitarianism influenced the other schools of thought that shaped Mead's philosophical scheme. For as we will come to see, early behaviorism and pragmatism, while rejecting extreme utilitarianism, nonetheless incorporated some of its basic tenets.

Darwinism

Charles Darwin's formulation of the theory of evolution influenced not only biological theory,[4] but also social thought.[5] For example, although such utilitarians as Herbert Spencer had long held the view that competition and struggle will produce the best social order, their argument carried more authority when seemingly supported by biological theory. The view that a species' profile is shaped from the competitive struggle with other species attempting to occupy an environmental niche was highly compatible with utilitarian notions. As a result of this superficial compatibility, utilitarianism was to be carried to absurd extremes in the late 19th and early 20th centuries by a group of thinkers who became known as "Social Darwinists."[6] From their viewpoint, social life is a competitive struggle in which the "fittest" will be the best able to "survive" and prosper.[7] Hence, those who enjoy privilege in a society deserve these benefits because they are the "most fit," whereas those who have the least wealth are less fit and worthy. Obviously, Social Darwinism was a gross distortion of the theory of evolution, but its flowering illustrates the extent to which Darwin's theory represented an intellectual bombshell in Europe and America in the 19th and early 20th centuries.

Other social theorists borrowed Darwin's ideas more cautiously. George Herbert Mead was to use the theory as a broad metaphor for understanding the processes by which the unique capacities of humans emerge. For Mead, all animals, including humans, must seek to adapt and adjust to an environment, and hence, many of the attributes that

---

[4] Charles Darwin, *On the Origin of Species* (London: Murry, 1859).

[5] See, for example, William G. Sumner, *What Social Classes Owe Each Other* (New York: Harper & Bros., 1883).

[6] Richard Hofstadter, *Social Darwinism in American Thought, 1860–1915* (Philadelphia: University of Pennsylvania Press, 1945).

[7] It was Spencer who first used the phrase "survival of the fittest" which apparently influenced Darwin, as the latter acknowledges in *On the Origin of Species*. Other early American sociologists, such as William Graham Sumner, took this idea to extremes.

an organism comes to reveal are the product of its efforts to adapt to a particular environment. In distant past, therefore, the unique capacities of humans for language, for mind, for self, and for normatively regulated social organization emerged as a result of selective pressures on the ancestors of humans for these unique capacities.

But Mead was not so much interested in the origins of humans as a species as in the development of the infant human from an asocial to social creature. For at birth, Mead argued, an infant is not a human. It acquires the unique behavioral capacities of humans only as it seeks to adapt to a social environment. Thus, just as the species as a whole acquired its distinctive characteristics through a process of "natural selection," so the infant organism develops its "humanness" through a process of "selection." Because the environment of a person is other people who use language, who possess mind and self, and who live in society, the young must adapt to this environment if they are to survive. And as they adapt and adjust, they acquire the capacity to use language, to reveal a mind, to evidence a sense of self, and to participate in society. Thus, Mead borrowed from Darwinian theory the metaphor of adaptation or adjustment as the key force shaping the nature of humans.[8] This metaphor was given its most forceful expression in the works of scholars who developed a school of thought known as "pragmatism."

Pragmatism

Mead is frequently grouped with pragmatists, such as Charles Pierce, William James, and John Dewey. Yet although Mead was profoundly influenced by James and Dewey, his theoretical scheme is only partially in debt to pragmatism.[9] For as we have emphasized, Mead took his ideas from a variety of sources, and pragmatism is only one of them.

The American scientist and philosopher Charles Pierce first developed the ideas behind pragmatism in an article entitled "How to Make Our Ideas Clear," which appeared in *Popular Science Monthly* in 1878.[10]

---

[8] Mead also reacted to Darwin's later efforts to understand emotions in animals. See Charles Darwin, *The Expression of Emotions in Man and Animals* (London: Murry, 1872). Mead used this analysis as his "straw man" in developing his own theory of "gestures" and "interaction."

[9] For relevant summaries of pragmatism, see Charles Morris, *The Pragmatic Movement in American Philosophy* (New York: George Braziller, 1970); and Edward C. Moore, *American Pragmatism: Pierce, James, and Dewey* (New York: Columbia University Press, 1961).

[10] For Pierce's general works, see Charles Sanders Pierce, *The Collected Papers of Charles Sanders Pierce*, 8 vol. (Cambridge, Mass.: Harvard University Press, 1931–1958). Pierce's "How to Make Our Ideas Clear" is in vol. 5, pp. 248–71.

But it was not until William James delivered a lecture in 1898 entitled "Philosophical Conceptions and Practical Results" that pragmatism became an acknowledged philosophical school.[11] And as John Dewey developed his "instrumentalism," pragmatism became a center of philosophical controversy in America during the early decades of this century. Pragmatism was primarily concerned with the process of thinking and how it influences the action of individuals, and vice versa. While pragmatists were each to carry its banner in different directions, the central thrust of this philosophical school is to view thought as a process that allows humans to adjust, adapt, and achieve goals in their environment.

Thus, pragmatists became concerned with symbols, language, and rational thinking as well as with the way action in the world is influenced by humans' mental capacities. Pierce saw pragmatism as concerned with "self-controlled conduct" and conduct "controlled by adequate deliberation," and hence, pragmatism was based upon:

> . . . a study of that experience of the phenomena of self-control which is common to all grown men and women; and it seems evident that to some extent, at least, it must always be so based. For it is to conceptions of deliberate conduct that pragmatism would trace the intellectual purport of symbols; and deliberate conduct is self-controlled conduct.[12]

For Pierce, then, pragmatism stressed the use of symbols and signs in thought and self-control, a point of emphasis that Mead was later to adopt. James and Dewey supplemented Pierce's emphasis by stressing that the process of thinking is intimately connected to the process of adaptation and adjustment. James stressed that "truth" is not absolute and enduring; rather, he argued that scientific as well as lay conceptions of truth are only as enduring as their ability to help people adjust and adapt to their circumstances.[13] Truth, in other words, is determined only by its "practical results." Dewey similarly emphasized the significance of thinking for achieving goals and adjusting to the environment. Thought, whether lay or scientific, is an "instrument" that can be used to achieve goals and purposes.[14]

Pragmatism emerged as a reaction to, and an effort to deal with, a number of scientific and philosophical events of the 19th century. First,

---

[11] This lecture was delivered at Berkeley, California. See also: William James, *Pragmatism* (Cambridge: Harvard University Press, 1975).

[12] Morris, *Pragmatic Movement*, p. 11.

[13] William James, *The Meaning of Truth: A Sequel to "Pragmatism"* (New York: Longmans, Green, 1909).

[14] John Dewey, *Human Nature and Conduct* (New York: Henry Holt, 1922).

the ascendance of Newtonian mechanics posed the question of whether all aspects of the universe, including human thought and action, could be reduced to invariant and mechanistic laws. To this challenge, pragmatists argued that such laws do not make human action mechanistic and wholly determinative, but rather, these laws are instruments to be used by humans in achieving goals.[15] Second, the theory of evolution offered the vision of continuity in life processes. To this idea, pragmatists added the notion that humans as a species, and as individuals, are engaged in a process of constant adjustment and adaptation to their environment and that thought represents the principal means of achieving such adjustment. Third, the doctrines of utilitarians presented a calculating, rational, and instrumental view of human action. To this perspective, pragmatists were highly receptive, although their concern was with the process of thought and how it is linked to action. Fourth, the ascendance of the scientific method with its emphasis on the verification of conceptual schemes through experienced data presented a consensual view of "proper" modes of investigation. To this point of emphasis, the pragmatists responded that all action involves an act of verification as people's thoughts and conceptions are "checked" against their experiences in the world. For the pragmatist, human life is a continuous application of the "scientific method" as people seek to cope with the world around them.[16]

Pragmatism thus represents the first distinctly American philosophical system. Mead was presonally tied to several of its advocates, while being intellectually involved in the debate surrounding the system and its critics. He clearly was influenced by the pragmatist's concern with the process of thinking and with the importance of symbols in thought. He accepted the metaphor that thought and action involve efforts to adjust and adapt to the environment. And he embraced the notion that such adaptation involves a continuous process of experiential verification of thought and action. In many ways, utilitarianism and Darwinism came to Mead through pragmatism, and hence to some extent, Mead must be considered a pragmatist. Yet Mead was also a behaviorist, and if his social psychology is to be given a label, it is more behavioristic than pragmatic.

Behaviorism

As a psychological perspective, behaviorism began from insights derived from observations of an accident. The Russian physiologist Ivan

---

[15] In particular, see John Dewey, *The Quest for Certainty* (New York: Minton, Balch, 1925); or James, *Meaning of Truth*.

[16] See, Morris, *Pragmatic Movement*, pp. 5–11.

Petrovich Pavlov discovered that experimental dogs associated food with the person bringing the food.[17] He observed, for instance, that dogs on whom he was performing secretory experiments would secrete saliva not only when presented food, but also when they heard their feeder's footsteps approaching. After considerable delay and personal agonizing,[18] Pavlov undertook a series of experiments on animals to understand such "conditioned responses." From these experiments, he developed several principles that later were to be incorporated into behaviorism. These include: (1) A stimulus consistently associated with another stimulus producing a given physiological response will, by itself, elicit that response. (2) Such conditioned responses can be extinguished when gratifications associated with stimuli are no longer forthcoming. (3) Stimuli that are similar to those producing a conditioned response can also elicit the same response as the original stimulus. (4) Stimuli that increasingly differ from those used to condition a particular response will decreasingly be able to elicit this response. Thus, Pavlov's experiments exposed the principles of conditioned responses, extinction, response generalization, and response discrimination. While Pavlov clearly recognized the significance of these findings of human behavior, his insights came to fruition in America under the tutelage of Edward Thorndike and John B. Watson— the founders of behaviorism.[19]

Edward Lee Thorndike conducted the first laboratory experiments on animals in America. In the course of these experiments, he observed that animals would retain response patterns for which they are rewarded.[20] For example, in experiments on kittens placed in a puzzle box, Thorndike found that they would engage in trial-and-error behavior until emitting that response allowing them to escape. And with each placement in the box, the kittens would engage in less trial-and-error behavior, thereby indicating that the gratifications associated with a response allowing the kitten to escape caused the kitten to learn and retain this response. From these and other studies, which were conducted at the same time as Pavlov's, Thorndike formulated three prinicples or laws: (1) the "law of effect" which holds that acts in a situation producing gratification will be more likely to occur in the future when that situation recurs;

---

[17] See, for relevant articles, lectures, and references, I. P. Pavlov, *Selected Works*, ed. K. S. Kostoyants, trans. S. Belsky (Moscow: Foreign Languages Publishing House, 1955); and *Lectures on Conditioned Reflexes*, 3d ed., trans. W. H. Gantt (New York: International Publishers, 1928).

[18] I. P. Pavlov, "Autobiography" in *Selected Works* pp. 41–44.

[19] For an excellent summary of their ideas, see Robert I. Watson, *The Great Psychologists*, 3d ed. (Philadelphia: Lippincott, 1971), pp. 417–46.

[20] Edward L. Thorndike, "Animal Intelligence: An Experimental Study of the Associative Processes in Animals," *Psychological Review Monograph*, Supplement 2, (1898).

(2) the "law of use" which states that situation-response connection is strengthened with repetitions and practice; and (3) the "law of disuse" which argues that the connection will weaken when practice is discontinued.[21]

These laws overlap with those presented by Pavlov, but there is one important difference. Thorndike's experiments were conducted by animals engaged in free trial-and-error behavior, whereas Pavlov's work was on the conditioning of physiological—typically glandular—responses in a tightly controlled laboratory situation. Thorndike's work could thus be seen as more directly relevant to human behavior in natural settings.

John B. Watson was only one of several thinkers to recognize the significance of Pavlov's and Thorndike's work,[22] but he soon became the dominant advocate of what was becoming explicitly known as "behaviorism." Watson's opening shot for the new science of behavior was fired in an article entitled, "Psychology as the Behaviorist Views It":

> Psychology as the behaviorist views it is a purely objective experimental branch of natural science. Its theoretical goal is the prediction and control of behavior. Introspection forms no essential part of its methods, nor is the scientific value of its data dependent upon the readiness with which they lend themselves to interpretation in terms of consciousness. The behaviorist, in efforts to get a unitary scheme of animal response, recognize no dividing line between man and brute.[23]

Watson thus became the advocate of the extreme behaviorism against which Mead so vehemently reacted.[24] For Watson, psychology is the study of stimulus-response relations and the only admissible evidence is overt behavior. Psychologists are to stay out of the "mystery box" of human consciousness and to study only observable behaviors as they are connected to observable stimuli. Mead rejected this assertion and argued that just because an activity such as thinking is not directly observable does not mean that it is not behavior. For as Mead was to

---

[21] See: Edward L. Thorndike, *The Elements of Psychology* (New York: Seiler, 1905), *The Fundamentals of Learning* (New York: Teachers College Press, 1932), and *The Psychology of Wants, Interests, and Attitudes* (New York: D. Appleton, 1935).

[22] The others included: Max F. Meyer, *Psychology of the Other-One* (Columbus: Missouri Book, 1921); and Albert P. Weiss, *A Theoretical Basis of Human Behavior* (Columbus: Adams, 1925).

[23] J. B. Watson, "Psychology as the Behaviorist Views It," *Psychological Review* 20 (1913):158–77. For other basic works by Watson, see *Psychology from the Standpoint of a Behaviorist*, 3d ed. (Philadelphia: Lippincott, 1929); *Behavior: An Introduction to Comparative Psychology* (New York: Henry Holt, 1914).

[24] For example, in his *Mind, Self and Society* (Chicago: University of Chicago Press, 1934), Mead has 18 references to Watson's work.

argue, covert thinking and the capacity to view onself in situations are nonetheless behaviors, and hence, are subject to the same laws as overt behaviors.

Mead thus rejected extreme behaviorism, but accepted its general principle: behaviors are learned as a result of gratifications associated with them. In accordance with the views of pragmatists, and consistent with Mead's Darwinian metaphor, the gratifications of humans typically involve adjustment to a social environment. And most important, some of the most distinctive behaviors of humans are covert, involving thinking, reflection, and self-awareness. In contrast to Watson's behaviorism, Mead was to postulate what some have called a *social behaviorism*. From this perspective, covert and overt behaviors are to be understood in terms of their capacity to produce adjustment to society.

In sum, we can conclude that Mead borrowed the broad assumptions from a number of intellectual perspectives, particularly utilitarianism, Darwinism, pragmatism, and behaviorism. Utilitarians and pragmatists emphasized the process of thinking and rational conduct; utilitarians and Darwinists stressed the importance of competitive struggle and selection of attributes; Darwinists and pragmatists argued for the importance of adaptation and adjustment to an understanding of thought and action; and behaviorists presented a view of learning as the association of behaviors with gratification-producing stimuli. Each of these general ideas became a part of Mead's theoretical scheme, but as Mead synthesized these ideas, they took on new meaning.

Mead was not only influenced by these general intellectual perspectives; he also borrowed specific concepts from a variety of scholars, only some of whom worked within these general perspectives. By taking specific concepts, reconciling them with each other, and then incorporating them into the metaphors of these four general perspectives, Mead was able to produce a major theoretical breakthrough.

WILHELM WUNDT AND G. H. MEAD

Even a casual reading of Mead's written work and posthumously published lectures reveals a large number of citations to the German psychologist Wilhelm Wundt.[25] Wundt is often given credit for being the father of psychology, since by the 1860s, he was conducting a series of experiments that could be clearly defined as psychological in nature. And in

---

[25] In *Mind, Self, and Society* alone, there are over 20 references to Wundt's ideas.

the 1870s, he was one of the first, along with the American, William James, to establish a psychological laboratory.

Mead studied briefly in Germany, although not in Heidelberg where Wundt had established his laboratory and school of loyal followers. Yet there can be little doubt that Wundt's eminence prompted Mead to read his works carefully.[26] At first glance, it might appear that Mead, the philosopher, would find little of interest in Wundt's voluminous output. Most of Wundt's laboratory work deals with efforts to understand the structure of consciousness—a point of emphasis not conducive to Mead's insistence on mind as a process. However, Wundt was also a philosopher, social psychologist, and sociologist. Although Wundt would write strictly psychological books like *Physiological Psychology*, he also founded the journal *Philosophical Studies*, in which he published his laboratory studies. Indeed, he saw little reason to distinguish psychology from philosophy. He also was to devote many pages in his *Outlines of Psychology* to gestures, language, self-consciousness, mental communities, customs, myths, and child development—all topics likely to interest the philosopher and social psychologist, George Herbert Mead. Moreover, his *Elements of Folk Psychology* was one of the first distinctly social-psychological studies, examining the broad evolutionary development of human thought and culture. Thus, Wundt was a scholar of great range and enormous productive energy. Mead would apparently find much in the work of Wundt to stimulate his own thought.

Wundt's View of Gestures

In much of his work, Mead devoted considerable space to Wundt's view of "gestures" and "speech."[27] Mead argued that Wundt was the first to recognize that gestures represent signs marking the course of ongoing action and that animals use these signs as ways of adjusting to each other. Human language, Wundt had argued, represents only an extension of this basic process in lower animals, since common and consensual meanings were, over the course of human evolution, given

---

[26] For basic references on Wundt's work, see Wilhelm Wundt, *Principles of Physiological Psychology* (New York: Macmillan, 1904; originally published in 1874); *Lectures on Human and Animal Psychology*, 2d ed. (New York: Macmillan, 1894; originally published in 1892), *Outlines of Psychology*, 7th ed. (Leipzig: Engleman, 1907; originally published in 1896); and *Elements of Folk Psychology; Outlines of a Psychological History of the Development of Mankind* (London: George Allen, 1916).

[27] See, for a more complete discussion, Wilhelm Wundt, *The Language of Gestures* (Hague: Mouton, 1973).

to signs. And as human mental capacities had grown, such gestures could be used for deliberate communication and interaction.

All of these points of emphasis, while greatly distorted by Wundt's poor ethnographic accounts, were to be incorporated in altered form into Mead's scheme.[28] Gestures were to be viewed as the basis for communication and interaction, and language was to be defined as gestures that carry common meanings. And as Wundt had implied, humans are unique creatures, and society is possible only by virtue of language and its use to create customs, myths, and other symbol systems.

Wundt's View of "Mental Communities"

Mead did not give Wundt credit for inspiring more than a sociological vision of gestures and language. Yet sprinkled throughout Wundt's work are ideas that bear considerable resemblance to those developed by Mead. One such idea is what Wundt termed the *mental community*.[29] Wundt saw the development of speech, self-consciousness, and mental activity in children as emerging out of interaction with the social environment. Such interaction, he argued, makes possible identification with a mental community which guides and directs human action and interaction in ways that are functionally analogous to the regulation of lower animals by instincts. Such mental communities can vary in their nature and extensiveness, producing great variations in human action and patterns of social organization. Just as Durkheim in France had emphasized the significance of the "collective conscious," Wundt saw humans as regulated by a variety of "mental communities." Mead was, we suspect, to translate this notion of mental community into his vision of "generalized others" or "communities of attitudes" that regulate human action and organization.

In sum, then, Mead appears to have taken from Wundt two critical points. First, interaction is a process of gestural communication, with language being a more developed form of such communication. Secondly, social organization is more than a process of interaction among people, it is also a process of socialization in which humans acquire the ability to create and use mental communities to regulate their action and interaction. As we will come to see, these two points are at the core of Mead's theory of mind, self, and society.

---

[28] See, for example, Wundt, *Folk Psychology.*
[29] Wundt, *Outlines of Psychology*, pp. 296–98.

WILLIAM JAMES AND G. H. MEAD

By 1890, William James was the most prominent psychologist in America, attracting students and worldwide attention. Yet James was also a philosopher who, along with Dewey, became the foremost advocate of pragmatism. Mead borrowed from both James's philosophy and his psychology, incorporating the general thrust of James's philosophy and his specific views on consciousness and self-consciousness.

James's Pragmatism

In many ways, James was the most extreme of the pragmatists, advocating the view that there is no such thing as "absolute truth."[30] Truth is temporary and lasts only as long as it works, that is, only as long as it allows for adjustment and adaptation to the environment. James thus rejected the notion that truth involves a search for isomorphism between theoretical principles and empirical reality and that science represents an effort to increase the degree of isomorphism. For James, theories are merely "instruments" to be used for a time in an effort to facilitate adjustment. Hence, objective, permanent, and enduring truth cannot be found.

Mead never completely accepted this extreme position. Indeed, much of his work was directed at discovering some of the fundamental principles describing the basic relationship between individuals and society. Mead did, however, accept and embrace the pragmatic notion that human life is a constant process of adjustment and that the faculty for consciousness is the key to understanding the nature of this adjustment.

James's View of Consciousness

James defined psychology as the "science of mental life."[31] As a science, the goal of psychology is to understand the nature of mental processes—that is, the nature of "feelings, desires, cognitions, reasons, decisions, and the like."[32] His classic text, *The Principles of Psychology*, became the most important work in American psychology, since it sought to summarize what was then known about mental life. It also contained James's interpretation of mental phenomena, and by far the most important of these interpretations was James's conceptualization of conscious-

---

[30] James, *Meaning of Truth.*
[31] William James, *The Principles of Psychology* (New York: Henry Holt, 1890), p. 1.
[32] Ibid.

ness as a process. For James, consciousness is a "stream" and "flow," not a structure of elements, as Wundt had proposed.[33] Thus, for James, "mind" is simply a process of thinking, and it is with this simple fact that psychological investigation must begin:[34]

> The only thing which psychology has a right to postulate at the outset is the fact of thinking itself, and that must first be taken up and analyzed.

James then went on to list five characteristics of thought: (1) thought is personal and always, to some degree, idiosyncratic to each individual; (2) thought is always changing; (3) thought is continuous; (4) to the individual, it appears to deal with objects in an external world; and (5) it is selective and focuses on some objects to the exclusion of others.[35] Of these characteristics, Mead appears to have been most influenced by 4 and 5. For Mead, mind is to be seen as a process of selectively denoting objects and of responding to these objects. While the details of his conceptualization of thinking reflect Dewey's influence more than that of James, it is likely that this early discussion by James shaped Mead's emphasis on selective perception of objects in the environment.

Far more influential on Mead's thought than James's view of consciousness in general was James's conceptualization of "self-consciousness."[36] Here, Mead borrowed much and was directly influenced by James's recognition that one of the objects in the flow of consciousness is oneself.

James's View of "Self-consciousness"

James's examination of self began with the assertion that people recognize themselves as objects in empirical situations. He called this process the *empirical self* or *me*—the latter term being adopted by Mead in his examination of self-images. But James went on to describe various types of empirical selves that all people evidence: (1) the material self, (2) the social self, and (3) the spiritual self. Moreover, each type or aspect of self was seen by James as involving two dimensions: (1) self-feelings (emotions about oneself) and (2) self-seekings (actions which are prompted by each self). Not only are there types of selves, revealing variations with respect to self-feelings and self-seeking, but there is a hierarchy among the various selves. Thus, James offered an elaborate

---

[33] James had also developed the notion of a "stream of consciousness" in his *The Varieties of Religious Experience* (New York: Longmans, Green, 1902).

[34] James, *Principles of Psychology*, p. 224.

[35] Ibid., pp. 225–90.

[36] Ibid., pp. 291–401.

taxonomy of self-related processes, and although Mead's own conceptualization was sparse by comparison, he selectively borrowed from the entire scheme.

Types of Empirical Selves. For James, the "material self" embraces people's conceptions of their body as well as their other possessions, since both one's actual body and possessions evoke similar feelings and actions. The "social self" is, in reality, a series of selves which people have in different types of situations. Thus, one may have somewhat different self-feelings and action tendencies depending upon the type of social situation—whether work, family, club, community, and so on. For Mead, this vision of a "social self" was to become most important, for people's self-feelings and actions are, Mead was to argue, most influenced by their conception of themselves in social meetings. The "spiritual self" was not clearly described by James, but it appears to embody those most intimate feelings that people have about themselves—that is, their worth, their talents, their strengths, and their failings. In *The Principles of Psychology* James summarized his conceptualization of empirical selves, and its constituent dimension, with a table; which is shown in Table 21–1.[37]

TABLE 21–1
James's Conceptualization of Empirical Selves

The Empirical Life of Self is Divided into

	Material	*Social*	*Spiritual*
Self-seeking.	Bodily appetites and instincts Love of adornment, foppery, acquisitiveness, constructiveness, Love of home, and so on	Desire to please, be noticed, admired, and so on Sociability, emulation, envy, love, pursuit of honor, ambition, and so on	Intellectual, moral and religious aspiration, conscientiousness
Self-estimation.	Personal vanity, modesty, and so on Pride of wealth, fear of poverty	Social and family pride, vainglory, snobbery, humility, shame, and so on	Sense of moral or mental superiority, purity, and so on Sense of inferiority or of guilt

The Hierarchy of Empirical Selves. James felt that some aspects of different empirical selves are more important than others. As he noted:

[37] Ibid., p. 329.

> A tolerably unanimous opinion ranges the different selves of which a man may be 'seized and possessed,' and the consequent different orders of his self-regard, in an [sic] *hierarchical scale, with the bodily Self at the bottom, the spiritual Self at Top, and the extracorporeal material selves and the various social selves between.*[38]

Thus, some degree of unity among a person's self is achieved through their hierarchical ordering, with self-feelings and action tendencies being greatest for those selves high in the hierarchy. A further source of unity comes from the nonempirical self, or what James termed the *pure ego*.

The Pure Ego and Personal Identity. Above these empirical selves, James argued, is a unity. People have "a personal identity" or *pure ego* in that they have sense of continuity and stability about themselves as objects. Like all sensations, humans take their somewhat diverse empirical selves and integrate them, seeing in them continuity and sameness.[39] Mead was, no doubt, greatly influenced by this conception of a stable and unified self-conception. For as Mead was to argue, humans develop, over time, from their experiences in the empirical world, a more "unified" or "complete" self—that is, a stable self-conception. This stable self-conception, Mead was to emphasize, gives individuals a sense of personal continuity and their actions in society a degree of stability and predictability.

In sum, then, Mead's view of self as one of the distinctive features of humans was greatly influenced by William James's work. James was not as concerned as Mead was with understanding the emergence of self or in its consequences for the social order. But he provided Mead with several critical insights about the nature of self: (1) self is a process of seeing oneself as an object in the stream of conscious awareness; (2) self varies from one empirical situation to another, and yet (3) self also reveals unity and stability across situations. Mead never adopted James's taxonomy, but he took the broad contours of James's outline and demonstrated their significance for understanding the nature of human action, interaction, and organization.

CHARLES HORTON COOLEY AND G. H. MEAD

Mead and Charles Horton Cooley were approximately contemporaries, and early in their careers at the University of Michigan, they were colleagues. Their direct interaction was, no doubt, significant, but Cooley's

---

[38] Ibid., p. 313 (emphasis in original).
[39] Ibid., p. 334.

influence extended beyond their period of colleagial contact. Indeed, it is from Cooley that Mead was to adopt a number of critical insights into the origins and nature of self as well as its significance for social organization.

It must be admitted that Cooley's sociology is often vague, excessively mentalistic, and highly moralistic. Yet, we can observe several lines of influence on Mead in Cooley's recognition that (1) society is constructed from reciprocal interaction, (2) interaction occurs through the exchange of gestures, (3) self is created from, and allows for the maintenance of, patterns of social organization, and (4) social organization is possible by virtue of people's attachment to groups that link them to the larger institutions of society. We should, therefore, examine in more detail these lines of influence.

Cooley's View of Social Organization

Cooley held the view that society is an organic whole in which specific social processes work to create, maintain, and change networks of reciprocal activity.[40] Much as Mead was to argue, Cooley saw the "vast tissue" of society as constructed from diverse social forms—from small groups to large-scale social institutions. Yet, the cement that links these diverse forms together is the capacity of humans to interact with each other and to share common ideas and conceptions. Such interaction is dependent upon the unique capacities of humans to use gestures and language.

Cooley's View of Interaction

Cooley saw that humans have the ability to assign common meanings and interpretations to their gestures—whether these be words, bodily countenance, facial expressions, and other gestural emissions. In this way humans can communicate, and out of this communication, they establish social relations.

> By communication is here meant the mechanism through which human relations exist and develop—all the symbols of the mind, together with the means of conveying them through space and preserving them in time.[41]

Mead was to accept Cooley's view of social organization as constructed gestural communication. But more importantly, Cooley gave Mead a

---

[40] Charles Horton Cooley, *Social Process* (New York: Scribner's, 1918), p. 28.

[41] Charles Horton Cooley, *Social Organization: A Study of the Larger Mind* (New York: Scribner's, 1916), p. 61.

clue as to how gestural communication leads to interaction and organization. By reading each other's gestures, people are able to "read each other's mind"—that is, to see and interpret the dispositions of others. Hence;

> Society is an interweaving and interworking of mental selves. I imagine your mind . . . I dress my mind before yours and expect that you will dress yours before mine.[42]

Mead was to take this somewhat vague idea and translate it into an explicit view of interaction and social organization as a process of reading gestures, placing oneself mentally into the position of others, and adjusting conduct so as to cooperate with others. Moreover, Mead was to accept Cooley's recognition that "self" is the critical link in the creation and maintenance of society from patterns of reciprocal communication and interaction.

Cooley's View of Self

Cooley emphasized that humans have the capacity for self-consciousness. This capacity emerges out of interaction with others in groups, and once it exists, it allows people to organize themselves into society. Mead was to adopt the general thrust of this argument, although he was to make it considerably more explicit and coherent. Mead appears to have taken three distinct lines of argument from Cooley's somewhat vague and rambling discussion: (1) self as constructed from the *looking glass* of other people's gestures, (2) self as emerging out of interaction in groups, and (3) self as a basis for self-control, and hence, social organization. Each of these is examined below.

The "Looking-Glass Self." Cooley adopted William James's view of self as the ability to see and recognize oneself as an object. But he added a critical insight: humans use the gestures of others to see themselves. The images that people have of themselves are similar to reflections from a looking glass, or mirror; they are provided by the reactions of others to one's behavior. Thus, by reading the gestures of others, humans see themselves as an object:

> As we see our face, figure, and dress in the glass, and are interested in them because they are ours, ... so in imagination we perceive in another's

[42] Charles Horton Cooley, *Life and the Student* (New York: Alfred A. Knopf, 1927), p. 200.

mind some thought of our appearance, manners, aims, deeds, character, friends, and so on, and are variously affected by it.[43]

As people see themselves in the looking glass of other people's gestures, then, they (1) imagine their appearance in the eyes of others, (2) sense the judgment of others, and (3) have self-feelings about themselves. Thus, during the process of interaction, people develop self-consciousness and self-feelings. While Cooley did not develop the idea in any great detail, he implied that humans develop, over time and through repeated glances in the looking glass, a more stable sense of self.

The Emergence of Self. Cooley argued that the life history of an individual is evolutionary. Because their ability to read gestures is limited, young infants cannot initially see themselves as objects in the looking glass. But with time, practice, biological maturation, and exposure to varieties of others, children come to see themselves in the looking glass and they develop feelings about themselves. Such a process, Cooley felt, is inevitable as long as the young must interact with others, since as the young act on their environment, others will react and this reaction will be perceived.[44] It is through this process, as it occurs during infancy, childhood, and adolescence, that an individual's "personality" is formed. And as Mead was to argue, the existence of a more stable set of self-feelings gives human action stability and predictability, thereby facilitating cooperation with others.

Self and Social Control. Cooley saw self as only one aspect of consciousness in general. And thus, he divided consciousness into three aspects: (1) "self-consciousness" or self-awareness of, and feelings about, oneself; (2) "social consciousness" or a person's perceptions of, and attitudes toward, other people; and (3) "public consciousness" or an individual's view of others as organized in a "communicative group."[45] Cooley saw all three aspects of consciouness as "phases of a single whole."

Cooley never developed these ideas to any great degree, but Mead apparently saw much potential in these distinctions. For Mead, the capacity to see oneself as an object, to perceive the dispositions of others, and to assume the perspective of a broader "public" or "community" gives people a basis for stable action and cooperative interaction. It is because of these capacities, then, that society is possible.

---

[43] Charles Horton Cooley, *Human Nature and the Social Order* (New York: Scribner's, 1902), p. 184.

[44] Ibid., pp. 137–211.

[45] Cooley, *Social Organization*, p. 12.

Cooley's View of Primary Groups

Cooley argued that the most basic unit of society is the "primary group," which was defined as those associations characterized by "intimate face-to-face association and cooperation."

> They are primary in several senses but chiefly in that they are fundamental in forming the social nature and ideals of individuals. The result of intimate association, psychologically, is a certain fusion of individualities in a common whole, so that one's very self, for many purposes at least, is the common life and purpose of the group.[46]

Thus, the looking glass of gestures emitted by those in one's primary groups are the most important in the emergence and maintenance of self-feelings. Moreover, the link between individuals and the broader institutional structure of society is the primary group. Institutions could not, Cooley maintained, be maintained unless past traditions and public morals are given immediate relevance to individuals through intimacy of primary groups. Indeed, for Cooley, primary groups "are the springs of life, not only for the individual but for social institutions."[47]

Cooley's concept of the primary group appears to have influenced Mead in two ways. First, Mead retained Cooley's position that self emerges, in large part, by virtue of an individual's participation in face-to-face, organized activity. Second, Mead implicitly argued that one of the bridges between the individual and broader institutional structure of society is the small group, although Cooley's emphasis on this point was much greater than Mead's.

Thus, Mead was greatly influenced by the work of Charles Horton Cooley. Although much of his work is excessively moralistic and goes to mentalistic extremes, Mead saw the full implications of Cooley's ideas for understanding the nature of the relationship between the individual and society. As we will come to appreciate in the next chapter, Mead borrowed, extended, and integrated into a more coherent theory Cooley's views on gestures, interaction, self and its emergence, and social organization.

JOHN DEWEY AND G. H. MEAD

John Dewey and Mead were initially young colleagues at the University of Michigan, and when Dewey moved to the then new University of

---

[46] Ibid., p. 23.
[47] Ibid., p. 27.

Chicago in 1894, he invited Mead to join him in the Department of Philosophy and Psychology. Mead and Dewey were thus colleagues until 1905 when Dewey left for Columbia University. As colleagues, Dewey and Mead engaged in much dialogue, therefore, it is not surprising that their thought reveals many similarities. Yet it was Dewey who was the intellectual star of Chicago, and it was Dewey who wrote in many diverse areas and generated much attention, in and outside the academic world.[48] In contrast, the retiring Mead, who had great difficulty writing, was constantly in Dewey's shadow. But ironically, it is Mead who, in the long run, made the more important intellectual contribution to sociology.

Mead accepted the broad contours of Dewey's pragmatism, but a more important influence on Mead's thought was Dewey's conceptualization of thought and thinking. Thus, as Dewey extended his brilliance into philosophy, morals, education, methodology, the history of science, psychology, and virtually any area of inquiry that caught his interest,[49] Mead selectively borrowed several key ideas from Dewey's wide-ranging inquiries and incorporated them into a vision of what he was to term *mind*.

Dewey's Pragmatism

Dewey's pragmatism attacked the traditional dualisms of philosophy: knower and known, objects and thought of objects, and mind and external world. Dewey thought that this dualism is false and that the act of knowing and the "things" to be known are interdependent. Objects may exist in a world external to an individual, but their existence and properties are determined by the process of acting toward these objects. For Dewey, the basic process of human life consists of organisms acting

---

[48] Dewey's bibliography is over 75 pages long, indicating his incredible productivity.

[49] Dewey's most important works, in addition to those cited earlier, include: *Outlines of a Critical Theory of Ethics* (Ann Arbor: Register, 1891); *The Study of Ethics* (Ann Arbor: Register, 1894); *The School and Society* (Chicago: University of Chicago Press, 1900); *Studies in Logical Theory* (Chicago: University of Chicago Press, 1903); with James H. Tufts, *Ethics* (New York: Henry Holt, 1908); *How We Think* (Boston: D. C. Heath, 1910); *The Influence of Darwin on Philosophy* (New York: Henry Holt, 1910); *Democracy and Education* (New York: Macmillan, 1916); *Essays in Experimental Logic* (Chicago: University of Chicago Press, 1916); *Reconstruction in Philosophy* (New York: Henry Holt, 1920); *Experience and Nature* (La Salle, Ill.: Open Court, 1925); *Philosphy and Civilization* (New York: Minton, Balch, 1931); *Art as Experience* (New York: Minton, Balch, 1934); *A Common Faith* (New Haven: Yale University Press, 1934); *Logic: The Theory of Inquiry* (New York: Henry Holt, 1938); *Theory of Valuation* (Chicago: University of Chicago Press, 1939); *Problems of Men* (New York: Philosophical Library, 1946); and with A. F. Bentley, *Knowing and the Known* (Boston: Beacon Press, 1949).

on, and making inquiry into, their environment. Indeed, the history of human thought has been a quest for greater certainty about the consequences of action. In a scheme that resembles Comte's "law of the three stages," Dewey argued that religion represented the primitive way to achieve certainty; the classical world classified experience to achieve certainty, and the modern world now seeks to control nature through the discovery of its laws of operation.[50] With the development of modern science, Dewey argued, a new problem emerges: moral values can no longer be legitimated by God or by appeals to the natural order.[51]

Such is the philosophical dilemma that Dewey proposed and, then, resolved with his pragmatism. Values, morality, and other evaluational ideas are to be found in the action of people as they seek to cope with their environment. Value is discovered and found as people try to adjust and adapt to a problematic situation. Thus, when humans do not know the morality of a situation, they will seek to construct one and use it as an "instrument" to facilitate their adjustment to that situation. Value-oriented action is like all thought and action: it emerges from people's acts in a problematic situation. Mead was never to absorb the details of Dewey's "instrumentalism" or Dewey's almost frantic efforts to create the "good society."[52] But he did not adopt the view that thinking and thought arise from the process of dealing with problematic situations.

Dewey's View of Thinking

Dewey's pragmatism led him to a vision of thinking as a process involving: (1) blockage of impulses, (2) selective perception of the environment, (3) rehearsal of alternatives, (4) overt action, (5) assessment of consequences; then if a situation is still problematic, a new sequence of perception, rehearsal, and action, and so on until the problematic situation is eliminated.[53]

Mead was to adopt two aspects of this vision. First, he saw thinking as part of a larger process of action. Thinking occurs when an organism's impulses are blocked and when it is in maladjustment with its environment.[54] This line of argument became a part of Mead's theory

---

[50] Dewey, Quest for Certainty.

[51] Dewey, Influence of Darwin, p. 22.

[52] However, it should be emphasized that Mead's ideals paralleled those of Dewey and that he was occasionally drawn into various reform causes.

[53] See, for example, Dewey, Human Nature and Conduct and How We Think.

[54] Indeed, Mead appeared to borrow Dewey's exact terms in Human Nature and Conduct.

of motivation and "stages of the act." Second, thinking for Mead involved selective perception of objects, covert and imaginative rehearsal of alternatives, anticipation of the consequences of alternatives, and selection of a line of conduct. These behavioral capacities Mead was to term *mind*, and they were clearly adapted from Dewey's discussion of human nature and conduct.[55]

MEAD'S SYNTHESIS

We can now appreciate the intellectual world as Mead encountered it. The convergence of utilitarianism, pragmatism, Darwinism, and behaviorism gave Mead a general set of assumptions for understanding human behavior. The specific concepts of Wundt, James, Cooley, and Dewey gave Mead the necessary intellectual tools to understand that humans are unique by virtue of their behavioral capacities for mind and self. Conversely, mind and self emerge out of gestural interaction in society. But once they emerge, mind and self make for a distinctive form of gestural interaction and for an entirely revolutionary creation: symbolically regulated patterns of social organization. In broad strokes, such is the nature of Mead's synthesis. We can now examine the details of this synthesis in the next chapter. But we should remember that Mead, like most great intellects, built his synthesis on "the shoulders of giants."

---

[55] Ibid.

22

GEORGE HERBERT MEAD II:
THE BASIC WORKS

We are confronted with an initial problem in analyzing Mead's basic works. Most of Mead's major works are published notes of his course lectures in philosophy and social psychology. As such, the four posthumous books that constitute the core of Mead's thought are somewhat long and rambling. Moreover, with the exception of *Mind, Self, and Society,* his ideas are distinctly philosophical rather than sociological in tone.[1] Our goal in this chapter, therefore, is to pull from Mead's philosophical works key sociological insights, while devoting most of our analysis to the explicitly social-psychological work, *Mind, Self, and Society.* At the same time, we will make reference to some of Mead's published essays, which can supplement our analysis.

Our presentation will begin with an analysis of *Mind, Self, and Society,* supplemented by various essays and references to the other philosophical books. Then we will explore the sociologically significant ideas in *The Philosophy of the Act.* And we will close with a short statement on Mead's broader philosophical vision, as revealed in *The Philosophy of the Present* and *Movements of Thought in the Nineteenth Century,* especially as this vision applies to broader sociological concerns.

---

[1] The philosophical tone of his posthumously published lectures is revealed in the titles of the four books: *The Philosophy of the Present* (La Salle, Ill.: Open Court, 1959; originally published in 1932), *Mind, Self, and Society* (Chicago: University of Chicago Press, 1934), *Movements of Thought in the Nineteenth Century* (Chicago: University of Chicago Press, 1936), and *The Philosophy of the Act* (Chicago: University of Chicago Press, 1938). *Mind, Self, and Society,* contains a bibliography of Mead's published work (pp. 390–92).

MIND, SELF, AND SOCIETY

Mead's "book" on *Mind, Self, and Society* represents verbatim transcripts from his famous course on social psychology at the University of Chicago. While the notes come from the 1927 and 1930 versions of the course, the basic ideas on social interaction, personality, and social organization had been clearly developed a decade earlier.

At the time that Mead addressed his students, the behaviorism of J. B. Watson and others simply abandoned serious effort to understand consciousness, personality, and other variables in the "black box" of human cognition. Mead felt that such a "solution" to studying psychological processes was unacceptable.[2] Mead also felt that the opposite philosophical tendency to view "mind," "spirit," "will," and other psychological states as a kind of spiritual entity was untenable. What is required, he argued, is for mind and self, as the two most distinctive aspects of human personality, and for "society" as maintained by mind and self, to be viewed as part of ongoing social processes.

Mead's View of the "Life Process"

The Darwinian theory of evolution provided Mead with a view of life as a process of adaptation to environmental conditions. The attributes of a species, therefore, are the result of selection for those characteristics that allow for adaptation to the conditions in which a species finds itself. This theory provided Mead with a general metaphor for viewing life in general, and thus, with a broad perspective for analyzing humans. Pragmatism, as philosophical doctrine, represented one way of translating the Darwinian metaphor into principles for understanding human behavior: humans are "pragmatic" creatures who use their faculties for achieving "adjustment" to the world, and conversely, out of making adjustments to the world, much of what is unique to any individual arises. Dewey's pragmatism, termed *instrumentalism*, stressed the importance of critical and rational thought in making life-adjustments to the world, giving Mead a view of thinking as the basic adjustment by which humans survive. Behaviorism, as a prominent psychological school of thought, converged with this emphasis in pragmatism, since it emphasized that all animals tend to retain those responses to environmental stimuli that are rewarded or reinforced. While the processes of thinking were regarded

---

[2] As he observed with respect to Watson's efforts to deal with "subjective experience": John B. Watson's attitude was that of the Queen in *Alice in Wonderland*—"Off with their heads!"—there were no such things. (Mead, *Mind, Self, and Society*, pp. 2–3.)

as too "psychical" by behaviorists like Watson, the stress on the retention of behaviors that are reinforced was not inconsistent with Darwinian notions of adaptation and survival or with pragmatist ideas of response and adjustment. Even utilitarianism, especially that of such thinkers as Jeremy Bentham who emphasized the pleasure and pain principles, could be seen by Mead as compatible with the theory of evolution, behaviorism, and pragmatism. The utilitarian emphasis on "utility," "pleasure," and "pain" was certainly compatible with behaviorist notions of reinforcement; the utilitarian concern with rational thought and the weighing of alternatives was compatible with Dewey's instrumentalism and its concept of critical thinking; and the utilitarian view that order emerges out of competition among free individuals seemed to parallel Darwinian notions of struggle as the underlying principle of the biotic order.

Thus, the unique attributes of humans, such as their capacity to use language, their ability to talk to each other, and to themselves, their ability to view themselves as objects, and their capacity to reason, must all be viewed as emerging out of life process of adaptation and adjustment. Mind and self cannot be ignored, as behaviorists often sought to do, nor can they be seen as a kind of mystical and spiritual force that elevated humans out of the basic life processes influencing all species. Humans as species evolved like other life forms, and hence, their most distinctive attributes—mind, self, and society—must be viewed as emerging out of the basic process of adaptation. Further, each individual member of the human species is like the individuals of other species: what they are is the result of the common biological heritage of their species as well as their adjustment to the particulars of their environment.

Mead's Social Behaviorism

Mead did not define his work as *social* behaviorism, but subsequent commentators have used this term to distinguish his work from Watsonian behaviorism. In contrast to Watson, who simply denied the distinctiveness of subjective consciousness, Mead felt that it is possible to use broad behavioristic principles to understand "subjective behavior":

> Watson apparently assumes that to deny the existence of mind or consciousness as a psychical [sic] stuff, substance, or entity is to deny its existence altogether, and that a naturalistic or behavioristic account of it as such is out of the question. But, on the contrary, we may deny its existence as a psychical entity without denying its existence in some other sense at all; and if we then conceive of it functionally, and as a natural

rather than a transcendental phenomenon, it becomes possible to deal with it in behavioristic terms.[3]

If subjective experiences in humans are viewed as behavior, then it is possible to understand them in behavioristic terms. For the unique mental capacities of humans are a mode of behavior that arises from reinforcement processes that explain nonsubjective and overt behavior. Of particular importance for understanding the attributes of humans, then, is the reinforcement that comes from adaptation and adjustment to environmental conditions. At some point in the distant past, the unique mental capacities of humans, and the creation of society employing these capacities, emerged out of the process of natural selection under natural environmental conditions. But once the unique patterns of human organization are created, the "environment" for any individual is social—that is, it is an environment of other people to whom an individual must adapt and adjust.

Thus, social behaviorism stresses the processes by which individuals come to acquire a certain behavioral repertoire by virtue of their adjustments to ongoing patterns of social organization. Thus, the process of analysis begins with the observable fact that organized activity occurs and, then, attempts to understand the particular actions of individuals in terms of their adjustment to such organized activity:

> We are not, in social psychology, building up the behavior of the social group in terms of the behavior of separate individuals composing it; rather, we are starting out with a given social whole of complex group activity, into which we analyze (as elements) the behavior of each of the separate individuals composing it. We attempt, that is, to explain the conduct of the individual in terms of the organized conduct of the social group, rather than to account for the organized conduct of the social group in terms of the conduct of the separate individuals belonging to it.[4]

The behavior of individuals, not just their observable actions but also their internal behaviors of thinking, assessing, and evaluating, must be analyzed within a social context. For what is distinctively human emerges out of adjustment to ongoing social activity or "society." Thus, Mead's social behaviorism must be distinguished from the behavioristic approach of Watson[5] in two ways. First, the existence of inner subjective experiences is not denied or viewed as methodologically irrelevant,[6] but rather,

---

[3] Ibid., p. 10.

[4] Ibid., p. 7.

[5] And of course, the more recent version of B. F. Skinner and others of this stripe.

[6] That is, since they cannot be directly observed, they cannot be studied.

these experiences are viewed as behavior. Second, the behaviors of humans—including those distinctly human behaviors of mind and self—arise out of adaptation and adjustment to ongoing and organized social activity. Reinforcement is thus seen as that which facilitates adjustment and adaptation to society.

Mead's Behavioristic View of Mind

For any given individual, "mind" is a type of behavioral response that emerges out of interaction with others in a social context. Without interaction, mind could not exist:

> We must regard mind, then, arising and developing within the social process, within the empirical matrix of social interactions. We must, that is, get an inner individual experience from the standpoint of social acts which include the experiences of separate individuals in a social context wherein those individuals interact. The processes of experience which the human brain makes possible are made possible only for a group of interacting individuals: only for individual organisms which are members of a society; not for the organism in isolation from other individual organisms.[7]

Gestures and Mind. The social process in which mind emerges is one of communication with gestures. Mead gave the German psychologist Wilhelm Wundt credit for understanding the central significance of the gesture to communication and interaction. In contrast to Darwin, who had viewed gestures as expressions of emotions, Wundt recognized that a gesture is that part of ongoing behavior of one organism that stimulates behavior of another organism.[8] Mead took this basic idea and extended it in ways that became the basis for not only the emergence of mind and self but also for the creation, maintenance, and change of society.

Mead formulated the concept of the "conversation of gestures" to describe the simplest form of interaction. During action on the part of one organism, gestures are emitted that stimulate a response from a second organism. In turn, the response of the second organism involves emission of gestures which stimulate an "adjusted response" from the first organism. Then, if interaction still continues, the adjusted response of the first organism involves emitting gestures that result in yet another

---

[7] Mead, *Mind, Self, and Society*, p. 133.

[8] As Mead observed: "The term 'gesture' may be identified with these beginnings of social acts which are stimuli for the response of other forms." (Ibid., p. 43.)

adjustment of behavior by the second organism, and so on, as long as the two organisms continue to interact. Mead frequently termed this conversation of gestures the *triadic matrix*, because it involves three inter-related elements:

1. Gestural emission by one organism as it acts on its environment.
2. A response by another organism in the environment as it reacts to this gestural emission. This response then becomes a gestural stimulus to the acting organism.
3. An adjusted response by the acting organism that takes into account the gestural stimuli of the responding organism.

This triadic matrix constitutes the simplest form of communication and interaction among organisms. It is the form of interaction, Mead felt, that typifies "lower animals" and human infants. For example, if one dog growls, indicating to another dog that its about to attack, then the other will react, perhaps by running away, requiring the growling dog to adjust its response by chasing the fleeing dog or by turning else-where to vent its aggressive impulses. Or, to take another example, a hungry infant cries which, in turn, arouses a response in its mother (for example, the mother feeds the infant) that in turn results in an adjusted response by the infant.

Much of the significance of Mead's discussion of the triadic matrix is that the mentalistic concept of "meaning" is lodged in the interaction process rather than in "ideas" or other mentalistic notions that might reside outside interaction. If a gesture "indicates to another organism the subsequent behavior of a given organism, then it has meaning."[9] Thus, if a dog growls and another dog uses this gesture to predict an attack, then this gesture of growling has "meaning." Meaning is thus given a behavioristic definition: it is a kind of behavior—a gesture—of one organism that signals to another subsequent behavior of this organism. Meaning, therefore, need not involve complex cognitive or mental activity. A dog that runs away from another growling dog, Mead would assert, is reacting without "ideas" or "elaborate deliberation"; yet, the growl has meaning to the dog, since it uses the growl as an early indicator of what will follow. Thus, meaning is

> . . . not to be conceived, fundamentally, as a state of consciousness, or as a set of organized relations existing or subsisting mentally outside the field of experience into which they enter; on the contrary, it should be

---

[9] Ibid., p. 76.

conceived objectively, as having its existence entirely within this field itself.[10]

The significance of the conversation of gestures for ongoing activity resides in the fact that the triadic matrix, and associated meanings, allow organisms to adjust their responses to each other. Thus, as organisms use each other's gestures as a means for adjusting their respective responses, they become increasingly capable of organized and concerted conduct. Yet such gestural conversations limit the capacity of organisms to organize themselves and to cooperate with each other. But among humans, Mead asserted, a qualitatively different form of communication evolved. This is communication involving *significant symbols*. And Mead felt that it is the development of the capacity to use significant symbols that distinguishes the human from other species. And it is from the development of the capacity to use significant symbols in a maturing human infant that *mind* arises. In turn, as we will come to see, the existence of mind assures the development of self and the perpetuation and change of society.

Significant Symbols and Mind. The gestures of "lower organisms," Mead felt, do not call out the same response in the organism emitting a gesture and the one interpreting the gesture. As he observed, the roar of the lion does not mean the same thing to the lion and its potential victim. When organisms become capable of using gestures that evoke the same response in each other, then they are employing what Mead termed *significant* or *conventional* gestures. As Mead illustrated, if a person shouts the word "fire" in a movie theater, this gesture evokes the same response tendency (escape, fleeing, and so on) in the person emitting the gesture and in those receiving it. Such gestures, Mead felt are unique to humans and make possible their capacities for mind, self, and society.[11]

Significant symbols are, as Mead emphasized, the basis for language. Of particular significance are vocal significant symbols, because sounds can readily be heard by both sender and receiver, thus evoking a similar behavioral tendency. Other non-vocal gestures, however, are also significant in that they can come to evoke similar tendencies to act. Thus, a frown, glare, clenched fist, rigid stance, and the like can all become significant in that they serve as a stimulus to similar responses by senders and receivers. Thus, it is the human capacity for language—that is,

---

[10] Ibid., p. 78.

[11] However, the evidence is now clear that other higher primates can use such "significant gestures."

communication by significant symbols—that makes for the emergence of their unique capacities for mind and self. And it is not until an infant of the species acquires the rudimentary capacity for language that it can have a mind.

In what ways, then, does language make mind possible? Mead borrowed Dewey's vision of "reflective" and "critical" thinking, as well as the utilitarian's vision of "rational choice," in formulating his conceptualization of mind. For Mead, mind involves several behavioral capacities:

1. The capacity to denote objects in the environment with significant symbols.
2. The capacity to use these symbols as a stimulus to one's own response.
3. The capacity to read and interpret the gestures of others and use these as a stimulus for one's response.
4. The capacity to temporarily suspend or inhibit overt behavioral responses to one's own gestural denotations, or those of others.
5. The capacity to "imaginatively rehearse" alternative lines of conduct, visualize their consequences, and select that response that will facilitate adjustment to the environment.

Mind is thus a behavior, not a substance or entity. It is behavior that involves using significant symbols to stimulate responses, but at the same time, to inhibit or delay overt behavior so that potential responses can be covertly rehearsed and assessed. Mind is thus an "internal conversation of gestures" using significant symbols, since an individual with mind talks to itself. It uses significant symbols to stimulate a line of response; it visualizes the consequences of this response; and if necessary, it inhibits the response, and uses another set of symbols to stimulte alternative responses; and so on, until the organism is satisfied with its response and overtly pursues a given line of conduct.

This capacity for mind, Mead stressed, is not inborn. It depends upon a certain level of biological maturation in the central nervous system and cerebral cortex, but most important, it depends upon interaction with others and the acquisition of the ability to interpret and use their significant symbols. As Mead noted, feral children who are raised without significant symbols do not seem "human" because they have not had to adjust to an environment mediated by significant symbols, and hence, have not acquired the behavioral capacities for mind.

Role-Taking and Mind. Mind emerges in an individual because human infants, if they are to survive, must adjust and adapt to a social environment—that is, to a world of organized activity. At first, an infant is like a "lower animal" in that it responds reflexively to the gestures of others and emits gestures that do not evoke similar responses in it and those in the environment. But such a level of adjustment, Mead implied, is not efficient, nor adaptive. A baby's cry does not indicate what it wants, whether food, water, warmth, whatever, and by not reading accurately the vocal and other gestures emitted by others in their environment, the young can frequently create adjustment problems for themselves. Thus, with a metaphor that is both Darwinian and behavioristic, there is "selective pressure" for acquiring the ability to use and interpret significant gestures, and hence, those gestures that bring reinforcement—that is, adjustment to the environment—are likely to be retained in the response repertoire of the infant.

A critical process in using and interpreting significant gestures is what Mead termed "taking the role of the other" or *role-taking*. An ability to use significant symbols means that the gestures emitted by others in the environment allow a person to read or interpret the dispositions of these others. For example, an infant who has acquired the rudimentary ability to interpret significant symbols can use its mother's tone of voice, facial expressions, and words to imagine her feelings and potential actions—that is, to "take" her role or perspective. Role-taking is critical to the emergence of mind, for unless the gestures of others, and the disposition to act that these gestures reveal, can become a part of the stimuli that are used to covertly rehearse alternative lines of conduct, overt behavior will often produce maladjustment to the environment. For without the ability to assume the perspective of others with whom one must deal, it is difficult to adjust to, and coordinate responses with, these others.

Mead's concept of role-taking captures the essence of interaction among humans: the reading of each other's significant symbols in order to assume each other's perspective, and hence, to coordinate activity. Role-taking is fundamental to mind, but it is also the basis for the formation of self and the maintenance of society.[12]

Mead's Behavioristic View of Self

The Social Nature of Self. As a "social behaviorist," Mead emphasized that the capacity to view oneself as an object in the field of experi-

---

[12] For other published statements by Mead on the nature and operation of mind, see "Image and Sensation," *Journal of Philosophy* I (1904):604–7; "Social Consciousness and the Consciousness of Meaning," *Psychological Bulletin* 7 (1910):397–405; "The Mechanism of Social Consciousness," *Journal of Philosophy* 9 (1912):401–6; "Scientific Method and Individual Thinker," *Creative Intelligence* (New York: Henry Holt, 1917):176–227; "A Behavioristic Account of the Significant Symbols," *Journal of Philosophy* 19 (1922):157–63.

ence is a type of learned behavior. It is learned through interaction with others:

> The self is something which has a development; it is not initially there, at birth, but arises in the process of social experience and activity, that is, develops in the given individual as a result of his relations to that process as a whole and to other individuals within that process.[13]

Self emerges out of the capacity to use language and to take the role of the other. Borrowing the essentials of Cooley's "looking-glass self,"[14] Mead viewed the social self as emerging out of a process in which individuals read the gestures of others, or "take their attitudes," and derive an image or picture of themselves as a certain type of object in a situation. This image of oneself then acts as a behavioral stimulus, calling out certain responses in the individual. In turn, these responses of an individual cause further reactions on the part of others, resulting in the emission of gestures, that enable role-taking by an individual who then derives new self-images and new behavioral stimuli. Thus, like mind, self arises out of the triadic matrix of people interacting and adjusting their responses to each other. For the individual does not experience self directly, but only indirectly, through reading the gestures of others:

> The individual experiences himself, not directly, but only indirectly, from the particular standpoints of other individual members of the same social group, or from the generalized standpoint of the social group as a whole to which he belongs . . . and he becomes an object to himself only by taking the attitudes of other individuals toward himself within a social environment or context of experience and behavior in which both he and they are involved.[15]

The Structure of Self. Mead appeared to use the notion of "self" in several different ways. One usage involve viewing self as a "transitory image" of oneself as an object in a particular situation. Thus as people interact with each other, they role-take and derive self images of themselves in that situation. In contrast to this conceptualization, Mead also viewed self as a structure, or configuration of typical responses that people have toward themselves as objects. For "after a self has arisen, it in a certain sense provides for itself its social experiences."[16]

---

[13] Mead, *Mind, Self, and Society*, p. 135.

[14] Mead did reject many of the specifics in Cooley's argument about "the looking-glass self." See, for example, ibid., p. 173; "Cooley's Contribution to American Social Thought," *American Journal of Sociology* 35 (1929–30):385–407; and "Smashing the Looking Glass," *Survey* 35 (1915–16): 349–61.

[15] Mead, *Mind, Self, and Society*, p. 138.

[16] Ibid., p. 140.

These views are not, of course, contradictory. The process of deriving self-images leads to the crystallization of a "set attitudes" toward oneself as a certain type of object. As such, humans begin to interpret selectively the gestures of others in light of their attitudes toward themselves, and thus, their behaviors take on a consistency. For if the view of oneself as a certain type of object is relatively stable, and if we use self as an object like all other environmental objects as a stimulus for behavior, then overt behavior will reveal a degree of consistency across social situations.

Mead sometimes termed this development of stable attitudes toward oneself as an object, the *complete* or *unified* self. Yet, he recognized that this complete self is not a rigid structure and that it is not imperiously and inflexibly imposed on diverse interactions. Rather, in different social contexts various aspects of the complete self are more evident. Depending on one's audience, then, different "elementary selves" will be evident:

> The unity and structure of the complete self reflects the unity and structure of the social process as a whole; and each of the elementary selves of which it is composed reflects the unity and structure of one of the various aspects of that process in which the individual is implicated. In other words, the various elementary selves that constitute, or are organized into, a complete self are the various aspects of the structure of that complete self answering to the various aspects of the structure of the social process as a whole; the structure of the complete self is thus a reflection of the complete social process.[17]

In this passage a further insight into the structure of self is evident: while elementary selves are unified by a "complete self," people who experience a highly contradictory social environment with *dis*unity in the social process will also experience difficulty in developing a "complete self," or a relatively stable and consistent set of attitudes toward themselves as a certain type of object. To some extent, then, people present different aspects of their more complete and unified selves to different audiences, but when these audiences demand radically contradictory actions, then the development of a unified self-conception becomes problematic.

In sum, then, Mead's conceptualization is behavioristic in that he viewed seeing oneself as an object as a behavior that is unique to humans. Moreover, like other objects in one's environment, the self is a stimulus to behavior. And thus, as people develop a consistent view of themselves

---

[17] Ibid., p. 144.

as a type of object—that is, their self reveals a structure—their responses to this stable stimulus take on a consistency. However, Mead's conceptualization of the structure of self involved the recognition that the stability of self is, to a very great extent, a consequence of the unity and stability in the social processes from which the self arises.

Phases of the Self. Mead wanted to avoid connoting that the structure of self limited a person's repertoire of potential responses. While a unified self-conception provides considerable stability in, and predictability to, overt behaviors, there is always an element of spontaneity and unpredictability to action. This fact is inherent in the "phases of self" which were conceptualized by Mead in terms of the *I* and *me*.

The image of a person's behavior is what Mead termed the *me*. As such, the "me" represents the attitudes of others and the broader community as these influence an individual's retrospective interpretation of behavior. For example, if we talk too loudly in a crowd of strangers, we see the startled looks of others and we will become cognizant of general norms about voice levels and inflections when among strangers. These are "me" images that are received by reading the gestures of specific others in a situation and by role-taking, or assuming the attitude, of the broader community. In contrast to the "me" is the "I," which is the actual emission of behavior. If a person speaks too loudly, this is "I"; and when this person reacts to his or her loudness, the "me" phase of action in initiated. Mead emphasized that the "I" "can only be known in experience," since we must wait for "me" images to know just what the "I" did. People cannot know until after they have acted ("I") just how the expectations of others ("me") are actually carried out.

Mead's conceptualization of the "I" and "me" allowed him to conceptualize the self as a constant process of behavior and self-image. People act; they view themselves as objects; they assess the consequences of their action; they interpret other's reaction to their action; and they resolve how to act next. Then, they act again, calling forth new self-images of their actions. This conceptualization of the phases of self enabled Mead to accomplish several conceptual tasks. First, he left room for spontaneity in human action; if the "I" can only be known in experience, or through the "me," then one's actions are never completely circumscribed. Second, and as we will explore in more detail later, it gave Mead a way of visualizing the process of self control. Humans are, in Mead's view, cybernetic organisms who respond, receive feedback and make adjustment, and then respond again. In this way, Mead could emphasize that, like mind, self is a process of adaptation; it is a behavior in which an organism successively responds to itself as an object as it adjusts to its environment. And third, the "I" and "me" phases of self gave Mead a way to conceptualize variations in the extent to which the expectations of others and the broader community constrain action. The *relative values* of the "I" and "me," as he phrased the matter,[18] are a positve function of people's status in a particular situation. The more involved in a group, the greater the values of "me" images and the greater the control of "I" impulses. Conversely, the less the involvement of a person in a situation, the less salient "me" images, and hence, the greater the variation in that person's overt behavior.

The Emergence of Self. Mead devoted considerable attention to the emergence of self and self-conceptions in humans. This attention allowed him to emphasize again that the self is a social product and that it is a type of behavior that emerges from the efforts of the human organism to adjust and adapt to its environment. Self arises out of the same processes that lead to the development of "mind," while being dependent upon the behavioral capacities of mind.

For self to develop, a human infant must acquire the ability to use significant symbols. For without this ability, it is not possible to role-take with others and thereby develop an image of oneself by interpreting the gestures of others. Self is also dependent upon the capacities of mind, since people must be able to designate linguistically themselves as an object in their field of experience and to organize responses toward themselves as an object. Thus, the use of significant symbols, the ability to role-take, and the behavioral capacities of mind are all preconditions for the development of self, particularly a more stable self-conception or "unified" self.

Mead visualized self as developing in three stages, each one marked by an increased capacity to role-take with a wider audience of others. The *play* stage is marked by a very limited capacity to role-take. A child can assume the perspective of only one or two others at a time, and frequently, play involves little more than discourse and interaction with "imaginary companions" to whom the child talks as it enacts a particular role. Thus, a child who plays "mother" may also, at the same time, assume the role of its baby, and in fact, the child may move back and forth between the mother's and infant's role. The play stage is thus typified by the ability to assume the perspective of only a few others at a time.

With biological maturation and with practice at assuming the perspectives of others, a child eventually acquires the capacity to take the role

---

[18] Ibid., p. 199.

of multiple others engaged in ongoing and organized activity. The *game* is perhaps the most prototypical form of such role-taking, since in order to be a participant in a game, such as baseball, the child must assume the role of other players, anticipate how they will act, and coordinate responses with their likely course of action. Thus, the child begins to see itself as an object in an organized field and it begins to control and regulate its responses to itself and to others in such a way as to facilitate the coordination of activity. During this stage in the development of self, the number and variety of such game situations expands:

> There are all sorts of social organizations, some of which are fairly lasting, some temporary, into which the child is entering, and he is playing a sort of social game in them. It is a period in which he likes "to belong," and he gets into organizations which come into existence and pass out of existence. He becomes something which can function in the organized whole, and thus tends to determine himself in his relationship with the group to which he belongs.[19]

In both the play and game situations, individuals view themselves in relation to specific others. By role-taking with specific others lodged in particular roles, individuals derive images of themselves from the viewpoint of these others. Yet, the self, Mead contended, cannot be complete until a final stage of role-taking is reached: the capacity to assume the perspective of the *generalized other*. Mead saw the generalized other as a "community of attitudes" among members of an ongoing social collective. When an individual can view itself in relation to this community of attitudes and then adjust its conduct in accordance with the expectations of these attitudes, then it is role-taking with the generalized other. For Mead, the play and game represent the initial stages in the development of self, but in the final stage, the individual can generalize the varied attitudes of others and see itself and regulate its actions from a broader perspective.

Without this capacity to view oneself as an object in relation to the generalized other, behavior could only be situation-specific. For unless people can see themselves as objects implicated in a broader social process, their actions cannot reveal continuity across situations. Moreover, humans could not create larger societies, composed of multiple groupings, without the members of the society viewing themselves, and controlling their responses, in accordance with the expectations of the generalized other.[20]

---

[19] Ibid., p. 160.

[20] The similarity between Durkheim's notion of the collective conscience and Mead's conception of generalized other should be immediately apparent. But in contrast to

Mead recognized that in complex social systems, there can be multiple "generalized others." There can be a variety of broader perspectives from which an individual views itself and controls its behaviors. Moreover, a generalized other can represent the embodiment of collective attitudes of concrete and functioning groups, or it can be more abstract, pertaining to broad social classes and categories:

> In the most highly developed, organized, and complicated human social communities . . ., [the] various socially functional classes or subgroups of individuals to which any given individual belongs . . . are of two kinds. Some of them are concrete social classes or subgroups, such as political parties, clubs, corporations, which are all actually functional social units, in terms of which their individual members are directly related to one another. The others are abstract social classes or subgroups, such as the class of debtors and the class of creditors, in terms of which their individual members are related to one another only more or less indirectly, and which only more or less indirectly function as social units, but which afford or represent unlimited possibilities for the widening and ramifying and enriching of the social relations among all the individual members of the given society as an organized and unified whole.[21]

The capacity to take the role of multiple and diverse generalized others—from the perspective of a small group to that of a large category—enables diversely located individuals to engage in the processes self-evaluation, self-criticisms, and self-control in terms of broader criteria than those provided by specific others in concrete groups. Thus, by virtue of self-images derived from role-taking with specific others in concrete groups *and* from role-taking with generalized others that personify varying and multiple "communities of attitudes," people come to themselves as a particular type of object, with certain strengths, weaknesses, and other attributes, and become capable of regulating their responses in terms of this vision of themselves as a certain type of object. And as people come to see themselves, and consistently respond to themselves, in terms of their particular configuration of specific and generalized attitudes of others, they come to possess what Mead termed a "complete" and "unified" self.

Self and Society. With the term *mind* Mead labeled those behavioral capacities in organisms that allowed for the use of symbols to denote objects and to role-take, to use objects as a stimuli for various behaviors,

---

Durkheim, Mead provided the mechanism, role-taking and self-related behaviors, by which individuals become capable of viewing and controlling their actions in terms of the perspective of the collectivity.

[21] Mead, *Mind, Self, and Society*, p. 157.

to inhibit responses, to imaginatively rehearse alternative responses, and to select a line of conduct. Thus, mind allows for cooperation among individuals as they attempt to select lines of conduct that will facilitate cooperation. *Self* is the term Mead used to describe the behavioral capacity to see oneself as an object in the environment and to use a stable conception of oneself as a certain type of object as a major stimulus for organizing behavior. The capacity for mind and self arises out of, and continues to be dependent upon, the process of role-taking, since one's view of oneself as an object and one's capacity to select among alternative behaviors is possible through reading the gestures of others and determining their attitudes and dispositions.

In many ways, mind is the capacity for denoting alternatives, whereas self involves the capacity for ordering choices in terms of a consistent framework. An organism with only mind could visualize alternatives, but could not readily select among these alternatives. The capacity for self is what allows for the selection of behaviors among alternatives. And in so doing, self provides a source of stability and consistency in a person's behavior, while integrating that behavior into the social fabric, or society. Mead appears to have viewed several ways in which self provides for the integration of behavior into society.

First, the capacity to see oneself as an object in a field of objects allows for individuals to see themselves vis-à-vis other individuals. As such, they can see their place in the field of perception, and hence, adjust their responses (through the capacity for mind) so as to coordinate their activities.

Second, the emergence of a unified and complete self, or stable self-conception, means that individuals consistently place into their perceptual field a view of themselves as a certain type of object. This object becomes a stimulus to subsequent behaviors that reveal a consistency of response, since they are responses to the self as a type of object that has certain stable attributes. People's behavior across widely divergent situations thus reveals consistency, because they introject, to some degree, a stable self-conception of themselves as a certain type of object, and it is this object, as much as any of the objects peculiar to a situation, that serves as a stimulus to the organization of behavior in that situation. And the more rigid the self-conception, the more gestures of others are selectively interpreted and used to organize responses that are consistent with one's self-conception. The consequence for society of these self-related processes is that, as people's actions take on consistency from situation to situation or from time to time in the same situation, their behaviors become predictable, thereby making it easier for individuals to adjust to, and cooperate with, each other.

Third, the process of role-taking allows individuals to see themselves not only in relation to specific others in particular situations but also in relation to varieties of generalized others. Thus, by evaluating one's actions in terms of a generalized other, behaviors will take on consistency from situation to situation and from time to time. Moreover, to the degree that all participants to an interaction role-take with the same generalized other, they will approach and perceive situations within "common meanings" and they will be prepared to act in terms of the same perspective. By viewing themselves as objects in regard to the same set of expectations, then, people approach situations with common understandings that will facilitate their adjustment to each other.

A fourth, and related point, is that the capacity to role-take with varieties of generalized others allows individuals to elaborate patterns of social organization. Individuals are now liberated from the need for face-to-face interaction as the basis for coordinating their activities, for once they can role-take with varieties of generalized others, some of whom are abstract conceptions, they can come to guide their conduct in terms of a common perspective without directly role-taking with each other. Thus, the capacity to view oneself as an object, and to adjust responses, in relation to the perspective of an abstract generalized other greatly extends the potential scope of patterns of social organization.

Fifth, in addition to providing behavioral consistency and individual integration into extended networks of interaction, self also serves as a vehicle of social change. The phases of self—the *I* and *me* as Mead termed them—assure that individual behaviors will, to some degree, alter the flow of the social process. For even if "me" images reflect perfectly the expectations in a situation, and even if one's view of oneself as a certain type of object is totally congruent with these expectations, actual behavior—that is, the "I"—can deviate from what is anticipated in "me" images. This deviation, however small or great, forces others in the situation to adjust their behaviors, providing new "me" images to guide subsequent behaviors ("I")—and so on in the course of interaction that moves in and out of "I" and "me" phases. Of course, when expectations are not clear or are ambiguous, and when one's self-conception is at odds with the expectations of others, then "I" behaviors are likely to be less predictable, requiring greater adjustments on the part of others. Or, when the capacity to develop "me" images dictates changes in a situation for an individual, and this is often the case among individuals whose self-conception or generalized others are at odds, then even greater behavioral variance and social change can be expected at the "I" phase of action occurs. Thus, the inherent phases of self—the "I" and "me"— make inevitable change in patterns of interaction. Sometimes these changes are small and imperceptible, and only after the long accumulation of small adjustments is the fact of change noticeable.[22] At other times, the change is great, as when a person in political power initiates a new course of activity. In either case, Mead went to great lengths to emphasize that self not only provides a source of continuity and integration for human behavior; it also is a source of change in society.

In summary, then, Mead presented a behavioristic conception of self. Self is a behavioral capacity to see oneself as an object in situations and to assess and control oneself in relation to the expectations of wide varieties of others. As such, self augments the capacities of mind and further facilitates adjustment and adaptation to the ongoing life process. For while both mind and self arise out of interaction in society, their emergence as behavioral capacities allows for the creation, maintenance, and change of patterns of social organization. From Mead's perspective, then, "society" must be viewed as a social process that is dependent upon humans' unique behavioral abilities, mind and self.[23]

Mead's Conception of Society

As a social psychologist and philosopher, Mead was interested in the basic relationship between the individual and society. How does society make humans unique? And in what ways do the distinctive behavioral capacities of the species make human patterns of social organization unique? We have already examined Mead's view of how the distinctive features of humans—mind and self—emerge out of a process of adaptation to ongoing social process. In his analysis of "society," or patterns of social organization, Mead turned the question around, and attempted to visualize how society is created, maintained, and changed through the processes of interaction among organisms with minds and selves.

In emphasizing the connection between personality and society, Mead provided a valuable supplement to the more macro-structural analyses of European sociology. Yet the result is often a rather vague portrayal of society, since Mead had little interest in developing a coherent or

---

[22] Ibid., pp. 180, 202, and 216 for relevant statements.

[23] For Mead's explicitly published works on self, see "The Social Self," *Journal of Philosophy* 10 (1913):374–80; "The Genesis of the Self and Social Control," *International Journal of Ethics* 35 (1924–25):251–77; and "Cooley's Contribution."

detailed view of social structure. Thus, one does not find in Mead the sense of substructures and superstructures evident in Marx's works, nor does one find Weber's passion for constructing ideal types of structural relations. To some extent Mead and Durkheim converge, in that both are vitally concerned with the symbolic bases for social integration, but they diverge in that Durkheim tended to view integration in terms of cultural and social structures, while Mead saw integration in terms of the behavioral capacities of mind and self. Mead and Simmel reveal some affinity in that both were concerned with interaction, roles, and self, but Simmel's emphasis on the "forms of sociation" and Mead's interest in the mechanisms of symbolic interaction took them in different, but still compatible, directions.

What emerges from Mead's view of society, then, is not a vision of social structure and the emergent properties and forms of these structures. Rather, Mead reaffirms that patterns of social organization, whatever their form and profile, are mediated by human behavioral capacities for language, role-taking, mind, and self. Aside from a general view, stressed by all thinkers of his time, that societies are becoming more differentiated and complex, Mead offered only a few clues about the properties of social structures in human societies.

His analysis of society, therefore, is actually a series of statements on the underlying process that make coordination among individuals possible. As long as this fact is recognized, we can avoid severe criticism of Mead's fragmentary and superficial discussion of social evolution and morphology. For his real contribution resides in his understanding of the behavioral mechanism—role-taking by language-using organisms with minds and selves—by which humans are able to coordinate their activities and construct elaborate patterns of social organization.

The Process of Society.   For Mead, the term *society* was simply a way of denoting the fact that interactive processes can reveal stability and that humans act within a framework imposed by stabilized social relations. The key to understanding society lies in the use of language and the practice of role-taking by individuals with mind and self. For it is by means of the capacity to use and read significant gestures that individuals can role-take and use their mind and self to articulate their actions to specific others in a situation and to a variety of generalized others. Since generalized others embody the broader groups, organizations, institutions, and communities that mark the structure of society, they provide a common frame of reference for individuals to use in adjusting their conduct to each other.

Society is thus maintained by virtue of humans' ability to role-take with each other and to assume the perspective of generalized others. Mead implicitly argued that society as presented to any given individual represents a series of perspectives or "attitudes" which the individual assumes in regulating behavior. Some attitudes are those of others in one's immediate field; other perspectives are those of less-immediate groups; still other attitudes come from more remote social collectives; additional perspectives come from the abstract categories that are used as a frame of reference; and ultimately, the entire population using a common set of symbols and meanings constitutes the most remote generalized other. Thus, at any given time, an individual is role-taking with some combination of specific and generalized others. The attitudes embodied by these others are then used in the processes of mind and self to construct lines of conduct.

For Mead, then, the structure and dynamics of society concern those variables that influence the number, salience, scope, and proximity of "generalized others." Thus, by implication, Mead argued that to the degree individuals can accurately take the role of each other and assume the perspective of common generalized other(s), patterns of interaction will be stable and cooperative. Conversely, to the degree that role-taking is inaccurate and occurs with respect to divergent generalized other(s), interaction will be disrupted, and perhaps conflictual.[24]

From this perspective, the theoretical key to explaining patterns of social organization involves isolating those variables that influence (1) the accuracy of role-taking and (2) the convergence of generalized others. What might some of these variables be? Mead did not discuss these variables in any great detail, since he was not interested in building formal sociological theory. Rather, his concerns are more philosophic, and hence, stress recognizing the general nature of the processes underlying the maintenance of the social order. Yet in a number of places, he offered some clues about what variables influence the capacity of actors to role-take with the same generalized other.

One barrier to role-taking with the same generalized other is social differentiation.[25] As people play different roles, they experience different sets of expectations with others connected with these roles. Moreover, to the degree that differentiated roles exist within different structural units, the most immediate generalized others for these roles will be different. This is, of course, a somewhat different way of stating Comte's and Durkheim's concerns about the mal-integrative effects of differentia-

---

[24] Mead, *Mind, Self, and Society*, pp. 321–22.
[25] Ibid.

tion. Durkheim's conceptualization emphasized the "enfeeblement" of the collective conscience, and the resulting anomie and egoism, whereas Mead's conceptualization stressed the importance of role-taking with divergent generalized others. Mead's view, however, offers the recognition that people role-take with multiple generalized others, and thus, while the community of attitudes of two individuals' immediate groups may diverge somewhat, they may at the same time assume the perspective of a more remote, or even abstract, generalized other and use this community of attitudes as a common perspective for guiding their conduct. Unlike Durkheim, who saw structural units like "occupational groups" as necessary mediators between the "collective conscience" and the individual, Mead's formulation of mind and self implicitly argues that through the capacity to role-take with multiple and remote others, diversely located individuals can become integrated into a common social fabric. Thus, structural differentiation will tend, Mead appears to have argued, to force role-taking with more remote and abstract generalized others. And in this way, the dimensions of a society can be greatly extended, since people's interactions are mediated and regulated by reference to a common community of attitudes rather than by face-to-face interaction.

Also related to differentiation—indeed, it is a type of differentiation— is stratification.[26] Class barriers increase the likelihood that individuals in different classes will not share the same community of attitudes. And thus, to the degree that a system of hierarchical differentiation is to be integrated, role-taking with a more distant generalized other will supplement the community of attitudes peculiar to a particular social class.

Related to differentiation is the size of a plurality of actors.[27] As populations increase in size, it becomes increasingly likely that any two individuals will role-take with somewhat different perspectives in their interaction with specific others in their immediate groups. If a large population is to remain integrated, Mead appears to have argued, individuals will supplement their immediate communities of attitudes by role-taking with more abstract generalized others. Hence, as the size of interaction networks increases, it can be expected that these networks are integrated by role-taking with an ever-more abstract perspective or community of attitudes.

In sum, then, Mead's view of society is dominated by a concern with social-psychological mechanisms by which social structures are inte-

---

[26] Ibid., p. 327.
[27] Ibid., p. 326.

grated. For Mead, "society" is but a term for the processes of role-taking with varieties of specific and generalized others and the consequent coordination of action that is made possible by the behavioral capacities of mind and self. By emphasizing the processes underlying social structures, Mead presented a highly dynamic view of society. For not only is society created by role-taking but it can be changed by these same processes. Thus, as diverse individuals come into contact, role-take, and adjust their responses, they create a community of attitudes that they then use to regulate their subsequent actions. And as more actors are implicated, or as their roles become more differentiated, they generate additional perspectives to guide their actions. Similarly, because actors possess unique self-conceptions and because they role-take with potentially diverse perspectives, they often must restructure existing patterns as they come to adjust to each other.

Thus, we get little feeling in Mead's work for the majesty of social structure. Mead's conceptualization can perhaps be seen as a demystification of society, since society is nothing more than a process of role-taking by individuals who possess mind and self and who seek to make adjustments to each other. Yet, we should note that Mead did offer some partial views of social morphology—that is, of the structural forms created by role-taking. And we should briefly examine these more morphological conceptualizations of society.

The Morphology of Society.   Mead frequently used terms that carry structural connotations, with notions of *group, community, institution,* and *society* being the most common. To some degree these terms are used interchangeably to denote regularity in patterns of interaction among individuals. Yet at times, Mead appears to have had an image of basic structural units that compose a total society.

The term *society* was used by Mead in two senses. On the one hand, society simply refers to ongoing, organized activity. On the other hand, society pertains to geopolitical units such as nation-states. It is the former usage, however, that is the most frequent, and thus, we will retain the view that society is the term for ongoing and organized activity among pluralities of actors, whether this activity be that of a small group or of a total society.

Mead's use of the term *community* was ambiguous and often appeared to be the same as the concept of society. His most general usage appears to have been the following: a plurality of actors who share a common set of significant symbols, who perceive that they constitute a distinguishable entity, and who share a common generalized other, or "community of attitudes." As such, a community can be quite small or large, depending on whether people perceive that they constitute an entity. Yet Mead typically employed the concept of community to denote large pluralities of actors, and thus, other structural units were seen to operate within communities.

Within every community, there are certain general ways that people are supposed to act. These are what Mead defined as *institutions*.

> There are, then, whole series of such common responses in the community in which we live, and such responses are what we term "institutions." The institution represents a common response on the part of all members of the community to a particular situation.[28]

Institutions, Mead argued, are related, and thus, when people act in one institutional context, they implicitly invoke responses to others. As Mead emphasized:

> Institutions . . . present in a certain sense the life-habits of the community as such; and when an individual acts toward others in, say, economic terms, he is calling out not simply a single response but a whole group of related responses.[29]

Institutions represent only general lines of response to varying life-situations, whether economic, political, familial, religious, or educational. People take the role of the generalized other for each institution, and since institutions are interrelated, they also tend to call out appropriate responses for other institutions. In this way, people can move readily from situation to situation within a broader community, calling out appropriate responses and inhibiting inappropriate ones. One moves smoothly, for example, from economic to familial situations, since responses for both are called out in the individual during role-taking with one or the other.

Mead recognized that institutions, and the attendant generalized other, provide only a broad framework guiding people's actions. People belong to a wide variety of smaller units that Mead tended to call *groups*. Economic activity, for example, is conducted by different individuals in varying economic groups. Familial actions occur within family groups, and so on for all institutional activity. Groups reveal their own generalized others which are both unique and yet consistent within the community of attitudes of social institutions or of the broader community. Groups can vary enormously in terms of size, differentiation, longevity, and re-

---

[28] Ibid., p. 261.
[29] Ibid., p. 264.

strictiveness, but Mead's general point is that activity of individuals involves simultaneous role-taking with the generalized other in groups, clusters of interrelated institutions, and broad community perspectives.

The Culture of Society. Mead never used the concept of *culture* in the modern sense of the term. Yet his view of social organization as mediated by generalized others is consistent with the view that culture is a system of symbols by which human thought, perception, and action are mobilized and regulated. As with social structure or morphology, however, Mead was not interested in analyzing in detail the varieties of symbol systems that humans create and use to organize their affairs. Rather, he was primarily concerned with the more general insight that humans use significant symbols, or language, to create communities of attitudes. And, by virtue of the capacity for role-taking, humans regulate their conduct not only in terms of the attitudes of specific others but also in regard to generalized others who embody these communities of attitudes.

The concept of *generalized other* is Mead's term for what would now be seen as those symbol systems of a broader cultural system that regulate perception, thought, and action. Mead's generalized other is thus norms, values, beliefs and other such regulatory systems of symbols. Mead never made careful distinctions, for example, among values, beliefs, and norms, for he was interested only in isolating the basic processes of "society": individuals with mind and self role-take with varieties of generalized others in order to regulate their conduct and thus coordinate their actions.

Mead's conception of society, therefore, emphasizes the basic nature of the processes underlying ongoing social activity. He was not concerned, to any great degree, with the details of social structure or the components of culture. His great insight was that regardless of the specific structure of society, the process by which society is created, maintained, and changed is the same. Social organization is the result of behavioral capacities for mind and self as these allow actors to role-take with varieties of others and to thus regulate and coordinate their actions. It was this insight into the fundamental relationship between the individual and society that marks Mead's great contribution in *Mind, Self, and Society.* Before Mead's synthesis, we should emphasize, the nature of this relationship had not been conceptualized, as can best be illustrated by Durkheim's fumbling efforts to link mental thought to social and cultural structures.[30]

---

[30] See Chapter 16.

THE PHILOSOPHY OF THE ACT

Mead left numerous unpublished papers, many of which were published posthumously in *The Philosophy of the Act*.[31] Much of this work is not of great interest to sociologists, and yet, in the first essay, one on which the editors imposed the unfortunate title "Stages of the Act," Mead offered new insights that cannot be found in his other essays or in his lectures. In this piece, Mead presented a theory of human motivation that should be viewed as supplemental to his conceptualization of mind, self, and society.

Mead did not present his argument in terms of the concept *motivation*, but his intent is to understand why and how human action is initiated and given direction. For Mead, the most basic unit of behavior is "the act," and much of *The Philosophy of the Act* concerns understanding the nature of this fundamental unit. For ultimately, the behavior of an individual is nothing more than a series of acts, sometimes enacted singularly but more often emitted simultaneously. Thus, if insight into the nature of human behavior is to be achieved, it is necessary to comprehend the constituent components of behavior—that is, "acts."

In his analysis of the act, Mead retained his basic assumptions. Acts are part of a larger life-process of organisms adjusting to the environmental conditions in which they find themselves. And human acts are unique because of the capacities for mind and self. Thus, Mead's theory of motivation revolves around understanding how the behavior of organisms with mind and self and operating within society is initiated and directed. He visualized the act as composed of four "stages," although he emphasized that humans can simultaneously be involved in different stages of different acts. And he also recognized that acts vary in length, degree of overlap, consistency, intensity, and other variable states. But in his analysis of the stages of the act, he was more interested in isolating the basic nature of the act than in developing propositions about its variable properties.

Mead saw acts as consisting of four stages: (1) impulse, (2) perception, (3) manipulation, and (4) consummation.[32] These are not entirely discrete, for they often blend into each other, but they constitute distinctive phases involving somewhat different behavioral capacities. Our discussion

---

[31] Mead, *Philosophy of the Act*.

[32] For an excellent secondary discussion of Mead's stages of the act, see Tamotsu Shibutani, "A Cybernetic Approach to Motivation," in Walter Buckley, ed. *Modern Systems Research for the Behavioral Scientist* (Chicago: Aldine, 1968); and Tamotsu Shibutani, *Society and Personality, An Interactionist Approach to Social Psychology* (Englewood Cliffs, N.J.: Prentice-Hall, 1961), pp. 63–93.

will focus on each stage separately, but it should be emphasized that Mead did not view the stages of a given act as separable from each other or as isolated from the stages of other acts.

Impulse

For Mead, an *impulse* represents a state of disequilibrium or tension between an organism and its environment. While Mead was not concerned with varying states of impulses—that is, their direction, type, intensity—he did offer two implicit propositions: (1) The greater the degree of disequilibrium between an organism and its environment, the stronger is its impulse and the more likely is behavior to reflect this fact. (2) The longer an impulse persists, the more it will serve to initiate and guide behavior until it is consummated.

The source of disequilibrium for an organism can vary. Some impulses come from organic needs that are unfulfilled, while others come from interpersonal maladjustments.[33] Still others stem from self-inflicted reflections. And many are a combination of organic, interpersonal, and intrapsychic sources of tension. The key point is that impulses initiate efforts at their consummation, while giving the behavior of an organism a general direction. However, Mead was quick to point out that a state of disequilibrium can be eliminated in many different ways and that the specific direction of behavior will be determined by the conditions of the environment. For Mead, humans are not pushed and pulled around by impulses. On the contrary, an impulse is defined in terms of the degree of harmony with the environment, and the precise ways that it is consummated are influenced by the manner in which an organism is prepared to adjust to its environment.

For example, even seemingly organic drives such as hunger and thirst are seen as arising from behavioral adaptations to the environment. Hunger is often defined by cultural standards as to when meals are to be eaten and it arises when the organism has not secured food from the environment. And the way in which this disequilibrium will be eliminated is greatly constrained by the social world of the individual. The types of foods that are considered edible, the way they are eaten, and when they can be eaten will all be shaped by environmental forces as they impinge upon actors with mind and self. Thus, for Mead, an impulse initiates behavior and gives it only a general direction. The next stage of the act—perception—will determine what aspects of the environment

---

[33] For Mead's conceptualization of biologic needs, see the supplementary essays in *Mind, Self, and Society*, particularly essay 2.

are relevant for eliminating the impulse.

Perception

What humans see in their environment, Mead argued, is highly selective. One basis for selective perception is the impulse: people become attuned to those objects in their environment that are perceived to be relevant to the elimination of an impulse. But even here, past socialization, self-conceptions, and expectations from specific and generalized others all constrain what objects are seen as relevant to eliminating a given impulse. For example, a hungry Indian will not see a cow as a relevant object of food, but rather, will become sensitized to other potential food objects.

The process of *perception* thus sensitizes an individual to certain objects in the environment. As objects, they become stimuli for repertoires of behavioral responses. Thus, as an individual becomes sensitized to certain objects, he or she is prepared to behave in certain ways toward those objects. For Mead, then, perception is simply the arousal of potential responses to stimuli—that is, as the organism becomes aware of relevant objects, it also is prepared to act in certain ways. Humans thus approach objects with a series of hypotheses or notions about how certain responses toward objects can eliminate their state of disequilibrium.

Manipulation

The testing of these hypotheses—that is, the emission of behaviors toward objects—is termed *manipulation*. Because humans have mind and self, they can engage in covert as well as overt manipulation. A human can often covertly imagine the consequences of action toward objects for eliminating an impulse. Hence, humans frequently manipulate their world mentally, and only after imagining the consequences of various lines of action do they emit an overt line of behavior. At other times, humans manipulate their environment without deliberate or delayed thinking; they simply emit a line of behavior that is perceived as likely to eliminate an impulse.

What determines whether manipulation will be covert before it is overt? The key condition is what Mead saw as *blockage*. For Mead, blockage is a condition where the consummation of an impulse is inhibited or delayed. Blockage produces imagery and initiates the process of thinking. For example, breaking a pencil while writing (creating impulse or disequilibrium with the environment) leads to efforts at manipulation:

one actor may immediately perceive a pile of sharpened pencils next to the writing pad, pick up a new pencil, and continue writing without a moment's reflection. Another writer, who did not prepare a stack of pencils, may initially become attuned to the drawer of the desk, open it, search for a pencil, and generally start searching "blindly" for a pencil. At some point, frequently after a person has "wandered around unconsciously" for a while, the blockage of the impulse begins to generate conscious imagery and a person's manipulations become covert. Images of where one last left a pencil are now consciously evoked or the probable location of a pencil sharpener is anticipated. Thus, when the impulse, perception, and overt manipulation stages of the act do not lead to consummation, thinking occurs and manipulation becomes covert, utilizing the behavioral capacities of mind and self.

Thinking can also be initiated earlier in the act. For example, if perception does not yield a field of relevant objects, then blockage occurs at this stage, with the result that by virtue of the capacities for mind, an actor immediately begins covert thinking. Thus, thinking is a behavioral adaptation of an organism that is experiencing disequilibrium with its environment and that has been unable to perceive objects or manipulate behaviors in ways leading to consummation of an impulse.

In the process of thinking, then, an actor comes to perceive relevant objects; the actor may even role-take with the object if it is another individual or a group; a self-image may be derived and one may see self as yet another object; and then various lines of conduct are imaginatively rehearsed until a proper line of conduct is selected and emitted. Of course, if the selected behavior does not eliminate the impulse, the process starts over again and continues until the organism's behavior allows it to achieve a state of equilibrium with its environment.

The stage of manipulation is thus "cybernetic" in that it involves behavior, feedback, readjustment of behavior, feedback, readjustment, and so on until an impulse is eliminated.[34] Mead's vision of thinking as "imaginative rehearsal" and his conceptualization of the "I" and "me" phases of self fit into this more general cybernetic view of the act. Thinking involves imagining a line of behavior and then giving oneself the feedback as to the probable consequences of the behavior. The "I" and "me" phases of self involve deriving "me" images (feedback) from behaviors ("I") and then using these images to adjust subsequent behaviors. Thus, unlike many views of motivation, Mead saw acts as constructed from a succession of manipulations that yield feedback which, in turn,

---

[34] See Shibutani, "Cybernetic Approach," for a more detailed discussion.

is used to make subsequent manipulations. Motivation is thus a process of constant adjustment and readjustment of behaviors to restore equilibrium with the environment.

While Mead did not develop any formal propositions on the manipulatory stage of the act, he implicitly assumed that the more often an impulse is blocked, the more it grows in intensity and the more it consumes the process of thinking and the phases of self. Thus, individuals who have not eliminated a strong impulse through successful manipulation will have a considerable amount of their thinking and self-reflection consumed by imagery pertaining to objects and behaviors that might eliminate the impulse. For example, people who cannot satiate their hunger or sexual appetites or who cannot achieve the recognition that they feel they deserve are likely to devote a considerable, and ever-increasing, amount of their time in covert and overt manipulations in an effort to control their impulses.

Consummation

This stage of the act simply denotes the completion of an act through the elimination of the disequilibrium between an organism and its environment. As a behaviorist, Mead emphasized that successful *consummation* of acts by the emission of behaviors in relation to certain objects leads to the development of stable behavior patterns. Thus, general classes or types of impulses will tend to elicit particular lines of responses from an individual if these responses have been successful in the past in restoring equilibrium. Individuals will tend to perceive the same or similar objects as relevant to the elimination of the impulse and they will tend to use these objects as stimuli for eliciting certain lines of behavior. In this way, people develop stable behavioral tendencies to act upon their environment.

Mead's analysis of the stages of the act provides a useful supplement to his discussion of *Mind, Self, and Society*. We now have a better vision of why people initiate action and why behaviors take a certain direction. In many ways, Mead's conception of motivation represents a synthesis of diverse schools of thought. The stimulus-response, or reflex-arc, approach of J. B. Watson, and more recently of B. F. Skinner, is retained without the restrictive tendency to avoid the "black box" of human cognition. The gestalt psychology of Mead's time is retained through the emphasis of behavior as initiated by a desire to maintain harmony within a perceptual field of objects and relations. The psychoanalytic view of behavior as a reconciliation of impulses and ego-processes is retained in the emphasis on bio-social sources of disequilibrium and the stages of perception and covert manipulation by actors with mind and self. Moreover, Mead's emphasis on blockage, and how blockage increases the intensity of impulses, is consistent with the psychoanalytic view of the sources of disruptive emotional stages.

In sum, then, Mead's theory of motivation, much like his view of mind, self, and society, represents a synthesis of diverse and often contradictory viewpoints. The biologic individual is not ignored; the internal psychological processes of individuals are highlighted; and the relation of acts to the ongoing processes of society are still prominent. Mead's view of motivation is thus distinctly sociological, emphasizing the relationship of individuals to each other and to the social as well as physical environment. What drives actors and what shapes the course of their behaviors is this relationship of the organism to its environment. And for human actors, who by virtue of mind and self are able to live and participate in society, this environment is decidedly social. Therefore, humans initiate and direct their actions in an effort to achieve integration into the ongoing social process.

A NOTE ON MEAD'S BROADER PHILOSOPHY

Many of Mead's ideas are strictly philosophical, and in fact, his sociological insights are only a part of a broader philosophical view. Mead's viewpoint was never fully articulated, nor was it well integrated. But Mead's other two posthumous works, *Movements of Thought in the Nineteenth Century* and *The Philosophy of the Present*, provide a glimpse at Mead's broader vision.[35]

There are many fascinating themes in these works, but one of the most persistent is that all human activity represents an adjustment and adaptation to the world. In *Movements of Thought*, Mead traced the development of social thought from its early, prescientific phases to the contemporary modern, scientific stage. In a way that is reminiscent of Comte's "law of the three stages," Mead saw the great ideas of history as moving toward an ever more rational or scientific profile, because with the emergence of rational scientific thought, a better level of adaptation and adjustment to the world could be achieved.

The Philosophy of the Present is a somewhat disjointed series of essays that represent a more philosophical treatment of ideas contained in his social psychology, particularly in *Mind, Self, and Society*. Here again,

---

[35] See note 1 for full reference.

Mead emphasized that what is uniquely human is nothing but a series of particular behavioral capacities that have evolved from adaptations to the ongoing life-process. Much of the discussion addresses purely philosophical topics about the ontological status of consciousnesses of the past, present, and future, but between the lines Mead stressed that the capacities of mind and self do not necessitate a dualism between mind and body, because all of the unique mental capacities of humans are behaviors that are directed toward facilitating adjustment to the environment as it is encountered in the present.

For sociologists, Mead's general philosophy is not of great importance, except that it led him to develop a conception of the relation between the individual and society. Mead's contribution resides in his capacity to isolate the basic properties of the relation between the individual and society. And in his works are a series of models and principles that make his contribution decidedly theoretical. These more formal theoretical aspects of Mead's thought are examined in the next chapter.

23

GEORGE HERBERT MEAD III:
MODELS AND PRINCIPLES

THE BASIC THEORETICAL APPROACH

George Herbert Mead's *social* behaviorism marked a synthesis of utilitarian, pragmatist, behaviorist, and even Darwinian notions. Its basic premise is: behaviors that facilitate the adjustment and adaptation of organisms to their environment will be retained.

For any individual organism, its environment is society. Thus, the young infant must adjust to society, developing the behavioral capacities for language, role-taking, mind, and self. And for the mature individual, the continued use of these fundamental capacities is essential for ongoing adjustment and adaptation to society. The critical insight of Mead's social behaviorism is that the capacities for mind and self are behaviors. Moreover, these capacities assure that among humans much action will be covert and involve role-taking, reflective thinking, self-criticism, and self-assessment.

It is these behavioral capacities for mind and self that make humans distinctive. And it is out of interaction by actors with mind and self that society is possible. For a species that is not organized by instincts, as are ants and bees, the ability to role-take with each other and with broader perspectives, values, beliefs, and norms allows for the organization of the species into society. This behavioral ability also makes human social organization flexible, thereby facilitating the adjustment and adaptation of the species as a whole to the environment.

Thus, the acquisition of mind and self enables the individual to adapt to its social environment, while the flexible interactive abilities of individuals with mind and self facilitate the species' adaptation to the environment through the creation, maintenance, and change of society. It is within this basic framework that Mead's ideas must be viewed. As we saw in Chapter 21, Mead borrowed much from other scholars, but he combined their ideas in new ways into an approach that unraveled the basic nature of the relationships between the individual and society.

In his efforts, Mead did not explicitly develop models and theoretical principles. But he continues to inspire sociological theorizing precisely because a number of models and principles can be pulled from his work. To properly assess his theoretical legacy, then, we should try to make more explicit these implicit models and principles.

MEAD'S BASIC MODELS

Mead's implicit models are of two types: (1) those that represent the nature of action and interaction and (2) those that map the genesis of mind and self. The various models that can be constructed within these two general areas are delineated below.

The Act and Action

As a social behaviorist, Mead was concerned with why an organism should act upon its environment. We can recall from Mead's presentation of the "stages of the act" in *The Philosophy of the Act* that he saw action as involving four phases: (1) impulse, (2) perception, (3) manipulation, and (4) consummation.[1] For any given act, these phases represent a causal sequence, with a number of crucial feedback loops. These are represented in Figure 23–1.

For organisms with mind and self, the model of the act presented in Figure 23–1 is greatly complicated. Impulses are often the result of disequilibrium with other individuals or abstract "others." Perception of objects involves seeing oneself as an object. Manipulation is frequently covert, involving conscious recognition of self, active role-taking with various types of others, and imaginative rehearsal of alternatives as these are constrained by self and cognizance of different "communities of attitudes."[2] Thus, much human action involves covert behavior. This covert behavior, Mead argued, is most likely when blockage at any point

---

[1] George Herbert Mead, *The Philosophy of the Act* (Chicago: University of Chicago, 1938). See also, Tamotsu Shibutani, "A Cybernetic Approach to Motivation" in Walter Buckley, ed., *Modern Systems Research for the Behavioral Scientist* (Chicago: Aldine, 1968); Tamotsu Shibutani, *Society and Personality: An Interactionist Approach to Social Psychology* (Englewood Cliffs, N.J.: Prentice-Hall, 1961) pp. 63–93.

[2] George Herbert Mead, *Mind, Self, and Society* (Chicago: University of Chicago Press, 1934).

FIGURE 23–1
Mead's Model of the Act

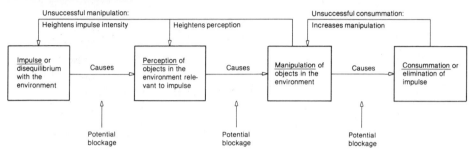

in the act is evident. For example, the inability to perceive relevant objects will heighten perceptual processes and set off covert manipulation, or thinking. When overt behavioral manipulation is unsuccessful, covert manipulation will ensue. And the longer an impulse goes unconsummated, the more it grows in intensity, thereby heightening perception, accelerating covert manipulation, and constraining overt behavior.

Mead's model of the act thus argues that the more blockage, the greater the causative weight of the arrows in Figure 23–1 connecting the stages of the act. Intense impulses cause heightened perception, and increased perception causes greater overt and covert manipulation. And the more the feedback arrows represent unsuccessful perception and manipulation for a given impulse, the greater the causal force of that impulse among an individual's present repertoire of impulses. This model of the act, then, allows for an understanding of how individuals can be "driven" to seemingly irrational or excessively emotional behavior, or it can provide insight into the dynamics of compulsive behavior. These behaviors would result from the blockage of powerful impulses that persist and escalate in intensity, thereby distorting an individual's perceptions, covert thinking, and overt behavior. For example, individuals, who, in their early years, were rejected by significant others, may have a powerful series of unconsummated impulses that distort their perception and manipulations to abnormal extremes. And given the fact that the unstable or abnormal self-conceptions of such individuals may distort the process of perception, as well as covert and overt manipulation, they may never be able to perceive that they have consummated their impulses in interpersonal relations.

Mead was not, unlike Freud or other clinicians and psychologists of his time, interested in types of abnormal behavior. He was more concerned with constructing a model that would denote the fundamental properties of human action, whether normal or abnormal. Mead's social behaviorism is often portrayed as overly rational, but this view does not take into account Mead's model of the act. This model contains the elements for emotional as well as rational action, and while Mead was not interested in assessing the consequences of various weights among the arrows in Figure 23–1, the model provides a valuable tool for those who are concerned with how various types of impulses, when coupled with different patterns of impulse blockage, will produce different forms of covert and overt behavior.

The Triadic Matrix and Interaction

Mead viewed human interaction as simply a more complex form of the triadic matrix.[3] Because organisms with mind and self can use language and role-take, the simple process of communication that is evident among "lower" organisms is altered. We can visualize this alteration by modeling Mead's view of the triadic matrix among nonhuman organisms and then comparing this simple model to one on human interaction.

In Figure 23–2, one organism with an impulse to act perceives another

FIGURE 23–2
Mead's Simple Model of Communication or the Triadic Matrix

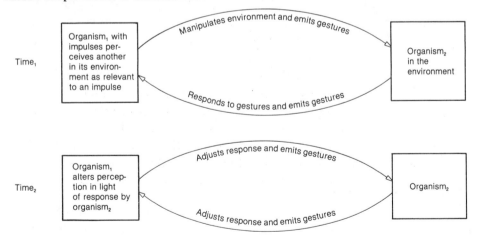

---

[3] Mead, *Philosophy of the Act.*

organism as relevant to the consummation of the impulse. As it begins to overtly manipulate or act on the environment, it will emit gestures that are perceived and interpreted by the other. The receiving organism then responds, and in so doing, emits gestures causing the first organism to adjust its responses and emit gestures that cause the other organism to alter further its responses, and so on, until the organisms are no longer cognizant of each other. We should emphasize that at no point, Mead argued, do the organisms need to share common meanings about their gestures. They can communicate and adjust responses simply by interpreting gestures, even though these gestures may not mean the same thing to both organisms.

Such was Mead's view of communication and interaction among animals that do not possess language, and hence, cannot role-take with each other. Once organisms become capable of emitting and receiving gestures that mean the same to all, they possess language, and with language, they can read consensual gestures and assume the perspective of each other. With role-taking, and the capacities for mind, they can covertly rehearse alternatives before overt behavior. With self, they can perceive of themselves as an object in their deliberations and they can assume the perspectives of a broader "community of attitudes" (generalized others) in their rehearsal of alternatives. Thus, among humans the triadic matrix is greatly complicated because human organisms no longer react automatically and unreflectively to each others' gestures. However, gestures mean the same thing to each organism and responses are often rehearsed and mediated through self conceptions and role-taking with a wide variety of others.

Yet Mead argued that the basic nature of interaction among humans is only a more elaborated version of the triadic matrix. Interaction still involves impulses, action, emission of gestures, and perception of gestures as disposing an organism to act in a certain way. The key difference between human and nonhuman communication and interaction is that the gestures are significant and that mind and self mediate the interpretation of, and reaction to, the gestures. This version of human interaction is summarized in Figure 23–3.

Figure 23–3 emphasizes that the essence of interaction among human beings involves (a) sending and receiving significant gestures, (b) role-taking on the basis of these gestures, (c) rehearsing alternative lines of response, and (d) introjecting oneself as an object and a variety of general perspectives into covert deliberations. For Mead, then, the elements delineated in Figure 23–3 are the key variables influencing interaction among humans.

FIGURE 23-3
Mead's Model of Human Interaction

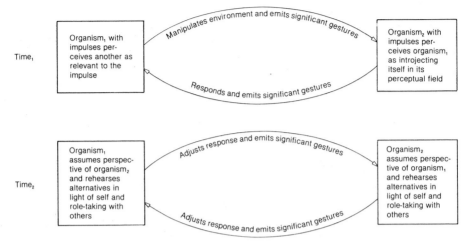

The Genesis of Mind

Humans are unique, Mead argued, because they possess mind and self. As we stressed in Chapter 22, mind involves several behavioral capacities: to denote objects in the environment with language, to inhibit overt responses, to weigh alternative responses to objects, to role-take with others by reading their gestures, and to select a line of conduct that facilitates cooperation with others and allows for adaptation to the environment. Mead stressed that mind is not inborn, but must be learned by virtue of interaction with others in society. Without the prior existence of society, or organized and ongoing activity, mind could not emerge in an individual.

Mead saw mind as developing in a sequence of phases, as is represented in Figure 23-4. Because an infant is dependent upon others, and in turn, these others are dependent for their survival upon society, mind develops out of the forced dependency of an infant on society. Since society is held together by actors who use language and who can role-take, the infant must seek to consummate its impulses in a world mediated by symbols. Through conscious coaching by others, and through simple trial and error, the infant comes to use significant symbols to denote objects relevant to satisfying its needs (such as food, mother, and so on). To consummate other impulses, the infant eventually must acquire greater capacities to use and understand language; once an infant can

500

FIGURE 23–4
Mead's Model on the Genesis of Mind

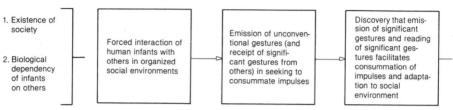

1. Existence of society

2. Biological dependency of infants on others

Forced interaction of human infants with others in organized social environments

Emission of unconventional gestures (and receipt of significant gestures from others) in seeking to consummate impulses

Discovery that emission of significant gestures and reading of significant gestures facilitates consummation of impulses and adaptation to social environment

Pre-conditions

use language, it can begin to read the gestures of others and call out in itself the dispositions of others. When a young child can role-take, it can soon begin to consciously think, reflect, and rehearse responses. In other words, it reveals the rudimentary behavioral abilities that Mead termed *mind*.

The causal arrows in Figure 23–4 actually represent a series of preconditions for the next stage of development. The model is "value added" in that certain conditions must be met before subsequent events can occur. Underlying these conditions is Mead's implicit vision of "social selection," which represents his reconciliation of learning theory principles with pragmatism and Darwinism. The development of abilities for language, role-taking, and mind are "selected for" as the infant seeks to consummate impulses in society. If the infant is to adjust and adapt to society, it must acquire the ability for minded behavior. And thus, as the infant seeks to adapt to its social environment, it learns those behaviors—first significant symbols, then role-taking, and eventually mind—that facilitate, to ever-increasing degrees, its adjustment to the social environment.

Thus, the model presented in Figure 23–4 underscores Mead's view that there is nothing mysterious or mystical about the human mind. It is a behavior that is acquired like other behavioral tendencies as a human organism attempts to adapt to its surroundings. And it is a behavioral capacity that is acquired in stages, with each stage setting the conditions for the next.

The Genesis of Self

In many respects, the emergence of mind is a precondition for the genesis of self. Yet the rudiments of self begin with an organism's ability to role-take, for it can then derive self-images or see itself as an object

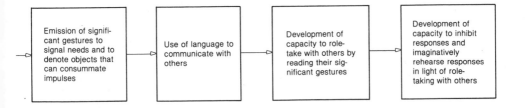

toward whom others have certain dispositions to act. The complete development of self, however, is only possible with mind, since an individual must be capable of seeing itself as an object in relation to ongoing deliberations about how to act in a given situation. Mead's model for the genesis of self is presented in Figure 23–5.

Figure 23–5 is more complex than the other models, because Mead appeared to use the notion of "self" in several related ways. First, Mead saw the development of self as a process of role-taking with increasingly varied and generalized "others." This facet of self is represented at the top of Figure 23–5, because increasing acuity at role-taking influences the other aspects of self (this is emphasized by the vertical arrows connecting the boxes at each stage in the emergence of self). Second, Mead visualized self as a process of self-control, as he emphasized in his notion of the "I" and "me" phases of self and in his view of the "manipulative" stage of the acts (see previous chapter). This facet of self involves the growing ability to read the gestures of others, to inhibit inappropriate responses in relation to these others, and to adjust responses in a way that will facilitate interaction. But in its more advanced stages, self-control also comes to include the capacity to assume the "general" perspective or "community of attitudes" of specific groups, and eventually, of the broader community. The process of self-control thus represents the extensions of the capacities for mind, and it is for this reason that the precondition for self—that is, the "incipient capacity for mind" at the left of the model—is seen to tie almost directly into the self-control aspect of self. Third, self was also seen by Mead as involving the emergence of a self-conception, or stable disposition to act toward oneself as a certain type of object. Such a stable self-conception evolves out of the accumulation of self-images and self-evaluations with reference to specific, and then increasingly generalized, others.

FIGURE 23–5
Mead's Model of the Genesis of Self

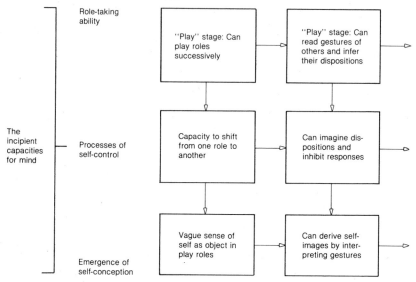

Thus, in reading Mead's model, the arrows that move from left to right denote the development of each aspect of self. The arrows that move down the columns stress Mead's emphasis on the role-taking process and on how developments in the ability to role-take influence the etiology of self-control processes and self-conceptions. Of course, we might also draw arrows back up the columns since, to some extent, self-control processes and self-conceptions influence role-taking abilities. But the arrows, as they are currently drawn, appear to capture best, we feel, Mead's vision of causal processes in the initial emergence of those multiple behavioral capacities that he subsumed under the label *self*.

MEAD'S THEORETICAL PRINCIPLES

When cast in models, Mead's ideas offer considerable insight into the causal sequences of events involved in action, interaction, and social organization among actors with the capacities for mind and self. A recasting of his scheme into theoretical principles, however, offers a somewhat different view of Mead's thought. For when his ideas are expressed as abstract principles, a series of fundamental relationships in the social world are exposed. While causal connections are not always lost in trans-

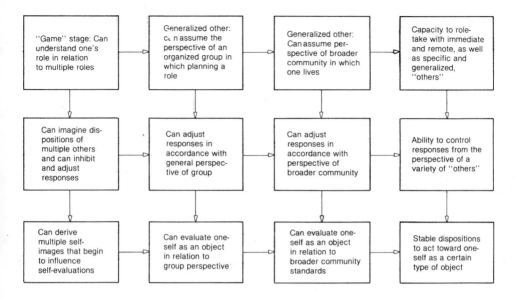

lating Mead's ideas into abstract principles, they become less central to the theoretical analysis, since the emphasis in abstract principles is on establishing basic and fundamental affinities in the world among classes of events.

We can best appreciate Mead's theoretical principles by recognizing that Mead sought to show how human action, interaction, and organization are qualitatively unique, and yet, extensions of behavioral processes evident in other species. Thus, Mead initially postulated principles of action and interaction in general and then attempted to show how the emergence of the behavioral capacities for mind and self make human action and interaction unique and how this uniqueness arises out of, and at the same time allows for, the creation, maintenance, and change of society. Thus, we will first seek to examine Mead's general principles of action and interaction, and then, attempt to explore his general principles of *human* action, interaction, and social organization.

Principles of Animal Action

In *The Philosophy of the Act*, Mead presented several general principles of action—that is, of what is involved in initiating and giving direction to behavior in all animals. As we saw in Chapter 22, his ideas are expressed as "stages" and can be modeled. But these ideas can also be expressed as a series of basic principles of action, as is done below:

1. The greater is the degree of maladjustment of an organism to its environment, the stronger are its impulses.
2. The greater is the intensity of an organism's impulse, the greater is the organism's perceptual awareness of objects that can potentially consummate the impulse and the greater is its manipulation of objects in the environment.
    2a. The more maladjustment stems from unconsummated organic needs, the greater is the intensity of the impulse.
    2b. The longer an impulse goes unconsummated, the greater is the intensity of the impulse.
3. The more impulses have been consummated by the perception and manipulation of certain classes of objects in the environment, the more likely are perceptual and behavioral responses to be directed at these and similar objects when similar impulses arise.

These three principles summarize Mead's social behaviorism. Action emerges out of adjustment and adaptation problems encountered by an organism. Behavior is directed at restoring equilibrium between the organism and the environment. The essence of behavior involves perception and manipulation of objects. And successful perception and manipulations are retained in the behavioral repertoire of organisms. As Mead argued, it is from this behavioral base that human action emerged, but the capacities for mind, self, and society require, as we will document shortly, additional theoretical principles if the distinctive qualities of human action are to be understood. But to appreciate fully these additional principles, we need first to summarize Mead's general principles of interaction among animals without mind, self, and society.

Principles of Animal Interaction

Mead's view of interaction can be modeled as a causal sequence of events over time, as was done earlier, or it can be expressed by the following two principles:

4. The more organisms seek to manipulate objects in their environment in an effort to consummate impulses, the greater is

the visibility of gestures that they emit during the course of their action.

5. The greater the number and visibility of gestures emitted by acting organisms, the more likely are these organisms to respond to each other's gestures and to adjust responses to each other.

These two principles underscore Mead's view that the essence of interaction involves (a) an organism emitting gestures as its act on the world, (b) another organism responding to these gestures and hence emitting its own gestures as it seeks to consummate its impulses, and (c) readjustments of responses by each organism on the basis of the gestures emitted. Mead termed the process the *triadic matrix*, and as we emphasized, it can occur without cognitive manipulations and without the development of common meanings. Indeed, as Mead argued, it is only among humans with mind and self, living in society, that this fundamental interactive process involves cognitive manipulations, normative regulation, and shared meanings.

Principles of Human Action, Interaction, and Organization

Critical to understanding Mead's view of human action, interaction, and organization is the recognition that humans develop mind and self out of their participation in society. We should first review Mead's formulation of principles on the development of mind and self, and then we can see how these two behavioral capacities alter the principles of human action, interaction, and organization.

Principles of the Emergence of Mind. Any particular individual is born into a society of actors with mind and self. And as will become evident shortly when we turn to principles of human action, interaction, and organization, actors with mind and self are able to create, maintain, and change society by virtue of the symbol-using and role-taking abilities allowed by mind and self. Mind, self, and human society were thus seen by Mead as intimately connected, and in fact, he saw that it is difficult to talk about one without addressing the other two. Nevertheless, we must jump into this web of interconnections at some point, and hence we can begin by isolating Mead's view of socialization and the emergence of mind. This view assumes the prior existence of society and adult actors with mind and self, and it is into this social milieu that young infants who do not possess these behavioral capacities must adapt and adjust. And in attempting to understand how infants come to adjust to adult actors and to society, Mead offered a series of important principles describing the fundamental properties of the socialization process. The first set of these principles, dealing with the emergence of mind, are summarized below:

6. The more an infant must adapt to its environment composed of organized collectivities of actors, the more likely is the infant to be exposed to significant gestures.

7. The more an infant must seek to consummate its impulses in an organized social collectivity, the more likely is the learning of how to read and use significant gestures to have selective value for consummating the infant's impulses.

8. The more an infant can come to use and read significant gestures, the greater is its ability to role-take with others in its environment, and hence, the greater is its capacity to communicate its needs and to anticipate the responses of others on whom it is dependent for the consummation of impulses.

9. The greater is the capacity of an infant to role-take and use significant gestures, the greater is its capacity to communicate with itself.

10. The greater is the capacity of an infant to communicate with itself, the greater is its ability to covertly designate objects in its environment, inhibit inappropriate responses, and select a response that will consummate its impulses and thereby facilitate its adjustment.

11. The greater is the ability of an infant to reveal such minded behavior, the greater is its ability to control its responses and, hence, to cooperate with others in ongoing and organized collectivities.

These propositions should be read in two ways. First, each proposition, by itself, expresses a fundamental relationship in the nature of human development. For example, proposition 6 states that human infants are, by virtue of being born into society, inevitably exposed to a collage of significant gestures; or proposition 7 states that since infants must consummate impulses in a world of significant gestures, they will learn to read and use these gestures as a means of increasing their adjustment. Thus, each proposition states that one variable condition, stated in the first clause of the proposition, will lead to the development of another capacity, which is stated in the second clause of the proposition, in the maturing human infant. Second, the sequence of six propositions should be viewed as marking "stages" in the genesis of a critical behavioral capacity, mind. For Mead, mind emerges out of a connected series of fundamental processes and the entire set of propositions summarizes this emergence.

Principles of the Emergence of Self. As the capacities for mind begin to emerge, self also becomes evident. However, the full development of self is, like the development of mind, the result of a series of fundamental processes. These processes are summarized by the following propositions:

12. The more a young actor can engage in minded behavior, the more it can read significant gestures, role-take, and communicate with itself.

13. The more a young actor can read significant gestures, role-take, and communicate with itself, the more it can see itself as an object in any given situation.

14. The more diverse the specific others with whom a young actor can come to role-take, the more it can increasingly come to see itself as an object in relation to the dispositions of multiple others.

15. The more generalized the perspective of others with whom a young infant can come to role-take, the more it can increasingly come to see itself as an object in relation to general values, beliefs, and norms of increasingly larger collectivities.

16. The greater stability in a young actor's images of itself as an object in relation to both specific others and generalized perspectives, the more reflexive is its role-taking and the more consistent are its behavioral responses.

    16a. The more the first self-images derived from role-taking with others have been consistent and noncontradictory, the greater is the stability, over time, of an actor's self-conception.

    16b. The more self-images derived from role-taking with generalized perspectives are consistent and noncontradictory, the greater is the stability, over time, of an actor's self-conception.

17. The more a young actor can reveal stability in its responses to itself as an object, and the more it can see itself as an object in relation to specific others as well as generalized perspectives, the greater is its capacity to control its responses and, hence, to cooperate with others in ongoing and organized collectivities.

These propositions document Mead's view of certain fundamental relationships among role-taking acuity, self-images of the self as an object, and the capacity for social control. They also summarize Mead's conceptualization of the sequence of events involved in generating a "unified" self in which an individual adjusts its responses in relation to (a) a stable self-conception, (b) specific expectations of others, and (c) general values, beliefs, and norms.

As the consecutive numbering of the propositions underscores, the development of mind and self is a continuous process. And once mind and self in individual human organisms have emerged and developed, the nature of action and interaction as well as patterns of social organization among humans is qualitatively different from that of non-human organisms. Yet Mead would emphasize that there is nothing mysterious or mystical about this qualitative difference. Indeed, even though human action, interaction, and organization are distinct by virtue of the capacity for mind, self, and symbolically mediated organization into society, this distinctiveness has been built upon a base common to all acting organisms. The elaboration of this base necessitates, of course, new principles to describe the nature of human action, interaction, and organization. And it is in the elaboration of these additional principles that Mead provided a number of critical insights into how and why humans create, maintain, and change patterns of social organization.

Principles of Human Action and Interaction. The emergence of mind and self complicate somewhat Mead's view of the act as involving impulse, perception, and manipulation as well as his notion of the triadic matrix as a simple process of actors emitting and reading gestures as they adjust their responses to each other. Indeed, the complications introduced into the processes of action and interaction make for an entirely new way to organize a species into society.

In regard to action, Mead noted one additional principle to account for the distinctive features of human acts:

18. **The greater is the intensity of impulses of humans with mind and self, (a) the more likely is perceptual awareness of objects that can potentially consummate the impulse to be selective, (b) the more likely is manipulation to be covert, and (c) the more likely are both perception and manipulation to be circumscribed by a self-conception, expectations of specific others, and the generalized perspective of organized collectivities.**

When action, as described in proposition 18, above, occurs in a social context with others, it then becomes overt interaction. But we should emphasize that even isolated acts, where others are not physically present, involve interaction with symbolically invoked others and generalized perspectives. The capacities for mind and self, Mead argued, assure that humans will invoke the dispositions of others and broader communities of attitudes to guide behavior during the course of their acts, even if specific others are not physically present and even if others do not directly react to one's behaviors. But when others are present, the use of significant symbols and role-taking becomes more direct and immediate, requiring several supplementary propositions on *inter*action:

19. The more humans with mind and self seek to consummate impulses in the presence of others, the more likely are they to emit overt significant gestures and the more likely are they to read the significant gestures of others and, hence, the greater their role-taking activity.

20. The more humans role-take with each other, the more likely is the course of their interaction to be guided by the specific disposition of others present in a situation, by the self-images of the self as a certain type of object in the situation, and by the generalized perspective of the organized collectivity in which they are participating.

These three principles of action and interaction summarize the fundamental relationships that Mead saw as inhering in the triadic matrix of humans (see Figure 23–3). When stated as principles, rather than as a causal model, the key relationships among impulses, significant gestures, role-taking, self-conceptions, expectations of others, and generalized perspectives are highlighted. For Mead, impulses are related to action; action occurs in a context of others, and hence, is related to interaction; interaction occurs through role-taking which, in turn, produces self-images, awareness of the dispositions of others, and cognizance of generalized perspectives. Such is the nature of human action and interaction among organisms with mind and self who must seek to consummate their impulses within the framework imposed by ongoing patterns of social organization. Thus, principles 18, 19, and 20 can be interpreted as Mead's "laws" of action and interaction among humans.

By comparing these laws to his general principles of action and interaction among nonhuman organisms (see propositions 1 through 5 in the sections on nonhuman action and interaction), we can see that these principles on humans represent extensions of those on nonhumans. For Mead saw both continuity and discontinuity in the behavioral capacities of humans. On the one hand, humans were seen by Mead as just another animal, subject to certain behavioral principles, while on the other hand, they were viewed as revealing unique behavioral capacities for mind, self, and social organization, thereby necessitating new theoretical principles. We have now summarized Mead's principles on the emergence of mind and self as well as those on action and interaction. These principles place into context Mead's vision of how society is created, maintained, and changed. For as a philosopher and social psychologist, rather than a structural sociologist, Mead had a distinctively social-psychological view of social organization. Yet this vision supplements and complements the structural perspective developed in Europe by such figures as Spencer, Marx, Weber, and Durkheim.[4] While each of these scholars sought to uncover some of the social-psychological dynamics of macro-social structures, none was able to achieve the insights that Mead developed on the fundamental social-psychological properties underlying patterns of social organization.

Principles of Human Social Organization. Since interaction among humans is possible by virtue of role-taking abilities, and since society involves stabilized patterns of interaction, society for Mead is ultimately a process of (*a*) role-taking with various "others" and (*b*) using the dispositions and perspectives of these others for self-evaluation and self-control. The nature and scope of society, Mead implicitly argued, are a dual function of the number of specific others and the abstractness of the generalized others with whom individuals can role-take. In many ways, Mead viewed society as a "capacity" for various types of role-taking. If actors can role-take with only one other at a time, then the capacity for society is limited, but once they can role-take with multiple others, and then, with generalized others, their capacity for society is greatly extended. These fundamental relationships are summarized in Mead's two basic propositions on the dynamics underlying society:

21. **The more actors can role-take with pluralities of others, and use the dispositions of multiple others as a source of self-evaluation and self-control, the greater is their capacity to create and maintain patterns of social organization.**

22. **The more actors can role-take with the generalized perspective of organized collectivities, and use this perspective as a source of self-evaluation and self-control, the greater is their capacity to create and maintain patterns of social organization.**

---

[4] See earlier chapters.

If actors cannot meet the conditions specified in these two "laws" of social organization, then instability and change in patterns of interaction are likely. Actors who cannot role-take with multiple others at a time, and use the dispositions of these others to see themselves as objects and to control their responses, will not be able to coordinate their responses as well as actors who can perform such role-taking. And actors who cannot role-take with the general norms, beliefs, values, and other symbol systems of organized groups, and use these to view themselves and to regulate their actions, will not be able to extend patterns of social organization beyond immediate face-to-face contact. For it is only after actors can role-take with a broader "community of attitudes," and use a common set of expectations to guide their conduct, that extended and indirect patterns of social organization become possible.

In addition to these two basic principles, Mead elaborated several propositions on role-taking with generalized others. Since the scope of society is ultimately a positive function of role-taking abilities with generalized others, Mead apparently felt it necessary to specify some of the variables influencing the relations among role-taking, generalized others, and the nature of society. Three variables are most prominent in Mead's scheme: (1) the degree to which actors can hold a *common* generalized other, (2) the degree of *consistency* among multiple generalized others, and (3) the degree of *integration* among different types and layers of generalized others. These variables were implicitly incorporated by Mead into additional principles of social organization.

23. The more actors can role-take with a common and generalized perspective, and use this common perspective as a source of self-evaluation and self-control, the greater is their capacity to create and maintain cohesive patterns of social organization.

In this principle, the ability to role-take with a common perspective (norms, values, beliefs, and other symbolic components) is linked to the degree of cohesiveness in patterns of social organization. Thus, unified and cohesive patterns of organization are maintained, Mead argued, by a common collective perspective. On this score, Mead came close to Durkheim's emphasis on the need for a "common" or "collective" conscience. But in contrast to Durkheim, Mead was able to tie this point of emphasis to the theory of human action and interaction, and hence, he was in a position to specify the mechanisms by which individual conduct is regulated by a "generalized other" or "collective conscience."

Much like Durkheim, Mead also recognized that the size of a population and its differentiation into roles influence the degree of commonality of the generalized other. These variables can be expressed as two subpropositions:

> 23a. The more similar is the position of actors, the more likely are they to be able to role-take with a common and generalized perspective.
>
> 23b. The smaller is the size of a population of actors, the more likely are these actors to role-take with a common and generalized perspective.

Naturally, the converse of propositions 3, 3a, and 3b could signal difficulties in achieving unified and cohesive patterns of social organization. If the members of a population cannot role-take with a common generalized other, then cohesive social organization will be more problematic. And if a population is large and/or highly differentiated, role-taking with a common generalized other will be more difficult.

Like Durkheim, Mead recognized that a common generalized other becomes increasingly tenuous with growing size and differentiation of a population. For large differentiated populations there are multiple "generalized others," since people participate in many different organized collectivities. These considerations led Mead to view consistency of generalized others as related to how extensive differentiation of social structure could become.

> 24. The more actors can role-take with multiple but consistent generalized perspectives, and the more they can use these perspectives as a source of self-evaluation and self-control, the greater is their capacity to differentiate roles and extend the scope of social organization.

In this principle, Mead argued that if the basic profile of norms, values, and beliefs of different groupings in which individuals participate are not contradictory, then differentiation does not lead to conflict and degeneration of social organization. On the contrary, multiple and consistent generalized others allow for functional differentiation of roles and groups which, in turn, expands the scope (size, territory, and other such variables) of society. Of course, if generalized others are contradictory, then conflictual relations are likely, thereby limiting the extent of social organization.

But much like Durkheim, Mead recognized that symbolic components of culture exist at different levels of generality. Some are highly abstract and cut across diverse groupings, while others are tied to specific groups and organizations. Mead distinguished between "abstract" generalized others and concrete "organized" others to denote this facet of symbolic organization. And like Durkheim, Mead saw that the scope of social organization is limited by how well "abstract others" (values and beliefs, for example) are integrated with more concrete "organized others" (particular norms and doctrines of concrete groups, social classes, organizations, and regions, for example). Large-scale social organization, Mead felt, is dependent upon common and highly abstract values and beliefs that are integrated with the specific perspectives of differentiated collectivities. The concept of integration, Mead appeared to argue, involves more than consistency and lack of contradiction; it denotes the fact that the specific generalized others of particular organized collectivities represent concrete applications of the abstract generalized other. The abstract generalized other sets the parameters for less-abstract perspectives, thereby assuring not just consistency between the two but also integration where the tenets of each are interrelated.

It is in this recognition that Mead's argument came close to that of Durkheim. We can visualize this similarity in the following proposition:

25. **The more actors can simultaneously role-take with a common and abstract perspective, and at the same time role-take with a variety of specific perspectives of particular collectivities that are integrated with the abstract perspective, and the more these integrated perspectives can be a source of self-evaluation and self-control, the greater is their capacity to extend the scope of social organization.**

As with propositions 1 through 24, the converse of this 25th proposition can point to some of the conditions producing conflict and change. To the degree that abstract and specific perspectives are not integrated, actors will potentially have different interpretations of situations, and to the degree that they come into contact, the probability for conflict will be increased.

These five principles summarize Mead's vision of the basic properties of social organization. For society to exist at all, actors must be able to role-take with multiple others and with generalized others (principles 21 and 22). For a highly cohesive organization to exist and persist, actors must be able to role-take a common generalized other (principle 23). For somewhat less-cohesive but more differentiated and extensive patterns of social organization to be viable, actors must be able to role-take with multiple, but nevertheless noncontradictory, generalized others (principle 24). And for large-scale and highly extensive patterns of organization, actors must role-take with well-integrated abstract and specific generalized others (principle 25).

MEAD IN RETROSPECT

Mead's ideas continue to influence sociological theory and research because, more than any of the early American social thinkers, his ideas penetrated to the core of social reality. His principles of action and interaction as well as those on mind and self capture the essence of these phenomena. While his principles on social structure are noticeably lacking in structural referents, they do point to a critical process underlying the nature and scope of social structures, whatever their specific form.

In our review of Mead's models and principles, we have sought to emphasize those aspects of his larger philosophical scheme that are of direct relevance to sociological theorizing. We have not summarized the whole of Mead's thought, only its sociological content. Yet, Mead's sociological insights are probably his most enduring, and hence, this and the previous chapters have documented the emergence, essence, and theoretical significance of the most important aspects of Mead's work.

In particular, our concern has been with Mead's theoretical significance. And while Mead's models are useful in communicating his vision of causality, we feel that it is in his more abstract theoretical principles that his contribution becomes most clearly evident. Each of these principles provides, we feel, a host of suggestive leads for both theoretical and research activity. By making these principles explicit, we hope that they can renew interest in Mead's theory of mind, self, and society.

PART IV

The Legacy: Problems
and Prospects for
Contemporary
Sociological Theory

24

THE SUBSTANTIVE AND STRATEGIC LEGACY

SUBSTANCE AND STRATEGY

In the previous chapters, we have summarized the basic models and principles of sociology's early masters. In particular, we have stressed their more abstract principles since these represent the enduring contribution of Spencer, Marx, Pareto, Weber, Durkheim, Simmel and Mead. Thus, if we were to summarize the substantive theoretical legacy of the masters, we would list, and perhaps catalogue and combine, the propositions presented in each of their "models and "principles." Such an exercise is perhaps unnecessary at this point, since the propositions have already been stated clearly. But in order to facilitate easy reference to these principles, they are listed for each scholar in the appendix to this chapter. It is our belief that these principles represent sociology's substantive legacy from its first masters. To phrase the matter differently, these principles are the legacy of our first 100 years as a formal scientific disciple. We believe that this is an impressive legacy that can continue to inform modern sociologists. We hope this legacy will continue to be consulted.

In generating, if only implicitly, the principles listed in the appendix, each theorist employed a somewhat unique theoretical strategy. We can review the respective strategies of our intellectual forefathers and gain considerable insight into why and how the propositions listed in the Appendix were developed. Moreover, we can see how our current approaches to theory building compare with those employed earlier in the history of the discipline. Such comparisons can perhaps tell us what we are doing right and, of course, what we are doing wrong.

THEORETICAL STRATEGIES, 1830–1930[1]

To assess the diverse strategies of sociology's early pioneers, we need some common reference points that can facilitate comparison. Below is a list of key issues around which diverse theoretical strategies revolve:

1. *Abstract Principles:* Should, or can, sociological theory resemble theory in physics? Can we develop abstract statements of fundamental relations among social phenomena, without regard to causality and without concern for historical epochs?

2. *Causality:* To what extent should sociological theory be concerned with discerning the causes of phenomena? Must sociology's abstract statements uncover causal connections?

3. *Typology and Classification:* To what degree should sociological theory employ abstract or concrete typologies of social phenomena? Should these be constructed prior to theoretical statements?

4. *Structural Affinities:* Should sociological theory be devoted to understanding the covariance of specific types of social structures (such as how changes in the economy are associated with changes in kinship and religion)? Or should theory seek to understand the more abstract properties of social interaction and organization common to all types of social structures (such as the principles of hierarchy, ecological distribution, mobility, and the like)?

5. *Meta-theoretical Supposition:* To what extent must sociology begin with a series of assumptive statements on the "nature of social reality" before theory can be developed? Can theory be developed only after creating an extensive metaphysical system?

6. *Induction versus Deduction:* Should detailed observations of social events precede and inspire the development of theory? Or should theory be articulated first, and then tested against the empirical facts?

On each of these issues, theorists are likely to take a stand. Table 24–1 represents in tabular form the position of each scholar discussed in this book on the six issues. By reading down the columns of the table, certain strategic trends are evident. First, the enthusiasm associated with the post-Newtonian vision of the 18th and early 19th centuries soon faded. Comte's advocacy of a "social physics" was not followed

---

[1] This section is a revised version of of Jonathan H. Turner, "Sociology as a Theory Building Enterprise: Detours from the Early Masters," *Pacific Sociological Review* 22 (October 1979); 446–69.

and the search for the abstract laws of the social universe was replaced by other concerns. Second, theorists became increasingly concerned with causality and functions. Whether Marx's economic determinism or Weber's tracing of historical causes, much theoretical activity revolved around assessing causality. Moreover, Spencer's functionalism was adopted by Durkheim and considered to be a key element in any sociological explanation. While Pareto, Simmel, and Mead were not greatly concerned with causality, they were by 1930 less influential than those who advocated an emphasis on causality. And hence, a concern with causality came to dominate modern sociological inquiry. Third, induction as a tool for theory development appears to have become the dominant emphasis. Fourth, metaphysical assumptions appear to have become more elaborated as notions of dialectics, function, cycles, equilibrium, and behaviorism were introduced as a central dynamic or property of the social universe.

These trends are, of course, far from unambiguous. But if we look at the most influential of these theorists at the dawn of the modern era, it is clear that *(a)* cause and function are dominant concerns and *(b)* the development of abstract laws is seen as awaiting the completion of "logically prior" activities, whether empirical descriptions, statements of assumptions, elaboration of typologies, or other preliminary activities.

As a result of these trends, modern sociology lost, we feel, much of the Newtonian vision of Comte and Spencer. Moreover, it took as a guideline the less-interesting facets of the work of Marx, Durkheim, Weber, and Mead. For example, Marx's argument against universal principles that transcended time and place was accepted, as was his one-sided determinism; Weber's penchant for typology and causal analysis became a prominent role model for those "doing theory"; Durkheim's functional preachings became gospel to many; and Mead's statements on *in*determinism spawned an anti-Newtonian vision of social science. Those who rejected causality and function, such as Pareto, or those who sought to articulate the principles of generic social forms, such as Simmel, did not begin to exert an influence on modern sociology until later, after sociologists were committed to causal and functional analysis as well as extensive typologizing.

THE LOST PROMISE: A CONCLUDING COMMENT

One of the themes of this book—indeed, the major motivation for writing these pages—has been our conviction that theory in sociology has lost its early theoretical vision. At a time when sociology has made

TABLE 24-1.
Diverse Theoretical Strategies of the Early Masters

	Degree of emphasis on:					
	Abstract laws	*Causality*	*Typologies*	*Structural affinities*	*Meta-theory*	*Induction versus deduction*
Auguste Comte (1798–1857)	Sociology can emulate physics and seek invariant laws of the social universe.	Concern with causality will detract from the search for laws.	Useful in describing stages of societal development.	Useful in showing how structures change together during societal development.	Organismic analogy: social phenomena reveal systemic properties.	Theory must be based on observation, and vice versa.
Herbert Spencer (1820–1903)	Sociology must seek the laws of the social universe, as these can be deduced from the law of cosmic evolution.	Should be concerned with causality, but must be secondary to search for laws.	Useful in describing stages of societal development and in capturing the cyclical dynamics of social systems.	Useful in creating a data base for inducing and testing theories. Engaged in a life-long effort to describe social structures of diverse types of societies.	1. Organismic analogy: social phenomena reveal systemic properties; 2. Implicit functionalism: appropriate to analyze needs of the social system met by a particular structure.	Theory must be based on observation, and vice versa.
Karl Marx (1818–1883)	Laws of distinctive historical epochs can be discovered and used to ana-	Must be concerned, since laws will be causal statements of economic deter-	Not as important as laws which describe the dynamics of a historical epoch.	Will reflect causal connections. Can be used to discover laws of each epoch.	1. Dialectics: structures contain the very properties that lead to their transformation.	Laws of a historical epoch can be induced from observations of the relations of pro-

	...lyze events in that epoch. Universal laws for all times and places cannot be discovered.	...minism.			2. Conflict–change: change is the result of conflict among super- and subordinate classes. 3. Sub- and super-structure: economic variables determine cultural and social patterns.	duction, and/or through praxis.
Max Weber (1864–1920)	Not concerned.	Should trace the causal relations among social phenomena.	Typologies, or ideal types, are the essence of sociological description.	The goal of sociology is to show how empirical structures covary and, if possible, are causally connected.	1. Action is meaningful and must be understood at this level. 2. Action creates emergent patterns which are amenable to sociological analysis.	Conceptual work is to be induced from a careful examination and comparison of empirical cases.
Émile Durkheim (1858–1917)	Regularities in human organization can be articulated.	First and final causes must always be assessed—that is, the antecedent conditions and functions of a phenomena must be determined.	Useful in capturing the variable states of phenomena.	Necessary to discovering social patterns. Few such affinities actually articulated.	1. Organismic analogy: phenomena reveal systemic properties. 2. Explicit functionalism: necessary to determine the integrative needs served by social phenomena.	Observations on empirical and historical events to form the basis for causal and functional statements.

TABLE 24-1 *(continued)*

Vilfredo Pareto (1848–1923)	Sociology can emulate physics and discover the invariant laws of social organization and change.	Analysis of one-way causality will inhibit sociological inquiry. Must focus on mutual connections of phenomena.	Useful in describing variable states of phenomena.	Social phenomena vary together, and hence, empirical descriptions of the patterns of covariance critical to sociological analysis are possible.	1. Social phenomena reveal equilibrium tendencies. 2. Change reveals cyclical patterns.	Theory must be based upon observations, and vice versa.
Georg Simmel (1858–1918)	Laws of sociation can be discovered. Little concern with explicit articulation.	Not concerned.	Not concerned.	Necessary to unraveling the basic forms of social interaction. Few actually developed.	Social phenomena reveal underlying forms which can be described.	Implicit inductive emphasis.
George Herbert Mead (1863–1931)	The fundamental nature of the relationship between individuals and patterns of social organization can be articulated. Little concern with formal laws, however.	Not concerned.	Not concerned.	Not concerned, except to show that mind, self, and society are interrelated.	1. Mind and self are behaviors. 2. Social organization cannot exist without mind and self, and vice versa.	Advocated neither, but scheme is implicitly deductive.

great strides in developing techniques for collecting and analyzing data, the discipline is in a state of theoretical confusion. As a result, theory does not guide data collection, and often seems irrelevant to interpreting data.

It is our contention that the first vision of sociological theory was the most correct: the search for the basic laws of the social universe. But sociology rarely maintains Comte's vision on this matter. If we examine the principles stated in the Appendix to follow, there is reason to believe that we have, as a discipline, come close to discovering some of the "laws" or "first principles" of the social universe. And yet, most sociologists continue to believe that the discovery of such laws is not possible or that it must await a variety of "prior" activities. Our view is that neither position is true. Moreover, both views arrest modern sociologists' theoretical imagination in ways that become a self-fulfilling prophecy. If we do not believe that abstract laws are discoverable, then we certainly will not find them. If we take only those principles of the masters articulated in this book, and seek to refine them, we would be close to realizing Comte's dream of a "social physics." Unfortunately, in the place of Comte's dream, we have a series of theoretical "orientations."[2] These are the topics of the last chapter.

APPENDIX

HERBERT SPENCER'S THEORETICAL PRINCIPLES

Principles of System Growth and Differentiation

1. The larger is a social system, the greater will be its level of structural differentiation.
2. The greater is the rate of growth of a social system, the greater is its rate and degree of structural differentiation.

---

[2] A number of books discuss these "orientations." See for relevant discussions: Jonathan H. Turner, *The Structure of Sociological Theory* (Homewood, Ill.: Dorsey Press, 1974, 1978); George Ritzer, *Sociology: A Multiple Paradigm Science* (Boston: Allyn & Bacon, 1975); Don Martindale, *The Nature and Types of Sociological Theory* (Boston: Houghton Mifflin, 1960); Alvin Boskoff, *The Mosaic of Sociological Theory* (New York: Thomas Y. Crowell, 1972); Percy Cohen, *Modern Sociological Theory* (New York: Basic Books, 1968); M. J. Mulkay, *Functionalism and Exchange and Theoretical Strategy* (New York: Schocken Books, 1971); Walter Wallace, *Sociological Theory* (Chicago: Aldine, 1969); Graham C. Kinloch, *Sociological Theory: Its Development and Major Paradigms* (New York: McGraw-Hill, 1977); Leon H. Warshay, *The Current State of Sociological Theory* (New York: David McKay, 1975); Margaret M. Poloma, *Contemporary Sociological Theory* (New York: Macmillan, 1979).

3. The more growth in the numbers of members in a social system is concentrated, the more likely is that growth to be accompanied by high rates of structural differentiation.

4. The more growth and differentiation at one point in time has resulted in structural integration of system units, the more likely is that system to grow and differentiate further at a subsequent point in time.

Principles of Internal System Differentiation

5. The more a social system has initiated the process of structural differentiation, the more likely is the initial axes of differentiation to be between regulatory and operative structures.

6. The more a social system has differentiated separate regulatory and operative structures, and the greater is the volume of activity in that system, the more likely are separate mediating structures involved in distributive processes to become differentiated from regulatory and operative structures.

7. The more differentiated are the three major axes in a social system, the greater are its integrative problems, and hence, the more likely are relations of mutual interdependence and centralized authority to develop in that system.

8. The greater is the degree of differentiation along the regulatory axes, the more likely is differentiation to occur initially between structures dealing with (a) the external environment and (b) internal activities, and only after the differentiation of a and b is differentiation of regulatory structures for facilitating the exchange of resources likely to occur.

9. The greater is the degree of differentiation along the operative axes, the more likely are diverse activities to become spatially separated and localized.

10. The greater is the degree of differentiation along the distributive axes, (a) the greater is the rate of movement of materials and information in the system, (b) the greater is the variety and volume of materials and information distributed in the system, and (c) the higher is the ratio of information to materials distributed in the system.

11. The greater is the degree of external environmental threat to a differentiating system, the greater is the degree of internal control exercised by the regulatory system.

12. The greater is the degree of threat to system stability posed by

dissimilar units, the greater is the degree of internal control exercised by the regulatory system.

13. The greater is the degree of control by the regulatory system, the more is growth and differentiation of operative and distributive structures circumscribed by the narrow goals of the regulatory system.

14. The more operative and regulatory structures are circumscribed by centralized regulatory structures, the more likely are they, over time, to resist such control, and the more they resist, the more likely is control to decrease.

15. The less operative and distributive processes are circumscribed by centralized regulatory structures, the greater are problems of internal integration, and the more likely is the regulatory system to increase efforts at centralized control.

The Principle of Differentiation and Adaptation

16. The greater is the degree of structural differentiation in a system, and the greater is its level of internal integration, the greater is its adaptive capacity.

KARL MARX'S THEORETICAL PRINCIPLES

Principles of Social Organization

1. The greater is the level of technological resources available to members of a population, the greater is their productive activity; and conversely, the greater is the productive activity of a population, the more likely is the level of technology to increase, setting into motion increased productivity.

2. The greater is the level of productive activity among members of a population, the more likely is that population to reveal high levels of social differentiation; and conversely, the greater is the level of social differentiation, the more likely is productivity to increase, setting into motion pressures for increased differentiation.

3. The greater are the levels of productivity and social differentiation in a system, the greater is the capacity of that system to support a larger population, and by implication, the larger is the population, the greater are the pressures for increased productivity and social differentiation.

4. The larger is the population and the greater is the degree of social

differentiation, the more is integration among members of that population achieved, at least in the short run, through the rank differentiation and concentration of power.

5.   The greater are the levels of rank differentiation and concentration of power, the more likely are belief and normative systems to be controlled by those with power and used to legitimize the inequalities in the distribution of scarce resources that are associated with rank differentiation.

Principles of Inequality and Change in Social Systems

6.   The more unequal is the distribution of scarce resources in a system, the greater will be the conflict of interest between dominant and subordinate segments in that system.

   6a.   The more those with power use this power to consolidate their control over other resources, the more unequal is the distribution of scarce resources in a system.

   6b.   The more those with power seek to limit the upward mobility of those in lower ranks, the more unequal is the distribution of scarce resources in a system.

7.   The more subordinate segments become aware of their true collective interests, the more likely are they to question the legitimacy of the unequal distribution of scarce resources.

   7a.   The more social changes wrought by dominant segments disrupt existing relations among subordinates, the more likely are the latter to become aware of their true collective interests.

   7b.   The more practices of dominant segments create alienative dispositions among subordinates, the more likely are the latter to become aware of their true collective interests.

   7c.   The more members of subordinate segments can communicate their grievances to each other, the more likely are they to become aware of their true collective interests.

      7c1.   The greater is the spatial concentration of members of subordinate groups, the more likely are they to communicate their grievances.

      7c2.   The more subordinates have access to educational media, the more diverse the means of their communication, and the more likely are they to communicate their grievances.

7d. The more subordinate segments can develop unifying systems of beliefs, the more likely are they to become aware of their true collective interests.

  7d1. The greater is the capacity to recruit or generate ideological spokespersons, the more likely is ideological unification.

  7d2. The less is the ability of dominant groups to regulate the socialization processes and communication networks in a system, the more likely is ideological unification.

8. The more subordinate segments of a system are aware of their collective interests, the greater is their questioning of the legitimacy in the distribution of scarce resources, and the more likely are they to organize and initiate overt conflict against dominant segments of a system.

  8a. The more the deprivations of subordinates move from an absolute to a relative basis, the more likely are they to organize and initiate conflict.

  8b. The less is the ability of dominant groups to make manifest their collective interests, the more likely are subordinate groups to organize and initiate conflict.

  8c. The greater is the ability of subordinate groups to develop a leadership structure, the more likely are they are to organize and initiate conflict.

9. The more subordinate segments are unified by a common belief and the more developed their political leadership structure, the more the dominant and subjugated segments of a social system will become polarized.

10. The more polarized are the dominant and subjugated, the more violent will be the ensuing conflict.

11. The more violent is the conflict, the greater will be the structural change of the system and the redistribution of scarce resources.

MAX WEBER'S THEORETICAL PRINCIPLES

Principles of Charismatic Leadership and Authority

1. The lower is the level of integration in a social system, the more likely are incumbents in that system to articulate their grievances,

and hence, the more likely are they to be receptive to the influence of charismatic leaders.

2. The less effective is a charismatic leader in resolving the grievances of incumbents in a system, the more likely are integrative problems to escalate, and hence, the more likely is a leader's authority to decrease; and conversely, the more effective is a charismatic leader in resolving the grievances of incumbents in a system, the more likely are integrative problems to decrease, and hence, the more likely is a charismatic leader's authority to endure.

3. The more effective a charismatic leader is in resolving system incumbents' grievances, the more likely is that leader to change the existing social structural arrangements as well as the cultural values and psychological orientations of system incumbents.

4. The longer is the duration of charismatic authority, the more likely are decision-making tasks to be transferred to an administrative staff, and hence, the more likely is the relationship between the leader and system incumbents to be transformed from one based upon charisma into one based upon law or tradition.

Principles of Stratification

5. The more status differences are based on ascriptive criteria and the more salient such criteria are, then the greater is the range of discrimination against those having different life-styles.

6. The lower is the rate of technological change in a system, the more stable is the stratification system and the higher is the level of social integration; and conversely, the higher is the rate of technological change in a system, then the less stable is the stratification system and the lower is the level of social integration.

Principles of Conflict and Social Change

7. The continuity in patterns of social organization is a positive function of the degree of legitimacy given to political authority, and the degree of legitimacy of political authority is a negative function of the following:

    7a. The degree of correlation of status, classes, and power, with the degree of correlation being a negative function of rationality in, and complexity of, patterns of organization.

    7b. The degree of discontinuity in social hierarchies, with the

degree of discontinuity being a negative function of rationality in, and complexity of, patterns of social organization.

7c. The degree to which upward mobility for lower ranking
units is blocked, with the degree of blockage being a negative function of rationality in, and complexity of, patterns
of social organization.

8. The degree of change in patterns of social organization is a positive
function of conflict, and the degree of conflict is a positive function
of the following:

8a. The degree of polarization of status, class, and power
groups, with the degree of polarization being a positive
function of 7a, 7b, and 7c.

8b. The availability of charismatic leaders who oppose the existing distribution of power.

GEORG SIMMEL'S THEORETICAL PRINCIPLES

Principles of Social Exchange

1. The more actors perceive as valuable each other's respective resources, the more likely is an exchange relationship to develop
among these actors.

2. The greater is the intensity of an actor's needs for a resource of
a given type and the less available is that resource, the greater is
the value of that resource to the actor.

3. The more an actor perceives as valuable the resources of another
actor, the greater is the power of the latter over the former.

4. The more "liquid" are an actor's resources, the greater will be
the exchange options and alternatives, and hence, the greater will
be the power of that actor in social exchanges.

5. The more actors in a social exchange manipulate the situation in
an effort to misrepresent their needs for a resource and/or conceal
the availability of resources, the greater is the level of tension in
that exchange and the greater is the potential for conflict.

Principles on the Use of Generalized and Symbolic Media

6. The greater is the degree of differentiation in a social system, the
greater will be the use of generalized and symbolic media of social
exchange, and vice versa.

7. The greater is the use of generalized and symbolic media of exchange in a social system, the greater will be:

    7a. The volume of exchange relations.

    7b. The rate of social exchange.

    7c. The scope of social exchange.

    7d. The accumulation of value in social exchange.

    7e. The continuity of interaction and exchange.

    7f. The multiplicity of social ties and exchanges.

    7g. The differentiation of power to regulate social relations and exchanges.

8. The greater is the use of generalized and symbolic media of exchange in a social system, the greater will be:

    8a. The options of individuals.

    8b. The diversity of individuals.

and the less will be:

    8c. The attachment of individuals to objects, others, and groups.

Principles of Social Conflict

9. The greater is the degree of emotional involvement of parties to a conflict, the more likely is the conflict to be violent.

    9a. The greater is the respective solidarity among members of conflicting parties, the greater is the degree of their emotional involvement.

    9b. The greater is the previous harmony between members of conflicting parties, the greater is the degree of their emotional involvement.

10. The more a conflict is perceived by members of conflict groups to transcend individual aims and interests, the more likely is the conflict to be violent.

11. The more conflict is perceived as a means to an end, the less likely is the conflict to be violent.

12. The less violent and more frequent is the conflict among social units in a differentiated social system, the more likely is the conflict to:

    12a. Allow units to release hostilities before they accumulate to extremely high levels.

    12b. Encourage the creation of norms to regulate the conflict.

    12c. Encourage the development of authority and judiciary systems to regulate the conflict.

13. The more violent are intergroup hostilities and the more frequent is conflict among groups, the less likely are group boundaries to disappear.

14. The more violent is the conflict, the more likely is centralization of power in the conflict groups.

15. The more violent is the conflict, the greater will be the internal solidarity of conflict groups, especially if:

    15a. The conflict group is small.

    15b. The conflict group represents a minority position.

    15c. The conflict group is engaged in self-defense.

16. The more violent and the more prolonged is the conflict between groups, the more likely is the formation of coalitions among previously unrelated groups in a system.

17. The more prolonged is the threat of violent conflict between groups, the more enduring are the coalitions of each of the conflict parties.

Principles of Group Affiliation

18. The greater is the degree of social differentiation, the less likely are group affiliations to be concentric and the more likely are they to be multiple and across diverse groups.

19. The more group affiliations cut across diverse groups, the greater is:

    19a. The distinctiveness of individual personality.

    19b. The freedom of individuals.

    19c. The potential for role-conflict.

ÉMILE DURKHEIM'S THEORETICAL PRINCIPLES

Principles of System Differentiation

1. The greater is the concentration of a population, the greater is the degree the social contact among its members, and hence, the greater is the rate of interaction among members of that population.

    1a. The greater is the size of a population, the more likely is it to be concentrated.

    1b. The more pronounced are the ecological barriers confronting a population, the more likely is it to be concentrated.

2. The greater are the rates of interaction among a concentrated population, the greater is the level of competition over scarce resources among members of that population.

2a.   The greater is the number and diversity of communication channels available to members of a population, the more likely are these members to interact and, hence, compete.

2b.   The more available and the greater is the variety of transportation facilities in a system, the more likely are members of this system to interact and, hence, compete.

3.   The greater is the competition for resources among members of a population in a social system, the more likely are they to become socially differentiated.

3a.   The more bounded is a population, the more likely is competition over scarce resources to result in social differentiation.

3a1.   The more pronounced are geographical or ecological boundaries, the more bounded is a population.

3a2.   The more politically organized is a system, the more bounded is a population.

3b.   The more symbolically unified is a population, the more likely is competition over scarce resources to result in social differentiation.

Principles of System Integration

4.   The greater is the degree of system differentiation in a social system, the more generalized are the values, beliefs, and other evaluational symbols in that system.

5.   The greater is the degree of differentiation and value-generalization in a social system, the more likely is normative specification of evaluational premises for relations within and between social units in that system.

6.   The greater is the degree of differentiation and value-generalization in a social system, the more likely are subgroups to form around similar or related role activities in that system.

7.   The greater is the degree of differentiation and value-generalization in a social system, the more likely is coordination of activity to be centralized in that system.

8.   The greater is the degree of centralized authority in a differentiated social system revealing subgroups, the more likely are subgroups to become centers of counterauthority mitigating the centralized authority of that system.

9.   The greater is the degree of differentiation and value-generalization in a social system, the more likely is the distribution of scarce

resources to correspond to the unequal distribution of talents among members of that system.

10. The greater is the degree of differentiation and value-generalization in a social system, the more likely are sanctions against deviance to be restitutive than punitive in that system.

Principles of Deviance

11. The greater is the degree of structural differentiation and value-generalization without a corresponding degree of normative specification in a social system, the greater is the level of anomie, and hence, the greater is the rate of deviance in that group.

12. The greater is the degree of structural differentiation and value-generalization without a corresponding degree of subgroup formation in a social system, the greater is the level of egoism, and hence, the greater is the rate of deviance in that system.

Principles of System Mal-integration

13. The greater is the differentiation and value-generalization in a social system, and the less the degree of normative specification, then the greater is the level of anomie, and hence, the more likely are individuals to be poorly integrated into that system.

14. The greater is the differentiation and value-generalization in a social system, and the less the formation of subgroups, then the greater is the level of egoism, and hence, the more likely are individuals to be poorly integrated into that system.

15. The greater is the differentiation and value-generalization in a social system, and the less the normative specification of relations among social units, then the less is the coordination of units, and hence, the less integrated is that system.

16. The greater is the differentiation and generalization of values in a social system, and the less the centralization of authority, then the less is the coordination of units, and hence, the less integrated is that system.

17. The greater is the differentiation, value-generalization, and centralization of authority in a social system, and the less the countervailing power of subgroups, then the greater is the level of tensions between those with and without power, and hence, the less integrated is that system.

18. The greater is the differentiation and value-generalization in a social system, the less the correlation perceived to exist between the distribution of scarce resources and talents, then the greater is the level of tensions between those with and without resources, and hence, the less integrated is that system.

VILFREDO PARETO'S THEORETICAL PRINCIPLES

Principles of Political Oscillation

1. The greater is the degree of decentralized decision-making in a system, the greater is the use of co-optation as a means of social control.
2. The more continued is the use of co-optation as a means of social control in a system, the greater are the number and diversity of control activities and the more coordination and control rest upon voluntary compliance.
3. The greater are the number and diversity of control activities and the more coordination and control rest upon voluntary compliance in decentralized systems, the more likely are problems of coordination and control to increase.
4. The more problematic coordination and control become in decentralized systems, the more likely are efforts at consolidation and centralization of power to increase.
5. The greater is the degree of centralization of power, the more likely is force, or the threat of force, to be used as a means of social control.
6. The greater and more prolonged is the use of force as a means of social control in a system, the more likely, over the long run, are system units to resist centralized power and to initiate pressures for the decentralization of power.

Principles of Economic Oscillation

7. The greater is capital investment, the greater is the level of productivity in a social system.
8. The more rapid is the rate of increase in productivity in a social system, the greater is the relative investment in facilities producing consumer goods and services as opposed to investment in capital-producing facilities.

9. The greater is the relative commitment of resources to production of consumer goods and services, the more likely is capital depletion.

10. The greater is the rate of capital depletion in a system, the more likely are investment and productivity to decline.

11. The greater are decreases in investment and productivity in a system, the greater is the long-term accumulation of capital.

12. The greater is the accumulation of capital in a system, the more likely is the level of investment in new and diverse productive facilities to increase.

Principles of Cultural Oscillation

13. The more cultural values, and attending beliefs, are "liberal" in profile, the more diverse and less constraining are cultural directives (and attending beliefs).

14. The more diverse and less constraining are cultural directives (and attending beliefs), the greater is the level, over time, of ambiguity in—and conflict among—them, and the more equivocal and less utilitarian they become as guides for behavior.

15. The greater is the level of ambiguity in, and conflict among, cultural directives (and attending beliefs), the more likely are efforts at creating coherence among cultural directives to be initiated.

16. The more efforts at creating coherence among cultural directives persist, the more likely are cultural values, and attending beliefs, to assume a "traditional" profile.

17. The more values, and attending beliefs, are traditional in profile, the more likely are cultural directives, over time, to come into conflict with actual experiences and structural conditions.

18. The more traditional cultural directives come into conflict with actual experiences and structural conditions, the more likely are efforts at creating consistency between existential conditions and cultural directives to be initiated.

19. The more efforts at creating consistency persist, the more likely are cultural values, and attending beliefs, to assume a "liberal" profile.

Principles Relating to Basic Properties of Social Systems

20. The greater is the level of production and decentralization in a system, and the greater is the rate of movement of cultural directives

toward a liberal profile, then the greater are the number of exploiters and avenues for co-optive exploitation in that system.

21. The greater the number of exploiters and avenues of exploitation in a decentralized system, then the more likely are inequities to increase and the greater is the level of alienation among nonelites in that system.

22. The greater is the level of alienation of nonelites in a system, the more likely are they to become aware of inequalities, to resist exploitation, and to debunk cultural beliefs.

23. The greater are the efforts of nonelites to resist exploitation by decentralized elites, the more likely are elites to begin centralizing power and using coercive force.

24. The more power becomes centralized in a predominantly decentralized system and the more productivity becomes contracted in a previously expanding economic system, then the greater are the number of avenues of exploitation abolished, the more equitable becomes distribution of rewards, and the more likely are cultural directives to become traditional in profile.

25. The greater is the degree of centralization and decrease in productivity in a system, and the greater is the rate of movement of cultural directives toward a traditional profile, then the greater is the level of exploitation through appropriation of resources by a few elites.

26. In predominantly centralized systems, the greater is the level of exploitation by centralized elites, the more likely are inequalities to increase, the greater is the level of alienation of nonelites, and the more likely are nonelites to become aware of inequalities, to resist exploitation, and to debunk cultural beliefs.

27. The greater are the efforts of nonelites to resist exploitation by a centralized elite, the more likely are elites to become decentralized, the more likely are co-optive means of exploitation to be initiated, and the more likely are beliefs to shift toward a liberal profile.

28. The more decentralized a predominantly centralized system becomes, and the greater the rate of economic expansion and diversification in a previously contracted economy, the less exploitive-power centralized elites have and the more equitable the distribution of resources.

29. The greater is the level of productivity and decentralization in a system, the greater is the level of upward mobility and the larger is the elite population in that system.

30. The greater is the rate of upward mobility in a decentralized system,

the more recruitment is selective, and hence, the more elites become homogeneous and "liberal" in their values and beliefs.

31. The more homogeneous and liberal is the elite population in a decentralized system, the less able is it to deal with escalating integrative problems in a decentralized system and the less able is it to select its recruits, and hence, the more heterogeneous the elite becomes.

32. The greater are integrative problems in a decentralized system, the greater are the pressures for centralization of power, decreased productivity, and traditional cultural directives.

   32a. The greater is the gap between declining productivity and opportunities, on the one hand, and increasingly liberal cultural directives, on the other, the greater are the integrative problems of a system.

   32b. The more decreased productivity reduces the resources available for co-optation, the greater are the integrative problems of a system.

   32c. The more inequalities have increased alienative dispositions among nonelites, the greater are the integrative problems of a system.

   32d. The greater is the diversification of production and distribution of power, the less able are elites to use force effectively, and hence, the greater are the integrative problems of a system.

33. The more pressures for centralization of power, productive contraction, and traditionalism are successful, the less is the rate of upward mobility and the less available are opportunities for nonelites.

34. The less are the opportunities of nonelites, and the greater is the use of force by elites, the greater are the alienative dispositions of nonelites and the greater is their frustration over the lack of opportunity, and hence, the greater are the pressures for decentralization, expanded productivity, and liberal cultural directives.

35. The greater is the level of production in a system, the greater is the number and diversity of productive units and, hence, the greater are the pressures for decentralization of power and liberal cultural directives, and vice versa.

36. The greater is the level of political decentralization, the greater is the reliance on co-optation as a means of social control, and hence, the greater are the pressures for liberal beliefs and expanded productivity as a means of co-optation, and vice versa.

37. The more "liberal" the beliefs, the less people save and accumulate capital, and hence, the more rapidly investment leads to depletion of available capital and economic contraction.
38. The more decentralized and productive a system, the greater are its integrative problems, and hence, the more likely are pressures for centralization, reduced productivity, and traditional cultural directives as means of social control.
39. The more is a system centralized, restricted in its productivity, and traditional in its cultural directives, the greater are pressures for either, or both, decentralization and expanded productivity.

GEORGE HERBERT MEAD'S THEORETICAL PRINCIPLES

Principles of Animal Action

1. The greater is the degree of maladjustment of an organism to its environment, the stronger are its impulses.
2. The greater is the intensity of an organism's impulse, the greater is the organism's perceptual awareness of objects that can potentially consummate the impulse and the greater is its manipulation of objects in the environment.
    2a. The more maladjustment stems from unconsummated organic needs, the greater is the intensity of the impulse.
    2b. The longer an impulse goes unconsummated, the greater is the intensity of the impulse.
3. The more impulses have been consummated by the perception and manipulation of certain classes of objects in the environment, the more likely are perceptual and behavioral responses to be directed at these and similar objects when similar impulses arise.

Principles of Animal Interaction

4. The more organisms seek to manipulate objects in their environment in an effort to consummate impulses, the greater is the visibility of gestures that they emit during the course of their action.
5. The greater the number and visibility of gestures emitted by acting organisms, the more likely are these organisms to respond to each other's gestures and to adjust responses to each other.

Principles on the Emergence of Mind

6. The more an infant must adapt to an environment composed of organized collectivities of actors, the more likely is the infant to be exposed to significant gestures.
7. The more an infant must seek to consummate its impulses in an organized social collectivity, the more likely is the learning of how to read and use significant gestures to have selective value for consummating the infant's impulses.
8. The more an infant can come to use and read significant gestures, the greater is its ability to role-take with others in its environment, and hence, the greater is its capacity to communicate its needs and to anticipate the responses of others on whom it is dependent for the consummation of impulses.
9. The greater is the capacity of an infant to role-take and use significant gestures, the greater is its capacity to communicate with itself.
10. The greater is the capacity of an infant to communicate with itself, the greater is its ability to covertly designate objects in its environment, inhibit inappropriate responses, and select a response that will consummate its impulses and thereby facilitate its adjustment.
11. The greater is the ability of an infant to reveal such minded behavior, the greater is its ability to control its responses and, hence, to cooperate with others in ongoing and organized collectivities.

Principles on the Emergence of Self

12. The more a young actor can engage in minded behavior, the more it can read significant gestures, role-take, and communicate with itself.
13. The more a young actor can read significant gestures, role-take, and communicate with itself, the more it can see itself as an object in any given situation.
14. The more diverse the specific others with whom a young actor can come to role-take, the more it can increasingly come to see itself as an object in relation to the dispositions of multiple others.
15. The more generalized the perspective of others with whom a young infant can come to role-take, the more it can increasingly come to see itself as an object in relation to general values, beliefs, and norms of increasingly larger collectivities.
16. The greater stability in a young actor's images of itself as an object

in relation to both specific others and generalized perspectives, the more reflexive is its role-taking and the more consistent are its behavioral responses.

16a. The more the first self-images derived from role-taking with others have been consistent and noncontradictory, the greater is the stability, over time, of an actors self-conception.

16b. The more self-images derived from role-taking with generalized perspectives are consistent and noncontradictory, the greater is the stability, over time, of an actor's self-conception.

17. The more a young actor can reveal stability in its responses to itself as an object, and the more it can see itself as an object in relation to specific others as well as generalized perspectives, the greater is its capacity to control its responses and, hence, to cooperate with others in ongoing and organized collectivities.

Principles of Human Action and Interaction

18. The greater is the intensity of impulses of humans with mind and self, (a) the more likely is perceptual awareness of objects that can potentially consummate the impulse to be selective, (b) the more likely is manipulation to be covert, and (c) the more likely are both perception and manipulation to be circumscribed by a self conception, expectations of specific others, and the generalized perspective of organized collectivities.

19. The more humans with mind and self seek to consummate impulses in the presence of others, the more likely are they to emit overt significant gestures and the more likely are they to read the significant gestures of others and, hence, the greater their role-taking activity.

20. The more humans role-take with each other, the more likely is the course of their interaction to be guided by the specific disposition of others present in a situation, by the self-images of the self as a certain type of object in the situation, and by the generalized perspective of the organized collectivity in which they are participating.

Principles of Human Social Organization

21. The more actors can role-take with pluralities of others, and use the dispositions of multiple others as a source of self-evaluation

and self-control, the greater is their capacity to create and maintain patterns of social organization.

22. The more actors can role-take with the generalized perspective of organized collectivities, and use this perspective as a source of self-evaluation and self-control, the greater is their capacity to create and maintain patterns of social organization.

23. The more actors can role-take with a common and generalized perspective, and use this common perspective as a source of self-evaluation and self-control, the greater is their capacity to create and maintain cohesive patterns of social organization.

    23a. The more similar is the position of actors, the more likely are they to be able to role-take with a common and generalized perspective.

    23b. The smaller is the size of a population of actors, the more likely are these actors to role-take with a common and generalized perspective.

24. The more actors can role-take with multiple but consistent generalized perspectives, and the more they can use these perspectives as a source of self-evaluation and self-control, the greater is their capacity to differentiate roles and extend the scope of social organization.

25. The more actors can simultaneously role-take with a common and abstract perspective, and at the same time role-take with a variety of specific perspectives of particular collectivities that are integrated with the abstract perspective, and the more these integrated perspectives can be a source of self-evaluation and self-control, the greater is their capacity to extend the scope of social organization.

25

THE EMERGENCE OF MODERN THEORETICAL PERSPECTIVES

"ON THE SHOULDERS OF GIANTS"

In all of the preceding chapters, our goal has been to communicate sociology's theoretical legacy. As is evident, this is a rich legacy, filled with insightful models and abstract theoretical principles. It is on the base laid by the masters examined in the previous chapters that modern sociological theory has been built. Indeed, to paraphrase Newton and many others who have recognized a debt to their predecessors, "if we have seen farther, it is by standing on the shoulders of giants." Some might contend that modern sociologists have not seen farther; rather, we remain in "the shadows of giants." Others would object to such a cynical conclusion. We suspect that modern theorists have "seen farther," but not as far as they could. The reason for this "shortsightedness" is, we feel, a lack of complete appreciation for the formal elegance and sophistication of early work in sociology. We hope our efforts in this book have contributed, even if only in a modest way, to communicating the theoretical power of our first masters' work.

In this last chapter, we will seek to outline in general terms the various directions that the masters' works have taken modern sociologists. To do so, we will analyze the substance and strategy of the five dominant theoretical perspectives in sociology: functionalism, conflict theory, exchange theory, interactionism, and phenomenology.[1]

---

[1] For more detailed accounts of these, and other, modern perspectives, see Jonathan H. Turner, *The Structure of Sociological Theory* (Homewood, Ill.: Dorsey Press, 1974, 1978) © 1974, 1978 The Dorsey Press.

542

THE SUBSTANTIVE ASSUMPTIONS OF MODERN THEORETICAL PERSPECTIVES

The Emergence of Functional Theory in Sociology

As we saw in Chapter 2, Auguste Comte first articulated a clear vision of a "science of society." In seeking legitimacy for this new science, Comte saw sociology as growing out of biology, for both sociology and biology are concerned with "organic bodies." Yet Comte was quick to assert that while "biology has hitherto been the guide and preparation for sociology . . . , sociology will in the future . . . [provide] the ultimate systematization of Biology."[2]

Comte went on to make a number of analogies between social and biological "organisms." He argued that social structures could be "decomposed anatomically" into "elements, tissues, and organs" and that it is possible to treat the "Social Organism" as "definitely composed of the Families which are the true elements or cells, next the classes or castes which are its proper tissues, and lastly of the cities and communes which are its real organs."[3]

This line of analogizing formally initiated what was in the 20th century to become known as "functionalism" and "structural-functionalism." For if social systems are "like biological organisms," then it is appropriate to ask: What is "the function" of a particular social structure for the survival and operation of the body social? It was Herbert Spencer who began to codify this line of reasoning in the latter half of the last century.

As we outlined in Chapters 3 to 5, Spencer's sociological works owe much to his earlier analysis of biological processes.[4] Indeed, throughout his work, one finds a persistent comparison between the organization of organic and "super-organic" bodies. But, he went much further than Comte and argued that sociological analysis of functions must seek to understand the "need" served by a social structure. That is, to determine the "function" of a structure, it is necessary to know the "need" of the social whole that it meets. Such needs are the "survival requisites" of the social whole; they are what must be done if the social whole is to remain viable.

While Émile Durkheim was highly critical of both Comte and

---

[2] Auguste Comte, *System of Positive Polity* (London: Burt Franklin, 1875), pp. 239–40.

[3] Ibid., pp. 241–42.

[4] In particular, his monumental *Principles of Biology*. For a more detailed review of the origins and profile of functionalism, see Jonathan H. Turner and Alexandra Maryanski, *Functionalism* (Menlo Park, Calif.: Benjamin/Cummings, 1978).

Spencer, he retained the critical elements of their functionalism. Indeed, he contributed to this perspective by distinguishing "causal" from "functional" analysis. For Durkheim stressed that sociological explanations must involve two elements: (1) an understanding of the causes of a particular social form and (2) an assessment of its functions for the integration of the social whole.[5]

Thus, by the turn of the century, much sociological and anthropological analysis was "functional" in its approach. This approach embodied the following elements:

1. Social systems are composed of interconnected parts.
2. Social systems confront external and internal problems of survival.
3. Such problems of survival can be visualized as the "needs" or "requisites" of the system.
4. Social systems and their constituent parts can only be understood by assessing how a part contributes to meeting the needs or requisites of the systemic whole.

These are the basic elements of all functional analyses. But they have been taken in many different directions over the last decades. Anthropologists used the elements as a way to interpret data on traditional societies, for by understanding the function of a cultural item, such as a religious ritual or kinship pattern, then that item could be explained.[6] Other anthropologists and sociologists took a more analytical approach and began to construct typologies of "system needs" and to catalogue structures in terms of the needs that they meet.[7] Still others argued that "needs" varied from one empirical system to another and that only after empirically establishing a system's requisites could an analysis of functions (and dysfunctions) of structures for meeting these needs be undertaken.[8]

For many decades, functional analyses dominated sociology and anthropology. But in recent years, functional analysis has come under heavy attack. Yet much anthropological and sociological work, both theoretical

---

[5] Émile Durkheim, *The Division of Labor in Society* (Glencoe, Ill.: Free Press, 1947; originally published in 1893); and *The Rules of the Sociological Method* (Glencoe, Ill.: Free Press, 1950; originally published in 1895).

[6] For an early illustration of this approach, see A. R. Radcliff-Brown, "Structure and Function in Primitive Society," *American Anthropologist* 37 (July–September 1935).

[7] See, for example, Talcotte Parsons, *The Social System* (Glencoe, Ill.: Free Press, 1951); and Bronislaw Malinowski, *A Scientific Theory of Culture* (Chapel Hill: University of North Carolina Press, 1944).

[8] See, for example, Robert K. Merton, "Manifest and Latent Functions" in *Social Theory and Social Structure* (New York: Free Press, 1968).

and empirical efforts, is still decidedly functional. Thus, one of the major legacies of the masters was functionalism which, for all of its acknowledged deficiencies, forced theorists to view the social world as composed of systems of interconnected parts and to construct theories about the basic properties of such systems.

The Emergence of Conflict Theory

Conflict was a prominent concern among 19th-century scholars. Indeed, the tumultuous eruptions that accompanied the industrial revolution in Europe gave the analysis of conflict processes an immediate relevance. Even the founders of functionalism with their emphasis on integrated social systems evidence an implicit concern with conflict, since they all were vitally interested in those conditions that mitigate conflict and promote integration.

Yet despite this pervasive concern with conflict, modern conflict theory owes its primary inspiration to one scholar, Karl Marx, and only to a lesser extent to others, such as Georg Simmel. For it is in Marx's work that we first see the guiding assumptions of conflict sociology. These include:

1. All social systems reveal inequalities in the distribution of scarce and valuable resources.
2. Such inequalities inevitably and inexorably create conflicts of interests among system units.
3. Such conflicts of interest will, over time, generate overt conflict among those who possess, and those who do not possess, valuable resources.
4. These conflicts will result in reorganization of the social system, creating new patterns of inequality that will serve as the next fulcrum for conflict and change.

Most modern conflict theories employ these assumptions and then seek to develop models and principles for specifying the conditions under which inequalities lead to varying forms of conflict and social change. The major variables are not much different than those originally proposed by Marx: inequality is usually seen as a function of productivity, size, and political centralization. Conflict is viewed as the result of subordinates withdrawing legitimacy from the system. Such withdrawal is related to the degree of inequality, the level of upward social mobility, the availability of grievance channels, and the strength of unifying cultural symbols, such as values and beliefs. In turn, the withdrawal of legitimacy is viewed as escalating subordinates' emotions to a point that they seek to become organized. Such emotional arousal is conceived to be a function of coercive acts by elites, the degree of alienation of key institutional positions, and the escalation of perceived deprivations. This arousal is then typically seen as leading to organization of subordinates to pursue conflict. The degree of violence of the conflict is usually viewed as a positive function of ecological concentration of subordinates, the availability of targets for violent actions, and the lack of clear leadership, unifying symbols, networks of communication, and articulation of interests.[9]

While this brief cataloging does not capture all of the variables employed by conflict theorists, virtually every conflict analysis embodies most of these variables. But, despite this commonality, conflict theory has become quite diverse in recent decades. Some scholars have sought to translate into more abstract and formal terms Marx's[10] or Simmel's[11] ideas; others have focused on specific conflict processes, such as society-wide revolutions; still others have extended the conflict view to the level of the "world system"; and another group has begun to apply a conflict perspective to more micro processes in groups and organizations.[12]

Thus, conflict theories focus on one of the most pervasive social processes in human systems: conflict. But they also provide indirect insights on another pervasive set of processes: social integration and cooperation. For by understanding the conditions that generate conflict, we have gained insight into what does not generate conflict. That is, the converse of those conditions producing conflict will provide us with many fruitful leads into the conditions that promote integration and cooperation. Hence, conflict is not a parochial perspective that focuses on one process; it takes us into the heart of sociological inquiry and allows us to visualize how and why patterns of social organization are created, maintained, and changed.

---

[9] Here is where Simmel's insights proved to be more powerful than Marx's, since Marx felt that violence is positively related to organization. Simmel showed that this was not necessarily the case and, in fact, that violence is most likely when the deprived are only incipiently organized, but emotionally aroused.

[10] See, for example, Ralf Dahrendorf, "Toward a Theory of Social Conflict," *Journal of Conflict Resolution* 2 (June 1958):170–83; and Jonathan H. Turner, "Marx and Simmel Revisited," *Social Forces* 53 (June 1975):723–29, and "A Strategy for Reformulating the Dialectical and Functional Theories of Conflict," *Social Forces*, 53 (March 1975):433–44.

[11] See, for example, Lewis A. Coser, *The Functions of Social Conflict* (Glencoe, Ill.: Free Press, 1956); and Turner, *Structure of Sociological Theory*, pp. 127–58.

[12] For a listing of these references for various directions, see Turner, *Structure of Sociological Theory* p. 180.

The Emergence of Exchange Theory

The explicit roots of exchange theory begin with classical economics of the 18th century. Working under the banner of "utilitarianism," the social world was conceptualized as a kind of open marketplace in which rational actors competed with each other and chose the best means to maximize their "utilities" (or gratifications). The basic metaphor of social life as the exchange of valued resources was retained in the explicitly sociological and anthropological thought of the 19th century. Herbert Spencer and Émile Durkheim both saw exchange as a critical dimension of social life. And George Herbert Mead adopted the utilitarian perspective and then adapted it to his social behaviorism. And Georg Simmel in his *Philosophy of Money* articulated an exchange perspective. Yet we could not proclaim any of the 19th-century founders of sociology to be impetus behind modern exchange theory. Rather exchange theory is a more recent perspective which owes its inspiration to a variety of sources, ranging from economics through sociology and anthropology to behaviorism in psychology.[13] As a result of this diversity exchange theorists often employ different vocabularies and stress somewhat different variables. But common to all exchange theories are the following assumptions:

1. All actors possess resources that they will expend in order to receive valued resources from other actors.
2. All actors make calculations as to the reward value or utility of resources that other actors have to offer and as to the costs that they must incur in the loss of their resources and the loss of alternative resources from other actors. Such calculations are made in terms of:
   a. The needs and/or goals of actors.
   b. The availability of resources in the environment.
   c. The level and value of actors' own resources.
3. All actors make calculations in order to receive from other actors resources that exceed in value or utility those resources that must be expended.
4. Social relations involve a constant process of exchange of resources among actors and both the dynamics and statics of social relations

---

[13] See ibid., p. 278. For a list of references representing the diversity of the sociological perspectives on exchange, see Harry C. Bredemeier, "Exchange Theory," in Tom Bottomore and Robert A. Nisbet, eds., *A History of Sociological Analysis* (New York: Basic Books, 1978), p. 454–56.

are to be explained by reference to the degree of balance or imbalance in such exchanges of resources among actors.

These assumptions have been translated into a wide variety of abstract principles. Such principles emphasize that exchanges of valued resources create pressures for the differentiation of social systems into ranks and that such rank differentiations create, under conditions similar to those listed by conflict theorists, conflict and change. In fact, we might view conflict theory as a special case of exchange theory—that is, a theory that specifies what is likely to occur in social systems where exchange relations have become dramatically asymmetrical, with some actors hoarding resources at the expense of others.

Yet exchange theorists examine many topics other than conflict. Moreover, one can see applications of exchange principles[14] in many diverse empirical contexts, from the analysis of interaction in dyads and small groups to discussions of national and international politics. Thus, exchange theory represents a prominent strategy in contemporary sociology to unify empirical inquiry and conceptual effort under one theoretical perspective.

The Emergence of Interactionist Theory

With the exception of Georg Simmel's analysis of interaction or "sociation" and examination of the "web of group affiliations" as well as with Max Weber's concern over the "subjective meaning" attached to social action, European sociology of the 19th century was decidedly "macro" in emphasis. It focused on large-scale events and processes—evolution, revolution, differentiation, integration, and other processes where the attributes of individuals and specific processes of interaction could be ignored, or at least subordinated to a concern with the structural properties of the world. Only in America were scholars seeking to examine systematically how the attributes of individuals are connected to ongoing social patterns and how specific interactive mechanisms made society a viable entity. As we emphasized in Chapters 21 to 23, this line of inquiry culminated in the work of George Herbert Mead. And it is out of his synthesis that modern interactionist theorizing was born.

For Mead, as for modern-day interactionists, the emphasis is on how the process of interaction mediates between the attributes of the individ-

---

[14] See Turner, *Structure of Sociological Theory,* and Jonathan H. Turner and Charles Powers "Theory and Political Sociology" in *Handbook of Political Sociology,* vol. 1 (New York: Plenam, 1981) for summaries of these principles.

ual and society. On the one hand, ongoing patterns of social organization are seen as constructed from people's capacities to read each other's gestures, to rehearse alternative lines of conduct, to visualize themselves as objects, and to become cognizant of broader cultural expectations. On the other hand, individual capacities for reflective thought, role-playing, and self are viewed as the result of prolonged socialization and other interactive experiences in existing patterns of social organization.

Modern interactionists tend to develop theoretical models and principles about specific social processes,[15] such as role-playing, techniques and strategies of interaction, deviant behavior, socialization, social control, and other processes in the social world. Rarely do interactionists study structures, such as community, organizations, societies, and even small groups, per se; rather their emphasis is always on the specific interactive processes that lead to the construction, maintenance, or change of a particular structure. While some interactionists firmly believe that macro structures like class, community, bureaucracy, and society are only understandable in terms of their constituent processes of interaction, most modern interactionists recognize that their theoretical efforts revolve around the micro processes that underlie patterns of social organization.[16] As a consequence, interactionism is a theoretical perspective within which a great deal of diverse theoretical effort and empirical work are conducted. There is no coherent interactionist "theory of" the social universe. Instead, there are a series of "theories about" specific processes in the social world. Such theories are guided by the general thrust of Mead's synthesis, but each elaborates on Mead's insights in ways that allow for more complete understanding of the specific topics under investigation.

The Emergence of Phenomenological Theory

In many respects, phenomenological theorizing has emerged independently of the early scholars discussed in this book. Weber's concern with action "at the level of meaning" and Mead's enphasis on the process of role-taking have exerted some influence on phenomenological theoriz-

---

[15] For some prominent examples, see Edwin M. Lemert, *Social Pathology* (New York: McGraw-Hill, 1951); Edwin H. Sutherland, *Principles of Criminology* (Philadelphia: Lippincott, 1939); Ralph H. Turner and Lewis Killian, *Collective Behavior* (Englewood Cliffs, N.J.: Prentice-Hall, 1972); and Erving Goffman, *The Presentation of Self in Everyday Life* (Garden City, N.Y.: Doubleday, 1959).

[16] For an exception to this recognition, see Herbert Blumer, *Symbolic Interactionism: Perspective and Method* (Englewood Cliffs, N.J.: Prentice-Hall, 1969).

ing. But, even if we give some credit to early theorists, phenomenology has emerged as a reaction against current theoretical perspectives.[17]

The nature of this reaction differs somewhat depending upon which variant of phenomenology is being analyzed. But all phenomenological theorizing questions and challenges with varying degrees of intensity, the underlying assumptions of the other four theoretical perspectives in sociology, including:

1. There exists "out there" a reality, sui generis, that exists independently of human consciousness and thought.
2. This external reality can be understood with the methods and tools of science.
3. While scientists' subjective states and biases can influence "what they see out there" in the world, these biases can be overcome.

Phenomenologists question these implicit assumptions of "normal science" by postulating an alternative vision. The subjective world of human actors is the major topic of social science inquiry. What exists "out there" in an "external world" is not known independently of states of consciousness, and hence, the logically prior topic of inquiry is understanding the properties and processes of human consciousness. Thus, all phenomenological perspectives view the processes of consciousness as the key topic of empirical and conceptual inquiry. Just whether there is a world "out there" existing independently of subjective consciousness is "bracketed" or suspended as a secondary issue. As an alternative, the more sociologically inclined phenomenologists, who work under labels such as "ethnomethodology" and "cognitive sociology,"[18] argue that the real topic of sociological inquiry is:

1. The processes by which people come to feel that they participate in a common reality.

2. The interpersonal practices by which people come to believe that an external reality exists "out there."

Such a line of inquiry is not just an adjunct to interactionism. For most phenomenologists believe that the only reality is the techniques and rules by which people construct a sense of reality. There is no reality

---

[17] In particular, Edmund Husserl and Alfred Shutz are the founders of modern phenomenology; see Turner, *Structure of Sociological Theory*, pp. 393–403 for a summary of their work. Also, see Kurt H. Wolff, "Phenomenology and Sociology" in Bottomore and Nisbet, eds., *History of Sociological Analysis*, pp. 499–556.

[18] See ibid., pp. 405–21, for a review of these sociological phenomenologies.

"out there"; the only reality is the activity of people trying to convince each other that there is an external world "out there."

MODERN THEORETICAL STRATEGIES

These five theoretical perspectives have dominated conceptual work in sociology. Each implies a strategy for "doing theory" and, hence, guides the efforts of many theorists and researchers. One way to visualize the strategic differences in these modern perspectives is to repeat the exercise performed in the last chapter by comparing the four perspectives with respect to the following issues:

1. Concern with developing highly abstract, timeless, and context-free laws.
2. Concern with tracing causality.
3. Concern with developing classification schemes, or typologies.
4. Concern with covariance among empirical structures—that is, with structural affinities.
5. Concern with developing an extensive system of metaphysics, or meta-theoretical assumptions.
6. Concern with either inductive or deductive reasoning.

Following the format employed in the last chapter, Table 25–1 compares the perspectives along these six dimensions.[19]

It is immediately evident in Table 25–1 that only exchange theory is unambiguously committed to visualizing social phenomena in terms of abstract laws. Other perspectives equivocate on this issue: some argue that laws of the social universe cannot be discovered in light of the spontaneity of human action; others hold that "laws" will be temporal and bound by the empirical conditions of a particular historical epoch; still others maintain that prior conceptual work, such as developing exhaustive typologies, must precede a concern for abstract law; and others argue that sociological laws are about a nonexistent reality.

Thus, modern theoretical strategies deviate considerably from Comte's vision of a "social physics."[20] This detour represents a great intellectual tragedy. We have lost a common vision as to what theory in sociology

---

[19] A version of this table originally appeared in Jonathan H. Turner, "Sociology as a Theory Building Enterprise: Detours from the Early Masters," *Pacific Sociological Review* 22 (October 1979):448–49.

[20] The current alternative theoretical perspectives have deviated even further from sociology's original vision. For a review of these alternatives, see Scott G. McNall, ed., *Theoretical Perspectives in Sociology* (New York: St. Martin's Press, 1979).

TABLE 25–1.
Diverse Theoretical Strategies of Dominant Orientations

	Abstract Laws	Causality	Typologies	Structural Affinities	Meta-theory	Induction versus Deduction
Functionalism	Sociology must do considerable preliminary conceptual work before these can be adequately articulated.	The discovery of how system parts cause variations in states of system whole is essential.	The development of typologies that capture the variable features of the social world is a necessary prerequisite for theory.	Description of empirical correlations among structures is essential.	Implicit organismic analogy: social phenomena must be analyzed as systems of interrelated parts, with assessment of consequences of parts for social whole.	Both induction and deduction are essential, although emphasis tends to be on developing abstract statements from which deductions to empirical cases are to be made.
Conflict theory	Disagreement over this issue: 1. Marxists stress temporal boundaries of abstract laws; 2. non-Marxists more concerned with laws of conflict.	Conditions causing conflict are the major focus of theoretical activity.	Not considered vitally important, although typologies on types of conflict abound.	Essential to understanding conditions producing conflict.	1. Dialectic: distribution of power in structures produces conflicts. 2. Conflict-change: conflict is major source of system change.	Rhetoric of deduction, but most analyses confined to empirical descriptions of specific empirical cases—historical and contemporary.
Exchange theory	Abstract principles of exchange process are essential to theoretical activity in sociology.	Causality is less essential than explanation by "covering laws" of exchange.	Few.	Few; concern is more with articulation of laws.	Social reality is structured around the exchange of rewards.	Emphasis is on deductive explanation.

Interactionism	Disagreement over this issue: 1. some argue that creative capacities of actors render the search for laws either useless, or always provisional; 2. others see the development of the laws of socialization, social control, and interaction as essential.	Causes of various personality types and modes of interaction are central to analysis; heavy emphasis on causes of deviance and personality.	Few.	Few; concern is more with micro processes.	Social reality is built from, and maintained through, symbolic interaction.	Emphasis is on induction from empirical observations.
Phenomenology	Disagreement, although majority hold that laws of the processes by which people develop and construct a "sense" of a common reality can be articulated.	The causes of interactive processes that produce a common sense of reality is a dominant concern.	Virtually none; emphasis is on processes in situations.	None: emphasis is on processes in situations. Existence of social structures is bracketed out of analysis.	Social reality is constructed from methods used by people to construct a sense, or presumption, that they share the same world.	Emphasis on induction of folk methods from actual empirical observations.

can and should be, and as a result, we are often not respected by other sciences. Indeed, we often do not respect ourselves as a science. It is our view that sociology must rekindle the vision of Comte and begin to seek and articulate the abstract laws of the social universe.

We wrote this book to show, perhaps only in a crude and modest way, that the early masters articulated some intriguing principles. We should use these principles, and with the vision of a young Comte, we should begin to search for the generic properties of the social world and to articulate abstract principles that allow us to understand the operation of these properties. This is what a "science of society" should be, as the founder of sociology recognized so clearly in his early years.

NAME INDEX

SUBJECT INDEX

This book has been set CAP in 10 and 9 point Avanta, leaded 3 points. Part numbers are 24 point Compano and part titles are 20 point Compano. Chapter numbers are 44 point Times Roman and chapter titles are 16 point Compano. The size of the type page is 27 by 46 picas.